W9-BAO-460

Linux:
The Complete Reference
Third Edition

Richard Petersen

Osborne/**McGraw-Hill**

Berkeley   New York   St. Louis   San Francisco
Auckland   Bogotá   Hamburg   London   Madrid
Mexico City   Milan   Montreal   New Delhi   Panama City
Paris   São Paulo   Singapore   Sydney
Tokyo   Toronto

Osborne/**McGraw-Hill**
2600 Tenth Street
Berkeley, California 94710
U.S.A.

For information on translations or book distributors outside the U.S.A., or to arrange bulk purchase discounts for sales promotions, premiums, or fundraisers, please contact Osborne/**McGraw-Hill** at the above address.

Linux: The Complete Reference, Third Edition

34567890 DOC DOC 90198765432109

ISBN 0-07-212164-5

Publisher

    Brandon A. Nordin

Associate Publisher and Editor-in-Chief

    Scott Rogers

Acquisitions Editor

    Jane Brownlow

Project Editor

    Betsy Manini

Editorial Assistant

    Tara Davis

Technical Editor

    Eric Richardson

Copy Editors

    Robert Campbell and Dennis Weaver

Proofreaders

    Stefany Otis

    Valerie Perry

Indexer

    Valerie Robbins

Computer Designers

    Roberta Steele

    Jani Beckwith

    Ann Sellers

Illustrators

    Beth Young

    Brian Wells

This book has been composed in Corel VENTURA.

Dedicated
to my brothers,
George, Robert, and Mark

About the Author...

Richard Petersen holds an M.L.I.S. in Library and Information Studies. He currently teaches Unix and C/C++ courses at the University of California, Berkeley.

About the Technical Reviewer

Eric Richardson is a professional Webmaster for Nabisco Inc. He has expertise with all versions of SunOS and Solaris along with SCO UNIX and the BSD variants. He is also an experienced computer-book and magazine author and technical reviewer.

Contents at a Glance

Contents

Part I

Introduction

Part II

Environments

Part III

Internet

Part IV

Servers

Part V

Applications

Part VI

System Administration

Part VII

Appendix

Acknowledgments

I would like to thank all those at Osborne/McGraw-Hill who made this book a reality: in particular, Jane Brownlow, acquisitions editor, for her continued encouragement and analysis as well as her management of such a complex project; Eric Richardson, the technical editor, whose analysis and suggestions proved very insightful and helpful; Tara Davis, editorial assistant, who provided needed resources and helpful advice; Bob Campbell and Dennis Weaver, copyeditors, for their excellent job editing as well as insightful comments; and project editor Betsy Manini who incorporated the large number of features found in this book as well as coordinated the intricate task of generating the final version. Thanks also to Scott Rogers who initiated the project.

Special thanks to Linus Torvalds, the creator of Linux, and to those who continue to develop Linux as an open, professional, and effective operating system accessible to anyone. Thanks also to the academic community whose special dedication has developed Unix as a flexible and versatile operating system. I would also like to thank professors and students at the University of California, Berkeley, for the experience and support in developing new and different ways of understanding operating system technologies.

I thank my parents, George and Cecelia, and my brothers, George, Robert, and Mark, for their support and encouragement with such a difficult project. I also thank Valerie and Marylou, and my nieces and nephews, Aleina, Larisa, Justin, Christopher, and Dylan, for their support and deadline reminders.

Introduction

The Linux operating system has become a viable alternative for anyone with a PC. It brings all the power and flexibility of a Unix workstation as well as a complete set of Internet applications and a fully functional desktop interface. All of this can easily be installed on any PC or workstation. This book is designed not only to be a complete reference on Linux, but also to provide clear and detailed explanations of Linux features. No prior knowledge of Unix is assumed; Linux is an operating system anyone can use.

This third edition of this book identifies five major Linux topics; Environments, the Internet, Servers, Applications, and Administration. Gnome and the K Desktop Environment (KDE) are two new desktop Graphical User Interfaces (GUI) for Linux, noted for their power, flexibility, and ease-of-use. These are complete desktop environments that are more flexible than either Windows or the Mac/OS. They support standard desktop features such as menus, taskbars, and drag-and-drop operations. But they also provide virtual desktops, panel applets and menus, and Internet-capable file managers. Gnome and KDE have become standard components in almost every Linux system. Both were designed with software development in mind, providing a firm foundation that has encouraged the development of a massive number of new applications for these interfaces. Both Gnome and KDE have become integrated components of Linux, with applications and tools for every kind of task and operation. Instead of treating Gnome and KDE as separate entities, Gnome and KDE tools and applications are presented throughout the book. For example, Gnome and KDE mail clients are discussed in that chapter on Internet mailers, along with other mail clients. Gnome and KDE FTP clients, editors, graphic tools, administration tools, among others are also handled in those respective chapters.

Linux is also a fully functional Unix operating system. It has all the standard features of a powerful Unix system, including a complete set of Unix shells such as BASH, TCSH, and the Z-shell. Those familiar with the Unix interface can use any of these shells, with the same Unix commands, filters, and configuration features.

For the Internet, Linux has become a platform for very powerful Internet applications. You not only can use the Internet with Linux, but also become a part of it, creating your own Web, FTP, and Gopher sites. Other users can access your Linux systems, several at the same time, using different services. You can also use very powerful Gnome, KDE, and Unix clients for mail and news. Linux systems are not limited to the Internet. You can use it on any local intranet, setting up an FTP or Web site for your network. The OpenLinux and Red Hat Linux system provided with this book comes equipped with a variety of fully functional FTP and Web servers already installed and ready to use. All you need to do is add the files you want onto your site.

A wide array of applications operates on Linux. Many personal versions of commercial applications are available for Linux free of charge, such as WordPerfect, Star Office, and Sybase database. You can download them directly from the Internet. Numerous Gnome and KDE applications are continually released through their respective Web sites. The GNU public licensed software provides professional-level applications such as programming development tools, editors and word processors, as well as numerous specialized applications such as those for graphics and sound. A massive amount of software is available at online Linux sites where you can download applications and then easily install them onto your system.

Linux has the same level of administration features that you find on standard Unix systems as well as many user-friendly interfaces that make any administration task a simple matter of choosing an item on a menu or clicking a checkbox. It has the same multiuser and multitasking capabilities. You can set up accounts for different users and each can access your system at the same time. Each user can have several programs running concurrently. With Linux you can control access, set up network connections, and install new devices. Most distributions like Red Hat, OpenLinux, and SuSE include very powerful and easy-to-use, window-based configuration utilities like Linuxconf and COAS that you can use to perform system administration tasks such as installing printers, adding users, and establishing new network connections.

Since this book is really five books in one:

■ an Internet book
■ a Gnome and KDE book
■ a Server book

- an Applications book
- an Administration book

how you choose to use it depends upon how you want to use your Linux system. Almost all Linux operations can be carried out using either the Gnome or KDE interface. You do not have to use the Unix command line interface at all. You can focus on the Gnome and KDE chapters and their corresponding tools and applications in the different chapters throughout the book. On the other hand, if you want to delve deeper into the Unix aspects of Linux, you can check out the Shell chapters and the corresponding shell-based applications in other chapters. If you only want to use Linux for its Internet services, then concentrate on the Internet clients and servers, most of which are already installed for you. If you want to use Linux as a multiuser system servicing many users or integrate it into a local network, you can use the detailed system, file, and network administration information provided in the administration chapters. None of these tasks are in any way exclusive. If you are working in a business environment, you will probably make use of all three aspects. Single users may concentrate more on the desktops and the Internet features, whereas administrators may make more use of the Unix features.

This book is designed to help you start using Linux quickly.

- In **Part I**, after a streamlined installation procedure for both Red Hat and OpenLinux taking about 30 minutes or less, basic Gnome and KDE interface operations and system configuration task are discussed. Here you learn the essentials of using both Gnome and KDE. System configuration tasks like mounting CD-ROMs and adding new user accounts are presented with the easiest methods, without much of the complex detail described in the administration chapters that is unnecessary for basic operations.

- In **Part II**, you are introduced to the different kinds of user environments available for Linux, starting with KDE and Gnome. Different features such as applets, the Panel, and configuration tools are described in detail. With either of these interfaces, you can run all your applications using icons, menus, and windows. At any time, you can open up a terminal window through which you can enter standard Linux commands on a command line. Linux makes a distinction between a desktop and a window manager. A window manager controls basic window operations like window appearance, movement, and elements. You have a variety of very powerful Linux window managers to choose from, such as AfterStep, WindowMaker, and Enlightenment. You can also choose to use just the standard Unix command-line interface to run any of the standard Unix commands. The remaining chapters in this section discuss the BASH shell and its various file, directory, and filter commands.

- In **Part III**, the book discusses in detail the many Internet applications you can use on your Linux system. OpenLinux automatically installs mail, news, FTP, and Web browser applications, as well as FTP and Web servers. Both KDE and Gnome come with a full set of mail, news, FTP clients, and Web browsers.

These are described in detail along with Netscape communicator, now an integrated part of all Linux systems. On your CD-ROM there are other mail clients, newsreaders, and Internet tools that you can easily install from your desktop. In addition, the book describes Internet clients like IglooFTP and Balsa that you can download from Internet sites and install on your system.

■ **Part IV** discusses Internet servers, including FTP, Web, Gopher, and DNS servers. Internet servers have become integrated components of most Linux systems. Both the standard wu-ftpd FTP server and the newer ProFTPD server with its directive format are presented. ProFTPD covers features like guest and virtual FTP sites. The Apache Web server chapter covers standard configuration directives like those for automatic indexing as well as the newer virtual host directives. Apache GUI configuration tools like comanche are also presented. The different Gopher servers like GN are discussed with their respective configurations. Configuration files and features for the Domain Name System and its BIND server are examined in detail along with features like virtual domains and IP aliases. With Linux you can easily set up your own Domain Name server for a home or small local network. The sendmail mail server, INN news server, the Squid proxy server, the ht:/DIG and WAIS search servers are also examined.

■ **Part V** reviews applications available for Linux, beginning with Office suites like Start Office and KOffice. The different database management systems available are then discussed along with the Web site locations where you can download them. Software installation has been simplified with the Red Hat Package Management System (RPMS). There are several GUI tools like the KDE kpackage and Gnome gnomeRPM that you can use to easily install and uninstall software, much as you would with the Windows install wizard. A variety of different text editors are also available, including several Gnome and KDE editors, as well as the Vim (enhanced VI), gvim (graphical Vi), GNU Emacs, and XEmacs editors.

■ **Part VI** discusses file system, system, network, and X Window System administration, respectively. These chapters emphasize the use of special GUI system management tools like Linuxconf, COAS, and the Red Hat control panel that you can operate from the desktop or command line. You can use them to set up your network, add users, and configure devices such as printers. Linuxconf also lets you configure your Internet servers. There are also a detailed descriptions of the configuration files used in management and how to make entries in them.

First, different file system tasks are covered such as mounting file systems, selecting device names, accessing DOS files, as well as the various network file system interfaces like NFS for Unix, Samba for Windows file systems, and NetaTALK for AppleTalk networks. System administration tasks like managing users and groups, installing devices, and monitoring your system presentations include both the GUI tools you can use for these tasks and the underlying configurations files and commands. Using, updating, and configuring the Linux kernel with its modules is covered in detail along with procedures for installing new kernels. Various aspects of network administration are discussed such as network connections and routes, Domain Name services, Hostname designations, IP virtual hosts, and IP masquerading. X Window System topics cover the XFree86 servers, window manager configuration, X Window System startup methods like the display manager, and X Window System configuration commands. The discussion of XFree86 servers includes a detailed explanation of the **/etc/XF86Config** configuration file used to configure your card.

■ Finally, there is an Appendix covering what is available on the CD-ROMs included with this book.

Note

This book includes numerous tables that list different commands and their options. In many cases, you will find them placed at the end of the section or chapter where they are referenced so that you can easily locate and refer to them.

The Complete Reference

Part I

Introduction

Chapter 1

Introduction to Linux

L inux is an operating system for PC computers and workstations that now features
a fully functional graphical user interface (GUI), just like Windows and the Mac
(though more stable). Linux was developed in the early 1990s by Linus Torvald,
along with other programmers around the world. As an operating system, it performs
many of the same functions as Unix, Mac, Windows, and Windows NT. However,
Linux is distinguished by its power and flexibility. Most PC operating systems, such
as Windows, began their development within the confines of small restricted personal
computers, which have only recently become more versatile machines. Such operating
systems are constantly being upgraded to keep up with the ever-changing capabilities
of PC hardware. Linux, on the other hand, was developed in a very different context.
Linux is a PC version of the Unix operating system that has been used for decades on
mainframes and minicomputers and is currently the system of choice for workstations.
Linux brings the speed, efficiency, and flexibility of Unix to your PC, taking advantage
of all the capabilities that personal computers can now provide. Along with its Unix
capabilities comes powerful networking features, including support for Internet, intranet,
Windows, and AppleTalk networking. As a standard, Linux is distributed with very fast,
efficient, and stable Internet servers such as the Web, FTP, and Gopher servers, along with
domain name, proxy, news, mail, and indexing servers. In other words, it has everything
you need to set up, support, and maintain a full functional network.

Now with both Gnome and K Desktop, Linux also provides GUI interfaces with that
same level of flexibility and power. Unlike Windows and the Mac, you can choose the
interface you want and then customize it further, adding panels, applets, virtual desktops,
and menus, all with full drag-and-drop capabilities and Internet-aware tools. On your
desktop, a file manager window can access any Internet site, letting you display Web
pages and download files with a few simple mouse operations. To print a file, just drag
it to a Printer icon.

Linux does all this at a great price. It is free, including the network servers and GUI
desktops. Unlike the official Unix operating system, Linux is distributed freely under a
GNU General Public License as specified by the Free Software Foundation, making it
available to anyone who wants to use it. Linux is copyrighted and is not public domain.
However, a GNU public license has much the same effect as being in the public
domain. The license is designed to ensure that Linux remains free and, at the same time,
standardized. There is only one official Linux. GNU stands for Gnu's Not Unix and is a
project initiated and managed by the Free Software Foundation to provide free software
to users, programmers, and developers. The list of software available under the GNU
Public License is extensive, including environments, programming languages, Internet
tools, and text editors.

The fact that Linux is free sometimes gives people the mistaken impression that
it is somehow less than a professional operating system. Linux is, in fact, a PC and
workstation version of Unix. Many consider it far more stable and much more powerful
than Windows. It is this power and stability that has made it an operating system of
choice as a network server.

To truly appreciate Linux, you need to understand the special context in which the Unix operating system was developed. Unix, unlike most other operating systems, was developed in a research and academic environment. In universities and research laboratories, Unix is the system of choice. Its development paralleled the entire computer and communications revolution over the past several decades. Computer professionals often developed new computer technologies on Unix, such as those developed for the Internet. Though a very sophisticated system, Unix was designed from the beginning to be flexible. The Unix system itself can be easily modified to create different versions. In fact, many different vendors maintain different official versions of Unix. IBM, Sun, and Hewlett-Packard all sell and maintain their own versions of Unix. People involved in research programs will often create their own versions of Unix, tailored to their own special needs. This inherent flexibility in the Unix design in no way detracts from its quality. In fact, it attests to its ruggedness, allowing it to adapt to practically any environment. It is in this context that Linux was developed. Linux is, in this sense, one other version of Unix—a version for the PC. Its development by computer professionals working in a research-like environment reflects the way Unix versions have usually been developed. The fact that Linux is publicly licensed and free reflects the deep roots that Unix has in academic institutions, with their sense of public service and support. Linux is a top-rate operating system accessible to everyone, free of charge.

As a way of introducing Linux, this chapter discusses Linux as an operating system, the history of Linux and Unix, the overall design of Linux, and Linux distributions. It also discusses online resources for documentation, software, and newsgroups as well as Web sites with the latest news and articles on Linux. Web and FTP site listings are placed in tables for easy reference at the end of this chapter. Here you can find sites for different distributions, Linux publications, software repositories, and Linux development as well as for office suites and commercial databases.

Operating Systems and Linux

An *operating system* is a program that manages computer hardware and software for the user. Operating systems were originally designed to perform repetitive hardware tasks. These tasks centered around managing files, running programs, and receiving commands from the user. You interact with an operating system through a user interface. This user interface allows the operating system to receive and interpret instructions sent by the user. You only need to send an instruction to the operating system to perform a task, such as reading a file or printing a document. An operating system's user interface can be as simple as entering commands on a line, or as complex as selecting menus and icons on a desktop.

An operating system also manages software applications. To perform different tasks, such as editing documents or performing calculations, you need specific software applications. An editor is an example of a software application. An editor allows you to edit a document, making changes and adding new text. The editor itself is a program consisting of instructions to be executed by the computer. To use the program, it must first be loaded into computer memory, and then its instructions executed. The operating system controls the loading and execution of all programs, including any software applications. When you want to use an editor, you simply instruct the operating system to load the editor application and execute it.

File management, program management, and user interaction are traditional features common to all operating systems. Linux, like all versions of Unix, adds two more features. Linux is a multiuser and multitasking system. As a multitasking system, you can ask the system to perform several tasks at the same time. While one task is being done, you can work on another. For example, you can edit a file while another file is being printed. You do not have to wait for the other file to finish printing before you edit. As a multiuser system, several users can log into the system at the same time, each interacting with the system through his or her own terminal.

Operating systems were originally designed to support hardware efficiency. When computers were first developed, their capabilities were limited and the operating system had to make the most of them. In this respect, operating systems were designed with the hardware in mind, not the user. Operating systems tended to be rigid and inflexible, forcing the user to conform to the demands of hardware efficiency.

Linux, on the other hand, is designed to be flexible, reflecting its Unix roots. As a version of Unix, Linux shares the same flexibility designed for Unix, a flexibility stemming from Unix's research origins. The Unix operating system was developed by Ken Thompson at AT&T Bell Laboratories in the late 1960s and early 1970s. It incorporated many new developments in operating system design. Originally, Unix was designed as an operating system for researchers. One major goal was to create a system that could support the researchers' changing demands. To do this, Thompson had to design a system that could deal with many different kinds of tasks. Flexibility became more important than hardware efficiency. Like Unix, Linux has the advantage of being able to deal with the variety of tasks any user may face.

This flexibility allows Linux to be an operating system that is accessible to the user. The user is not confined to limited and rigid interactions with the operating system. Instead, the operating system is thought of as providing a set of highly effective tools that the user can make use of. This user-oriented philosophy means that you can configure and program the system to meet your specific needs. With Linux, the operating system becomes an *operating environment*.

History of Linux and Unix

As a version of Unix, the history of Linux naturally begins with Unix. The story begins in the late 1960s when there was a concerted effort to develop new operating system techniques. In 1968, a consortium of researchers from General Electric, AT&T Bell Laboratories, and the Massachusetts Institute of Technology carried out a special operating system research project called MULTICS (MULTiplexed Information Computing System). MULTICS incorporated many new concepts in multitasking, file management, and user interaction. In 1969, Ken Thompson, Dennis Ritchie, and the researchers at AT&T Bell Laboratories developed the Unix operating system, incorporating many of the features of the MULTICS research project. They tailored the system for the needs of a research environment, designing it to run on minicomputers. From its inception, Unix was an affordable and efficient multiuser and multitasking operating system.

The Unix system became popular at Bell Labs as more and more researchers started using the system. In 1973, Dennis Ritchie collaborated with Ken Thompson to rewrite the programming code for the Unix system in the C programming language. Dennis Ritchie, a fellow researcher at Bell Labs, developed the C programming language as a flexible tool for program development. One of the advantages of C is that it can directly access the hardware architecture of a computer with a generalized set of programming commands. Up until this time, an operating system had to be specially rewritten in a hardware-specific assembly language for each type of computer. The C programming language allowed Dennis Ritchie and Ken Thompson to write only one version of the Unix operating system that could then be compiled by C compilers on different computers. In effect, the Unix operating system became transportable—able to run on a variety of different computers with little or no reprogramming.

Unix gradually grew from one person's tailored design to a standard software product distributed by many different vendors, such as Novell and IBM. Initially, Unix was treated as a research product. The first versions of Unix were distributed free to the computer science departments of many noted universities. Throughout the 1970s, Bell Labs began issuing official versions of Unix and licensing the systems to different users. One of these users was the Computer Science department of the University of California, Berkeley. Berkeley added many new features to the system that later became standard. In 1975, Berkeley released its own version of Unix, known by its distribution arm, Berkeley Software Distribution (BSD). This BSD version of Unix became a major contender to the AT&T Bell Labs version. Other independently developed versions of Unix sprouted up. In 1980, Microsoft developed a PC version of Unix called Xenix. AT&T developed several research versions of Unix, and in 1983 they released the first commercial version, called System 3. This was later followed by System V, which became a supported commercial software product. You can find more information on Unix in *UNIX: The Complete Reference*, written by the Unix experts at AT&T Laboratories, Kenneth Rosen, Douglas Host, James Farber, and Richard Rosinski (Osborne/McGraw-Hill, 1999).

At the same time, the BSD version of Unix was developing through several releases. In the late 1970s, BSD Unix became the basis of a research project by the Department of Defense's Advanced Research Projects Agency (DARPA). As a result, in 1983, Berkeley released a powerful version of Unix called BSD release 4.2. It included sophisticated file management as well as networking features based on TCP/IP network protocols—the same protocols now used for the Internet. BSD release 4.2 was widely distributed and adopted by many vendors such as Sun Microsystems.

The proliferation of different versions of Unix led to a need for a Unix standard. Software developers had no way of knowing what versions of Unix their programs would actually run on. In the mid-1980s, two competing standards emerged, one based on the AT&T version of Unix and the other on the BSD version. In bookstores today you will see many different books on Unix for one or the other version. Some specify System V Unix, while others focus on BSD Unix.

AT&T moved Unix to a new organization, called Unix System Laboratories, that could focus on developing a standard system, integrating the different major versions of Unix. In 1991, Unix System Laboratories developed System V release 4, which incorporated almost all the features found in System V release 3, BSD release 4.3, SunOS, and Xenix. In response to System V release 4, several other companies, such as IBM and Hewlett-Packard, established the Open Software Foundation (OSF) to create their own standard version of Unix. There were then two commercial standard versions of Unix—the OSF version and System V release 4. In 1993, AT&T sold off its interest in Unix to Novell. Unix Systems Laboratories became part of Novell's UNIX Systems Group. Novell issued its own versions of Unix based on System V release 4, called UnixWare, designed to interact with Novell's NetWare system. Unix Systems Laboratories is currently owned by the Santa Cruz Operation. With Solaris, Sun has introduced System V release 4 onto its Sun systems. Two competing graphical user interfaces (GUIs) for Unix, called Motif and OpenLook, have been merged into a new desktop standard called the Common Desktop Environment (CDE).

Throughout much of its development, Unix remained a large and demanding operating system requiring a workstation or minicomputer to be effective. Several versions of Unix were designed primarily for the workstation environment. SunOS was developed for Sun workstations, and AIX was designed for IBM workstations. However, as personal computers became more powerful, efforts were made to develop a PC version of Unix. Xenix and System V/386 are commercial versions of Unix designed for IBM-compatible PCs. AUX is a Unix version that runs on the Macintosh. It is a testament to Unix's inherent portability that it can be found on almost any type of computer: workstations, minicomputers, and even supercomputers. This inherent portability made possible an effective PC version of Unix.

Linux was originally designed specifically for Intel-based personal computers. It started out as a personal project of a computer science student named Linus Torvald at the University of Helsinki. At that time, students were making use of a program called Minix that highlighted different Unix features. Minix was created by Professor Andrew Tannebaum and widely distributed over the Internet to students around the world. Linus's intention was to create an effective PC version of Unix for Minix users. He called it Linux, and in 1991 released version 0.11. Linux was widely distributed over the Internet, and in the following years other programmers refined and added to it, incorporating most of the applications and features now found in standard Unix systems. All the major window managers have been ported to Linux. Linux has all the Internet utilities, such as FTP, telnet, and SLIP. It also has a full set of program development utilities, such as C++ compilers and debuggers. Given all its features, the Linux operating system remains small, stable, and fast. In its simplest format, it can run effectively on just 4MB of memory.

Though Linux has developed in the free and open environment of the Internet, it adheres to official Unix standards. Due to the proliferation of Unix versions in the previous decades, the Institute of Electrical and Electronics Engineers (IEEE) developed an independent Unix standard for the American National Standards Institute (ANSI). This new ANSI-standard Unix is called the Portable Operating System Interface for Computer Environments (POSIX). The standard defines how a Unix-like system needs to operate, specifying details such as system calls and interfaces. POSIX defines a universal standard that all Unix versions must adhere to. Most popular versions of Unix are now POSIX compliant. Linux was developed from the beginning according to the POSIX standard.

Linux Overview

Like Unix, Linux can be generally divided into three major components: the kernel, the shell environment, and the file structure. The *kernel* is the core program that runs programs and manages hardware devices such as disks and printers. The *environment* provides an interface for the user. It receives commands from the user and sends those commands to the kernel for execution. The *file structure* organizes the way files are stored on a storage device such as a disk. Files are organized into directories. Each directory may contain any number of subdirectories, each holding files. Together, the kernel, the environment, and the file structure form the basic operating system structure. With these three, you can run programs, manage files, and interact with the system.

Environments: Shells, Desktops, and Window Managers

An environment provides an interface between the kernel and the user. It can be described as an interpreter. It interprets commands entered by the user and sends them to the kernel. Linux provides several kinds of environments: desktops, window managers, and command line shells. Each user on a Linux system has his or her own user interface. Users can tailor their environments to their own special needs, whether they be shells, window managers, or desktops. In this sense, for the user, the operating system functions more as an operating environment, which the user can control.

The shell interface is very simple. It usually consists of a prompt at which you type a command and then press ENTER. In a sense, you are typing the command on a line; this line is often referred to as the *command line*. You will find that the commands entered on the command line can become very complex. Over the years, several different kinds of shells have been developed. Currently, there are three major shells: Bourne, Korn, and C-shell. The Bourne shell was developed at Bell Labs for System V. The C-shell was developed for the BSD version of Unix. The Korn shell is a further enhancement of the Bourne shell. Current versions of Unix, including Linux, incorporate all three shells, allowing you to choose the one you prefer. However, Linux uses enhanced or public domain versions of these shells: the Bourne Again shell, the TC-shell, and the Public Domain Korn Shell. When you start your Linux system, you will be placed in the Bourne Again shell, an updated version of the Bourne shell. From there, you can switch to other shells as you wish.

As an alternative to a command line interface, Linux provides both desktops and window managers. These use graphical user interfaces (GUIs) based on the X-Windows system developed for Unix by the Open Group consortium (**www.opengroup.org**). A window manager is a reduced version of a desktop, supporting only window operation, but still lets you run any application. A desktop provides a complete GUI much like Windows and the Mac. You have windows, icons, and menus, all managed through mouse controls. Currently, there are two desktops freely available and included with most distributions of Linux: Gnome and KDE.

File Structure: Directories and Files

In Linux, files are organized into directories, much as they are in Windows. The entire Linux file system is one large interconnected set of directories, each containing files. Some directories are standard directories reserved for system use. You can create your own directories for your own files, as well as easily move files from one directory to another. You can even move entire directories and share directories and files with other users on your system. With Linux, you can also set permissions on directories and files, allowing others to access them or restricting access to you alone.

The directories of each user are in fact ultimately connected to the directories of other users. Directories are organized into a hierarchical tree structure, beginning with an initial root directory. All other directories are ultimately derived from this first root directory. Figure 1-1 shows an example of this tree-like, hierarchical file structure. You can actually travel throughout the system, entering any directory that may be open to you. This interconnectivity of the file structure makes it easy to share data. Several users could access the same files.

The root directory is a special directory that you will need to make use of when you first set up your Linux system. Linux is a multiuser system. You could have several users sharing the same operating system. However, the operating system itself resides in programs placed in special directories beginning with the root directory. These are sometimes referred to as *system directories*. In Figure 1-1, the system directories are those just below the root: **bin**, **man**, and **usr**. There are many others. System directories are described in Chapter 9.

Desktops

With the K Desktop Environment (KDE) and the GNU Network Object Model Environment (Gnome), Linux now has a completely integrated GUI interface. You can perform all your Linux operations entirely from either interface. Previously, Linux did

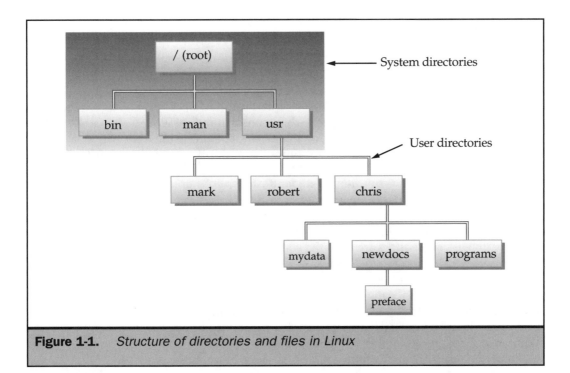

Figure 1-1.   *Structure of directories and files in Linux*

support window managers that provided some GUI functionality, but they were usually restricted to window operations. KDE and Gnome are fully operational desktops supporting drag-and-drop operations letting you drag icons to your desktop and set up your own menus on an Applications panel. Both rely on an underlying X-Windows system, which means that as long as they are both installed on your system, applications from one can run on the other desktop. You can run KDE programs like the KDE mailer or newsreader, on the Gnome desktop. Gnome applications like the gFTP client can run on the KDE desktop. You can even switch file managers, running the KDE file manager on Gnome. You will lose some desktop functionality such as drag-and-drop operations, but the applications will run fine.

Both desktops can run any X-Windows system program as well as any cursor-based program like Emacs and Vi, which were designed to work in a shell environment. At the same time, there are a great many applications written just for those desktops and included with your distributions. The K Desktop has a complete set of Internet tools along with editors and graphic, multimedia, and system applications. Gnome has slightly fewer applications, but a great many are currently in the works. Check their Web sites at **www.gnome.org** and **www.kde.org** for new applications. As new versions are released, they will include new software.

Linux Software

Linux was developed as a cooperative effort over the Internet. No company or institution controls Linux. Software developed for Linux reflects this background. Development often takes place when Linux users decide to work on a project together. When completed, the software is posted at an Internet site. Any Linux user can then access the site and download the software. The potential for Linux-based software is explosive. Linux software development has always operated in an Internet environment. It is global in scope, enlisting programmers from around the world. The only thing you need to start a Linux-based software project is a Web site.

Most Linux software is copyrighted under a GNU public license provided by the Free Software Foundation, and is often referred to as GNU software (see **www.gnu.org**). GNU software is distributed free provided it is freely distributed to others. GNU software has proven to be very reliable and effective. Many of the popular Linux utilities such as C compilers, shells, and editors are all GNU software applications. You will find installed with your Linux distribution the GNU C++ and Lisp compilers, Vi and Emacs editors, BASH and TCSH shells, as well as TeX and Ghostscript document formatters. Many other GNU software applications are available at different Internet sites and are listed in Table 1-7 (located with all the other tables at the end of this chapter). Chapter 4 and Chapter 24 describe in detail the process of downloading software applications from Internet sites and installing them on your system.

Lately, major software companies are also developing Linux versions of their most popular applications. Netscape provides a Linux version of their popular Web browser that is now included as standard on most Linux distributions. There is also a Linux version of Sun's Java Development Kit (JDK) available through **ftp.blackdown.org**. Corel has developed a Linux version of WordPerfect, and Oracle provides a Linux version of its Oracle database. (At present, there do not seem to be any plans for Microsoft applications.)

Until recently, however, many of these lacked a true desktop interface. That has changed dramatically with the introduction of the K Desktop Environment (KDE) and the GNU Network Object Management Environment (Gnome). These desktops are not merely interfaces. They both provide very extensive, flexible, and powerful development libraries that software developers can use to create almost any kind of application, which they are.

One of the most important features of Linux, as well as all Unix systems, is its set of Internet clients and servers. The Internet was designed and developed on Unix systems. Internet clients and servers such as those for FTP and the Web were first implemented on BSD versions of Unix. DARPANET, the precursor to the Internet, was set up to link Unix systems at different universities across the nation. Linux contains a full set of Internet clients and servers including mail, news, FTP, Web, and proxy clients and servers.

Software packages are distributed either in compressed archives or in RPM packages. RPM packages are those archived using the Red Hat Package Manager. Compressed archives have an extension like **.tar.gz** or **.tar.Z**, whereas RPM packages have an **.rpm** extension. For OpenLinux and Red Hat, it is best to download the RPM package versions of software from their FTP sites. Whenever possible, you should try to download software from a distribution's FTP site. However, you could also download the source version and compile it directly on your system. This has become a very simple process, almost as simple as installing the compiled versions (see Chapter 4).

Distributions, like OpenLinux and Red Hat also have a large number of mirror sites from which you can also download their software packages. Red Hat mirror sites are listed at **www.redhat.com/mirrors.html**. Most Linux Internet sites that provide extensive software archives have mirror sites, like **www.kernel.org** that holds the new Linux kernels. If you have trouble connecting to a main FTP site, try one of its mirrors.

Online Information Sources

Extensive online resources are available on almost any Linux topic. The tables at the end of this chapter list sites where you can obtain software, display documentation, and read articles on the latest developments. Many Linux Web sites provide news, articles, and information about Linux. Several are based on popular Linux magazines, such as **www.linuxjournal.org** and **www.linuxgazzette.org**. Others operate as Web portals for Linux, such as **www.linux.com**, **www.linuxworld.org**, and **www.linux.org**. Some specialize in particular topics, such as **kernelnotes.org** for news on the Linux kernel and **www.linuxgames.org** for the latest games ported for Linux. You can find their Web site addresses listed in Table 1-4 at the end of this chapter.

Distribution FTP and Web sites such as **www.calderasystems.com** and **www.redhat.com** provide extensive Linux documentation and software. The **www.gnome.org** site holds software and documentation for the Gnome desktop, and **www.kde.org** holds software and documentation for the KDE desktop. The tables at the end of this chapter list many of the available sites. You can find other sites through resource pages that hold links to other Web sites—for example, the Linux on the World Wide Web at **http://metalab.unc.edu/LDP/links.html**.

Documentation

Linux documentation has also been developed over the Internet. Much of the documentation currently available for Linux can be downloaded from Internet FTP sites. A special Linux project called the Linux Documentation Project (LDP) headed by Matt Welsh is currently developing a complete set of Linux manuals. The documentation, at its current level, is available at the LDP home site at **http://metalab.unc.edu/LDP/**.

An extensive number of mirrors are maintained for the Linux Documentation Project. You can link to any of them through a variety of sources such as the LDP home site **www.linux.org** and **www.linuxjournal.org**. The documentation includes a user's guide, an introduction, and administration guides. They are available in text, PostScript, or Web page format. Table 1-3 lists these guides. You can find briefer explanations in what are referred to as HOW-TO documents. HOW-TO documents are available for different subjects such as installation, printing, and e-mail. The documents are available at Linux FTP sites, *usually* in the directory **/pub/Linux/doc/HOW-TO**.

You can find a listing of different Linux information sites in the file **META-FAQ** located at Linux FTP sites, usually in the directory **/pub/Linux/doc**. On the same site and directory, you can also download the Linux Software Map, LSM. This is a listing of most of the software currently available for Linux. Also, many software companies have Web sites that provide information about their Linux applications. Several of these are listed in Tables 1-7 and 1-8.

In addition to FTP sites, there are also Linux Usenet newsgroups. Through your Internet connection, you can access Linux newsgroups to read the comments of other Linux users and post messages of your own. There are several Linux newsgroups, each beginning with **comp.os.linux**. One of particular interest to the beginner is **comp.os.linux.help**, where you can post questions. Table 1-6 lists the different Linux newsgroups available on Usenet.

Most of the standard Linux software and documentation currently available is already included on your Red Hat and OpenLinux CD-ROMs. HOW-TO documents are all accessible in HTML format, so you can view them easily with your Web browser. However, in the future, you may need to directly access Linux Internet sites for up-to-date information and software.

Linux Distributions

Although there is only one standard version of Linux, there are actually several different releases. Different companies and groups have packaged Linux and Linux software in slightly different ways. Each company or group then releases the Linux package, usually on a CD-ROM. Later releases may include updated versions of programs or new software. Some of the more popular releases are Red Hat, OpenLinux, SuSE, and Debian. Several distributions, such as Caldera and Red Hat, also offer their systems bundled with commercial software.

Red Hat

Red Hat Linux is currently the most popular Linux distribution. It originated with the RPM package system used on several distributions that automatically installs and removes software packages. Red Hat is also providing much of the software development for the Gnome desktop. However, it also supports KDE. Its distribution includes both Gnome and KDE. Red Hat, like Caldera, maintains software alliances with major companies like Oracle, IBM, and Sun. The Red Hat distribution of Linux is available online at numerous FTP sites. It maintains its own FTP site (**ftp.redhat.com**), along with one dedicated to updates (**updates.redhat.com**) and third-party software (**contrib.redhat.com**). Currently it supports Sparc, Intel, Alpha, PPC, ARM, Mac m68K, and SGI platforms. See **www.redhat.com** for more information.

OpenLinux

Caldera OpenLinux is designed for corporate commercial use. The OpenLinux CD-ROM included with this book contains Caldera's complete OpenLinux Linux system and software packages including all the GNU software packages, as well as the X-Windows managers, Internet servers, WordPerfect 8.0, and the K Desktop. However, it does not presently include Gnome. It is POSIX compliant, adhering to Unix standards. Caldera distributes its OpenLinux system free of charge. Caldera also offers a line of commercial and proprietary Linux packages that are not included here. Such proprietary, licensed software packages are not freely distributable. They include such products as Partition Magic, Star Office, AdabasD database, and the Novell NetWare client. See the Caldera Web site at **www.calderasystems.com** for more information. Presently, it supports only the Intel platform.

SuSE

Originally a German language–based distribution, SuSE has become very popular throughout Europe, and is currently one of the fastest growing distributions world-wide. Its current distribution includes both KDE and Gnome. Its distributions include WordPerfect, Star Office, and KOffice. It also bundles commercial products like AdabasD and the Linux Office Suite. Currently, it only supports Intel platforms. For more information, see **www.suse.com**.

Debian

Debian Linux is an entirely noncommercial project, maintained by a group of volunteer programmers. It does, however, incorporate support for commercial products in its distribution. Debian currently maintains software associations with Corel and Sun, among others. Currently it supports Alpha, Intel, Mac m68K, and Sparc platforms. For more information, see **www.debian.org**.

Slackware

Slackware is available from numerous Internet sites, and you can order the CD from Walnut Creek software. It includes both Gnome and KDE. The Slackware distribution takes special care to remain as closely Unix compliant as possible. Currently, it supports only Intel platforms. See **www.slackware.com** for more information.

Infomagic

Infomagic distributes bundled sets of Linux software. The Linux Developers Resource set includes the four major distributions, Red Hat, OpenLinux, SuSE, and Slackware. The Linux Archive set contains mirrors of Linux archive sites including KDE, Gnome, Xfree86, and GNU. Currently it supports only the Intel platform. See **www.infomagic.com** for more information.

LinuxPPC

The LinuxPPC distribution provides versions of Linux designed exclusively for use on PowerPC machines. The distribution will run on any PowerPC machine, including IBM, Motorola, and Apple systems (including G3 and iMac machines). It provides support for the USB on Mac systems. Its current distribution includes the Gnome desktop and the Enlightenment window manager. See **www.linuxppc.com** for more information.

TurboLinux

TurboLinux is distributed by Pacific HiTech, providing English, Chinese, and Japanese versions. It includes several of its own packages, such as TurboPkg for automatically updating applications, the TurboDesk desktop, and the Cluster Web Server. Like Red Hat, it supports RPM packages. It is currently widely distributed in East Asia. Currently, TurboLinux only supports the Intel platform, but a PowerPC version is in development. See **www.turbolinux.com** for more information.

Linux Resources

The tables at the end of this section list various Linux resources available on the Internet. Many of these sites have links to other popular sites. Table 1-1 lists the Web sites for several of the more popular Linux distributions. Also listed here are Linux kernel sites that provide the newest releases of the official Linux kernel. These sites have corresponding FTP sites, listed in Table 1-2, where you can download updates and new releases, as well as third-party software packaged for these distributions. For those not listed, check their Web sites for FTP locations. Linux documentation provided by the Linux Documentation Project (LDP) are listed, along with their Internet sites, in Table 1-3. Currently there are many Linux Web sites that provide news, information, and articles on Linux developments, as well as documentation, software links, and other resources. These are listed in Table 1-4. Desktop and window manager sites are listed in Table 1-5. The Gnome and KDE sites are particularly helpful for documentation, news, and software that you can download for those desktops. Table 1-6 lists some of the Usenet Linux newsgroups you can check out and, in particular, post questions to.

The following tables also list different sites for Linux software. Repositories and archives for Linux software are listed in Table 1-7 along with several specialized sites, such as those for commercial and game software. Table 1-8 lists sites for office suites and databases. Most of these sites provide free personal versions of their software for Linux that you can download directly and install on your Linux system. Sites for Internet server software available for Linux are listed in Table 1-9. Most of these, such as Red Hat and OpenLinux, are already included on distribution CD-ROMs. However, you can obtain news, documentation, and recent releases directly from the server's Web sites. Table 1-10 lists different sites of interest for Linux programming, including Perl, Tcl/Tk, and Linux kernel sites.

When downloading software packages, always check to see if there are versions packaged for your particular distribution. For example, Red Hat will use RPM packages. Many sites will provide packages for the different popular distributions such as Red Hat, Caldera, and Debian. For others, first check the distribution FTP sites for a particular package. For example, a Red Hat package version for ProFTPD is located at the **contrib.redhat.com** FTP site. Another good place for locating RPM packages for particular distributions is **rpmfind.net**.

URL	Internet Site
www.redhat.com	Red Hat Linux
www.calderasystems.com	OpenLinux (Caldera)
www.suse.com	SuSE Linux
www.debian.org	Debian Linux
www.infomagic.com	Infomagic
www.linuxppc.com	LinuxPPC (Mac PowerPC version)
www.turbolinux.com	Turbo Linux (Pacific Hi-Tech)
www.slackware.com	Slackware Linux Project
www.kernel.org	The Linux Kernel

Table 1-1.   *Linux Distributions and Kernel Sites*

URL	Internet Site
ftp.redhat.com	Red Hat Linux
updates.redhat.com	Red Hat Linux updates
contrib.redhat.com	Software packaged for Red Hat Linux
ftp.calderasystems.com	OpenLinux (Caldera)
ftp.suse.com	SuSE Linux
ftp.debian.org	Debian Linux
ftp.linuxppc.com	LinuxPPC (Mac PowerPC version)
ftp.turbolinux.com	Turbo Linux (Pacific Hi-Tech)

Table 1-2.   *Linux Distribution FTP Sites*

Sites	Description
http://metalab.unc.edu/LDP/	LDP Web site
ftp://metalab.unc.edu/pub/linux/docs/LDP/	LDP FTP site
http://hibase.cs.hut.fi/~liw/linux/sag/	System Administrator's Guide home page (also at LDP Web site)
Guides	**Document Format and Web Sites**
Linux Installation and Getting Started Guide	DVI, PostScript, LaTeX, PDF, and HTML
Linux User's Guide	DVI, PostScript, HTML, LaTeX, and PDF
Linux System Administrator's Guide	PostScript, PDF, LaTeX, and HTML
Linux Network Administrator's Guide	DVI, PostScript, PDF, and HTML
Linux Programmer's Guide	DVI, PostScript, PDF, LaTeX, and HTML
The Linux Kernel	HTML, LaTeX, DVI, and PostScript
Linux Kernel Hacker's Guide	**khg.redhat.com/** (link through LDP Web site), DVI, PostScript and HTML
Linux HOWTOs	HTML, PostScript, SGML, and DVI
Linux FAQs	HTML, PostScript, and DVI
Linux Man Pages	Man page format

Table 1-3. *Linux Documentation Project*

URL	Internet Site
metalab.unc.edu/LDP/	Web site for Linux Documentation Project
www.lwn.net	Linux Weekly News
www.linux.com	Linux.com
www.linuxtoday.com	Linux Today

Table 1-4. *Linux Information and News Sites*

URL	Internet Site
www.linuxpower.org	Linux Power
www.linuxfocus.org	Linux Focus
www.linuxworld.org	Linux World
www.linuxmall.org	Linux Mall
www.linuxjournal.org	Linux Journal
www.linuxgazette.org	Linux Gazette
www.linux.org	Linux Online
www.li.org	Linux International Web site
www.uk.linux.org	Linux European Web site
www.kernelnotes.org	Latest news on the Linux kernel
slashdot.org	Linux forum
webwatcher.org	Linux Web site watcher
www.linux.com	Linux news

Table 1-4.   *Linux Information and News Sites* (continued)

URL	Internet Site
www.gnome.org	Gnome Web site
www.kde.org	K Desktop Environment Web site
www.x11.org	X-Windows system Web site, with links
www.fvwm.org	FVWM window manager
www.windowmaker.org	Window Maker window manager
www.enlightenment.org	Enlightenment window manager
www.afterstep.org	AfterStep window manager
www.blackbox.org	Blackbox window manager
www.lesstif.org	Hungry Programmers OSF/Motif

Table 1-5.   *Linux Desktops and Window Managers*

URL	Internet Site
www.themes.org	Desktop and Window manager themes, including KDE and Gnome
www.xfree86.org	Xfree86, GNU version of the X-Windows system provided for Linux

Table 1-5. *Linux Desktops and Window Managers* (continued)

Newsgroup	Description
comp.os.linux.announce	Announcements of Linux developments
comp.os.linux.development.apps	For programmers developing Linux applications
comp.os.linux.development.system	For programmers working on the Linux operating system
comp.os.linux.hardware	Linux hardware specifications
comp.os.linux.admin	System administration questions
comp.os.linux.misc	Special questions and issues
comp.os.linux.setup	Installation problems
comp.os.linux.answers	Answers to command problems
comp.os.linux.help	Questions and answers for particular problems
comp.os.linux.networking	Linux network questions and issues

Table 1-6. *Usenet Newsgroups*

URL	Internet Site
www.uk.linux.org/Commercial.html	Linux Commercial Vendors Index
www.db.erau.edu/linux	Linux archive
http://www.happypenguin.org/	Linux Game Tome
www.linuxgames.org	Linux games
www.linuxquake.com	Quake
http://www.xnet.com/~blatura/linapps.shtml	Linux applications and utilities page
freshmeat.net	New Linux software
www.linuxlinks.com	Linux links
filewatcher.org	Linux FTP site watcher
metalab.unc.edu/LDP/links.html	Linux links
rpmfind.net	RPM package repository
www.gnu.org	GNU archive
www.opensound.com	Open sound system drivers
www.blackdown.org	Web site for Linux Java
www.fokus.gmd.de/linux	Woven goods for Linux
metalab.unc.edu	Mirror site for Linux software and distributions
www.linuxapps.com	Linux applications with search engine

Table 1-7.   *Linux Software Archives, Repositories, and Links*

URL	Software
Databases	
www.oracle.com	Oracle database
www.sybase.com	Sybase database
www.software.ibm.com/data/db2/linux	IBM database
www.informix.com/linux	Informix database
www.cai.com/products/ingres.htm	Ingress II
www.softwareag.com	AdabasD database
www.mysql.com	MySQL database
www.ispras.ru/~kml/gss	The GNU SQL database
www.postgresql.org	The PostgreSQL database
www.fship.com/free.html	Flagship (interface for xBase database files)
koffice.kde.org	Katabase (KOffice desktop database)
gaby.netpedia.net	Gaby (Gnome desktop personal database)
Office Software	
koffice.kde.org	KOffice
linux.corel.com	WordPerfect
www.stardivision.com	Star Office
www.gnome.org/gw.html	Gnome Workshop Project
www.redhat.com	Applixware (commercial)

Table 1-8.   *Database and Office Software*

URL	Server
www.apache.org	Apache Web server
www.proftpd.org	ProFTPD FTP server
www.isc.org	Internet Software Consortium: BIND, INN, and DHCPD
www.sendmail.org	Sendmail mail server
www.squid.org	Squid proxy server
www.samba.org	Samba SMB (Windows network) server
boombox.micro.umn.edu/pub/gopher	Gopher server
www.eudora.com/free/qpop.html	Qpopper POP3 mail server

Table 1-9. *Network Servers*

URL	Internet Site
www.linuxprogramming.org	Linux programming resources
www.scriptics.com	Tk/Tcl Products
java.sun.com	Sun Java Web site
www.perl.com	Perl Web site with Perl software
www.blackdown.org	Sun's Java Development Kit for Linux
developers.gnome.org	Gnome developer's Web site
www.openprojects.nu	Open Projects Network
developer.kde.org	Developer's library for KDE

Table 1-10. *Linux Programming*

The
Complete
Reference

Chapter 2

Installing Red Hat Linux

This chapter describes the installation procedure for the Red Hat. The installation includes the Linux operating system, a great many Linux applications, and a complete set of Internet servers. Different Linux distributions usually have their own installation programs. The Red Hat installation program is designed to be efficient and brief while installing as many features as possible. Certain features, such as Web server support, would ordinarily require specialized and often complex configuration operations. Red Hat automatically installs and configures many of these features.

Red Hat provides a very detailed installation manual both on the CD-ROM provided with this book and at its Web site. The manual consists of Web pages that you can view using any browser. They include detailed figures and step-by-step descriptions. It is advisable for you to check this manual before you install. This chapter presents all the steps in the installation process but is not as detailed as the Red Hat manual. On the CD-ROM, the Red Hat Installation manual is located at:

```
doc/rhmanual/manual/index.htm
```

On the Red Hat Web site at **www.redhat.com**, click Support and choose the Installation Guides, Manuals, & FAQs entry. This presents a menu on which the first entry is the Red Hat Linux 6.0 Installation Guide.

Installing Linux involves several steps. First, you need to determine whether your computer meets the basic hardware requirements. These days, most Intel-based PC computers do. If you want to have your Linux system share a hard drive with another operating system, you may need to repartition your hard disk. There are several different options for partitioning your hard drive, depending on whether or not it already contains data you need to preserve.

Red Hat supports several methods for installing Linux. You can install from a Local source such as CD-ROM or a hard disk, or from a network or Internet source. For a network and Internet source, Red Hat supports NFS, FTP, and HTTP installations. With FTP you can install from an FTP site, and with HTTP you can install from a Web site. NFS lets you install over a local network. For a Local source, you can install from CD-ROM or a hard disk. In addition you can start the installation process by booting from your CD-ROM, from a DOS system, or from boot disks that can the use the CD-ROM or hard disk repository. Red Hat documentation covers each of these methods in detail. This chapter deals with the installation using the CD-ROM provided by this book and a boot disk created from a boot image on the CD-ROM. This is the most common approach.

Once the installation program begins, you simply follow the instructions, screen by screen. Most of the time you will only need to make simple selections or provide yes and no answers. The installation program progresses through several phases. First, you create Linux partitions on your hard drive, and then you install the software packages. After that you can configure your network connection, and then your X Window System for graphical user interface support. Both X-Windows and network configurations can be performed independently at a later time.

Once your system is installed, you are ready to start it and log in. You will be logging into a simple command line interface. From the command line, you can then invoke X-Windows, which will provide you with a full graphical user interface.

You have the option of installing just the operating system, the system with a standard set of applications, or all the software available on the CD-ROM. If you choose a standard installation, you can add the uninstalled software packages later. Chapter 3 and Chapter 24 describe how you can use the GnomeRPM utility or the Red Hat Package Manager to install, or even uninstall, the software packages.

Hardware, Software, Information Requirements

Before installing Linux, you need to be sure that your computer meets certain minimum hardware requirements. You will also need to have certain specific information ready concerning your monitor, video card, mouse, and CD-ROM drive. All the requirements are presented in detail in the following sections. Be sure to read them carefully before you begin installation. During the installation program, you will need to provide responses based on the configuration of your computer.

Hardware Requirements

Listed here are the minimum hardware requirements for installing a Linux system:

- A 32-bit Intel-based personal computer. An Intel or compatible 80386, 80486, or Pentium microprocessor is required.

- A 3 ½-inch floppy disk drive.

- At least 32MB RAM, though 64MB are recommended.

- At least 1GB free hard disk space; 1 to 2GB are recommended. You will need at least 1.2GB to load and make use of all the software packages on your CD-ROM. The Standard installation of basic software packages takes 500MB, plus 32 to 64MB for swap space. If you have less than 500MB, you can elect to perform a minimum install, installing only the Linux kernel without most of the applications. You could later install the applications you want one at a time.

- A 3 ½-inch, DOS-formatted, high-density (HD) floppy disk drive, to be used to create a install disk.

- A CD-ROM drive.

- Two empty DOS-formatted, 3 ½-inch, high-density (HD) floppy disks.

If you plan to use the X-Windows graphical user interface, you will also need:

- A video graphics card
- A mouse or other pointing device

Software Requirements

There are only a few software requirements. If you intend to install using the floppy disks, you need an operating system from which you can create them. The DOS operating system is required to allow you to prepare your installation disks. Using a DOS system, you can access the CD-ROM and issue DOS-like commands to create your installation disks. Any type of DOS will do, and you can even use the same commands on OS/2. However, you do not need DOS to run Linux. Linux is a separate operating system in its own right.

If you want to have Linux share your hard disk with another operating system, Windows for example, you will need certain utilities to prepare the hard disk for sharing. For Windows, you need either the **defrag** and **fips** utilities or disk management software like Partition Magic 4.0. The **fips** utility is provided on your CD-ROM. It essentially frees up space by reducing the size of your current extended or primary partition. Defrag and **fdisk** are standard DOS utilities, usually located in your **dos** directory. Defrag is used with **fips** to defragment your hard disk before **fips** partitions it. This collects all files currently on the partition into one area, leaving all the free space grouped in one large chunk. If you are installing on a new empty hard drive and you want to use part of it for Windows, you can use **fdisk** to set up your Windows partitions. All these tasks can also be carried out using Partition Magic 4.0, a commercial product that now supports Linux partitions.

Information Requirements

Part of adapting a powerful operating system like Linux to the PC entails making the most efficient use of the computer hardware at hand. To do so, Linux requires specific information about the computer components that it is dealing with. For example, special Linux configuration files are tailored to work with special makes and models of video cards and monitors. Before installing Linux, you will need to have such information on hand. The information is usually available in the manual that came with your hardware peripherals or computer.

CD-ROM, Hard Disk, and Mouse Information

- For some older SCSI CD-ROM drives, you will need the manufacturer's name and model.

- Decide how much of your hard drive (in megabytes) you want to dedicate to your Linux system. If you are sharing with Windows, decide how much you want for Windows and how much for Linux.

- Decide how much space you want for your swap partition. Your swap partition must be between 16MB and 64MB, with 32MB appropriate for most systems. It is used by Linux as an extension of your computer's RAM.

- Find the make and model of the mouse you are using. Linux supports both serial and bus mice. Most mice are supported, including Microsoft, Logitech, and Mouse Systems.

- Know what time zone you are in and what your hardware clock is set to. This can be either Greenwich Mean Time (GMT) or your local time zone.

- Know which serial port your mouse is using: COM1, COM2, or none if you use the PS/2 mouse port.

Video and Monitor Information

Though most monitors and video cards are automatically configured during installation, you will still need to provide the manufacturer make and model. Find out the manufacturer for your monitor and its model, such as Iiyama VisionMaster 450, or NEC E500. Do the same for your video card, for example Matrox Millennium G200, or ATI XPERT@Play 98 (you can find a complete list of supported cards at **www.xfree86.org**). For some very recent ones and some older uncommon ones you may need to provide certain hardware specifications. It is advisable to have this information on hand if possible, just in case. At the end of the installation process you will be presented with lists of video cards and monitors from which to choose your own. These lists are very extensive. However, in case your card or monitor is not on the list, you will need to provide certain hardware information about them. If the configuration should fail, you can always do it later using an X Window System configuration utility such as Xconfigurator and XF86Setup. Of particular importance is the monitor information, including the vertical and horizontal refresh rates.

Video Card Information:

- What is the make and model of your video card?
- What chipset does your video card use?
- How much memory is on your video card?

Monitor Information:

- What is the manufacturer and model of your monitor? Linux supports an extensive list of monitors, covering almost all current ones. You will only have to select yours from the list. If, however, your monitor is not on this list , you will need to provide the following information. Be sure it is correct. Should you enter a horizontal or vertical refresh rate that is too high, you can seriously damage your monitor. You can choose a generic profile, or you can enter information for a custom profile. To do that, you will need the following information:
  - The horizontal refresh rate in Hz
  - The vertical refresh rate in Hz

Network Configuration Information

Except for deciding your hostname, you do not have to configure your network during installation. You can put configuration off to a later time and use network configuration utilities like Linuxconf or netcfg to perform network configuration. However, if the information is readily available, the installation procedure will automatically configure your network, placing needed entries in the appropriate configuration files. If you are on a network, you will have to obtain most of this information from your network administrator. If you are setting up a network yourself, you will have to determine each piece of information. If you are using a dial-up Internet service provider, you configure your network access using a PPP dial-up utility like kppp or Linuxconf after you have installed the system. The installation program will prompt you to enter in these values:

■ Decide on a name for your computer (this is called a *hostname*). Your computer will be identified by this name on the Internet. Do not use "localhost"; that name is reserved for special use by your system.

■ Your domain name.

■ The IP (Internet Protocol) address assigned to your machine. Every host on the Internet is assigned an IP address. This address is a set of four numbers, separated by periods, which uniquely identifies a single location on the Internet, allowing information from other locations to reach that computer.

■ Your network IP address. This address is usually the same as the IP address, but with an added 0.

■ The netmask. This is usually 255.255.255.0 for class C IP addresses. If, however, you are part of a large network, check with your network administrator.

■ The broadcast address for your network. Usually, your broadcast address is the same as your IP address with the number 255 added at the end.

■ If you have a gateway, you will need the gateway (router) IP address for your network.

■ The IP address of any name servers that your network uses.

■ NIS domain and IP address if your network uses an NIS server.

Upgrade Information for Currently Installed Linux Systems

If you already have installed another version of Linux such as OpenLinux or Red Hat, you may have personalized your system with different settings that you would like to keep. If you choose the Upgrade option, rather than Install, during the installation process, then these settings will be kept. However, upgrade only works for Red Hat kernel 2.0 and above (Red Hat 5.0 and up). For earlier versions, you will have to save your settings first. You may want to back up these settings anyway as a precaution.

These settings are held in configuration files that you can save to a floppy disk and then use on your new system, in effect, retaining your original configuration (if you use **mcopy** be sure to use the **-t** option). There also may be directories and files of data you may want to preserve such as Web pages used for a Web site. You may also want to save copies of software packages you have downloaded. For these and for large directories it is best to use the following **tar** operation.

```
tar cvMf /dev/fd0  directory-or-package
```

Make copies of the following configuration files and any other files you want to restore. You only need to copy the ones you want to restore.

Files	Description
/etc/XF86Config	X-Windows configuration file
/etc/lilo.conf	Boot manager configuration file
/etc/hosts	IP addresses of connected systems
/etc/resolv.conf	Domain name server addresses
/etc/fstab	File systems mounted on your system
/etc/passwd	Names and passwords of all users on your system
/home/user	Any home directories of users with their files on your system, where *user* is the user name. (For a large number of files use **tar cfM/dev/fd0/home/user**)
.netscape	Each **home** directory has its own **.netscape** subdirectory with Netscape configuration files such as your bookmark entries
Web site pages and FTP files	You may want to save any pages used for a Web site or files on an FTP site you are running. These are located at **/home/httpd/** and **/home/ftpd**

Once you have installed your system, you can mount the floppy disk and copy the saved files from the floppy to your system, overwriting those initially set up. If you use the **/etc/XF86Config** file from your previous system, you will not have to run XF86Setup to set up X-Windows. The **/etc/XF86Config** file includes all the X-Windows setup information.

If you want to restore the **/etc/lilo.conf** file from your previous system, you will also have to install it using the following command.

```
# lilo /etc/lilo.conf
```

To restore archives that you saved on multiple disks using the **tar** operation, place the first disk in the floppy drive and use the following command.

```
tar xvMf   /dev/fd0
```

Opening Disk Space for Linux Partitions for Shared Hard Disks

If you are using an entire hard drive for your Linux system or if you are upgrading a currently installed Linux system and want to use the same partitions, you can skip this section and go on to installing Linux. If, however, your Linux system is going to share a hard drive with your Windows or DOS system, you will need to organize your hard drive so that part of it is used for DOS and the remaining part is free for Linux installation. How you go about this process depends on the current state of your hard disk. If you have a new hard disk and you are going to install both Windows and Linux on it, you only need to be sure to install Windows on only part of the hard drive, leaving the rest free for Linux. This means specifying a size smaller than the entire hard disk for your Windows partition that you set up during the Windows install procedure. You could also use fdisk to manually create partitions for Windows that will take up only a part of the hard disk. However, if you want to install Linux on a hard disk that already have Windows installed on the entire hard disk, you need to resize your primary or extended partition, leaving part of the disk free for Linux. The objective in each situation is to free up space for Linux. When you install Linux, you will then partition and format that free space for use by Linux.

A hard disk is organized into partitions. The partitions are further formatted to the specifications of a given operating system. When you installed Windows, you first needed to create a primary partition for it on your hard disk. If you have only one disk on your hard drive, then you only have a primary partition. To add more partitions, you created an extended partition and then, within that, logical partitions. For example, if you have C, D, and E disks on your hard drive, your C disk is your primary partition and the D and E disks are logical partitions set up within in your extended partition. You then used the DOS **format** operation to format each partition into a Windows disk, each identified by a letter. For example, you may have divided your disk into two partitions, one formatted as the C disk and the other as the D disk. Alternatively, you may have divided your hard disk into just one partition and formatted it as the C disk. In order to share your hard drive with Linux, you will need to free up some space by either reducing their size or deleting some of those partitions.

First, decide how much space you will need for your Linux system. You will probably need a minimum of 1GB, though more is recommended. As stated earlier, the basic set of Linux software packages takes up 500MB, whereas the entire set of software packages, including all their source code file, takes 1.2GB. In addition, you will need space for a Linux swap partition used to implement virtual memory. This takes between 16 and 32MB.

Once you have determined the space you need for your Linux system, you can then set about freeing up that space on your hard drive. To see what options are best for you, you should first determine what your partitions are and their sizes. You can do this with the fdisk utility. To start this utility, type **fdisk** at the DOS prompt, and press ENTER.

```
C:\> fdisk
```

This brings up the menu of fdisk options.

1. Choose option 4 to display a list of all your current partitions and the size of each.

2. Press ESC to leave the fdisk utility.

You can use the DOS defrag and Linux fips utilities to reduce the size of the partitions, creating free space from unused space on your hard drive.

1. You should first make a backup of your important data for safety's sake.

2. First, check if you already have enough unused space on your hard drive that can be used for Linux.

3. If you do not, you will have to delete some files. When Windows creates and saves files, it places them in different sectors on your hard disk. Your files are spread out across your hard disk with a lot of empty space in between. This has the effect of fragmenting the remaining unused space into smaller sections, separated by files. The defrag utility performs a defragmentation process that moves all the files into adjoining space on the hard disk, thereby leaving all the unused space as one large continuous segment.

Once you have defragmented your disk, you can use the fips utility to create free space using part or all of the unused space. The fips utility is a version of fdisk designed to detect continuous unused space and remove it from its current Windows partition, opening unpartitioned free space that can then be used by Linux. All your Windows partitions and drives remain intact with all their data and programs. They are just smaller.

To run the defrag utility, enter the command **defrag**. This is a DOS command usually found in the **dos** or **windows** directory. You can also run it from Windows.

```
C:\>  windows\defrag
```

The defrag utility will display a screen with colored blocks representing the different sectors on your hard disk. It will carry out an optimization of your hard disk, moving all your used sectors, your data and programs, together on the hard disk. This may take a few minutes. When it is complete, you will see the used sectors arranged together on the screen. You can then exit the defrag utility.

Now you are ready to run the fips utility to actually free up space. The fips utitlity is located on your RedHat Linux CD-ROM, also in the directory named **dosutils**. Change to your CD-ROM drive and run the fips utility. In the following example, the CD-ROM drive is drive E.

```
C:\> e:
E:\> \dosutils\fips
```

The fips utility will display a screen showing the amount of free space. Use your arrow keys to make the space smaller if you do not need all your free space for Linux. You should leave some free space for your Windows programs. Then press ENTER to free the space.

Creating the Red Hat Boot Disks

You can install Red Hat using an install disk whose image is located on the Red Hat CD-ROM. You create the install disk using the MSDOS program **rawrite** and a install disk image. The install disk has to be created on a computer that runs DOS. There are install disk images for local installation (**boot.img**), installing from an network source like a Web site (**netimage.img**), and installing with PCMCIA support (**pcmcia.img**). Begin by first starting your computer and entering **DOS**. Then perform the following steps.

Insert the Red Hat CD-ROM into your CD-ROM drive. At your DOS prompt, change to your CD-ROM drive, using whatever the letter for that drive may be. For example, if your CD-ROM drive is the E drive, just type **e:** and press ENTER. Once you have changed to the CD-ROM drive, you then need to change to the \images directory. The Install disk images are there, **boot.img**, **pcmia.img**, and **netboot.img**. The **rawrite** command is in the **dosutils** directory, \dosutils\rawrite.

To create the install disk, insert a blank floppy disk into your floppy drive. Now start the **rawrite** command. The **rawrite** command will actually write the disk image to your floppy disk. The **rawrite** command will first prompt you for the name of the disk image file you want to copy. Enter the full name of the install image file (in this example **boot.img**). It will then ask you to enter the letter of the floppy drive where you put your floppy disk. On many systems this will be the A drive.

```
E:\> cd images
E:\col\launch\floppy > e:\dosutils\rawrite
Enter source file name: boot.img
Enter destination drive (A or B) and press ENTER: a
```

Press ENTER to confirm that you have a blank floppy disk in the drive. The `rawrite` command will then copy the image file to your floppy disk, creating your install disk. When it finishes, remove your disk from the floppy drive. This is the disk that the installation procedure described later refers to as the Install diskette. If you need to create a network boot disk, use **netimage.img** instead. For PCMCIA support use **pcmcia.img**.

Installing Linux

Installing Linux involves several processes, beginning with creating Linux partitions, then loading the Linux software, configuring your X-Windows interface, installing the Linux Loader (LILO) that will boot your system, and creating new user accounts. The installation program is a screen-based program that takes you through all these processes, step by step, as one continuous procedure. Use TAB, the arrow keys, SPACEBAR, and ENTER to make selections. You can always move back to the previous screen by pressing the ESC key. There is very little you have to do other than make selections and choose options. Some screens, such as the monitor screen, will provide a list of options from which you make a selection. Others will just ask you to choose OK or Cancel, buttons that you can select using the TAB key and pressing ENTER. In a few cases you will be asked for information you should already have if you followed the steps earlier in this chapter. You are now ready to begin installation. The steps for each part of the procedure are delineated in the following sections. It should take you no more than an hour.

Booting the Computer and Creating Linux Partitions

If you followed the instructions in the first part of the chapter, you have freed up space on your hard drive and created your install and module disks, and you are now ready to create your Linux partitions. To do this, you will need to boot your computer using the install disk that you made earlier. When you start your computer, the installation program will begin, and through that you can access the Linux fdisk utility with which you will create your Linux partitions.

You can start the installation using one of several methods. If your computer can boot from the CD-ROM, you can start the installation directly from the CD-ROM. Just place the Red Hat CD-ROM in the CD-ROM drive before you start your computer. If you have a DOS system installed on your hard drive, you can start up DOS and then use the **autoboot.bat** command in the **dosutils** directory to start the installation, as shown here. You have to execute this command from a DOS system, not the Windows DOS window. Only DOS can be running for this command to work.

```
e:\dosutils\autoboot.bat
```

If neither of these options are feasible for you, you can use the install floppy disk (see the previous section on creating a boot disk). This is perhaps the most fail-safe method of installing Linux. Insert the Linux install disk into your floppy drive and reboot your computer. It is best to perform a cold boot, turning off the computer completely and then turning it on again with the install disk in the floppy drive.

The installation program will start, presenting you with an Introduction screen. After a moment, the following prompt will appear at the bottom of your screen:

```
boot:
```

1. Press ENTER. (If necessary, you can enter boot parameters as described in the Red Hat manual). Configuration information will fill your screen as the installation program attempts to detect your hardware components automatically.

2. The first screen displays a list of languages. Use the arrow keys to move to the language entry you want. Then press the TAB key to select the OK button, and press ENTER.

3. A screen is displayed that shows a list of keyboards. Choose your keyboard from the list and press ENTER.

4. Your system is then probed to see if you require PCMCIA support. If so, you can then put your PCMCIA support disk in your floppy drive.

5. A screen then is displayed that lets you choose your installation method. You can install from your Local CD-ROM or a hard disk. For the CD-ROM provided with this book, select Local CD-ROM. (With a netboot disk you can also choose NFS over a network, FTP from an FTP site, or HTML from a Web site.)

6. You are then prompted to insert your Red Hat CD-ROM. Your system then detects the type of CD-ROM you have. If it cannot do so, it will ask you to select yours from a list. If you have an IDE CD-ROM and the system fails to detect it, it may be because it is not connected on the default HDC device interface. You will have to restart the installation, providing the CD-ROM device name at the boot prompt.

```
Boot: linux hdX=cdrom
```

Replace the X with one of the following letters, depending on the interface the unit is connected to, and whether it is configured as master or slave: a—First IDE controller master, b—First IDE controller slave, c—Second IDE controller master, d—Second IDE controller slave.

As an alternative to the CD-ROM installation, you can copy the entire cdrom to a Window partition (one large enough), and then install using that partition instead of the CD-ROM. You need to know the device name of the partition and the directory to copied the CD-ROM files to. When asked to choose the installation method, you can select hard disk. You then have to specify the partition name and the directory.

7. Once your CD-ROM is detected, the next screen asks whether you want to Install or Upgrade. Use Install for a new Linux system and Upgrade to upgrade an existing Red Hat system (kernel 2.0 or later, only).

8. The next screen asks you to choose an Installation Class. You can choose from Workstation, Server, or Custom. Be sure to choose Custom, particularly if you are using a shared disk or upgrading Linux. Workstation erases all Linux partitions, and Server erases all partitions, including DOS and Windows.

9. You are then asked if you have any SCSI adapters. If you say yes, then a list of adapters is presented you can choose from.

10. You are now ready to set up Linux partitions and format them. The next screen asks you to choose a disk partitioning utility. You can choose either Disk Druid or Linux fdisk. Use the TAB key to move to the button you want.

Disk Druid is a Red Hat utility for creating Linux partitions. The fdisk performs the same function but uses a command line interface. Both are described here. If you use **fdisk**, you still have to use Disk Druid to specify a installation directory.

Disk Druid

When you select Disk Druid, you are presented with a screen showing two sections and buttons for operations at the bottom, as shown in Figure 2-1. The top section is the Current Disk Partitions section. Each line here represents a disk partition. All the disk partitions currently set up on your hard disk are shown. If you have only DOS partitions set up, only those partitions are shown. As you create Linux partitions, they will also be shown. Each line in this section has five different fields:

- Mount point
- Partition's device name (like hda1 or hda3)
- Minimum size requested when it was created
- Actual space allocated
- Partition type

The mount point indicates where the partition will be mounted when Red Hat Linux is installed and running.

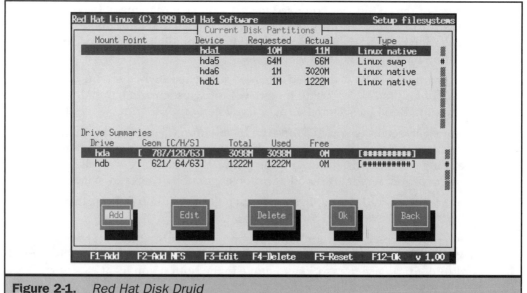

Figure 2-1.   *Red Hat Disk Druid*

The lower section is the Drive Summaries section that shows the hard disks on your system. If you have only one hard disk, there will be only one entry. The Used field shows how much space has been allocated for defined partitions, and the Free field shows how much is free.

Use the buttons at the bottom to add and delete partitions, and change partition attributes. Once you have created your partitions, you can use the OK button to effect them.

> **Caution**   *Be careful of the Delete button. If you have DOS partitions, you do not want to accidentally delete them.*

Use the Back button to quit Disk Druid without effecting any changes.

To create a Linux partition:

1. Select the Add button (use Tab to move to it and then press ENTER). This opens an Edit Disk Partition window as shown in the following illustration of the Edit Disk Partition window, with boxes for entering the mount point, the size of the partition in megabytes, the partition type, and the hard drive it is to be created on. You can also have the partition size grow to fill the remainder of the free space on the drive.

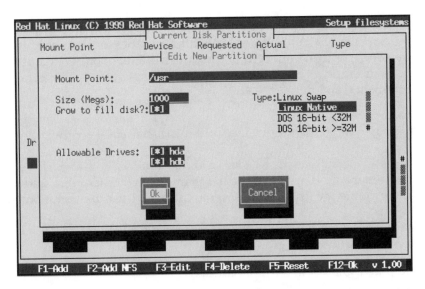

2. You will have to first create a Linux swap partition of 32 or 64MB. Select the Linux Swap type. Use the arrow keys to move to that entry in the Type list. The swap partition has no mount point. When finished, tab to the OK button and press the SPACEBAR.

3. For the main Linux partition be sure to select the Linux Native type. The mount point is the root directory represented with just a slash (not **/usr** as shown in the above illustration). Set the size and select the hard drive. When finished, tab to the OK button and press the SPACEBAR.

4. Then, on the Disk Druid screen, tab to the OK button and press the SPACEBAR.

Using fdisk

Instead of Disk Druid you can use fdisk to set up your partitions (you also use fdisk for the LISA installation of OpenLinux). The initial screen displays a list of hard disks on your system.

1. Choose the hard disk where you want the partition. If you have more than one, use the arrow keys to move to the one you want.

2. Press ENTER to continue. You are then asked if you want to change your partition table.

3. Press Y to select Yes.

You are now in the Linux fdisk program. You will be taking the free space that you created earlier and partitioning and formatting it for your Linux operating system. Or, if you are using your entire hard disk for Linux, you will be creating all the partitions for that hard disk.

You need to create at least two Linux partitions: The main partition and the swap partition. The partitions have different types that you need to specify. Linux fdisk is a line-oriented program. It has a set of one-character commands that you simply press. Then you may be prompted to type in certain information and press ENTER.

> **Tip** *If you run into trouble during the fdisk procedure, you can press **q** at any time, and you will return to the previous screen without any changes having been made.*

No changes are actually made to your hard disk until you press **w**. This would be your very last command. It makes the actual changes to your hard disk and then quits fdisk, returning you to the installation program. Table 2-1 lists the commonly used fdisk commands.

Perform the following steps to create your Linux partitions. You will first be creating the swap partition.

1. Press **p** to display your current partitions.

2. Press **n** to define a new partition. You will be asked if it is a primary partition.

   a) Press **p** to indicate that it is a primary partition.

   b) Enter the partition number for the partition you are creating.

   c) Enter the beginning cylinder for the partition. This is the first number in parentheses at the end of the prompt.

   d) You are then prompted to enter the last cylinder number or size of the partition. This determines the size of the partition. Alternatively, you can enter the size in megabytes by entering a **+** before the number and an **M** after it; **+32M** specifies a partition of 32MB. In this case, you do not need to determine the last cylinder number.

   e) Enter a size for the swap partition, between 16MB and 32MB.

3. Press **t** to indicate that you want to set the type for the Linux partition. Enter the partition number, and then at the Hex code prompt enter **82**. This is the type for the Linux swap partition.

4. Press **n** to define another new partition and **p** to mark it as a primary partition.

   a) Enter the partition number for the partition you are creating.

   b) Enter the beginning cylinder for the partition; this is the first number in parentheses at the end of the prompt.

   c) You are then prompted to enter the last cylinder number. You can either enter the last cylinder you want for this partition or enter a size.

   d) You can enter the size as **+1000M** for 1GB.

■ Remember that a standard install uses at least 1GB. Anywhere from 1000MB to 2000MB would be appropriate, though; if you have the space, you can make it larger.

■ Bear in mind that the size cannot exceed your free space. Also, recall that the full package with all source code files will take 1.4GB.

e) The default type for a Linux partition is 83. You will not have to set it. If your Linux system will use several hard disks, then you need to create a partition on each of them.

You can create other Linux partitions for different components of your systems. For example, you could create a separate partition to hold software that you could mount on the **/usr** directory, or a partition to hold user directories and their files that you could mount on the **/home** directory.

Press **w** to write out the changes to the hard disk, and then ENTER to continue.

The following is a sample run of the fdisk program, showing you the interface and the commands you will need to use to create your partitions. When specifying the size of main Linux partitions, you can specify a cylinder number as shown in this example, or just the size you want with a preceding **+**, such as **+500** for a 500MB partition. Notice that when you are prompted to enter the first cylinder, the first available cylinder is listed in the prompt. You can use that (205 and then 238 in this example).

```
Command (m for help): p

Disk /dev/hda: 32 heads, 63 sectors, 827 cylinders
Units = cylinders of 2016 * 512 bytes

   Device Boot   Begin    Start    End    Blocks   Id  System
/dev/hda1            1        1    204    205600+   6  DOS 16-bit>=32M
/dev/hda4          537      537    826    292320    5  Extended
/dev/hda6          543      543    826    286240+   6  DOS 16-bit>=32M

Command (m for help): n
Command action
   l   logical (5 or over)
   p   primary partition (1-4)
p
Partition number (1-4): 2
First cylinder (205-827): 205
Last cylinder or +size or +sizeM or +sizeK ([205]-536): +32

Command (m for help): n
Command action
   l   logical (5 or over)
```

```
    p    primary partition (1-4)
p
Partition number (1-4): 3
First cylinder (238-827): 238
Last cylinder or +size or +sizeM or +sizeK ([238]-536): 536


Command (m for help): p


Disk /dev/hda: 32 heads, 63 sectors, 827 cylinders
Units = cylinders of 2016 * 512 bytes

    Device Boot    Begin    Start     End    Blocks   Id  System
/dev/hda1              1        1     204   205600+    6  DOS 16-bit     >=32M
/dev/hda2            205      205     237    33264    83  Linux native
/dev/hda3            238      238     536   301392    83  Linux native
/dev/hda4            537      537     826   292320     5  Extended
/dev/hda6            543      543     826   286240+    6  DOS 16-bit     >=32M

Command (m for help): t
Partition number (1-6): 2
Hex code (type L to list codes): 82
Changed system type of partition 2 to 82 (Linux swap)

Command (m for help): a
Partition number (1-6): 3

Command (m for help): p


Disk /dev/hda: 32 heads, 63 sectors, 827 cylinders
Units = cylinders of 2016 * 512 bytes

Device Boot        Begin    Start     End    Blocks   Id  System
/dev/hda1              1        1     204   205600+    6  DOS 16-bit     >=32M
/dev/hda2            205      205     237    33264    82  Linux swap
/dev/hda3    *       238      238     536   301392    83  Linux native
/dev/hda4            537      537     826   292320     5  Extended
/dev/hda6            543      543     826   286240+    6  DOS 16-bit     >=32M

Command (m for help): w
The partition table has been altered!
Calling ioctl() to re-read partition table
(reboot to insure the partition table has been updated)
Syncing disks.
```

A screen warns you that your partition table has been changed. Press ENTER, and you then return to the screen displaying your system's hard disks. The entry "1. No further disk changes" at the top will be highlighted. At this point you can press ENTER to continue, unless you have other hard disks on your system that you also want to partition.

Note that if you already have old Linux partitions that you no longer want, you can use Linux **fdisk** to delete them. Remember, only a Linux fdisk can safely delete a Linux partition First, press **p** to display the partitions so you can determine the partition number of the Linux partition you want to remove. Then enter **d**, and you will be prompted for the partition number to delete.

*Be very careful to give the correct number. If you accidentally enter the one for your DOS partition, you will be instructing **fdisk** to delete it, erasing everything on it. If this should happen, you can always press **q** to abandon the fdisk sessions, instead of **w**, so that no changes will be made and nothing will be deleted. Then, at the hard disk selection screen, you can select your hard disk again and start over.*

When you are finished with **fdisk**, the Disk Druid is invoked and displays your partitions. You have to then use Disk Druid to enter in the mount point for your Linux Native partitions. Use the arrow keys to select the Linux partition, and then tab to the Edit button. This opens a Edit Disk Partition window for that Linux partition. Enter a mount point in the Mount Point box, such as / for the root directory.

Command	Action
a	Toggle a bootable flag
l	List known partition types
m	List commands
n	Add a new partition
p	Print the partition table
q	Quit without saving changes
t	Change a partition's system ID
w	Write table to disk and exit

Table 2-1. *A List of Commonly Used fdisk Commands*

INTRODUCTION

Installing Packages

The next screen then formats your Swap space, and the next screen formats your Linux Native partitions.

A Components to Install window then displays the software components you want installed on your system. You can choose from servers, development packages, desktops like Gnome and KDE, X Window System, file managers, and so on. You can find a complete listing of Red Hat packages in Appendix D of the Red Hat manual.

1. To install all packages, select the Everything entry at the bottom of the list.

2. If you want to further refine your installation by selecting individual packages, you can select the Select Individual Packages entry. This will then display a list of package groups, which you can then expand to individual packages by selecting and pressing ENTER. F1 displays information about a particular package.

3. Tab to the OK button when you are finished.

Once you have selected your packages, your Linux partitions are formatted and the packages are installed. A progress bar shows the progress.

After your packages are installed, the next screen displays a list of mice. Choose the one that describes your type of mouse.

Networking

The next screen lets you configure your network interface. Use this if you are connected to a network, such as with an Ethernet card. If you use a dial-up ISP, skip this section.

■ If you select Yes, then the next screen asks you to select a boot protocol.

■ You can choose from static IP addressing, DHCP, or BOOTP. If you choose static IP, then the next screen shows boxes where you can enter your IP address, Netmask, Gateway, and Primary name server. The next screen shows boxes for the Domain name, hostname, secondary and tertiary name servers.

Finishing Installation

To complete your installation, you'll address these final issues:

1. The next screen then asks you to select a time zone.

2. You select the services you want to start whenever your system boots up. Here, will be listed Internet servers like Web and FTP servers, as well as daemons like kerneld, which manages your kernel modules. To find out what a service does, move to it with the arrow keys and press F1.

3. The next several screens let you configure your printer.

    a) First select a printer connect (local for one connected to your PC).

b) The next screen displays the default queue and spool directory for the printer. Usually, you only have to accept these settings, tab to OK, and press ENTER.

c) The next screen displays the default device name. Again accept the default.

d) The Configure Printer screen then lists the types of printers that Linux currently supports. Move through the list to find yours.

e) The following screen lets you set the page size and resolution.

f) The final screen displays all the printer information, asking you to verify it.

4. At the Root Password screen, you enter the password for the root user account. There are two boxes. Repeat your password in the second box. Be sure not to forget it. You need it to log in. The password must be at least six characters long. You can make it simple at this point, as you can always change it later.

5. The next screen lets you set authentication information, enabling NIS (if you have it on your network), shadow passwords, and MD5 password encoding.

6. You are then asked to create a boot disk. This is always advisable, as you can use the boot disk to start Linux if, for some reason, it cannot boot from the hard disk. For example, if you have a shared disk with Windows on it and use LILO to boot one or the other, then if you were to install a new version of Windows, you would lose the LILO boot record and be unable to use it to start Linux. In this case, you could use the boot disk to start Linux, log in as the root user, and execute the **lilo** command to reinstall the LILO boot record.

7. In the next series of screens, you configure and install LILO. Use this for a shared disk where you have Windows and Linux on the same disk, or for a computer with several hard drives where Windows may be on one and Linux, on another. LILO will prompt you to enter in the system you want to start (usually, DOS for Windows and Linux for Linux).

■ The first screen asks you where you want to install LILO. You are given the choice of the Master Boot Record or the first sector on the boot partition. Always choose the Master Boot Record, unless you are already have a boot loader installed on it as in the case of OS/2 boot manager.

■ The next screen shows your bootable partitions. If you have a Windows partition, it will be shown with a partition type of DOS. Linux partitions will have a partition type of Linux. Both the DOS partition and Linux partition will already have labels assigned to them. The entry with an asterisk in the Default column is the default system. This is the system automatically started by LILO if no other is specified at the boot prompt when your computer starts up. To change the default, move to the partition you want to make the default and press F2. If you want to edit an entry, say to change its label or add any startup parameters, select it and tab to the Edit button. Once you are finished making any changes, tab to the OK button and press ENTER.

X Window System Configuration

The installation program then runs Xconfigurator to install and configure the
X Window System on your Linux system. At this point, installation of Red Hat Linux
is complete. Should Xconfigurator hang in its installation, you can just restart your
computer and boot into Linux, with the command line interface. You can then log
in as root and install and configure the X Window System using one of several
configuration utilities such as XF86Setup, Xconfigurator, or XF86config.

Xconfigurator first probes your system in an attempt to determine what type of
video card you have. Failing that, Xconfigurator will present a list of video cards.

1. Select your video card from the list and press ENTER.

2. If your video card does not appear on the list, XFree86 may not support it.
   However, if you have technical knowledge about your card, you may choose
   Unlisted Card and attempt to configure it by matching your card's video
   chipset with one of the available X servers.

   Once you have selected your video card, the installation program installs the
   appropriate XFree86 server, and Xconfigurator presents a list of monitors,
   shown in the next illustration.

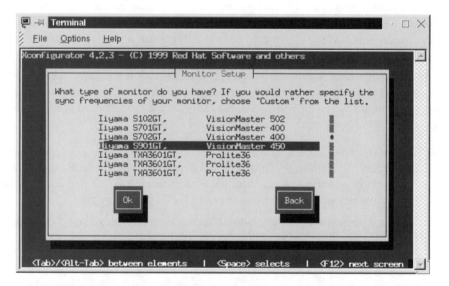

3. If your monitor appears on the list, select it and press ENTER.

4. If it is not on the list, select Custom. This displays a screen where you enter the
   horizontal sync range and vertical sync range of your monitor (these values are
   generally available in the documentation which accompanies your monitor, or
   from your monitor's vendor or manufacturer).

- Be very careful to enter the correct horizontal and vertical frequencies. If you enter values too high, it is possible you may overclock your monitor and damage or destroy it.

- Do not select a monitor *similar* to your monitor unless you are certain that the monitor you are selecting does not exceed the capabilities of your monitor.

The next screen prompts you for the amount of video memory installed on your video card. If you are not sure, please consult the documentation accompanying your video card. It will not damage your video card to choose more memory than is available, but the XFree86 server may not start correctly if you do.

If the video card you selected has a video clock chip, Xconfigurator will presents a list of clock chips. The recommended choice is No Clockchip Setting, since XFree86 can automatically detect the proper clock chip.

In the next screen, Xconfigurator prompts you to select the video modes you wish to use. These are screen resolutions you may want to use. You can select one or more moving to it and pressing the SPACEBAR. Xconfigurator will then start the X Window System and display a dialog asking if you can see it.

Xconfigurator then generates an X Window System configuration file called **/etc/X11/XF86Config**. It is this file that the X Window System uses to start up.

The last screen asks you to choose whether you want the X Window System to start up automatically whenever you start Linux.

- If you choose this entry, then when you start, the Gnome Desktop Manager (GDM) will start and display a login screen where you can enter the user name and password.

  1. A Sessions menu in the Options menu lets you choose whether to start KDE, Gnome, or the Another Level window manager.

  2. The default is Gnome. When you log in, Gnome will automatically start up. When you log out of Gnome, the GDM login window is redisplayed.

  3. Select Shutdown from the Options menu to shut down Linux.

- If you do not choose this option, then you will start up with the command line interface.

  1. Enter the user name at the login prompt and the password at the password prompt to log in.

  2. Use the **startx** command to start Gnome and **switchdesk** to switch to KDE or Another Level.

  3. The **logout** command logs out, and CTRL-ALT-DEL will shut down Linux.

The final screen congratulates you on successfully installing Linux and asks you to remove your boot disk, if you used one. Tab to the OK button and press ENTER to reboot and start Linux. After a few minutes your system will reboot automatically. When your system restarts, the login prompt or the GDM login screen will appear, depending upon whether you chose to have the X Window System start up automatically. You can then log into your Linux system using a login name and a password for any users you have set up.

- If you log in as the root user, you can perform administrative operations such as installing new software or creating more users.

- To log in as the root user, enter **root** at the login prompt, and the root user password at the password prompt.

If you are upgrading from a previously installed Linux system and have saved configuration files that you want to use, you can restore them now. Mount the floppy disk where you saved these files and copy the configuration files to your new system. You can also restore any **tar** archived files and packages with the **tar xvMf/dev/fd0** command.

When you are finished, log out of your account using the command **logout** on the command line interface or by selecting Log Out from the Gnome Main Menu. You then need to shut down the entire system.

- From the GDM login window, select Shutdown from the Options menu.

- From the command line interface, hold down the CTRL and ALT keys and press DEL (CTRL-ALT-DEL). It is very important that you always use CTRL-ALT-DEL to shut down the system; never turn it off as you do with DOS.

Should your Linux system fail to boot at any time, you can use the boot disk that you created to perform an emergency boot. You can also use the install disk, and at the boot prompt, enter: **boot rw root=** with the device name of the root Linux partition. For example, if your root Linux partition is **/dev/hda4**, then you would enter **boot rw root=/dev/hda4** as shown here:

```
boot> boot rw root=/dev/hda4
```

The
Complete
Reference

Chapter 3

Installing OpenLinux

This chapter describes the installation procedure for the OpenLinux CD-ROM provided with this book. The installation includes the Linux operating system, a great many Linux applications, and a complete set of Internet servers. Different Linux distributions usually have their own installation programs. The Caldera OpenLinux installation program is designed to be efficient and brief while installing as many features as possible.

OpenLinux provides a very detailed installation manual both on the CD-ROM provided with this book and at its Web site, along with extensive documentation. The manual consists of Web pages that you can view using any browser. They include detailed figures and step-by-step descriptions. It is advisable for you to check this manual before you install. This chapter presents all the steps in the installation process but is not as detailed as the OpenLinux manual.

You can easily view the documentation and installation guide located on your OpenLinux CD-ROM using any Windows system. Start Windows and then place the CD-ROM in the CD-ROM drive. This automatically starts the Caldera Systems OpenLinux tools window with several choices. Select the Browse This CD-ROM entry. This then opens your Web browser and displays a Welcome page with options for Online Docs, Frequent Questions, and Special Offers. Select Online Docs. This will actually access the documentation on your CD-ROM. You do not have to be connected to the Internet. The Online Docs page lists the entries for documentation. For the OpenLinux installation guide, select the first entry. This will give you detailed instructions on preparing for installation, a step-by-step description of the process, and initial configuration information.

OpenLinux 2.2 Getting Started Guide

Bear in mind that the chapters referring to PartitionMagic do not apply to the version of OpenLinux provided by this book. This CD-ROM does not include PartitionMagic or BootMagic. You have to use the **defrag** and **fips** utilities described in Chapter 2 to set up partitions for hard disks that will share both Windows and Linux.

On the Caldera Web site at **www.calderasystems.com**, click Support and choose the Online Support Resources. This displays a list of online resources. Click Caldera Systems Online Manuals & Documentation to display a list of online documentation, including the OpenLinux 2.2 Getting Started Guide.

Installing Linux involves several steps. First, you need to determine whether your computer meets the basic hardware and software requirements. These days, most Intel-based PC computers do. Then you will then need certain technical specifications about the hardware you use, such as your monitor type and the type of chips used in your video card. This kind of information is available in the manuals that came with the hardware. If you are connected to a local area network with a network card like Ethernet, you will have to know whether automatic network configuration is provided by DHCP or BOOTP, or know the network IP addresses and domain names for your computer and network.

If you want to have your Linux system share a hard drive with another operating system, you may need to resize your hard disk partitions. For a hard disk with existing Windows partitions, you use the Windows **defrag** utility to reorganize your file space and then use **fips** in the **col\tools\fips** directory on your OpenLinux CD-ROM to resize your partitions, freeing up space for Linux. See Chapter 2 for a discussion on preparing Windows partitions to share a hard disk with Linux.

You then need to prepare a boot disk with which you will start the installation program. Once the installation program begins, you simply follow the instructions, screen by screen. There are two installation programs that you can use, Lizard and LISA. Lizard is a new program with a much better interface, whereas LISA is an older program. The only disadvantage to using Lizard exists for those who want to have both Windows and Linux on the same hard disk. Unlike LISA, Lizard does not install LILO, the boot loader that lets you select which system to use, Linux or Windows. However, this is very easily remedied by running LISA after you install Linux, and having it just set up and install LILO. The Lizard install process is so much better than LISA that you will find it easier to use Lizard and just install LILO later.

The installation program progresses through several phases. First you create Linux partitions on your hard drive, and then you install the software packages. After that you can configure your network connection and then your X-Windows server for graphical user interface support. Both X-Windows and network configurations can be performed independently at a later time.

You have the option of installing just the operating system, the system with a standard set of applications, or all the software available on the CD-ROM. If you choose a standard installation, you can add the uninstalled software packages later. Chapter 4 describes how you can use the COAS utility or the Red Hat Package Manager to install, or even uninstall, the software packages.

Creating the OpenLinux Install Disks from Windows

The OpenLinux CD-ROM provided with this book is based on an enhanced version designed to install from a Windows system. This CD-ROM cannot do that. You need to create an install disk and boot the install disk to start the installation process. However, you can easily create the install disks using the Windows startup window for OpenLinux installation. Start Windows, and then put your OpenLinux CD-ROM in your CD-ROM drive. Windows automatically detects the CD-ROM and launches the Caldera Systems OpenLinux tools. This displays a window listing several options, including Browse The CD, View Our Website, and Install Products. Select Install Products. Of the options listed on this window, you can only choose one:

```
Create Floppy Install Disks
```

This window then displays four entries, two for Lizard installation disks and two for LISA. In each case, you will have to create two floppy disks, an install disk and a modules disk. The modules disk is for any kernel modules that may be needed for specialized hardware such as some SCSI adapters. For most systems, you will not need to use it. It is preferable to use the Lizard install process. For this just click the Create Lizard Install Disk to create your Lizard install disk, and for the Lizard modules disk, click Create Lizard Modules Disk. If you want to use LISA instead, you use the LISA entries to create LISA install and modules disks.

When you click a create disk entry, a DOS window opens up labeled **rawrite**. The window displays a prompt at which you enter your destination drive. On most systems, your floppy drive is your A drive. First place an empty formatted DOS disk in your floppy drive. Then enter the drive letter for your floppy drive and press ENTER. The install disk image for Lizard is then copied to the floppy disk. Do the same for the modules disk. As a precaution, you might also want to create the LISA disk, should you have trouble with Lizard.

Creating the OpenLinux Install Disks from DOS

If you do not have Windows, then you can use a DOS system to create your install disks. You create the Install disk using the MS-DOS program **rawrite** and an install disk image. On the OpenLinux CD-ROM, the LISA install disk images are in the **col\launch\lisa\floppy** directory with **install.144** being the install image and **modules.144** the modules image.You can use the **rawrite** command in this directory in DOS to create the disk images. The Lizard install disks are located in **col\launch\floppy** and have the same file names. You can also use the **rawrite** command to create the disks. Insert the OpenLinux CD-ROM into your CD-ROM drive. At your DOS prompt, change to your CD-ROM drive, using whatever the letter for that drive may be. For example, if your CD-ROM drive is the E drive, just type **e:** and press ENTER. Once you have changed to the CD-ROM drive, you then need to change to the **\col\launch\floppy** directory to create Lizard install disks. For LISA install disks you change to the **\col\launch\lisa\floppy** directory. The Install disk images are there, as well as the **rawrite** command you use to create the disks. Several install image files are designed for different types of floppy disks. Most PCs support 1.44MB floppy disks. For these you use the **install.144** image file.

To create the install disk, insert a blank floppy disk into your floppy drive. Now start the **rawrite** command, which will actually write the disk image to your floppy disk. The **rawrite** command will first prompt you for the name of the disk image file you want to copy. Enter the full name of the install image file (in this example **INSTALL.144**). The program will then ask you to enter the letter of the floppy drive where you put your floppy disk. On many systems this will be the A drive.

```
E:\> cd col\launch\floppy
E:\col\launch\floppy > rawrite
Enter source file name: INSTALL.144
Enter destination drive (A or B) and press enter: A
```

Press ENTER to confirm that you have a blank floppy disk in the drive. The **rawrite** command will then copy the image file to your disk, creating your install disk. When it finishes, remove your disk from the floppy drive. This is the disk that the installation procedure described later refers to as the Install disk.

You should also create a modules disk. This disk contains kernel modules that support certain hardware components. Most systems will not need to use the modules disk. But some, particularly those with SCSI components, may need to use it. Repeat the same process to make a modules disk. For example, for a 1.44MB floppy disk you would use the **modules.144** disk image.

Installing Linux with Lizard

Installing Linux involves several processes, beginning with creating Linux partitions, then loading the Linux software, configuring your X-Windows interface, installing the Linux Loader (LILO) that will boot your system, and creating new user accounts. The Lizard and LISA install procedures perform the same tasks but use radically different interfaces. Both are described in this chapter, beginning with Lizard (Linux Installation Wizard).

Lizard provides a full-screen interface with mouse support that lets you easily select entries and move to the next screen much as you would using a Window install wizard. Each screen has a right pane that describes in detail the actions to be taken in the current screen. For each screen there is also a Help button that will display detailed context help about the task performed by a particular screen. When you are finished with a screen, click its Next button to move to the next one. Much of the installation process is automatic, such as detecting your hardware components and X Window System configuration. There are very few entries that you actually have to make.

If you are installing Linux on a hard disk that it will share with another system such as Windows, then be sure you have already freed up space on the disk. See the Chapter 2 on preparing the hard disk.

Insert the Linux boot disk into your floppy drive and reboot your computer and the CD-ROM into the CD-ROM drive. When the installation begins, OpenLinux opens a graphical display. Configuration information will fill your screen as the installation program attempts to detect your hardware components automatically. Should Linux have a problem identifying one of your components, that fact will be listed here. For example, OpenLinux will automatically detect your CD-ROM and know that you are using it to install OpenLinux. After the hardware detection is complete, the Caldera logo appears.

The next screen displays a list of languages to choose from. If your mouse is not working at this point, use the TAB and arrow keys to make your selection, though on most systems you can use your mouse.

The next screen configures your mouse so that you can use it to make selections in the following screen. First, move your mouse. Then select the type of port your mouse is connected to, PS/2 or Serial (most Pentium II systems have PS/2 mice). If you have a serial mouse, then select the serial port it is connected to, usually the first serial port, **/dev/ttyS0** (COM1). Then, from the drop-down menu, select the entry that best describes your mouse. You can even check your mouse by clicking the keys on the keypad. Click Next when you are finished to go to the next screen.

On the Installation Target screen you select the kind of partitions you want to install Linux on. If you are sharing the hard disk between Linux and Windows, always select Custom. With this option you can then create Linux partitions in the free space on your hard disk. Be very careful to select Custom before you select Next. If Lizard finds no Linux partitions, it automatically selects Entire Hard Disk. You have to manually select Custom to ensure that your Windows partitions remain intact. If you accidentally move to the next screen, you are asked to choose a hard disk to prepare for Linux. There is a Back button on this screen you can use to get back to the Installation Target screen. If you want to just overwrite Linux partitions you already set up for an older version of Linux already installed on your hard disk, you can select Prepared Partitions. If you are installing Linux by itself on the entire hard disk, select Entire Hard Disk.

If you selected Custom, the Partition Hard Disk screen shown in Figure 3-1 is displayed. This shows entries for all the partitions on your hard drive. There are fields for the size, system type, mount point, and whether it is bootable or not. Your Windows partitions will have a DOS/Windows type. Linux partitions will have a Linux type, and Linux swap partitions will have a Swap type. The first IDE hard drive will have a device name of **hda**, and the first SCSI hard drive will have a device name of **sda**. Partition numbers are attached to the device name. The first partition in the IDE hard drive is **hda1**, the second is **hda2**, the third, **hda3**, and so on. The first partition in a SCSI disk is **sda1**, the second, **sda2**, and so on.

You will see an entry for the swap and Linux partitions, but you still have to define them and set their sizes. Double-click the entry to display a window where you can enter the size and the mount point. A top section labeled Partition Boundaries will have two boxes, a left one labeled Start and the right one labeled End. To set the size, you will use these two boxes, one with the starting cylinder and the second for the ending cylinder (a cylinder is a segment of space on your hard disk). You specify the size of a partition by selecting its start and ending cylinders.

You should leave the Start value untouched, as this is determined automatically for you; it is the hard disk's first empty cylinder. The End cylinder can have any number larger than the first cylinder. As you enter a number for the end cylinder, you will see the size in megabytes displayed next to it. The partition should be from 300MB for the smallest installation to at least 2GB for the largest installation. The smallest OpenLinux

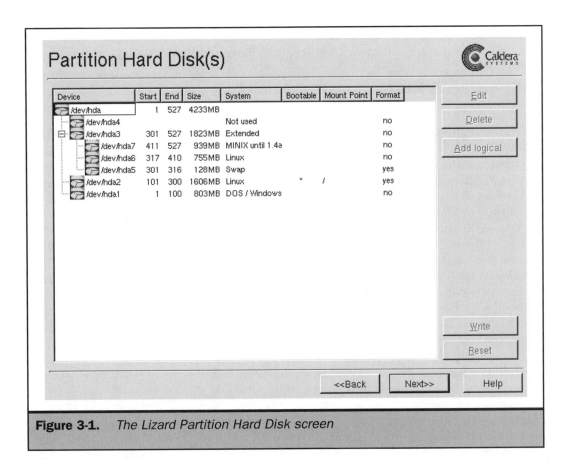

Partition Hard Disk(s)

Device	Start	End	Size	System	Bootable	Mount Point	Format
/dev/hda	1	527	4233MB				
/dev/hda4				Not used			no
/dev/hda3	301	527	1823MB	Extended			no
/dev/hda7	411	527	939MB	MINIX until 1.4a			no
/dev/hda6	317	410	755MB	Linux			no
/dev/hda5	301	316	128MB	Swap			yes
/dev/hda2	101	300	1606MB	Linux	*	/	yes
/dev/hda1	1	100	803MB	DOS / Windows			no

Edit
Delete
Add logical

Write
Reset

<<Back   Next>>   Help

Figure 3-1.   *The Lizard Partition Hard Disk screen*

installation is 160MB, and the largest, 1.4GB. Be sure to specify the mount point. If you want to use more than one Linux partition, you can add them here. When you are finished, click Next.

You then select the System Type. This can be linux, dos, or swap. For a Linux partition select the linux type, and swap for your Swap partition. For a Mount Point, you would usually select /.

If you have trouble setting up your partition, you can always use LISA to create them with the Linux **fdisk** utility.

1. Start the installation process with the LISA floppy disk and follow the instructions in the next section up and including the point of creating your Linux partitions (see Chapter 2 for instructions on using **fdisk**).

2. You will then have to restart your system, but you can then use Lizard. Take out the LISA disk and put the Lizard one back in.

3. When you get to the Installation Target screen, you can then skip the Custom Partitions screen and select the Prepared Partitions entry instead.

4. If the Prepared Partitions entry will not let you select it, then your partitions were not set up. Redo the process and make sure you write the partition configuration in **fdisk**.

The Select Root Partition screen will list your Native and Swap Linux partition. If you have only one Linux partition, it will be shown and selected. If you have several, you can choose on which to install your Linux system.

The Partition Information screen is used to format your Linux partitions. The screen shows the Linux partitions you set up on your hard drive. To format them, click the Format Chosen Partitions button at the bottom of the screen.

You are now ready to install OpenLinux. The Select Installation screen lets you choose a minimal (160MB), recommended (500MB), or full (1.4GB) installation. Click the one you want. Recommended is selected by default. When you click Next, the installation process will begin as packages are copied over to your Linux partitions. As packages are copied, you can continue with the remainder of the installation process. You will see a progress bar at the bottom of the screen showing the current percentage installed. Once the installation of the packages begins you will notice that the install procedure for the next step may become sluggish. This is nothing to be concerned about. Just wait for a response.

You now configure your X Window System interface. On the next screen you select the type of keyboard you use and its language.

Lizard then automatically determines the type of video card you have and, in the Select Video Card screen shown in Figure 3-2, displays it along with minimum configuration specifications. The Card Type window will hold the make and model of your video card. The Video RAM check boxes will indicate the Video RAM on the card.

1. Click the Probe button to have Lizard detect the full settings for your card, such as the actual amount of memory it has.

2. A message box will warn you that the screen will go blank for a few seconds as your card is probed. Choose Probe in the message box to continue.

3. When probing is finished, another message box tells you probing was successful. If the Video RAM on your card is more than what is selected on the panel, you can select the correct size. Click OK to return to the Video Card screen.

4. Click Next to continue.

On the Select Monitor screen you select the type of monitor you have. The screen displays an extensive list of monitor brand names.

1. Scroll through the list until you find the brand name for your monitor, such as NEC or Iiyama.

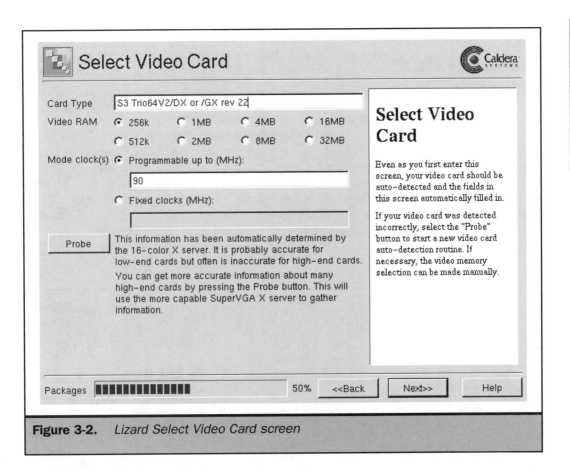

Figure 3-2. *Lizard Select Video Card screen*

2. Then click the + check box to the left of the brand name. This expands to a list of all monitor models for that brand.

3. Select the one for your monitor. When you select a monitor, the hardware specification boxes at the bottom of the screen are automatically filled.

4. If your monitor is not on the list, then enter its hardware specification in the boxes at the bottom of the screen.

5. You need to enter the horizontal and vertical sync ranges. Be sure these do not exceed the actual ranges of your monitor, or you could damage it.

The next screen lets you select your video mode. Here you can choose from all the possible entries that your card supports. Fields specify the resolution, color depth, refresh rate, and horizontal sync. A standard 15-inch monitor usually uses an 800 × 600 resolution and a 24-bit color depth, whereas 17- and 19-inch monitors use a 1024 × 768 resolution and a 24-bit color depth. Newer cards support a 32-bit color depth. Newer monitors can easily support 85 Hz refresh rates, whereas older ones may only go as high as 60 Hz. Once you select your mode, choose the color depth from the button at the bottom of the screen. You can click Test to see how the mode will be displayed on your monitor.

The Set Root Password screen shows two prompts for entering the password for the root user, the user that performs system administration functions.

The Set Login Names screen then lets you define users for your system. You can always define them later when you have your system running. At the boxes provided enter the user's real name, login name, password, and login shell. Then click Add User to add the user. You can add as many users as you want.

The Set Up Networking screen shown in Figure 3-3 then lets you enter network information. First enter a fully qualified host name for your computer in the Hostname box in the lower half of the screen. Include the host and domain name as in **turtle.mytrek.com**.

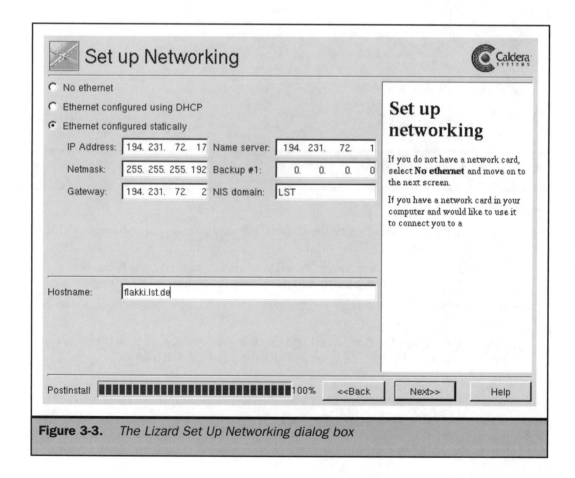

Figure 3-3.   *The Lizard Set Up Networking dialog box*

At the top of the screen are boxes for network addresses needed if you are connected to a local area network with an Ethernet card. If you use a dial-up ISP, you can skip this part. If your network provides network configuration with DHCP, select its entry at the top of the window. If you have to enter the network information yourself, select Ethernet Configured Statically. Then enter the IP address, name server, gateways, and netmask addresses.

In the Choose Time Zone screen, select your time zone from the drop-down list and whether your hardware clock is local or GMT.

The next screen provides entertainment as you wait for your packages to finish installing. When the progress bar at the bottom reaches 100 percent, click Finish.

The installation is finished; your system will reboot with Linux.

Using Lizard to install, automatically install the K Display Manager (KDM). Whenever Linux starts, it will display a login window with boxes for the login name and password. To log in as the root user, enter **root** and the root password you specified during installation. This will start the K desktop automatically. When you log out of the K desktop, you return to the KDM window. Click the Shutdown button to shut down the system.

If you have installed both Linux and Windows on your system, either on the same hard disk or on different ones if you have more than one, you will now have to install the LILO boot loader that will let you select the system you want to use by default whenever you boot your system. Follow the instructions in the following section to install LILO.

Installing LILO with LISA

If you used Lizard to install OpenLinux, you can then use the Linux Installation and System Administration (LISA) program to install the LILO boot loader, if Linux is sharing your hard disks with another system like Windows. First log in as the root user. This will start up the K Desktop. LISA is a screen-based utility that you run from the command line interface. You can either click the terminal icon in the KDE panel to start a terminal window and then run LISA there, or you can switch to the command line interface with the CTRL-ALT-F1 keys. This provides a much larger screen. Use CTRL-ALT-F7 to return to Gnome.

LISA is a simple menu-driven tool that you start from the command line or a terminal window by entering the command **lisa**.

```
# lisa
```

The UP ARROW and DOWN ARROW keys move from one menu entry to another. Use the TAB key to move from one button to another. RIGHT ARROW and LEFT ARROW let you select either the Call or Continue button. You know you've selected a button if its letters are white. To select a menu entry, move to the entry you want, make sure the

Call button is selected, and then press ENTER. The Continue button will move back to the previous menu.

The System Configuration entry in the LISA main menu brings you into other menus for adding to or changing features of your system configuration.

1. Select the Configure boot manager entry. This will start the LILO configuration. You will be first asked what partition you want to install LILO on. A screen is displayed showing partitions where you can install LILO. You should always choose the Master Boot Record, unless you are already using a boot loader for another system like OS/2. In that case choose the first Linux partition.

2. The next screen then shows your bootable partitions and asks you to choose the system you want to start as a default. This is usually Linux or DOS. The Linux system is identified as **/vmlinuz** (Linux kernel image). Your DOS or Windows 95 system will include the term DOS with Windows in it.

3. You are then asked to enter a label for that system. A default term will be displayed for you; DOS for DOS/Windows 95 and Linux for Linux. To use the default label, choose OK by pressing ENTER. You can backspace and type in another name if you wish.

4. If you choose the Linux system, then any special hardware boot parameters that you had to specify are displayed. If you had no special hardware configuration problems, this entry will be blank. Choose OK to continue.

5. You can now make additional entries for other operating systems. The screen will list all the systems on your hard drives, DOS as well as Linux. If you have both DOS and Linux on your system, you now need to choose the other operating system. For example, if you choose DOS for your default system, you would now have to choose your Linux system, and vice versa (the Linux system is labeled **/vmlinuz)**.

6. Choose the other operating system, DOS or Linux. You are then prompted to enter a name for this other operating system. If you are now choosing Linux, the term Linux will be displayed for you and you can just choose OK. Otherwise, enter the label you want to give this other operating system. You can repeat the steps for adding new labels for as many operating systems as you have. Most people would have no more than two, DOS and Linux. If, however, you should have a third operating system on your hard disk, choose its partition and repeat the previous steps.

7. Once you have finished making entries, choose the entry No Further Entries To Add To LILO, and then press ENTER.

8. Your **lilo.conf** file will then be displayed. This is the file that actually configures LILO. You will see entries for Linux and other operating systems that you entered such as DOS. Press ENTER to confirm installation of LILO.

9. You are then asked to install LILO as configured. Press Y or ENTER to do so.

10. When LILO finishes its installation, press ENTER to continue.

11. You may then be asked to mark the LILO partition as active. Press ENTER to do so.

12. You can then select the Continue button to return to the main menu. You can now log out and shut down. When you restart, you will be prompted by LILO with a boot prompt. Enter in the label of the system you want to start.

Once LILO is installed, you will first be presented with a boot prompt whenever you start your computer. At the prompt, enter the label for the system you want, such as Linux or DOS. These are labels that were assigned in the LILO install process. If you enter nothing, then after a few moments, the default system starts.

```
boot: linux
```

Installation Using LISA

The LISA installation program is a screen-based program that takes you through all these processes, step by step, as one continuous procedure. You will be able to use your mouse, as well as the arrow keys, SPACEBAR, and ENTER. You can always move back to the previous screen by pressing the ESC key. There is very little you have to do other than make selections and choose options. Some screens, such as the monitor screen, will provide a list of options from which you make a selection. Others will just ask you to choose YES or NO for which you can enter a **y** or **n**, or use the mouse click. In a few cases you will be asked for information you should already have if you followed the steps earlier in this chapter. The information you should have before you start is listed in the previous section on required information. You are now ready to begin installation. The steps for each part of the procedure are delineated in the following sections. It should take you no more than an hour.

If you followed the instructions in the first part of the chapter, you have freed up space on your hard drive if needed and created your install and modules disks, and you are now ready to create your Linux partitions. To do this, you will need to boot your computer using the LISA install disk that you made earlier. When you start your computer, the installation program will begin, and through that you can access the Linux **fdisk** utility with which you will create your Linux partitions.

Insert the Linux install disk into your floppy drive and reboot your computer. The installation program will start, presenting you with an Introduction screen. After a moment, the prompt "boot:" will appear at the bottom of your screen.

1. Press ENTER. Configuration information will fill your screen as the installation program attempts to detect your hardware components automatically. Should Linux have a problem identifying one of your components, that fact will be listed here. The auto-detection messages will fill up several screens.

2. A list of languages then appears. Choose a language and press ENTER.

3. A screen is displayed that shows a list of keyboards. Choose your keyboard from the list and press ENTER.

4. If your system has Plug and Play cards, be sure to disable them at this point by selecting the Disable Plug And Play Cards entry. Plug and Play cards can cause problems with Linux installations and hardware interfaces. Most systems have at least one Plug and Play card, usually the modem or sound card.

5. If your system is connected to a network that supports the bootp protocol, you can choose to have the network automatically perform the network configuration for your system. If your network includes Caldera Linux systems that support Caldera's netprobe utility, you can use the netprobe to perform the network configuration instead of bootp.

6. Then the hardware on you particular system is automatically detected and the detected hardware is displayed. This screen provides a detailed description of all the hardware that the auto-detection process identified. Check to make sure all your hardware is listed. Select the Continue button to continue.

7. You are then asked if all the hardware has been correctly recognized. If all your hardware is correctly detected, select YES by pressing Y to continue installation. If not, you can select NO at the bottom of the screen.

8. You then have the option to automatically attempt detection with the auto-probe utility or to manually detect unrecognized hardware. If you select NO to the auto-probing, then you will be placed in the Kernel Module Manager, where you can load specific hardware modules used to detect and configure your hardware. In the Kernel Module Manager you first choose the type of hardware support you need and then choose a module you want loaded. If needed enter any hardware parameters.

9. Next you are asked to create or change a Linux partition. The first time you install, you will have to create the Linux partition where your OpenLinux system is to be installed. Press Y to choose YES to create a Linux partition. The partitions have to be a type 83, ext2, Linux partition. In this case, press N and continue on to format those partitions. Skip to **fdisk** procedures and start installing OpenLinux.

10. A list of hard disks on your system is then displayed. Choose the hard disk where you want the partition. If you have more than one, use the arrow keys to move to the one you want. Press ENTER to continue.

11. You are then asked if you want to change your partition table. Press Y to select YES.

You are now in the Linux **fdisk** program. You will be taking the free space that you created earlier and partitioning and formatting it for your Linux operating system. Or if you are using your entire hard disk for Linux, you will be creating all the partitions for that hard disk. You need to create at least two Linux partitions: the main partition and the swap partition. The partitions have different types that you need to specify. Linux **fdisk** is a line-oriented program. It has a set of one-character commands that you simply press. Then you may be prompted to type in certain information and press ENTER. If you run into trouble during the **fdisk** procedure, you can press Q at any time, and you will return to the previous screen without any changes having been made. No changes are actually made to your hard disk until you press W. This would be your very last command. It makes the actual changes to your hard disk and then quits **fdisk**, returning you to the installation program. See Chapter 2 for a description of the process used to create Linux partitions with **fdisk**. Use the same procedure described in that chapter in the **fdisk** section.

The next screen prompts you to reboot your computer. Recall that your Linux install disk is still in your floppy disk drive. If it is not, insert it now. Press ENTER to reboot. You will begin installation all over again, but your hard disk partitions will now be ready. Continue with the next section to perform installation.

Now that you have created your Linux partitions, you are ready to install your Linux system. As before, introductory information is displayed and a boot prompt appears at the bottom of the screen. You will be repeating the hardware detection step, but this time you will skip partitioning because it is already done, and you will continue with the actual installation of the Linux system.

1. When asked to change your partition table, this time, press N or ENTER.

2. The next screen displays the partition you created for your Linux swap space. By selecting it, you will format it. Be sure the Linux swap partition is selected. It will have a type of 82. Press ENTER to format your swap space.

3. In the next screen, you are given three choices—CD-ROM, hard disk, or network—from which to install Linux. Choose CD-ROM to install the OpenLinux Lite system included with this text.

4. Once you choose CD-ROM, a list of CD-ROM drives, with yours highlighted, will be displayed. You have to confirm that this is your CD-ROM drive. If not, look through the list to find yours and click it.

5. Recall the device name given to your CD-ROM earlier. Press ENTER to confirm your CD-ROM drive. (If it is not listed, you will have to start over and enter the hardware specification for it when the boot prompt appears.)

Alternatively, you can use the hard disk option if you should have difficulty accessing your CD-ROM. You could copy the CD-ROM to a DOS partition and then install from there. The network install allows you to access the OpenLinux CD-ROM remotely, across a network such as an NFS network. You could also have the CD-ROM copied to a hard drive partition and then load it from there across a network. If you choose a hard drive install, you have to specify the hard disk partition and the directory where the copy of the CD-ROM was placed. The value **/dev/hda1** indicates the first partition. If you choose a network install, you have to specify the server address and the directory path where the Linux CD-ROM is located.

1. The list of partitions on your hard disk is again displayed. The partition you created for your Linux main partition should already be highlighted, and it will have a type of 83. Be sure the main Linux partition is highlighted. Then press ENTER to format it.

2. You can have Linux check for defective sectors while it formats, if you wish. Wait a moment for the partition to be formatted.

3. Next, you are asked to choose an install option. There are several choices, dependent largely on the amount of space you have.

4. If you are performing a standard or minimal install, you are then asked to choose an X Window System graphics server. A full install installs all the servers automatically. You can choose the standard SVGA server and a specialized accelerated server tailored to specific chipsets used in different video cards. The name of the chipset is included in the name of the accelerated server (S3 for S3 chipset). In most cases, select the SVGA server. (See Chapter 29 for a complete listing of the X Windows System servers.)

5. It takes approximately 15 to 30 minutes for a standard installation. During this time a screen will appear showing the progress of the installation, indicating the percentage completed and each package as it is installed. The Linux screen saver will be active, so after a while your monitor will go dark. To reactivate the screen, just press either the SHIFT, CTRL, or ALT key.

6. A screen will prompt you for a hostname for your computer. If your computer does not already have a hostname, you can decide on one yourself and enter it. (If your computer is already connected to a network, it will probably have a hostname. In that case, check with your network administrator for the hostname, if you do not know it.) Type in the hostname for your system and press ENTER.

7. You are then asked if you have a network card. If you have a network card, choose YES and you will then be asked the following questions. If you are not connected to a network, press N to choose NO and continue with the steps under Final Configuration. (If you have a standalone PC, you are probably not connected to a network.)

8. You are asked to confirm that your network device is eth0. This is the default device for an Ethernet setting. Choose the default, or if your network is not Ethernet, choose NO.

9. You are then prompted for your network information:
   - Enter your IP address.
   - Enter your netmask. A default is shown that works for most configurations.
   - Enter the broadcast address for your network.

10. You are then asked if you have a router or gateway system on your network. If so, enter the IP address of that router or gateway. If not, press N to choose NO.

11. Indicate whether you have a DNS name server. If so, enter the IP address of that name server. (Many Internet service providers have DNS name servers.)

12. You are then asked if you have an NIS system. Choose YES to configure it. Otherwise, choose NO. To configure NIS, you will need to enter your NIS domain and the IP address of your NIS server.

13. The next two screens ask you to choose whether your hardware clock is on local or Greenwich Mean Time. You also enter the time zone for your system. Local time would be the more common choice for PC users. DOS systems usually operate according to local time. However, Greenwich Mean Time (GMT) is the standard for Unix computers and will provide better interoperability with other Unix computers on the Internet, worldwide.

14. The next screen will list a series of mouse types. Choose the type for your mouse and press ENTER. Most current systems use a PS/2-type mouse.

15. The next screen prompts you to choose the port you are using for your mouse. Select the port (usually COM1 for a serial mouse) and press ENTER.

16. You are then prompted to set up your printer. You are first presented with a list of printer drivers, each bearing the name of a printer. Use your arrow keys to select one. Then select the printer port (usually the first parallel port). Choose the default printer resolution (for many printers this is 300 × 300). Choose a default paper size (usually letter).

17. You are then asked to enter a password for the superuser (root user). Make it simple and easy to remember. You will have to log in as the root user many times to configure your system, performing administrative operations such as installing software or configuring applications. At the Password prompt, enter the root user password you decide on. Enter it again at the Retype prompt.

18. You are then prompted to enter another password, this one for a normal user account called col. Create a password and enter it, then re-enter it for confirmation.

The next screen displays the Boot Setup Analysis for LILO, the Linux Loader. LILO will start your Linux system when you boot up. However, if you have more than one operating system on your hard disk, LILO will allow you to choose the one you want to start. LILO will designate one of the operating systems as the default to start up if one is not specified. So if you have both DOS and Linux on your hard disk, LILO will let you choose the one you want to use.

1. The next screen then lists the partitions where you can install LILO. You can select the Master Boot Record (MBR) or the first Linux partition. Always choose the Master Boot Record, unless you already have another boot loader installed there. In that case you can choose the first Linux partition.

2. The next screen asks you to choose the system you want to start as a default. This is usually Linux or DOS. The Linux system is identified as **/vmlinuz** (Linux kernel image). Your DOS or Windows 95 system will include the term DOS with Windows at the end. Choose the system you want to start as a default.

3. You are then asked to enter a label for that system. A default term will be displayed for you; DOS for DOS/Windows 95 and Linux for Linux. To use the default label, choose OK by pressing ENTER. You can backspace and type in another name if you wish. If you choose the Linux system, then any special hardware boot parameters that you had to specify are displayed. If you had no special hardware configuration problems, this entry will be blank. Choose OK to continue.

4. You can now make additional entries for other operating systems. The screen will list all the systems on your hard drives, DOS as well as Linux. If you have both DOS and Linux on your system, you now need to choose the other operating system. For example, if you choose DOS for your default system, you would now have to choose your Linux system, and vice versa (the Linux system is labeled **/vmlinuz**).

5. Choose the other operating system, DOS or Linux. You are then prompted to enter a name for this other operating system. If you are now choosing Linux, the term Linux will be displayed for you and you can just choose OK. Otherwise, enter the label you want to give this other operating system. You can repeat the steps for adding new labels for as many operating systems as you have. Most people would have no more than two, DOS and Linux. If, however, you should have a third operating system on your hard disk, choose its partition and repeat the previous steps.

6. Once you have finished making entries, choose the entry No Further Entries To Add To LILO, and then press ENTER.

7. Your **lilo.conf** file will then be displayed. This is the file that actually configures LILO. You will see entries for Linux and other operating systems that you entered such as DOS. Press ENTER to confirm installation of LILO.

8. You are then asked to install LILO as configured. Press Y or ENTER to do so. When LILO finishes its installation, press ENTER to continue.

9. Then you are asked to mark the LILO partition as active. Press ENTER to do so. You can edit **lilo.conf** later if you wish, but be very careful when doing so (see Chapter 27).

You will now complete the last steps of configuration.

1. You are provided with a list of services that will boot up automatically whenever Linux is started. Included is the Apache Web Server. All those available for OpenLinux Lite are already selected. You can deselect an entry by using the arrow keys to move to that entry and pressing the SPACEBAR. Press ENTER to continue.

2. You are then asked whether you want to configure your X-Windows server. It is best to answer NO at this point. Then finish the installation process. Configuring X-Windows can be complicated, and the system could crash if done improperly. This would corrupt the installation, and you would have to start over. Press N or ENTER to choose NO and finish the installation.

You have now completed your installation. A notice to that effect will be displayed. Remove the boot floppy in your disk drive and press ENTER. After a few minutes your system will reboot automatically. When your system restarts, the login prompt will appear. You can then log into your Linux system using a login name and a password for any users you have set up. During installation, you already set up a root user and a user named col. You can log into either one of these. If you log in as the root user, you can perform administrative operations such as installing new software or creating more users. To log in as the root user, type **root** at the prompt and press ENTER. Then type the root user password at the password prompt and press ENTER. If, at any time, you try to run a program and receive an error such as a notice of a missing file, use LISA to check if the package is installed. If not, then install it. See Chapter 4 about how to log in and out of your system.

If you are upgrading from a previously installed Linux system and have saved configuration files that you want to use, you can restore them now. Mount the floppy disk where you saved these files and copy the configuration files to your new system. You can also restore any **tar** archived files and packages with the **tar xvMf/dev/fd0** command.

When you are finished, log out of your account using the command **logout**.

```
$ logout
```

You then need to shut down the entire system. Whenever you are ready to shut down the system, hold down the CTRL and ALT keys and press DEL (CTRL-ALT-DEL). It is very important that you always use CTRL-ALT-DEL to shut down the system; never turn it off as you do with DOS.

Should your Linux system fail to boot at any time, you can use the Install disk that you created to perform an emergency boot. Put the Install disk in your floppy drive and start up your computer. At the boot prompt, enter **boot rw root=** with the device name of the root Linux partition. For example, if your root Linux partition is **/dev/hda4**, then you would enter **boot rw root=/dev/hda4** as shown here:

INTRODUCTION

```
boot> boot rw root=/dev/hda4
```

Configuring the X Window System with XF86Setup

You still have to install the X Window System so that you can use your K Desktop. You can do this with **Xconfigurator**, **XF86Setup**, or **xf86config**. **Xconfigurator** was discussed in the previous chapter. **xf86config** is a simple line-based configuration utility. **XF86Setup** provides a full-screen interface for configuring X. This is the interface described here. If you have trouble with it, try the other utilities. First you log in as the root user. (At the LILO prompt, enter **linux** and press ENTER to start Linux.)

Before you can use the X Window System, you have to configure your mouse, keyboard, graphics card, and monitor to support your Xs interface. To configure the X Window System, you use the **XF86Setup** program. This is a full-screen graphics user interface in which you simply click buttons and menu entries to choose options. You can run it at any time should you need to reconfigure your X interface. With the **XF86Setup** program, this is a very simple process. Configuring your graphics card is a simple matter of choosing it from a list.

Before you start **XF86Setup**, check your monitor hardware documentation for the vertical and horizontal frequency of your monitor. The frequencies could be single numbers or ranges. For example, the synchronization frequencies for an NEC 3V are 31–50 for horizontal and 55–90 for vertical. To start the **XF86Setup** program, enter the **XF86Setup** command at the shell prompt. The **XF86Setup** program is located in the **/usr/X11R6/bin** directory. It will create an X-Windows configuration file called **/etc/XF86Config** that will be used to run X-Windows on your system.

```
$ /usr/X11R6/bin/XF86Setup
```

If your **XF86Setup** does not start, the reason may be that not all the XFree86 libraries were loaded during the installation. Use the LISA utility and select the Software Management entry, then the entry to Install Packages. Then select those beginning with the term XFree86 packages, if they are not already installed. You should then be able to start **XF86Setup**. If you still can't, try using **XF86Config**.

You are then asked to enter graphics mode. Press ENTER.

You are now in the **XF86Setup** program. There are five configuration tasks, each indicated by a button on the top row of the **XF86Setup** window. The buttons are labeled: Mouse, Keyboard, Card, Monitor, and Other. Each button brings up a screen for configuring that task. At the bottom of the screen are three buttons: Abort, Done, and Help. Abort will cancel the entire **XF86Setup** without making any changes. If you are at all unsure about any of the configuration options, you can simply click Abort to end the program safely and then start it up later. When you are finished with all the configuration tasks, click Done to save your configuration and end the **XF86Setup** program. You will then be ready to start K Desktop with the **kde** command.

To bring up the Mouse screen, you can press ENTER or ALT-M. When the Mouse screen first appears, a list of keyboard commands are presented. It is advised not to use your mouse until you have configured it. Instead, you can use the keyboard command to select entries on the screen.

The Mouse screen lists a series of mouse brands. These are indicated by a row of buttons at the top of the screen under the label Select Mouse Protocol. Microsoft is a protocol that most mice are compatible with. Most standard mice are Microsoft serial. Choose the brand for your mouse. You can then set different features such as the number of buttons or the baud rate. Default settings are already entered. For the mouse device path use **begin/dev/psaux** for a PS/2 mouse, **/dev/ttyS0** refers to the first serial port, **/dev/ttyS1**, to the second, and so on. The value **/dev/ttyS0** is already selected and is usually the port used for a mouse. The b key sets the baud rate. The **e** command emulates a middle button on a two-button mouse, and the **c** command enables Chordmiddle, the middle button on a three-button mouse. When finished, press A to select the Apply button in the lower-right corner. Your mouse is then configured and ready to use with the rest of the configurations.

Click Keyboard to bring up the Keyboard screen. There are drop-down menus for selecting the keyboard model and the language you use. You can also set different control key positions or just use the defaults. When finished, select the Apply button located below the picture of the keyboard.

Two screens are used for graphics card configurations: a Detailed Setup screen and a Card List screen. Ordinarily, you will only have to use the Card List screen. To begin, click the Card tab. If you have not previously run **XF86Setup**, you will immediately be placed in the Card List screen. If you have previously run the **XF86Setup** program, the Detailed Setup screen will display first. In the lower-right corner of the screen is a button labeled Card List. Choose this button to bring up the Card List screen.

The Card List screen lists most video cards currently available. To the right is a slider bar that you can use to move through the list. Find the video card that your system uses. Select it by clicking it, and then click the README File button to read information about the server for this card (see Figure 3-4). You can then continue on to the Monitor screen.

If your card is not listed, then choose the Detailed Setup. This brings up the Detailed Setup screen, where you can perform a detailed setup of your card. On the Detailed Setup screen, you will see a row of buttons on the top indicating the different X-Windows servers. Below them are drop-down menus for selecting your chipset, RAMDAC, and clock chip. There are drop-down menus for selecting the keyboard model and the language you use. Click Monitor to bring up the Monitor screen. To configure your monitor, you only need to set the horizontal and vertical frequency ranges. However, it is critically important that these settings be correct. An incorrect frequency can damage your monitor (see Figure 3-5).

Before you choose a monitor frequency (Hz), check your hardware documentation. If you set the frequency higher than the one your monitor supports, you can cause serious damage.

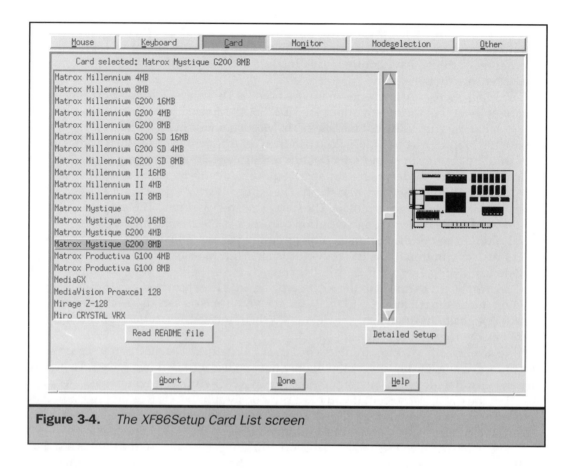

Figure 3-4.   *The XF86Setup Card List screen*

There are boxes at the top of the screen labeled Horizontal and Vertical. Here, you can enter your horizontal and vertical frequencies. After you type in a frequency number, press ENTER to have it entered. You will see the frequency represented on the associated bar. If your monitor supports ranges for each entry, you enter them separated by a dash. For example, a multisync monitor might have a horizontal frequency range of 30–90 and a vertical frequency range of 50–130. Below the vertical and horizontal boxes, a vertical and horizontal graph will show the ranges you entered. In a box in the center of the screen is a list of common monitor types. You can click one to select a standard set of frequencies. However, under no condition should you take these frequencies as valid. Always check your monitor documentation for the correct frequencies.

Click Modeselection to bring up the Modes selection screen. This displays a list of possible screen resolutions that your video card can display. Select the ones you want to use by clicking them. The bottom of the screen displays a set of buttons indicating the number of colors you want displayed. The setting 24 bmp displays 16 million colors

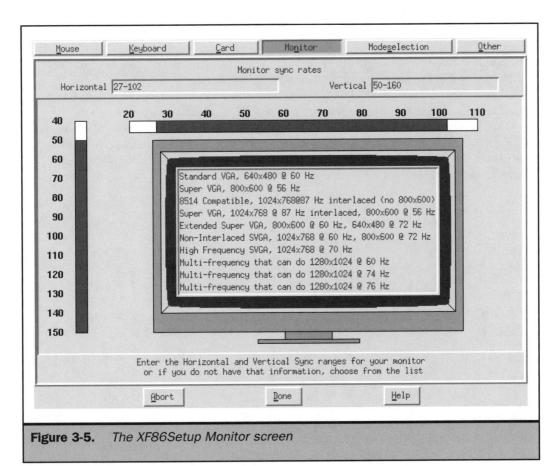

Figure 3-5.   *The XF86Setup Monitor screen*

(a common standard for many current video cards), 16 bmp displays 32 thousand colors, and 8 displays 256 colors.

Click Other to bring up the Optional Server Settings. This lists a set of five options, the first two of which are already selected. Ordinarily, you will not have to change anything on this screen. The first option allows you to end an X Window System session from the keyboard with CTRL-ALT-BACKSPACE. The second lets you change video modes with the CTRL-ALT-+ keys (the + key is the one on the keypad). You can easily switch between different resolutions. The third lets you exit the server cleanly, and the fourth and fifth allow changes in video, mouse, and keyboard configurations from remote workstations.

Upon finishing your X Window System configuration, choose the Done button at the bottom of the screen. X-Windows starts up, and you are then presented with three buttons: Run **xvidtune**, Save The Configuration And Exit, or Abort. If the X Window System fails to start, the reason may be that your XFree86 server was not installed.

Return to the command line and start up LISA with the **lisa** command to install the server you need.

Choose to save the configuration and exit. (You can run **xvidtune** later to tune your monitor display should you need to, though most users won't.)

You can start up the X Window System with the **kde** command. This command actually starts up the X Window System and the KDE desktop. You will see the K Desktop displayed on your screen. If the display is smaller or larger than you like, you may want to change the video resolution using the keyboard command CTRL-ALT-+. This places you in a higher resolution. CTRL-ALT-- places you in a lower resolution where images appear larger.

Chapter 4

Interface Basics and System Configuration

To start using Linux, you will need to know how to access your Linux system and, once you are on the system, how to execute commands and run applications. Accessing Linux involves more than just turning on your computer. Once Linux is running, you have to log into the system using a predetermined login name and password. Once on the system, you can start executing commands and running applications. You can then interact with your Linux system using either a command line interface or a graphical user interface (GUI). The Linux systems use desktops to provide a fully functional GUI, with which you can use windows, menus, and icons to interact with your system.

It is very easy to obtain information quickly about Linux commands and utilities while logged into the system. Linux has several online utilities that provide information and help. You can access an online manual that describes each command, or obtain help that provides more detailed explanations of different Linux features. A complete set of manuals provided by the Linux Documentation Project is on your system and available for you to print or browse through.

To make effective use of your Linux system you will need to know how to configure certain features. Administrative operations like adding users, specifying network settings, accessing CD-ROM drives, and installing software can now be performed with user-friendly system tools.

This chapter will discuss how to access your Linux system, including logging in and out of user accounts as well as starting the system and shutting it down. Linux commands and utilities are also covered, along with basic operations of the Gnome and KDE desktops. The chapter ends with an explanation of basic system administration operations, such as creating new user accounts and installing software packages.

User Accounts

You never directly access a Linux system. Instead, Linux sets up an interface through which you can interact. A Linux system can actually set up and operate several user interfaces at once, accommodating several users simultaneously. In fact, you can have many users working off the same computer running a Linux system. To a particular user, it appears as if he or she is the only one working on the system. It is as if Linux can set up several virtual computers, and each user can then work on his or her own virtual computer. Such virtual computers are really individually managed interfaces whereby each user interacts with the Linux system.

These user interfaces are frequently referred to as accounts. Unix, which Linux is based on, was first used on large minicomputers and mainframes that could accommodate hundreds of users at the same time. Using one of many terminals connected to the computer, users could log into the Unix system using their login names and passwords. All of this activity was managed by system administrators. To gain access to the system, you needed to have a user interface set up for you. This was commonly known as "opening an account." A system administrator would create the account on the Unix system, assigning a login name and password for it. You then used your account to log in and use the system.

Each account is identified by a login name with access protected by a password. Of course, you can access any account if you know its login name and password. On your Linux system, you can create several accounts, logging into different ones as you wish. Other people can access your Linux system, making use of login names and passwords you provide for them. In effect, they will have their own accounts on your system. Recall that in the previous chapter on installing Linux, you created a login name and password for yourself. These are what you will use to access Linux regularly. When you created the login name and password, you were actually creating a new user account for yourself.

You can, in fact, create other new user accounts using special system administration tools. These tools become available to you when you log in as the root user. The *root user* is a special user account reserved for system administration tasks such as creating users and installing new software. Basic system administration operations are discussed briefly in this chapter, and in detail in Chapters 26, 27, and 28. For now, you will only need your regular login name and password.

Accessing Your Linux System

To access and use your Linux system, you must carefully follow required startup and shutdown procedures. You do not simply turn off and turn on your computer. If you have installed the Linux Loader, LILO, then when you turn on or reset your computer, LILO will first decide what operating system to load and run. You will see the following prompt; enter **linux** to start up the Linux operating system:

```
LILO: linux
```

If, instead, you wait a moment or press the ENTER key, LILO will load the default operating system. (Recall that earlier you designated a default operating system.) If you want to run Windows instead, LILO will give you a moment at the prompt to type in the name you gave for Windows, such as **dos** or **win**.

You can think of your Linux operating system as operating on two different levels, one running on top of the other. The first level is when you start your Linux system and the system loads and runs. It has control of your computer and all its peripherals. However, you still are not able to interact with it. After Linux starts, it will display a login prompt, waiting for a user to come along and log into the system to start using it. To gain access to Linux, you first have to log in.

You can think of logging in and using Linux as the next level. Now you can issue commands instructing Linux to perform tasks. You can use utilities and programs such as editors or compilers, even games. However, depending upon a choice you made during installation, you may be either interacting with the system using a simple command line interface or using the desktop directly. There are both command line login prompts and Graphical login windows.

■ In the case of Red Hat, if you choose to use a graphical interface at the end of the installation, you are presented with a graphical login window at which you enter your login and password. If you choose not to use the graphical interface, you will be presented with a simple command line prompt to enter your login name.

■ In the case of OpenLinux, if you use Lizard to install, then you automatically use the graphical login, whereas with LISA you are given the command line login.

On the command line interface, you are presented with a simple prompt such as a $ or # symbol. You type in a command and press ENTER to have the system perform actions. You can start up the GUI desktop from the command line interface, if you wish. In Linux, the command **startx** will start the X Window System along with a GUI that will then allow you to interact with the system using windows, menus, and icons. On Red Hat, the **startx** command starts the Gnome desktop by default, though you can configure it to start up other window managers like WindowMaker. On OpenLinux, you use the **kde** command to start the KDE desktop. Once you shut down the GUI interface, you will return to your command line interface, still logged in. You then have to log out from your account when you are finished.

Shutting down from a command line interface involves several steps. If you are using the GUI started from the command line interface, you first need to exit the GUI, returning to the command line interface. Then you log out of your account and return to the system's login prompt. Logging out does *not* shut down the system. It is still running and has control of your machine. You then need to tell the system to shut itself down by issuing a shutdown command: Hold down the CTRL and ALT keys and press the DEL key (CTRL-ALT-DEL). The system shuts itself down and reboots. When rebooting starts, only then can you turn off your computer. Alternatively, you can log in as the root user and issue a shutdown command. The **-h** option simply shuts down the system, whereas the **-r** option shuts down the system and then reboots it. In the next example, the system is shut down after five minutes. To shut down the system immediately, you can use **+0** or the word **now** (see Chapter 27 for more details).

```
# shutdown -h +5
```

With the graphical login, your X Window System starts up immediately and displays a login window with boxes for a user login name and a password. When you enter your login name and password and click the OK or GO button, your default GUI starts up. On Red Hat this is Gnome, and on OpenLinux and SuSE this is KDE. On Red Hat you can easily change this to KDE or another window manager. When you quit your GUI, you are also logging out of your account. The login window is then redisplayed. To shut down, you simply select the Shutdown entry in the Options menu, or click Shutdown.

Graphical logins are handled by a display manager. The display manager manages the login interface along with authenticating a user password and login name, and starting up a selected desktop. Both Gnome and KDE provide their own display managers called the Gnome Display Manager (GDM) and the K Display Manager (KDM) respectively. Both are based on the X Display Manager (XDM) that originally provided graphical login services.

Should there ever be problems using the X Window System display of the GUI interface, you can force a shutdown of the X Window System and the GUI with the CTRL-ALT-BACKSPACE keys. Also, from the Display Manager you can shift to the command line interface with the CTRL-ALT-F1 keys and shift back to the X Window System with the CTRL-ALT-F7 keys.

Gnome Display Manager: GDB

When the Gnome Display Manager starts up, it shows a login window with boxes for login and password, shown in the following illustration. There are two buttons below the boxes, one for Login and the other for Options. To log in, just enter your login name and password and then click Login. In the case of Red Hat, the Gnome desktop is then started up. When you log out from the desktop, you return to the GDM login window. To shut down your Linux system, click Options to display a pop-up menu, select System, and from System choose Reboot or Halt.

Clicking Options displays a pop-up menu that shows entries for Sessions, Languages, and System. You use the Sessions menu to select the desktop or window manager you want to start up. The following illustration of GDM Sessions shows the default entries for Red Hat's GDM. Here you can select KDE to start up the K Desktop instead of Gnome.

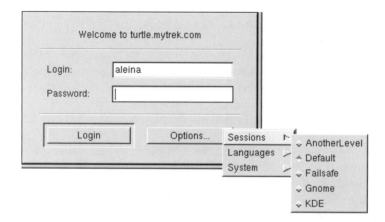

K Desktop Display Manager: KDM

On systems that use the KDE Display Manager, the login window also shows boxes for login and password. To log in, enter your login name and password and then click Go. Your GUI starts up. When you log out of your GUI, you return to the KDM login screen. To shut down the system, click Shutdown to display a shutdown dialog from which you can choose to shut down, restart the X server, or shift to the console mode (command line interface).

You can use the Sessions drop-down menu to select the GUI to use. On OpenLinux there is only an entry for the KDE. KDM also display icons for different users defined on the system at the top of its login window. You can click a user's icon to have that user's name automatically entered in the login box. The root user will have the image of a conductor. To log in as root, just click it and you will see the word root appear in the login box. Then enter the root user password in the password box.

If you log in as the root user to the KDE desktop, you can then use the KDM Configuration Manager shown in Figure 4-1 to configure the KDM interface. Select KDM Login Manager from the Applications menu in the Settings menu. Here you can select what background picture to use, the color of the login window, the icons to use for particular users, and the logo you want displayed. The Sessions panel lets you select what GUIs you want to access, provided they are installed on your system.

Command Line Interface

For the command line interface, you will initially be given a login prompt. The system is now running and waiting for a user to log in and use it. You can enter your user name and password to use the system. The login prompt will be preceded by the hostname you gave your system. In this example, the hostname is **turtle**. When you are finished using Linux, you first **logout**. Linux will then display the login prompt, waiting for you or another user to log in again. This is the equivalent of the login window provided by the display manager.

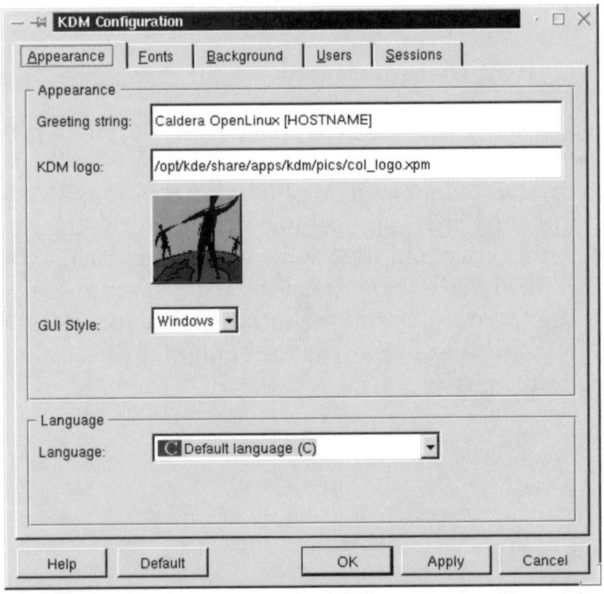

Figure 4-1.   *The KDM Configuration Manager*

```
Red hat Linux release 6.0 (Hedwig)
Kernel 2.2.5-15 on i686

turtle login:
```

Should you want to turn off your computer, you must first shut down Linux. If you don't, you could require Linux to perform a lengthy systems check when it starts up again. You shut down your system by holding down both the CTRL and ALT keys and pressing the DEL key, CTRL-ALT-DEL. You will see several messages as Linux shuts itself down. Linux will then reboot your computer. During the reboot process, you can turn off your computer. The following steps include all the startup and shutdown procedures for the command line interface.

1. Boot your computer.

2. At the LILO prompt type **linux** and press ENTER. (Or just press ENTER if Linux is your default.)

3. After a few messages, the login prompt appears, and you can log into the system and use it.

4. At the login prompt you can also shut down the system with CTRL-ALT-DEL. The login prompt will reappear after you log out.

5. You can now turn off your computer.

Once you log in, you can enter and execute commands. After you have finished, you need to log out of the system before you shut it down. You do not have to shut down the system if you don't want to. You will be presented with a login prompt, and you could then log in using a different user name, or log in as the root user.

Logging into your Linux account involves two steps: entering your user name and then your password. You already know what the login prompt looks like. Type in the login name for your user account. If you make a mistake, you can erase characters with the BACKSPACE key. In the next example, the user enters the user name richlp and is then prompted to enter the password.

```
Red hat Linux release 6.0 (Hedwig)
Kernel 2.2.5-15 on i686

turtle login: richlp
Password:
```

When you type in your password, it will not appear on the screen. This is to protect your password from being seen by others. If you enter either the login or password incorrectly, the system will respond with the error message "Login incorrect" and will ask for your login name again, starting the login process over. You can then reenter your login name and password.

Once you have entered your user name and password correctly, you are logged into the system. Your command line prompt will be displayed, waiting for you to enter a command. Notice that the command line prompt is a dollar sign, $, not a sharp sign, #. The $ is the prompt for regular users, whereas the # sign is the prompt solely for the root user. In this version of Linux, your prompt will be preceded by the hostname and the directory you are in. Both will be bounded by a set of brackets.

```
[turtle /home/richlp]$
```

To end your session, you issue the **logout** command. This returns you to the login prompt, and Linux waits for another user to log in.

```
$ logout
```

Once logged into the system, you have the option of starting an X Window System GUI such as Gnome or KDE and using it to interact with your Linux system. You start the X GUI by entering **startx** on the command line. On OpenLinux you use the **kde** command to start KDE. On Red Hat, you can use the **switchdesk** command, while in your desktop, to switch between Gnome, KDE, or the FVWM window manager (open a terminal window to enter it). You make your selection and then quit the desktop to return to the command line interface. When you start up the GUI again, the desktop you selected will be used.

Gnome Desktop

The Gnome desktop shown in Figure 4-2 initially displays a panel at the bottom of the screen and any icons for folders and Web pages initially set up by your distribution. For Red Hat you will see several Web page icons and a folder for your home directory. The panel at the bottom of the screen will contain icons for starting applications such as Netscape (the Netscape logo) and the Help system (the question mark logo). You can start applications using the main menu, which you display by clicking the Gnome icon (the image of a bare foot print) located on the left side of the panel.

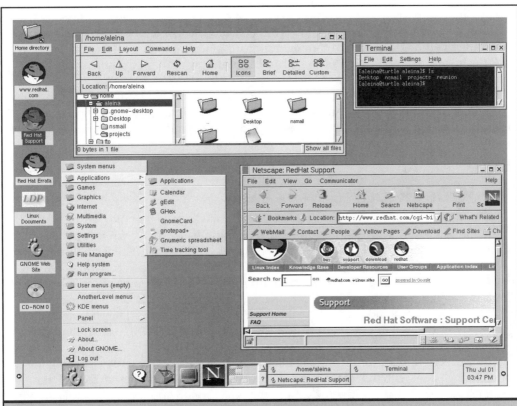

Figure 4-2.   *The Gnome desktop*

When you click the folder for your home directory on your desktop or select the File Manager entry on the main menu, a file manager window opens showing your home directory. You can display files in your home directory and use the up arrow button to move to the parent directory. Back and Forward buttons move through previously displayed directories. In the location window you can enter the pathname for a directory to move directly to it. The file manager is also Internet aware. You can use it to access remote FTP directories and display or download their files (though it cannot display Web pages).

To move a window, click and drag its title bar or right-click its other borders. Each window supports Maximize, Minimize, and Close buttons, as well as a stick pin. Double-clicking the title bar will reduce the window to just its title bar; you can redisplay the window with another double-click. The desktop supports full drag-and-drop capabilities. You can drag folders, icons, and applications to the desktop or other file manager window open to other folders. The move operation is the default drag operation. Ctrl-click to copy files and middle-click to create links. In most cases, you would use links for desktop icons.

The Control Panel also contains a pager for desktop areas. This appears as four squares. Clicking a square moves you to that area. You can think of the desktop work area as being four times larger than your monitor screen, and you can use the pager to display different parts. You can configure your Gnome interface, setting features such as the background using the Gnome Control Panel. Click the image of a toolbox on the panel. To execute a command using the command line interface, you open a Terminal window. Click the image of a monitor on the panel. In that window at the $ prompt you can type in your command.

To quit the Gnome desktop, select the logout entry at the bottom of the main menu. If you entered from a login window you be logged out of your account and return to the login window; if you started Gnome from the command line, you will return to the command line prompt, still logged into your account.

The K Desktop

The KDE desktop shown in Figure 4-3 initially displays a panel at the bottom of the screen and any icons for folders and Web pages initially set up by your distribution. In the upper-left corner you will see folder icons labeled Autostart, Trash, and Templates. When a user starts KDE for the first time, the KDE Setup Wizard is run, displaying a series of four windows advising you to set up icons for KDE Web pages as well as CD-ROM and printer icons. Initially, the KDE wizard lets you choose a theme such as a Windows, KDE standard, or Mac theme. You can change this later if you wish. The next windows ask if you want to add icons for your CD-ROM, printer, and links to certain Web sites like the KDE Web site.

You can start applications using the main menu, which you display by clicking the button in the panel with the large K on a cogwheel. It is located on the left side of the panel. When you click the folder for your home directory on your panel (icon of a folder

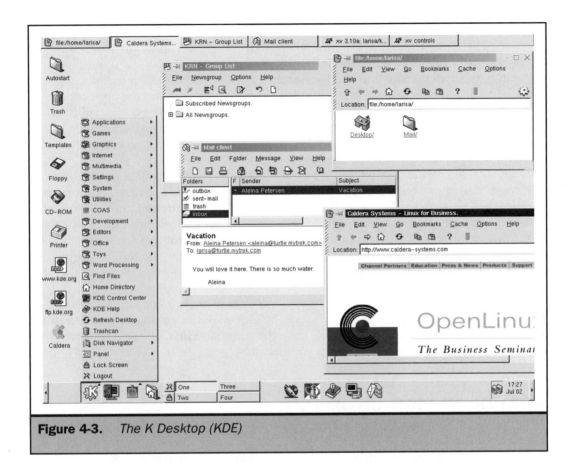

Figure 4-3.   *The K Desktop (KDE)*

with a house on it) or select the File Manager entry on the main menu, a file manager
window opens showing your home directory. You can display files in your home
directory and use the up arrow button to move to the parent directory. Back and Forward
buttons move through previously displayed directories. In the location window you can
enter the pathname for a directory to move directly to it. The file manager is also Internet
aware and a fully functional Web browser. You can use it to access remote Web and FTP
sites, displaying Web pages or downloading files from an FTP site.

To move a window, click and drag its title bar or click and drag its other borders.
Each window supports Maximize, Minimize, and Close buttons, as well as a stick pin.
Double-clicking the title bar will reduce the window to just its title bar, which can
redisplay with another double-click. The desktop supports full drag-and-drop
capabilities. You can drag folders, icons, and applications to the desktop or to another
file manager window open to other folders. Clicking the cogwheel in the right corner
of a file manager window will open a duplicate window.

Selection of an icon in a file manager window is different than in other GUIs. To select an item, Ctrl-click, instead of making a single left-click. The single left-click is the same as a double-click on other GUIs, executing the item or opening it with its associated application. So if you single-click on a folder icon, you open the folder (as opposed to simply selecting it). If you single-click a file, you start up the application using that file. To select items, be sure to Ctrl-click them. To unselect a selected item, Ctrl-click it again. When you click and drag a file to the desktop or another file manager window, a pop-up menu appears that then lets you choose whether you want to move, copy, or create a link for the item.

The panel also contains a pager for virtual desktops. This appears as four squares. Clicking a square moves you to that desktop. You can think of the virtual desktops as separate desktops, and you can use the pager to move to the different ones. To execute a command using the command line interface, you open a Console window. Click the image of a monitor on the panel. In that window at the $ prompt you can type in your command. You can modify your KDE interface at any time using the KDE Control Center. Click the image of a monitor with a circuit board on the panel, or select the KDE Control Center from the main menu.

To quit the KDE desktop, select the logout entry at the bottom of the main menu. If you entered from a login window, you will be logged out of your account and return to the login window; if you started KDE from the command line, you will return to the command line prompt, still logged into your account.

Command Line Interface

When using the command line interface, you are given a simple prompt at which you type in your command. Even with a GUI, you will sometimes need to execute commands on a terminal window command line. Linux commands make extensive use of options and arguments. Be careful to place your arguments and options in their correct order on the command line. The format for a Linux command is the command name followed by options and then by arguments, as shown here:

```
$ command-name   options   arguments
```

An option is a one-letter code preceded by a dash that modifies the type of action the command takes. Options and arguments may or may not be optional, depending on the command. For example, the **ls** command can take an option **-s**. The **ls** command displays a listing of files in your directory, and the **-s** option adds the size of each file in blocks. You would enter the command and its option on the command line as:

```
$ ls -s
```

An *argument* is data that the command may need to execute its task. In many cases it will be a file name. An argument is entered as a word on the command line after any options. For example, to display the contents of a file, you can use the **more** command with the file's name as its argument. The **more** command used with the file name **mydata** would be entered on the command line as:

```
$ more mydata
```

The *command line* is actually a buffer of text that you can edit. Before you press ENTER, you can perform editing commands on the existing text. The editing capabilities provide a way for correcting mistakes you may make when typing in a command and its options. The BACKSPACE and DEL keys allow you to erase the character just typed in. With this character-erasing capability, you can BACKSPACE over the entire line if you wish, erasing what you have entered. CTRL-U erases the whole line and lets you start over again at the prompt.

You can also use UP ARROW to redisplay your previously executed command. You can then reexecute that command or edit it and execute the modified command. You'll find this very helpful when you have to repeat certain operations over and over, such as editing the same file. It is also helpful when you've already executed a command that you had entered incorrectly.

Help and Online Documentation

A great deal of help is already installed on your system, as well as accessible from online sources. Both the Gnome and KDE desktops feature Help systems that use a browser-like interface to display help files. To start KDE Help, click the book icon in the panel. Here you can select from the KDE manual, the Linux Man pages, or the GNU info pages. KDE help features browser capabilities, including bookmarks and history lists for documents you view.

To start the Gnome Help browser, click the icon with the question mark in the panel. You can then choose from the Gnome user guide, Man pages, and info pages. It also features bookmarks and history lists.

Both Gnome and KDE, along with other applications such as Linuxconf, also provide context-sensitive help. Each KDE and Gnome application features detailed manuals that will be displayed using their respective Help browsers. Also, applications like Linuxconf feature detailed context-sensitive help. Most panels on Linuxconf have help buttons that will display detailed explanations for the operations on that panel.

In addition, extensive help is provided online. The Red Hat desktop displays Web page icons for support pages, including online manuals and tutorials. OpenLinux provides the same kind of support on the Caldera Web site.

When you start up your browser, a default Web page lists links for documentation both on your own system and at the Caldera and Red Hat Web sites. To use the Caldera and Red Hat Web sites, you first have to be connected to the Internet. However, your CD-ROM and your system contain extensive documentation showing you how to use the desktop and take you through a detailed explanation of Linux applications, including the Vi editor and shell operations. The links to this documentation are listed here. Other documentation provides detailed tutorials on different Linux topics.

On your system, the **/usr/doc** directory contains documentation files installed by each application. There are subdirectories with the names of installed Linux applications that contain documentation such as README files. You can access the complete set of HOW-TO text files in the **/usr/doc/HOWTO** directory. The HOW-TO series contains detailed documentation on all Linux topics from hardware installation to network configuration. In addition, **/doc/HOWTO/HTML** holds documentation in the form of Web pages that you display with a Web browser. (Use LISA to install the HOW-TO HTML package.)

There is also online documentation for GNU applications such as the gcc compiler and the Emacs editor. You can access this documentation by entering the command **info**. This brings up a special screen listing different GNU applications. The **info** interface has its own set of commands. You can learn more about it by entering **info info**. Typing **m** opens a line at the bottom of the screen where you can enter the first few letters of the application. Pressing ENTER brings up the info file on that application. You can also display info documents using either the Gnome or KDE help browsers.

You can also access the online manual for Linux commands from the command line interface using the **man** command. Just enter **man** with the command you want information on.

```
$ man ls
```

Pressing either the SPACEBAR or the **f** key will advance you to the next page. Pressing the **b** key will move you back a page. When you are finished, press the **q** key to quit the man utility and return to the command line. You activate a search by pressing either the slash, **/**, or question mark. A **/** will search forward and the **?** will search backward. When you press the **/**, a line will open at the bottom of your screen, and you then enter a word to search for. Press ENTER to activate the search. You can repeat the same search by pressing the **n** key. You don't have to reenter the pattern. Other utilities like Xman and Tkman provide a GUI front end for the Man pages. You can also use either the Gnome or KDE Help systems to display Man pages.

Red Hat Configuration

The official Red Hat configuration tool is Linuxconf. Red Hat also provides a collection of older configuration tools accessible through an Icon bar called the Control Panel. These are discussed in detail in Chapter 27. Red Hat, however, recommends that you use Linuxconf. Linuxconf supports three interfaces: an X Window System interface, a cursor-based interface, and a Web interface. You use the cursor-based interface from a Linux command line. You do not have to be running a GUI. The interface presents a full screen display on which you can use arrow keys, the TAB key, the SPACEBAR, and the ENTER key to make selections. With the Web-based interface you use your Web browser to make selections. Use the URL for your system with a :90 attached, as in turtle.mytrek.com:90.

Linuxconf provides an extensive set of configuration options, letting you configure features like user accounts and file systems, as well as your Internet servers, dial-up connections, and LILO. You can access the main Linuxconf interface with its entire set of configuration options, or use specialized commands that just display entries for a particular task, such as configuring users accounts or entering your network settings. The specialized commands include **userconf** for user accounts, **fsconf** for file systems, and **netconf** for networks. The main Linuxconf interface is discussed in Chapter 27. In all cases you need to log in as the root user. Configuration tools are only accessible by the root user.

Users: userconf

To add users on Red Hat, use the **userconf** command. If you are using Gnome or KDE, open a terminal window and enter the command **userconf** and press ENTER. You will see a window showing buttons for users and groups, as shown in Figure 4-4. Clicking User accounts will display a window listing all the users on your system. Click Add here to add a new user. This opens another window where you can enter the user login, home directory, and login shell, though you can use defaults for the last of these. You can use the other panels in this window to add mail aliases or set privileges such as allowing the user to mount a CD-ROM. When you are finished, another window opens that prompts you to specify a password for the user.

To change any settings for a user, just double-click its entry in the User Accounts window. This displays the User Information for this user. Click Passwd to change the password, if you wish.

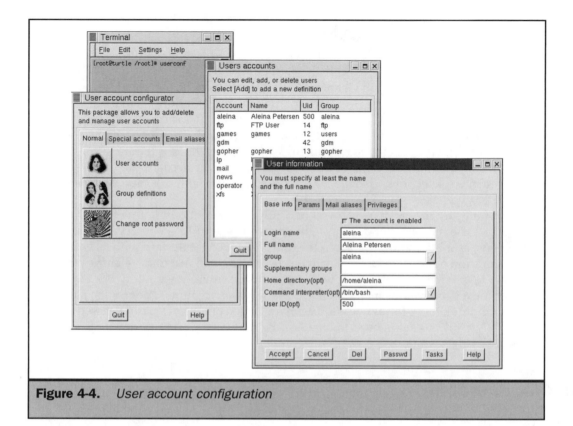

Figure 4-4. *User account configuration*

File Systems

Files and directories contained on different hardware devices such as floppy disks, CD-ROMs, and hard disk partitions are called *file systems*. The Linux partition you used to install your Linux system on is called the *root partition*. It contains the main file system with a directory tree starting from the root and spreading out to different system and user subdirectories. To access files on another file system, say a CD-ROM disc, you need to attach that file system to your main system. Attaching a file system is called mounting the file system. You first set up an empty directory to which you want to mount the file system. On Red Hat the **/mnt/cdrom** directory has already been reserved for mounting CD-ROMs, and the **/mnt/floppy** directory, for floppy disks.

Though you can mount a CD-ROM using Linuxconf, the Red Hat Gnome interface also provides a very simple method for mounting and unmounting a CD-ROM. On the Gnome desktop, you will see an icon labeled CD-ROM. Right-click it to display a pop-up menu with options to Mount the CD-ROM. Select the Mount option. You can then access the CD-ROM you placed in your CD drive by double-clicking the Gnome CD-ROM icon shown in the following illustration, or change to the **/mnt/cdrom** directory. Your CD-ROM drive remains locked until you select the Unmount entry that will now be displayed on the pop-up menu instead of Mount. If you do not see an icon for your CD-ROM, you will have to first make it user-mountable. Use **fsconf** or Linuxconf to select the local drive and double click on the cdrom entry in the Local volume window. Then on the options panel select the user mountable option. Click Act/Changes to register the change. Then right-click on the desktop and select Rescan Desktop Shortcuts from the pop-up menu.

To mount a file system using Linuxconf, you first start up Linuxconf with the **fsconf** command. This displays a Filesystem Configurator window with a button for the local drive. Click this button to display the local volume window. This lists the entries for all the file systems currently accessible on your system. To mount your CD-ROM, double-click the **/mnt/cdrom** entry to open a Volume specification window and click the Mount button. You can then access the contents of the CD-ROM at the **/mnt/cdrom** directory on your system. The CD-ROM remains locked until you click Umount.

You can also use the Local volume window to add new entries for mounting any Windows partitions that may be on your system's hard drives. Linux can directly access files on any Windows or DOS partition. Figure 4-5 shows the entries for a Windows partition (type v**fat**) to be mounted at the **/dose** directory. Should you have another CD-ROM drive on your system, you can add another entry for it (use the **iso9660** type).

Network

Network configuration differs depending on whether you are connected to a local area network (LAN) with an Ethernet card or you use a dial-up ISP connection. You had the opportunity to enter your LAN network settings during the installation process. You can configure either connection by accessing Linuxconf with the **netconf** command. This displays a the Network Configurator window that lists buttons for different network settings. (As an alternative to Linuxconf, you can use **netcfg** in the Control Panel or **kppp** as described in Chapter 28.)

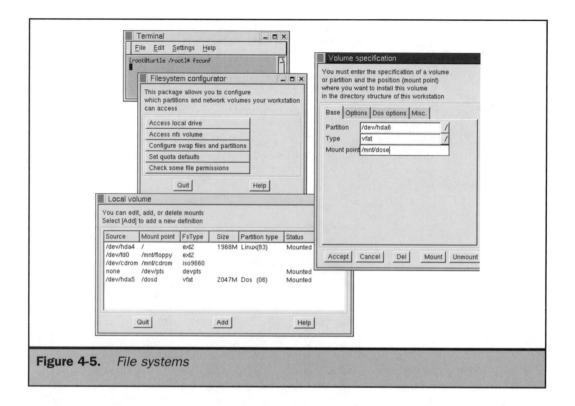

Figure 4-5. *File systems*

LAN

To configure a LAN connection, you click the Basic Host Information button to display the host configuration window. In the first adapter panel you can enter the IP address, network device, and the kernel module to use (the drivers for your Ethernet card). Then in the Network Configurator window click the Name Server Specification button to display the Resolver Configuration window, where you can enter the IP addresses for the Domain Name servers on your network (see Figure 4-6).

PPP

If you have a dialup connection to a Internet service provider (ISP), you need to configure a PPP interface. Almost all ISPs currently use PPP connections. Click the PPP/SLIP/PLIP button on the Network Configurator window. A window then opens that asks you to choose the type of interface you want. Select PPP. Then a small window opens displaying a ppp0 entry. Double-click it to display PPP interface

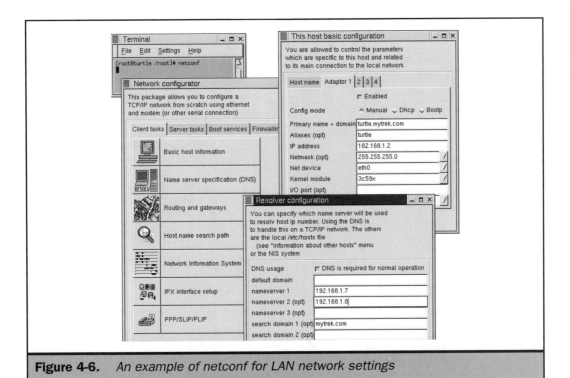

Figure 4-6.   *An example of netconf for LAN network settings*

window with panels for setting your modem connections, the phone number to dial, and the Expect and Send entries for your login name and password (see Figure 4-7). To activate a connection, click Connect. You can also use dial-up managers like **kppp**, **xisp**, and **gnomeppp** to set up and manage your PPP connections. (See Chapter 28.)

OpenLinux Configuration

On OpenLinux, you configure your system using the Caldera Open Administration System (COAS). You will find an entry for COAS in the root user KDE main menu and on the KDE Panel. COAS also supports a cursor-base interface that you can run from the command line by entering the command **coastool**. Use arrow keys, TAB, and ENTER keys to make selections.

Figure 4-7. *netconf for PPP dial-up connections*

Users

Under System Administration, select Account Administration. This displays a window showing your user accounts.

- To add a new user, select Add from the Actions menu. This opens an Edit User window where you can enter the user login name, the home directory, and the password.

- To edit a current user, double-click its entry to display its Edit User window (see Chapter 27 for more details).

File Systems

To mount file systems, select File System from the System Administration menu. This displays a File System window showing mountable devices on the left and the directories for mounted file systems on the right. To mount a file system, like a CD-ROM, select its device in left list and click Mount. An IDE CD-ROM will often have a device name like **hdc** or **hdd**. To check what a device is used for, click it and then click Info. When you mount a file system, a window opens showing the device name, the directory it will be mounted on, and the file system type (see Figure 4-8). For a new device, you will have to enter a directory and type. CD-ROMs have the type iso9660, and Linux floppy disks use **ext2**. Windows partitions have a type of vfat. You can further set options such as read only or user mountable. You can also elect to have it added to the **fstab** file, which then makes it a permanent entry and easier to mount again later.

LAN Networks

To configure a LAN connection, you select Network Administration from the COAS menu. You can then further select Ethernet Interfaces to enter your network settings. This displays a window where you can enter your IP, Gateway, Broadcast addresses, and Netmask, as well as the name of your Ethernet device. When finished, you can then select the Hostname Resolution entry in the Network Administration menu to open a window where you can enter your domain name server addresses.

PPP Dialup Connections

If you use a dial-up PPP connection to an ISP, you will need to use a PPP connection utility. Several are available, such as xisp and kppp. OpenLinux provides kppp, which you can access in the Utilities menu on your KDE main menu. The kppp utility is described in detail in Chapter 28. Click Setup on the kppp window to display a configuration window with tabbed panels for accounts, device, and modem settings.

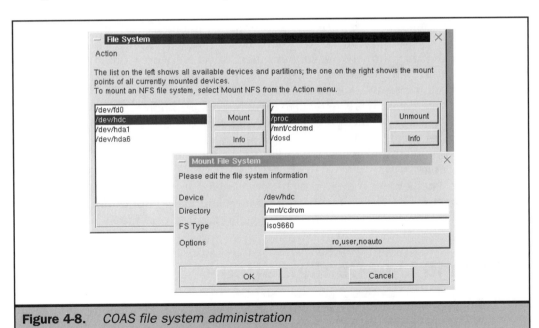

Figure 4-8.   *COAS file system administration*

Then click New in the Accounts panel to display a window of tabbed panels for entering your account connection information. The login script panel is where you enter your Expect/Send login and password strings.

SuSE Configuration

On SuSE, you configure your system using the Yet Another System Tool (YaST). You start YaST by entering the command **yast** on the command line. Use the arrow keys, TAB, and ENTER to make selections. On the main menu choose System Administration and press ENTER. This will display a submenu for different configuration options. For example, to set up your X Window System, select configure XFree86, and press ENTER. You can then choose from several X Window System configuration tools, including SaX, the SuSE XFree86 configuration tool. SaX provides a simple and easy-to-use interface for configuring your mouse, keyboard, video card, and monitor. You can use susewm to select the window manager you want to use. Select Settings of susewm from the System Administration menu to list a window with the different window managers available.

To add or edit users, select User Administration from the System Administration window and press ENTER. This displays a User administration window where you can edit or add new users. Press F3 to add a new user or select a current one. You can then make entries in the displayed fields. Use the Group Administration entry to add or change groups.

File system management is currently performed by manually editing the **/etc/fstab** file and using the **mount** command to mount and unmount file systems.

To add or change your network configuration, select Network Configuration from the System Administration menu, and then Basic Network Configuration. For an Ethernet connection press F5 then F6 and enter your IP address, netmask, and gateway. Press F4 to activate the network, and F10 to save the configuration. You then select Configure Nameserver to enter your name server addresses, and then Configure Network Services to specify the network service you want, such as inetd and NFS. For PPP use kppp on the KDE desktop or the command line form of pppd as shown in the next section.

To choose whether you want to start the system with the command line or the display manager (KDM), select Login configuration and make your choice.

You can also download Linuxconf, install it, and use it to configure your system.

Command Line Configuration

When logged in as the root user, you can also perform certain configuration operations from the command line. You can manually access system configuration files, editing them and making entries yourself. For example, the domain name server entries are kept in the **/etc/resolv.conf** file. You can edit this file and type in the addresses.

You can use the **useradd** command to add user accounts and the **userdel** command to remove them. One common operation performed from the command line is to change a password. Any user can change their own password with the **passwd** command. The command prompts you for your current password. After entering that and pressing ENTER, you are then prompted for your new password. After entering the new password, you are asked to reenter it. This is to make sure that you actually entered the password that you intended to enter. Because password characters are not displayed when you type them in, it is easy to make a mistake and press a wrong key.

```
$ passwd
Old password:
New password:
Retype new password:
$
```

File Systems

You can easily mount and unmount file systems with the **mount** and **umount** commands. To mount your CD-ROM you only have to enter the command **mount** and the directory **/mnt/cdrom**. You can then access the contents of the CD-ROM at the **/mnt/cdrom** directory.

```
$ mount /mnt/cdrom
```

When you are finished, unmount the CD-ROM with the **umount** command.

```
$ umount /mnt/cdrom
```

You can also manually mount and unmount floppy disks and hard disk partitions. See Chapter 26 for a detailed discussion.

Network

To configure a LAN connection, you make entries in network configuration files in the **/etc** directory (see Chapter 28). For a dial-up PPP connection you can manually invoke the **pppd** command to create such a connection. If, for some reason, you have not been able to set up your X Window System, you may have to set up such a connection (see Chapter 28 for more details). The following example shows how to make a very simple connection. The **connect** option instructs **pppd** to make a connection. It takes as its argument a Linux command that will actually make the connection—usually the **chat** command. You enter **pppd** followed by the **connect** option and the **chat** command with its expect-reply pairs. The entire **chat** operation is encased in single quotes. In the next example, the user invokes **pppd** with the **chat** operation. The modem is connected to port 2, **/dev/cua1**, and the speed is 57600 baud. Notice the single quotes around the entire **chat** operation with its expect-reply pairs.

```
# pppd connect  'chat -v "" ATDT5556666 ogin: mylogin  word: mypass'  /dev/cua1    57600
```

Modem Setup

If you have a modem connected to your PC, it will be connected to one of four communications ports. The PC names for these ports are COM1, COM2, COM3, and COM4. These ports can also be used for other serial devices such as your serial mouse (though not for PS/2 mice). Usually, your serial mouse is connected to COM1 and your modem is connected to COM2, though in many cases your modem may be connected to COM4. Find out which ports your modem and mouse are connected to; you'll need to know this to access your modem. On the PC, COM1 and COM3 share the same access point to your computer; the same is true of COM2 and COM4. For this reason, if you have a serial mouse connected to COM1 you should not have your modem on COM3. You could find your mouse cutting out whenever you used your modem. If your mouse is on COM1, then your modem should be either on COM2 or COM4.

In Linux, the four communications ports have different names than those used for the PC. Modem ports begin with the name **/dev/cua** with an attached number from 0 to 3. (Notice the numbering begins from 0, not 1.) The first port, COM1, is **/dev/cua0**, and **/dev/cua1** are the second ports. The third and fourth ports are **/dev/cua2** and **/dev/cua3**. In many Linux communication programs, you will need to know the port for your modem. This will be either **/dev/cua1** for COM2 or **/dev/cua3** for COM4.

Some communication programs try to access the modem port using just the name **/dev/modem**. It is meant to be an alias, another name, for whatever your modem port really is. If your system has not already set up this alias, you can easily create this alias using the **ln -s** command. On Red Hat you can use **modemtool** on the Control Panel in the System menu. The following would create an alias called modem for the COM2 port, **/dev/cua1**. If your modem port is **/dev/cua3**, you would use that instead. (You have to be logged in as root user to execute this command.) The following example sets up the **/dev/modem** alias for the second serial port, **/dev/cua1**.

```
# ln -s /dev/cua1  /dev/modem
```

Your **/dev/mouse** alias should already be set up for the port it uses. For a serial mouse this is usually the COM1 port, **/dev/cua0**. If the alias is not set up, or you need to change it, you can use the **ln -s** command. The following example sets up the **/dev/mouse** alias for the first serial port, **/dev/cua0**.

```
# ln -s /dev/cua0  /dev/mouse
```

Installing Software Packages

Now that you know how to start Linux and access the root user, you can install any other software packages you may want. Installing software is an administrative function performed by the root user. Unless you chose to install all your packages during your installation, only some of the many applications and utilities available for users on Linux were installed on your system. Both the Caldera and Red Hat distributions of Linux use the Red Hat Package Manager (RPM) to organize Linux software into packages that you can automatically install or remove. An RPM software package operates like its own installation program for a software application. A Linux software application will often consist of several files that need to be installed in different directories. The program itself will most likely be placed in a directory called **/usr/bin**, online manual files will go in another directory, and library files, in yet another. In addition, the installation may require modification of certain configuration files on your system. The RPM software packages on your Red Hat and OpenLinux CD-ROM will perform all these tasks for you. Also, if you should later decide that you don't want a specific application, you can uninstall packages to remove all the files and configuration information from your system (see Chapter 24 or more details).

The RPM packages on your CD-ROMs only represent a small portion of the software packages available for Linux. You can download additional software in the form of RPM packages from distribution contrib sites, such as **contrib.redhat.com** for Red Hat packages and the **contrib** directory in the OpenLinux FTP site at **ftp.calderasystem.com**. In addition, these packages are organized into **lib5** and **lib6** directories. The former refers to the packages using the older libraries, whereas **lib6** refers to those using the new GNU 2.x libraries. For Red Hat 6.0 and OpenLinux 2.2 you should use the **lib6** versions, though **lib5** versions will also work. There is also an extensive repository for RPM packages located at **http://rpmfind.net/**. Here, packages are indexed according to distribution, group, and name. It includes packages for every distribution including previous versions of those distributions. You can also locate many of the newest Linux applications from **freshmeat.net**. Here, you can link to the orginal development sites for these applications and download documentation and the recent versions.

Installing Packages on OpenLinux

To install packages from the OpenLinux CD-ROM, select Software Management from the COAS menu. This opens a window, as shown in the following illustration, that lists software packages by category. Packages are listed in the right-most column, with specific-to-general categories listed from right to left. Selecting different categories displays the packages in them.

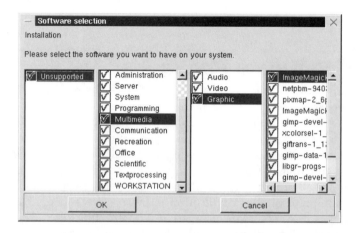

Alternatively, on the KDE desktop, you can also use kpackage to install packages. Select the Open entry in the File menu and move to the CD-ROM. It will be located in the **/mnt/cdrom** directory, and the RPM packages will be listed in the **Packages/RPMS** directory.

On the KDE desktop, you can install an RPM package simply by locating its RPM file on your system using the KDE file manager and then single-clicking its icon or name. This will automatically open kpackage with the RPM package loaded. It will be displayed on a window with panels for the package information and the list of files in it. At the bottom of the panels is an Install button. Click it to install the package.

As the KDE file manager is Internet aware, you can use this same method to both download and install RPM packages from FTP sites. Locate the FTP site with the file manager (enter its URL in the location box), and then locate your package. Once it is listed in the file manager window, just click it. It will be automatically downloaded, and then kpackage will start up showing the package (see Figure 4-9). Just click Install to install it.

Installing Packages on Red Hat

To install packages on Red Hat, you use the GnomeRPM utility or the Gnome file manager. Select the GnomeRPM entry in the Gnome main menu under Systems. With GnomeRPM you can locate packages on your file system. For your Red Hat CD-ROM, be sure to first mount the CD-ROM, then use GnomeRPM to access the **/mnt/cdrom/ RedHat/RPMS** directory. There you will find your packages listed. Choose the ones you want to install. GnomeRPM will list packages already installed. You can select them to view their details and file list.

Instead of GnomeRPM, you can use the Gnome file manager to install RPM packages. This is actually easier to do for individual packages. Use the file manager window to access the directory with your package. Then right-click the package name or icon. In the pop-up menu you can select the Install option to install the package. You can use this same method for FTP sites. The Gnome file manager is Internet aware. You can enter a URL for an FTP site in its location box to access the site. When you have

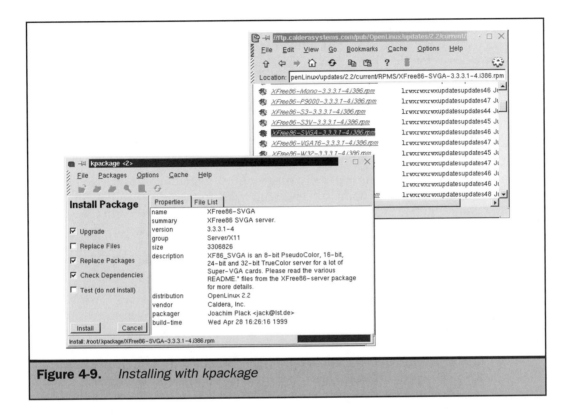

Figure 4-9. *Installing with kpackage*

located the package, right-click it and select Install or Update. The file is downloaded and then automatically installed on your system.

Command Line Installation

If you do not have access to the desktop or you would prefer to work from the command line interface, you can use the **rpm** command to manage and install software packages. The command name stands for the Red Hat Package Manager. It is the command that actually performs installation, removal, and verification of software packages. In fact, both K package and GnomeRPM use the **rpm** command to install and remove packages. Each software package is actually an RPM package, consisting of an archive of software files and information about how to install those files. Each archive resides as a single file with a name that ends with **.rpm**, indicating that it is a software package that can be installed by the Red Hat Package Manager.

You can use the **rpm** command to either install or uninstall a package. It uses a set of options to determine what action to take. Table 3-1 lists the set of **rpm** options. The **-i** option will install the specified software package, and the **-U** option will update a package. With an **-e** option, **rpm** will uninstall the package. A **q** placed before an **i**

(**-qi**) will query the system to see if a software package is already installed and display information about the software (**-qpi** will query an uninstalled package file). The **-h** option provides a complete list of **rpm** options. A helpful one is the **--nodeps** option, that will install without performing dependency checks . The syntax for the **rpm** command is as follows (*rpm-package-name* is the name of the software package that you want to install):

    rpm *options* rpm-package-name

The software package name is usually very lengthy, including information about version and release date in its name. All end with **.rpm**. In the next example, the user installs the linuxconf package using the **rpm** command. Notice that the full file name is entered. To list the full name, you can use the **ls** command with the first few characters and an asterisk, **ls linuxconf***. You can also use the * to match the remainder of the name, as in **linuxconf-1.16*.rpm**. In most cases, you will be installing packages with the **–U** option, update. Even if the package is not already installed, **–U** will still install it.

    $ rpm -Uvh linuxconf-1.16r-1-1.i386.rpm

When RPM performs an installation, it first checks for any dependent packages. These are other software packages with programs that the application you are installing needs to use. If other dependent packages need to be installed first, then RPM will cancel the installation and list those packages. You can install those packages, and then repeat the installation of the application. In a few situations such as a major distribution update where packages may be installed out of order, it will be alright to install without dependency checks. For this you use the **–nodeps** option. This assumes though that all the needed packages are being installed.

To find out if a package is already installed, use the **-qi** option with **rpm**. The **-q** stands for query. To obtain a list of all the files that the package has installed, as well as the directories it installed to, you use the **-ql** option.

To query package files, you add the **p** option. The **-qpi** option will display information about a package, and **-qpl** will list the files in it. The following example lists all the files in the Linuxconf package.

    $ rpm -qpl linuxconf-1.16r-1-1.i386.rpm

To remove a software package from your system, first use **rpm -qi** to make sure it is actually installed. Then, use the **-e** option to uninstall it. As with the **-qi** option, you do not have to use the full name of the installed file. You only need the name of the application. In the next example, the user removes the xtetris game from the system:

```
$ rpm  -e  xtetris
```

-U	Update package
-i	Install package
-e	Remove package
-qi	Display information for an installed package
-ql	Display file list for installed package
-qpi	Display information from an RPM package file (used for uninstalled packages)
-qpl	Display file list from an RPM package file (used for uninstalled packages)

Updating Distributions

New versions of distributions are often released every 6 to 12 months. In the meantime, new updates are continually being prepared for particular software packages. These are posted as updates that you can download from a distribution's FTP site and install on your system. These will include new versions of applications, servers, and even the kernel. Downloading and installing updates is a fairly straightforward process, made even easier with the Gnome and KDE desktops. An important update you may need to perform is to update the xFree86 packages. If you install a new video card or monitor and the current xFree86 package does not support it, chances are that the new one will. Just download those packages from the distribution update sites and install them with the RPM update operation, as shown here.

```
$ rpm -Uvh  --nodeps  XFree86*rpm
```

Updating Red Hat

RPM update packages are kept in the Red Hat update site at **updates.redhat.com** and its mirror sites. You can access the site, locate the updates for your distribution version, and then download them to your system. Then you can install them using an RPM utility like GnomeRPM, or the **rpm** command using the update option, **-U**. Perhaps the easiest way to do this is to use the Gnome file manager to first download the files (see Figure 4-10).

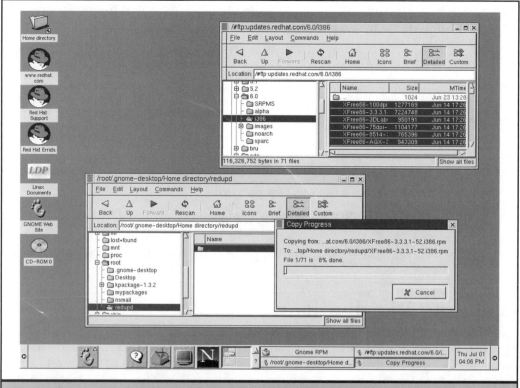

Figure 4-10.   *Downloading updates on the Gnome desktop*

1. First open a file manager window, then enter the URL for the Red Hat update site in its location box, and access the update site. For Red Hat 6.0, the updates will be in the **6.0** directory.

2. Within that directory move to the **current** directory. There you will see the list of all the updates.

3. Download any new ones, or all of them if this is the first update for your version. To download, open another file manager window and create a new directory to hold your update. Open that directory. Then just select and drag the update files from the file manager window for the update site to that new directory. You may not need all the files. In the case of kernel updates, you will only need the kernel file for your processor, either i386, i586 (Pentium), or i686 (Pentium II).

4. As files are downloaded, a dialog box displays the file name and the percentage downloaded.

Once the update is downloaded, you can open a Terminal window, change to that new directory. You open a Terminal window by clicking the Monitor icon in the panel. Then use the **cd** command to change to that directory. If the directory name is **redup**, you would enter:

 # cd redup

Then issue the following **rpm** update command. The **nodeps** options uses two dashes. If you just want to start by installing certain packages, you can refine your installation, as shown in the previous example for XFree86.

```
$ rpm -Uvh  --nodeps  *rpm
```

Alternatively, you can open the GnomeRPM utility and then open the dialog for installing packages. From the file manager window displaying the packages, you can drag and drop the files to the GnomeRPM install dialog. You may receive errors messages noting dependency requirements. You can usually safely ignore these. If you also receive install conflicts, you may be trying to install two versions of the same package. In that case you will have to install one or the other.

Updating OpenLinux

To update OpenLinux, you can perform much the same kind operation.

1. Use the KDE file manager window to access the OpenLinux update directory located at the Caldera FTP site at **ftp.calderasystems.com**. Be sure to view any readme files for any special instructions on installing the updates.

2. Then open another file manager window to a new directory where you want to store your update files.

3. Select all the files and then drag and drop them to that new file manager window. A dialog box will appear as each file is downloaded, showing the percentage of the download (see Figure 4-11).

4. Once the download is complete, you individually install packages with kpackage, or use the **rpm** command.

   ■ If there are many files, as there are for the 2.2 update, you may want to use the **rpm** command.

- Open a Terminal window by clicking the Monitor icon in the panel.

- Then use the **cd** command to change to that directory. If the directory name is **caldup**, you would enter:

```
# cd caldup
```

- Then use the **rpm** command with the **-Uvh** options and ***rpm** to select all the RPM packages at once.

You can refine the install using more refined file-name matching.

```
# rpm -Uvh --nodeps   *rpm
```

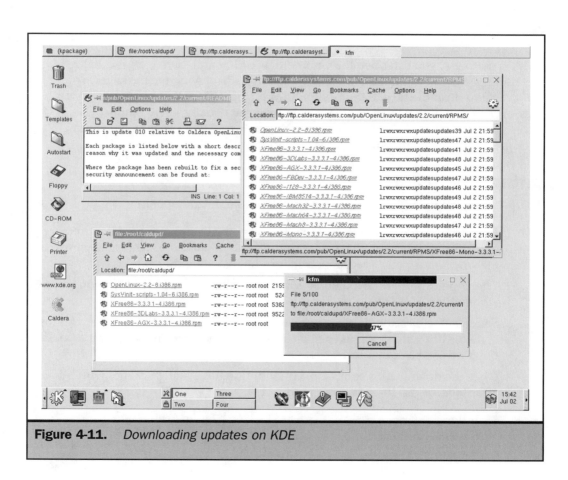

Figure 4-11.   *Downloading updates on KDE*

The
Complete
Reference

Linux

Part II

Environments

The
Complete
Reference

Chapter 5

The K Desktop Environment: KDE

The K Desktop Environment (KDE) is a network transparent desktop that includes the standard desktop features such as a window manager and file manager as well as an extensive set of applications that cover most Linux tasks. It is an Internet-aware system that includes a full set of integrated network/Internet applications, including a mailer, a newsreader, and a Web browser. The file manager doubles as a Web and FTP client, letting you access Internet sites directly from your desktop. KDE aims to provide a level of desktop functionality and ease of use found in MAC/OS and Windows systems, combined with the power and flexibility of the Unix operating system. Though the Unix system has long been prevalent in scientific and server applications, it has not been used extensively by ordinary users due to its somewhat difficult interface. KDE aims to make Unix and Linux systems as easy to use for the ordinary user as Windows and MAC/OS systems, and then some. It bears an interface that will be familiar to users of Window 98 and Windows 2000.

The KDE desktop is developed and distributed by the KDE project. This a large, open group of hundreds of programmers around the world. KDE is entirely free and open software provided under a GNU public license. It is available free of charge along with its source code. KDE development is managed by a core group: The KDE Core Team. Anyone can apply, though membership is based on merit. KDE applications are developed using the Compound Document Framework called KOM/OpenParts. To allow applications to share object such as images, spreadsheets, and documents, a desktop like KDE uses a technology for managing distributed objects called CORBA, the Common Object Request Broker Architecture. KDE has added to CORBA an additional object management capability called KOM (K Object Manager). KOM provides functionality not found in the CORBA standard. KOM/OpenParts allows developers to develop KDE applications quickly. You can think of it as similar to IBM/Apple's SOM/OpenDoc or Microsoft's DCOM/OLE/ActiveX.

Numerous applications written specifically for KDE are easily accessible from the desktop. These include editors, photo and paint image applications, spreadsheets, and office applications. Such applications usually have the letter "k" as part of their name—for example, **kedit** or **kpaint**. Table 5-4 provides a listing of commonly used KDE applications. On a system administration level, KDE provides several tools for configuring your system. With **kuser**, you can manage user accounts, adding new ones or removing old ones. The **kppp** application lets you easily connect to remote networks with PPP (Point-to-Point Protocol) protocols using a modem. Practically all your Linux tasks can be performed from the KDE desktop. Currently, KDE is developing an office application suite called KOffice, based on KDE's KOM/OpenParts technology. KOffice includes a presentation application, a spreadsheet, an illustrator, and a word processor, among other components. A variety of tools are provided with the KDE desktop for your use. These include calculators, console windows, notepads, and even software package managers. Of course, let's not forget games. Table 5-4 provides a current listing, though these will be added to with new KDE releases. KDE applications feature a built-in Help application. Choosing the Contents entry in the Help menu starts the

KDE Help viewer. The Help viewer provides a Web page–like interface with links for navigating through the Help documents.

KDE was initiated by Matthias Ettrich in October 1996. It has an extensive list of sponsors, including SuSE, Caldera, Red Hat, O'Reilly, DLD, Delix, Live, Linux Verband and others. It is designed to run on any Unix implementation, including Linux, Solaris, HP-UX, and FreeBSD. The official KDE Web site is **www.kde.org**. The site provides news updates, download links, and documentation. KDE software packages can be downloaded from the KDE FTP site at **ftp.kde.org** and its mirror sites. There are several KDE mailing lists for users and developers, announcements, administration, and other topics. See the KDE Web site to subscribe.

Qt and Harmony

KDE uses as its library of GUI tools the Qt library developed and supported by Troll Tech (**www.troll.no**). Qt is considered one of the best GUI libraries available for Unix/Linux systems. Using Qt has the advantage of relying on a commercially developed and supported GUI library. Also, using the Qt libraries drastically reduced the development time for KDE. Troll Tech provides the Qt libraries as open source software that is freely distributable. There are, however, certain restrictions. Qt-based (KDE) applications must be free and open sourced, with no modifications made to the Qt libraries. If you develop an application with the Qt libraries and want to sell it, then you have to buy a license from Troll Tech. In other words, the Qt library is free for free applications, but not for commercial ones.

The Harmony Project is currently developing a free alternative to the Qt libraries. Harmony will include all Qt functionality as well as added features such as mutlithreading and theming. It will be entirely compatible with any KDE applications developed using Qt libraries. Harmony will be provided under the GNU library public license (LGPL). See **www.harmony.org** for more information.

KDE Desktop

One of KDE aims is to provide users with a consistent integrated desktop, where all applications use GUI interfaces. To this end, KDE provides its own window manager (kwm), file manager (kfm), program manager, and desktop panel. You can run any other X Window System compliant application such as Netscape in KDE, as well as any Gnome application. In turn, you can also run any KDE application (see Figure 5-1), including the kfm file manager, with any other Linux window manager like Blackbox, Afterstep, and even Enlightenment. You can even run KDE applications in Gnome.

When you first start KDE, the initial file manager window is displayed on your screen showing your current working directory. At the bottom of the screen is the KDE panel. Located on the panel are icons for menus and programs, as well as buttons for different desktop screens. The icon for the Applications Starter shows a large "K" on a

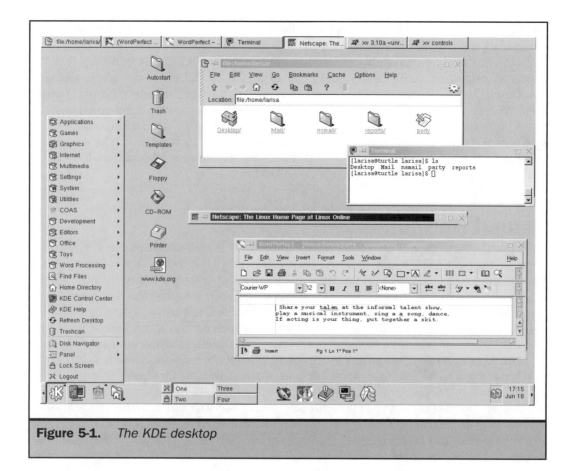

Figure 5-1. The KDE desktop

cog wheel with a small arrow at the top indicating that it is a menu. Click on this to display the menu listing all the applications you can run. The Applications Starter operates somewhat like the Start menu in Windows. The standard KDE applications that were installed with the KDE can be accessed through this menu. You will find entries for different categories such as Internet, Systems, Multimedia, and Utilities. These submenus will list KDE applications that you can use. For example, to start the KDE mailer, select the Mail Client entry in the Internet submenu. At the top of the screen is a taskbar showing buttons for different programs you are running or windows you have open. This is essentially a docking mechanism that lets you change to a window or application just by clicking on its button. To quit KDE, you can select the Logout entry in the Applications Starter menu. You can also right-click anywhere on the desktop and select the Logout entry from the pop-up menu. If you leave any KDE or X11 applications or windows open when you quit, they will automatically be restored when you start up again.

Three icons are initially displayed in the upper-right corner of the desktop. The Trash icon operates like the Recycle Bin in Windows or the trash can on the Mac. Drag items to it to hold them for deletion. The AutoStart folder holds programs you want automatically started whenever KDE starts. The Templates folder holds templates for easily creating documents. You can place default document files here, such as default files for Web links, makefiles, or editor files. The panel will initially show small icons for the Applications Starter, window list, your **home** directory, a terminal window, and buttons for virtual desktops, among others. The Window List icon looks like several grouped windows. It displays a list of all open windows and the desktop they are on. The Home Directory icon shows a folder with a house. Click on it to open a file manager window showing your **home** directory. The Help Viewer icon is an image of a book. The Terminal Window icon will be a picture of two computer monitors. Click on this to open a terminal window where you can enter Linux shell commands.

The desktop supports drag-and-drop operations. For example, to print a document, drag it to the Printer icon. You can place any directories on the desktop by simply dragging them from a file manager window to the desktop. You can also create new ones on the desktop by right-clicking anywhere on the desktop and selecting New, then Directory from the pop-up menu. All items that appear on the desktop are located in the **Desktop** directory in your **home** directory. There you will find the **Trash**, **Templates**, and **AutoStart** directories, along with any others that you place on the desktop. To configure your desktop, either click on the Desktop icon located on the right of your panel, or right-click on the desktop and select the Display Properties entry. This displays a window with several tabbed panels for different desktop settings, such as the background or style.

kdelink Files

On the KDE desktop, special files called *kdelink files* are used to manage a variety of tasks, including device management, Internet connections, program management, and document types. You create a kdelink file by right-clicking on the desktop and then selecting New. From this menu, you choose the type of kdelink file you want to create. Application is for launching applications. The File System Devices option creates a kdelink file that can mount devices on your system such as CD-ROMs and floppy disks. The MIME Types option is for kdelink files that are used to define new MIME types and their associated applications. The Internet Address entry lets you define a simple kdelink file that you can use to access a Web or FTP site. The application, device, and MIME type functions are covered in later sections.

You can create a kdelink file (see Figure 5-2) that holds an Internet URL address and then use that kdelink file to directly access that site. You can place the kdelink file on your desktop or put it in your panel, where it is easily accessible. You can configure the file to display any icon you choose. In effect, you can have an icon on your desktop that you can click on to immediately access a Web site. When you click on the URL kdelink file, the file manager will start up and access that address, displaying the Web page. For FTP sites, it will perform an anonymous login and display the **remote** directory.

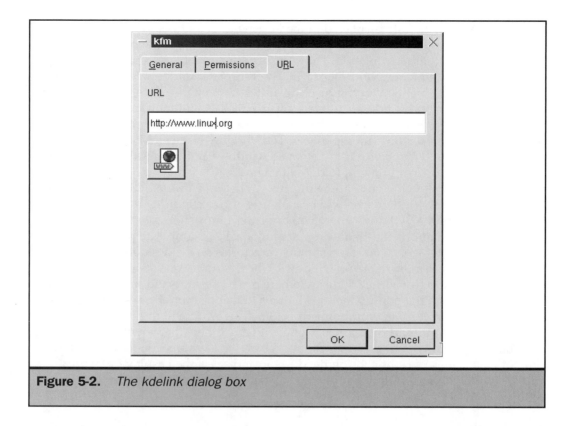

Figure 5-2. *The kdelink dialog box*

To create a URL kdelink file, right-click on the desktop and select the New menu. You then have three possible kinds of URL kdelink files to choose from. They are all URL kdelink files but have different defaults, depending on what you want to use it for. There are entries for an FTP, a Web, and a generic Internet address: FTP URL, World Wide Web URL, and Internet kAddresss (URL). For a Web URL, you would select World Wide Web URL. A window will appear that displays a box with the name **WWWUrl.kdelink** (for FTP, this will be **FTPUrl.kdelink**, and for the Internet address it will be **URL.kdelink**) (shown in Figure 5-2). Replace the prefix, in this case **WWWUrl**, with a name of your own choosing. Be sure to keep the **.kdelink** extension (this is important). For example, to create a kdelink file for the KDE themes Web site, you would enter something like **kdethemes.kdelink**. A kdelink dialog box for URL access will then be displayed. This dialog box has three tabbed panels: General, Permissions, and URL. On the General panel will be the name of your kdelink file. Go to the URL panel. There, you will see a box labeled "URL" with a default Web URL already in it. Replace it with the URL you want. For example, for KDE themes the URL would be **http://kde.themes.org**. Be sure to include the protocol, such as **http://** or **ftp://**. An Icon button on this panel will show the icon that will be displayed for this kdelink file on your desktop. The default will be a Web World icon. You can change it if you wish by clicking on the Icon button to open a window that lists icons you can choose from. Click OK when you are finished. The kdelink file will then appear on your desktop with that icon. Click on it to access the Web site. An alternative and easier way to create a URL kdelink file is to simply drag a URL from a Web page displayed on the file manager to your desktop. A kdelink file will be automatically generated with that URL. To change the default icon used, you can right-click on the file and choose Properties to display the kdelink dialog box. Click on the Icon button to choose a new icon.

KDE Windows

A KDE window has the same functionality that you find in other window managers and desktops. You can resize the window by clicking and dragging any of its corners or sides. A side will extend the window in that dimension, whereas a corner will extend both height and width at the same time. You will notice that the corners are slightly enhanced. The top of the window has a title bar showing the name of the window. This will be the program name in the case of applications, and current directory name for the file manager windows. The active window will have the title bar highlighted. Figure 5-3 shows an example of a KDE window.

To move the window, click its title bar and drag it where you want. In the right side of the title bar are small buttons for closing, minimizing, or maximizing the window. The button with the X will close the window. The one with a small box will maximize the window, letting the window take up the entire screen. Click on the button again to restore the window to its previous size. Clicking on the Maximize button with the middle or right mouse button will maximize vertically or horizontally. The button showing a simple period will minimize it. On KDE, when you minimize a window it is no longer displayed on the desktop, but its button entry remains in the taskbar at the top of the screen. Click on that button to redisplay the window. You can also reduce a window to its title bar by double-clicking on the title bar. To restore the window, double-click on the title bar again.

On the left side of the title bar are two buttons: a Window button and a Stick Pin button. Clicking the Window button displays a drop-down menu with entries for window operations such as closing or resizing the window. The Stick Pin button next to it is used to have a window appear on all your virtual desktops, no matter which one you change to. In effect, the window sticks on the screen when you change to another virtual desktop. When active, only its head will appear, as if you pushed a stick pin into the desktop. When not active, a side view stick-pin image is shown, making it appear as if it has been laid on its side. Below the title bar, menus for the particular application are displayed. Toolbars may also be displayed, such as the navigation toolbar used for the file manger.

As a multitasking operating system, Linux lets you run several applications at the same time. This means that you can have several applications open and running on

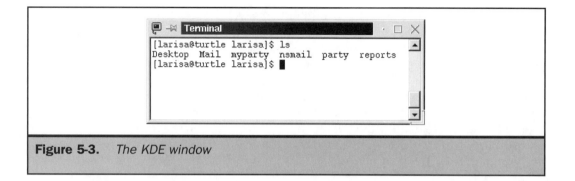

Figure 5-3.   *The KDE window*

your desktop, each with their own window. You can switch between them by moving
from one window to another. When an application is open, a button for it is placed in
the taskbar at the top of the desktop. You can switch to that application at any time by
clicking on its Taskbar button. From the keyboard, you can use the ALT-TAB key
combination to display a list of current applications. Holding down the ALT key and
sequentially pressing TAB moves you through the list. You can hide an application at
any time by clicking on its window's Minimize button. The Taskbar button entry for it
will remain. Click on this to restore the application.

Table 5-1 shows the KDE keyboard shortcuts.

Keypresses	Effect
ALT-ESC or CTRL-ESC	"Current Session"-manager with Logout button
ALT-TAB and ALT-SHIFT-TAB	Traverse the windows of the current desktop
CTRL-TAB and CTRL-SHIFT-TAB	Traverse the virtual desktops
ALT-F2	Open small command-line window
ALT-F3	Window operation menu
ALT-F4	Close window
CTRL-F[1–8]	Switch to a particular virtual desktop
CTRL-ALT-ESC	Force shutdown of X Windows

Table 5-1.   *KDE Keyboard Shortcuts*

Virtual Desktops

KDE, as with most Linux window managers, supports virtual desktops. In effect, this extends the desktop area for you to work on. You could have Netscape running on one desktop and be using a text editor in another. KDE can support up to eight virtual desktops, though the default is four. The KDE panel holds a button for each virtual desktop. The buttons are displayed with the names One, Two, Three, and Four (see the following illustration). As you shall see, you can change these names to whatever you want. To move from one desktop to another, just click on its button. Clicking on Three will display the third desktop, and clicking on One will move you back to the first desktop.

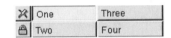

Normally, when you open an application on a particular desktop, it will appear only in that desktop. When you move to another desktop, the application will disappear from your screen. Moving back will again show the application. For example, if you open kmail on the third desktop and then move to the second desktop, kmail will disappear from your screen. Moving back to the third desktop will cause kmail to appear again. Selecting the Taskbar button for an application will also switch you to the desktop that the application is open on. For example, clicking on the kmail Taskbar button will switch to the third desktop. You can also use the Window list menu in the panel to display a listing of all open windows in each desktop. Selecting a window entry will move to that desktop. If you want an application to appear on all desktops, no matter which one you move to, click on its window's Pin button in the upper-left corner.

Should you want to move a window to a different desktop, first open the window's menu by clicking on the Window button in the upper-left corner. Then, select the To Desktop entry, which then lists the available desktops. Choose the one you want. You can also right-click on the window's title bar to display the window's menu.

Most window managers use a pager to let you switch from one desktop to another. KDE also has a pager, which is not initially displayed. To display the pager, select Desktop Pager from the System menu in the Applications Starter menu. A four-squared rectangle is displayed, one for each desktop. Click a rectangle to move to that desktop.

You can also configure KDE so that if you move the mouse over the edge of a desktop screen, it will automatically move to the adjoining desktop. You need to imagine the desktops arranged in a four-square configuration, with two top desktops next to each other and two desktops below them. You enable this feature by selecting the Active Desktop Borders entry in the Desktop panel in the KDE Control Center.

To change the number of virtual desktops you use the KPanel configuration window. From the Applications Starter menu, select Panel and then Configure. On the KPanel configuration window, select the Desktop panel. You will see entries for the current desktops. The visible bar controls the number of desktops. Slide this to the right to add more, and to the left to reduce the number. The width bar controls the width of the desktop buttons on the panel. You can change any of the desktop names by clicking on a name and entering a new one.

You can also configure desktop features such as color background for each virtual desktop. In the Applications Starter menu, select Settings and then Desktop. From this menu, you can choose various features to change. Selecting Background displays a Display Settings window. A list of virtual desktops will be shown. Select the one whose background you want to change. You can then choose from colors and wallpaper. You can select wallpaper from a preselected list or choose your own.

KDE Panel and Applications Starter

The KDE panel (shown below) is located at the bottom of the screen. Through it you can access most KDE functions. The panel includes icons for menus, directory windows, specific programs, and virtual desktops. At the left end of the panel is an icon with a large K on a cog wheel. This is the icon for the KDE Application Starter. Click on this icon to display the menu of applications you run. From the KDE menu, you can access numerous submenus for different kinds of applications. You can also open the Application Starter with the ALT-F1 key.

To add an application to the panel, select the Add application entry in the panel submenu located in the Applications Starter. This menu will display all installed KDE applications. To add a button for an application to the panel, just click on the application entry. You can also drag applications from a File Manager window to the panel directly and have them automatically placed in the panel. The panel only displays kdelink files. When you drag and drop a file to the panel, a kdelink file for it is automatically generated.

To configure the panel position and behavior, right-click on the panel and select the configure entry. This displays a panel configuration dialog box with several tabbed panels. The Positions panel lets you specify the edges of the screen where you want your panel and taskbar displayed. You can also enlarge or reduce it in size. On the Options panel you can set auto-hide options for the panel and taskbar. The Desktops panel is used for configuring your virtual desktops, letting you add more desktops and rename the current ones.

You can add or remove menu items in your Applications Starter menu using the Edit Menus program. Right-click on its K icon and select Configure. This launches the Edit Menus window, displaying the Applications Starter menu to the right and a menu button to the left labeled Empty. To add a new item, just drag this button to the Launcher menu. You can even place it in a submenu. To enter a label and an application for it to start, you right-click on the button. This displays a dialog box with fields for the application program, menu item name, and the MIME types to be associated with the program. You can also specify if you want the program opened in a terminal window. For example, to create a menu entry for the notorious Vi editor, drag the Empty button to the Launcher menu. Right-click on it and enter **vi** as the command and **The Vi Editor** as the name. Click the check box for "Open in terminal window," as Vi is a shell-based program. Before you quit, be sure to select Save from the File menu. You will then see an entry for The Vi editor in the Applications Starter menu. You can also delete entries using Edit Menus. On Red Hat systems, when you first start Edit Menus, you will find that there is another menu item under the empty item that is labeled Red Hat Menus. These are menus already set up for all your applications that were installed by Red Hat. You can place all these menus on the Applications Starter by just dragging this button to the Starter menu. You will then see an entry for Red Hat menus that will expand to numerous submenus.

KDE Themes

For your desktop, you can select a variety of different themes. A theme changes the look and feel of your desktop, affecting the appearance of GUI elements such as scrollbars, buttons, and icons. For example, you use the Mac OS theme to make your K desktop look like a Macintosh. Themes for the K desktop can be downloaded from the **kde.themes.org** Web site. Information and links for themes for different window managers can be found at **www.themes.org**. You can use the KthemeMgr program to install and change your themes.

The KDE Help System

The KDE Help viewer provides a browser-like interface for accessing and displaying both KDE Help files and Linux man and info files. You can start the Help system either by selecting its entry in the Applications Starter menu or by right-clicking on the desktop and selecting the Help entry (see Figure 5-4). You can use a URL format to access man and info pages, info: and man:. For example, man:cp will display the man page for the **cp** command. A navigation toolbar lets you move through previously viewed documents. KDE Help documents use an HTML format with links you can

Figure 5-4. *The KDE Help System*

click on to access other documents. Initially, the KDE Help system will display a list of contents with links for access in the KDE applications index for application documentation, the system man pages, and system info directory where you can access info documents for TeX, emacs, gcc, among others. The **Back** and **Forward** commands move you through the list of previously viewed documents. **Prev**, **Next**, **Up**, and **Top** are use for man and info documents. These are arranged in a tree that you can move up and down through. The KDE Help system provides an effective search tool for searching for patterns in Help documents, including man and info pages. Select the Search entry to display a page where you can enter your pattern. You can also click on the small icon in the toolbar of a page with a spyglass.

Applications

You can start an application in KDE in several ways. If there is an entry for it in the Applications Starter menu, you can just select that entry to start the application. Some applications also have buttons on the KDE panel that you can click on to start them. The panel already holds several of the commonly used programs such as the kmail and kcalendar. You can also use the file manager to locate a file that uses that application or the application program itself. Clicking on its icon will start the application. Alternatively you can open a shell window and enter the name of the application at the shell prompt and press ENTER to start an application. You can also use the ALT-F2 key to open a small window consisting of a box for entering a single command. You can use the UP and DOWN ARROW keys to display previous commands, as well as use the RIGHT and LEFT ARROW keys and the BACKSPACE keys to edit any of them. Press ENTER to execute a command.

You can also access applications directly from your desktop. To access an application from the desktop, you either create a kdelink or standard link file that will link to the original application program. With a kdelink file, you can choose your own icon and specify a tooltip comment. You can also use a kdelink file to start a shell-based application running in its own terminal window. A standard link, on the other hand, is a simple reference to the original program file. Using a link will start the program directly with no arguments. To create a standard link file, locate the application on your file system, usually in the **/usr/bin** or **/usr/sbin** directory. Then, click and drag the application icon to your desktop. In the pop-up menu, select Link. The link will have the same icon as the original application. Whenever you then click on that icon, you can select Start from the pop-up menu to start the application.

To create a kdelink file, you right-click anywhere on the empty desktop, select New from the pop-up menu, and then choose Application. Enter the name for the program and a kdelink file for it will appear on the desktop with that name. A kfm dialog box then opens with four panels: General, Permissions, Execute, and Application. The General panel will display the name of the link with the extension **.kdelink**. To specify the application that the kdelink file will run, go to the Execute panel and either enter the application's program name in the Execute box or click Browse to select it. KDE applications are often located in the **/usr/bin** directory and begin with "k". To select an icon image for the kdelink file, click on the Cog icon. The "Select icon" window is displayed, listing icons for you to choose from. To run a shell-based program such as Vi or Pine, click the "Run in terminal" check box and specify any terminal options. Certain KDE program can minimize to a small icon while they are running, which can be displayed in the panel. This is referred to as "Swallowing on the panel." Enter the name of the program in that Execute box.

On the Permissions panel, be sure to set execute permissions so that the program can be run. In the Application panel, you can specify the type of documents that will be associated with this application. The bottom of the panel shows two lists. The left list is for MIME types you want associated with this program, and the right list is the listing of available MIME types to choose from. To add a MIME type, select an entry in the right list and click the Left Arrow button. Use the Right Arrow button to remove a MIME type. On the panel, you also specify the comment, the file manager program name, and the name in your language. The comment is the Help note that will appear when you pass your mouse over the icon. For the file manager program name, enter the name followed by a semicolon (;). This is the name used for the link, should you use the file manger to display it; kdelinks do not have to reside on the desktop. You can place them in any directory and access them through the file manager. You can later make changes to a kdelink file by right-clicking on its icon and selecting Properties from the pop-up menu. This again displays the kfm dialog box for this file. You can change its icon and even the application that it runs. You can download other icons from **icons.themes.org**.

You can have KDE automatically display selected directories or start certain applications whenever it starts up. To do so, you place links for these windows and applications in the **AutoStart** directory. You will see the AutoStart folder displayed on your desktop. To place a link for a directory in the AutoStart folder, first locate the Directory icon using the file manager. Then, click and drag the icon to the AutoStart folder. From the pop-up menu that then appears, select Link (not Copy or Move). Whenever you start KDE, that directory will be displayed in a file manager window. You can do the same for applications and files. Locate the application with the file manager and click and drag it to the AutoStart folder, selecting Link. For a file, do the same. Whenever KDE starts, those applications will automatically start. For files, the application associated with it will start using that file. For example, to automatically start kmail, click and drag its icon to the AutoStart folder, selecting Link.

Mounting CD-ROMs and Floppy Disks from the Desktop

With KDE, you can create icons on your desktop that you can use to easily access a CD-ROM or floppy disk using these icons. The icons are kdelink files. These are special files that can perform a variety of tasks, including accessing devices such as CD-ROMs. Once you have set up a kdelink file for your CD-ROM you can access a CD-ROM disk, by just placing it in your CD-ROM drive and clicking on the CD-ROM icon. The file manager window will open, displaying the contents of the CD-ROM's top-level directory. You can also right-click on the icon to display a pop-up menu with an entry to mount the disk. When the CD-ROM holds a mounted CD disk, the CD-ROM icon will display a small red rectangle on its image. Unlike Windows systems, the CD-ROM disk will remain locked in the CD-ROM drive until you unlock it. To unmount the CD, right-click on the CD-ROM's icon and select Unmount from the pop-up menu. You can then open the CD-ROM drive and remove the CD.

To access a floppy disk, you can perform a similar operation using the Floppy Disk icon. Place the floppy disk in the disk drive and click on the Floppy Disk icon. This displays a file manager window with the contents for floppy disk. Alternatively, you can right-click on the icon to display a pop-up menu with an entry to mount the disk. Once mounted you can access it, copying files to and from the disk. Be careful not to remove the disk unless you first unmount it. To unmount the disk, right-click on its icon and select Unmount from the icon's pop-up menu. There is one added operation you can perform with a floppy disk. If you put in a blank disk, you can format it. There are several file system formats to choose from, including MS-DOS. To format a standard Linux file system, you select the ext2 entry.

A kdelink that you use for your CD-ROM is a special kind of kdelink file designed for file system devices. To create one, first right-click anywhere on the desktop and select New and then File System Device. A window appears prompting you for a file name for the kdelink file. It will show a default name **device.kdelink**. Replace **device** with the name you want, and be sure to keep the **.kdelink** extension. For example, for a CD-ROM you could have **cdrom.kdelink**. The kdelink icon will then appear on your desktop with a question mark, indicating that the device is not yet configured. Right-click on this icon and select the Properties entry. In the Properties window, change to the Device panel and in the box labeled Device, enter the full path name for the device (see Figure 5-5). Devices are located in the **/etc/dev** directory. A device name for an IDE CD-ROM is usually **/etc/dev/hdc**. For the mount point, enter in the directory where you want the device to be mounted. For a CD-ROM, this is usually **/mnt/cdrom**.

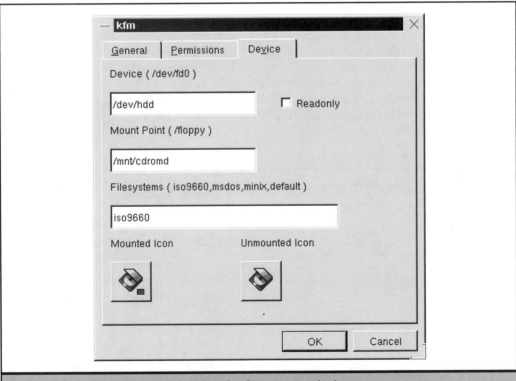

Figure 5-5.   *The kdelink dialog box for file system devices*

See the file administration chapter, Chapter 26, for a discussion on devices and file systems. You can then select images for Unmounted and Mounted icons. To select the Mounted icon, click on the Mounted icon to display a list of icons from which to choose. Do the same for the Unmounted icon. The kdelink file does not perform the necessary system administration operations that will allow access to the CD-ROM by ordinary users. Normally, only the systems administrator (root user) can mount or unmount CD-ROMs and floppy disks. You will also have to make sure there is an entry in the **/etc/fstab** file for the CD-ROM or floppy drive. If not, you will have to add one. Such operations are fairly easy to perform using the file system management tools provided by COAS on OpenLinux, Linuxconf and fsconf on RedHat, and YaST on SuSE. Check Chapters 4 and 26, on the procedures to use.

KDE File Manager and Internet Client: kfm

The KDE file manager is a multifunctional utility with which you can manage files, start programs, browse the Web, and download files from remote sites (see Figure 5-6). Traditionally, the term "file manager" was used to refer to managing files on a local hard disk. The KDE file manger extends its functionality well beyond this traditional function. It is Internet capable, seamlessly displaying remote file systems as if they were your own, as well as viewing Web pages with browser capabilities.

A KDE file manager window consists of a menu bar, a navigation toolbar, a location field, a status bar, and a pane of file and directory icons for the current working directory. When you first display the file manager window, it will display the file and subdirectory icons for your **home** directory. The files listed in a directory can be viewed in several different ways. You can view files and directories as icons, small icons, or in a detailed listing. The detailed listing provides permissions, owner, group,

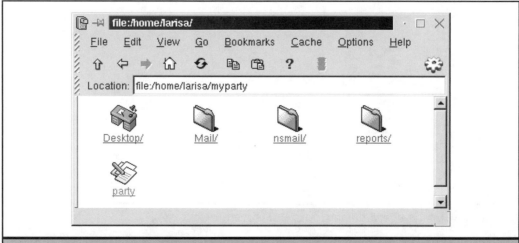

Figure 5-6. *KDE file manager*

and size information. Permissions are the permissions controlling access to this file (see Chapter 8). Configuration files are not usually displayed. These are files beginning with a period and are often referred to as "dot" files. To have the file manager display these files, select Show Dot Files from the View menu.

To search for files, select the Find entry in the File menu. This opens a dialog box with which you can search for file names using wildcard matching symbols such as asterisk (*). Click on the small image of a looking glass in the toolbar to run the search, and on the stoplight to stop it (see Figure 5-7). The search results are displayed in a pane in the lower half of the search window. You can click on a file and have it open with its appropriate application. Text files will be displayed by the kwrite text editor, and images by kview. Applications will be run. The search program also lets you save your search results for later reference. You can even select files from the search and add them to an archive.

You can open a file either by clicking on it or by selecting it and then choosing the Open entry in the File menu. A single-click opens the file, not a double-click. If you just want to select the file or directory, you need to hold down the CTRL key while you click

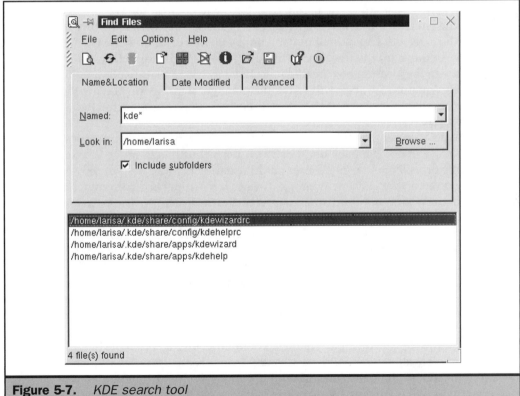

Figure 5-7.   *KDE search tool*

it. A selection is performed with a CTRL-click. If the file is a program, that program will start up. If it is a data file such as text file, then the associated application will be run using that data file. For example, if you click on a text file, then the kwrite application will start displaying that file. If kfm cannot determine the application to use, it opens a dialog box prompting you to enter in the application name. You can click on the Browse button on this box to use a directory tree to locate the application program you want.

The file manager can also extract tar archives and install RPM packages. An archive is a file ending in either **.tar.gz**, **.tar**, or **.tgz**. Clicking on the archive will list the files in it. You can extract a particular file by simply dragging it out of the window. Clicking on a text file will display it with kwrite, and clicking on an image file will display it with kview. Selecting an RPM package will open it with the kpackage utility that you can then use to install the package.

Moving Through the File System

A single-click on a Directory icon will move to that directory and display its file and Subdirectory icons. Unlike other interfaces, KDE does not use double-clicking to open a directory. To move back up to the parent directory, you click on the Up Arrow button located on the left end of the navigation toolbar. A single-click on a Directory icon moves you down the directory tree a directory at a time, and by clicking on the Up Arrow button you can move up the tree. To move directly to a specific directory, you can enter its path name in the location box located just above the pane that displays the File and Directory icons. Figure 5-6 shows the KDE file manager window displaying the current directory. You can also use several keyboard shortcuts to perform such operations as listed in Table 5-2.

Like a Web browser, the file manager remembers the previous directories it has displayed. You can use the Back and Forward Arrow buttons to move through this list of prior directories. For example, a user could use the Location field to move to the **~/birthday** directory, and use it again to move to the **~/reports** directory. Clicking on the Back Arrow button would display the ~/**birthday** directory. Then, clicking on the Forward Arrow button would move back to the ~/**reports** directory. You can move directly to your **home** directory by clicking on the Home button. This has the same effect as the **cd** command in the shell. If there are particular directories that you know you will want to access again, you can bookmark them, much as you do a Web page. Just open the directory and select the Add Bookmarks entry in the Bookmarks menu. An entry for that directory will be placed in the file manager's Bookmark menu. To move to the directory again, just select its entry in the Bookmark menu. This is very helpful for directories you will be frequently using or for directories you have to access that have lengthy or complex path names. Bookmarks also apply to individual files and applications. You can even bookmark desktop icons. To bookmark a file, first select a file and then choose the Add Bookmarks entry in the Bookmark menu. Later, selecting that bookmark will open that file. You can do the same thing with applications, where

Keypresses	Description
ALT-LEFT ARROW	Back in History
ALT-RIGHT ARROW	Forward in History
ALT-UP ARROW	One directory up
ENTER	Open a file/directory
ESC	Open a pop-up menu for the current file
LEFT/RIGHT/UP/DOWN ARROWS	Move among the icons
SPACEBAR	Select/unselect file
PAGE UP	Scroll up fast
PAGE DOWN	Scroll down fast
RIGHT ARROW	Scroll right (on WWW pages)
LEFT ARROW	Scroll left (on WWW pages)
UP ARROW	Scroll up (on WWW pages)
DOWN ARROW	Scroll down (on WWW pages)
CTRL-C	Copy selected file to Clipboard
CTRL-V	Paste files from Clipboard to current directory
CTRL-S	Select files by pattern
CTRL-T	Open a terminal in the current directory
CTRL-L	Open new location
CTRL-F	Find files
CTRL-W	Close window

Table 5-2.   *KDE File Manager Keyboard Shortcuts*

selecting the application's bookmark will start the application. Each bookmark is a file placed in your **.kde/share/apps/kfm/bookmarks** directory. You can go to this directory and change the names of any of the files and they will appear as changed on your Bookmark menu. These files are kdelink files. To change their names, right-click on the file and select Properties from the pop-up menu. In the dialog box that is displayed, you will see that the file name is the full path name with a **.kdelink** extension on a panel tabbed General. You can replace the path name with one of your own choosing, but keep the **.kdelink** extension—for example, **myreport.kdelink**. This bookmark would then appear as **myreport**. The path name used to access the file is actually on the URL panel.

To help you navigate from one directory to another, you can use the Location field or the directory tree. In the Location field, you can enter the path name of a directory, should you know it, and press ENTER. The file manager will then display that directory. The directory tree provides a tree listing all directories on your system and in your **home** directory. You can activate the directory tree by selecting Show Tree entry in the View menu. The directory tree will have three main entries: **Root**, **My Home**, and **Desktop**. The **Root** entry will display the directories in tree starting from the system root directory. The **My Home** entry displays directories starting from your **home** directory, and the **Desktop** entry displays the files and links on your desktop. Click on a side triangle to expand a directory entry, and click on a down triangle of an expanded directory entry to hide it.

Internet Access

The KDE file manager doubles as a Web browser and FTP client. It includes a box for entering either a path name for a local file or a URL for a Web page on the Internet or your intranet. A navigation toolbar can be used to display previous Web pages or previous directories. When accessing Web page, the page is displayed as on any Web browser. With the navigation toolbar, you can move back and forth through the list of previously displayed pages in that session. This feature is particularly convenient for displaying local Web pages, such as documentation in HTML format. Most Linux distributions provide extensive documentation in the form of Web pages that you can easily access and display using a KDE file manager window. Red Hat and OpenLinux Web page documentation is located at **/usr/doc/HTML**. Figure 5-8 shows the KDE file manager window operating as a Web browser, displaying a Web page.

The KDE file manager also operates as an FTP client. When you access an FTP site, you navigate the remote directories as you would your own. The operations to download a file are the same as copying a file on your local system. Just select the file's icon or entry in the file manager window and drag it to a window showing the local directory you want it downloaded to. Then, select the Copy entry from the pop-up menu that appears.

By default, KDE will attempt an anonymous login. If you want to perform a nonanonymous login as a particular user, add the user name with an **@** symbol before the FTP address. You will then be prompted for the user password. For example, the following entry will log in to the **ftp.mygames.com** server as the **chris** user:

```
ftp://chris@ftp.mygames.com
```

Figure 5-8.   *File manager as Web browser*

Copy, Move, Delete, and Archive Operations

To perform an operation on a file or directory, you first have to select it. In KDE, to select a file or directory, you hold down the CTRL key while clicking on the file's icon or listing. To select more than one file, continually hold down the CTRL key while you click on the files you want. Alternatively, you can use the keyboard arrow keys to move from one file icon to another, and then use the spacebar to select the one you want.

To copy and move files, you can use the standard drag-and-drop method with your mouse. To copy a file, you locate it using the file manager. Open another file manager window to the directory that you want the file copied to. Then, click and drag the File icon to that window (be sure to keep holding down the mouse button). A pop-up menu will appear with selections for Move, Copy, or Link. Choose Copy. To move a file to another directory, follow the same procedure, but select Move from the pop-up menu. To copy or move a directory, use the same procedure as for files. All the directory's files and subdirectories will also be copied or moved.

You can also move or copy files using the Copy and Paste commands. First, use a CTRL-click to select a file or directory (hold the CTRL key down while clicking on the File icon). Either select the Copy entry from the Edit menu or click on the Copy button in the navigation bar. Change to the directory you want to copy the selected file to. Then, either select Paste from the Edit menu or click on the Paste button. Follow the same procedure for moving files, using the Move entry from the Edit menu or the Move button in the navigation toolbar. Most of the basic file manager operations can be selected from a pop-up menu that is displayed whenever you right-click on a file or directory. Here, you will find entries for copying, moving, and deleting the file as well as navigating to a different directory.

It is important to distinguish between a copy of a file or directory and a link. A copy creates a duplicate, whereas a link is just another name for the same item. Links are used extensively as ways of providing different access points to the same document. If you want to access a file using an icon on your desktop, it is best to create a link on the desktop rather than a copy. With a copy, you would have two different documents, whereas with a link you are accessing and changing the same document. To create a link on your desktop, just click and drag the File icon from the directory window to the desktop and select Link from the pop-up menu. Clicking on the link will bring up the original document. Deleting the link will only remove the link, not the original document. You can create links for directories or applications using the same procedure. You can also place links in a directory. Just click and drag the files you want to link to into that directory and select Link from the pop-up menu.

You delete a file by removing it immediately or placing it in a Trash folder to delete later. To delete a file, select it and then choose the Delete entry in the Edit menu. You can also right-click on the icon and select Delete. To place a file in the Trash folder, just click and drag it to the Trash icon on your desktop, or select Move to Trash from the Edit menu. You can later open the Trash folder and delete the files. To delete all the files in the Trash folder, right-click on the Trash icon and select Empty Trash Bin from the pop-up menu. To restore any files in the Trash bin, open the Trash bin and drag them out of the Trash folder.

Each file and directory has properties associated with it that include permissions, the file name, and its directory. To display the properties window for a given file, right-click on the file's icon and select the Properties entry. On the General panel, you will see the name of the file displayed. To change the file's name, replace name there with a new one. Permissions are set on the Permissions panel. Here, you can set read, write, and execute permissions for user, group, or other access to the file. (See Chapter 8 for a discussion of permissions.) The group entry lets you change the group for a file.

.directory

KDE will automatically search for and read an existing **.directory** file located in a directory. A **.directory** file holds KDE configuration information used to determine how the directory is displayed. You can create such a file in a directory and can place settings in it to set the display features for the file manager, such as the icon to use it to display the directory folder.

KDE Configuration: KDE Control Center

With the KDE Control Center you can configure your desktop and system, changing the way it is displayed and the features it supports (see Figure 5-9). You can open the

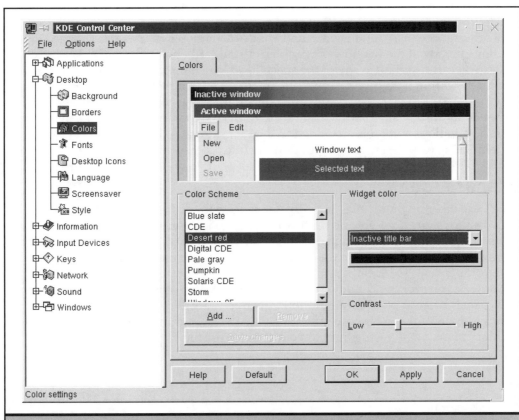

Figure 5-9.   *KDE Control Center*

Control Center directly to a selected component by selecting its entry in the Applications Starter Settings menu. The Settings menu displays a submenu listing the configuration categories. Select a category and then the component you want. For example, to configure your screen saver, select the screen saver config entry in the Desktop menu located in the Settings menu. The Control Center can be directly started by either clicking on the Control Center icon in the panel, or selecting Control Center from the Applications Starter menu.

The Control Center window is divided into two panes. The left one shows a tree view of all the components you can configure. They are arranged into categories whose titles you can expand or shrink. The Applications heading hold entries for configuring the KDE file manager's Web browser features as well as its file management operations. Under Desktop, you can set different features for displaying and controlling your desktop. For example, the Background entry lets you select a different background color or image for each one of your virtual desktops. Other desktop entries let you configure components such as the screen saver, the language used, and the window style. There are entries that let you configure your mouse, key mappings, network connections, sound events, and window components. You can change key bindings for any of the window operations, or standard operations such as cut and paste. You can also change any of the specialized key mappings such as ALT-TAB key that moves through your open applications, CTRL-TAB that moves through your virtual desktops, or ALT-F2 that display a dialog box for executing commands. Configuration components are actually modules. In future releases, more modules will be included as more applications and tools are added to the K desktop. See the Help viewer for a current listing of K desktop configuration modules.

.kde/share/config

Your **.kde** directory holds files and directories used to maintain your KDE desktop. The **.desktops** directory holds KDE link files whose icons are displayed on the desktop. Configuration files are located in the **.kde/share/config** directory. Here, you will find the general KDE configuration file **kfmrc** as well as configuration files for different KDE components. The **krootwmrc** file holds configuration commands for your root window, **kwmrc** for the window manager, **ksoundrc** for sound, and **kcmpanelrc** for your panel. You can place configuration directives directly in any of these files—for example, to have the left mouse button display the Applications Starter menu on the desktop, place the following lines in your **krootwmrc** file:

```
[MouseButtons]

Left=Menu
```

MIME Types

As you install new kinds of programs, they may use files of a certain type. In that case, you would have to register the type with KDE so that it can be associated with a given application or group of applications. For example, the MIME type for **.gif** images is **image/gif**, which is associated with image viewing programs. You use a kdelink file to create a new MIME type for KDE. Right-click on the desktop and select MIME from the New menu. Type in the name for the kdelink file, keeping the **.kdelink** extension, and click OK. The Properties dialog box will then appear with three panels: General, Permissions, and Bindings. Click on the Bindings tab and then enter the possible extensions for the file type, using an asterisk (*) to match the prefix. For example ***.gif; *.GIF** would match any file ending with **.gif**. Type in a comment and then the MIME type, such as **image/gif**. Select a default application and an icon to use for files of that type.

KDE Directories and Files

Most distributions will install KDE in the **/opt/kde** directory on your system. This is the default directory, though you can specify another if you wish. KDE core programs along with KDE applications are held in the **/opt/kde/bin** directory. When KDE is installed, the **/opt/kde/bin** path is added to your **PATH**, telling your system where KDE programs can be found. In addition, the **KDEDIR** system variable should be set in your **.bash_profile** file to make accessing KDE applications easier. KDE libraries are located in the **/opt/kde/lib** directory and Web programs for the KDE file manger Web interface are located in **/opt/kde/cgi-bin**. KDE also has its own **man** directory, **/opt/kde/man**, and **include** directory with header files for use in compiling and developing KDE applications.

The directories located in **/opt/share** contain files used to configure your KDE environment. (See Table 5-3.) The **/opt/share/applnk** directory maps its files to the Applications Launcher menu. Its directories and subdirectories appear as menu items and submenus on the main menu. Their contents consist of kdelink files, one for each menu entry. The **/opt/share/apps** file contains files and directories set up by KDE applications. **/opt/share/mimelnk** holds MIME type definitions. The **/opt/share/config** directory contains the configuration files for particular KDE applications. For example, **kfmrc** holds configuration entries for displaying and using the kfm file manager. These are the system-wide defaults that can be overridden by user's own configurations in their own **.kde/share/config** directory. The **/opt/share/icons** directory holds the default icons used on your KDE desktop and by KDE applications. The **/opt/share** directory also holds files for other configuration elements such as wallpaper, toolbars, and languages.

The **.kde** directory holds a user's own KDE configuration for the desktop and its applications. The **.kde/share** directory holds user versions of the **/opt/kde/share** directories, specifying user configurations for menus, icons, MIME types, sounds, and applications. The **.kde/share/config** directory holds configuration files with a user's own configuration specifications for their use of KDE applications. For example, **desktop4rc** holds display configurations the user set up for the fourth virtual desktop.

The **.kde/share/icons** directory holds the icons for a user's particular themes, and **/.kde/share/sounds** holds sound files. **.kde/share/applnk** holds the kdelink files for the menu entries in the Personal section of the Applications Launcher menu that were added by the user. In a user's **home** directory, the **.kderc** file contains current desktop configuration directives for resources such as key bindings, colors, and window styles.

Each user has a **Desktop** directory (see Table 5-3) that holds KDE link files for all icons and folders on the user's desktop. These include the AutoStart, Trash, and Template folders. The AutoStart folder holds links to applications that will be automatically started up whenever KDE starts. The Trash folder holds files you want to delete, and the Templates folder holds default kdelink files that you can use as a basis for creating particular kdelink files.

System Configuration Using KDE

KDE provides some system administration tools, though for most tasks it is preferable to use Linuxconf, COAS, or YaST. You can easily run Linuxconf or any of the Red Hat or OpenLinux system tools on your KDE desktop. You can access the KDE system administration tools through the root desktop. Log in as the root user and start KDE. You will find system tools in both the System and Utilities menu in the Applications Starter menu. The **kuser** file provides a KDE interface for managing users on your system. You can add or remove users, or set permissions for current ones. The

System KDE Directories	Description
/opt/kde/bin	KDE programs
/opt/kde/lib	KDE libraries
/opt/kde/cgi-bin	Web programs for the KDE file manager Web interface
/opt/kde/man	KDE **man** directory
/opt/kde/include	Header files for use in compiling and developing KDE applications
/opt/kde/share/config	KDE desktop and application configuration files
/opt/kde/share/applnk	kdelink files used to build the main menu
/opt/kde/share/apps	Files used by KDE applications

Table 5-3.   *KDE Installation Directories*

/opt/kde/share/icons	Icons used in KDE desktop and applications
/opt/kde/share/sounds	Sounds used in KDE desktop and applications
/opt/kde/share/doc	KDE Help system
/usr/doc/kde	KDE documentation
KDEDIR	System variable that holds KDE directory, **KDEDIR=/opt/kde**
User KDE Directories	
.kde/share/config	User KDE desktop and application configuration files for user specified features
.kde/share/applnk	kdelink files used to build the user's personal menu entries on the KDE main menu
.kde/share/apps	Directories and files used by KDE applications.
.kde/share/icons	Icons used in user KDE desktop and applications, such as the ones for the user-specified theme
.kde/share/sounds	Sounds used in KDE desktop and applications
.kderc	User configurations directives for desktop resources
Desktop	Holds kdelink files for icons and folders displayed on the user's KDE desktop
Desktop/Templates	Template kdelink files
Desktop/Trash	Trash folder for files marked for deletion
Desktop/AutoStart	Applications automatically started up with KDE.

Table 5-3.   *KDE Installation Directories* (continued)

K desktop provides two utilities for viewing and managing your processes: the KDE Task Manager (KTop) and the KDE Process Manager (**kpm**). The SysV Init Editor is a version of the System V Init Manager (see Chapter 16). You can use it to start and stop servers and determine what run level they will start at. (See Chapter 27 on system administration for a more detailed discussion on administration tasks.) With **kppp**, you can connect to the Internet using a modem. You would use **kppp** to connect to an Internet service provider (ISP) that supports the PPP protocols. The **kppp** file is discussed in more detail in the chapter on network administration, Chapter 28. The **kpackage** file lets you manage the RPM packages you have installed (see Chapter 24). You can use it to install new packages, see the ones that are installed, and easily display information about the package. With **kpackage**, you can list the files in a particular package and display the release information. You can even display text files such as Readme and configuration files. This is an easy what to find out exactly where an application's program and configuration files are installed on your system.

Updating KDE

Currently, new versions of KDE are being released frequently, sometimes every few months. KDE releases are designed to let users easily upgrade their older versions. Be sure to obtain the release for your particular distributions (though you can install from the source code if you wish). Packages tailored for various distributions can be downloaded through the KDE Web site at **www.kde.org** or directly from the KDE FTP site at **ftp.kde.org** and its mirror sites. RPM packages for OpenLinux and Red Hat should be obtained from their respective FTP sites (**ftp.calderasystems.com** and **updates.redhat.com**).

First log in as the root user and then create a directory to hold the KDE files. Then connect to an FTP site. You can use a Web browser such as Netscape, but it is preferable to use an FTP client such as FTP, IglooFTP, or even the KDE file manager. Download the files for the new version to your new directory. For Red Hat and OpenLinux, these will be a series of RPM package files. To download using FTP, be sure to turn off prompts with the prompt command and use **mget *** to download all the files at once. With GUI FTP clients like IglooFTP, you may be able to select the entire directory at once to download. With the KDE file manager, select the files and just drag them to a window open to the local directory and select Copy from the pop-up menu.

Current KDE releases from the KDE FTP site feature an install script called **install-kde**. For distributions that use RPM packages, you first install the kde-installer package. This installs the install script. Then execute the following command. The various KDE packages will be installed in proper order, replacing or upgrading older versions. For RPM packages obtained from Red Hat and OpenLinux, you can simply install the KDE packages along with any other RPM updated packages.

```
rpm -Uvh kde-installer-1.1.1-*rh*.i386.rpm
install-kde-1.1.1
```

To install a particular KDE RPM package manually, you use the **rpm** command with the **-Uvh** options. This example installs the kdenetwork package.

```
Rpm -Uvh  kdenetwork-1.1.1pre2.2.i386.rpm
```

KDE Applications and Tools

Provided here for your convenience, Table 5-4 lists the KDE applications currently available. Most are distributed with the current release of KDE and are included with the Red Hat and OpenLinux distributions. Some of the newer applications are accessible on the KDE Web site at **www.kde.org**.

Tip   *Check the Web site periodically for new KDE applications, since a large number of them are currently under development. Keep in mind that the Red Hat and OpenLinux collections may not be entirely consistent. Some packages found in one distribution may not be found in the other.*

Core	Description
kaudio	Audio server
kbgndwm	Background module for KWM
kcontrol	Central control panel
kdehelp	Help browser
kdm	Replacement for xdm
kfind	Find tool
kfm	File manager with integrated Web browser
kfontmanager	Tool for managing fonts
kmenuedit	Editor for menu entries for **kpanel** and **ktaskbar**
konsole	X Terminal
kpanel	Desktop panel
kpager	Pager module for KWM
krootwm	KWM module for root window handling
kscreensaver	Screen saver package
kstart	A tiny utility to launch legacy applications with special KDE features
kvt	Terminal emulation

Table 5-4.   *KDE Applications*

Core	Description
kwm	The KDE window manager
kwmcom	Communication tool for KWM
kwmpager	Pager module for KWM

Development	Description
kdevelop	Integrated Development Environment (IDE)

Office	Description
kticker	Downloads news headlines and displays
korganizer	Organizer
karm	Time-management utility
kcalc	Scientific calculator
kedit	Simple text editor
khexdit	Simple hex editor
kjots	Note-taking utility
knotes	Post-it™-like application

Games	Description
kabalone	Puzzle
kasteroids	Asteroids game
kblackbox	Logic game
kmahjongg	Mah Jongg
kmines	Minesweeper
konquest	Multiplayer strategy game
kpat	Patience card game
kpoker	Poker game

Table 5-4. *KDE Applications* (continued)

Games	Description
kreversi	Reversi (Othello)
ksame	Same game
kshisen	Shisen
ksmiletris	Tetris™-like game
ksnake	Snake
ksirtet	Tetris™
Kglchess	GNU-Chess

Graphics	Description
kdvi	TeX DVI file viewer
kfax	Fax file viewer
kfract	Fractals generator
kghostview	PostScript viewer
kiconedit	Icon editor
kpaint	Paint program
kgnuplot	Replacement for the gnuplot_x11
ksnapshot	Desktop and windows image capture
kview	Image viewer for **.gif/.jpeg**
kmoon	Phases of the moon
kworldwatch	A clock with the world

Multimedia	Description
kmedia	Mediatool-compliant media player
kmid	Midi/karaoke file player using external synth, fm, awe and gus devices
kmidi	Midi to wav player/converter

Table 5-4.   *KDE Applications* (continued)

Multimedia	Description
kmix	Sound device mixer
kscd	Simple CD player

Network	Description
karchie	Archie client
kbiff	Biff utility-mail notification
kexpress	Newsreader
kfinger	Finger client
Caitoo	Download files from the Internet
kmail	Mail user agent
knu	Front end for several network utilities
korn	Multiple-mailbox mail notification
kppp	Dialer and front end to pppd
korn	Multifolder new mail monitor
krn	Usenet news reader
ksirc	Chat client
ktalkd	Enhanced Unix talk
kWebMaker	HTML editor
knetmon	Displays the active users in a network

Administration	Description
kfloppy	A DOS ext2fs Floppy formatter
kdat	Tar-based tape archiver
kpackage	Manage RPM and Debian packages
ksysv	Editor for SysV-style init configuration
kuser	A user administration tool
Kcrontab	Cron table front end

Table 5-4.   *KDE Applications* (continued)

Administration	Description
klpq	Displays entries in your print queue
kpackage	Handles RPM and Debian packages
kthememgr	Theme manager
Mouspedometa	Measures your desktop mileage
ark	Utility for dealing with compressed files
kljettool	Config tool for HP LaserJets and other PJL printers
kpm	Process status manager
ktop	System monitor

Table 5-4.   *KDE Applications* (continued)

Chapter 6

Gnome

The GNU Network Object Model Environment, known as Gnome, is a powerful and easy-to-use environment consisting primarily of a panel, a desktop, and a set of GUI tools with which program interfaces can be constructed. Unlike KDE, its aim is not so much to provide a consistent interface as to provide a flexible platform for the development of powerful applications.

The core components of the Gnome desktop consist of a panel for starting programs and desktop functionality. Other components normally found in a desktop such as a file manager, Web browser, and window manager are provided by Gnome-compliant applications. Gnome provides libraries of Gnome GUI tools that developers can use to create Gnome applications. Programs can be said to be Gnome compliant that use buttons, menus, and windows that adhere to a Gnome standard. For a file manager the Gnome desktop uses a new Gnome version of Midnight Commander. Window managers as well can be Gnome compliant. The Gnome desktop does not have its own window manager as KDE does. It uses any Gnome-compliant window manager. Currently the Enlightenment window manager is the one commonly used for the Gnome desktop.

Gnome is completely free under the GNU Public License with no restrictions. You can obtain the source directly from the Gnome Web site at **www.gnome.org**. Gnome uses the Common Object Request Broker Architecture (CORBA), which allows software components to interconnect, regardless of the computer language in which they are implemented or kind of machine they are running on. The Gnome implementation of CORBA is called ORBit.

You can find out more about Gnome at its Web site at **www.gnome.org**. The site provides a detailed software map of current Gnome projects with links to their development sites. It also maintains extensive mailing lists for Gnome projects that you can subscribe to. The site provides online documentation such as the Gnome User's Guide and FAQs. If you want to develop Gnome programs, check the Gnome developer's Web site at **developer.gnome.org**. The site provides tutorials, programming guides, and development tools. The site also includes detailed online documentation for the GTK+ library, Gnome widgets, and the Gnome desktop.

GTK+

GTK+ is the widget set used for Gnome applications. Its look and feel was originally derived from Motif. The widget set is designed from the ground up for power and flexibility. For example, buttons can have labels, images, or any combination thereof. Objects can be dynamically queried and modified at run time. It also includes a theme engine that lets users change the look and feel of applications using these widgets. At the same time, the GTK+ widget set remains small and efficient.

The GTK+ widget set is entirely free under the Library General Public License (LGPL). The LGPL allows developers to use the widget set with proprietary as well as free software. The widget set also features an extensive set of programming language bindings including C++, Perl, Python, Pascal, Objective C, Guile, and Ada. Internationalization is fully supported, permitting GTK+-based applications to be used with other character sets such as those in Asian languages. The drag-and-drop functionality supports both Xdnd and Motif protocols, allowing drag-and-drop operations with other widget sets that support these protocols, such as Qt and Motif.

The Gnome Interface

The Gnome interface consists of the panel and a desktop, as shown in Figure 6-1. The panel appears as a long bar across the bottom of the screen. It holds menus, program buttons, and applets. An applet is a small program designed to be run within the panel. On the panel there will be a button with a large barefoot imprint on it. This is the Gnome applications menu, the main menu. The menu operates like the Start menu in Windows, listing entries for applications you can run on your desktop. You

Figure 6-1. *Gnome*

ENVIRONMENTS

can display panels horizontally or vertically and have them automatically hide, to show you a full screen.

The remainder of the screen is the desktop. Here you can place directories, files, or programs. You can create them on the desktop directly or drag them from a file manager window. A click-and-drag operation with the middle mouse button lets you create links on the desktop to installed programs. Initially the desktop will only hold an icon for your home directory. Clicking it will open a file manager window to that directory.

From a user's point of view, you can think of the Gnome interface as having four components: the desktop, the panel, the main menu, and the file manager. In its standard default configuration, the Gnome desktop will display a folder icon for your home directory in the upper-left corner. Some distributions may include other icons such as links to the Gnome Web site or to the Linux Documentation site. Initially, a file manager window will open on the desktop displaying your home directory. The panel will have several default icons: the main menu (bare foot), the Terminal program (monitor), the Gnome Help System (question mark), the Gnome Control Center (toolbox), the Gnome pager (squares), and a clock. Many distributions will also include the Netscape Web browser.

To start a program, you can select its entry in the main menu, click its application launcher button in the panel (if there is one), double-click its icon in either the desktop or the file manager window, or drag a data file to its icon. You can also select the Run Program entry in the main menu to open a small window where you can type in the program name.

To quit Gnome, you select the Logout entry in the main menu. You can also add a Logout button to the panel that you could use instead. To add the Logout button, right-click the panel and select the Add Logout Button entry. A Logout button will appear in the panel. When you log out, the Logout dialog box is displayed. You have three options. The first, Logout, will just quit Gnome, returning you to your command line shell still logged into your Linux account. The Halt option will not only quit Gnome but also shut down your entire system. The Reboot entry will shut down and reboot your system. The Logout entry is selected by default. Halt and Reboot are only available to the root user. If normal users execute them, they will be prompted to enter the root user password in order to shut down. You can also elect to retain your desktop by clicking the "Save current setup" check box. This will reopen any programs or directories that were still open when you logged out. Window managers that are Gnome compliant will also quit when you log out of Gnome. You will then have to separately quit a window manager that is not Gnome compliant after logging out of Gnome.

The Gnome Help system shown in Figure 6-2 provides a browser-like interface for displaying the Gnome user's manual, Man pages, and info documents. It features a toolbar that lets you move through the list of previously viewed documents. You can even bookmark specific items. A Web page interface lets you use links to connect to different documents. You can easily move the manual, or the list of Man pages and

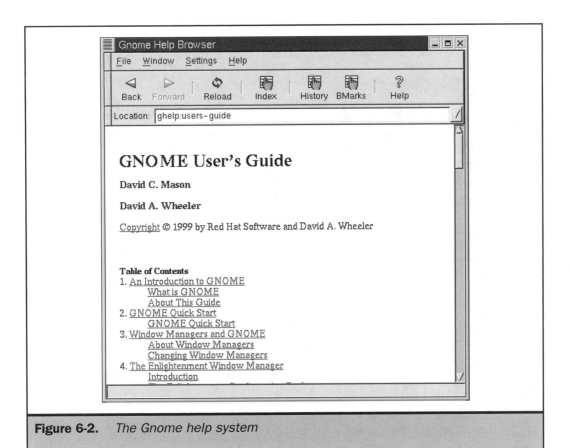

Figure 6-2.   *The Gnome help system*

info documents. In the location box you can place entries to directly access specific documents. Special URL-like protocols are supported for the different types of documents: **ghelp**: for Gnome help, **man**: for Man pages, and **info**: for the info documents.

The Gnome Desktop

The Gnome desktop provides you with all the capabilities of GUI-based operating systems (see Figure 6-3). You can drag files, applications, and directories to the desktop and back to Gnome-compliant applications. Should the desktop stop functioning, you can restart it by starting up the Gnome file manager. The desktop is actually a back end process in the Gnome file manager. But you do not have to have the file manager open to use the desktop.

ENVIRONMENTS

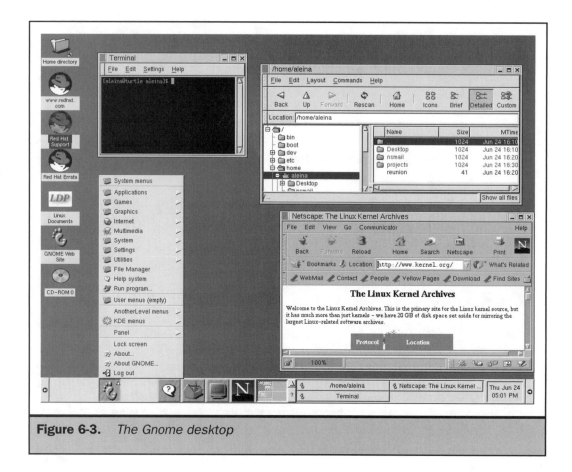

Figure 6-3. *The Gnome desktop*

Though the Gnome desktop supports drag-and-drop operations, these work only for applications that are Gnome or Motif compliant. You can drag any items from a Gnome-compliant application to your desktop, and vice versa. Any icon for an item that you drag from a file manager window to the desktop will also appear on the desktop. However, the default drag-and-drop operation is a move operation. If you select a file in your file manager window and drag it to the desktop, you are actually moving the file from its current directory to the **.gnome-desktop** directory, which is located in your home directory and holds all items on the desktop (notice that it is a dot file). In the case of dragging directory folders to the desktop, the entire directory and its subdirectories would be copied to the **.gnome-desktop** directory.

In most cases, you will only want to create on the desktop another way to access a file without moving it from its original directory. You can do this by creating a link or a program launcher, instead of moving the file. To create a link, drag the file while holding down the middle mouse button. When you release the mouse button, a pop-up menu will appear with entries for copy, move, or link. Select the link entry. A copy of the icon will appear with a small arrow in the right corner indicating that it is a link. You can then click this link to start the program, open the file, or open the directory, depending on what kind of file you linked to. To create a program launcher, right-click anywhere on the desktop and choose the Create Launcher applet entry. This opens a dialog where you can enter the program name, select an icon for it, and set its permissions.

You can then use that icon to access the item directly. This is often used for starting common programs. For example you can middle-click-and-drag the Netscape icon to the desktop and select Link from the pop-up menu to create a link icon for Netscape. Double-clicking the icon will start Netscape. You can do the same with files. In this case their respective program will be started. If the item is a directory, then the file manager will start up, opened to that directory. If you want to have an application placed on your desktop that is not Gnome compliant, you can manually place a link to it in your home directory's **.gnome-desktop** directory.

As an alternative to the desktop, you can drag any program, file, or directory to the panel; a program button launcher applet will be automatically created for it on the panel. The item is not moved or copied. You can also right-click anywhere on the empty desktop to display a menu some of whose entries will start applications. The entries for this menu are listed in Table 6-1. You will notice an entry for a new directory. Bear in mind that this entry creates a new directory on your desktop, specifically your **.gnome-desktop** directory.

The desktop will also display icons for any drives that you have access to such as a CD-ROM or floppy drive, provided they are user mountable. You can easily make a drive user mount table with Linuxconf (System menu). Select the Access Local Drive entry and then select the drive and the Options panel for that drive. On this panel select the User Mountable option. If you do not have Linuxconf, you will have to make the appropriate entry in the **fstab** file, adding "user" to the options field for that device.

You can mount file systems on these devices by right-clicking their icons and choosing the Mount Device entry. For example, to mount a CD-ROM disk, right-click the CD-ROM icon and select the Mount Device entry. You can then access the disk in the CD-ROM drive by either double-clicking it or right-clicking and selecting the Open entry. A file manager window will open to display the contents of the CD-ROM disk. To unmount a CD-ROM, just right-click the CD-ROM icon and select the Unmount Device entry. You can then safely remove the CD-ROM disk. You can use the Eject Device entry to open your CD-ROM tray. The same procedure works for floppy disks, using the floppy disk icon. Be sure not to remove a mounted floppy disk until you have first unmounted it, selecting the Unmount Device entry in the pop-up menu. If for some reason not all your devices are showing up, you can have Gnome rescan your system for them. Right-click anywhere on the empty desktop to display a pop-up menu. From the menu select Recreate Desktop Shortcuts.

ENVIRONMENTS

Options	Description
New | Terminal	Launches a new Gnome Terminal window that will navigate to the ~/.**gnome-desktop** directory
New | Directory	Creates a new directory on your desktop
New | Launcher	Places a new application launcher on the desktop. Uses the Application Launcher dialog to have you specify the application and its properties
New | [application]	Some Gnome applications will place entries in the New menu to let you easily start new sessions for those applications
Arrange Icons	Arranges your desktop icons
Create New Window	Launches a new Gnome File Manager window showing your Home directory
Rescan Mountable Devices	Rescans the mountable devices on your machine and displays an icon for any new devices
Rescan Desktop	Rescans the files in your ~/.**gnome-desktop** directory

Table 6-1.   *The Gnome Desktop Menu*

Usually a window manager will extend a desktop into several areas that appear as different screens. Gnome's drag-and-drop operation will work on desktop areas that are provided by a Gnome-compliant window manager. Gnome does not directly manage desktop areas, though you can use the Gnome pager to move to them. You use the window manager configuration tool to configure them. In addition, most window managers also support virtual desktops. Instead of being extensions of the same desktop area, virtual desktops are separate entities. Gnome does not support its drag-and-drop capabilities on virtual desktops. It is aware of only a single desktop with multiple areas. An area is an extension of a desktop, making it larger than the screen, whereas virtual desktops are entirely separate entities. KDE implements virtual desktops, whereas Gnome supports desktop operations only on desktop areas. The Gnome pager, however, does support virtual desktops, creating icons for each in the panel, along with task buttons for any applications open on them. You can use the Gnome pager to move to different virtual desktops and their areas.

Window Managers

Gnome will work with any window manager. However, desktop functionality such as drag-and-drop capabilities and the Gnome pager will only work with window managers that are Gnome compliant. Currently only the Enlightenment window manager is completely Gnome compliant, though others such as FVWM, IceWin, and Window Maker are partially compliant and soon will be fully so. Check a window manager's documentation to see if it is Gnome compliant.

Enlightenment employs much the same window operations as used on other window managers. You can resize a window by clicking any of its sides or corners and dragging. You can move the window with a click-and-drag operation on its title bar. You can also right-click and drag any border to move the window, as well as ALT-click anywhere on the window. The upper-right corner lists the Maximize, Minimize, and Close buttons. If the Gnome pager is running in your panel, then Minimize creates a button for the window in the panel that you can click to restore it. If the Gnome pager is not present, then the window will iconify, minimizing to an icon on the desktop. You can click the upper-left corner of a window to display a window menu with entries for window operations. These include a desktop entry to move the window to another desktop area and the Stick option, which displays the window no matter what desktop area you move to.

You can also access the Enlightenment desktop menu. To display the menu, middle-click anywhere on the desktop (hold both mouse buttons down at the same time for a two-button mouse). A pop-up menu will appear with submenus for Gnome, user, and other applications as well as the Desktop, Themes, and Enlightenment configuration. You can use this menu to start any application, if you wish. With the desktop menus you move to different desktop areas and virtual desktops. The Themes menu lets you choose different Enlightenment themes (these are separate from KDE themes). Enlightenment also has extensive configuration options discussed in the "Enlightenment" section.

If you have several window managers installed on your system, then you can change from one to the other using the Window Manager capplet in the Gnome Control Center. The term *capplet* is used for a control applet, a module used to configure your desktop. Select the Control Center entry in the main menu to start the Control Center. In the Control Center window select Window Manager, listed under Desktop in the tree on the left. A panel is displayed listing your window managers. Initially only Enlightenment will be listed. To add others to the list, click the Add button on the right side of the panel. This opens a window that prompts you to enter an identifying name for the window manager, the command that starts the window manager, and any configuration tool it may use. If the window manager is Gnome compliant, you can click the button Window Manager Is Session Managed. Once you have finished making your entries and click OK, then the new window manager will appear in the list on the Control Center panel. Select it and click Try to run that window manager. If you want to run the window manager's configuration tool, click the Run Configuration Tool button.

ENVIRONMENTS

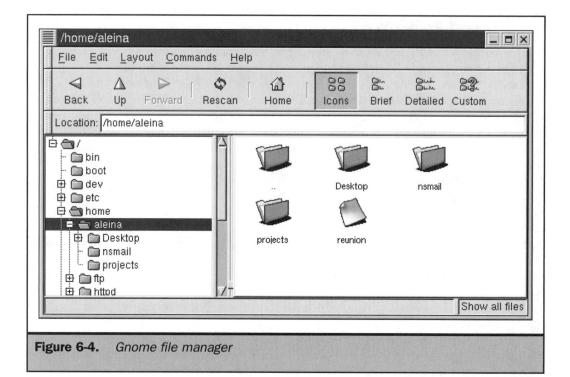

Figure 6-4. *Gnome file manager*

The Gnome File Manager

Gnome uses GNU Midnight Commander (GMC, shown in Figure 6-4) for its file manager. This is the Midnight Commander file manager with a Gnome front end. The GMC window consists of a menu bar, a toolbar, a location box, and two panes. The left pane displays a directory tree from which you can directly select directories. The right pane is the Directory view, which displays the files and subdirectories for the currently selected directory. The directory tree maps all the directories on your system, starting from the root directory. You can expand or shrink any directory by clicking the + or – symbol before its name. Select a directory by clicking the directory name. The contents of that directory are then displayed in the right-hand pane, the Directory view.

The Directory view has several viewing options. You can view a directory's contents as icons, a brief list, a detailed list, or a custom view. You select the different options from the Layout menu or by clicking their respective buttons in the toolbar. The brief list simply provides the name, whereas the detailed list provides the name, permissions, size, date, owner, and group. For a custom view you can select the informational fields you want displayed for your files. In all the list views, buttons are displayed for each field across the top of the Directory View pane. You can use these buttons to sort the lists according to that field. For example, to sort the files by Date, click the Date button, to sort by size, click the Size button. You can also select a field from the Sort By entry in the Layout menu.

The GMC file manager operates similar to a Web browser. It maintains a list of previously viewed directories; you can move back and forth through that list using the toolbar buttons. The left arrow button moves you to the previously displayed directory, and the right arrow button moves you to the next displayed directory. The up arrow button will move you to the parent directory, and the Home button moves you to your home directory. To use a pathname to go directly to a given directory, you can type the pathname in the Location box and press ENTER. GMC is also Internet aware. You can use the location box to access an FTP site and display the directories on that remote site and drag-and-drop files to another file manager window to download them to your system. Be sure to include the FTP protocol specification, **ftp://**.

To open a subdirectory, you can double-click its icon or single-click the icon and select Open from the File menu. If you want to open a separate GMC window for that directory, click the middle mouse button on the directory's icon (for two-button mice, click the right and left buttons at the same time).

As a Gnome-compliant file manager, Midnight Commander supports GUI drag-and-drop operations for copying and moving files. To move a file or directory, just click and drag from one directory to another, as you would on Windows or Mac interfaces. The move operation is the default drag-and-drop operation in Gnome. To copy a file, hold the CTRL key down while you click the item and drag it.

If you click and drag a file with the middle mouse button, then when you reach the destination and lift up on the mouse button, a pop-up menu appears (see Table 6-2) listing several options: Copy, Move, Link, or Cancel drag. This is a convenient way to create a link to a file such as an application. Just click and drag with the middle mouse button and then choose Link from the pop-up menu.

You can also perform file operations on a file by right-clicking its icon and selecting the action you want from the pop-up menu that appears. For example, to delete an item, right-click it and select the Delete entry from the pop-up menu. To move a file, select the Move entry. This displays a dialog box where you can change the pathname of the file you want to rename. A Browse button lets you use a directory tree to select a new directory location. The Advanced Options panel in this dialog box lets you select a Preserve Symlinks option. With this option, any symbolic links to this file will be changed to point to the new location. To copy a file, you can select Copy from the pop-up menu and use the dialog to select the new location for the copy and a new name if you wish. The destination directory displayed in the Move, Copy, or Links menu is that of the currently active file manger window. To move a file from one directory to another, just open a file manger window to that new dirctory, click it, then, in your source window, right-click directly on the file icon for the file you are moving. The location box in the Move window will show the pathname for the directory whose file manger window you just selected. The same process works for Copy and Link operations. For example, to create a link in the **presents** directory to the **party** file in the

Options	Description
Open	Open the file with its associated application
Open With	Select an application to open this file with
View	View the file with a basic text viewer
Edit	Use an editor to edit the file
Copy	Copy the file to the clipboard so that it can be pasted elsewhere
Delete	Delete the file
Move	Display the Move dialog with which you can move the file
Properties	Display the Properties dialog box for this file. There are three panels: Statistics, Options, and Permissions

Table 6-2.   *The File Pop-Up Menu*

birthday directory, you open a file manger window for both the **birthday** and **presents** directory, click the **presents** directory, and then right-click the **party** file in the **birthday** directory and select the link entry. You will see the location box in the Link window showing the pathname for the **birthday** directory. Add in the name you want to give to the link file.

You can use this same procedure to rename a file. Right-click and select the Move entry from the pop-up menu. In the dialog, enter a new name for the file. You can also rename a file either by entering a new name in its Properties dialog box or by slowly clicking the name displayed under the icon. Use a right-click and select Properties from the pop-up menu to display the Properties dialog box.

File operations can be performed on a selected group of files and directories. There are several ways to select a group of items. You can click the first item and then hold down the SHIFT key while clicking the last item. You can also click and drag the mouse across items you want to select. To select separated items, hold the CTRL key down as you click the individual icons. If you want to select all the items in the directory, just choose the Select All entry in the Edit menu. You can also select files based on pattern matches on the file names. Choose the Select Files entry in the Edit menu. You can then enter a pattern using Linux file matching wildcard symbols such as * (see Chapter 8). For example, the pattern ***.c** would select all C source code files. You can then click and drag a set of items at once. This lets you copy, move, or even delete several files at once. To move files between directories, open two file manager windows to the respective directories. Then click and drag the items from one window to the other.

You can start any application in the file manager by double-clicking either the application itself or a data file used for that application. If a file does not have an associated application, you can right-click the file and select the Open With entry. A dialog box is then displayed where you can choose the application you want to open this file with. Drag-and-drop operations are also supported for applications. You can drag a data file to its associated application icon (say one on the desktop); the application will start up using that data file.

With the Properties dialog box you can view detailed information on a file and set options and permissions. A Properties box has three panels: Statistics, Options, and Permissions. The Statistics panel shows detailed information such as size, date, and ownership. The Options panel lets you set the open, view, and edit operations for this file. You can choose what application to open it with, which one to use to just view it, and which one to use to edit it. The Permissions panel shows the read, write, and execute permissions for user, group, and other as set for this file. You can change any of the permissions here, provided the file belongs to you.

You can set preferences for your GMC file manager in the Preferences dialog box. Access this dialog by selecting the Preferences item in the Edit menu. The Preferences dialog has five panels: File Display, Confirmation, Custom View, Caching, and VFS. On the File Display panel you can select such features as hiding or showing hidden (dot) files. The Confirmation panel is where confirmation checks are specified for deleting and overwriting files. The VFS (Virtual File System) panel lets you set options for accessing remote file systems such as FTP sites. You can specify an anonymous FTP password, a timeout period, and whether you have to use an FTP proxy server. The Caching panel lets you specify caching options for directory and FTP information. GMC will keep a copy of displayed directories for a given amount of time per session. This allows fast reload of previously displayed directories. You use the Custom View panel to select the fields you want displayed in your custom view of a directory listing. These are such fields as date, time, and permissions. You will have two panes, one listing possible fields (Possible Columns) and the other the fields you have chosen (Displayed Columns). Use the Add button to add a field to your list, the Remove button, to remove one. You can drag entries up or down in the Displayed Columns pane to reorder them.

The Gnome Panel

The panel is the center of the Gnome interface (see the following illustration). Through it you can start your applications, run applets, and access desktop areas. You can think of the Gnome panel as a type of tool you can use on your desktop. You can have several Gnome panels displayed on your desktop, each with applets and menus you have placed in them. In this respect, Gnome is very flexible, letting you configure your panels any way you want. You can customize a panel to fit your own needs, holding applets and menus of your own selection. You may add new panels, add applications to the panel, and add various applets.

You can hide the panel at any time by clicking either of the Hide buttons located on each end of the panel. The Hide buttons are thin buttons showing a small arrow. This is the direction in which the panel will hide. To redisplay the panel, move your mouse off the screen in that direction at the bottom of the screen. If you want the panel to automatically hide when you are not using it, select the Autohide option in the panel configuration window. Moving the mouse to the bottom of the screen will redisplay the panel. You can also move the panel to another edge of the screen by clicking and dragging it with your middle mouse button (both buttons simultaneously for two-button mice).

To add a new panel, select the Add New Panel entry in the Panel menu located in the main menu. You can choose from edge or corner panels. An edge panel is displayed across one of the edges of the screen. Your original panel is an edge panel. A corner panel is a smaller panel that does not extend across the entire screen. It only extends as far as it needs to, to contain whatever applets and menu button you place in it. It will be anchored on one corner of the screen. If you click the Hide button on the corner, you will hide the panel. But if you click the other Hide button, it will merely move the panel to the other corner. Clicking it again will hide the panel. You can change a panel's type at any time by right-clicking the panel and selecting the alternate configuration. Right-clicking, an edge panel will display a "Convert to edge panel" entry that you can use to change on the edge panel to a corner panel.

Adding Applications and Applets

It is very easy to add applications to a panel. For an application that is already in the main menu, you only need to go to its entry and right-click it. Then select the Add This Launcher To Panel entry. An application launcher for that application will be automatically added to the panel. Suppose you use gEdit frequently and would like to add its icon to the panel, instead of having to go through the main menu all the time. Right-click the gEdit menu entry and select the Add This Launcher To Panel option. The gEdit icon will appear in your panel.

To add an application icon not in the Mail menu, first right-click the panel to display the pop-up menu and select the Add New Launcher entry. This opens the Create Launcher Applet window for entering properties for the applications launcher. You will be prompted for the application name, the command that invokes it, and its type. To select an icon for your launcher, click the Icon button. This opens the icon picker window, listing icons you can choose from.

You can also group applications under a Drawer icon. Clicking the Drawer icon will display a list of the different application icons that you can then select. To add a drawer to your panel, right-click the panel and select the Add Drawer entry. If you want to add a whole menu of applications on the main menu to your panel, just

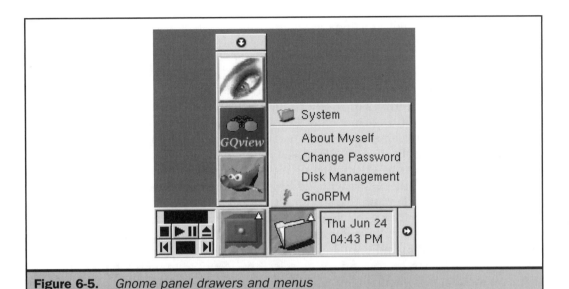

Figure 6-5.   *Gnome panel drawers and menus*

right-click the menu item and select the Add This As Drawer To Panel entry. The entire menu will appear as a drawer on your panel, holding icons instead of menu entries (see Figure 6-5). For example, suppose you want to place the Internet applications menu on your panel. Right-click the Internet item and select Add This As Drawer To Panel. A drawer will appear on your panel labeled Internet. Clicking it will display a pop-up list of icons for all the Internet applications.

A menu differs from a drawer in that a drawer holds application icons instead of menu entries. You can add menus to your panel much as you add drawers. To add a submenu in the main menu to your panel, just right-click the menu title and select the Add This As Menu To Panel entry. The menu title will appear in the panel; you can click it to display the menu entries.

You can also add directory folders to a panel. Just click and drag the folder icon from the file manager window to your panel. Whenever you click this folder button, a file manager window will open up, displaying that directory. You already have a folder button for your home directory. You can add directory folders to any drawer on your panel.

Main Menu

You open the main menu by clicking its button on the panel. The Main Menu button is a stylized picture of a bare foot. It will initially be located on the left side of your panel, the lower left-hand corner of your screen. You only need to single-click the Main Menu button. The menu will pop up much like the Start menu in Windows.

You can configure menus using the Menu Properties dialog. To change the properties for a menu on the panel, including the main menu, you right-click its icon in the panel and select the Properties entry. This displays the Menu Properties dialog, which has two sections: Menu Type and Main Menu. In the Main Menu section you can set properties for that main menu. Several possible submenus can be displayed on the main menu, either directly or in other submenus. You can choose from the System, User, Red Hat, KDE, and Debian menus. Red Hat and Debian menus are those used for specific Red Hat or Debian programs installed by those distributions that are not specifically Gnome applications. KDE is used for KDE applications, should the KDE desktop also be installed on your system.

You can customize the main menu, adding your own entries, with the Menu editor. The main menu is divided into two sections: the Systems menu and the User menu. The Systems menu, which can be changed only by the system administrator, the root user, will contain the default Gnome applications installed with Gnome. The User menu can be changed by individual users, adding entries for applications a user frequently runs. To start the Menu editor, select the Menu Editor entry in the Setting submenu located in the main menu. The Menu editor is divided into two panes, the left being a tree view of the main menu. You can expand or shrink any of the submenus. The right pane holds configuration information for a selected entry. There are two panels: basic and advanced. The basic panel displays the name, command, and application type, as well as the icon. You can click the icon to change it. You can also change the name, command, or type fields.

To add a new application, click the New Item button on the toolbar. The new item will be placed in the currently selected menu. Enter the name, command, and type information, and then select an icon. Then click the Save button to add the entry to the menu. You can move the menu item in the menu by clicking the up or down arrow button in the toolbar, or dragging it with the mouse. If you are a user, remember that you can only add entries to the User menu, not the Systems menu.

An easier way to add an application is to use the drag-and-drop method. Locate the application you want to add with the file manager, and then drag and drop its icon to the appropriate menu in the Menu editor. The entry will be made automatically using configuration information provided for that application by the file manager.

Panel Configuration

You use the Global Panel Configuration dialog to configure properties for all Gnome panels. Either right-click the panel and select Global Properties or select Global Properties in the Panel submenu in the main menu to display this dialog window. The Global Panel Configuration dialog has six tabbed panels: Animation, Launcher Icon, Drawer Icon, Menu Icon, Logout Icon, and Miscellaneous. With the animation panel you can enable panel animations, setting various options for them. The various Icon panels let you select the images you want to use to denote active or inactive elements, among other features such as border and depth. On the miscellaneous panel you set certain options such as allowing pop-up menus on the desktop, prompt before logout, or keep panel below windows.

To configure individual panels, you use the Panel Properties dialog. To display this dialog, you right-click the particular panel and select the This Panel Properties entry in the pop-up menu, or select This Panel Properties in the main menu's Panel menu. For individual panels you can set features for edge panel configuration and the background. The Panel Properties dialog includes a tabbed panel for each. On the Edge panel you can choose options for positioning an edge panel and for minimizing it, including the autohide feature. The Hide Buttons feature lets you hide the panel yourself.

On the Background panel you can change the background image used for the panel. You can select an image, have it scaled to fit the panel, and select a background color. For an image, you can also drag and drop an image file from the file manager to the panel, and that image will become the background image for the panel.

Gnome Applets

Applets are small programs that perform tasks within the panel. To add an applet, right-click the panel and select Add New Applet from the pop-up menu. This in turn will display other pop-up menus listing categories of applets with further listings of available applets. Select the one you want. For example, to add the clock to your panel, select Clock from the Utility menu. To remove an applet, right-click it and select Remove from panel.

Gnome features a number of helpful applets such as a CPU monitor and a mail checker. There are applets that monitor your system, such as the Battery Monitor, which checks the battery in laptops, CPU/MEM Usage, which shows a graph indicating your current CPU and memory usage, as well as separate applets for CPU and memory load: CPULoad and MemLoad. The Mixer applet displays a small scrollbar for adjusting sound levels. The CD player displays a small CD interface for playing music CDs.

For Network tasks there are MailCheck, PPP dialer, and Web Control applets. MailCheck checks for received mail. To configure it, you right-click it and select the Properties entry. You can set the frequency of checks as well as specify a more sophisticated mail checker to run such as fetchmail. The PPP dialer will set up a PPP connection to an ISP. This requires that you have a PPP dialer program such as gnomeppp already configured. Web Control lets you start your Web browser with a specified URL.

Several helpful utility applets provide added functionality to your desktop. The Clock applet can display time in 12- or 24-hour format. Right-click the Clock applet and select the Properties entry to change its setup. You use the Printer applet to print your files. To print a file, just drag its icon to the Printer applet. To configure the Printer applet, right-click it and select Properties. Here you can specify the printer name and the printer command to use, helpful if you have more than one printer.

The Drive Mount applet lets you mount a drive using a single click. You can create a Drive Mount applet for each device you have, such as a floppy drive and a CD-ROM. To mount a file system, all you have to do is click the appropriate Drive Mount icon in the panel. The applet will originally display a small image of a floppy drive. By default, the applet will mount the floppy drive. You can change its configuration to mount a CD-ROM, a hard drive, or a Zip drive, by first right-clicking an applet and selecting the Properties entry. This displays a Drive Mount Settings dialog. Here you can select the icon the applet should display and its mount point, the directory on your file system that it will be attached to. For a CD-ROM, this is usually **/mnt/cdrom**. You have four icons to choose from: Floppy, CDROM, Zip Disk, and Hard Drive. Select the one you want. Now you can just click the icon in the panel to mount the device. Normally only the root user can mount floppy disks or CD-ROMS. If you want to allow users to mount floppies or CD-ROM disc you have to set the appropriate permissions on these devices. You can easily use Linuxconf to do this (see Chapter 26 on File Administration).

Gnome Pager

The Gnome pager shown in the next illustration appears in the panel and shows a pager for your desktop areas as well as buttons for each window open on the desktop. A window may be part of an application such as Netscape or the file manager displaying a directory. The Gnome pager is a panel applet that works only in the panel. If it is not already active, you can activate it by right-clicking the panel and selecting Add New Applet from the pop-up menu. This in turn will display other pop-up menus listing categories of applets and their listings of available applets. Select the Utility category and in that menu select Gnome Pager.

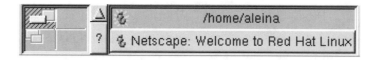

The Gnome pager is divided into two areas, the Pager view and the Task List view. The Pager view shows all your areas as small adjoining rectangles. Applications show up as small outlines in these rectangles. If you click the small arrow to the right of the Desktop view, the areas will be displayed with a listing of the applications on them. The task list arranges applications in a series of buttons, one for each open application (window). Clicking an application button moves you to that window.

To configure the pager, right-click it and select Properties to display the Gnome Pager Setting dialog. You can also click the small icon with the question mark. Here you can set the width of the task list, and the number of rows and columns. You can also control how the pager is displayed, suppressing either the Pager view or the task list, including icons in the task list, or using small pages for the desktop areas. Bear in mind that the window manager you are using may also have a pager you can use. Check your window manager documentation on how to activate it.

Quicklaunch

You can use the Quicklaunch applet in the panel to start programs. The Quicklaunch applet holds a collection of small icons for application launchers. Just click them to launch your application. The Quicklaunch applet can use only launchers that are already set up either on the main menu or on your desktop. To add a launcher to Quicklaunch, just drag and drop the launcher to the Quicklaunch applet in the panel. A small icon will be created for it in the Quicklaunch applet. For main menu items, just click an item and drag it to the Quicklaunch applet. Right-click a particular application's icon and select Properties to configure that launcher.

Gnome Configuration: Control Center

With the Gnome Control Center shown in Figure 6-6 you can configure different parts of your system using the *capplet* tools. You can think of capplets as modules or plugins that can be added to the Control Center to let you configure various applications. There are capplets for the core set of Gnome applications as well as for other applications for which developers may have written capplets. You can either start the Control Center directly or start up a particular capplet that will start the Control Center open to that capplet. To start the Control Center directly, select the Control Center entry in the System menu located in the main menu or on its applet in the panel (icon of a toolbox). The Control Center menu will also list the capplets currently available on your system. To start using a capplet, select the particular application capplet you want from the Control Center menu.

The Control Center window is divided into two panes. The left one is a tree view of the capplets available on your system. They are arranged into categories that you can expand or shrink. The left pane displays the panel for configuring that particular application. Just click the entry in the view tree for the application you want to configure, and its configuration panel will appear to the left.

Your Gnome system provides several desktop capplets that you can use to configure your desktop: Background, Screensaver, Theme Selector, and Window Manager. You use the Background capplet to select a background color or image, the Screensaver to select the screensaver images and wait time, the Theme selector to choose a theme, and the Window Manager to choose the window manager you want to use.

Gnome Edit Properties lets you to choose an editor to be your default editor for Gnome, the editor that the Gnome file manager will use to open text files. Gnome MIME types lets you specify MIME (Multipurpose Internet Mail Extensions) type entries for your system, associating given MIME types with certain applications. You

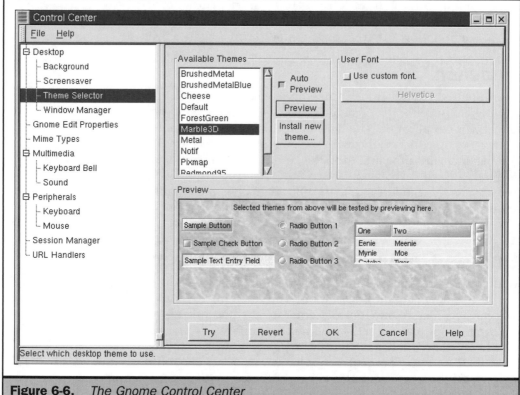

Figure 6-6. *The Gnome Control Center*

will notice that basic MIME type entries are already present. You can edit an entry and change its associated application. Also listed are Multimedia and Peripheral capplets. For the sound configuration you can select sound files to play for events in different Gnome applications. For your keyboard you can set the repeat sensitivity and click sound. You can configure mouse buttons for your right or left hand and adjust the mouse motion. With the Session Manager capplet you can configure certain Gnome session features, specifying non-Gnome programs to start up and whether you want a logout prompt.

Several User Interface capplets let you configure different interface components such as menus, toolbars, and status bars. There are capplets for setting these features for applications, dialogs, and the Multiple Document Interface (MDI). You can specify whether toolbars and menus can be detached, whether they have relief borders, and whether they include icons. For dialogs you can set features such as the arrangement of buttons or the position of the dialog on the screen when it appears. The default MDI used for Gnome is notebook. The notebook interface consists of tabbed panels that are used in many applications such as the Control Center. You can choose two other interfaces, toplevel and modal. You can also adjust the way the notebook interface displays its tabs.

Gnome sets up several configuration files and directories in your home directory. The **.gnome** directory holds configuration files for different desktop components such as **gmc** for the file manager, panel, for the panels, and **gmenu** for the main menu. The **.gtkrc** holds configuration directives for the GTK+ widgets. The **.gnome-desktop** holds all the items you've placed on your desktop.

Gnome Directories and Files

Most distributions will install Gnome binaries in the **/usr/bin** directory on your system. Gnome libraries are located in the **/usr/lib** directory. Gnome also has its own directories with header files for use in compiling and developing Gnome applications, **/usr/include/libgnome** and **/usr/include/libgnomeui**. The directories located in **/usr/share/gnome** contain files used to configure your Gnome environment. See Table 6-3 in the next section.

Gnome sets up several hidden directories that begin with ".gnome" and include a preceding period in the name. The **.gnome** holds files used to configure a user's Gnome desktop and applications. Here are located configuration files for the panel, Control Center, GnomeRPM, MIME types, and sessions, among others. The files **Gnome**, **GnomeHelp**, **Background**, and **Terminal** all hold Gnome configuration commands for how to display and use these components. For example, **Gnome** holds general display features for the desktop, and **GnomeHelp** specifies the history and bookmark files for the help system. Configuration files for particular Gnome applications are kept in the subdirectory **apps**. On Red Hat, the **redhat-apps** directory holds **.desktop** files that contain Gnome instructions on how to handle different Red Hat utilities such as **netcfg.** The **.gnome-desktop** holds any files, folders, or links that the user has dragged to the desktop. The **.gnome-help-browser** holds the Bookmark and History files for the Gnome Help System. These are the bookmarks and the list of previous documents the user consulted with the Gnome Help browser. The **.gtckrc** is the user configuration file for the GTK+ libraries. It contains current desktop configuration directives for resources such as keybindings, colors, and window styles.

Enlightenment

Currently, Gnome is distributed with the Enlightenment window manager. Enlightenment is fully Gnome compliant and also has its own display features and functionality. You can configure Enlightenment from within Gnome, by first selecting it in the Control Center's Window Manager panel. Then select Run Configuration Tool For Enlightenment. This will run the e-conf Enlightenment configuration program, displaying the Enlightenment configuration window shown in Figure 6-7.

ENVIRONMENTS

System Gnome Directories

/usr/bin	Gnome programs
/usr/lib	Gnome libraries
/usr/include/libgnome	Header files for use in compiling and developing Gnome applications
/usr/include/libgnomeui	Header files for use in compiling and developing Gnome User interface components
/usr/share/gnome/apps	Files used by Gnome applications
/usr/share/gnome/help	Files used by Gnome Help System
/usr/doc/gnome*	Documentation for various Gnome packages, including libraries
/etc/X11/gdm/gnomerc	Gnome configuration file invoked with the Gnome Display Manager (GDM)

User Gnome Directories

.gnome	Holds configuration files for the user's Gnome desktop and Gnome applications. Includes configuration files for the panel, Control Center, background, GnomeRPM, MIME types, and sessions
.gnome-desktop	Directory where files, directories, and links that you place on the desktop will reside
.gnome-help-browser	Contains Gnome Help System configuration files, including History and Bookmarks set up by the user
.gnome_private	The user private Gnome directory
.gtkrc	GTK+ configuration file
.mc	Configuration files for the Midnight Commander File Manager

Table 6-3.   *Gnome Configuration Directories*

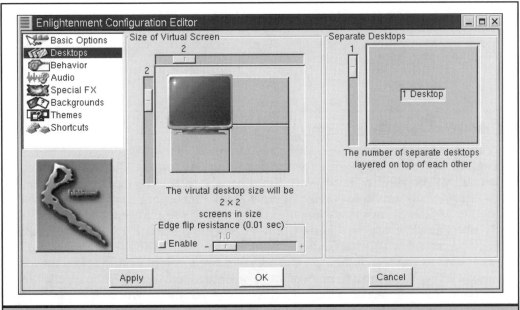

Figure 6-7. *Enlightenment configuration*

The Enlightenment Configuration window displays a list of configuration topics on the left and the panel for the selected topic on the right. Basic options set window displays, letting you select resize and move methods. With the Desktops option you can create virtual desktops and specify the number of desktop areas for each one. On the panel are two configuration tools. The left one, labeled Size Of Virtual Screen, is used to determine the number of desktop areas, and the right one, labeled Separate Desktops, is used to specify the number of virtual desktops. Recall, however, that the Gnome desktop is only supported on the first virtual desktop, not on any others. This means that drag-and-drop operations do not work on the other virtual desktops. They will, however, work on any of the desktop areas on that first virtual desktop. The Gnome pager will support all the virtual desktops, displaying rectangles for each in the panel. Other topics cover features such as sounds, special effects, window focus, keyboard shortcuts, and backgrounds. You can set different backgrounds for each virtual desktop.

The Themes panel lets you use an Enlightenment theme, of which there are many to choose from. Enlightenment is known for its magnificent themes. See **e.themes.org** for ones that you can download. To make a theme available, place it in your home directory's **.enlightenment/themes** directory. Make sure that file has an **.etheme** extension. Enlightenment maintains its own configuration directory called **.enlightenment** in your home directory. It contains subdirectories for themes, backgrounds, and windows.

Gnome Themes

You can display your Gnome desktop using different themes that change the appearance of desktop objects such as windows, buttons, and scrollbars. Gnome functionality is not affected in any way. There are a variety of themes that you can choose from. Many are posted on the Internet at **gtk.themes.org**. Technically, these are referred to as GTK themes that allow the GTK widget set to change their look and feel.

To select a theme, use the Gnome Control Center and select Themes in the Desktop listing. You can select a theme from the Available Themes list on the Configuration panel. The Auto Preview button lets you see an example of the theme. To use the theme, click Try. To install a theme you have downloaded from the Internet, click the Install New Theme button and locate the theme file. The theme will be installed on your system, and an entry for it will appear in the Available Themes list.

Updating Gnome

Currently, new versions of Gnome are being released frequently, sometimes every few months. Gnome releases are designed to let users easily upgrade their older versions. Be sure to obtain the release for your particular distributions (though you can install from the source code if you wish). Packages tailored for various distributions can be downloaded through the Gnome Web site at **www.gnome.org** or directly from the Gnome FTP site at **ftp.gnome.org** and its mirror sites. RPM packages for Red Hat can also be obtained from **updates.redhat.com**.

First log in as the root user and then create a directory to hold the Gnome files. Then connect to an FTP site. You can use a Web browser such as Netscape, but it is preferable to use an FTP client such as ftp, IglooFTP, or even the Gnome file manager. Download the files for the new version to your new directory. For Red Hat these will be a series of RPM package files. To download using the Gnome file manager, just enter the FTP URL in a file manager window's Location box to access the site. Move to the directory holding the Gnome files. Then select the files and drag and drop them in another file manager window that is open to the local directory where you want them placed. The files will be downloaded for you. To download using FTP, be sure to turn off prompts with the **prompt** command and use **mget *** to download all the files at once. Once they are downloaded, you can use the **rpm** command with the **–Uvh** option to install them or the GnomeRPM utility. Be sure to read any installation instructions first. These can be found in README or INSTALL files. You may have to install some packages before others.

To manually install a particular Gnome RPM package you use the **rpm** command with the **–Uvh** option or an RPM package utility like GnomeRPM (see Chapter 4 and 24). This example installs the games package.

```
rpm -Uvh gnome-games-1.1.1pre2.2.i386.rpm
```

Many of the most recent updates will be provided in the form of source files that you can download and compile. These are usually packages in compressed archives with **.tar.gz** extensions. At **ftp.gnome.org** these are currently located in **pub/Gnome/sources**. Check the Gnome Web site for announcements. For example, a new version of the Gnome core programs could be:

```
ftp.gnome.org/pub/GNOME/sources/gnome-core/gnome-core-1.0.7.tar.gz
```

Once you have downloaded the archive, use the **tar** command with the **xvzf** options to decompress and extract it. In the directory generated use the **./configure**, **make**, and **make install** commands to create and install the programs.

```
tar xvzf gnome-core-1.0.7.tar.gz
```

Gnome Applications and Tools

Table 6-4 lists the Gnome applications currently available. Most are distributed with the current release of Gnome and included with the Red Hat distribution. Some of the newer applications are accessible on the Gnome Web site at **www.gnome.org**. Check the Web site for new applications. A large number of Gnome applications are currently under development.

Core	Description
Afterstep Clock Applet	NeXT-like clock
gnome-core	Contains the Gnome panel and applets, the help browser desktop properties, and other essential Gnome utilities
gnome-help-browser	Browses HTML, GNU info, and Man pages
gnome-libs	Main set of support libraries
GNotes!	Panel applet to create yellow notes on your desktop
GNU Midnight Commander	Gnome file manager
LibGTop	A library that fetches information about the running system
ORBit	CORBA ORB
Development Tools	**Description**
CvsRpmBuilder	CVS to RPM builder
Dylan Gnome Bindings	Gnome bindings for the Dylan programming language
gbuild	Bash script to update code modules from CVS
gIDE	GTK-based integrated development environment for the C compiler
GJP	GTK-based Java classfile parser
Glade	GTK+ user interface builder
GNOME EDMA ClassBrowser	EDMA development tools
Gnome RPM Workstation	Creates spec files for RPM files
gnome-python	Bindings for python
gnome-standalone	Starting place for new Gnome development
GNOMEBook	Gnome-compliant document-oriented interface
gnometool	Maintains Gnome from CVS

Table 6-4. *Gnome Software*

Development Tools	Description
GRAD	Visual programming environment
gtk–	C++ wrapper for GTK+
java-gnome	Bindings for Java applications
libglade	Library to load GLADE interfaces at runtime
MEGIDO	Pascal-based Linux oriented RAD tool
Perl/GTK	Bindings for Perl
Pharmacy	Gnome-compliant front end to CVS
PiGTK	Pike interface for GTK+ 1.1
TOM/gtk	Bindings for TOM
V/Gtk	GTK+ port of the V library
VDK	C++ wrapper of GTK+ Library
wxWindows/Gtk	Toolkit with Python bindings
Internet Tools	**Description**
ac	Apache configuration tool
AMCL	MUD client
AQSS	Recursive online HTTP searcher
Crescendo	TinyFugue MUD client
DPS-FTP	FTP client, like Bulletproof FTP
Express	Web browser
ganesha	Locates a file using ftpsearch
gfinger	Finger client
gFTP	Multithreaded FTP client
gHostLookup	Returns machine IP address
gIPSC	Subnet calculator
Gnome Darxite Monitor	Panel applet for Darxite daemon
gnome-ppp	PPP-dialup network app

Table 6-4.   *Gnome Software* (continued)

Internet Tools	Description
gnome-vnc	A VNC (virtual network computing) viewer
Gpppsetup	Version of pppsetup
GSmbClient	Gnome version of smbclient
GtkNeighborhood	A GTK smbclient front end
GTransferManager	Retrieves multiple files from the Web
gVN	Gnome Visual Network, which allows you to manage an intranet or a small network
IglooFTP	Graphical and user-friendly FTP client
litespeed	FTP client much like ws_ftp
Mnemonic	Web browser with GTK front end
PopApp	Checks your POP3 account for mail
screem	A Web site editing/management program
Web Studio	Web development
Wsnitch	HTTP proxy
XSitecopy	Sitecopy is for copying locally stored Web sites to remote Web servers
Xwhois	Searches global NIC whois databases
Mail Clients	**Description**
Balsa	E-mail reader
Gmail	Light/stable/fast e-mail client
LinPopUp	Port of Winpopup
Mahogany	E-mail client
Math and Science Tools	**Description**
AutoDOC	OBD-II compatible scan tool
DND	Molecular Dynamics Simulation of the Molecule

Table 6-4. *Gnome Software* (continued)

Math and Science Tools	Description
gcad	2-D CAD program
genius	Arbitrary precision integer and multiple-precision floating-point calculator
GINA	Gnu INstrumentation Architecture
GNOME Particle Simulator	A general multiparticle simulator (3-D)
gnuclid	Euclidean geometry exploration program
Guppi	Gnome/GNU Useful Production Interface
Loci	Framework for linking biocomputing programs
moiss	Quantum Monte Carlo program
Nightfall	Interactive astronomy application for fun, education, and science
Snurbs	Simple NURBS Library and Viewer
superficie	Visualize 3-D surfaces
Network Talk Clients (IRC/ICQ/etc)	Description
gicq	ICQ-compatible instant messaging client
GMasqDialer	Gnome/GTK client for masqdialer server
GnomeICU	Internet Communication Utility for Gnome based on the ICQ protocol
GNU Talk	Plugin replacement for standard talk/talkd
gtkFAIM	Gnome-based client for AOL Instant Messenger
GtkICQ	GTK-based ICQ client
irssi	IRC client that can work in Gnome panel
X-Chat	IRC client
yagIRC	Yet Another GTK+ IRC client

Table 6-4. *Gnome Software* (continued)

Productivity	Description
Achtung	Presentation program similar to PowerPoint
Electric Eyes	Image viewer based on imlib
Gaby	Small personal databases manager using GTK+ Gnome
Gaspell	A Gnome front end to Aspell, which is an Open Source spell checker
gBibTeX	BibTeX front end
GBurn!	GTK/Gnome interface for burning CD-R
gEdit	Lightweight text editor
Gfax	Pop-up fax application for Gnome
ggv	PostScript viewer
gimp	Image program (like Photoshop)
gnofin	Tracks checking and savings accounts
gnome-pilot	A daemon for pilot synchronization
gnome-pim	Gnome personal information management programs; includes GnomeCalendar and GnomeAddressbook
gnome-utils	Contains Gnome time tracker, searching tool, calculator, and others
GnomeCalendar	Electronic business card
GnomePGP	Gnome front end for GNU Privacy Guard
Gnotepad	Simple notepad
Gnucash	Personal finance package
GnuGradeBook	Tracks students' progress (for teachers)
Gnumeric	Gnome spreadsheet
GnuPaghe	Wages place simulation
Go	Word processor

Table 6-4.   *Gnome Software* (continued)

Productivity	Description
gpattern	Create tilable patterns
gquest	Learning, editing, and printout of questionnaires
GQview	Simple image viewer
graphtool	Produces BMP graphs
GWP	Hungry Programmers word processor, Xword

Sound Tools	Description
Audio File Library	Elegant API for accessing a variety of audio file formats
Audiotechque	Multitrack audio editor/discombobulator
Electric Ears	Audio player/editor
esound	Mixes multiple digitized audio streams and samples together
G-Sox	Sox sound processing
gnome-media	Contains the gtcd CD player, gmix, gnomeovision, and extace
Gstring	Guitar tuner
gTune	Guitar/any instrument tuner
gtuner	Radio card tuner
gvoice	Library wrapping IBM ViaVoice, allowing connection of arbitrary spoken words to callbacks and GTK signals
mixer-applet	Tiny little mixer for panel
Sonic Flow	Library for a parametric EQ
Sound Monitor applet	Shows VU meter or scope of the output of the ESD daemon
TCD	Gnome CD player with CDDB
Voodoo Tracker	Digital studio tracker

Table 6-4. *Gnome Software* (continued)

System Utilities	Description
cpanel	Configurator Panel is a tool to set up network cards, printers, modems, and partitions
cromagnon	Gnome crontab manager
gdialog	Gnome port of the "dialog" utilities
gdm	Display Manager Gnome
gfdisk	Disk partition program
GFile	File manager
ginetd-config	Inetd services editor
gLaptop	Gnome applet that will have suspend/standby buttons, battery meter, and hot-swap functionality for laptops
GNOME Printer Queue	The Gnome Printer Queue
gnome-admin	System administration tools
gnome-apt	Gnome front end for the next-generation Debian package manager
GnoRPM	RPM front end for Gnome
grpm	Red Hat's Gnome RPM manager
gstripchart	Generates a strip chart of various system parameters
GtkSamba	Configures Samba
GtkZip	Maintains your Iomega Zip drive disks under Linux
gtop	Gnome system monitor
guiTAR	Archive tool
gxsnmp	Network management package
gxTar	Gnome/GTK front end to common archive utilities under Unix

Table 6-4. *Gnome Software* (continued)

System Utilities	Description
Jade	Terminal program
LKM	Linux Kernel Manager, GUI for compiling and setting up the Linux kernel
logview	Views and monitors system logs
Merlins Clock Applet	A Gnome panel clock applet
Mini-Commander	Adds a command line to the panel

Window/Session/ Desktop Managers	Description
Blackbox GNOME compliance patch	Adds Gnome compliance to the window managers
GNOME Panel	Program is responsible for launching other applications
GnoWM	Window manager utilizing GTK+
gtkwm	Window manager using GTK
mosquito	Window manager for Gnome
xglock	Launcher of xlock

Miscellaneous	Description
BakaSub	Subtitling program for Linux
Battery Meter Applet	Analog-like battery meter
carnegie	Class scheduler
Character Picker	Allows accented characters
Xunzip	Uncompressing utility
gAlarm	Alarm
gEuroCalc	Calculator to convert European currencies to EURO
GHex	A binary file editor

Table 6-4.   *Gnome Software* (continued)

Miscellaneous	Description
Giram	GPLed 3-D Modeler
GNOME Comp-jugador	Conjugator of Spanish verbs
GNOME Disk Catalog	Catalog Zip disks, CD-ROMs, and floppies
GNOME Portfolio Manager	Simple portfolio management
gnome-db	Database access for GNU applications
GNU Photo (gphoto)	Retrieves and organizes images from digital cameras
GnuSniff	Network packet sniffer
Gpasman	Password manager
gUE	GUI for emulators (games)
gufe	GUI for setting options for command line utilities
gvbox	ISDN answering machine
ImageShaker	Image processing program
Java Interactive Environment	3-D interface bound to Gnome
k2gmenu	Converts a KDE menu structure into a Gnome menu structure
Millennium	Countdown timer that displays the time left to the millennium
Mnemonic-Core	Message handler
SkyApp	Weather data and forecasts
sview	Displays text word by word RSVP
Videobase	Tracks the movies you have or have not seen
Websearch Applet	Searches the Web
Word Inspector	"Dict" dictionary program
Xsteak	Dictionary for Unix Systems

Table 6-4. *Gnome Software* (continued)

Chapter 7

The X Window System
and Window Managers

Instead of the command line interface, you can use an X Window System (X) GUI to interact with your Linux system. With such an interface you can use icons, windows, and menus to issue commands and run applications. Unlike PC-based GUIs such as Windows or the Mac OS, Linux and Unix systems divide the GUI into three separate components: the X Window System, window managers, and program/file managers. The X Window System, also known as X and X11, is an underlying standardized graphic utility that provides basic graphic operations such as opening windows or displaying images. A window manager handles windowing operations such as resizing and moving windows. Window managers vary in the way windows are displayed, using different borders and window menus. All, however, use the same underlying X graphic utility. A file manager handles file operations using icons and menus, and a program manager runs programs, often allowing you to select commonly used ones from a taskbar. Unlike window managers, file and program managers can differ greatly in their capabilities. In most cases, different file and program managers can run on the same window manager.

All Linux and Unix systems use the same standard underlying X graphics utility. This means, in most cases, that an X Window System–based program can run on any of the window managers and desktops. X Window System–based software is often found at Linux or Unix FTP sites in directories labeled **X11**. You can download these packages and run them on any window manager running on your Linux system. Some may already be in the form of Linux binaries that you can download, install, and run directly. Netscape is an example. Others will be in the form of source code that can easily be configured, compiled, and installed on your system with a few simple commands. Some applications, such as Motif applications, may require special libraries.

With a window manager, you can think of a window as taking the place of a command line. Operations you perform through the window are interpreted and sent to the Linux system for execution. Window managers operate off the underlying X Window System, which actually provides the basic window operations that allow you to open, move, and close windows as well as display menus and select icons. FVWM2 and AfterStep manage these operations, each in its own way, providing their own unique interfaces. The advantage of such a design is that you can have different window managers that can operate on the same Linux system. In this sense, Linux is not tied to one type of graphical user interface (GUI). On the same Linux system, one user may be using the FVWM window manager, another may be using the Xview window manager, and still another, the Enlightenment window manager, all at the same time. You can find out detailed information about different window managers available for Linux from the X11 Web site at **www.X11.org**. The site provides reviews, screenshots, and links to home sites, as well as a comparison table listing the features available for the different window managers.

Window, File, and Program Managers

With a window manager you can use your mouse to perform windowing operations such as opening, closing, resizing, and moving windows. Several window managers are available for Linux (see Table 7-3). Some of the more popular ones are Enlightenment (**enlightenment**), Window Maker (**wmaker**), AfterStep (**afterstep**), and the Free Virtual Window Manager 2.0 (FVWM2). FVWM2, written by Robert Nation, is used as the default window manager on most Linux systems. It is easy to use, powerful, and flexible. Window Maker and AfterStep are originally based on the NeXTSTEP interface used for the NeXT operating system. Enlightenment is the default window manager for Gnome.

Window managers operate through the underlying X graphics utility. The X Window System actually provides the basic operations that allow you to open, move, and close windows as well as display menus and select icons. Window managers manage these operations each in their own way, providing different interfaces from which to choose. All window managers, no matter how different they may appear, use X Window System tools. In this sense, Linux is not tied to one type of graphical user interface. On the same Linux system, one user may be using the FVWM2 window manager, another may be using Enlightenment, and yet another, Window Maker.

Window managers originally provided only very basic window management operations such as opening, closing, and resizing of windows. Their features have been enhanced in the more sophisticated window managers such as Window Maker and Enlightenment to include support for virtual desktops, docking panels, and themes that let users change the look and feel of their desktop. However, to work with files and customize applications, you need to use file and program managers. With a file manager, you can copy, move, or erase files within different directory windows. With a program manager, you can execute commands and run programs using taskbars and program icons. A desktop program will combine the capabilities of window, file, and program managers, providing a desktop metaphor with icons and menus to run programs and access files. Gnome and the K Desktop are two such desktop programs. See Table 7-3 for a listing of window managers and desktops along with their Web sites where you can obtain more information.

Several window managers have been enhanced to include many of the features of a desktop. The window managers included with many Linux distributions have program management capabilities in addition to window handling. FVWM2 and AfterStep have a taskbar and a workplace menu that you can use to access all your X programs. With either the menu or the taskbar, you can run any X program directly from FVWM2. Window Maker provides a NeXTSTEP interface that features a docking panel for your applications with drag-and-drop support. You can drag files to the application icon to start it with that file.

Using just a window manager, you can run any X program. Window managers have their own workspace menu and taskbar. You can also run any X program from an Xterm terminal window. There you can type the name of an X application; when you press ENTER, the X application will start up with its own window. It is best to invoke an X application as a background process by adding an ampersand after the command. A separate window will open for the X application that you can work in.

Window Managers

Instead of the command line interface, you can use an X window manager and file manager, which will allow you to interact with your Linux system using windows, buttons, and menus. Window managers provide basic window management operations such as opening, closing, and resizing windows, and file managers allow you to manage and run programs using icons and menus. The X Window System supports a variety of window managers. Several of these are listed in Table 7-3, along with Web sites that you can download them from.

Windows and Icons

You run applications, display information, or list files in windows. A window is made up of several basic components. The outer border contains resize controls. There are also various buttons with which you can control the size of a window or close the window. Inside the outer border are the main components of the window: the title bar, which displays the name of the window; the menu, through which you can issue commands; and the window pane, which displays the contents of a window. You can change a window's size and shape using buttons and resize areas. The resize areas are the corner borders of the window. Click and hold a resize area and move the mouse to make the window larger or smaller in both height and width. You can make the window fill the whole screen using a maximize operation. Most window managers include a small button in the upper-right corner that you can click to maximize the window. To reduce the window to its original size, just click the Maximize button again. If you want to reduce the window to an icon, click the Minimize button. It's the small square with a dot in the center next to the Maximize button. Once you have reduced the window to an icon, you can reopen it later by double-clicking that icon.

You can move any window around the desktop by selecting either its title bar or its border (not a corner). Move your mouse pointer to the window's title bar; then click and hold it while you move your mouse pointer. You will see the window move. When you have reached the position you want, release the mouse button. Just clicking the title bar will move the window to the front of any overlapping windows. The same process holds true for borders. Move the mouse pointer to the edge of the window until you see the pointer transform into a small straight line. Then click and hold that edge, and move the mouse pointer. You will see the entire window move.

Applications that have been designed as X programs will have their own menus, buttons, and even icons within their windows. You execute commands in such X applications using menus and icons. If you are running an application such as an editor, the contents of the window will be data that the menus operate on. If you are using the file manager, the contents will be icons representing files and directories. The desktop file manager is discussed in Chapter 8 on directories and files. Some windows, such as terminal windows, will not have menus.

You can have several windows open at the same time. However, only one of those windows will be active. The active window will have dark borders, and the inactive windows will have light borders. On some window managers, just moving your mouse pointer to a particular window makes it the active window, rendering all others inactive. On others you need to click its title bar. Most window managers let the user configure the method for making the window active. In FVWM2, overlapping windows sometimes cause confusion. Making a window active does not automatically bring it to the front. An active window could still be partially hidden by other overlapping windows. To bring a window to the front, you need to click that window's title bar. Clicking anywhere else on the window would only make it the active window, not bring it to the front. Icons represent either applications you can run or data files for those applications. They appear on your desktop window and within file manager windows, with the name of the file or application below them. To run an application, just double-click its icon.

Themes

Many window managers such as Enlightenment, Window Maker, AfterStep, and FVWM2 support themes. Themes change the look and feel for widgets on your desktop, providing different background images, animation, and sound events. With themes, users with the same window manager may have desktops that appear radically different. The underlying functionality of the window manager does not change. You can easily download themes from Web sites and install them on your window manager. New ones are constantly being added. Information and links to window manager theme sites can be found at **http://themes.org**.

Workspace Menu

Most window managers provide a menu through which you can start applications, perform window configurations, and exit the window manager. Window managers give it different names. Enlightenment calls it the applications menu, Window Maker refers to it as the root-window menu, and FVWM2 calls it the workplace menu. In this chapter it is referred to as the workspace menu. This menu is usually a pop-up menu that you can display by clicking anywhere on the desktop. The mouse button you use differs with window managers. Enlightenment uses a middle-click, whereas Window Maker uses a right-click, and FVWM2 uses a left-click. Many of the entries on this workspace menu lead to submenus that in turn may have their own submenus. For example, applications will bring up a submenu listing categories for all your X programs. Selecting the graphics item will bring up a list of all the X graphic programs on your system. If you choose Xpaint, the Xpaint program will then start up. On some window managers you will find entries for window configuration and themes. Here will be items and submenus for configuring your window manager. For example, both AfterStep and Enlightenment have menus for changing your theme.

Desktop Areas and Virtual Desktops

Initially, you may find desktop areas disconcerting—they provide a kind of built-in enlargement feature. You will discover that the area displayed on your screen may be only part of the desktop. Moving your mouse pointer to the edge of your screen moves the screen over the hidden portions of the desktop. You will also notice a small square located on your desktop or in your window manager's icon bar, taskbar, or panel. This is called the *pager*, and you use it to view different areas of your virtual desktop. The pager will display a rectangle for every active virtual desktop. Some window managers such as FVWM2 will display only two, others like AfterStep will have four, and others like FVWM will start out with only one.

Each desktop rectangle will be divided into smaller squares called desktop areas. You can think of each desktop area as a separate extension of your desktop. It's as if you have a very large desk, only part of which is shown on the screen. The active part of the desk is a highlighted square, usually in white. This is the area of the desktop currently displayed by your screen. A desktop can have as many as 25 squares, though the default is usually 4. You can click one of the squares in the rectangle to move to that part of your desk. You could place different windows in different parts of your desk and then move to that part when you want to use them. In this way, everything you want on your desktop does not have to be displayed on your screen at once, cluttering it up. If you are working on the desktop and everything suddenly disappears, it may be that you accidentally clicked one of the other squares. Certain items will always be displayed on your screen, no matter what part of the virtual desktop you display. These are called "sticky" items. The pager is one, along with taskbars or panels. For example, the taskbars and icon bars pager will always show up on your screen no matter what part of the virtual desktop you are viewing. Windows by default are not sticky, though you can make them sticky.

Most window managers also support virtual desktops. A desktop includes all the desktop areas, along with the items displayed on them such as icons, menus, and windows. Window managers such as Enlightenment, AfterStep, and FVWM2 allow you to use several virtual desktops. Unlike desktop areas that just extend a desktop, virtual desktops are separate entities. Most pagers will display the different virtual desktops as separate rectangles, each subdivided into their respective desktop areas. To move to a virtual desktop, you click its rectangle. In some window managers, such as Window Maker, you select the desktop from a list. Window managers will provide entries on their main menus for selecting virtual desktops and even moving windows from one desktop to another. Use a window manager's configuration program or configuration files to specify the number of virtual desktops you want.

Panels, Buttonbars, Taskbars, and Window Lists

A panel displays buttons for frequently used X Window System commands. Popular panels include Wharf and Zharf for AfterStep and FVWM2, the Clip on Window Maker, and GoodStuff for FVWM. Each icon on the panel will display an image and the name of a program. Just click the button to start that program. For example, to open an Xterm window, just click the icon labeled Xterm. Each window manager has different ways to add applications to the panel. Adding an entry in Window Maker is as simple as dragging an application's icon to the docking panel. In most cases you can just edit the panel entries in the window manager configuration files. For example, the entries beginning with the keyword ***GoodStuff** will configure the GoodStuff panel in FVWM2 configuration files. In addition, some window managers support button bars with small icons for applications. A taskbar shows tasks that are running, and it can hold menu buttons for displaying menus. The FVWM2 taskbar features a Start menu for applications and lists buttons for current tasks. Windows can be minimized to the taskbar, much like docking in Windows 95. Open windows will also be listed in the taskbar. Most window managers also provide a window list. Window lists are handy if you have work spread across different desktop areas and virtual desktops. Selecting a window entry in the window list will move you directly to that window and its virtual desktop/area.

The Terminal Window: Xterm

From within a Linux window manager you can open a special window called a *terminal* window, which will provide you with a standard command line interface. You can then enter commands on a command line with options and arguments at the prompt displayed in this window. You can use any of several programs to create a terminal window, the most commonly used one being a program called Xterm. Rxvt is an alternative terminal window program that is a stripped-down version of Xterm, lacking some configuration and emulation features, but smaller and faster. Most window manager workspace menus and panels have entries for starting a terminal window with either Xterm or Rxvt. An entry may be labeled with one of those names or an icon of a monitor.

Once opened, the window will display a shell prompt, usually the $, where you can enter Linux commands just as you would on the command line. You will see any results of your commands displayed within the terminal window, followed by a shell prompt indicating the beginning of the command line. An Xterm window supports several text-handling features. To the left of the window is a scroll bar that you can use to scroll back to view previously displayed text. As text moves off the top of the screen, you can scroll back to see it. This is particularly helpful if you are displaying directories with a large number of files that will not fit on one screen. Xterm also lets you copy text and paste it to the command line. You use the left mouse button to copy text and the second mouse button to paste it. You can copy any of the text previously displayed, such as previous commands or output from those commands. To copy text, click and hold down the left mouse button while dragging it across the text you want to copy, letting up when you reach the end. Also, double-clicking will select a word, and a triple-click will select a line. If you want to extend the selected text, use the third mouse button. Once you have selected text, click the second mouse button. This automatically pastes the text to the end of the command line. Repeating clicks repeats the paste. The copy-and-paste operation is particularly helpful for constructing a complex command from previous ones. You can also copy and paste across different terminal windows.

The terminal window has the special capability of being able to run any X program from its command line. The terminal window operates within the X Window System environment. To run any X program, just open an Xterm window and enter the command, terminating it by pressing ENTER. The X program will then start up in its own window. For example, to run Netscape you could open a terminal window and type the command **netscape**. A new window will open up running Netscape. You can open as many terminal windows as you want and then start an X program from each. However, closing a terminal window will also close the program started from it.

You will notice that the terminal window in which you entered the X command appears to suspend itself. There is no following prompt after you press ENTER to run the program. That is because the terminal window is currently busy running the X program you just executed. You can free the terminal window to execute other commands while that program is running by invoking the program with an ampersand (&). Technically, this places it in the background as far as the terminal window is concerned (see Chapter 8). But you are free to move to that X program's window and run it there. The following example would run Netscape, freeing the terminal window to run other commands. Notice the prompt:

L 7-1

```
$ netscape  &
```

When you are finished using the terminal window, close it by typing the command **exit** on the command line. Each terminal window is its own shell, and **exit** is the command to end a shell. (Shells are discussed in detail in Chapter 8.) Figure 7-1 shows the terminal window. The user has entered several commands, and the output is displayed in the window. As you reach the bottom of the window, the text displayed will scroll up, line by line, just as a normal terminal screen would. You can, of course, use the window controls to make the terminal window larger or smaller. You can even minimize it to an icon and later reopen it.

An Xterm window has four menus: the main menu, a VT options menu, a VT font menu, and a Tektronix window options menu. To bring up the main menu, hold down the CTRL key and click the left mouse button. For the VT options menu, hold down the CTRL key and click the second (right or middle) mouse button. To bring up the font

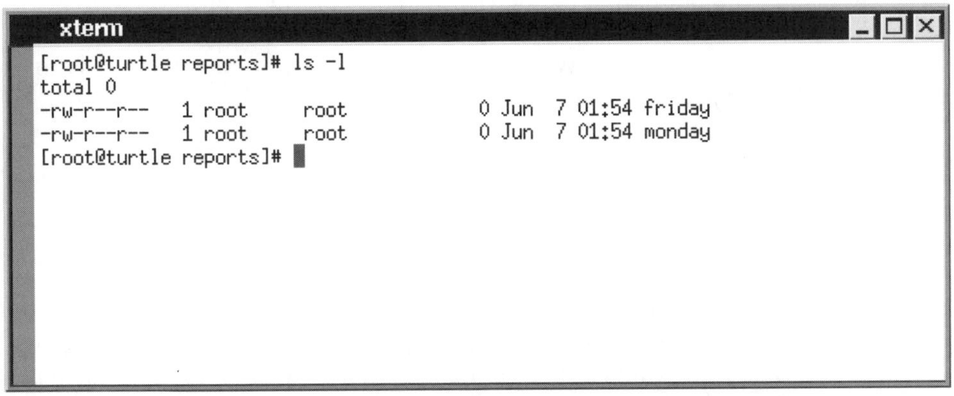

Figure 7-1.   *The terminal window*

menu, use the CTRL key and the third mouse button. You can then set the font and size of characters displayed. The terms *second mouse button* and *third mouse button* can be confusing. On a two-button mouse, the second button is the right button, and the third button is the left and right buttons held down at the same time. On a three-button mouse, the second button is the middle button, and the third button is the rightmost button.

X Window System Multitasking

One of the most useful features of your Linux X Window System interface is its capability to open several operations at the same time, each with its own window. Notice that in the command line interface you can only work on one task at a time (there is an exception discussed in Chapter 8 dealing with what are called *background processes*). You issue a command and after it executes, you can execute another. In the X Window System you can have several different applications running at once. Moving your mouse pointer from one window to another effectively moves you from one application to another. This feature of the X Window System illustrates one of the most useful capabilities of Linux: concurrency, the capability to have several processes operating at the same time. In your X Window System interface, you can have several applications running at the same time, each with its own window.

This feature can be easily illustrated using terminal windows. You can have several terminal windows open at the same time, each with its own command line. From the window manager's Main menu you can open terminal windows. Each terminal window will have its own command line, and moving your mouse pointer from one window to another moves you from one command line to another. You can type a command in the active window and execute it. You can then move to another terminal window and type in another command. Each terminal window operates independently of the other. If you issue a command that takes a while to execute, and you move to another window, you will notice that the command in the window you just left is still executing.

File Managers

A file manager uses directory windows that allow you to use menus, icons, and windows to manage files and directories. A directory is displayed as a window, with files displayed as icons. Directories are usually represented by icons that look like folders. You open a directory and examine the files in it, just as you would open a folder and examine its contents. A directory window has menus for performing standard file and directory operations such as opening or deleting a file. Most file managers can also display files as lists providing details like the sizes and dates. Desktop file managers such as gmc in Gnome and kfm in KDE support drag-and-drop operations where you can copy or move files with a click-and-drag operation from one file manager window to another. You can also use gmc and kfm without their desktop interface, running on any window manager, though Gnome and KDE still have to be installed on your system. Xfm is another popular file manager that provides basic directory and file operations.

Desktops

A Desktop is an integrated program and file manager, providing you with menus and icons with which you can manage your files, run programs, and configure your system. Two desktops currently included in most Linux distributions are the K Desktop Environment (KDE) and the Gnome. They provide easy access to Internet tools as well as the many Linux programs written for them or for the X Window System. You will be able to take full advantage of all desktop features, such as toolbars, configuration utilities, file management windows, and automatic history lists. KDE includes its own window manager with its desktop, though you can use any window manager. Gnome uses a separate window manager, though it should be Gnome compliant like Enlightenment. Currently, OpenLinux provides only the KDE desktop. Red Hat provides both KDE and Gnome. To switch between the two, you use the desktop switching tool, **switchdesk**. The interfaces vary, but both include certain basic features. Desktop drag-and-drop operations are supports. A panel holds an application's starter menu, small utility programs, and icons for starting programs. The desktops also include an Internet-aware file manager that can access FTP sites and, in the case of KDE, operate as a Web browser. For each directory, you can open a window that shows all the files in that directory, displayed as icons. You can then run applications by double-clicking their icons (for KDE you single-click), or you can move the icons out of the file manager window and onto the desktop for easier access. By selecting different windows, menus, and icons on your screen using a mouse, you can run the application associated with the icon, opening a new window for it.

Starting Window Managers

As noted in Chapter 4, either the X window system is started automatically using a display manager with a login window or from the command line by entering the **startx** command. Your X Window System server will then load, followed immediately by the window manager. You exit the window manager by choosing an exit or quit entry in the desktop workspace menu. The display manager and some window managers, like FVWM2 and Window Maker, will give you the option of starting other window managers. If you get into trouble and the window manager hangs, you can forcibly exit the X Window System with the keys CTRL-ALT-BACKSPACE.

The window manager that you will start is the default one set up by your Linux distribution when you installed your system. Many distributions now use as their default either Gnome or KDE. For Gnome and the K Desktop different window managers are used, kwm for the K Desktop and Enlightenment for Gnome. You can run Gnome or KDE applications on most window managers. To have Gnome use a particular window manager, you need to select it using the Gnome Control Center. It is possible to use a window manager in place of kwm for KDE. Check the window manager's Web site for current information on Gnome and KDE compatibility. Currently, Enlightenment is fully Gnome compliant, and AfterStep and Window Maker are nearly so. Normally, distributions will include several window managers on their CD-ROM that you can install and run on your system. Red Hat provides Window Maker, Enlightenment, AfterStep, kwm, and FVWM2, with FVWM2 being the default.

To use a different window manager, first install it. RPM packages will install with a default configuration for the window manager. If you are installing from source code you compiled, follow the included installation instructions. You can then configure Gnome or DE to use that window manager, provided it is compliant with them. Alternatively, you can configure your system to start a particular window manager without either desktop. To do this, you have to place an entry for your window manager in an X Window System startup file. There are different startup files for the display manager and the **startx** command. The startup file for the display manager is called **/etc/X11/xdm/Xsession** and the one for the **startx** command is called **/etc/X11/xinit/xinitrc**. For **startx**, users can also set up their own **.xinitrc** file in their home directories in place of the system's **xinitrc** file. Modifying these files can be a complex process. The procedure is described in detail in Chapter 29.

Window managers will provide default configuration files and include utilities for changing your configuration. Red Hat features a customized configuration of FVWM2 called AnotherLevel, carried out using M4 macros. You can also use the **wmconfig** program to generate workspace menu entries for different window managers. Currently AfterStep and FVWM2 are supported. Both AfterStep and Window Maker use the GNUstep configuration standard, placing configuration files in a directory named **GNUstep** in a user's home directory. The common X Window System and window manager configuration files are listed in Tables 7-1 and 7-2 for your Linux system and user home directories respectively.

Path	Description
/etc/X11	The X Window System configuration directory
/etc/X11/xinit	The directory that contains system default X Window System startup files
/etc/X11/xinit/xinitrc	The default startup file for the X Window System
/etc/X11/xinit/kdeinitrc	The default startup file for the X Window System used by the **kde** command on OpenLinux. The KDE version of **xinitrc**
/etc/X11/xinit/.Xclients	The default startup file for user X client programs (Red Hat)
/etc/X11/xinit/Xresources	The default display configuration for X components and programs
/etc/X11/wmconfig	The window manager menu configuration defaults
/etc/X11/GNUstep	Configuration files for Window Maker and AfterStep
/etc/X11/fvwm2	Configuration files for FVWM2
/etc/X11/AnotherLevel	The Red Hat configuration for FVWM2 window manager

Table 7-1.   *X Window System and Window Manager Directories and Files*

Files	Description
.xinitrc	The user startup file for the X Window System
.Xcients	The user startup file for X client programs (Red Hat)
.Xsessions	The user startup file for X client programs
.Xresources	The user display configuration for X components and programs
.kdeinitrc	The OpenLinux version of **xinitrc** for KDE, used by the **kde** command
.wm_style	The user's preferred window manager as set by wmconfig
.wmconfig	The user's preferred window manager menu display configuration defaults
Desktop	The user desktop files and directories shown on the desktop display
.kde	The user KDE configuration files
.enlightenment	The user Enlightenment window manager configuration files
.fvwm2rc	The user FVWM2 window manager configuration file

Table 7-2.   *The User X Window System and Window Manager Configuration Files*

Window Managers for Linux

Several of the more popular Linux window managers are the Free Virtual Window Manager 2.0 (fvwm2), Enlightenment (**enlightenment**), Window Maker (**wmaker**), Blackbox (**blackbox**), IceWin, Xview (**olwm**),TWM, FVWM95 (fvwm95), LessTif (**mwm**), AfterStep (**afterstep**), and Motif (**mwm**). All except Motif are free. Most are easily configurable and provide theme support. Enlightenment is currently the default window manager for Gnome. AfterStep and Window Maker are based on the NeXTSTEP interface. Xview is the Linux version of the Sun System's OpenLook interface. FVWM2 is the replacement for the original FVWM window manager, which was until recently the standard window manager used by most Linux distributions. FVWM95 is a variation of FVWM that provides a Windows 95–like interface. LessTif is a free Motif clone that provides a Motif interface and will run many Motif applications. TWM is an older window manager that provides basic windowing capabilities. AfterStep, Window Maker, FVWM2, TWM, and Enlightenment are included with most major distributions, including Red Hat and OpenLinux. The other window managers you can download from their Web sites, Linux sites, or the Red Hat contrib site, **contrib.redhat.com**. You can download and install recent versions of any window manager as they become available. Most window managers are GNU public-licensed software—they are yours free of cost.

Enlightenment

Enlightenment aims to provide a highly configurable graphical shell for a user's work environment. It is still undergoing development, though releases are very stable. It is currently the default window manager distributed with Gnome. You can download new releases from the Enlightenment Web site at **www.enlightenment.org**, which also includes documentation. RPM packages for Red Hat and OpenLinux are available on their respective FTP sites. Enlightenment has the same window operations as used on other window managers. You can resize a window by clicking and dragging any of its sides or corners. You can move the window with a click-and-drag operation on its title bar. You can also right-click and drag any border to move the window. The upper-right corner lists the Maximize, Minimize, and Close buttons. The Minimize button will minimize to an icon on the desktop. You can click the upper-left corner of a window to display a window menu with entries for window operations. These include a Desktop entry to move the window to another desktop area and the Stick option, which displays the window no matter what desktop area you move to.

To access the Enlightenment workspace menu, middle-click anywhere on the desktop (hold both mouse buttons down at the same time for a two-button mouse). There will be entries for applications as well as the desktop, themes, and Enlightenment configuration. With the desktop menus, you move to different desktop areas and virtual desktops. The themes menu lets you choose different Enlightenment themes. Enlightenment also has extensive configuration options, discussed in a later section.

To configure Enlightenment, use its GUI configuration tool. The Enlightenment Configuration window displays a list of configuration topics on the left and the panel for the selected topic on the right. Basic options set window displays, letting you select resize and move methods. With the Desktops option you can create virtual desktops and specify the number of desktop areas for each one. Other topics cover features such as sounds, special effects, window focus, keyboard shortcuts, and backgrounds as seen in Figure 7-2. You can set different backgrounds for each virtual desktop. The Themes panel lets you use an Enlightenment theme, of which there are many to choose from. Enlightenment is known for its impressive themes. See **e.themes.org** for ones that you can download. To make a theme available, place it in your home directory's **.enlightenment/themes** directory. Make sure that file has a **.etheme** extension. Enlightenment maintains its own configuration directory in your home directory called **.enlightenment**. It contains subdirectories for themes, backgrounds, and windows.

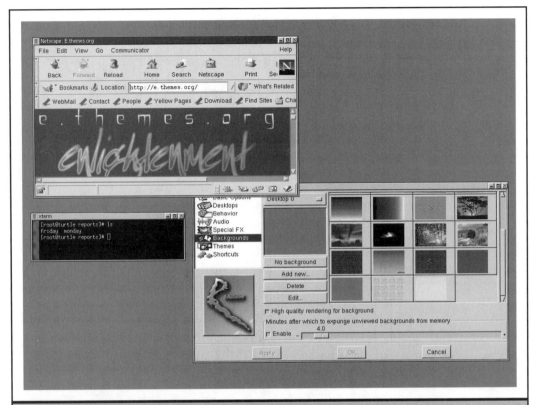

Figure 7-2.   *The Enlightenment window manager*

AfterStep

Originally based on the NeXTSTEP interface used on the NeXT operating system, AfterStep has evolved into a window manager in its own right (see Figure 7-3). It includes the advantages of the NeXTSTEP interface, while adding features of its own. AfterStep began as a continuation of the BowMan window manager, which, in turn, was based on FVWM. It is available for free under the GNU Public License. You can download AfterStep from the AfterStep Web site (**www.afterstep.org**) or obtain the RPM version from the Red Hat and Caldera FTP sites.

Windows, menus, and icons are intentionally similar to NeXTSTEP. Clicking anywhere on the desktop will display the workspace menu. Clicking and dragging a menu title will tear it off from the menu and let it stick to the desktop. To start applications, you can also access features from an icon bar called Wharf. It is initially displayed on the left side, though can be placed on any edge. Double-click an

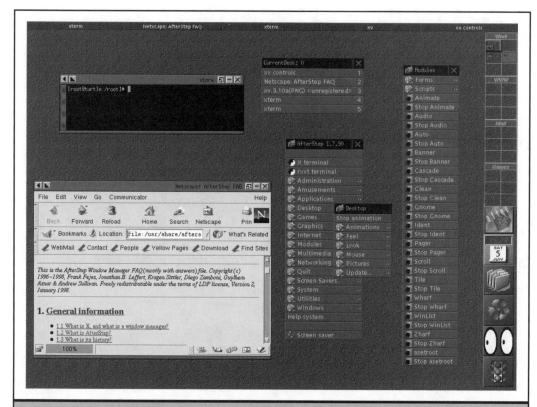

Figure 7-3. *The AfterStep window manager*

application's icon to start it. Wharf can contain folders that themselves expand to rows of application icons. There is also a Windows list that maintains a list of all open windows. The pager will initially display pages for four virtual desktops, each with four desktop areas. These will appear above Wharf. Click a desktop or a desktop area to move to it.

AfterStep includes an extensive set of modules and support themes. You can download themes from the **as.themes.org** Web site. The AfterStep Web site contains documentation, themes, and current releases. It also maintains links to sites that provide added material such as the AfterStep configuration guide, applets, and themes. AfterStep is ICCCM (Inter-Client Communications Conventions Manual), Gnome, and KDE compliant. To start AfterStep, use the command **afterstep** where your X-Windows configuration files start your window manager (usually **.xinitrc** or **.Xsession**). The AfterStep configuration files are located in the directory **GNUstep/Library/AfterStep** in a user's home directory. Configuration follows the GNUstep/Library standard. Separate configuration files are used for different components such as Wharf, Pager, and other modules and applications. A standard configuration is included with the installation, and you can download others from AfterStep sites. Most AfterStep material, including the current release, can be downloaded from the AfterStep FTP site at **ftp.afterstep.org**.

Window Maker

Window Maker is designed to closely emulate NeXTSTEP. It includes additional support for GNUstep applications. GNUstep is an attempt to develop a GNU version of Next's OpenStep API. Window Maker plans to be Gnome and KDE compliant (see the Web site for current status). The Window Maker Web site at **www.windowmaker.org** provides online documentation, links, screenshots, and new releases. You can download the newest version directly from **ftp.windowmaker.org**.

A right-click will display the root-window menu (workspace). A middle-click will display a window list of currently opened windows. You can make frequently used menus "stick" to the desktop by dragging the title bar of the menu. This will make a Close button appear in the menu title bar. If you want to close the menu, just click that button. Docked icons are listed in an icons bar. Initially this is shrunk to the GNUstep logo. Click and drag the logo to display the dock. To start an application, just double-click its icon. Whenever you start an application, a small icon for it, known as an appicon, is placed on the desktop. To add that application to the dock, just drag this icon to it. The dock icons support drag-and-drop operations. Just drag a file to an application's icon to start the application with that file. Window Maker supports multiple desktops, which it calls workspaces. You use the Workspaces menu to create new workspaces and change to current ones. There is also a workspace-dependent dock called the Clip, where you can have different clips of programs for each workspace.

You resize windows using a resize bar at the bottom of a window. You can move the window by dragging the title bar. To the left of the title bar is a miniaturizing window that reduces the window to a miniature window with its own title bar. To restore the window, double-click its miniature. To maximize the window, hold the CTRL key down while you double-click the title bar. Do the same to restore it. See Figure 7-4.

Window Maker also supports themes. You can download Window Maker themes from **wm.themes.org**. To install a theme, extract its archive in your **GNUstep/Library/WindowMaker/Themes** directory. Then from the root-window menu, select Themes and choose the theme from the list. Window Maker also features an extensive number of dock applications specifically designed to run within the dock (like Gnome applets in the panel). For example you can run a miniature network interface monitor, a POP3 mail checker, or, of course, a CD player.

Window Maker is configured using a GUI configuration utility, WPrefs. There is also a wmakerconf utility that automatically generates the configuration files. Configuration files are kept in your **GNUstep/WindowMaker** directory. Attributes for different applications are kept in the **GNUstep/Defaults** directory. For example, the entries for the application's menu are kept in the **GNUstep/Defaults/WMRootMenu** file.

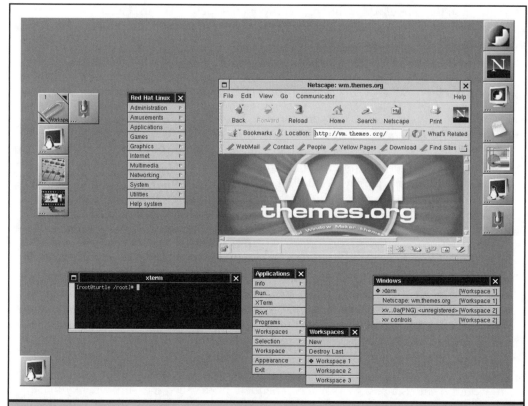

Figure 7-4.   *The Window Maker window manager*

Blackbox

The Blackbox window manager is designed to be simple and fast. It provides multiple workspaces and small menus. Its source code can be compiled using just a C++ compiler and the X11 development libraries. It uses no special graphic libraries. It is nearly compliant with the Inter-Client Communications Conventions Manual (ICCCM). Though it has an interface similar to Window Maker, it is an entirely original program written in C++ sharing no common code with any other window manager. Blackbox was written by Brad Hughes, who currently maintains it. Blackbox provides support for KDE and Motif, but not Gnome. Blackbox also supports themes. You can download Blackbox themes from **blackbox.themes.org**. You can find out more about Blackbox from its Web site, **blackbox.wiw.org**. Blackbox comes with a standard configuration, though you can set up your own in a **.blackboxrc** configuration file.

scwm

The Scheme-Configurable Window Manager (scwm) provides powerful customization capabilities using a configuration language based on Guile Scheme. Originally based on FVWM2, it has developed its own capabilities while maintaining compatibility with FVWM2, including support for FVWM2 modules. With Guile Scheme, it is fully programmable. Configurations can be made and implemented while running the window manager, without having to restart it. You can find out more about scwm at **http://huis-clos.mit.edu/scwm**.

IceWM

The IceWM window manager supports many of the same features as FVWM, including themes. You can obtain recent releases, screenshots, and themes from the IceWM Web page currently at **http://www.kiss.uni-lj.si/~k4fr0235/icewm/**. IceWM features a taskbar where open windows and running applications are docked. A sequence of labeled buttons represents different desktops. Click one to move to that desktop. To the left is a Linux button that you can click to display the Workspace menu. Next to the Linux button is a Window List button to display your open windows. Windows have Minimize, Maximize, and Close buttons in the upper-right corner. Resize borders are on every corner of a window. Clicking anywhere on the desktop will display the workspace menu. Configuration can be performed using the IcePref configuration tool.

FVWM and FVWM2

The current version, FVWM2, supports features such as the taskbar, workplace menu, modules, and themes. Modules are small programs that can be loaded and run dynamically. FVWM2 replaces FVWM, which is no longer under development. You can obtain newer versions of FVWM2 as they come out, from the FVWM2 Web page, currently located at **www.fvwm.org**. RPM packages of the new FVWM2 versions are also available at the Red Hat and Caldera FTP sites. You can download FVWM2 themes from **fvwm.themes.org**.

The new version of FVWM is called FVWM2 for FVWM version 2.0. FVWM2 is usually the default window manager for most distributions, used when you have not specified a window manager (Gnome or KDE specify their own window managers). FVWM2 extends the capabilities of FVWM to provide better configuration files, allows customization of individual windows, and provides better module support. There are modules for a taskbar that adds Windows 95–like docking and Start menu capabilities. FVWM2 supports virtual desktops and desktop areas. FVWM2 also supports the Wharf icon bar. A pager display lets you move from one desktop to another. Clicking anywhere on the desktop will display a workplace menu. To quit FVWM2, select the Quit entry from this menu. See Figure 7-5.

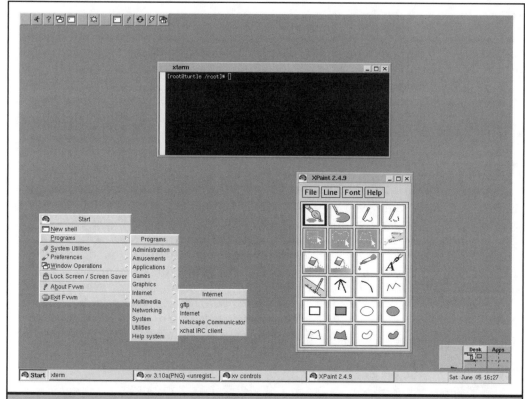

Figure 7-5. The FVWM2 window manager with Red Hat AnotherLevel

When the FVWM window manager starts up, it will execute its own configuration file, performing tasks such as displaying buttons on the FVWM taskbar, setting up entries in the workplace menu, and determining what programs to initially start up, if any. The default configuration file is **/etc/X11/fvwm2/system.fvwm2rc**. The configuration file for the older FVWM window manager is **/etc/X11/fvwm/ system.fvwmrc**. You can modify any of these files to configure your FVWM window manager as you wish. For example, if you want to set the number of virtual desktops, you can modify the DeskTopNum entry in this file. Changes to this file are global for all users. Individual users can create their own **.fvwm2rc** files in their home directories and edit entries to customize their window managers. To start, users can copy the **system.fvwm2rc** file to their home directories as their **.fvwm2rc** file to use as a basis for their own configurations. The following entry determines the number of desktop areas to support in a virtual desktop. It is measured by the number of squares on the length and width, so 3 × 3 would be nine desktop areas.

```
DeskTopSize 2x2
```

Red Hat uses the AnotherLevel configuration for FVWM2 to create a custom FVWM2 desktop with Red Hat icons and menus. AnotherLevel uses a set of M4 macro files located in the **/etc/X11/AnotherLevel** directory. Different configuration features are organized into separate files such as **fvwm2rc.keys.m4** for key bindings and **fvwm2rc.modules.m4** for modules used. The **fvwm2rc.defines.m4** file holds definitions for many configuration values, including the number of virtual desktops and the number of areas set up for them. Values are defined using macros:

```
# NUM_DESKTOPS is number of desktops -- each desktop is DESKTOP_SIZE panes
define('NUM_DESKTOPS',2)

# DESKTOP_SIZE is a geometry specifying horizontal desktop x vertical desktops
# So 3x3 gives 9 panes per desktop
define('DESKTOP_SIZE',2x2)
```

To create your own customized AnotherLevel, copy the **fvwm2rc.defstyles.m4** and **fvwm2rc.defines.m4** files to your home directory as **.fvwm2rc.defstyles.m4** and **.fvwm2rc.defines.m4**. Workspace menus are defined using **wmconfig**. The **wmconfig** application configuration is located in **/etc/X11/wmconfig**. You can copy this directory to your home directory as **.wmconfig** and then change the entries in those files as you wish; adding, changing, or removing application entries.

Xview: olwm and olvwm

Xview is the implementation of Sun System's OpenLook interface. Those familiar with OpenLook will find that the Linux version runs in much the same way. You can download Xview from the **metalab.unc.edu** FTP site. The Xview archive files are located in the **/pub/Linux/libs/X/xview** directory, currently **xview-3.2p1.4. bin.tar.gz**. This Xview package includes both the olwm and olvwm window managers as well as several utilities such as a clock and text editor. The olvwm version of Xview supports a virtual desktop.

The Xview package many distributions provide, contains a set of shared libraries that provide OpenLook menus, buttons, and other widgets. These are used in many Linux applications. Though applications that use these Xview widgets do not have to use the Xview window manager, they do use the Xview libraries. So you can run applications like the textedit Xview editor in the FVWM window manager. The buttons and menus that textedit uses are Xview widgets, though it can operate in an FVWM window. Sucn an Xview package is not the full Xview window manager. It is a subset of libraries with a few popular applications.

To install the full Xview window manager, first download its tar archive from **metalab.unc.edu**. If your distribution previously installed the Xview package, you will need to remove the **/usr/openwin** directory. Then unpack the Xview package you downloaded with the **tar xvf** command. This creates a subdirectory named **usr** in your current directory. In this **usr** directory is a subdirectory named **openwin**, which you move into the **/usr** directory (notice the forward slash).

```
# mv usr/openwin   /usr
```

Then run the **ldconfig** command on the **/usr/openwin/lib** directory. This sets up the Xview libraries.

```
# ldconfig /usr/openwin/lib
```

Make sure a **/usr/openwin/lib** entry is in the **/etc/ld.so.config** file. Because the Xview archive is not an RPM package, you have to perform the installation tasks yourself, such as moving files to the right directory and running **ldconfig**. Other window managers can be obtained in RPM format that will automatically install and configure their files for you. You then place an entry for starting olvwm in either the **.xinitrc** or **.xsession** file.

When you first bring up the olvwm window manager, you will be presented with a blank screen and a pager with six squares displayed in the upper-left corner. Double-click any square to move to that screen. To bring up the Xview workspace menu, click anywhere on the screen with the right mouse button. The workspace menu is a pinnable menu. You will see a picture of a push-pin at the top. If you click it, the workplace menu will remain displayed at that place on the screen. Click the pin again to be able to remove the workplace menu. The "X11 Progs" entry in the workspace menu automatically lists installed X11 programs, and the "Xview Progs" entry lists all Xview programs (those installed in **/usr/openwin/bin**).

Window components are slightly different from other window managers, though they serve much the same function. Menus are displayed with the right mouse button. On the workspace menu, you bring up submenus by right-clicking the small triangle to the right of a menu item. To move windows and pinned menus, you click and drag with the left mouse button on the very edge of the window. See Figure 7-6.

Xview components are installed in the **/usr/openwin** directory. Here you will find subdirectories such as **/usr/openwin/bin** that hold Xview programs and **/usr/openwin/lib** that hold Xview libraries. When the X Window System starts up, it has to have a shell variable called OPENWINHOME set to the Xview directory, **/usr/openwin**. Such assignments should also be placed in the repsective X startup files like **.xinitrc** or **.xsession**.

The **/usr/openwin/lib** directory contains the menu files used to display the Xview workspace menu and its submenus. You can add entries to these menus if you wish. An entry consists of the label to be displayed followed by the action to take. For example, to add an entry to the workspace menu for Netscape, you would place the following entry in the **openwin-menu** file. The Xview Man pages have a detailed explanation of Xview menus and the kind of entries you can make.

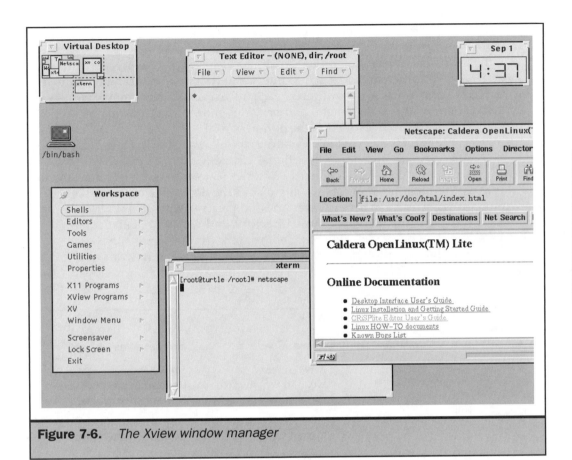

Figure 7-6.   *The Xview window manager*

```
"Netscape"      exec /usr/bin/netscape.
```

FVWM95 and qvwm

FVWM95 and qvwm are Linux window managers that have a Windows 95 user interface, complete with taskbar and Start menu. Window components are the same. You can even minimize windows to the taskbar. FVWM95 is based on the FVWM2 window manager, using much of the same source code, and like FVWM2, it supports modules. Currently, it does not have a file manager, but one is under development. It is called explorer and will operate like the file manager in Windows 95. The FVWM95 Web page is currently located at **ftp://mitac11.uia.ac.be/html-test/fvwm95.html**.

The FVWM95 window manager has several window modules that provide capabilities similar to FVWM. It has a button bar, in addition to the Windows 95 taskbar, that operates like the FVWM taskbar. There are buttons for frequently used programs such as Xterm. It also has a pager that operates like the FVWM pager, giving you a six-section virtual desktop. A mini-button bar brings up a small taskbar with just a few of the programs. A pager module displays a much larger pager depicting four desktops labeled for different tasks such as Internet and development. You can move from desktop to desktop as well as different sections in each. Clicking anywhere on the screen background will pop up a menu that provides entries for frequently used utilities, as well as the modules such as the button bars.

The qvwm program is a very stable Windows 95–like window manager that was developed with original code. A fully functional virtual window manager with a nine-pane pager, qvwm provides standard Windows 95 features such as a Start menu and shortcuts. Shortcuts are moveable to any part of the desktop. However, it is a work in progress currently in beta release. An RPM package with qvwm Linux binaries is available in the Red Hat contrib directory, and you can obtain the most recent version of the source code downloaded from the qvwm mirror site at **http://www-masuda.is.s.u-tokyo.ac.jp/~kourai/qvwm/index-en.html**, or from the home page listed in Table 7-3.

Window Manager	Command	Description	Internet Sites
AfterStep	**afterstep**	Based on the NeXTSTEP interface	**www.afterstep.org** **ftp.afterstep.org** **afterstep.themes.org**
amiwn	**amiwn**	An Amiga window manager interface	**www.lysator.liu.se/ ~marcus/amiwn.html**
Blackbox	**blackbox**	Simple and fast window manager	**blackbox.wiw.org** **blackbox.themes.org**
Enlightenment	**enlightenment**	Window manager supporting themes	**www.enlightenment.org** **e.themes.org**
eXode		Enhanced X Open Desktop	**http://www.simplicity.net/ exode/**
FVWM2	**fvwm2**	The Free Virtual Window Manager	**www.fvwm.org** **fvwm.themes.org**
FVWM95	**fvwm95**	Windows 95 interface	**ftp://mitac11.uia.ac.be/ html-test/fvwm95.html**

Table 7-3. *Window Managers*

Window Manager	Command	Description	Internet Sites
Gnome	**gnome-session**	GNU Network Object ModelEnvironment	**www.gnome.org** **ftp.gnome.org** **gnome.themes.org**
IceWM	**icewm**	Ice window manager	**www.kiss.uni-lj.si/ ~k4fr0235/icewm/**
The K Desktop	**startkde**	The K Desktop Environment	**www.kde.org** **ftp.kde.org** **kde.themes.org**
LessTif	**mwm**	A clone of Motif	**www.lesstif.org**
Macintosh-like Virtual Window Manager	**mlvwm**	A clone of the Macintosh interface	**http://www2u.biglobe.ne.jp/ ~y-miyata/mlvwm.html**
Motif	**mwm**	Motif window manager	
Q Virtual Window Manager	**qvwm**	Windows 95 interface	**qvwm.kuntrynet.com**
Scheme-Configurable Window Manager	**scwm**	Highly configurable, based on FVWM2	**huis-clos.mit.edu/scwm**
TWM	**twm**	Tom's window manager	
Window Maker	**wmaker**	Originaly based on NeXTSTEP	**www.windowmaker.org** **ftp.windowmaker.org** **wm.themes.org**
Xview	**olwm** **olvwm**	The Xview window manager (OpenLook)	**metalab.unc.edu/pub/ Linux/libs/X/xview**
X11.org	X Window System Web site	Detailed window manager and desktop information	**www.x11.org**
Themes.org	Themes Web site	Window manager themes and links	**http://themes.org**

Table 7-3. *Window Managers* (continued)

LessTif: mwm

LessTif is a Motif clone designed to run any Motif program. It describes itself as the Hungry Programmers' version of OSF/Motif. It is currently source compatible with OSF/Motif® 1.2; that is, the same source code will compile with either LessTif or Motif. LessTif is provided free under the GNU Library General Public License (LGPL). You can download it from the LessTif Web site at **www.lesstif.org**. You can also download RPM versions from the Red Hat contrib site, **contrib.redhat.com**. The Web site also provides documentation and a listing of applications that currently work under LessTif. You invoke LessTif with the command **mwm**. It uses a global configuration file **/etc/X11/mwm/system.mwmrc** and a user configuration file **.mwmrc**. Currently, LessTif does not run all Motif programs. The project is still under development, but it provides the same window management look and feel as that of Motif. Plans are to provide compatibility first with Motif 1.2 and then with version 2.0.

Motif

Motif is proprietary software that you have to purchase from a vendor for about $150. Motif and Xview were the two major competing window interfaces provided for Unix, representing two different window standards. These two standards have been recently integrated into a new GUI standard for Unix called the Common Desktop Environment (CDE).

The Common Desktop Environment (CDE)

The Common Desktop Environment (CDE) provides a common set of desktop interface standards that were proposed by Hewlett-Packard, Novel, IBM, and Sun in 1995. It was designed to merge OpenLook and Motif into one standard interface that could be used on all versions of Unix. Commercial versions of CDE such as TriTeal CDE are available for Linux (**www.triteal.com**). The CDE desktop provides an interface somewhat similar to Gnome and KDE. Along with window and desktop support it provides a panel for launching applications. Most CDE desktops include a set of CDE applications such as a file manager, a mail client, and a text editor. Like other desktops and window managers, CDE supports virtual desktops. Help is context sensitive, letting you display information about a component by clicking a help entry in its pop-up menu.

The
Complete
Reference

Chapter 8

Shell Operations

The shell is a command interpreter that provides a line-oriented interactive interface between the user and the operating system. You enter commands on a command line, and they are then interpreted by the shell and sent as instructions to the operating system. This interpretive capability of the shell provides for many sophisticated features. For example, the shell has a set of wildcard characters that can generate file names. It can redirect input and output. It can also run operations in the background, freeing you to perform other tasks.

Several different types of shells have been developed for Linux: the Bourne Again shell (BASH), the Public Domain Korn shell (PDKSH), the TCSH shell, and the Z-shell. All shells are available for your use, although the BASH shell is the default. You only need one type of shell to do your work. This chapter discusses the BASH shell that shares many of the same features as other shells.

The Command Line

When you log into Linux, you are presented with a command line interface. This consists of a single line into which you enter commands with any of their options and arguments. A shell *prompt*, such as the one shown here, marks the beginning of the command line:

```
$
```

Linux installs with the Bourne Again shell, commonly referred to as the BASH shell. The BASH shell has a dollar sign prompt; but Linux has several other types of shells, each with its own prompt. The different types of shells are discussed at length beginning with Chapter 15.

When the system prompt appears, you are logged into the system. The prompt designates the beginning of the command line. You are now ready to enter a command and its arguments at the prompt. In the next example, the user enters the **date** command, which displays the date. The user types the command on the first line and then presses ENTER to execute the command.

```
$ date
Sun July 7 10:30:21 PST 1999
```

When you log in, you are actually placed into the shell, which interprets the commands you enter and sends them to the system. The shell follows a special *syntax* for interpreting the command line. The first word entered on a command line must be the name of a command. The next words are options and arguments for the command.

Each word on the command line must be separated from the others by one or more spaces or tabs.

```
$ Command     Options     Arguments
```

An *option* is a one-letter code preceded by a dash that modifies the type of action that the command takes. One example of a command that has options is the **ls** command. The **ls** command, with no options, displays a list of all the files in your current directory. It merely lists the name of each file with no other information.

With a **-l** option, the **ls** command will modify its task by displaying a line of information about each file, listing such data as its size and the date and time it was last modified. In the next example, the user enters the **ls** command followed by a **-l** option. The dash before the **-l** option is required. Linux uses it to distinguish an option from an argument.

```
$ ls -l
```

Another option, **-a**, lists all the files in your directory, including what are known as hidden files. *Hidden files* are often configuration files and always have names beginning with a period. For this reason they are often referred to as *dot files*. In most cases, you can also combine options. You do so by preceding the options with an initial dash and then listing the options you want. The options **-al**, for example, will list information about all the files in your directory, including any hidden files. Another option for the **ls** command is **-F**. With this option, the **ls** command displays directory names with a preceding slash so that you can easily identify them.

```
$ ls -al
```

Most commands are designed to take arguments. An *argument* is a word that you type in on the command line after any options. Many file management commands take file names as their arguments. For example, if you only wanted the information displayed for a particular file, you could add that file's name after the **-l** option:

```
$ ls -l mydata
```

The command line is actually a buffer of text that you can edit. Before you press ENTER, you can perform editing commands on the text you have entered. The editing capabilities are limited, but they do provide a way to correct mistakes. The BACKSPACE and DEL keys allow you to erase the character just typed in. With this character-erasing capability, you can backspace over the entire line if you wish, erasing what you have entered. The CTRL-U key combination erases the whole line and lets you start over again at the prompt. In the next example, the user types **datl** instead of **date**. Using BACKSPACE, the user erases the **l** and then enters an **e**.

```
$ datl
$ dat
$ date
```

The shell you will start working in is the BASH shell, your default shell. This shell has special command line editing capabilities that you may find very helpful as you learn Linux. You can easily modify commands you have entered before executing them, moving anywhere on the command line and inserting or deleting characters. This is particularly helpful for very complex commands. You can use the CTRL-F or RIGHT ARROW key to move forward a character, the CTRL-B or LEFT ARROW key to move back a character. CTRL-D or DEL deletes the character the cursor is on, and CTRL-H or BACKSPACE deletes the character before the cursor. To add text, you just use the arrow keys to move the cursor to where you want to insert text and type in the new characters. At any time, you can press ENTER to execute the command. For example, if you make a spelling mistake when entering a command, rather than re-entering the entire command, you can use the editing operations to correct the mistake.

You can also use the UP ARROW key to redisplay your previously executed command. You can then re-execute that command or edit it and execute the modified command. You'll find this capability very helpful when you have to repeat certain operations over and over, such as editing the same file. It is also helpful when you've already executed a command that you had entered incorrectly. In this case you would be presented with an error message and a new, empty command line. By pressing the UP ARROW key you can redisplay your previous command, make corrections to it, and then execute it again. This way, you would not have to enter the whole command over again.

The BASH shell keeps a list, called a *history list*, of your previously entered commands. You can display each command in turn on your command line by pressing the UP ARROW key. The DOWN ARROW key will move you down the list. You can modify and execute any of these previous commands when you display them on your command line. This history feature is discussed in more detail in Chapter 15.

Some commands can be very complex and take some time to execute. When you mistakenly execute the wrong command, you can interrupt and stop such commands with the interrupt keys—CTRL-C or DEL.

You can enter a command on several lines by typing a backslash just before you press ENTER. The backslash "escapes" the ENTER key, effectively continuing the same command line to the next line. In the next example, the **cp** command is entered on three lines. The first two lines end in a backslash, effectively making all three lines one command line.

```
$ cp -i \
mydata \
newdata
```

Wildcards and File Name Arguments: *, ?, [ ]

File names are the most common arguments used in a command. Often you may know only part of the file name, or you may want to reference several file names that have the same extension or begin with the same characters. The shell provides a set of special characters called wildcards that search out, match, and generate a list of file names. The wildcard characters are the asterisk, question mark, and brackets (*, ?, []). Given a partial file name, the shell uses these matching operators to search for files and generate a list of file names found. The shell replaces the partial file name argument with the list of matched file names. This list of file names can then become the arguments for commands such as **ls** that can operate on many files. Table 8-1, at the end of the next section, lists the shell's wildcard characters.

The asterisk, *, references files beginning or ending with a specific set of characters. You place the asterisk before or after a set of characters that form a pattern to be searched for in file names. If the asterisk is placed before the pattern, file names that end in that pattern are searched for. If the asterisk is placed after the pattern, file names that begin with that pattern are searched for. Any matching file name is copied into a list of file names generated by this operation. In the next example, all file names beginning with the pattern "doc" are searched for and a list generated. Then all file names ending with the pattern "day" are searched for and a list generated.

```
$ ls
doc1 doc2 document docs mydoc monday tuesday
$ ls doc*
doc1 doc2 document docs
$ ls *day
monday tuesday
$
```

File names often include an extension specified with a period and followed by a single character. The extension has no special status. It is only part of the characters making up the file name. Using the asterisk makes it easy to select files with a given extension. In the next example, the asterisk is used to list only those files with a .c extension. The asterisk placed before the .c constitutes the argument for **ls**.

```
$ ls *.c
calc.c main.c
```

It is possible to use * with the **rm** command to erase several files at once. The asterisk first selects a list of files with a given extension, or beginning or ending with a given set of characters, and then presents this list of files to the **rm** command to be erased. In the next example, the **rm** command erases all files beginning with the pattern "doc":

```
$ rm doc*
```

The asterisk by itself matches all files. If you use a single asterisk as the argument for an **rm** command, all your files will be erased. In the next example, the **ls ***command lists all files, and the **rm *** command erases all files.

```
$ ls *
doc1 doc2 document docs mydoc myletter yourletter
$ rm *
$ ls
$
```

Use the * wildcard character carefully and sparingly with the **rm** command. The combination can be very dangerous. A misplaced * in an **rm** command without the **-i** option could easily erase all your files. The first command in the next example erases only those files with a .c extension. The second command, however, erases all files. Notice the space between the asterisk and the period in the second command. A space in a command line functions as a *delimiter*, separating arguments. The asterisk is considered one argument, and the .c, another. The asterisk by itself matches all files and, when used as an argument with the **rm** command, instructs **rm** to erase all your files.

```
$ rm *.c
$ rm * .c
```

The question mark, **?**, matches only a single incomplete character in file names. Suppose you want to match the files **doc1** and **docA**, but not **document**. Whereas the asterisk will match file names of any length, the question mark limits the match to just one extra character. The next example matches files that begin with the word "doc" followed by a single differing letter.

```
$ ls
doc1 docA document
$ ls doc?
doc1 docA
```

Whereas the * and ? wildcard characters specify incomplete portions of a file name, the brackets, [], allow you to specify a set of valid characters to search for. Any character placed within the brackets will be matched in the file name. Suppose you want to list files beginning with "doc" but only ending in *1* or *A*. You are not interested in file names ending in *2*, or *B*, or any other character. Here is how it's done:

```
$ ls
doc1 doc2 doc3 docA docB docD document
$ ls doc[1A]
doc1 docA
```

You can also specify a set of characters as a range, rather than listing them one by one. A dash placed between the upper and lower bounds of a set of characters selects all characters within that range. The range is usually determined by the character set in use. In an ASCII character set, the range "a–g" will select all lowercase alphabetic characters from *a* through *g* inclusive. In the next example, files beginning with the pattern "doc" and ending in characters *1* through *3* are selected. Then those ending in characters *B* through *E* are matched.

```
$ ls doc[1-3]
doc1 doc2 doc3
$ ls doc[B-E]
docB docD
```

You can combine the brackets with other wildcard characters to form very flexible matching operators. Suppose you only want to list file names ending in either a **.c** or **.o** extension, but no other extension. You can use a combination of the asterisk and brackets: ***[co]**. The asterisk matches all file names, and the brackets match only file names with extension **.c** or **.o**.

```
$ ls *.[co]
main.c  main.o  calc.c
```

At times, a wildcard character is actually part of a file name. In these cases, you need to quote the character by preceding it with a backslash in order to reference the file. In the next example, the user needs to reference a file that ends with the **?** character, **answers?**. The **?** is, however, a wildcard character and would match any file name beginning with "answers" that has one or more characters. In this case, the user quotes the **?** with a preceding backslash in order to reference the file name.

```
$ ls answers\?
answers?
```

Standard Input/Output and Redirection

When Unix was designed, a decision was made to distinguish between the physical implementation and the logical organization of a file. Physically, Unix files are accessed in randomly arranged blocks. Logically, all files are organized as a continuous stream of bytes. Linux, as a version of Unix, has this same organization. Aside from special system calls, the user never references the physical structure of a file. To the user, all files have the same organization—a byte stream. Any file can be easily copied or appended to another because all files are organized in the same way. In this sense, there is only one standard type of file in Linux, the byte-stream file. Linux makes no implementational distinction between a character file and a record file, or a text file and a binary file.

This logical file organization extends to input and output operations. The data in input and output operations is organized like a file. Data input at the keyboard is placed in a data stream arranged as a continuous set of bytes. Data output from a command or program is also placed in a data stream and arranged as a continuous set of bytes. This input data stream is referred to in Linux as the *standard input*, and the output data stream is called the *standard output*.

Because the standard input and standard output have the same organization as that of a file, they can easily interact with files. Linux has a redirection capability that lets you easily move data in and out of files. You can redirect the standard output so that, instead of displaying the output on a screen, you can save it in a file. You can also redirect the standard input away from the keyboard to a file, so that input is read from a file instead of from your keyboard.

When a Linux command is executed that produces output, this output is placed in the standard output data stream. The default destination for the standard output data stream is a device, in this case, the screen. *Devices*, such as the keyboard and screen, are treated as files. They receive and send out streams of bytes with the same organization as that of a byte-stream file. The screen is a device that displays a continuous stream of bytes. By default, the standard output will send its data to the screen device, which will then display the data.

For example, the **ls** command generates a list of all file names and outputs this list to the standard output. This stream of bytes in the standard output is then directed to the screen device. The list of file names is then printed on the screen. The **cat** command also sends output to the standard output. The contents of a file are copied to the standard output whose default destination is the screen. The contents of the file are then displayed on the screen.

Redirecting the Standard Output: > and >>

Suppose that instead of displaying a list of files on the screen, you would like to save this list in a file. In other words, you would like to direct the standard output to a file rather than the screen. To do this, you place the output redirection operator, **>** (greater-than sign), and the name of a file on the command line after the Linux command. Table 8-2, at the end of this section, lists the different ways you can use the redirection operators. In the next example, the output of the **cat** command is redirected from the screen device to a file.

```
$ cat myletter > newletter
```

The redirection operation creates the new destination file. If the file already exists, it will be overwritten with the data in the standard output. You can set the **noclobber** feature to prevent overwriting an existing file with the redirection operation. In this case, the redirection operation on an existing file will fail. You can overcome the **noclobber** feature by placing an exclamation point after the redirection operator. The next example sets the **noclobber** feature for the BASH shell and then forces the overwriting of the **oldletter** file if it already exists.

```
$ set -o noclobber
$ cat myletter >! oldletter
```

Though the redirection operator and the file name are placed after the command, the redirection operation is not executed after the command. In fact, it is executed before the command. The redirection operation creates the file and sets up the redirection before it receives any data from the standard output. If the file already exists, it will be destroyed and replaced by a file of the same name. In effect, the command generating the output is executed only after the redirected file has been created.

In the next example, the output of the **ls** command is redirected from the screen device to a file. First the **ls** command lists files, and in the next command, **ls** redirects its file list to the **listf** file. Then the **cat** command displays the list of files saved in **listf**. Notice that the list of files in **listf** includes the **listf** file name. The list of file names generated by the **ls** command will include the name of the file created by the redirection operation, in this case, **listf**. The **listf** file is first created by the redirection operation, and then the **ls** command lists it along with other files. This file list output by **ls** is then redirected to the **listf** file, instead of being printed on the screen.

```
$ ls
mydata intro preface
$ ls > listf
$ cat listf
mydata intro listf preface
```

Errors occur when you try to use the same file name for both an input file for the command and the redirected destination file. In this case, because the redirection operation is executed first, the input file, since it exists, is destroyed and replaced by a file of the same name. When the command is executed, it finds an input file that is empty.

In the **cat** command shown next, the file **myletter** is the name for both the destination file for redirected output and the input file for the **cat** operation. As shown in the next example, the redirection operation is executed first, destroying the **myletter** file and replacing it with a new and empty **myletter** file. Then the **cat** operation is executed and attempts to read all the data in the **myletter** file. However, there is now nothing in the **myletter** file.

```
$ cat myletter > myletter
```

You can also *append* the standard output to an existing file using the **>>** redirection operator. Instead of overwriting the file, the data in the standard output is added at the end of the file. In the next example, the **myletter** and **oldletter** files are appended to the **alletters** file. The **alletters** file will then contain the contents of both **myletter** and **oldletter**.

```
$ cat myletter >> alletters
$ cat oldletter >> alletters
```

The Standard Input

Many Linux commands can receive data from the standard input. The standard input itself receives data from a device or a file. The default device for the standard input is the keyboard. Characters typed into the keyboard are placed in the standard input, which is then directed to the Linux command. The **cat** command without a file name argument reads data from standard input. When you type in data on the keyboard, each character will be placed in the standard input and directed to the **cat** command.

The **cat** command will then send the character to the standard output—the screen device—which displays the character on the screen. When you try this, you will find that as you enter a line, that line will immediately be displayed on the screen. This is due to the line buffering method used in many Linux systems. *Line buffering* requires that a user type in an entire line before any input is sent to the standard input. The **cat** command receives a whole line at a time from the standard input, and it will immediately display the line. In the next example, the user executes the **cat** command without any arguments. As the user types in a line, it is sent to the standard input, which the **cat** command reads and sends to the standard output:

```
$ cat
This is a new line
This is a new line
for the cat
for the cat
command
command
^D
$
```

The **cat** operation will continue until a CTRL-D character (**^D**) is entered on a line by itself. The CTRL-D character is the end-of-file character for any Linux file. In a sense, the user is actually creating a file at the keyboard and ending it with the end-of-file character. Remember, the standard input, as well as the standard output, have the same format as any Linux file.

If you combine the **cat** command with redirection, you have an easy way of saving what you have typed to a file. As shown in the next example, the output of the **cat** operation is redirected to the **mydat** file. The **mydat** file will now contain all the data typed in at the keyboard. The **cat** command, in this case, still has no file arguments. It will receive its data from the standard input, the keyboard device. The redirection operator redirects the output of the **cat** command to the file **mydat**. The **cat** command has no direct contact with any files. It is simply receiving input from the standard input and sending output to the standard output.

```
$ cat > mydat
This is a new line
for the cat
command
^D
$
```

Just as with the standard output, you can also redirect the standard input. The standard input may be received from a file rather than the keyboard. The operator for redirecting the standard input is the less-than sign, **<**. In the next example, the standard input is redirected to receive input from the **myletter** file rather than the keyboard device. The contents of **myletter** are read into the standard input by the redirection operation. Then the **cat** command reads the standard input and displays the contents of **myletter**.

```
$ cat < myletter
hello Christopher
How are you today
$
```

You can combine the redirection operations for both standard input and standard output. In the next example, the **cat** command has no file name arguments. Without file name arguments, the **cat** command receives input from the standard input and sends output to the standard output. However, the standard input has been redirected to receive its data from a file, and the standard output has been redirected to place its data in a file.

```
$ cat < myletter > newletter
```

Common Shell Symbols	Execution
ENTER	Execute a command line
;	Separate commands on the same command line
'command'	Execute a command
[]	Match on a class of possible characters in filenames
\	Quote the following character. Used to quote special characters
|	Pipe the standard output of one command as input for another command
&	Execute a command in the background
!	History command

Table 8-1. *Shell Symbols*

Wildcard Symbols	Execution
*	Match on any set of characters in filenames
?	Match on any single character in filenames
Redirection Symbols	**Execution**
>	Redirect the standard output to a file or device, creating the file if it does not exist and overwriting the file if it does exist
>!	The exclamation point forces the overwriting of a file if it already exits. This overrides the `noclobber` option
<	Redirect the standard input from a file or device to a program
>>	Redirect the standard output to a file or device, appending the output to the end of the file
Standard Error Redirection Symbols	**Execution**
2>	Redirect the standard error to a file or device
2>>	Redirect and append the standard error to a file or device
2>&1	Redirect the standard error to the standard output
>&	Redirect the standard error to a file or device
|&	Pipe the standard error as input to another command

Table 8-1. *Shell Symbols* (continued)

Pipes: |

You will find yourself in situations in which you need to send data from one command to another. In other words, you will want to send the standard output of a command to another command, not to a destination file. Suppose you want to send a list of your file names to the printer to be printed. You need two commands to do this: the **ls** command to generate a list of file names and the **lpr** command to send the list to the printer. In effect, you need to take the output of the **ls** command and use it as input for the **lpr** command. You can think of the data as flowing from one command to another. To form such a connection in Linux, you use what is called a pipe. The *pipe operator*, |, (vertical bar character) placed between two commands forms a connection between them. The standard output of one command becomes the standard input for the other. The pipe operation receives output from the command placed before the pipe and sends this data as input to the command placed after the pipe. As shown in the next example, you can connect the **ls** command and the **lpr** command with a pipe. The list of file names output by the **ls** command is piped into the **lpr** command.

```
$ ls | lpr
```

You can combine the pipe operation with other shell features such as wildcard characters to perform specialized operations. The next example prints only files with a **.c** extension. The **ls** command is used with the asterisk and ".c" to generate a list of file names with the **.c** extension. Then this list is piped to the **lpr** command.

```
$ ls *.c | lpr
```

In the previous example, a list of file names was used as input, but it is important to note that pipes operate on the standard output of a command, whatever that might be. The contents of whole files or even several files can be piped from one command to another. In the next example, the **cat** command reads and outputs the contents of the **mydata** file, which are then piped to the **lpr** command.

```
$ cat mydata | lpr
```

Suppose you want to print out data you are typing in from the keyboard instead of data from a file. The **cat** command without any arguments reads data from the standard input. In the next example, **cat** takes input from the keyboard instead of a file and pipes the output to the **lpr** command. The **cat** command is executed before the **lpr** command, so you first enter your data for the **cat** command on the keyboard, ending with the end-of-file, CTRL-D. The input for a piped byte stream may come from any source.

```
$ cat | lpr
This text will
be printed
^D
$
```

Linux provides **cat** with a **-n** option that outputs the contents of a file, adding line numbers. If you want to print your file with line numbers, you must first use the **cat** command with the **-n** option to output the contents of the file with line numbers added. You then pipe this output to the **lpr** command for printing, for example:

```
$ cat -n  mydata | lpr
```

You do much the same thing for displaying a file with line numbers. In this case, the numbered output is usually piped to the **more** command for screen-by-screen examination. You can even specify several files at once and pipe their output to the **more** command, examining all the files. In the next example, both **mydata** and **preface** are numbered and piped to the **more** command for screen-by-screen examination.

```
$ cat -n mydata preface | more
```

Linux has many commands that generate modified output; the **cat** command with the **-n** option is only one. Another is the **sort** command. The **sort** command takes the contents of a file and generates a version with each line sorted in alphabetic order. It works best with files that are lists of items. Commands like **sort** that output a modified version of its input are referred to as filters. Filters are discussed in detail in Chapter 14. They are often used with pipes. In the next example, a sorted version of **mylist** is generated and piped into the **more** command for display on the screen. Note that the original file, **mylist**, has not been changed and is not itself sorted. Only the output of **sort** in the standard output is sorted.

```
$ sort mylist | more
```

You can, of course, combine several commands, connecting each pair with a pipe. The output of one command can be piped into another command, which, in turn, can pipe its output into still another command. Suppose you have a file with a list of items that you want to print out both numbered and in alphabetical order. To print the numbered and sorted list, you can first generate a sorted version with the **sort** command and then pipe that output to the **cat** command. The **cat** command with the **-n** option then takes as its input the sorted list and generates as its output a numbered, sorted list, which can then be piped to the **lpr** command for printing. The next example shows the command.

```
$ sort mylist | cat -n | lpr
```

The standard input piped into a command can be more carefully controlled with the standard input argument, **-**. When you use the dash as an argument for a command, it represents the standard input. Suppose you would like to print a file with the name of its directory at the top. The **pwd** command outputs a directory name, and the **cat** command outputs the contents of a file. In this case, the **cat** command needs to take as its input both the file and the standard input piped in from the **pwd** command. The **cat** command will have two arguments: the standard input as represented by the dash and the file name of the file to be printed.

In the next example, the **pwd** command generates the directory name and pipes it into the **cat** command. For the **cat** command, this piped-in standard input now contains the directory name. As represented by the dash, the standard input is the first argument to the **cat** command. The **cat** command copies the directory name and the contents of the **mylist** file to the standard output, which is then piped to the **lpr** command for printing. If you want to print the directory name at the end of the file instead, simply make the dash the last argument and the file name the first argument, as in **cat mylist -** .

```
$ pwd | cat - mylist | lpr
```

Redirecting and Piping the Standard Error: >&, 2>

When you execute commands, it is possible that an error could occur. You may give the wrong number of arguments, or some kind of system error could take place. When an error occurs, the system will issue an error message. Usually such error messages are displayed on the screen, along with the standard output. However, Linux distinguishes between standard output and error messages. Error messages are placed in yet another standard byte stream called the *standard error*. In the next example, the **cat** command is given as its argument the name of a file that does not exist, **myintro**. In this case, the **cat** command will simply issue an error:

```
$ cat myintro
cat : myintro not found
$
```

Because error messages are in a separate data stream than the standard output, error messages will still appear on the screen for you to see even if you have redirected the standard output to a file. In the next example, the standard output of the **cat** command is redirected to the file **mydata**. However, the standard error, containing the error messages, is still directed to the screen.

```
$ cat myintro > mydata
cat : myintro not found
$
```

You can redirect the standard error as you can the standard output. This means that you can save your error messages in a file for future reference. This is helpful if you need a record of the error messages. Like the standard output, the standard error has for its default destination the screen device, but you can redirect the standard error to any file or device that you choose using special redirection operators. In this case, the error messages will not be displayed on the screen.

Redirection of the standard error relies on a special feature of shell redirection. You can reference all the standard byte streams in redirection operations with numbers. The numbers 0, 1, and 2 reference the standard input, standard output, and standard error, respectively. By default, an output redirection, **>**, operates on the standard output, 1. However, you can modify the output redirection to operate on the standard error by preceding the output redirection operator with the number 2. In the next example, the **cat** command again will generate an error. The error message is redirected to the standard byte stream represented by number 2, the standard error.

```
$ cat nodata 2> myerrors
$ cat myerrors
cat : nodata not found
$
```

You can also append the standard error to a file by using the number 2 and the redirection append operator, **>>**. In the next example, the user appends the standard error to the **myerrors** file, which then functions as a log of errors.

```
$ cat nodata 2>> myerrors
```

Command	Execution
ENTER	Execute a command line
;	Separate commands on the same command line
command\\ *opts args*	Enter backslash before carriage return in order to continue entering a command on the next line

Table 8-2. *The Shell Operations*

ENVIRONMENTS

Command	Execution
`'command'`	Execute a command
BACKSPACE CTRL-H	Erase the previous character
CTRL-U	Erase the command line and start over
CTRL-C	Interrupt and stop a command execution

Special Characters for Filename Generation	Execution
*	Match on any set of characters
?	Match on any single characters
[]	Match on a class of possible characters
\	Quote the following character. Used to quote special characters

Redirection	Execution
command > *filename*	Redirect the standard output to a file or device, creating the file if it does not exist and overwriting the file if it does exist
command < *filename*	Redirect the standard input from a file or device to a program
command >> *filename*	Redirect the standard output to a file or device, appending the output to the end of the file
command >! *filename*	In the C-shell and the Korn shell, the exclamation point forces the overwriting of a file if it already exits. This overrides the **noclobber** option
command 2> *filename*	Redirect the standard error to a file or device in the Bourne shell
command 2>> *filename*	Redirect and append the standard error to a file or device in the Bourne shell

Table 8-2.   *The Shell Operations* (continued)

Redirection	Execution
command **2>&1**	Redirect the standard error to the standard output in the Bourne shell
command **>&** *filename*	Redirect the standard error to a file or device in the C-shell

Pipes	Execution
command | *command*	Pipe the standard output of one command as input for another command
command |**&** *command*	Pipe the standard error as input to another command in the C-shell

Background Jobs	Execution
&	Execute a command in the background
fg *%jobnum*	Bring a command in the background to the foreground or resume an interrupted program
bg	Place a command in the foreground into the background
CTRL-Z	Interrupt and stop the currently running program. The program remains stopped and waiting in the background for you to resume it
notify *%jobnum*	Notify you when a job ends
kill *%jobnum* **kill** *proccessnum*	Cancel and end a job running in the background
jobs	List all background jobs. The **jobs** command is not available in the Bourne shell, unless it is using the jsh shell
ps	List all currently running processes including background jobs
at *time date*	Execute commands at a specified time and date. The time can be entered with hours and minutes and qualified as am or pm

Table 8-2.   *The Shell Operations* (continued)

Shell Variables

You define variables within a shell, and such variables are known—logically enough—as *shell variables*. There are many different shells. Some utilities, such as the mailx utility, have their own shells with their own shell variables. You can also create your own shell using what are called shell scripts. You have a user shell that becomes active as soon as you log in. This is often referred to as the login shell. Special system variables are defined within this login shell. Shell variables exist as long as your shell is active, that is, until you exit the shell. For example, logging out will exit the login shell. When you log in again, any variables that you may need in your login shell will have to be defined once again.

Definition and Evaluation of Variables: =, $, set, unset

You define a variable in a shell when you first use the variable's name. A variable's name may be any set of alphabetic characters, including the underscore. The name may also include a number, but the number cannot be the first character in the name. A name may not have any other type of character, such as an exclamation point, an ampersand, or even a space. Such symbols are reserved by the shell for its own use. Also, a name may not include more than one word. The shell uses spaces on the command line to distinguish different components of a command such as options, arguments, and the name of the command.

You assign a value to a variable with the assignment operator, **=**. You type in the variable name, the assignment operator, and then the value assigned. Do not place any spaces around the assignment operator. The assignment **operation poet = Virgil**, for example, will fail. (The C-shell has a slightly different type of assignment operation that is described in the section on C-shell variables later in this chapter.) You can assign any set of characters to a variable. In the next example, the variable **poet** is assigned the string **Virgil**.

```
$ poet=Virgil
```

Once you have assigned a value to a variable, you can then use the variable name to reference the value. Often you use the values of variables as arguments for a command. You can reference the value of a variable using the variable name preceded by the **$** operator. The dollar sign is a special operator that uses the variable name to reference a variable's value, in effect, evaluating the variable. Evaluation retrieves a variable's value, usually a set of characters. This set of characters then replaces the variable name on the command line. Wherever a **$** is placed before the variable name, the variable name is replaced with the value of the variable. In the next example, the shell variable **poet** is evaluated and its contents, **Virgil**, are then used as the argument for an **echo** command. The **echo** command simply echoes or prints a set of characters to the screen.

```
$ echo $poet
Virgil
```

You must be careful to distinguish between the evaluation of a variable and its name alone. If you leave out the **$** operator before the variable name, all you have is the variable name itself. In the next example, the **$** operator is absent from the variable name. In this case, the **echo** command has as its argument the word "poet", and so prints out "poet".

```
$ echo poet
poet
```

The contents of a variable are often used as command arguments. A common command argument is a directory path name. It can be tedious to retype a directory path that is being used over and over again. If you assign the directory path name to a variable, you can simply use the evaluated variable in its place. The directory path you assign to the variable is retrieved when the variable is evaluated with the **$** operator. The next example assigns a directory path name to a variable and then uses the evaluated variable in a copy command. The evaluation of **ldir** (which is **$ldir**) results in the path name **/home/chris/letters**. The copy command evaluates to **cp myletter /home/chris/letters**.

```
$ ldir=/home/chris/letters
$ cp myletter $ldir
```

You can obtain a list of all the defined variables with the **set** command. The next example uses the **set** command to display a list of all defined variables and their values.

```
$ set
poet   Virgil
ldir   /home/chris/letters/old
$
```

If you decide that you do not want a certain variable, you can remove it with the **unset** command. The **unset** command "undefines" a variable. The next example undefines the variable **poet**. Then the user executes the **set** command to list all defined variables. Notice that **poet** is missing.

```
$ unset poet
$ set
ldir   /home/chris/letters/old
$
```

Shell Scripts: User-Defined Commands

You can place shell commands within a file and then have the shell read and execute the commands in the file. In this sense, the file functions as a shell program, executing shell commands as if they were statements in a program. A file that contains shell commands is called a *shell script*.

You enter shell commands into a script file using a standard text editor such as the Vi editor. The **sh** or **.** command used with the script's file name will read the script file and execute the commands. In the next example, the text file called **lsc** contains an **ls** command that displays only files with the extension **.c**.

```
lsc

ls *.c
```

```
$ sh lsc
main.c calc.c
$ . lsc
main.c calc.c
```

You can dispense with the **sh** and **.** commands by setting the executable permission of a script file. When the script file is first created by your text editor, it is only given read and write permission. The **chmod** command with the **+x** option will give the script file executable permission. (Permissions are discussed in Chapter 7.) Once it is executable, entering the name of the script file at the shell prompt and pressing ENTER will execute the script file and the shell commands in it. In effect, the script's file name becomes a new shell command. In this way, you can use shell scripts to design and create your own Linux commands. You only need to set the permission once. In the next example, the **lsc** file's executable permission for the owner is set to on. Then the **lsc** shell script is directly executed like any Linux command.

```
$ chmod u+x lsc
$ lsc
main.c calc.c
```

Just as any Linux command can take arguments, so also can a shell script. Arguments on the command line are referenced sequentially starting with **1**. An argument is referenced using the **$** operator and the number of its position. The first argument is referenced with **$1**, the second, with **$2**, and so on. In the next example, the **lsext** script prints out files with a specified extension. The first argument is the extension. The script is then executed with the argument **c** (of course, the executable permission must have been set).

lsext

```
ls *.$1
```

```
$ lsext c
main.c calc.c
```

In the next example, the commands to print out a file with line numbers have been placed in an executable file called **lpnum**, which takes a file name as its argument. The command to print out the line numbers is executed in the background.

lpnum

```
cat -n $1 | lp &
```

```
$ lpnum mydata
```

You may need to reference more than one argument at a time. The number of arguments used may vary. In **lpnum** you may want to print out three files at one time and five files at some other time. The **$** operator with the asterisk, **$***, references all the arguments on the command line. Using **$*** allows you to create scripts that take a varying number of arguments. In the next example, **lpnum** is rewritten using **$*** so that it can take a different number of arguments each time you use it.

lpnum

```
cat -n $* | lp &
```

```
$ lpnum mydata preface
```

Jobs: Background, Kills, and Interruptions

In Linux, you not only have control over a command's input and output but also over its execution. You can run a job in the background while you execute other commands. You can also cancel commands before they have finished executing. You can even interrupt a command, starting it up again later from where you left off. Background operations are particularly useful for long jobs. Instead of waiting at the terminal until a command has finished execution, you can place it in the background. You can then continue executing other Linux commands. You can, for example, edit a file while other files are printing.

Canceling a background command can often save you a lot of unnecessary expense. If, say, you execute a command to print out all your files and then realize you have some very large files you do not want to print out, you can reference that execution of the print command and cancel it. Interrupting commands is rarely used, and sometimes, it is unintentionally executed. You can, if you want, interrupt an editing session to send mail, and then return to your editing session, continuing from where you left off. The background commands as well as commands to cancel and interrupt jobs are listed in Table 8-2.

In Linux, a command is considered a *process*—a task to be performed. A Linux system can execute several processes at the same time, just as Linux can handle several users at the same time. There are commands to examine and control processes, though they are often reserved for system administration operations. Processes actually include not only the commands a user executes but also all the tasks the system must perform to keep Linux running.

The commands that users execute are often called jobs in order to distinguish them from system processes. When the user executes a command, it becomes a job to be performed by the system. The shell provides a set of job control operations that allow the user to control the execution of these jobs. You can place a job in the background, cancel a job, or interrupt one.

You execute a command in the background by placing an ampersand on the command line at the end of the command. When you do so, a user job number and a system process number are displayed. The user job number, placed in brackets, is the number by which the user references the job. The system process number is the number by which the system identifies the job. In the next example, the command to print the file **mydata** is placed in the background.

```
$ lpr mydata &
[1]   534
$
```

You can place more than one command in the background. Each is classified as a job and given a name and a job number. The command **jobs** will list the jobs being run in the background. Each entry in the list will consist of the job number in brackets, whether it is stopped or running, and the name of the job. The **+** sign indicates the job currently being processed, and the **–** sign indicates the next job to be executed. In the next example, two commands have been placed in the background. The **jobs** command then lists those jobs, showing which one is currently being executed.

```
$ lpr intro &
[1]  547
$ cat *.c > myprogs &
[2]  548
$ jobs
[1]  +  Running  lpr intro
[2]  -  Running  cat *.c > myprogs
$
```

If you wish, you can place several commands at once in the background by entering the commands on the command line, separated by an ampersand, **&**. In this case, the **&** both separates commands on the command line and executes them in the background. In the next example, the first command, to **sort** and redirect all files with a **.l** extension, is placed in the background. On the same command line, the second command, to print all files with a **.c** extension, is also placed in the background. Notice that the two commands each end with **&**. The **jobs** command then lists the **sort** and **lpr** commands as separate operations.

```
$ sort *.l > ldocs & lpr *.c &
[1]  534

[2]  567
$ jobs
[1]  +  Running  sort *.l > ldocs
[2]  -  Running  lpr
$
```

After you execute any command in Linux, the system will tell you what background jobs, if you have any running, have been completed so far. The system will not interrupt any operation, such as editing, to notify you about a completed job. If you want to be notified immediately when a certain job ends, no matter what you are doing on the system, you can use the **notify** command to instruct the system to tell you. The **notify** command takes as its argument a job number. When that job is finished, the system will interrupt what you are doing to notify you that the job has ended. The next example tells the system to notify the user when job 2 has finished.

```
$ notify %2
```

You can bring a job out of the background with the foreground command, **fg**. If there is only one job in the background, the **fg** command alone will bring it to the foreground. If there is more than one job in the background, you must use the job's number with the command. You place the job number after the **fg** command, preceded with a percent sign. There is also a **bg** command that places a job in the background. This command is usually used for interrupted jobs. In the next example, the second job is brought back into the foreground. You may not immediately receive a prompt again, because the second command is now in the foreground and executing. When the command is finished executing, the prompt will appear, and you can execute another command.

```
$ fg %2
cat *.c > myprogs
$
```

If you want to stop a job that is running in the background, you can force it to end with the **kill** command. The **kill** command takes as its argument either the user job number or the system process number. The user job number must be preceded by a percent sign, **%**. You can find out the job number from the **jobs** command. In the next example, the **jobs** command lists the background jobs; then job 2 is canceled.

```
$ jobs
[1]  +  Running  lpr intro
[2]  -  Running  cat *.c > myprogs
$ kill %2
$
```

You can also cancel a job using the system process number, which you can obtain with the **ps** command. The **ps** command displays a great deal more information than the **jobs** command does. It is discussed in detail in Chapter 27 on systems administration. The next example lists the processes a user is running. The PID is the system process number, also known as the process ID. TTY is the terminal identifier. The time is how long the process has taken so far. COMMAND is the name of the process.

```
$ ps
PID       TTY        TIME       COMMAND
523       tty24      0:05       sh
567       tty24      0:01       lpr
570       tty24      0:00       ps
```

You can then reference the system process number in a **kill** command. Use the process number without any preceding percent sign. The next example kills process 567.

```
$ kill 567
```

You can interrupt a job and stop it with the CTRL-Z command. This places the job to the side until it is restarted. The job is not ended; it merely remains suspended until you wish to continue. When you're ready, you can continue with the job in either the foreground or the background using the **fg** or **bg** command. The **fg** command will restart an interrupted job in the foreground. The **bg** command will place the interrupted job in the background.

There will be times when you need to place a job that is currently running in the foreground into the background. However, you cannot move a currently running job directly into the background. You first need to interrupt it with CTRL-Z, and then place it in the background with the **bg** command. In the next example, the current command to list and redirect **.c** files is first interrupted with a CTRL-Z. Then that job is placed in the background.

```
$ cat *.c > myprogs
^Z
$ bg
```

Filters and Regular Expressions

Filters are commands that read data, perform operations on that data, and then send the results to the standard output. Filters generate different kinds of output, depending on their task. Some filters only generate information about the input, other filters output selected parts of the input, and still other filters output an entire version of the input, but in a modified way. Some filters are limited to one of these, while others have options that specify one or the other. You can think of a filter as operating on a stream of data; receiving data and generating modified output. As data is passed through the filter, it is analyzed, screened, or modified.

The data stream input to a filter consists of a sequence of bytes that can be received from files, devices, or the output of other commands or filters. The filter operates on the data stream but does not modify the source of the data. If a filter receives input from a file, the file itself is not modified. Only its data is read and fed into the filter.

The output of a filter is usually sent to the standard output. It can then be redirected to another file or device, or piped as input to another utility or filter. All the features of redirection and pipes apply to filters. Often data will be read by one filter and its modified output piped into another filter. Data could easily undergo several modifications as it is passed from one filter to another. However, it is always important to realize that the original source of the data is never changed.

Many utilities and filters use patterns to locate and select specific text in your file. Sometimes, you may need to use patterns in a more flexible and powerful way, searching for several different variations on a given pattern. There is a set of special characters that you can include in your pattern to enable a flexible search. A pattern that contains such special characters is called a *regular expression*. Regular expressions can be used in most filters and utilities that employ pattern searches such as Ed, **sed**,

awk, **grep**, and **egrep**. Though many of the special characters used for regular expressions are similar to the shell wildcard characters, they are used in a different way. Shell wildcard characters operate on file names. Regular expressions search text.

In Linux, as in Unix, text files are organized into a series of lines. For this reason, many editors and filters are designed to operate on a text file line by line. The very first Unix editor, Ed, is a line editor whose commands reference and operate on a text file one line at a time. Other editing utilities and filters operate on text much the same way as the Ed line editor. In fact, the Ed editor and other editing filters use the same set of core line editing commands. The editing filters such as **sed** and **diff** use those same line-editing commands to edit filter input. An edit filter receives lines of text as its input and performs line-editing operations on them, outputting a modified version of the text. There are three major edit filters: **tr**, which translates characters; **diff**, which outputs editing information about two files; and **sed**, which performs line editing operations on the input. Table 8-4, at the end of this section, lists the different editing filters.

Using Redirection and Pipes with Filters

Filters send their output to the standard output and so, by default, display their output on the screen. The simplest filters merely output the contents of files. You have already seen the **cat** commands. What you may not have realized is that **cat** is a filter. It receives lines of data and outputs a version of that data. The **cat** filter receives input and copies it out to the standard output, which, by default, is displayed on the screen. Commonly used filters are listed in Tables 8-3 and 8-4.

You can save the output of a filter in a file or send it to a printer. To do so, you need to use redirection or pipes. To save the output of a filter to a file, you redirect it to a file using the redirection operation, **>**. To send output to the printer, you pipe the output to the **lpr** utility, which will then print it. In the next command, the **cat** command pipes its output to the **lpr** command, which then prints it.

```
$ cat complist | lpr
```

Other commands for displaying files, such as **more**, may seem to operate like a filter, but they are not filters. You need to distinguish between filters and device-oriented utilities such as **lpr** and **more**. Filters send their output to the standard output. A device-oriented utility such as **lpr**, though it receives input from the standard input, sends its output to a device. In the case of **lpr**, the device is a printer; for **more**, the device is the terminal. Such device-oriented utilities may receive their input from a filter, but they can only output to their device.

All filters accept input from the standard input. In fact, the output of one filter can be piped as the input for another filter. However, many filters also accept input directly from files. Such filters can take file names as their arguments and read data directly from those files. The **cat** and **sort** filters operate in this way. They can receive input from the standard input or use file name arguments to read data directly from files.

One of the more powerful features of **cat** is that it can combine the contents of several files into one output stream. This output can then be piped into a utility or even another filter, allowing the utility or filter to operate on the combined contents of files as one data stream. For example, if you want to view the contents of several files at once, screen by screen, you must first combine them with the **cat** filter and then pipe the combined data into the **more** filter. The **more** command is, then, receiving its input from the standard input. In the following set of examples, the **cat** filter copies the contents of **preface** and **intro** into a combined output. In the first example, this output is piped into the **more** command. The **more** filter then allows you to view the combined text, screen by screen. In the second, the output is piped to the printer using the **lpr** command, and in the third, the output is redirected to a file called **frontdata**.

```
$ cat preface intro | more
$ cat preface intro | lpr
$ cat preface intro > frontdata
```

Types of Filter Output: wc, spell, and sort

The output of a filter may be a modified copy of the input, selected parts of the input, or simply some information about the input. Some filters are limited to one of these, while others have options that specify one or the other. The **wc**, **spell**, and **sort** filters illustrate all three kinds of output. The **wc** filter merely prints out counts of the number of lines, words, and characters in a file. The **spell** filter selects misspelled words and outputs only those words. The **sort** command outputs a complete version of the input, but in sorted order. These three filters are listed in Table 8-3, at the end of this section, with their more commonly used options.

The **wc** filter takes as its input a data stream, which is usually data read from a file. It then counts the number of lines, words, and characters (including the newline character, found at the end of a line) in the file and simply outputs these counts. In the next example, the **wc** command is used to find the number of lines, words, and characters in the **preface** file.

```
$ wc preface
6      27     142     preface
```

The **spell** filter checks the spelling of words in its input and outputs only those words that are misspelled.

```
$ spell foodlistsp
soop
vegetebels
```

Using redirection, you can save those words in a file. With a pipe, you can print them out. In the next example, the user saves the misspelled words to a file called **misspell**.

```
$ spell foodlistsp > misspell
```

You can pipe the output of one filter into another filter, in effect applying the capabilities of several filters to your data. For example, suppose you only want to know how many words are misspelled. You could pipe the output of the **spell** filter into the **wc** filter, which would count the number of misspelled words. In the next example, the words in the **foodlistsp** file are spell-checked, and the list of misspelled words is piped to the **wc** filter. The **wc** filter, with its **–w** option, then counts those words and outputs the count.

```
$ spell preface | wc -w
2
```

The **sort** filter outputs a sorted version of a file. It is a very useful utility with many different sorting options. These options are primarily designed to operate on files arranged in a database format. In fact, **sort** can be thought of as a powerful data manipulation tool, arranging records in a database-like file. This chapter examines how **sort** can be used to alphabetize a simple list of words. The **sort** filter sorts, character by character, on a line. If the first character in two lines is the same, then **sort** will sort on the next character in each line. You can, of course, save the sorted version in a file or send it to the printer. In the next example, the user saves the sorted output in a file called **slist**.

```
$ sort foodlist > slist
```

Command	Execution
cat *filenames*	Displays a file. It can take file names for its arguments. It outputs the contents of those files directly to the standard output, which, by default, is the screen.
tee *filename*	Copies the standard input to a file while sending it on to the standard output. It is usually used with another filter and allows you to save output to a file while sending the output on to another filter or utility.

Table 8-3. *Filters*

Command	Execution
head *filename*	Displays the first few lines of a file. The default is ten lines, but you can specify the number of lines.
tail *filename*	Displays the last lines in a file. The default is ten lines, but you can specify the number of lines **$ tail** *filenames*.
wc *filename*	Counts the number of lines, words, and characters in a file and outputs only that number. Options: **c** Counts the number of characters in a file. **l** Counts the number of lines in a file. **w** Counts the number of words in a file.
spell *filename*	Checks the spelling of each word in a file and outputs only the misspelled words.
sort *filename*	Outputs a sorted version of a file.
cmp *filename filename*	Compares two files, character by character, checking for differences. It stops at the first difference it finds and outputs the character position and line number.
comm *filename filename*	Compares two files, line by line, and outputs both files according to lines that are similar and different for each.
grep *pattern filenames*	Searches files for a pattern and lists any matched lines. Options: **i** Ignores upper- and lowercase differences. **c** Only outputs a number—the count of the lines with the pattern. **l** Displays the names of the files that contain the matching pattern. **n** Outputs the line number along with the text of those lines with the matching pattern. **v** Outputs all those lines that do not contain the matching pattern.

Table 8-3.   *Filters* (continued)

Command	Execution
fgrep *patterns file-list*	Searches files in the file list for several patterns at the same time. It executes much faster than either **grep** or **egrep**; however, **fgrep** cannot interpret special characters. It cannot search for regular expressions.
egrep *pattern file-list*	Searches files in the file list for the occurrence of a pattern. Like **fgrep**, it can read patterns from a file. Like **grep**, it can use regular expressions, interpreting special characters. However, unlike **grep**, it can also interpret extended special characters such as **?**, **|**, and **+**.
pr	Outputs a paginated version of the input, adding headers, page numbers, and any other specified format.
cpio	Copies files to an archive and extracts files from an archive. It has two modes of operation: one using the **-o** option to copy files to an archive, and the other using the **-i** option to extract files from an archive. When copying files to an archive, you need to first generate the list of file names using a command such as **ls** or **find**. *generated-filenames* **| cpio -o >** *archive-file* **cpio -i** *filenames* **<** *archive-file*

Table 8-3. *Filters (continued)*

Command	Execution
sed *editing-command file-list*	Outputs an edited form of its input. The **sed** editor takes as an argument an editing command and a file list. The editing command is executed on input read from files in the file list. Then **sed** outputs an edited version of the files. The editing commands are line editing commands similar to those used for the Ed line editor.
	n With this option, **sed** does not output lines automatically. This option is usually used with the **p** command to output only selected lines.
	f *filename* With this option, **sed** reads editing commands *filename*.

Table 8-4. *Edit Filters*

Line Commands	(You need to quote any new line characters if you are entering more than one line.)
a	Appends text after a line.
i	Inserts text before a line.
c	Changes text.
d	Deletes lines.
p	Prints lines.
w	Writes lines to a file.
r	Reads lines from a file.
q	Quits the **sed** editor before all lines are processed.
n	Skips processing to next line.
s/_pattern/replacement/_	Substitutes matched pattern with replacement text.
g **s/**_pat/rep_**/g**	Global substitution on a line.
p **s/**_pat/rep_**/p**	Outputs the modified line.
w **s/**_pat/rep_**/w** _fname/_	Writes the modified line to a file.
pattern/	A line can be located and referenced by a pattern.
diff _filename filename_	Compares two files and outputs the lines that are different as well as the editing changes needed to make the first file the same as the second file.
f1-linenum **a** _f2-line1, f2-line2_	Appends lines from file2 to after _f1-linenum_ in file1.
f1-line1, f1-line2 **d** _f1-linenum_	Deletes the lines in file1.
f1-line1, f1-line2 **c** _f2-line1, f2-line2_	Replaces lines in file1 with lines in file2.
b	Ignores any trailing or duplicate blanks.
c	Outputs a context for differing lines. Three lines above and below are displayed.

Table 8-4.   _Edit Filters_ (continued)

Line Commands	(You need to quote any new line characters if you are entering more than one line.)
e	Outputs a list of Ed editing commands that, when executed, change the first file into an exact copy of the second file.
tr *first-character-list second-character-list*	Outputs a version of the input in which characters in the first character list that occur in the input are replaced in the output by corresponding characters in the second character list.

Table 8-4.   *Edit Filters* (continued)

Searching Files: grep and fgrep

The **grep** and **fgrep** filters search the contents of files for a pattern. They then inform you of what file the pattern was found in and print out the lines in which it occurred in each file. Preceding each line is the name of the file the line is in. The **grep** filter can search for only one pattern, whereas **fgrep** can search for more than one pattern at a time. The **grep** and **fgrep** filters, along with their options, are described in Table 8-3.

The **grep** filter takes two types of arguments. The first argument is the pattern to be searched for; the second argument is a list of file names, which are the files to be searched. You enter the file names on the command line after the pattern. You can also use special characters, such as the asterisk, to generate a file list.

```
$ grep pattern filenames-list
```

In the next example, the **grep** command searches the lines in the **preface** file for the pattern "stream".

```
$ grep stream preface
  consists of a stream of
```

If you want to include more than one word in the pattern search, you enclose the words within single quotation marks. This is to quote the spaces between the words in the pattern. Otherwise, the shell would interpret the space as a delimiter or argument on the command line, and **grep** would try to interpret words in the pattern as part of the file list. In the next example, **grep** searches for the pattern "text file".

```
$ grep 'text file' preface
A text file in Unix
text files, changing or
```

If you use more than one file in the file list, **grep** will output the name of the file before the matching line. In the next example, two files, **preface** and **intro**, are searched for the pattern "data". Before each occurrence, the file name is output.

```
$ grep data preface intro
preface: data in the file.
intro: new data
```

As mentioned earlier, you can also use shell wildcard characters to generate a list of files to be searched. In the next example, the asterisk wildcard character is used to generate a list of all files in your directory. This is a simple way of searching all of a directory's files for a pattern.

```
$ grep data *
```

The special characters are often useful for searching a selected set of files. For example, if you want to search all your C program source code files for a particular pattern, you can specify the set of source code files with a ***.c**. Suppose you have an unintended infinite loop in your program and need to locate all instances of iterations. The next example searches only those files with a **.c** extension for the pattern "while" and displays the lines of code that perform iterations.

```
$ grep while *.c
```

Regular Expressions

Regular expressions allow you to match possible variations on a pattern, as well as patterns located at different points in the text. You can search for patterns in your text that have different ending or beginning letters, or you can match text that is at the beginning or end of a line. The regular expression special characters are the circumflex, dollar sign, asterisk, period, and brackets: **^**, **$**, *****, **.**, **[]**. The circumflex and dollar sign match on the beginning and end of a line. The asterisk matches repeated characters, the period matches single characters, and the brackets match on classes of characters. Regular expressions are used extensively in many Linux filters and applications to perform searches and matching operations. The Vi and Emacs editors and the **sed**, **diff**, **grep**, and **gawk** filters all use regular expressions.

To match on patterns at the beginning of a line, you enter the circumflex symbol ^ followed immediately by a pattern. The ^ special character makes the beginning of the line an actual part of the pattern to be searched. In the next example, **^consists** matches on the line beginning with the pattern "consists".

```
^consists
consists of a stream of
```

The next example uses the **$** special character to match patterns at the end of a line.

```
such$
 be used to create such
```

The period is a special character that matches any one character. Any character will match a period in your pattern. The pattern **b.d** will find a pattern consisting of three letters. The first letter will be *b*, the third letter will be *d*, and the second letter can be any character. It will match on "bid", "bad", "bed", "b+d", or "b d", for example. Notice that the space is a valid character (so is a tab).

For the period special character to have much effect, you should provide it with a context—a beginning and ending pattern. The pattern **b.d** provides a context consisting of the preceding *b* and the following *d*. If you specified **b.** without a *d*, then any pattern beginning with *b* and having at least one more character would match. The pattern would match on "bid", "bath", "bedroom", and "bump", as well as "submit", "habit", and "harbor".

The asterisk special character, *****, matches on zero or more consecutive instances of a character. The character matched is the one placed before the asterisk in the pattern. You can think of the asterisk as an operator that takes the preceding character as its operand. The asterisk will search for any repeated instances of this character. Here is the syntax of the asterisk special character:

```
c*    matches on zero or more repeated occurrences of whatever
      the character c is:
c cc ccc cccc  and so on.
```

The asterisk comes in handy when you need to replace several consecutive instances of the same character. The next example matches on a pattern beginning with *b* and followed by consecutive instances of the character *o*. This regular expression will match on "boooo", "bo", "boo", and "b".

```
bo*
     book
     born
     booom
     zoom     no match
```

The `.*` pattern used by itself will match on any character in the line; in fact, it selects the entire line. If you have a context for `.*`, you can match different segments of the line. A pattern placed before the `.*` special characters will match the remainder of the line from the occurrence of the pattern. A pattern placed after the `.*` will match the beginning of the line up until the pattern. The `.*` placed between patterns will match any intervening text between those patterns on the line. In the next example, the pattern `.*and` matches everything in the line from the beginning up to and including the letters "and". Then the pattern `and.*` matches everything in the line from and including the letters "and" to the end of the line. Finally, the pattern `/o.*F/` matches all the text between and including the letters *o* and *F*.

```
.*and     Hello to you and to them Farewell

and.*     Hello to you and to them Farewell

o.*F      Hello to you and to them Farewell
```

Because the `*` special character matches zero or more instances of the character, you can provide a context with zero intervening characters. For example, the pattern `I.*t` matches on "It" as well as "Intelligent".

Suppose that instead of matching on a specific character or allowing a match on any character, you need to match only on a selected set of characters. For example, you might want to match on words ending with an *A* or *H*, as in "seriesA" and "seriesH", but not "seriesB" or "seriesK". If you used a period, you would match on all instances. Instead, you need to specify that *A* and *H* are the only possible matches. You can do so with the brackets special characters.

You use the brackets special characters to match on a set of possible characters. The characters in the set are placed within brackets and listed next to each other. Their order of listing does not matter. You can think of this set of possible characters as defining a class of characters, and characters that fall into this class are matched. You may notice that the brackets operate much like the shell brackets. In the next example, the user searches for a pattern beginning with "doc" and ending with either the letters *a*, *g*, or *N*. It will match on "doca", "docg", or "docN", but not on "docP".

```
doc[agN]
    List of documents
    doca docb
    docg docN docP
```

The brackets special characters are particularly useful for matching on various suffixes or prefixes for a pattern. For example, suppose you need to match on file names that begin with the pattern "week" and have several different suffixes, as in **week1**, **week2**, and so on. To match on just those files with suffixes 2, 4, and 5, you enclose those characters within brackets. In the next example, notice that the pattern **week[245]** matches on **week2** and **week4**, but not on **week1**.

```
week[245]
    week2 weather
    reports on week4
    week1 reports        no match
```

The brackets special characters are also useful for matching on a pattern that begins in either upper- or lowercase. Linux distinguishes between upper- and lowercase characters. The pattern "computer" is different from the pattern "Computer"; "computer" would not match on the version beginning with an uppercase C. To match on both patterns, you need to use the brackets special characters to specify both *c* and *C* as possible first characters in the pattern. Place the uppercase and lowercase versions of the same character within brackets at the beginning of the pattern. For example, the pattern **[Cc]omputer** searches for the pattern "computer" beginning with either an uppercase *C* or a lowercase *c*.

You can specify a range of characters within the brackets with the dash. Characters are ranged according to the character set that is being used. In the ASCII character set, lowercase letters are grouped together. Specifying a range with **[a-z]** selects all the lowercase letters. In the first example shown next, any lowercase letter will match the pattern. More than one range can be specified by separating the ranges with a comma. The ranges **[A-Za-z]** select all alphabetic letters, both upper- and lowercase.

```
doc[a-z]        doca docg docN docP
doc[A-Za-z]     doca docg docN docP
```

Character	Match	Operation
^	Start of a line	References the beginning of a line
$	End of a line	References the end of a line
.	Any character	Matches on any one possible character in a pattern
*	Repeated characters	Matches on repeated characters in a pattern
[]	Classes	Matches on classes of characters (a set of characters) in the pattern

Though shell file matching characters allow you to match on file names, regular expressions allow you to match on data within files. Using **grep** with regular expressions, you can locate files and the lines in them that match a specified pattern. You can use special characters in a **grep** pattern, making the pattern a regular expression. **grep** regular expressions use the *****, **.**, and **[]** special characters, as well as the **^** and **$** special characters.

Suppose that you want to use the long form output of **ls** to display just your directories. One way to do this is to generate a list of all directories in the long form and pipe this list to **grep**, which can then pick out the directory entries. You can do this by using the **^** special character to specify the beginning of a line. Remember that in the long form output of **ls**, the first character indicates the file type. A **d** represents a directory, an **l** represents a symbolic link, and **a** represents a regular file. Using the pattern **^d**, **grep** will match only on those lines beginning with a *d*.

```
$ ls -l | grep '^d'
drwxr-x---  2  chris 512 Feb 10 04:30  reports
drwxr-x---  2  chris 512 Jan 6  01:20  letters
```

If you only want to list those files that have symbolic links, you can use the pattern **^l**:

```
$ ls -l | grep '^l'
lrw-rw-r-- 1 chris  group 4    Feb 14   10:30  lunch
```

Be sure to distinguish between the shell wildcard character and special characters used in the pattern. When you include special characters in your **grep** pattern, you need to quote the pattern. Notice that regular-expression special characters and shell wildcard characters use the same symbols: the asterisk, period, and brackets. If you do not, then any special characters in the pattern will be interpreted by the shell as shell wildcard characters. Without quotes, an asterisk would be used to generate file names rather than being evaluated by **grep** to search for repeated characters. Quoting the pattern guarantees that **grep** will evaluate the special characters as part of a regular expression. In the next example, the asterisk special character is used in the pattern as a regular expression and in the file name list as a shell wildcard character to generate file names. In this case, all files in the current directory will be searched for patterns with zero or more *s* after "report".

```
$ grep 'reports*' *
mydata: The report was sitting on his desk.
weather: The weather reports were totally accurate.
```

The brackets match on either a set of characters, a range of characters, or a non-match of those characters. For example, the pattern **doc[abc]** matches on the patterns "doca", "docb", and "docc", but not on "docd". The same pattern can be specified with a range: **doc[a-c]**. However, the pattern **doc[^ab]** will match on any pattern beginning with "doc", but not ending in *a* or *b*. Thus, "docc" will be retrieved, but not "doca" or "docb". In the next example, the user finds all lines that reference "doca", "docb", or "docc".

```
$ grep 'doc[abc]' myletter
File letter doca and docb.
We need to redo docc.
```

Certain Linux utilities such as **egrep** and **awk** can make use of an extended set of special characters in their patterns. These special characters are **|**, **( )**, **+**, and **?**, and are listed here:

Character	Execution
*pattern	pattern*	Logical OR for searching for alternative patterns
(pattern)	Parentheses for grouping patterns
char+	Searches for one or more repetitions of the previous character
char?	Searches for zero or one instance of the previous character

The **+** and **?** are variations on the ***** special character, whereas **|** and **( )** provide new capabilities. Patterns that can use such special characters are referred to as full regular expressions. The Ed and Ex standard line editors do not have these extended special characters. Only **egrep**, which is discussed here, and **awk** have extended special characters.

The **+** sign matches one or more instances of a character. For example, **t+** matches at least one or more *t*s, just as **tt*** does. It will match on "sitting" or "biting", but not "ziing". The **?** matches zero or one instance of a character. For example, **t?** matches on one *t* or no *t*s, but not "tt". The expression **it?i** will match on "ziing" and "biting" but not "sitting". In the next examples, repeated *n* characters followed by an *e* is searched for. With the **+** special character, the regular expression **an+e** will match on one or more instances of *n* preceded by *a* and followed by *e*. The "ane" is matched in "anew", and "anne" is matched on "canned".

The **|** and **( )** special characters operate on pattern segments, rather than just characters. The **|** is a logical OR special character that specifies alternative search patterns within a single regular expression. Though part of the same regular expression, the patterns are searched for as separate patterns. The search pattern **create|stream** will search for either the pattern "create" or "stream".

```
create|stream
  consists of a stream of
  be used to create such
```

The **egrep** command combines the capabilities of **grep** and **fgrep**. Like **fgrep**, it can search for several patterns at the same time. Like **grep**, it can evaluate special characters in its patterns and can search for regular expressions. However, unlike **grep**, it can evaluate extended special characters such as the logical OR operator, **|**. In this respect, **egrep** is the most powerful of the three search filters.

To search for several patterns at once, you can either enter them on the command line separated by a newline character as **fgrep** does, or you can use the logical OR special character in a pattern to specify alternative patterns to be searched for in a file. The patterns are actually part of the same regular expression, but they are searched for as separate patterns. The pattern **create|stream egrep** will search for either the pattern "create" or the pattern "stream".

```
$ egrep 'create|stream' preface
consists of a stream of
  be used to create such
```

Chapter 9

The Linux File Structure

In Linux, all files are organized into directories that, in turn, are hierarchically connected to each other in one overall file structure. A file is referenced not just according to its name, but also according to its place in this file structure. You can create as many new directories as you want, adding more directories to the file structure. The Linux file commands can perform sophisticated operations such as moving or copying whole directories along with their subdirectories. You can use file operations such as **find**, **cp**, **mv**, and **ln** to locate files and copy, move, or link them from one directory to another. Desktop file managers, such as kfm and Midnight Commander used on the K and Gnome desktops, perform the same operations using icons, windows, and menus.

Together, these features make up the Linux file structure. This chapter will first examine different types of files as well as file classes. Then, the chapter examines the overall Linux file structure and how directories and files can be referenced using path names and the working directory. The last part of the chapter discusses the different file operations such as copying, moving, and linking files, as well as file permissions.

Linux Files

You can name a file using any alphabetic characters, underscores, and numbers. You can also include periods and commas. However, a number cannot begin a file name, and except in certain special cases, you should never begin a file name with a period. Other characters, such as slashes, question marks, or asterisks (*), are reserved for use as special characters by the system and cannot be part of a file name. File names can be as long as 256 characters.

You can include an extension as part of a file name. A period is used to distinguish the file name proper from the extension. Extensions can be useful for categorizing your files. You are probably familiar with certain standard extensions that have been adopted by convention. For example, C source code files always have an extension of **.c**. Files that contain compiled object code have a **.o** extension. You can, of course, make up your own file extensions. The following examples are all valid Linux file names:

```
preface
chapter2
New_Revisions
calc.c
intro.bk1
```

There are also special initialization files that are used to hold shell configuration commands. These are the hidden, or "dot" files, referred to in Chapter 5 that begin with a period. Dot files have predetermined names. Recall that when you use **ls** to display your file names, the dot files will not be displayed. To include the dot files, you need to use **ls** with the **-a** option. Dot files are discussed in more detail in Chapter 10 on shell configuration.

As shown in Figure 9-1, the **ls -l** command displays detailed information about a file. First the permissions are displayed, followed by the number of links, the owner of the file, the name of the group the user belongs to, the file size in bytes, the date and time the file was last modified, and the name of the file. The group name indicates the group that is being given group permission. In Figure 9-1, the file type for **mydata** is that of an ordinary file. There is only one link, indicating that the file has no other names and no other links. The owner's name is **chris**, the same as the login name, and the group name is **weather**. There are probably other users who also belong to the weather group. The size of the file is 207 bytes. It was last modified on February 20, at 11:55 A.M. The name of the file is **mydata**.

If you want to display this detailed information for all the files in a directory, simply use the **ls -l** command without an argument.

```
$ ls -l
-rw-r--r--  1  chris  weather 207  Feb 20  11:55  mydata
-rw-rw-r--  1  chris  weather 568  Feb 14  10:30  today
-rw-rw-r--  1  chris  weather 308  Feb 17  12:40  monday
```

All files in Linux have one physical format—a byte stream. A *byte stream* is just a sequence of bytes. This allows Linux to apply the file concept to every data component in the system. Directories are classified as files, and so are devices. Treating everything as a file allows Linux to organize and exchange data more easily. The data in a file can be sent directly to a device such as a screen, because a device interfaces with the system using the same byte-stream file format as regular files.

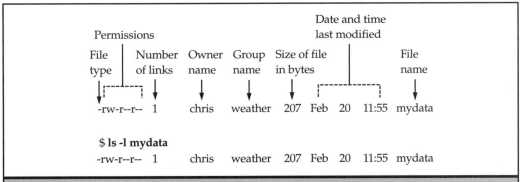

Figure 9-1. *File Information displayed using the **-l** option for the **ls** command*

This same file format is used to implement other operating system components. The interface to a device such as the screen or keyboard is designated as a file. Other components, such as directories, are themselves byte-stream files, but they have a special internal organization. A directory file contains information about a directory, organized in a special directory format. Since these different components are treated as files, they can be said to constitute different file types. A character device is one file type. A directory is another file type. The number of these file types may vary according to your specific implementation of Linux. However, there are four common types of files: ordinary files, directory files, character device files, and block device files. Though you may rarely reference a file's type, it can be useful when searching for directories or devices. Later in the chapter, you will see how to use the file type in a search criterion with the **find** command to specifically search for directory or device names.

Though all ordinary files have a byte-stream format, they may be used in different ways. The most significant difference is between binary and text files. Compiled programs are examples of binary files. However, even text files can be classified according to their different uses. You can have files that contain C programming source code or shell commands, or even a file that is empty. The file could be an executable program or a directory file. The Linux **file** command helps you determine what a file is used for. It examines the first few lines of a file and tries to determine a classification for it. The **file** command looks for special keywords or special numbers in those first few lines, but it is not always accurate. In the next example, the **file** command examines the contents of two files and determines a classification for them:

```
$ file monday reports
monday:      text
reports:      directory
```

To illustrate the variety of classifications, the **file** command in the next example examines a C source code file, an executable file, and an empty file:

```
$ file calc.c proj newdata
calc.c:      C program text
proj:      executable
newdata:      empty
```

If you need to examine the entire file byte by byte, you can do so with the **od** command. The **od** command performs a dump of a file. By default, it prints out every byte in its octal representation. However, you can also specify a character, decimal, or hexadecimal representation. The **od** command is helpful when you need to detect any special character in your file, or if you want to display a binary file. If you perform a character dump, then certain nonprinting characters will be represented in a character notation. For example, the carriage return will be represented by a \n. Both the **file** and **od** commands, with their options, are listed in Table 9-1.

Commands	Execution
`file`	Examines the first few lines of a file to determine a classification
`-f` *filename*	Reads the list of file names to be examined from a file
`od`	Prints out the contents of a file byte by byte in either octal, character, decimal, or hexadecimal; octal is the default
`-c`	Outputs character form of byte values; nonprinting characters have a corresponding character representation
`-d`	Outputs decimal form of byte values
`-x`	Outputs hexadecimal form of byte values
`-o`	Outputs octal form of byte values

Table 9-1.   *The file and od Commands*

ENVIRONMENTS

The File Structure

Linux organizes files into a hierarchically connected set of directories. Each directory may contain either files or other directories. In this respect, directories perform two important functions. A directory holds files, much like files held in a file drawer, and a directory connects to other directories, much like a branch in a tree is connected to other branches. With respect to files, directories appear to operate like file drawers, with each drawer holding several files. To access files, you open a file drawer. However, unlike file drawers, directories can contain not just files, but other directories. In this way, a directory can connect to another directory.

Because of the similarities to a tree, such a structure is often referred to as a *tree structure*. However, it could more accurately be thought of as an upside-down bush rather than a tree. There is no trunk. The tree is represented upside down, with the root at the top. Extending down from the root are the branches. Each branch grows out of only one branch, but it can have many lower branches. In this respect, it can be said to have a *parent-child structure*. In the same way, each directory is itself a subdirectory of one other directory. Each directory may contain many subdirectories, but is itself the child of only one parent directory.

Figure 9-2 illustrates the hierarchical file structure. Beginning with the *root* directory at the top, other directories branch out. Each directory has several other directories or files, but a directory can only have one parent directory. The directory **chris**, for example, has two subdirectories: **reports** and **programs**. However, **chris** itself is connected to only one parent directory, the directory called **home**.

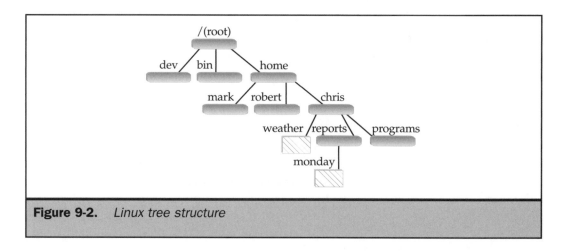

Figure 9-2.   *Linux tree structure*

The Linux file structure branches into several directories beginning with a root directory, /. Within the root directory there are several system directories that contain files and programs that are features of the Linux system. The root directory also contains a directory called **home** that may contain the **home** directories of all the users in the system. Each user's **home** directory, in turn, will contain the directories the user has made for his or her use. Each of these could also contain directories. Such nested directories would branch out from the user's **home** directory, as shown in Figure 9-3.

Home Directories

When you log in to the system, you are placed within your **home** directory. The name given to this directory by the system is the same as your login name. Any files you create when you first log in will be organized within your **home** directory. However,

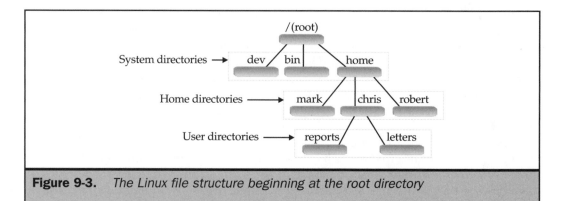

Figure 9-3.   *The Linux file structure beginning at the root directory*

within your **home** directory, you can create more directories. You can then change to these directories and store files in them. The same is true for other users on the system. Each user has his or her own **home** directory, identified by the appropriate login name. They, in turn, can create their own directories.

You can access a directory either through its name or by making it the default directory. Each directory is given a name when it is created. You can use this name in file operations to access files in that directory. You can also make the directory your default directory. If you do not use any directory names in a file operation, then the default directory will be accessed. The default directory is referred to as the *working directory*. In this sense, the working directory is the one you are currently working from.

When you log in, the working directory is your **home** directory, usually having the same name as your login name. You can change the working directory by using the **cd** command to designate another directory as the working directory. As the working directory is changed, you can move from one directory to another. Another way to think of a directory is as a corridor. In such a corridor, there are doors with names on them. Some doors lead to rooms; others lead to other corridors. The doors that open to rooms are like files in a directory. The doors that lead to other corridors are like other directories. Moving from one corridor to the next corridor is like changing the working directory. Moving through several corridors is like moving through several directories.

Path Names

The name that you give to a directory or file when you create it is not its full name. The full name of a directory is its *path name*. The hierarchically nested relationship among directories forms paths, and these paths can be used to unambiguously identify and reference any directory or file. In Figure 9-4, there is a path from the root directory, /, through the **home** directory to the **robert** directory. There is another path from the root directory through the **home** and **chris** directories to the **reports** directory. Though parts of each path may at first be shared, at some point they differ. Both the directories **robert** and **reports** share the two directories, **root** and **home**. Then they differ. In the **home** directory, **robert** ends with **robert**, but the directory **chris** then leads to **reports**. In this way, each directory in the file structure can be said to have its own unique path. The actual name by which the system identifies a directory will always begin with the root directory and consist of all directories nested above that directory.

In Linux, you write a path name by listing each directory in the path separated by a forward slash, /. A slash preceding the first directory in the path represents the root. The path name for the **robert** directory is **/home/robert**. The path name for the **reports** directory is **/home/chris/reports**. Path names also apply to files. When you create a file within a directory, you give the file a name. However, the actual name by which the system identifies the file is the file name combined with the path of directories from

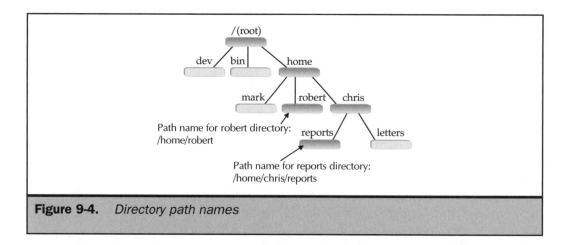

Figure 9-4. *Directory path names*

the root to the file's directory. In Figure 9-5, the path for the **weather** file consists of the root, **home**, and **chris** directories and the file name **weather**. The path name for **weather** is **/home/chris /weather** (the root directory is represented by the first slash).

Path names may be absolute or relative. An *absolute path name* is the complete path name of a file or directory beginning with the root directory. A *relative path name* begins from your working directory; it is the path of a file relative to your working directory. Using the directory structure described in Figure 9-5, if **chris** is your working directory, the relative path name for the file **monday** is **/reports/monday**. The absolute path name for **monday** is **/home/chris/reports/monday**.

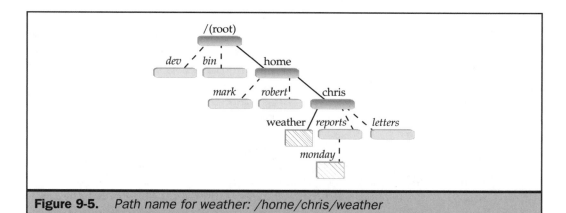

Figure 9-5. *Path name for weather: /home/chris/weather*

System Directories

The root directory that begins the Linux file structure contains several system directories. The system directories contain files and programs used to run and maintain the system. Many contain other subdirectories with programs for executing specific features of Linux. For example, the directory **/user/bin** contains the various Linux commands that users execute, such as **cp** and **mv**. The directory **/bin** holds interfaces with different system devices, such as the printer or the terminal. Table 9-2 lists the basic system directories, and Figure 9-6 shows how they are organized in the tree structure.

Directory	Function
/	Begins the file system structure—called the *root*
/home	Contains users' **home** directories
/bin	Holds all the standard commands and utility programs
/usr	Holds those files and commands used by the system; this directory breaks down into several subdirectories
/usr/bin	Holds user-oriented commands and utility programs
/usr/sbin	Holds system administration commands
/usr/lib	Holds libraries for programming languages
/usr/doc	Holds Linux documentation
/usr/man	Holds the online manual **man** files
/usr/spool	Holds spooled files, such as those generated for printing jobs and network transfers
/sbin	Holds system administration commands for booting the system
/var	Holds files that vary, such as mailbox files
/dev	Holds file interfaces for devices such as the terminals and printers
/etc	Holds system configuration files and any other system files

Table 9-2. *Standard System Directories in Linux*

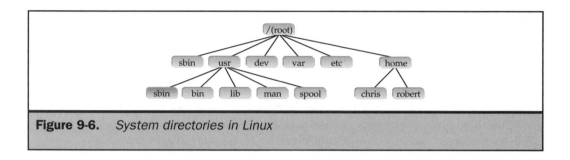

Figure 9-6. *System directories in Linux*

Listing, Displaying, and Printing Files: ls, cat, more, and lpr

One of the primary functions of an operating system is the management of files. You may need to perform certain basic output operations on your files, such as displaying them on your screen or printing them out. The Linux system provides a set of commands that perform basic file management operations such as listing, displaying, and printing files, as well as copying, renaming, and erasing files. These commands are usually made up of abbreviated versions of words. For example, the **ls** command is a shortened form of *list* and lists the files in your directory. The **lpr** command is an abbreviated form of *line print* and will print a file. The **cat** and **more** commands display the contents of a file on the screen. Table 9-3 (at the end of this section) lists these commands with their different options. When you log in to your Linux system, you may want a list of the files in your **home** directory. The **ls** command, which outputs a list of your file and directory names, is useful for this. The **ls** command has many possible options for displaying file names according to specific features. These are discussed in more detail at the end of the chapter.

Displaying Files: cat and more

You may also need to look at the contents of a file. The **cat** and **more** commands display the contents of a file on the screen. **cat** stands for *concatenate*. It is actually a very complex and versatile command, as described in Chapter 7. Here it is used in a very limited way, displaying the text of a file on the screen:

```
$ cat mydata
computers
```

The **cat** command outputs the entire text of a file to the screen at once. This presents a problem when the file is large because its text quickly speeds past on the screen. The **more** command is designed to overcome this limitation by displaying one screen of text at a time. You can then move forward or backward in the text at your leisure. You invoke the **more** command by entering the command name followed by the name of the file that you want to view.

```
$ more mydata
```

When **more** invokes a file, the first screen of text is displayed. To continue to the next screen, you press the **f** key or the SPACEBAR. To move back in the text, you press the **b** key. You can quit at any time by pressing **q**.

Printing Files: lpr, lpq, and lprm

With the printer commands like **lpr** and **lprm** you can perform printing operations like printing files or canceling print jobs (see Table 9-3). When you need to print files, use the **lpr** command to send files to the printer connected to your system. In the next example, the user prints the **mydata** file:

```
$ lpr mydata
```

If you want to print out several files at once, you can specify more than one file on the command line after the **lpr** command. In the next example, the user prints out both the **mydata** and **preface** files:

```
$ lpr mydata preface
```

Printing jobs are placed in a queue and printed one at a time in the background. You can continue with other work as your files print. You can see the position of a particular printing job at any given time with the **lpq** command. This command gives the owner of the printing job (the login name of the user who sent the job) the print job ID, the size in bytes, and the temporary file in which it is currently held. In this example, the owner is *chris* and the print ID is 00015:

```
$ lpq
Owner      ID        Chars      Filename
chris      00015      360       /usr/lpd/cfa00015
```

Should you need to cancel an unwanted printing job, you can do so with the **lprm** command. This command takes as its argument either the ID number of the printing job or the owner's name. The **lprm** command will then remove the print job from the print queue. For this task, **lpq** is very helpful, for it will provide you with the ID number and owner of the printing job that you need to use with **lprm**. In the next example, the print job 15 is canceled:

```
$ lprm   00015
```

You can have several printers connected to your Linux system. One of these will be designated the default printer, and it is to this printer that **lpr** will print, unless another printer is specified. With **lpr**, you can specify the particular printer you want your file printed on. Each printer on your system will have its own name. You can specify which printer to use with the **-P** option followed by that printer's name. In the next example, the file **mydata** is printed on the *evans1* printer:

```
$ lpr -Pevans1 mydata
```

Command or Option	Execution
ls	This command lists file and directory names: **$ ls**
cat	This filter can be used to display a file. It can take file names for its arguments. It outputs the contents of those files directly to the standard output, which, by default, is directed to the screen: **$ cat** filenames
more	This utility displays a file screen by screen. It can take file names for its arguments. It outputs the contents of those files to the screen, one screen at a time: **$ more** filenames
+num	Begins displaying the file at page *num*
numf	Skips forward *num* number of screens
numb	Skips backward *num* number of screens
d	Displays half a screen
h	Lists all **more** commands
q	Quits **more** utility
lpr	Sends a file to the line printer to be printed; a list of files may be used as arguments
-P *printer-name*	Selects a specific printer
lpq	Lists the print queue for printing jobs
lprm	Removes a printing job from the printing queue

Table 9-3.   *Listing, Displaying, and Printing Files*

Managing Directories: mkdir, rmdir, ls, cd, and pwd

You can create and remove your own directories, as well as change your working directory, with the **mkdir**, **rmdir**, and **cd** commands. Each of these commands can take as their argument the path name for a directory. The **pwd** command will display the absolute path name of your working directory. In addition to these commands, the special characters represented by a single dot (.), a double dot (..), and a tilde (~) can be used to reference the working directory, the parent of the working directory, and the **home** directory, respectively. Taken together, these commands allow you to manage your directories. You can create nested directories, move from one directory to another, and use path names to reference any of your directories. Those commands commonly used to manage directories are listed in Table 9-4.

Command	Execution
mkdir	Creates a directory: $ **mkdir reports**
rmdir	Erases a directory: $ **rmdir letters**
ls -F	Lists a directory name with a preceding slash: $ **ls -F** **today /reports /letters**
ls -R	Lists a working directory as well as all subdirectories
cd *directory name*	Changes to the specified directory, making it the working directory. The **cd** command without a directory name changes back to the home directory: $ **cd reports** $ **cd**
pwd	Displays the path name of the working directory: $ **pwd** **/home/chris/reports**
directory name / filename	A slash, /, is used in path names to separate each directory name. In the case of path names for files, a slash separates the preceding directory names from the file name: $ **cd /home/chris/reports** $ **cat /home/chris/reports/mydata**

Table 9-4.   *Directory Commands*

ENVIRONMENTS

Command	Execution

..	References the parent directory. You can use it as an argument or as part of a path name:
	`$ cd ..`
	`$ mv ../larisa oldletters`

.	References the working directory. You can use it as an argument or as part of a path name:
	`$ ls .`
	`$ mv ../aleina .`

~/*pathname*	The tilde, ~, is a special character that represents the path name for the **home** directory. It is useful when you need to use an absolute path name for a file or directory:
	`$ cp monday ~/today`
	`$ mv tuesday ~/weather`

Table 9-4.   *Directory Commands* (continued)

You create and remove directories with the **mkdir** and **rmdir** commands. In either case, you can also use path names for the directories. In the next example, the user creates the directory **reports**. Then, the user creates the directory **letters** using a path name.

```
$ mkdir reports
$ mkdir /home/chris/letters
```

You can remove a directory with the **rmdir** command followed by the directory name. In the next example, the user removes the directory **reports** with the **rmdir** command. Then, the directory **letters** is removed using its path name.

```
$ rmdir reports
$ rmdir /home/chris/letters
```

You have seen how to use the **ls** command to list the files and directories within your working directory. However, to distinguish between file and directory names, you need to use the **ls** command with the **-F** option. A slash is then placed after each directory name in the list.

```
$ ls
weather reports letters
$ ls -F
weather reports/ letters/
```

The **ls** command will also take as an argument any directory name or directory path name. This allows you to list the files in any directory without having to first change to that directory. In the next example, the **ls** command takes as its argument the name of a directory, **reports**. Then the **ls** command is executed again, only this time the absolute path name of **reports** is used.

```
$ ls reports
monday tuesday
$ ls /home/chris/reports
monday tuesday
$
```

Within each directory, you can create still other directories—in effect, nesting directories. Using the **cd** command, you can change from one directory to another. However, there is no indicator that tells you what directory you are currently in. To find out what directory you have changed to, use the **pwd** command to display the name of your current working directory. The **pwd** command displays more than just the name of the directory—it displays the full path name, as shown in the next example. The path name displayed here consists of the **home** directory, **dylan**, and the directory it is a part of, **home**. Each directory name is separated by a slash. The root directory is represented by a beginning slash.

```
$ pwd
/home/dylan
```

As you already know, you can change directories with the **cd** command. Changing to a directory makes that directory the working directory, which is your default directory. File commands such as **ls** and **cp**, unless specifically told otherwise, will operate on files in your working directory.

When you log into the system, your working directory is your **home** directory. When a user account is created, the system also creates a **home** directory for that user. When you log in, you are always placed in your **home** directory. The **cd** command allows you to make another directory the working directory. In a sense, you can move from your **home** directory into another directory. This other directory then becomes the default directory for any commands and any new files created. For example, the **ls** command will now list files in this new working directory.

The **cd** command takes as its argument the name of the directory you want to change to.

```
$ cd directory-name
```

In the next example, the user changes from the **home** directory to the **props** directory. The user issues a **pwd** command to display the working directory.

```
$ pwd
/home/dylan
$ cd props
$ pwd
/home/dylan/props
$
```

You can also change to another directory by using its full path name. In the next example, the **cd** command takes as its argument the path name for the **letters** directory:

```
$ cd /home/chris/letters
$ pwd
/home/chris/letters
$
```

Notice that when you create a new directory, you are already in a working directory. Any directories that you then create are nested within that working directory. The working directory within which you create a new directory and the new directory itself take on a parent-child relationship. The working directory is the parent of the newly created directory. If, within the **home** directory, the user creates a **props** directory, then the **home** directory is the parent of the **props** directory, and **props** is the child of the **home** directory.

You can use a double dot symbol, **..**, to represent a directory's parent. It literally represents the path name of the parent directory. You can use the double dot symbol with the **cd** command to move back up to the parent directory, making the parent directory the current directory. In the next example, the user moves to the **props** directory and then changes back to the **home** directory:

```
$ cd props
$ pwd
/home/dylan/props
$ cd ..
$ pwd
/home/dylan
```

If you want to change back to your **home** directory, you only need to enter the **cd** command by itself, without a file name argument. You will change directly back to the **home** directory, making it once again the working directory. In the next example, the user changes back to the **home** directory:

```
$ cd
```

Referencing the Working and Parent Directories: . and ..

A directory will always have a parent (except, of course, for the root). For example, in the next listing, the parent for **thankyou** is the **letters** directory. When a directory is created, two entries are made: one represented with a dot, **.**, and the other represented by a double dot, **. .** . The dot represents the path names of the directory, and the double dot represents the path name of its parent directory. The double dot, used as an argument in a command, references a parent directory. The single dot references the directory itself. In the next example, the user changes to the **letters** directory. The **ls** command is used with the **.** argument to list the files in the **letters** directory. Then, the **ls** command is used with the **..** argument to list the files in the parent directory of **letters**, the **chris** directory.

```
$ cd letters
$ ls .
thankyou
$ ls ..
weather letters
$
```

You can use the single dot to reference your working directory, instead of using its path name. For example, to copy a file to the working directory retaining the same name, the dot can be used in place of the working directory's path name. In this sense, the dot is another name for the working directory. In the next example, the user copies the **weather** file from the **chris** directory to the **reports** directory. The **reports** directory is the working directory and can be represented with the single dot.

```
$ cd reports
$ cp /home/chris/weather  .
```

The **. .** symbol is often used to reference files in the parent directory. In the next example, the **cat** command displays the **weather** file in the parent directory. The path name for the file is the **. .** symbol followed by a slash and the file name.

```
$ cat ../weather
raining and warm
```

You can use the **cd** command with the **..** symbol to step back through successive parent directories of the directory tree from a lower directory. In the next example, the user is placed in the **thankyou** directory. Then, the user steps back up to the **chris** directory by continually using the command **cd ..**.

```
$ pwd
/home/chris/letters/thankyou
$ cd ..
$ pwd
/home/chris/letters
$ cd ..
$ pwd
/home/chris
```

There are many times when you will use both the **..** and **.** as arguments to a command. For example, with **letters** as the working directory, **weather** can be copied down to **letters** referencing the **chris** directory with **..** and the **letters** directory with **.**.

```
$ cp ../weather .
```

Using Absolute and Relative Path Names: ~

As mentioned earlier, you can reference files and directories using absolute and relative path names. However, each has its limitations. Though an absolute path name can reference any file or directory, it is usually lengthy and complex, making it difficult to use. A relative path name is often simpler and easier to use, but it is limited in the number of files it can reference. Usually, you will use relative path names whenever possible and absolute path names only when necessary. Some shells provide a way to abbreviate part of an absolute path name.

The relative path name starts from the working directory. In the next example, the **ls** command is used first with the relative path name and then with the absolute path name of **thankyou**. The working directory is the user's **home** directory, **chris**, and the relative path name of the **thankyou** directory is **letters/thankyou**. The absolute path name of the **thankyou** directory is **/home/chris/letters/thankyou**.

```
$ ls letters/thankyou
larisa
$ ls /home/chris/letters/thankyou
larisa
$
```

Relative path names can only reference files in subdirectories of the working directory. The subdirectories can be nested to any depth, but their paths must branch from the working directory. Suppose you need to reference a directory that is higher up in the directory tree or off in another branch from the working directory. For example, given **letters** as the working directory, suppose you want to display a file in a directory that is not a subdirectory of **letters**—say, the **reports** directory. In this case, you have to use the absolute path name for **reports**. In the next example, the user references the file **monday** in the **reports** directory using its absolute path name:

```
$ cat /home/chris/reports/monday
```

You also need to use an absolute path name when referencing directories higher in the directory tree than the working directory. Given **thankyou** as the working directory, suppose the user wants to display a file in your **home** directory, **/home/chris**. The **chris** directory is not a subdirectory of **thankyou** and cannot be referenced with a relative path name. In this case, the user would have to use the absolute path name to reference a file in his **home** directory. In the next example, the user is in the **thankyou** directory and wants to display a file, **weather**, in the **home** directory, **/home/chris**. To do so, the user needs to use an absolute path name for **weather**:

```
$ pwd
/home/chris/letters/thankyou
$ cat /home/chris/weather
raining and warm
$
```

The absolute path name from the root to your **home** directory could be especially complex and, at times, even subject to change by the system administrator. To make it easier to reference, you can use a special character, the tilde (~), which represents the absolute path name of your **home** directory. In the next example, the user references the **weather** file in the **home** directory by placing a tilde and slash before **weather**:

```
$ pwd
/home/chris/letters/thankyou
$ cat ~/weather
raining and warm
$
```

You must specify the rest of the path from your **home** directory. In the next example, the user references the **monday** file in the **reports** directory. The tilde represents the path to the user's **home** directory, **/home/chris**, and then the rest of the path to the **monday** file is specified.

```
$ cat ~/reports/Monday
```

File and Directory Operations: find, cp, mv, rm, and ln

As you create more and more files, you may want to back them up, change their names, erase some of them, or even give them added names. Linux provides you with several file commands that allow you to search for files, copy files, rename files, or remove files (see Table 9-6 later on in the chapter). If you have a large number of files, you can also search them to locate a specific one. The commands are shortened forms of full words, consisting of just two characters. The **cp** command stands for *copy* and copies a file, **mv** stands for *move* and will rename or move a file, **rm** stands for *remove* and will erase a file, and **ln** stands for *link* and will add another name for a file. One exception to this rule is the **find** command, which performs searches of your file names to find a file.

Searching Directories: find

Once you have a large number of files in many different directories, you may need to search them to locate a specific file or files of a certain type. The **find** command allows you to perform such a search. The **find** command takes as its arguments directory names followed by several possible options that specify the type of search and the criteria for the search. The **find** command then searches within the directories listed and their subdirectories for files that meet these criteria. The **find** command can search for a file based on its name, type, owner, and even the time of the last update.

```
$ find directory-list -option  criteria
```

The **-name** option has as its criteria a pattern and instructs **find** to search for the file name that matches that pattern. To search for a file by name, you use the **find** command with the directory name followed by the **-name** option and the name of the file.

```
$ find directory-list -name filename
```

The **find** command also has options that merely perform actions, such as outputting the results of a search. If you want **find** to display the file names it has found, you simply include the **-print** option on the command line along with any other options. The **-print** option instructs **find** to output to the standard output the names of all the files it locates. In the next example, the user searches for all the files in the **reports** directory with the name **monday**. Once located, the file, with its relative path name, is printed out.

```
$ find reports -name monday -print
reports/monday
```

The **find** command will print out the file names using the directory name specified in the directory list. If you specify an absolute path name, the absolute path of the found directories will be output. If you specify a relative path name, only the relative path name is output. In the previous example, the user specified a relative path name, **reports**, in the directory list. Located file names were output beginning with this relative path name. In the next example, the user specifies an absolute path name in the directory list. Located file names are then output using this absolute path name.

```
$ find /home/chris -name monday -print
/home/chris/reports/monday
```

If you want to search your working directory, you can use the dot in the directory path name to represent your working directory. The double dot would represent the parent directory. The next example searches all files and subdirectories in the working directory, using the dot to represent the working directory. If you are located in your **home** directory, this is a convenient way to search through all of your own directories. Notice that the located file names are output beginning with a dot.

```
$ find . -name weather -print
./weather
```

You can use shell wildcard characters as part of the pattern criteria for searching files. However, the special character must be quoted in order to avoid evaluation by the shell. In the next example, all files with the **.c** extension in the **programs** directory are searched for:

```
$ find programs -name '*.c' -print
```

You can also use the **find** command to locate other directories. In Linux, a directory is officially classified as a special type of file. Though all files have a byte-stream format, some files, such as directories, are used in special ways. In this sense, a file can be said to have a file type. The **find** command has an option called

-type that searches for a file of a given type. The **-type** option takes a one-character modifier that represents the file type. The modifier that represents a directory is a **d**. In the next example, both the directory name and the directory file type are used to search for the directory called **thankyou**:

```
$ find /home/chris -name thankyou -type d -print
/home/chris/letters/thankyou
$
```

File types are not really so much different types of files as they are the file format applied to other components of the operating system, such as devices. In this sense, a device is treated as a type of file, and you can use **find** to search for devices and directories, as well as ordinary files. Table 9-5 lists the different types available for the **find** command's **-type** option.

Command or Option	Execution
find	Searches directories for files based on search criteria. This command has several options that specify the type of criteria and actions to be taken.
-name *pattern*	Searches for files with *pattern* in the name.
-group *name*	Searches for files belonging to this group *name*.
-size *numc*	Searches for files with the size *num* in blocks. If **c** is added after *num*, then the size in bytes (characters) is searched for.
-mtime *num*	Searches for files last modified *num* days ago.
-newer *pattern*	Searches for files that were modified after the one matched by *pattern*.
-print	Outputs the result of the search to the standard output. The result is usually a list of file names, including their full path names.
-type *filetype*	Searches for files with the specified file type.
b	Block device file.

Table 9-5.   *The find Command*

Command or Option	Execution
c	Character device file.
d	Directory file.
f	Ordinary (regular) file.
p	Named pipes (fifo).
l	Symbolic links.

Table 9-5. *The find Command* (continued)

Copying Files

To make a copy of a file, you simply give **cp** two file names as its arguments. The first file name is the name of the file to be copied—the one that already exists. This is often referred to as the *source file*. The second file name is the name you want for the copy. This will be a new file containing a copy of all the data in the source file. This second argument is often referred to as the *destination file* (see Table 9-6). The syntax for the **cp** command follows:

```
$ cp source-file destination-file
```

In the next example, the user copies a file called **proposal** to a new file called **oldprop**:

```
$ cp proposal oldprop
```

When the user lists the files in that directory, the new copy will be among them.

```
$ ls
proposal  oldprop
```

It is possible that you could unintentionally destroy another file with the **cp** command. The **cp** command generates a copy by first creating a file and then copying data into it. If another file has the same name as the destination file, then that file is destroyed and a new file with that name is created. In a sense, the original file is overwritten with the new copy. In the next example, the **proposal** file is overwritten by the **newprop** file. The **proposal** file already exists.

```
$ cp newprop  proposal
```

Most Linux distributions configure your system to detect this overwrite condition. If not, you can use the **cp** command with the **-i** option to detect it. With this option, **cp** will first check to see if the file already exists. If it does, you will then be asked if you wish to overwrite the existing file. If you enter **y**, the existing file will be destroyed and a new one created as the copy. If you enter anything else, it will be taken as a negative answer and the **cp** command will be interrupted, preserving the original file.

```
$ cp -i  newprop  proposal
Overwrite proposal?  n
$
```

To copy a file from your working directory to another directory, you only need to use that directory name as the second argument in the **cp** command. The name of the new copy will be the same as the original, but the copy will be placed in a different directory. Files in different directories can have the same names. Because they are in different directories, they are registered as different files.

```
$ cp filenames directory-name
```

To copy a file from the **home** directory to a subdirectory, simply specify the directory's name. In the next example, the file **newprop** is copied from the working directory to the **props** directory:

```
$ cp newprop props
```

The **cp** command can take a list of several file names for its arguments, so you can copy more than one file at a time to a directory. Simply specify the file names on the command line, entering the directory name as the last argument. All the files are then copied to the specified directory. In the next example, the user copies both the files **preface** and **doc1** to the **props** directory. Notice that **props** is the last argument.

```
$ cp preface doc1 props
```

You can use any of the wildcard characters to generate a list of file names to use with **cp** or **mv**. For example, suppose you need to copy all your C source code files to a given directory. Instead of listing each one individually on the command line, you could use a * character with the **.c** extension to match on and generate a list of C source code files (all files with a **.c** extension). In the next example, the user copies all source code files in the current directory to the **sourcebks** directory:

```
$ cp *.c sourcebks
```

If you want to copy all the files in a given directory to another directory, you could use ***.*** to match on and generate a list of all those files in a **cp** command. In the next example, the user copies all the files in the **props** directory to the **oldprop** directory. Notice the use of a **props** path name preceding the ***.*** special characters. In this context, **props** is a path name that will be appended before each file in the list that *.* generates.

```
$ cp props/*.* oldprop
```

You can, of course, use any of the other special characters, such as **.**, **?**, or **[]**. In the next example, the user copies both source code and object code files (.c and .o) to the **projbk** directory:

```
$ cp *.[oc] projbk
```

When you copy a file, you may want to give the copy a different name than the original. To do so, place the new file name after the directory name, separated by a slash.

```
$ cp filename directory-name/new-filename
```

In the next example, the file **newprop** is copied to the directory **props** and the copy is given the name **version1**. The user then changes to the **props** directory and lists the files. There is only one file, and it is called **version1**.

```
$ cp newprop props/version1
$ cd props
$ ls
version1
```

When you want to copy a file from a child directory such as **props** to a parent directory, you need to specify the name of the child directory. The first argument to **cp** is the file name to be copied. This file name must be preceded by the name of the child directory and separated by a slash. The second argument is the name the file will have in the parent directory.

```
$ cp child-directory-name/filename    new-filename
```

ENVIRONMENTS

In the next example, the file **version1** is copied from the directory **props** up to the **home** directory:

```
$ cp props/version1    version1
```

Suppose, however, you have changed your working directory to that of a child directory and then want to copy a file from the child directory up to the parent. You need some way to reference the parent. You can do so using the double dot symbol, which represents the path name of the parent directory.

```
$ cp filename ..
$ cp filename ../new-filename
```

For example, if **props** is your current working directory and you want to copy the file **version1** from **props** up to its parent (in this case, the user's **home** directory), you need to use the double dot symbol in the second argument of the **cp** command.

```
$ cp version1 ..
```

If you want to give the copy of **version1** a new name, add the new name in the second argument, preceding it with a slash.

```
$ cp version1   ../newversion
```

Moving Files

You can use the **mv** command either to change the name of a file or to move a file from one directory to another. When using **mv** to rename a file, you simply use the new file name as the second argument. The first argument is the current name of the file that you are renaming.

```
$ mv original-filename    new-filename
```

In the next example, the **proposal** file is renamed with the name **version1**:

```
$ mv proposal version1
```

As with **cp**, it is very easy for **mv** to erase a file accidentally. When renaming a file, you might accidentally choose a file name that is already used by another file. In this case, that other file will be erased. The **mv** command also has a **-i** option that will check first to see if a file by that name already exists. If it does, then you will be asked first if you want to overwrite it. In the next example, a file already exists with the name **version1**. The overwrite condition is detected and you are asked whether or not you want to overwrite that file.

```
$ ls
proposal version1
$ mv -i  version1   proposal
Overwrite proposal?   n
$
```

You can move a file from one directory to another by using the directory name as the second argument in the **mv** command. In this case, you can think of the **mv** command as simply moving a file from one directory to another, rather than renaming the file. After you move the file, it will have the same name as it had in its original directory, unless you specify otherwise.

```
$ mv filename directory-name
```

In the next example, the file **newprop** is moved from the **home** directory to the **props** directory:

```
$ mv newprop props
```

Should you want to rename a file when you move it, you can specify the new name of the file after the directory name. The directory name and the new file name are separated by a forward slash. In the next example, the file **newprop** is moved to the directory **props** and renamed as **version1**:

```
$ mv newprops props/version1
$ cd props
$ ls
version1
```

A file can just as easily be moved from a child directory back up to the parent directory by specifying the child directory's name before the file name.

```
$ mv props/version1   version1
```

ENVIRONMENTS

Suppose, however, you have changed your working directory to that of a child directory and then want to move a file from the child directory up to the parent. As with the **cp** command, you can use the double dot symbol to reference the parent directory.

```
$ mv filename ..
$ mv filename ../new-filename
```

If **props** is your current working directory and you want to move **version1** from **props** up to its parent—the **home** directory—then you can use the double dot symbol as the second argument of the **mv** command.

```
$ mv version1 ..
```

If you want to give the **version1** file a new name in the parent directory, you need to add the new name in the second argument, preceding it with a slash.

```
$ mv version1 ../oldprop
```

The actual name of a file is its file name preceded by its directory path. When **tuesday** was moved to the **reports** directory, its path name was actually changed. The full name of the **monday** file changed from **/home/chris/tuesday** to **/home/chris /reports/tuesday**. Its path name now includes the directory **reports**. In this sense, renaming a file is more like moving it.

You could just as easily use an absolute path name. In the next example, **today** is moved to the **reports** directory and given a new name, **tuesday**. Notice that the absolute path name is used for the file name argument in both the **mv** and **ls** commands.

```
$ mv today /home/chris/reports/tuesday
$ ls /home/chris/reports
monday tuesday
$
```

As with the **cp** command, the **mv** command can also move several files at once from one directory to another. You only need to enter the file names on the command line. The destination directory is always the last name you enter. In the next example, the user moves both the files **wednesday** and **friday** to the **lastweek** directory.

```
$ cp wednesday friday lastweek
```

You can also use any of the special characters described in Chapter 5 to generate a list of file names to use with **mv**. In the next example, the user moves all source code files in the current directory to the **newproj** directory:

```
$ mv *.c newproj
```

If you want to move all the files in a given directory to another directory, you can use ***.*** to match on and generate a list of all those files. In the next example, the user moves all the files in the **reports** directory to the **repbks** directory:

```
$ mv reports/*.*   repbks
```

Moving and Copying Directories

You can also copy or move whole directories at once. Both **cp** and **mv** can take as their first argument a directory name, allowing you to copy or move subdirectories from one directory into another. The first argument is the name of the directory to be moved or copied, and the second argument is the name of the directory within which it is to be placed. The same path name structure that is used for files applies to moving or copying directories.

You can just as easily copy subdirectories from one directory to another. To copy a directory, the **cp** command requires that you use the **-r** option. The **-r** option stands for *recursive*. It directs the **cp** command to copy a directory as well as any subdirectories it may contain. In other words, the entire directory subtree, from that directory on, will be copied. In the next example, the **thankyou** directory is copied to the **oldletters** directory. There are now two **thankyou** subdirectories, one in **letters** and one in **oldletters**.

```
$ cp -r letters/thankyou oldletters
$ ls -F letters
/thankyou
$ ls -F oldletters
/thankyou
```

Suppose that instead of copying a directory, making it a subdirectory of another directory, you just want to copy its files over. To copy all the files in one directory to another, you need to specify their file names. The asterisk (*) special character will match all the file and directory names within a directory. To copy all the files in the **letters** directory to **oldletters**, you use the asterisk as your first argument in order to generate a list of all the file names in **letters**. If you need to specify a path name for the first argument, you can do so and place the asterisk at the end. In the next example, all the files in the **letters** directory are copied to the **oldletters** directory. A path name is specified for **letters**, and the asterisk at the end of the path name matches all files in the **letters** directory.

```
$ cp letters/* oldletters
```

In order to include the subdirectories in **letters** in the copy operation, you need to use the **-r** option with **cp**.

```
$ cp -r letters/* oldletters
```

The ~ Special Character

You have already seen how you can use the tilde (~) to represent the absolute path name of the **home** directory. For example, to copy a file from a lower directory back to the **home** directory, you can use the tilde in place of the **home** directory's absolute path name. In the next example, the user changes to the **reports** directory and then copies the file **monday** from the **reports** directory up to the **home** directory:

```
$ cd reports
$ cp monday ~
```

To give a new name to the copied file when copying up to the **home** directory, place the new name after a **~/**. In the next example, the file **monday** is copied back up to the **home** directory and the copy is given the name **today**.

```
$ cp monday ~/today
```

The tilde is used in the same way for arguments in the **mv** command. In the next example, the file **monday** is moved from the **reports** directory back up to the **home** directory.

```
$ mv monday ~
```

If you are renaming a file while moving it to the **home** directory from a lower directory, the new name of the file is preceded by a tilde and a slash, **~/**. In the next example, there is a change to the **reports** directory, and then the file **monday** is moved back up to the **home** directory and renamed as **today**.

```
$ cd reports
$ mv monday ~/today
```

The tilde can be used wherever you would use the path name for the **home** directory. In the next example, previously described **mv** and **ls** commands are executed with the tilde:

```
$ mv weather ~/reports/monday
$ ls ~/reports
monday
$
```

Erasing a File: The rm Command

As you use Linux, you will find that the number of files you use increases rapidly. It is easy to generate files in Linux. Applications such as editors, and commands such as **cp**, easily create files. Eventually, many of these files may become outdated and useless. You can then remove them with the **rm** command. In the next example, the user erases the file **oldprop**:

```
$ rm oldprop
```

The **rm** command can take any number of arguments, allowing you to list several file names and erase them all at the same time. You just list them on the command line after you type **rm**.

```
$ rm proposal version1 version2
```

Be careful when using the **rm** command. It is irrevocable. Once a file is removed, it cannot be restored. Suppose, for example, you enter the **rm** command by accident while meaning to enter some other command, such as **cp** or **mv**. By the time you press ENTER and realize your mistake, it is too late. The files are gone. To protect against this kind of situation, you can use the **rm** command's **-i** option to confirm that you want to erase a file. With the **-i** option, you are prompted separately for each file and asked whether or not to remove it. If you enter **y**, the file will be removed. If you enter anything else, the file is not removed. In the next example, the **rm** command is instructed to erase the files **proposal** and **oldprop**. It then asks for confirmation for each file. The user decides to remove **oldprop** but not **proposal**.

```
$ rm -i proposal oldprop
Remove proposal? n
Remove oldprop? y
$
```

Table 9-6 lists the different file commands.

Command	Execution
cp *filename filename*	Copies a file. The **cp** command takes two arguments: the original file and the name of the new copy. You can use path names for the files in order to copy across directories: `$ cp today reports/monday`
cp -r *dirname dirname*	Copies a subdirectory from one directory to another. The copied directory will include all its own subdirectories: `$ cp -r letters/thankyou oldletters`
mv *filename filename*	Moves (renames) a file. **mv** takes two arguments: the first is the file to be moved. The second argument can be the new file name or the path name of a directory. If it is the name of a directory, then the file is literally moved to that directory, changing the file's path name: `$ mv today /home/chris/reports`
mv *dirname dirname*	Moves directories. In this case, the first and last arguments are directories: `$ mv letters/thankyou oldletters`
ln *filename filename*	Creates added names for files referred to as links. A link can be created in one directory that references a file in another directory: `$ ln today reports/monday`
rm *filenames*	Removes (erases) a file. Can take any number of file names as its arguments. Literally removes links to a file. If a file has more than one link, you need to remove all of them in order to finally erase a file: `$rm today weather weekend`

Table 9-6.   *File Operations*

Links: The ln Command

You can give a file more than one name using the **ln** command. You might want to reference a file using different file names to access it from different directories. The added names are often referred to as *links*.

The **ln** command takes two arguments: the name of the original file and the new, added file name. The **ls** operation will list both file names, but there will be only one physical file.

```
$ ln original-file-name added-file-name
```

In the next example, the **today** file is given the additional name **weather**. It is just another name for the **today** file.

```
$ ls
today
$ ln today weather
$ ls
today weather
```

You can give the same file several names by using the **ln** command on the same file many times. In the next example, the file **today** is given both the name **weather** and **weekend**:

```
$ ln today weather
$ ln today weekend
$ ls
today weather weekend
```

You can use the **ls** command with the **-l** option to find out if a file has several links. The **ls** command with **-l** lists several pieces of information, such as permissions, the number of links a file has, its size, and the date it was last modified. In this line of information, the first number, which precedes the user's login name, specifies the number of links a file has. The number before the date is the size of the file. The date is the last time a file was modified. In the next example, the user lists the full information for both **today** and **weather**. Notice that the number of links in both files is 2. Furthermore, the size and date are the same. This suggests that both files are really different names for the same file.

```
$ ls -l today weather
-rw-rw-r-- 2  chris   group 563  Feb  14   10:30   today
-rw-rw-r-- 2  chris   group 563  Feb  14   10:30   weather
```

This still does not tell you specifically what file names are linked. You can be somewhat sure if two files have exactly the same number of links, sizes, and modification dates, as in the case of the files **today** and **weather**. However, to be certain, you can use the **ls** command with the **-i** option. With the **-i** option, the **ls** command lists the file name and its inode number. An *inode number* is a unique number used by the system to identify a specific file. If two file names have the same inode number, they reference the exact same file. They are two names for the same file. In the next example, the user lists **today, weather,** and **larisa.** Notice that **today** and **weather** have the same inode number.

```
$ ls -i today weather larisa
1234 today     1234 weather     3976 larisa
```

The added names, or links, created with **ln** are often used to reference the same file from different directories. A file in one directory can be linked to and accessed from another directory. Suppose you need to reference a file that is in the **home** directory from within another directory. You can set up a link from that directory to the file in the **home** directory. This link is actually another name for the file. Because the link is in another directory, it can have the same name as the original file.

To link a file in the **home** directory to another directory, use the name of that directory as the second argument in the **ln** command.

```
$ ln filename directory-name
```

In the next example, the file **today** in the **chris** directory is linked to the **reports** directory. The **ls** command will list the **today** file in both the **chris** directory and the **reports** directory. In fact, there is only one copy of the **today** file, the original file in the **home** directory.

```
$ ln today reports
$ ls
today reports
$ ls reports
today
$
```

Just as with the **cp** and **mv** commands, you can give another name to the link. Simply place the new name after the directory name, separated by a slash. In the next example, the file **today** is linked to the **reports** directory with the name **wednesday**. There is still only one actual file, the original file called **today** in the **chris** directory. However, **today** is now linked to the directory **reports** with the name **wednesday**. In this sense, **today** has been given another name. In the **reports** directory, the **today** file goes by the name **wednesday**.

```
$ ln today reports/wednesday
$ ls
today reports
$ ls reports
wednesday
$
```

You can easily link a file in any directory to a file in another directory by referencing the files with their path names. In the next example, the file **monday** in the **reports** directory is linked to the directory, **chris**. Notice that the second argument is an absolute path name.

```
$ ln monday /home/chris
```

To erase a file, you need to remove all of its links. The name of a file is actually considered a link to that file. Hence the command **rm** that removes the link to the file. If you have several links to the file and remove just one of them, the others stay in place and you can reference the file through them. The same is true even if you remove the original link—the original name of the file. Any added links will work just as well. In the next example, the **today** file is removed with the **rm** command. However, there is a link to that same file called **weather**. The file can then be referenced under the name **weather**.

```
$ ln today weather
$ rm today
$ cat weather
The storm broke today
and the sun came out.
$
```

Symbolic Links and Hard Links

Linux supports what are known as symbolic links. Links, as they have been described so far, are called *hard links*. Though hard links will suffice for most of your needs, they suffer from one major limitation. A hard link may fail when you try to link to a file on some other user's directory. This is because the Linux file structure can be physically segmented into what are called *file systems*. A file system can be made up of any physical memory device or devices, from a floppy disk to a bank of hard disks. Though the files and directories in all file systems are attached to the same overall directory tree, each file system will physically manage its own files and directories. This means that a file in one file system cannot be linked by a hard link to a file in another file system. If you try to link to a file on another user's directory that is located on another file system, your hard link will fail.

To overcome this restriction, you use symbolic links. A *symbolic link* holds the path name of the file it is linking to. It is not a direct hard link, but rather information on how to locate a specific file. Instead of registering another name for the same file as a hard link does, a symbolic link can be thought of as another symbol that represents the file's path name. It is another way of writing the file's path name.

You create a symbolic link using the **ln** command with the **-s** option. In the next example, the user creates a link called **lunch** to the file **/home/george/veglist**:

```
$ ln -s lunch /home/george/veglist
```

If you list the full information about a symbolic link and its file, you will find that the information displayed is different. In the next example, the user lists the full information for both **lunch** and **/home/george/veglist** using the **ls** command with the **-l** option. The first character in the line specifies the file type. Symbolic links have their own file type represented by a l. The file type for **lunch** is l, indicating that it is a symbolic link, not an ordinary file. The number after the term *group* is the size of the file. Notice that the sizes differ. The size of the **lunch** file is only four bytes. This is because **lunch** is only a symbolic link—a file that holds the path name of another file—and a path name takes up only a few bytes. It is not a direct hard link to the **veglist** file.

```
$ ls lunch /home/george/veglist
lrw-rw-r-- 1   chris    group 4     Feb  14    10:30    lunch
-rw-rw-r-- 1   george   group 793   Feb  14    10:30    veglist
```

To erase a file, you need to remove only its hard links. If there are any symbolic links left over, they will not be able to access the file. In this case, a symbolic link would hold the path name of a file that no longer exists.

Unlike hard links, you can use symbolic links to create links to directories. In effect, you can create another name with which you can reference a directory. However, if you use a symbolic link for a directory name, bear in mind that the **pwd** command always displays the actual directory name, not the symbolic name. In the next example, the user links the directory **thankyou** with the symbolic link **gifts**. When the user uses **gifts** in the **cd** command, the user is actually changed to the **thankyou** directory. The **pwd** command will display the path name for the **thankyou** directory.

```
$ ln -s /home/chris/letters/thankyou  gifts
$ cd gifts
$ pwd
/home/chris/letters/thankyou
$
```

If you want to display the name of the symbolic link, you can access it in the **cwd** variable. The **cwd** variable is a special system variable that holds the name of a directory's symbolic link, if there is one. Variables such as **cwd** are discussed in Chapter 15. You display the contents of **cwd** with the command **echo $cwd**.

```
$ pwd
/home/chris/letters/thankyou
$ echo $cwd
/home/chris/gifts
```

File and Directory Permissions: chmod

Each file and directory in Linux contains a set of permissions that determines who can access them and how. You set these permissions to limit access in one of three ways: you can restrict access to yourself alone, you can allow users in a predesignated group to have access, or you can permit anyone on your system to have access; and, you can control how a given file or directory is accessed. A file and directory may have read, write, and execute permission. When a file is created, it is automatically given read and write permissions for the owner, allowing you to display and modify the file. You may change these permissions to any combination you want. A file could have read-only permission, preventing any modifications. It could also have execute permission, allowing it to be executed as a program.

There are three different categories of users that can have access to a file or directory: the owner, the group, or others. The *owner* is the user who created the file. Any file that you create, you own. You can also permit your group to have access to a file. Often, users are collected into *groups*. For example, all the users for a given class or project could be formed into a group by the system administrator. It is possible for a user to give access to a file to other members of the group. Finally, you can also open up access to a file to all other users on the system. In this case, every user on your system could have access to one of your files or directories. In this sense, every other user on the system makes up the *others* category.

Each category has its own set of read, write, and execute permissions. The first set controls the user's own access to his or her files—the owner access. The second set controls the access of the group to a user's files. The third controls the access of all other users to the user's files. The three sets of read, write, and execute permissions for the three categories— owner, group, and other—make a total of nine types of permissions.

As you saw in the previous section, the **ls** command with the **-l** option displays detailed information about the file, including the permissions. In the next example, the first set of characters on the left is a list of the permissions that have been set for the **mydata** file.

```
$ ls -l mydata
-rw-r--r-- 1 chris weather 207 Feb 20 11:55 mydata
```

An empty permission is represented by a dash, **-**. The read permission is represented by *r*, write by *w*, and execute by *x*. Notice that there are ten positions. The first character indicates the file type. In a general sense, a directory can be considered a type of file. If the first character is a dash, a file is being listed. If it is *d*, information about a directory is being displayed.

The next nine characters are arranged according to the different user categories. The first set of three characters is the owner's set of permissions for the file. The second set of three characters is the group's set of permissions for the file. The last set of three characters is the other users' set of permissions for the file. In Figure 9-7, the **mydata** file has the read and write permissions set for the owner category, the read permission only set for the group category, and the read permission set for the other users category. This means that, though anyone in the group or any other user on the system can read the file, only the owner can modify it.

You use the **chmod** command to change different permission configurations. This command takes two lists as its arguments: permission changes and file names. You can specify the list of permissions in two different ways. One way uses permission symbols and is referred to as the *symbolic method*. The other uses what is known as a *binary mask* and is referred to as either the *absolute* or the *relative method*. Of the two, the symbolic method is the more intuitive and will be presented first. Table 9-7, at the end of the chapter, lists options for the **chmod** command.

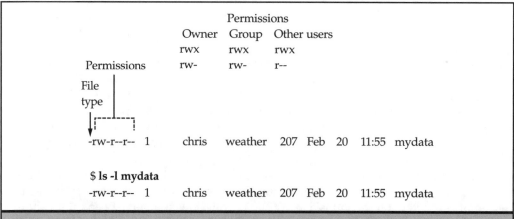

Figure 9-7.   *Owner, group, and other file permissions: r stands for read permission, w for write, and x for execute; a dash is a permission that is off*

ENVIRONMENTS

Command or Option	Execution
`chmod`	Changes the permission of a file or directory.
Options	
`+`	Adds a permission.
`-`	Removes a permission.
`=`	Assigns an entire set of permissions.
`r`	Sets read permission for a file or directory. A file can be displayed or printed. A directory can have the list of its files displayed.
`w`	Sets write permission for a file or directory. A file can be edited or erased. A directory can be removed.
`x`	Sets execute permission for a file or directory. If the file is a shell script, it can be executed as a program. A directory can be changed to and entered.
`u`	Sets permissions for the user who created and owns the file or directory.
`g`	Sets permissions for group access to a file or directory.
`o`	Sets permissions for access to a file or directory by all other users on the system.
`a`	Sets permissions for access by the user, group, and all other users.
`s`	Set User ID and Group ID permission; program owned by owner and group.
`t`	Sets sticky bit permission; program remains in memory.
`chgrp` *groupname filenames*	Changes the group for a file or files.
`chown` *user-name filenames*	Changes the owner of a file or files.
`ls -l` *filename*	Lists a file name with its permissions displayed.
`ls -ld` *directory*	Lists a directory name with its permissions displayed.
`ls -l`	Lists all files in a directory with its permissions displayed.

Table 9-7.   *File and Directory Permission Operations*

Setting Permissions: Permission Symbols

As you might have guessed, the symbolic method of setting permissions uses the characters *r*, *w*, and *x* for read, write, and execute, respectively. Any of these permissions can be added or removed. The symbol to add a permission is the plus sign, **+**. The symbol to remove a permission is the minus sign, **-**. In the next example, the **chmod** command adds the execute permission and removes the write permission for the **mydata** file. The read permission is not changed.

```
$ chmod +x-w mydata
```

There are also permission symbols that specify each user category. The owner, group, and others categories are represented by the *u*, *g*, and *o* characters, respectively. Notice that the owner category is represented by a *u* and can be thought of as the user. The symbol for a category is placed before the read, write, and execute permissions. If no category symbol is used, all categories are assumed, and the permissions specified are set for the user, group, and others. In the next example, the first **chmod** command sets the permissions for the group to read and write. The second **chmod** command sets permissions for other users to read. Notice that there are no spaces between the permission specifications and the category. The permissions list is simply one long phrase with no spaces.

```
$ chmod g+rw mydata
$ chmod o+r mydata
```

A user may remove permissions as well as add them. In the next example, the read permission is set for other users, but the write and execute permissions are removed.

```
$ chmod o+r-wx mydata
```

There is another permission symbol, *a*, that represents all the categories. The *a* symbol is the default. In the next example, both commands are equivalent. The read permission is explicitly set with the *a* symbol denoting all types of users: other, group, and user.

```
$ chmod a+r mydata
$ chmod +r mydata
```

One of the most common permission operations is setting a file's executable permission. This is often done in the case of shell program files, which are discussed in Chapters 8 and 16. The executable permission indicates that a file contains executable instructions and can be directly run by the system. In the next example, the file **lsc** has its executable permission set and then executed:

```
$ chmod u+x lsc
$ lsc
main.c lib.c
$
```

In addition to the read/write/execute permissions, you can also set ownership permissions for executable programs. Normally, the user that runs a program will own it while it is running, even though the program file itself may be owned by another user. The User ID permission allows the original owner of the program to always own it, even while another user is running the program. For example, most software on the system is owned by the root user but run by ordinary users. Some such software may have to modify files owned by the root. In this case, the ordinary user would need to run that program with the root retaining ownership so that the program could have the permissions to change those root-owned files. The Group ID permission works the same way except for groups. Programs owned by a group will retain ownership, even when run by users from another group. The program can then change the owner group's files.

To add both the User ID and Group ID permissions to a file, you use the **s** option. The following example adds the User ID permission to the **pppd** program, which is owned by the root user. When an ordinary user runs **pppd**, the root user will retain ownership, allowing the **pppd** program to change root-owned files.

```
#   chmod +s /usr/sbin/pppd
```

The User ID and Group ID permissions show up as an *s* in the execute position of the owner and group segments. User ID and Group ID are essentially variations of the execute permission, *x*. Read, write, and User ID permission would be *rws* instead of just *rwx*.

```
# ls -l /usr/sbin/pppd
-rwsr-sr-x   1 root      root          84604 Aug 14   1996
/usr/sbin/pppd
```

One other special permission provides efficient use of programs. The sticky bit will instruct the system to keep a program in memory after it finishes execution. This is useful for small programs that are used frequently by many users. The sticky bit permission is *t*. The sticky bit shows up as a *t* in the execute position of the other permissions. A program with read and execute permission with the sticky bit would have its permissions displayed as *r-t*.

```
# chmod +t  /usr/X11R6/bin/xtetris
# ls -l /usr/X11R6/bin/xtetris
-rwxr-xr-t  1 root     root         27428 Nov 19  1996
/usr/X11R6/bin/xtetris
```

Absolute Permissions: Binary Masks

Instead of permission symbols, many users find it more convenient to use the absolute method. The *absolute method* changes all the permissions at once, instead of specifying one or the other. It uses a binary mask that references all the permissions in each category. The three categories, each with three permissions, conform to an octal binary format. Octal numbers have a base-eight structure. When translated into a binary number, each octal digit becomes three binary digits. A binary number is a set of 1 and 0 digits. Three octal digits in a number translate into three sets of three binary digits, which is nine altogether—and the exact number of permissions for a file.

You can use the octal digits as a mask to set the different file permissions. Each octal digit applies to one of the user categories. You can think of the digits matching up with the permission categories from left to right, beginning with the owner category. The first octal digit applies to the owner category, the second to the group, and the third to the others category.

The actual octal digit that you choose will determine the read, write, and execute permissions for each category. At this point, you need to know how octal digits translate into their binary equivalents. The following table shows how the different octal digits, 0 to 7, translate into their three-digit binary equivalents. You can think of the octal digit first being translated into its binary form, and then each of those three binary digits being used to set the read, write, and execute permissions. Each binary digit is then matched up with a corresponding permission, again moving from left to right. If a binary digit is 0, the permission is turned off. If the binary digit is 1, the permission is turned on. The first binary digit sets the read permission on or off, the second sets the write permission, and the third sets the execute permission. For example, an octal digit 6 translates into the binary digits 110. This would set the read and write permission on, but set the execute permission off.

Octal	Binary
0	000
1	001
2	010
3	011

Octal	Binary
4	100
5	101
6	110
7	111

When dealing with a binary mask, you need to specify three digits for all three categories as well as their permissions. This makes it less versatile than the permission symbols. To set the owner execute permission on and the write permission off for the **mydata** file, as well as retain the read permission, you need to use the octal digit 5 (101). At the same time, you need to specify the digits for group and other users access. If these categories are to retain read access, you need the octal number 4 for each (100). This gives you three octal digits, 544, which translate into the binary digits 101 100 100.

```
$ chmod 544 mydata
```

One of the most common uses of the binary mask is to set the execute permission. As Chapter 8 describes, you can create files that contain Linux commands. Such files are called *shell scripts*. To have the commands in a shell script executed, you must first indicate that the file is executable—that it contains commands that the system can execute. There are several ways to do this, one of which is to set the executable permission on the shell script file. Suppose you just completed a shell script file and need to give it executable permission in order to run it. You also want to retain read and write permission, but deny any access by the group or other users. The octal digit 7 (111) will set all three permissions, including execute (you can also add 4-read, 2-write, and 1-execute to get 7). Using 0 for the group and other users denies them access. This gives you the digits 700, which are equivalent to the binary digits 111 000 000. In the next example, the owner permission for the **myprog** file is set to include execute permission:

```
$ chmod 700 myprog
```

If you want others to be able to execute and read the file but not change it, you can set the read and execute permissions and turn off the write permission with the digit 5 (101). In this case, you would use the octal digits 755, having the binary equivalent of 111 101 101.

```
$ chmod 755 myprog
```

For the ownership and sticky bit permissions, you add another octal number to the beginning of the octal digits. The octal digit for User ID permission is 4 (100); for Group ID, it is 2 (010); and for the sticky bit, it is 1 (001). The following example sets the User ID permission to the **pppd** program, along with read and execute permissions for the owner, group, and others:

```
#   chmod 4555 /usr/sbin/pppd
```

The following example sets the sticky bit for the **xtetris** program:

```
# chmod 1755   /usr/X11R6/bin/xtetris
```

The next example would set both the sticky bit and the User ID permission on the **xman** program. The permission 5755 has the binary equivalent of 101 111 101 101.

```
# chmod 5755 /usr/X11R6/bin/xman
# ls -l /usr/X11R6/bin/xman
-rwsr-xr-t   1 root      root        44364 Mar 26 04:28
/usr/X11R6/bin/xman
```

Directory Permissions

You can also set permissions on directories. The read permission set on a directory allows the list of files in a directory to be displayed. The execute permission allows a user to change to that directory. The write permission allows a user to create and remove his or her files in that directory. If you allow other users to have write permission on a directory, they can add their own files to it. When you create a directory, it is automatically given read, write, and execute permission for the owner. You may list the files in that directory, change to it, and create files in it.

Like files, directories have sets of permissions for the owner, the group, and all other users. Often, you may want to allow other users to change to and list the files in one of your directories, but not let them add their own files to it. In this case, you would set read and execute permissions on the directory, but not write permission. This would allow other users to change to the directory and list the files in it, but not create new files or copy any of their files into it. The next example sets read and execute permission for the group for the **thankyou** directory, but removes the write permission. Members of the group may enter the **thankyou** directory and list the files there, but they may not create new ones.

```
$ chmod g+rx-w letters/thankyou
```

Just as with files, you can also use octal digits to set a directory permission. To set the same permissions as in the previous example, you would use the octal digits 750, which have the binary equivalents of 111 101 000.

```
$ chmod 750 letters/thankyou
```

As you know, the **ls** command with the **-l** option will list all files in a directory. To list only the information about the directory itself, add a **d** modifier. In the next example, **ls -ld** displays information about the **thankyou** directory. Notice that the first character in the permissions list is *d*, indicating that it is a directory.

```
$ ls -ld thankyou
drwxr-x---  2  chris 512 Feb 10 04:30   thankyou
```

If you have files that you want other users to have access to, you need to not only set permissions for that file, but also make sure that the permissions are set for the directory that the file is in. Another user, in order to access your file, must first access the file's directory. The same applies to parents of directories. Though a directory may give permission to others to access it, if its parent directory denies access, the directory cannot be reached. In this respect, you have to pay close attention to your directory tree. To provide access to a directory, all other directories above it in the directory tree must also be accessible to other users.

Changing a File's Owner or Group: chown and chgrp

Though other users may be able to access a file, only the owner can change its permissions. If, however, you want to give some other user control over one of your file's permissions, you can change the owner of the file from yourself to the other user. The **chown** command transfers control over a file to another user. This command takes as its first argument the name of the other user. Following the user name, you can list the files you are giving up. In the next example, the user gives control of the **mydata** file to robert:

```
$ chown robert mydata
$ ls -l mydata
-rw-r--r--  1  robert weather 207  Feb  20 11:55  mydata
```

You can also, if you wish, change the group for a file, using the **chgrp** command. **chgrp** takes as its first argument the name of the new group for a file or files.

Following the new group name, you then list the files that you want changed to that group. In the next example, the user changes the group name for **today** and **weekend** to the **forecast** group. The `ls -l` command then reflects the group change.

```
$ chgrp forecast today weekend
$ ls -l
-rw-r--r--  1  chris weather 207  Feb  20 11:55  mydata
-rw-rw-r--  1  chris forecast 568  Feb  14 10:30  today
-rw-rw-r--  1  chris forecast 308  Feb  17 12:40  weekend
```

The Complete Reference

Linux

Chapter 10

Shell Features and Configuration

our different major shells are commonly used on Linux systems: the Bourne Again shell (BASH), the Public Domain Korn shell (PDKSH), the TCSH shell, and the Z-shell. The BASH shell is an advanced version of the Bourne shell, which includes most of the advanced features developed for the Korn shell and C-shell. TCSH is an enhanced version of the C-shell that was originally developed for BSD versions of Unix. PDKSH is a subset of the Unix Korn shell, whereas the Z-shell is an enhanced version of the Korn shell. Though their Unix counterparts differ greatly, the Linux shells share many of the same features. In Unix, the Bourne shell lacks many capabilities found in the other Unix shells. However, in Linux, the BASH shell incorporates all the advanced features of the Korn shell and C-shell, as well as the TCSH shell.

All four shells are available for your use, though the BASH shell is the default. All examples so far in this book have used the BASH shell. You log into your default shell, but you can change to another shell by entering its name. **tcsh** invokes the TCSH shell, **bash** the BASH shell, **ksh** the PDKSH shell, and **zsh** the Z-shell. You can leave a shell with the CTRL-D or **exit** command. You only need one type of shell to do your work. This chapter describes common features of the BASH shell such as history and aliases, as well as how to configure the shell to your own needs using shell variables and initialization files. The other shells share many of the same features and use similar variables and initialization files.

Command and File Name Completion

The BASH command line has a built-in feature that performs command and file name completion. If you enter an incomplete pattern as a command or file name argument, you can then press the TAB key to activate the command and file name completion feature, which will complete the pattern. If there is more than one command or file with the same prefix, the shell will simply beep and wait for you to add enough characters to select a unique command or file name. In the next example, the user issues a **cat** command with an incomplete file name. Upon pressing the TAB key, the system searches for a match and, when it finds one, fills in the file name. The user can then press ENTER to execute the command.

```
$ cat pre tab
$ cat preface
```

The shell can also perform file name completion to list the partially matching files in your current directory. If you press ESC followed by a question mark, ESC-?, the shell will list all the file names matching the incomplete pattern. In the next example, the ESC-? after the incomplete file name generates a list of possible file names. The shell then redraws the command line, and you can type in the complete name of the file you want, or type in distinguishing characters and press the TAB key to have the file name completed.

```
$ ls
document docudrama
$ cat doc escape ?
document
docudrama
$ cat docudrama
```

Command Line Editing

The BASH shell has built-in command line editing capabilities that let you easily modify commands you have entered before executing them. If you make a spelling mistake when entering a command, rather than reentering the entire command, you can use the editing operations to correct the mistake before executing the command. This is particularly helpful for commands that use arguments with lengthy path names. The command line editing operations are a subset of the Emacs editing commands (see Table 10-1). You can use CTRL-F or the RIGHT ARROW key to move forward a character, the CTRL-B or the LEFT ARROW key to move back a character. CTRL-D or DEL will delete the character the cursor is on. To add text, you just move the cursor to where you want to insert text and type in the new characters. At any time, you can press ENTER to execute the command. As described in the next section, you can also use the command line editing operations to modify history events—previous commands that you have entered.

Command Line Editing

CTRL-B or LEFT ARROW	Moves left one character (backward to the previous character)
CTRL-F or RIGHT ARROW	Moves right one character (forward to the next character)
CTRL-A	Moves to beginning of a line
CTRL-A	Moves to end of a line
ESC-F	Moves forward one word
ESC-B	Moves backward one word
DEL	Deletes the character the cursor is on

Table 10-1.   *Command Line Editing, History Commands, and History Event References*

Command Line Editing

BACKSPACE or CTRL-H	Deletes the character before the cursor
CTRL-D	Deletes the character after the cursor
CTRL-K	Removes (kills) the remainder of a line

History Commands

CTRL-N or DOWN ARROW	Moves down to the next event in the history list
CTRL-P or UP ARROW	Moves up to the previous event in the history list
ESC-<	Moves to beginning of the history event list
ESC->	Moves to end of the history event list
ESC-TAB	History event matching and completion
fc *event-reference*	Edits an event with the standard editor and then executes it: **options** –l List recent history events; same as **history** command –e *editor event-reference* Invokes a specified editor to edit a specific event

History Event References

! *event num*	References an event with event number
! *characters*	References an event with beginning characters
! **?***pattern***?**	References an event with a pattern in the event
! *–event num*	References an event with an offset from the first event
! *num–num*	References a range of events

Table 10-1.   *Command Line Editing, History Commands, and History Event References* (continued)

History

In the BASH shell, the history utility keeps a record of the most recent commands you have executed. The commands are numbered starting at 1, and there is a limit to the number of commands remembered—the default is 500. The history utility is a kind of short-term memory, keeping track of the most recent commands you have executed.

To see the set of your most recent commands, type **history** on the command line and press ENTER. A list of your most recent commands is then displayed, preceded by a number.

```
$ history
1 cp mydata today
2 vi mydata
3 mv mydata reports

4 cd reports
5 ls
```

Each of these commands is technically referred to as an "event." An event describes an action that has been taken—a command that has been executed. The events are numbered according to their sequence of execution. The most recent event has the highest number. Each of these events can be identified by its number or beginning characters in the command.

The history utility lets you reference a former event, placing it on your command line and allowing you to execute it. The easiest way to do this is to use the UP ARROW and DOWN ARROW keys to place history events on your command line one at a time. You do not need to display the list first with **history**. Pressing the UP ARROW key once will place the last history event on your command line. Pressing it again places the next history event on your command. Pressing the DOWN ARRROW key will place the previous event on the command line.

The BASH shell also has a history event completion operation invoked by the ESC-TAB command. Much like standard command line completion, you enter part of the history event that you want. Then you press ESC, followed by TAB. The event that matches the text you have entered will be located and used to complete your command line entry. If more than one history event matches what you have entered, you will hear a beep, and you can then enter more characters to help uniquely identify the event you want.

You can then edit the event displayed on your command line using the command line editing operations. The LEFT ARROW and RIGHT ARROW keys move you along the command line. You can insert text wherever you stop your cursor. With BACKSPACE and DEL, you can delete characters. Once the event is displayed on your command line, you can press ENTER to execute it.

You can also reference and execute history events using the ! history command. The ! is followed by a reference that identifies the command. The reference can be either the number of the event or a beginning set of characters in the event. In the next example, the third command in the history list is referenced first by number and then by the beginning characters:

```
$ !3
mv mydata reports
```

```
$ !mv
mv mydata reports
```

You can also reference an event using an offset from the end of the list. A negative number will offset from the end of the list to that event, thereby referencing it. In the next example, the fourth command, **cd mydata**, is referenced using a negative offset, and then executed. Remember that you are offsetting from the end of the list—in this case, event 5, up toward the beginning of the list, event 1. An offset of 4 beginning from event 5 places you at event 2.

```
$ !-4
vi mydata
```

If no event reference is used, then the last event is assumed. In the next example, the command ! by itself executes the last command the user executed—in this case, **ls**:

```
$ !
ls
mydata today reports
```

History Event Editing

You can also edit any event in the history list before you execute it. In the BASH shell, there are two ways to do this. You can use the command line editor capability to reference and edit any event in the history list. You can also use a history **fc** command option to reference an event and edit it with the full Vi editor. Each approach involves two very different editing capabilities. The first is limited to the commands in the command line editor, which edits only a single line with a subset of Emacs commands. However, at the same time, it allows you to reference events easily in the history list. The second approach invokes the standard Vi editor with all of its features, but only for a specified history event.

With the command line editor, not only can you edit the current command, but you can also move to a previous event in the history list to edit and execute it. The CTRL-P command then moves you up to the prior event in the list. The CTRL-N command will move you down the list. The ESC-< command moves you to the top of the list, and the ESC-> command moves you to the bottom. You can even use a pattern to search for a given event. The slash followed by a pattern searches backward in the list, and the question mark followed by a pattern searches forward in the list. The **n** command repeats the search.

Once you have located the event you want to edit, you use the Emacs command line editing commands to edit the line. CTRL-D will delete a character. CTRL-F or the RIGHT ARROW move you forward a character, and CTRL-B or the LEFT ARROW move you back a character. To add text, you position your cursor and type in the characters you want. Table 10-1 lists the different commands for referencing the history list.

If, instead, you want to edit an event using a standard editor, you need to reference the event using the **fc** command and a specific event reference, such as an event number. The editor used is the one specified by the shell as the default editor for the **fc** command. The next example will edit the fourth event, **cd reports**, with the standard editor and then execute the edited event:

```
$ fc 4
```

You can select more than one command at a time to be edited and executed by referencing a range of commands. You select a range of commands by indicating an identifier for the first command followed by an identifier for the last command in the range. An identifier can be the command number or the beginning characters in the command. In the next example, the range of commands 2 through 4 are edited and executed, first using event numbers and then using beginning characters in those events:

```
$ fc 2 4
$ fc vi c
```

The **fc** command uses the default editor specified in the **FCEDIT** special variable. Usually, this is the Vi editor. If you want to use the Emacs editor instead, you use the **-e** option and the term **emacs** when you invoke **fc**. The next example will edit the fourth event, **cd reports**, with the Emacs editor and then execute the edited event:

```
$ fc -e emacs 4
```

Configuring History: HISTFILE and HISTSAVE

The number of events saved by your system is kept in a special system variable called **HISTSIZE**. By default, this is usually set to 500. You can change this to another number by simply assigning a new value to **HISTSIZE**. In the next example, the user changes the number of history events saved to 10 by resetting the **HISTSIZE** variable:

```
$ HISTSIZE=10
```

The actual history events are saved in a file whose name is held in a special variable called **HISTFILE**. By default, this file is the **.bash_history** file. However, you can change the file in which history events are saved by assigning its name to the **HISTFILE** variable.

In the next example, the value of **HISTFILE** is displayed. Then a new file name is assigned to it, **newhist**. History events will then be saved in the **newhist** file.

```
$ echo $HISTFILE
.bash_history
$ HISTFILE="newhist"
$ echo $HISTFILE
newhist
```

Aliases

You use the **alias** command to create another name for a command. The **alias** command operates like a macro that expands to the command it represents. The alias does not literally replace the name of the command; it simply gives another name to that command. An **alias** command begins with the keyword **alias** and the new name for the command, followed by an equal sign and the command that the alias will reference. There can be no spaces around the equal sign. In the next example, **list** becomes another name for the **ls** command:

```
$ alias list=ls
$ ls
mydata today
$ list
mydata today
$
```

You can also use an alias to substitute for a command and its option. However, you need to enclose both the command and the option within single quotes. Any command that you alias that contains spaces must be enclosed in single quotes. In the next example, the alias **lss** references the **ls** command with its **-s** option, and the alias **lsa** references with the **-F** option. The **ls** command with the **-s** option lists files and their sizes in blocks, and the **ls** with the **-F** option places a slash before directory names. Notice that single quotes enclose the command and its option.

```
$ alias lss='ls -s'
$ lss

mydata 14    today  6    reports  1
$ alias lsa='ls -F'
$ lsa
```

```
mydata today /reports
$
```

You may often use an alias to include a command name with an argument. If you find yourself executing a command that has an argument with a complex combination of special characters on a regular basis, you may want to alias it. For example, suppose you often list just your source code and object code files—those files ending in either a **.c** or **.o**. You would need to use as an argument for **ls** a combination of special characters—***.[co]**. Instead, you could alias **ls** with the ***.[co]** argument, giving it a simple name. In the next example, the user creates an alias called **lsc** for the command **ls*.[co]**:

```
$ alias lsc='ls *.[co]'
$ lsc
main.c main.o lib.c lib.o
```

You can also use the name of a command as an alias. This can be helpful in cases where you should only use a command with a specific option. In the case of the **rm**, **cp**, and **mv** commands, the **-i** option should always be used to ensure that an existing file is not overwritten. Instead of constantly being careful to use the **-i** option each time you use one of these commands, the command name can be aliased to include the option. In the next example, the **rm**, **cp**, and **mv** commands have been aliased to include the **-i** option:

```
$ alias rm='rm -i'
$ alias mv='mv -i'
$ alias cp='cp -i'
```

The **alias** command by itself provides a list of all aliases in effect and their commands. You can remove an alias by using the **unalias** command. In the next example, the user lists the current aliases and then removes the **lsa** alias:

```
$ alias
lsa=ls -F
list=ls

rm=rm -i
$ unalias lsa
```

Controlling Shell Operations

The BASH shell has several features that allow you to control the way different shell operations work. For example, setting the **noclobber** feature prevents redirection from overwriting files. You can turn these features on and off like a toggle, using the **set** command. The **set** command takes two arguments: an option specifying on or off and the name of the feature. To set a feature on, you use the **-o** option, and to set it off, you use the **+o** option. Here is the basic form:

```
$ set -o feature        turn the feature on
$ set +o feature        turn the feature off
```

Three of the most common features are described here: **ignoreeof**, **noclobber**, and **noglob**. Table 10-2 (later in this chapter) lists these different features as well as the **set** command. Setting **ignoreeof** enables a feature that prevents you from logging out of the user shell with a CTRL-D. CTRL-D is not only used to log out of the user shell, but also to end user input that is entered directly into the standard input. It is used often for the mailx program or for utilities such as **cat**. You could easily enter an extra CTRL-D in such circumstances and accidentally log yourself out. The **ignoreeof** feature prevents such accidental logouts. In the next example, the **ignoreeof** feature is turned on using the **set** command with the **-o** option. The user can now only log out by entering the **logout** command.

```
$ set -o ignoreeof
$ ctrl-d
Use exit to logout
$
```

Setting **noclobber** enables a feature that safeguards existing files from redirected output. With the **noclobber** feature, if you redirect output to a file that already exists, the file will not be overwritten with the standard output. The original file will be preserved. There may be situations in which you use, as the name for a file to hold the redirected output, a name that you have already given to an existing file. The **noclobber** feature prevents you from accidentally overwriting your original file. In the next example, the user sets the **noclobber** feature on and then tries to overwrite an existing file, **myfile**, using redirection. The system returns an error message.

```
$ set -o noclobber
$ cat preface > myfile
myfile: file exists
$
```

There may be times when you want to overwrite a file with redirected output. In this case, you can place an exclamation point after the redirection operator. This will override the **noclobber** feature, replacing the contents of the file with the standard output.

```
$ cat preface >! myfile
```

Setting **noglob** enables a feature that disables special characters in the user shell. The characters *****, **?**, **[]**, and **~** will no longer expand to matched file names. This feature is helpful if you have special characters as part of the name of a file. In the next example, the user needs to reference a file that ends with the **?** character, **answers?**. First the user turns off special characters using the **noglob** feature. Now the question mark on the command line is taken as part of the file name, not as a special character, and the user can reference the **answers?** file.

```
$ set -o noglob
$ ls answers?
answers?
```

Environment Variables and Subshells: export

When you log in to your account, Linux generates your user shell. Within this shell, you can issue commands and declare variables. You can also create and execute shell scripts. However, when you execute a shell script, the system generates a subshell. You then have two shells, the one you logged into and the one generated for the script. Within the script shell, you could execute another shell script, which would have its own shell. When a script has finished execution, its shell terminates and you return to the shell it was executed from. In this sense, you can have many shells, each nested within the other. Variables that you define within a shell are local to it. If you define a variable in a shell script, then, when the script is run, the variable is defined with that script's shell and is local to it. No other shell can reference it. In a sense, the variable is hidden within its shell.

You can define environment variables in all types of shells including the BASH, Z-shell, and TCSH shells. However, the strategy used to implement environment variables in the BASH shell is different from that of the TCSH shell. In the BASH shell, environment variables are exported. That is to say, a copy of an environment variable is made in each subshell. For example, if the **myfile** variable is exported, a copy is automatically defined in each subshell for you. In the TCSH shell, on the other hand, an environment variable is defined only once and can be directly referenced by any subshell.

In the BASH shell, an environment variable can be thought of as a regular variable with added capabilities. To make an environment variable, you apply the **export** command to a variable you have already defined. The **export** command instructs the system to define a copy of that variable for each new shell generated. Each new shell will have its own copy of the environment variable. This process is called "exporting variables." It is a mistake to think of exported environment variables as global variables. A new shell can never reference a variable outside of itself. Instead, a copy of the variable with its value is generated for the new shell. You can think of exported variables as exporting their values to a shell, not themselves. For those familiar with programming structures, exported variables can be thought of as a form of "call by value."

Configuring Your Shell with Special Shell Variables

When you log in to your account, the system generates a shell for you. This shell is referred to as either your login shell or your user shell. When you execute scripts, you are generating subshells of your user shell. You can define variables within your user shell, and you can also define environment variables that can be referenced by any subshells that you generate. Linux sets up special shell variables that you can use to configure your user shell. Many of these special shell variables are defined by the system when you log in, but you define others yourself. See Table 10-2 for a list of the commonly used ones.

A reserved set of keywords is used for the names of these special variables. You should not use these keywords as the names of any of your own variable names. The special shell variables are all specified in uppercase letters, making them easy to identify. Shell feature variables are in lowercase. For example, the keyword **HOME** is used by the system to define the **HOME** variable. **HOME** is a special environment variable that holds the path name of the user's **home** directory. On the other hand, the keyword **noclobber**, covered earlier in the chapter, is used to set the **noclobber** feature on or off.

Common Special Variables

Many of the special variables that are automatically defined and assigned initial values by the system when you log in can be changed, if you wish. However, there are some special variables whose values should not be changed. For example, the **HOME** variable holds the path name for your **home** directory. Commands such as **cd** reference the path name in the **HOME** special variable in order to locate your **home** directory. Some of the more common of these special variables are described in this section. Other special variables are defined by the system and given an initial value that you are free to change. To do this, you redefine them and assign a new value. For example, the **PATH** variable is defined by the system and given an initial value; it contains the path names of directories where commands are located. Whenever you execute a command, the shell searches for it in these directories. You can add a new directory to be searched by redefining the **PATH** variable yourself so that it will include the new directory's path name. There are still other special variables that the system does not define. These are usually optional features, such as the **EXINIT** variable that allows you to set options for the Vi editor. You must define and assign a value to such variables each time you log in. You can obtain a listing of the currently defined special variables using the **env** command. The **env** command operates like the **set** command, but only lists special variables.

You can automatically define special variables using special shell scripts called "initialization files." An initialization file is a specially named shell script executed whenever you enter a certain shell. You can edit the initialization file and place in it definitions and assignments for special variables. When you enter the shell, the initialization file will execute these definitions and assignments, effectively initializing special variables with your own values. For example, the BASH shell's **.bash_profile** file is an initialization file that is executed every time you log in. It contains definitions and assignments of special variables. However, the **.bash_profile** file is basically only a shell script, which you can edit with any text editor such as the Vi editor; changing, if you wish, the values assigned to special variables. Instead of the name **.bash_profile**, the BASH shell initialization file may be called **.profile**, as it is in OpenLinux.

In the BASH shell, all the special variables are designed to be environment variables. When you define or redefine a special variable, you also need to export it in order to make it an environment variable. This means that any change you make to a special variable must be accompanied by an **export** command. You shall see that at the end of the login initialization file, **.bash_profile**, there is usually an **export** command for all the special variables defined in it.

The **HOME** variable contains the path name of your **home** directory. Your **home** directory is determined by the system administrator when your account is created. The path name for your **home** directory is automatically read into your **HOME** variable when you log in. In the next example, the **echo** command displays the contents of the **HOME** variable:

```
$ echo $HOME
/home/chris
```

The **HOME** variable is often used when you need to specify the absolute path name of your **home** directory. In the next example, the absolute path name of **reports** is specified using **HOME** for the **home** directory's path:

```
$ ls $HOME/reports
```

Some of the more common special variables are **SHELL**, **PATH**, **PS1**, **PS2**, and **MAIL**. The **SHELL** variable holds the path name of the program for the type of shell that you log into. The **PATH** variable lists the different directories to be searched for a Linux command. The **PS1** and **PS2** variables hold the prompt symbols. The **MAIL** variable holds the path name of your mailbox file. You can modify the values for any of them to customize your shell.

The **PATH** variable contains a series of directory paths separated by colons. Each time a command is executed, the paths listed in the **PATH** variable are searched one by one for that command. For example, the **cp** command resides on the system in the directory **/usr/bin**. This directory path is one of the directories listed in the **PATH** variable. Each time you execute the **cp** command, this path is searched and the **cp** command located. The system defines and assigns **PATH** an initial set of path names. In Linux, the initial path names are **/usr/bin** and **usr/sbin**.

The shell can execute any executable file, including programs and scripts that you have created. For this reason, the **PATH** variable can also reference your working directory; so if you want to execute one of your own scripts or programs in your working directory, the shell can locate it. There can be no spaces between the path names in the string. A colon with no path name specified references your working directory. Usually, a single colon is placed at the end of the path names as an empty entry specifying your working directory. For example, the path name **/usr/bin:/usr/sbin:** references three directories: **/usr/bin**, **/usr/sbin**, and your current working directory.

```
$ echo $PATH
/usr/bin:/usr/sbin:
```

You can add any new directory path you wish to the **PATH** variable. This can be very useful if you have created several of your own Linux commands using shell scripts. You could place these new shell script commands in a directory you created and then add that directory to the **PATH** list. Then, no matter what directory you are in, you can execute one of your shell scripts. The **PATH** variable will contain the directory for that script, so that directory will be searched each time you issue a command.

You add a directory to the **PATH** variable with a variable assignment. You can execute this assignment directly in your shell. In the next example, the user **chris** adds a new directory called **mybin** to the **PATH**. Though you could carefully type in the complete path names listed in **PATH** for the assignment, you can also use an evaluation of **PATH**, **$PATH**, in their place. In this example, an evaluation of **HOME** is also used to designate the user's **home** directory in the new directory's path name. Notice the empty entry between two colons, which specifies the working directory.

```
$ PATH=$PATH:$HOME/mybin:
$ export PATH
$ echo $PATH
/usr/bin:/usr/sbin::/home/chris/mybin
```

If you add a directory to **PATH** yourself while you are logged in, the directory would be added only for the duration of your login session. When you log back in, the login initialization file, **.bash_profile**, would again initialize your **PATH** with its original set of directories. The **.bash_profile** file is described in detail a bit later in the chapter. To permanently add a new directory to your **PATH**, you need to edit your **.bash_profile** file and find the assignment for the **PATH** variable. Then, you simply insert the directory, preceded by a colon, into the set of path names assigned to **PATH**.

The **PS1** and **PS2** variables contain the primary and secondary prompt symbols, respectively. The primary prompt symbol for the BASH shell is a dollar sign, **$**. You can change the prompt symbol by assigning a new set of characters to the **PS1** variable. In the next example, the shell prompt is changed to the **->** symbol:

```
$ PS1="->"
-> export PS1
->
```

You can change the prompt to be any set of characters, including a string, as shown in the next example:

```
$ PS1="Please enter a command: "
Please enter a command: export PS1
Please enter a command: ls
mydata /reports
Please enter a command:
```

The **PS2** variable holds the secondary prompt symbol, which is used for commands that take several lines to complete. The default secondary prompt is **>**. The added command lines will begin with the secondary prompt instead of the primary prompt. You can change the secondary prompt just as easily as the primary prompt, as shown here:

```
$ PS2="@"
```

Like the TCSH shell, the BASH shell provides you with a predefined set of codes that you can use to configure your prompt. With them you can make the time, your user name, or your directory path name a part of your prompt. You can even have your prompt display the history event number of the current command you are about to enter. Each code is preceded by a **** symbol. **\w** represents the current working directory, **\t** the time, and **\u** your user name. **\!** will display the next history event number. In the next example, the user adds the current working directory to the prompt:

```
$ PS1="\w $"
/home/dylan $
```

The codes must be included within a quoted string. If there are no quotes, the code characters are not evaluated and are themselves used as the prompt. **PS1=\w** will set the prompt to the characters **\w**, not the working directory. The next example incorporates both the time and the history event number with a new prompt:

```
$ PS1="\t \! ->"
```

The following table lists the codes for configuring your prompt.

\!	Current history number
\$	Use **$** as prompt for all users except the root user, which has the **#** as its prompt
\d	Current date
\s	Shell currently active
\t	Time of day
\u	User name
\w	Current working directory

If **CDPATH** is undefined, then when the **cd** command is given a directory name as its argument, it searches only the current working directory for that name. However, if **CDPATH** is defined, **cd** will also search the directories listed in **CDPATH** for that directory name. If the directory name is found, **cd** changes to that directory. This is helpful if you are working on a project in which you constantly have to change to directories in another part of the file system. To change to a directory that has a path name very different from the one you are in, you would need to know the full path name of that directory. Instead, you could simply place the path name of that directory's parent in **CDPATH**. Then, **cd** will automatically search the parent directory, finding the name of the directory you want. Notice that you assign to **CDPATH** the path name of the parent of the directory you want to change to, not the path name of the directory itself.

It is advisable to use the **HOME** variable to specify the home directory part of the path in any new path name added to **CDPATH**. This is because it is possible that the path name for your home directory could be changed by the system administrator during a reorganization of the file system. **HOME** will always hold the current path name of the **home** directory. In the next example, the path name **/home/chris/letters** is specified with **$HOME/letters**:

```
$ CDPATH=$CDPATH:$HOME/letters
$ export CDPATH
$ echo $CDPATH
:/home/chris/letters
```

The **EXINIT** variable holds editor commands with which to configure the Ex and Vi editors. When you invoke these editors, the commands in the **EXINIT** variable are executed. These commands usually set other commands that specify such features as line numbering or indentation. In the next example, the **EXINIT** variable is assigned an editor **set** command to execute. This **set** command sets line numbering and automatic indent. Notice that the two commands can be abbreviated and combined into one string.

```
$ EXINIT='set nu ai'
$ export EXINIT
```

Several shell special variables are used to set values used by network applications such as Web browsers or newsreaders. **NNTPSERVER** is used to set the value of a remote news server accessible on your network. If you are using an ISP, the ISP usually provides a news server that you can access with your newsreader applications. However, you first have to provide your newsreaders with the Internet address of the news server. This is the role of the **NNTPSERVER**. News servers on the Internet usually use the NNTP protocol. **NNTPSERVER** should hold the address of such a news server. For many ISPs, the news server address is a domain name that begins with **nntp**. The following example assigns the news server address **nntp.myservice.com** to the **NNTPSERVER** special variables. Newsreader applications will automatically obtain the news server address from **NNTPSERVER**. Usually, this assignment is placed in the shell initialization file, **.bash_profile**, so that it is automatically set each time a user logs in.

```
NNTPSERVER=nntp.myservice.com
export NNTPSERVER
```

Other special variables are used for specific applications. The **KDEDIR** variable holds the path name for the KDE Desktop program files. This is usually **/opt/kde**, but at the time of installation you can choose to install KDE in a different directory and then change the value of **KDEDIR** accordingly.

```
export KDEDIR=/opt/kde
```

Table 10-2 lists several commonly used special variables.

BAS Shell Special Variables	Description
HOME	Path name for user's home directory
LOGNAME	Login name
USER	Login name

Table 10-2.   *BASH Shell Special Variables and Features*

BAS Shell Special Variables	Description
SHELL	Path name of program for type of shell you are using
PATH	List of path names for directories searched for executable commands
PS1	Primary shell prompt
PS2	Secondary shell prompt
IFS	Interfield delimiter symbol
MAIL	Name of mail file checked by mail utility for received messages
MAILCHECK	Interval for checking for received mail
MAILPATH	List of mail files to be checked by mail for received messages
TERM	Terminal name
CDPATH	Path names for directories searched by **cd** command for subdirectories
EXINIT	Initialization commands for Ex/Vi editor
BASH Shell Features	
$ **set -+o** *feature*	Korn shell features are turned on and off with the **set** command; **-o** sets a feature on and **+o** turns it off: $ **set -o noclobber** *set noclobber on* $ **set +o noclobber** *set noclobber off*
ignoreeof	Disabled CTRL-D logout
noclobber	Does not overwrite files through redirection
noglob	Disables special characters used for file name expansion: *****, **?**, **~**, and **[]**

Table 10-2.   *BASH Shell Special Variables and Features* (continued)

Configuring Your Login Shell: .bash_profile

The **.bash_profile** file is the BASH shell's login initialization file, which can also be named **.profile**. It is a script file that is automatically executed whenever a user logs in.

The file contains shell commands that define special environment variables used to manage your shell. They may be either redefinitions of system-defined special variables or definitions of user-defined special variables. For example, when you log in, your user shell needs to know what directories hold Linux commands. It will reference the **PATH** variable in order to find the path names for these directories. However, first, the **PATH** variable must be assigned those path names. In the .bash_profile file, there is an assignment operation that does just this. Since it is in the .bash_profile file, the assignment is executed automatically when the user logs in.

Special variables also need to be exported, using the **export** command, in order to make them accessible to any subshells you may enter. You can export several variables in one **export** command by listing them as arguments. Usually at the end of the .bash_profile file there is an **export** command with a list of all the variables defined in the file. If a variable is missing from this list, you may not be able to access it. Notice the **export** command at the end of the .**profile** file in the example described next. You can also combine the assignment and **export** command into one operation as shown here for **NNTPSEVER**.

```
export NNTPSERVER=nntp.myservice.com
```

A copy of the standard .**bash_profile** file provided for you when your account is created is listed in the next example. Notice how **PATH** is assigned, as is the value of **$HOME**. Both **PATH** and **HOME** are system special variables that the system has already defined. **PATH** holds the path names of directories searched for any command that you enter, and **HOME** holds the path name of your **home** directory. The assignment **PATH=$PATH:$HOME/bin** has the effect of redefining **PATH** to include your **bin** directory within your **home** directory. So, your **bin** directory will also be searched for any commands, including ones you create yourself, such as scripts or programs. Notice that **PATH** is then exported so that it can be accessed by any subshells. Should you want to have your **home** directory searched also, you can use any text editor to modify this line in your .**bash_profile** file to **PATH=$PATH:$HOME\bin:$HOME**, adding **: $HOME** at the end. In fact, you can change this entry to add as many directories as you want searched.

.bash_profile

```
# .bash_profile

# Get the aliases and functions
if [ -f ~/.bashrc ]; then
 . ~/.bashrc
fi
```

```
# User specific environment and startup programs

PATH=$PATH:$HOME/bin
BASH_ENV=$HOME/.bashrc
USERNAME=""

export USERNAME BASH_ENV PATH
```

Your Linux system also has its own profile file that it executes whenever any user logs in. This system initialization file is simply called **profile** and is found in the **/etc** directory, **/etc/profile**. It contains special variable definitions that the system needs to provide for each user. A copy of the system's **.profile** file follows. Notice how **PATH** is redefined to include the **/usr/X11R6/bin** directory. This is the directory that holds the X Windows commands that you execute when using the desktop. Also, **PATH** includes the path name for the KDE Desktop programs, **/opt/kde/bin**. **HISTFILE** is also redefined to include a larger number of history events. An entry has been added here for the **NNTPSERVER** variable. Normally, a news server address is a value that needs to be set for all users. Such assignments should be made in the system's **/etc/profile** file by the system administrator, rather than in each individual user's own **.bash_profile** file. The **/etc/profile** file also executes any scripts in the directory **/etc/profile.d**. This design allows for a more modular structure. Rather than make entries by editing the **/etc/profile** file, you can just add a script to the **profile.d** directory. The scripts for the BASH shell have the extension **.sh**. For example, the **kde.sh** script in the **profile.d** directory checks for a definition of the **KDEDIR** variable and makes one if none is in effect.

/etc/profile

```
# /etc/profile

# System wide environment and startup programs
# Functions and aliases go in /etc/bashrc

PATH="$PATH:/usr/X11R6/bin:/opt/kde/bin:"
PS1="[\u@\h \W]\\$ "

ulimit -c 1000000
if [ 'id -gn' = 'id -un' -a 'id -u' -gt 14 ]; then
    umask 002
else
    umask 022
fi
```

```
USER='id -un'
LOGNAME=$USER
MAIL="/var/spool/mail/$USER"

HOSTNAME='/bin/hostname'
HISTSIZE=1000
HISTFILESIZE=1000
NNTPSERVER=nntp.myservice.com
export PATH PS1 HOSTNAME HISTSIZE HISTFILESIZE USER LOGNAME
MAIL NNTPSERVER

for i in /etc/profile.d/*.sh ; do
    if [ -x $i ]; then
        . $i
    fi
done

unset i
```

Your **.bash_profile** initialization file is a text file that can be edited by a text editor, like any other text file. You can easily add new directories to your **PATH** by editing **.bash_profile** and using editing commands to insert a new directory path name in the list of directory path names assigned to the **PATH** variable. You can even add new variable definitions. However, if you do so, be sure to include the new variable's name in the **export** command's argument list. For example, if your **.bash_profile** file does not have any definition of the **EXINIT** variable, you can edit the file and add a new line that assigns a value to **EXINIT**. The definition **EXINIT='set nu ai'** will configure the Vi editor with line numbering and indentation. You then need to add **EXINIT** to the **export** command's argument list. When the **.bash_profile** file executes again, the **EXINIT** variable will be set to the command **set nu ai**. When the Vi editor is invoked, the command in the **EXINIT** variable will be executed, setting the line number and auto-indent options automatically.

In the following example, the user's **.bash_profile** has been modified to include definitions of **EXINIT** and redefinitions of **PATH**, **CDPATH**, **PS1**, and **HISTSIZE**. The **PATH** variable has **$HOME**: added to its value. **$HOME** is a variable that evaluates to the user's **home** directory and the ending colon specifies the current working directory, allowing you to execute commands that may be located in either the **home** directory or the working directory. The redefinition of **HISTSIZE** reduces the number of history events saved, from 1,000 defined in the system's **.profile** file, to 30. The redefinition of the **PS1** special variable changes the prompt to include the path name of the current working directory. Any changes that you make to special variables within your

.bash_profile file will override those made earlier by the system's **.profile** file. All these special variables are then exported with the **export** command.

.bash_profile

```
# .bash_profile
# Get the aliases and functions
if [ -f ~/.bashrc ];
 then
    . ~/.bashrc
fi
# User-specific environment and startup programs
PATH=$PATH:$HOME/bin:$HOME:
ENV=$HOME/.bashrc
USERNAME=""
CDPATH=$CDPATH:$HOME/bin:$HOME
HISTSIZE=30
NNTPSERVER=nntp.myserver.com
EXINIT='set nu ai'
PS1="\w \$"
export USERNAME ENV PATH CDPATH HISTSIZE EXINIT PS1 NNTPSERVER/
```

Though **.profile** is executed each time you log in, it is not automatically re-executed after you make changes to it. The **.profile** file is an initialization file that is *only* executed whenever you log in. If you want to take advantage of any changes you make to it without having to log out and log in again, you can re-execute **.profile** with the dot (.) command. The **.profile** is a shell script and, like any shell script, can be executed with the . command.

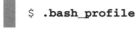

```
$ .bash_profile
```

Configuring the BASH Shell: .bashrc

The **.bashrc** file is a configuration file that is executed each time you enter the BASH shell or generate any subshells. If the BASH shell is your login shell, **.bashrc** is executed along with your **.bash_login** file when you log in. If you enter the BASH shell from another shell, the **.bashrc** file is automatically executed, and the variable and alias definitions it contains will be defined. Should you enter a different type of shell, then the configuration file for that shell will be executed instead. For example, if you were to enter the TCSH shell with the **tcsh** command, then the **.tcshrc** configuration file is executed instead of **.bashrc**.

The **.bashrc** shell configuration file is actually executed each time you generate a BASH shell, such as when you run a shell script. In other words, each time a subshell is created, the **.bashrc** file is executed. This has the effect of exporting any local variables or aliases that you have defined in the **.bashrc** shell initialization file. The **.bashrc** file usually contains the definition of aliases and any feature variables used to turn on shell features. Aliases and feature variables are locally defined within the shell. But the **.bashrc** file will define them in every shell. For this reason, the **.bashrc** file usually holds such aliases as those defined for the **rm**, **cp**, and **mv** commands. The next example is a **.bashrc** file with many of the standard definitions:

```
.bashrc

# Source global definitions
if [ -f /etc/bashrc ];
 then
    . /etc/bashrc
fi
set  -o ignoreeof
set  -o noclobber
alias rm 'rm -i'
alias mv 'mv -i'
alias cp 'cp -i'
```

Linux systems usually contain a system **.bashrc** file that is executed for all users. This may contain certain global aliases and features needed by all users whenever they enter a BASH shell. This is located in the **/etc** directory, **/etc/bashrc**. A user's own **.bashrc** file, located in the **home** directory, will contain commands to execute this system **.bashrc** file. The **. /etc/bashrc** command in the previous example of **.bashrc** does just that. You can add any commands or definitions of your own to your **.bashrc** file. If you have made changes to **.bashrc** and you want them to take effect during your current login session, you need to re-execute the file with either the **.** or the **source** command.

```
$ . .bashrc
```

The BASH Shell Logout File: .bash_logout

The **.bash_logout** file is also a configuration file, which is executed when the user logs out. It is designed to perform any operations you want done whenever you log out. Instead of variable definitions, the **.bash_logout** file usually contains shell commands that form a kind of shutdown procedure—actions you always want taken before you log out. One common logout command is to clear the screen and then issue a farewell message.

As with **.bash_profile**, you can add your own shell commands to **.bash_logout**. In fact, the **.bash_logout** file is not automatically set up for you when your account is first created. You need to create it yourself, using the Vi or Emacs editor. You could then add a farewell message or other operations. In the next example, the user has a **clear** and an **echo** command in the **.bash_logout** file. When the user logs out, the **clear** command will clear the screen, and then the **echo** command will display the message "Good-bye for now."

.bash_logout

```
clear
echo "Good-bye for now"
```

Other Initialization and Configuration Files

Each type of shell has its own set of initialization and configuration files. The TCSH shell used the **.login**, **.tcshrc**, and **.logout** files in place of **.bash_profile**, **.bashrc**, and **.bash_logout**. The Z-shell has several initialization files: **.zshenv**, **.zlogin**, **.zprofile**, **.zschrc**, and **.zlogout**. See Table 10-3 for a listing. Check the Man pages for each shell to see how they are usually configured. When you install a shell, default versions of these files are automatically placed in the **home** directories. Except for the TCSH shell, all shells use much the same syntax for variable definitions and assigning values (TCSH uses a slightly different syntax, described in its Man pages).

Configuration Directories and Files

Applications will often install configuration files in a user's **home** directory that contain specific configuration information that tailors the application to the needs of that particular user. This may take the form of a single configuration file that begins with a period, or a directory that contains several configuration files. The directory name will also begin with a period. For example, Netscape installs a directory called **.netscape** in the user's **home** directory that contains configuration files. On the other hand, the mailx applications use a single file called **.mailrc** to hold alias and feature settings set up by the user. Most single configuration files end in the letters **rc**. The **.gopher** uses a file called **.gopherc**. Entries in configuration files are usually set by the application, though you can usually make entries directly by editing the file. Applications have their own set of special variables that you can define and assign values to. You can list the configuration files in your **home** directory with the **ls -a** command.

BASH Shell	Function
.bash_profile	Login initialization file
.bashrc	BASH shell configuration file
.bash_logout	Logout name
TCSH Shell	
.login	Login initialization file
.tcshrc	TCSH shell configuration file
.logout	Logout file
Z-shell	
.zshenv	Shell login file (first read)
.zprofile	Login initialization file
.zlogin	Shell login file
.zshrc	Z-shell shell configuration file
.zlogout	Logout file
PDKSH Shell	
.profile	Login initialization file
.kshrc	PDKSH shell configuration file

Table 10-3. *Shell Configuration Files*

The Complete Reference

Linux

Part III

Internet

The
Complete
Reference

Chapter 11

Mailers

Your Linux system has electronic mail utilities known as "mailers" that allow you to send messages to other users on your system or other systems, such as those on the Internet. You can send and receive messages in a variety of ways, depending on type of mailer you use. Though all electronic mail utilities perform the same basic tasks of receiving and sending messages, they tend to have very different interfaces. There are mailers that operate on a desktop, such as KDE or Gnome. Others will run on any X Windows window managers. Several popular mailers were designed to use a screen-based interface and can run from just the command line. Other traditional mailers were developed for just the command line interface, requiring that you type your commands. Most mailers described here are included in standard Linux distributions and come in a standard rpm package for easy installation. For Web-based Internet mail services such as Hotmail, Lycos, and Yahoo, you use a Web browser instead of a mailer to access mail accounts provided by those services.

Local and Internet Addresses

Each user on a Linux system has a mail address, and whenever you send mail, you will be required to provide the address of the user to whom you are sending the message. For users on your local Linux system, addresses can consist of only the user's login name. However, when sending messages to users on other systems, you need to know not only the login name but also the address of the system they are on. Internet addresses require that the system address be uniquely identified.

Most systems have Internet addresses that you can use to send mail. Internet addresses use a form of addressing called "domain addressing." A system is assigned a domain name, which, when combined with the system name, gives the system a unique address. This domain name is separated from the system name by a period and may be further qualified by additional domain names. Here is the syntax for domain addresses:

```
login-name@system-name.domain-name
```

Systems that are part of a local network are often given the same domain name. The domain name for both the **garnet** and **violet** systems at U.C. Berkeley is **berkeley.edu**. To send a message to **chris** on the **garnet** system, you simply include the domain name:

```
chris@garnet.berkeley.edu.
```

In the next example, a message is sent to **chris**, located on the **garnet** system, using domain addressing:

```
$ mail chris@garnet.berkeley.edu < mydata
```

Early domain names reflect the fact that the Internet was first developed in the United States. They qualify Internet addresses by category such as commercial, military, or educational systems. The domain name **.com** indicates a commercial organization, whereas **.edu** is used for educational institutions. As the Internet developed into a global network, a set of international domain names was established. These domain names indicate the country in which a system is located—for example, **.fr** represents France, **.jp** represents japan, and **.us** represents the United States.

Mail Transport Agents: sendmail, smail

Mail is transported to and from destinations using mail transport agents. The **sendmail** and **smail** agents send and receive mail from destinations on the Internet or at other sites on a network. To send mail over the Internet, they use the Simple Mail Transfer Protocol (SMTP). The **sendmail** agent is smaller and easy to configure, whereas **smail** is more complex as well as more powerful. Most Linux distributions such as Red Hat and OpenLinux will automatically install and configure **sendmail** for you. Upon starting up your system, you can send and receive messages over the Internet.

Signature files: .signature

You can end your e-mail message with the same standard signature information, such as your name, Internet address or addresses, or farewell phrase. It is helpful to have your signature information automatically added to your messages. To do so, you need to create a signature file in your **home** directory and enter your signature information in it. A *signature file* is a standard text file that you can edit using any text editor. Mailers such as kmail will let you specify a file to function as your signature file. Others, such as Mail, expect the signature file to be named **.signature**.

The K Desktop Mailer: kmail

The K Desktop mailer, kmail, provides a full-featured GUI interface for composing, sending, and receiving mail messages. The kmail window displays three panes for folders, headers, and messages, as shown in Figure 11-1. The upper-left pane displays your mail folders. You have an inbox folder for received mail, an outbox folder for mail you have composed but not sent yet, and a sent-mail folder for messages you have previously sent. You can create your own mail folders and save selected messages in them if you wish. The top-right pane displays mail headers for the currently selected mail folder. You can use the scroll bar to the right to move through the list of headers. The headers are segmented according to fields, beginning with sender and subject. A color code is used to indicate read and unread messages. New messages are listed in

INTERNET

red. Read messages are green. A bullet symbol also appears at the beginning of unread message headers. To display a message, click on its header. The message is then displayed in the large pane below the header list. You can also send and receive attachments, including binary files. Pictures and movies that are received are displayed using the appropriate K Desktop utility. If you right-click on the message, a pop-up menu displays options for actions you may want to perform on it. You can move or copy it to another folder, or simply delete it. You can also compose a reply or forward the message.

The menus in the menu bar at the top of the window contain the commands and options you can use for managing your mail. An icon bar for commonly used mail commands is displayed below the menu bar. To get new mail, click on the icon showing a page with a question mark. To print a message, click on the Printer icon; to save one, just click on the Disk icon. If you hold the mouse over an icon, a short description of its function is displayed. The icon of an open book will open the kmail address book. Here, you can enter in a list of e-mail addresses. Also, a right-click on a displayed message will give you the option of automatically adding its e-mail address to your address book. You can use the Help button or Help menu to obtain more detailed descriptions of the different kmail features. The Help button will open the kmail Handbook, which provides easy reference to different operations.

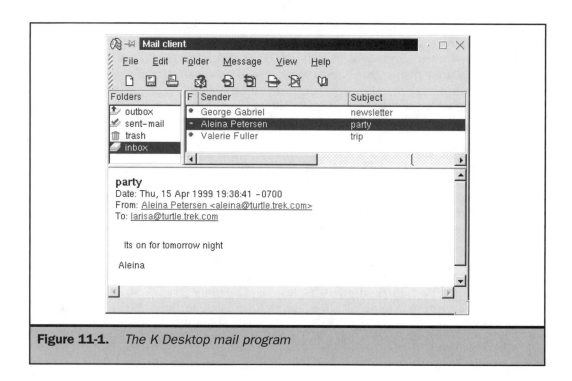

Figure 11-1.   *The K Desktop mail program*

You click on the Blank Page icon to compose and send a new message. If you want to compose a reply, select the header of the message you want to reply to and then just click on the icon showing a page with a single curved arrow on it. A message window will open up with the To entry already filled with the sender's address, the From entry with your address, and the Subject line with the sender's subject with a preceding "RE:". To forward a message, select the message's header and click on the icon showing a page with two curved arrows on it.

When you compose a message, a new window opens up with entries for the e-mail address, Carbon copy (Cc), and Subject (see Figure 11-2). A button with three dots is placed next to address entries like From and CC. Clicking on one of these buttons invokes your K address book, from which you can select an e-mail address. You enter the message in the body of the window. You can use any of the standard mouse-based editing capabilities to cut, copy, paste, and select text. All commands available to you for composing messages are listed in the menus in the menu bar at the top of the window. A button bar of commonly used functions is displayed just below the menu bar. To send the message, just click on the Envelope button. To attach a file, you can select the Attach entry in the Attach menu or click on the Paper Clip button. This menu also has entries for inserting the text of files into the message or appending a signature file. Other composition features, such as spell checking and encryption, are also supported. The standard message window does not display all the header entries unless you select All from the View menu. You can also individually select the fields

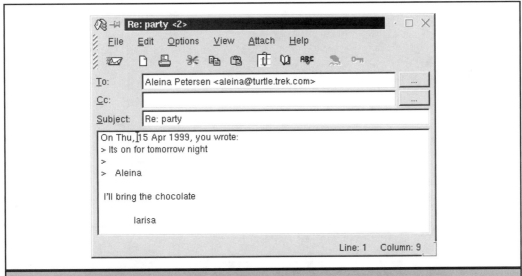

Figure 11-2.   *Composing a message in kmail*

you want displayed. The Options menu lets you mark a message as urgent or request a delivery confirmation.

To set up kmail to use with your mail accounts, you will have to enter account information. Select the Settings entry in the File menu. There will be several panels available on the Settings window that is then displayed (see Figure 11-3). For accounts, you select the Network panel. There are two sections on this panel, one for sending mail and one for receiving mail. In the sending mail section, enter in the SMTP server you use. If you have an ISP or are on a LAN, enter in the server name for your network. The default is the sendmail utility on your own Linux system. In the receiving mail section, you can add any mail accounts you may have. You may have more than one on mail servers maintained by your ISP or LAN. A configure window is displayed where you can enter login, password, and host information. The host is the name of the POP server this particular account uses.

Gnome Mailers: Balsa, Gmail, Mahogany, etc.

Several mailers are being adapted for use with the Gnome interface. Balsa is a Gnome mailer with extensive features, though it will operate under any window manager, including KDE, as long as Gnome is installed on your system. Balsa provides a

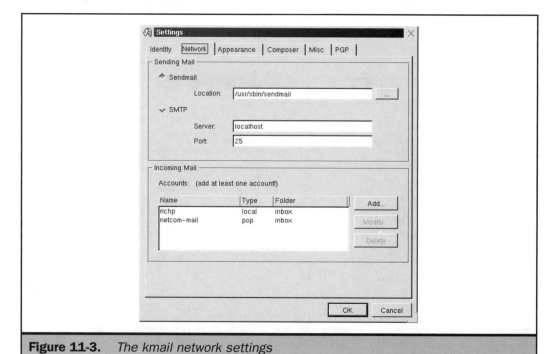

Figure 11-3. *The kmail network settings*

full-featured GUI interface for composing, sending, and receiving mail messages. The Balsa window displays three panes for folders, headers, and messages, as shown in Figure 11-4. The left-side pane displays your mail folders. You will initially have three folders: an inbox folder for received mail, an outbox folder for mail you have composed but not sent yet, and a trash folder for messages you have deleted. You can also create your own mail folders in which you can store particular messages. To place a message in a folder you have created, just click and drag the message header for that message to the folder.

The right side of the Balsa window consists of two panes. The top-right pane lists the message headers for currently selected folder. Message headers are displayed showing the subject, sender, and date. An Envelope icon indicates an unread message and a Trash Can icon indicates a message to be deleted. Headers are segmented into fields with buttons for the fields shown at the top of the pane. You can click on these buttons to sort headers by different fields such as subject or sender. To display a message, you click on it. It will be displayed in the pane below the message headers. You can click on the Right and Left Arrow icons in the icon bar to move through the header list.

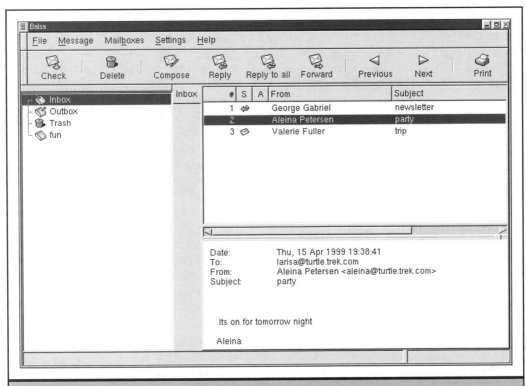

Figure 11-4. *Balsa*

To display message headers for a particular folder, you first have to open that folder. Double-clicking on the folder's icon will both open the folder and select it, having its headers displayed. You can also single-click on the folder's icon and select Open from the Mailbox menu. This will open the folder and display a button for it in the bar separating the folder pane from the right-side panes. You can open several folders at once, and each will have its own button in the bar. To have an open folder's message headers display, you can just click its button in this middle bar. To close a folder, select it and then choose the Close entry on the Mailbox menu.

You can access commands for managing your mail through the menus on the menu bar located at the top the Balsa window. An icon bar for commonly used mail commands is displayed below the menu bar. To retrieve new messages, just click on the Check icon or select the Get New Mail item in the File menu. To print a message, click its header and then on the Printer icon, and to delete a message, select its header and click on the Delete icon. The icons featuring envelopes are different forms of message composition: one for new messages, one for replies, and one for forwarding messages. Balsa also supports filters for automatically performing operations on received mail. You can create a filter that matches a specified string in a header field and then automatically perform an operation on that message. For example, you could have any message from a certain person automatically deleted or messages on a certain subject automatically printed.

To compose a message, you click on the Compose icon or select the New item on the Message menu. A new message window opens up with entries for the To, From, Subject, and Carbon copy (Cc) header fields, as shown in Figure 11-5. If you selected the Reply or Forward icons, then the To, From, and Subject fields will already be filled in with yours and the sender's address, and the sender's subject with a preceding Re: for replies and Fwd: for forwards. Fields that use addresses have a small Address Book button at the end of their fields. You can click on this button to use the address book to enter an address for a field. Enter the message in the body of the window. The standard GUI editing operations are supported, allowing you to use your mouse to select, cut, copy, and move text. To send the message, just click on the Send icon in the icon bar or select the Send entry in the File menu. There are also icons for operations such as selecting attachments or printing the message. Attachments added to a message are displayed in a pane just below the icon bar.

You can configure Balsa to access any number of mail accounts. Select the Preferences entry to bring up a window with panels for configuring Balsa (see Figure 11-6). The Mail Servers panel will show three sections, one for remote mailbox servers, another for local mail, and one for outgoing mail. In the remote mailbox servers section, you can add the server information for your network. Clicking on the Add button opens a mailbox configurator window where you can enter your account's user name and password, as well as the server name for that mailbox server. The mailbox name is any name you want to use to identify this mail service.

There are currently several Gnome-based mailers under development, including gmail, GnoMail, and N-tool. Check the Gnome Web site for more as they come out. Many are based on the Gnome-mailer libraries (camel) currently under development,

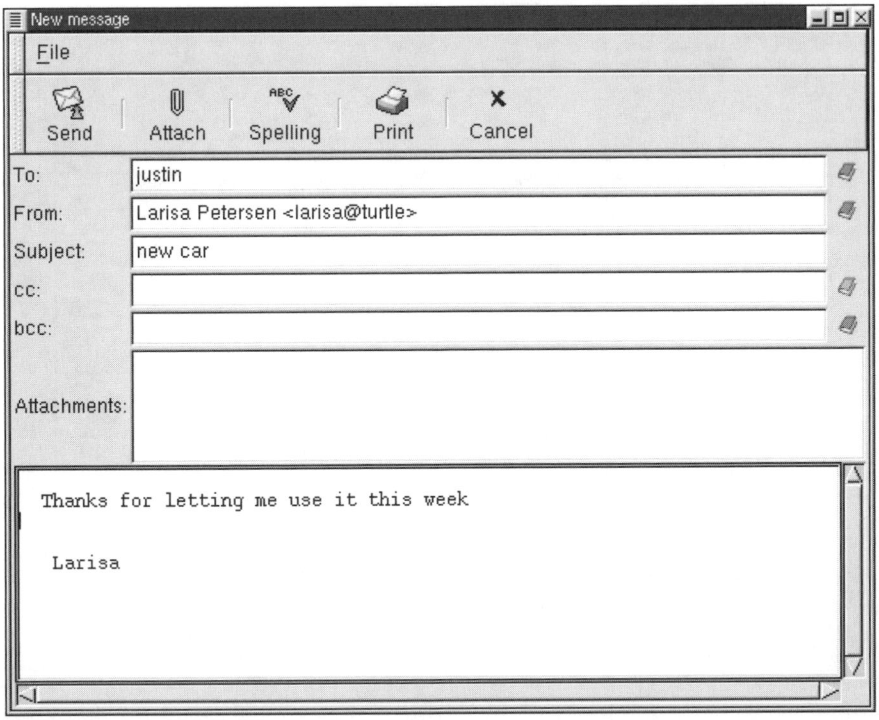

Figure 11-5. *A new message on Balsa*

which provide support for standard mail operations. Gmail is meant to be a light and fast e-mail client, supporting basic mail operations such as forwarding, replies, and mailboxes. Gnomail is yet another Gnome mail client that also uses the Gnome-mailer libraries. The N-tool is a Gnome mailer with Japanese language support, providing standard features including mailboxes and full MIME support. LinPopUp is a port of WinPopUp that operates on Samba-connected networks. It can send messages to users on Windows machines running WinPopUp.

The Mahogany mailer is a Gnome mailer that also has versions for other platforms. The Mahogany mailer window uses a format similar to Balsa. There are three panes: a left one for listing folders, and two others on the right side for headers and message text. The headers pane has buttons for sorting headers by different fields, such as subject or sender. Mail operations can be performed using the menus or the button bar at the top of the window. To compose a message, you can click on the Envelope button. This opens a window with entries for From, To, and Subject header fields. Mouse-based editing operations such as cut and paste are currently not supported, though you can invoke

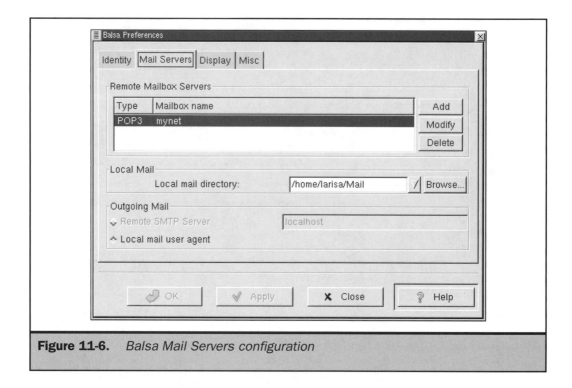

Figure 11-6. *Balsa Mail Servers configuration*

an external editor. A menu bar and icon bar at the top of the window list the different message operations you can perform, such as spell checking and printing.

X-window Mailers: Netscape and exmh

Though many of the newer mailers are being designed for either Gnome or the K Desktop, there are several mailers that were developed for use on X Windows and will operate under any window manager or desktop. The do not require either Gnome or the K Desktop. Two of the more popular are Netscape Messenger and exmh. The Emacs mailers are integrated into the Emacs environment, of which the Emacs editor is the primary application. They are, however, fully functional mailers. The GNU Emacs mailer can operate either with X Windows capabilities or with just a screen-based interface like Pine. The XEmacs mailer operates solely as an X Windows application.

Netscape Messenger

Netscape Communicator includes a mailer called Messenger. To use the mailer, you have to select the mail window item in Navigator's window menu or select the

Messenger icon in the Communicator window. Account information such as your mail server, user name, and password have to be entered in the Mail panel in the Preferences window, accessible from the Edit menu. Received messages are displayed in the Messenger window. The window is divided into two panes, the upper one listing headers of received messages, and the lower one for displaying messages, as shown in Figure 11-7. To display a message, click on its header. The icon bar displays icons for several common mail operations, such as sending, deleting, or forwarding messages.

To send a message, you click on the New Message icon. This opens a window that displays three sections. The middle section is for entering in the subject line and the bottom section is for entering in the text of your message. The top section switches between three alternate panes: address, attachments, and options. You can use the small buttons on the left side of the section to switch between panes. The address pane features a drop-down menu for selecting which address field you want to fill. There are entries for the To, From, Cc, and Bcc fields. The attachments pane will list files attached to this message. Use the Attachment's icon in the icon bar to add attachments. The options pane lists several options, such as priority, encryption, and receipts. For the text section, Messenger supports a wide range of composition features such HTML addresses, fonts, formatting, and spell checking. It supports standard GUI editing operations including cut and paste, though you use the ALT key instead of the CTRL key for keyboard equivalents.

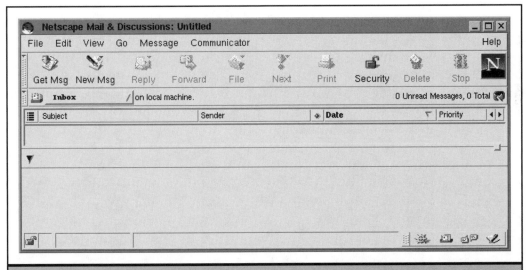

Figure 11-7. *Netscape Messenger*

exmh

An X Windows version of the MH mailer, exmh, is described later in this chapter. It displays a window with two panes (see Figure 11-8). The upper pane will list the headers for received mail and the lower pane will display a selected message. Above each pane is a button bar for various MH commands. These are the same as the commands for the MH mailer. To check for new mail, you press the Inc button on the top pane. Headers for unread messages are colored blue and the selected header is displayed in red. You can add new mailbox folders by pressing the New button.

To read a message, click on its header. It will be displayed in the lower pane. Buttons for managing a message are listed across the top of that pane. Long messages will be displayed screen by screen, and you can see the next screen by clicking on the More button. The Next and Previous buttons move you directly to the next or previous message. Comp, Reply, and Forward all open a new message window for composing

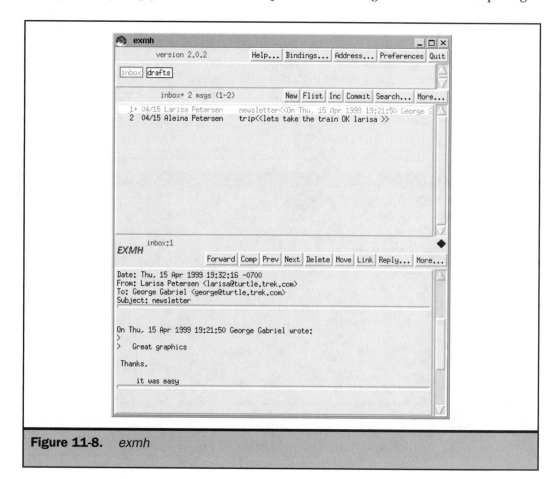

Figure 11-8. *exmh*

and sending a message. Comp is for new messages, and Reply and Forward will include your address, the sender's, and the current message's subject.

To compose a new message, you click on the Comp button in the lower pane. Header fields and their titles are listed from the top. Click next to a header title and enter its value. For example, to enter a value for the To field just click after "To" and type the address you want. A line below the header separates the header from the text of the message. Click below this line and enter your message. You can change any of the header fields and the text of your message at any time. Click on the Send button to send the message.

The Emacs mailer: GNU Emacs and XEmacs

The GNU version of Emacs includes a mailer along with other components such as a newsreader and editor. GNU Emacs is included on Red Hat distributions. Check the Emacs Web site at **www.emacs.org** for more information. When you start up GNU Emacs, menu buttons are displayed across the top of the screen. If you are running Emacs in an X Windows environment, then you will have full GUI capabilities and can select menus using your mouse. To access the Emacs mailer, select from the mail entries in the Tools menu. To compose and send messages, just select the Send Mail item in the Tools menu. This opens a screen with a prompt for To and Subject header entries (see Figure 11-9). You then type the message below them, using any of the Emacs editing capabilities (see Chapter 25). On the menu bar, a new menu is added labeled Mail. When you are ready to send the mail, choose the Send Mail entry in this menu. To read mail, select the Read Mail item in the Tools menu. This will display the first mail message received. Use entries in the Move menu to move to the next message or back to a previous one. Use entries in the Delete menu to remove a message. The Mail menu will list entries for message operations such as sending replies or forwarding the message. GNU Emacs is really a working environment within which you can perform a variety of tasks, with each task having its own buffer. When you read mail, a buffer is opened to hold the header list, and when you read a message, another buffer will hold the contents; when you compose a message, yet another buffer will hold the text you wrote. The buffers you have opened for mail, news, or editing notes or files will be listed in the Buffers menu. You can use this menu to switch between them.

XEmacs is another version of Emacs designed to operate solely with a GUI interface (**www.xemacs.org**). The Internet applications, which you can easily access from the main XEmacs button bar, includes a Web browser, a mail utility, and a newsreader. Currently, XEmacs is distributed on OpenLinux. Clicking the Mail button will bring up another window that will list received messages and also let you compose new ones. You can compose, reply, or print messages using buttons on the side of the window. To display a message, click on its header and press the SPACEBAR. You can display the headers by choosing the Display item in the Folder menu. When composing a message, you have full use of the Emacs editor with all its features, including spell checking and search/replace.

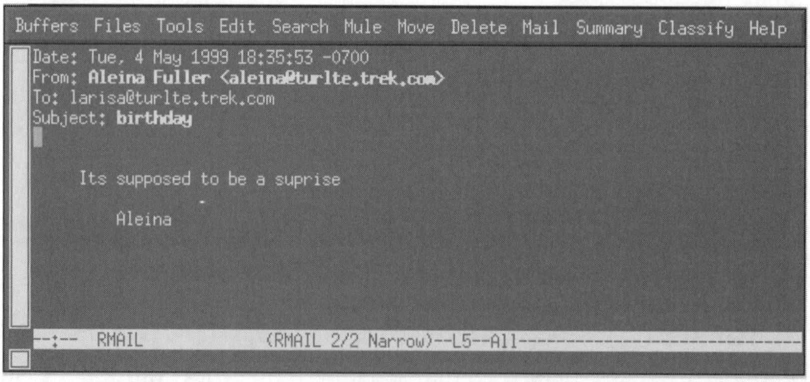

Figure 11-9. *Emacs mailer*

A new window is opened up that prompts you for the address and subject. When you are finished editing your message, choose Send and Exit in the Mail menu located at the end of the menu bar.

Screen-Based Mailers

There are several very powerful mailers available that you can invoke on the command line that provide a full-screen cursor-based interface. Menus are displayed on the screen whose entries you can select using your keyboard. Basic cursor movement is supported with arrow keys. Pine, Elm, and Mutt are all mailers that provide a screen-based interface. Though screen-based, the mailers are very capable. Pine, in particular, has an extensive set of features and options.

Pine

Pine stands for Program for Internet News and Email. If features full MIME support, letting you easily send messages, documents, and pictures. It has an extensive list of options, and has flexible Internet connection capabilities, letting you receive both mail and Usenet news. Pine also lets you maintain an address book where you can place frequently used e-mail addresses. You can find more information about Pine, including documentation and recent versions, from the Pine Information Center Web site at **www.washington.edu/pine**. The Pine newsgroup is **comp.mail.pine**, where you can post questions.

Pine runs from the command line using a simple cursor-based interface. Enter the `pine` command to start up Pine. Pine supports full-screen cursor controls. It displays a menu whose items you can select by moving the cursor with the arrow keys to the entry of your choice and pressing ENTER, as shown in Figure 11-10. Each item is labeled with a capital letter that you use to select it. The O command brings up a list of other Pine commands you can use.

To send a message, select the Compose Message item. This brings up a screen where you can enter your message. You are first taken through the different entries for the header, which prompts you for an e-mail address and subject. You can even attach files. Then, you type in the text of the message. A set of commands listed at the bottom of the screen specify different tasks. You can read a file with CTRL-R and cancel the message with CTRL-C. Use CTRL-X to send the message, as shown in Figure 11-11.

Pine organizes both sent and received messages into folders that you select using the Folder List entry on the main menu. The different available folders will be listed from left to right. Three folders are automatically set up for you; INBOX, sent-mail, and saved-messages. The INBOX folder holds mail that you have received but not yet read. Sent-mail is for messages you have sent to others, and saved-messages are messages you have read and want to keep. Use the LEFT and RIGHT ARROW keys to select the one you want and press ENTER. Selecting the INBOX folder will list the messages you have received. Headers for received messages will be displayed, and you can choose a specific header to view your message. The folder you select becomes your default folder. You can go back to it by selecting the Folder Index entry in the main menu.

```
PINE 3.95   MAIN MENU                           Folder: INBOX  0 Messages


        ?      HELP               -  Get help using Pine

        C      COMPOSE MESSAGE    -  Compose and send a message

        I      FOLDER INDEX       -  View messages in current folder

        L      FOLDER LIST        -  Select a folder to view

        A      ADDRESS BOOK       -  Update address book

        S      SETUP              -  Configure or update Pine

        Q      QUIT               -  Exit the Pine program




     Copyright 1989-1996.  PINE is a trademark of the University of Washington.
  ? Help                    P PrevCmd            R RelNotes
  O OTHER CMDS ? [Help]     N NextCmd            K KBLock
```

Figure 11-10. *Pine*

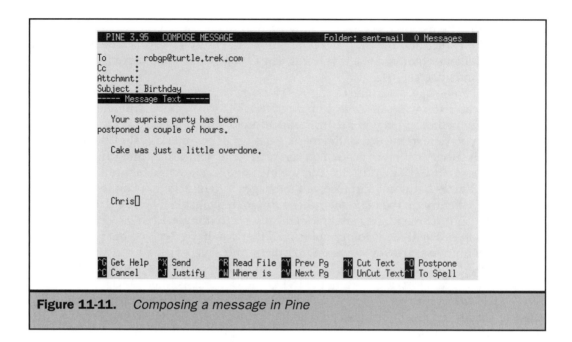

Figure 11-11. *Composing a message in Pine*

Mutt

Mutt incorporates many of the features of both Elm and Pine. It has an easy-to-use screen-based interface similar to Elm. Like Pine, it has an extensive set of features such as MIME support. You can find more information about Mutt from the Mutt Web page at **www.mutt.org**. Here, you can download recent versions of Mutt and access online manuals and help resources. On most distributions, the Mutt manual is located in the **/usr/doc** directory under Mutt. The Mutt newsgroup is **comp.mail.mutt** where you can post queries and discuss recent Mutt developments.

Mutt screens have an index mode and a pager mode. The index mode is used to display and manage message header lists, whereas the pager mode is used to display and compose messages (see Figure 11-12). Mutt screens support ANSI escape sequences for color coding, displaying commands, prompts, and selected entries in different colors. You invoke Mutt with the command **mutt** entered on a Linux shell command line. Mutt displays a list of common commands across the top of the screen. Pressing the single key listed before the command will execute that command. For example, pressing **q** will quit Mutt, **s** will save the current message, and **r** will let you send a reply to a message. Press the **?** key to obtain a complete listing of Mutt commands.

To compose a new message, press **m**. On the bottom line, you are then sequentially prompted to enter the address of the person to whom you are sending a message, the

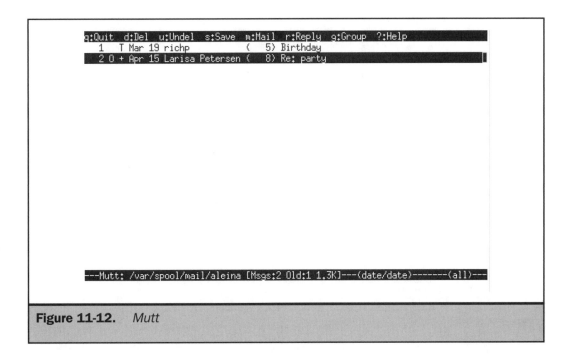

```
q:Quit  d:Del  u:Undel  s:Save  m:Mail  r:Reply  g:Group  ?:Help
   1   T Mar 19 richp            (   5) Birthday
   2 0 + Apr 15 Larisa Petersen  (   8) Re: party
```

```
---Mutt: /var/spool/mail/aleina [Msgs:2 Old:1 1.3K]---(date/date)-------(all)---
```

Figure 11-12. *Mutt*

subject line, and a carbon copy list. Then you are placed in the standard editor, usually Vi or Emacs, and you can use the editor to enter your message. If you are using Vi, you first have to press the **a** or **i** command before you can enter text. After entering your text, you press ESC to return to the Vi command mode. When you have finished entering your message, you save and exit Vi with the **ZZ** command. After editing the message, Mutt will display the header and a list of possible commands at the top of the screen. You can then edit the message again, or any of the header fields. With the **a** command, you can add attachments to the message, and with the **q** command you can cancel the message. Press **y** to send the message.

Headers for received mail are listed in the main screen upon starting Mutt. You can use the arrow keys to move from one to the next. The selected header will be highlighted. Press the ENTER key to display the contents of the message, as shown in Figure 11-13. This opens another screen showing the header fields and the text of the message. Long messages are displayed screen by screen. You can use the PAGE UP or SPACEBAR keys to move to the next screen, and the PAGE DOWN or – keys to move back to the previous screen. The commands for operations you can perform on the message are listed across the top of the screen. With the **r** command, you can compose and send a reply to the message, and the **d** command will delete the message. Once you have examined your message, you can use the **i** command to return to the main screen (**i** stands for index).

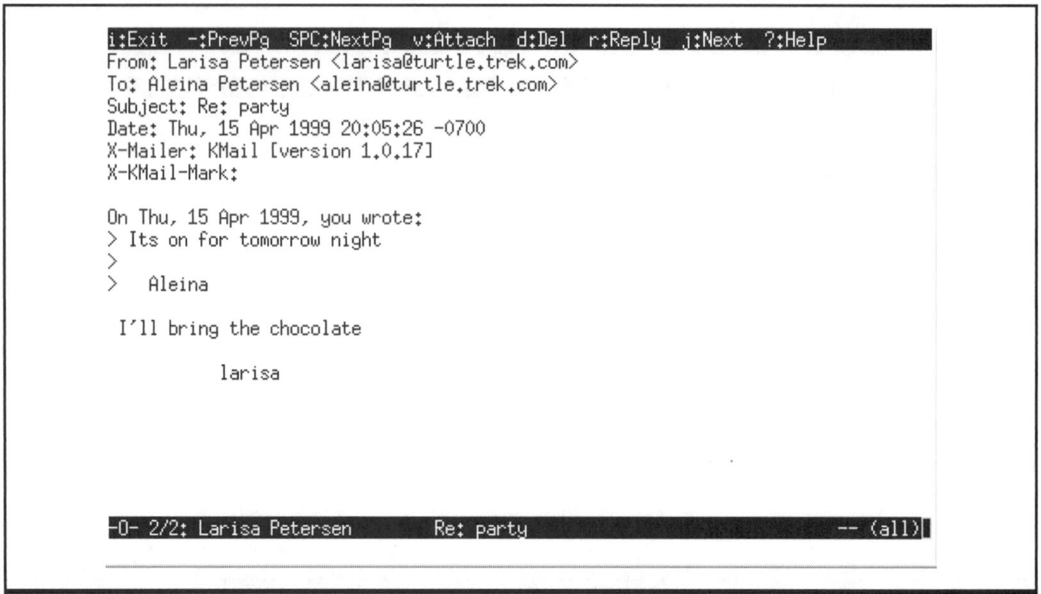

```
i:Exit  -:PrevPg  SPC:NextPg  v:Attach  d:Del  r:Reply  j:Next  ?:Help
From: Larisa Petersen <larisa@turtle.trek.com>
To: Aleina Petersen <aleina@turtle.trek.com>
Subject: Re: party
Date: Thu, 15 Apr 1999 20:05:26 -0700
X-Mailer: KMail [version 1.0.17]
X-KMail-Mark:

On Thu, 15 Apr 1999, you wrote:
> Its on for tomorrow night
>
>     Aleina

  I'll bring the chocolate

          larisa




-O- 2/2: Larisa Petersen          Re: party                          -- (all)
```

Figure 11-13.   *Reading Mutt messages*

Elm

Elm has a screen-oriented, user-friendly interface that makes mail tasks easy to execute. Messages are displayed one screen at a time, and you can move back and forth through the message screen by screen. The Elm newsgroup is **comp.mail.elm** where you can post queries for problems you may encounter. To send a message using Elm, you type **elm** along with the address of the person to whom you are sending the message. When you press ENTER, Elm will display the name of the person to whom you are sending the message and then prompt you for the subject. Elm displays the actual name of the person, not the address. At the subject prompt, you enter a subject. Then Elm prompts you for a carbon copy list. You can then enter the addresses of other users whom you want to have a copy of the message, or you can simply press ENTER if you do not want any carbon copies sent. Upon pressing ENTER at this point, you are placed in the standard editor, either Vi or Emacs, and you can use the editor to enter your message. After editing the message, Elm will prompt you for an action, at which time you can send it, quit without sending, edit the message again, or edit its headers, as shown here. Each option is listed with a single-letter command. The **h** option displayed in the Elm message menu is for editing the header. With this option, you can change any of the entries in your message header, and you can enter other header values, such as addresses for blind carbon copies.

> Please choose one of the following options by parenthesized letter:
>
> e)dit message, edit h)eaders, s)end it, or f)orget it

To receive mail using Elm, you enter **elm** by itself on the command line. Elm then displays a list of message headers representing messages you have received. The headers are displayed from the top of the screen. At the bottom of the screen is an information menu listing the different commands you can perform on the screen of message headers (see Figure 11-14). This list of headers is referred to in Elm as the *index*. If you have more than one screen of message headers, you can move to the next screen with the + key. You can also move back a screen with the – key. An Elm header displays the status, message number, date, name of the sender, number of lines in the message, and the subject. The message status is represented by a letter code. An **N** indicates a newly received message, and **O** indicates an old message—one that is still unread. The current header is either preceded by an arrow, **->**, or highlighted by the background. The arrow or highlight will move as you use arrow keys to move to the next or previous message header. To display the current message, you press ENTER. A new screen will appear in which the message is displayed. If the message is larger than a screen, you can move through it, screen by screen, using the same commands as those in the **more** utility. Pressing the SPACEBAR moves you to the next screen, and pressing **b** moves you back a screen. You can even search for particular patterns in the message. Once you have examined your message, you can use the **i** command to return to the header screen. The **i** stands for index, which is the term Elm uses to refer to the list of headers. You quit Elm by pressing the **q** key.

With Elm, you create any number of different mailbox files in which you can save your messages. The **c** command will prompt you for the name of a mailbox file. Simply

```
Mailbox is '/usr/spool/mail/rich/pete' with 3 messages
N 1  Gabriel Matoza       Feb 11   (5)     "Budget"
N 2  Aleina Petersen      Feb 12   (28)    "Birthday"
N 3  Marylou Carrion      Feb 14   (16)    "Homework"




    You can use any of the following commands by pressing the first character;
    d)elete or u)ndelete mail, m)ail a message, r)eply or f)orward mail, q)uit
    To read a message, press <return>. j = move down, k = move up, ? = help

Command:
```

Figure 11-14. *The Elm header list*

press the **c** key and the prompt appears. The prompt will display the name of the mailbox file used to hold received messages from the sender in the current message header. You can specify your own mailbox file by entering the name of the file preceded by an **=** sign. **=birthdays** will specify the **birthdays** mailbox file. Once you have changed to the other folder, the headers for all the messages in this mailbox file will be displayed, and you can display the messages, delete them from the file, or send replies. The folder's name will be displayed at the top of the screen.

Elm maintains an **.elm** directory in your home directory with which it will configure your use of Elm. Each time you invoke Elm, it generates a shell for your own use, within which you can define your own aliases and configuration variables. The **.elm** directory contains special configuration files in which you can place alias or variable definitions. You can set options either by entering assignments to the **.elmrc** file in your **.elm** directory, or by using the Options menu within in Elm (command **o** displays the options menu). Elm also lets you create mail aliases. You can create aliases either by using the Alias menu within the utility, or by entering aliases in the **aliases.text**. file in the **.elm** directory.

Command Line Mailers

Several mailers use a simple command line interface. They can be run without any other kind of support such as X Windows, desktops, or cursor support. They are simple and easy to use, but include an extensive set of features and options. Two of the more widely used mailers of this type are Mail and MH (Mail Handler). Mail is the mailx mailer that was developed for the Unix system. It is considered a kind of default mailer that can be found on all Unix and Linux systems. You can also use the Emacs mailer from the command line, as described in the previous section, "The Emacs mailer: GNU Emacs and XEmacs."

Mail

What is known now as the Mail utility was originally created for BSD Unix and called, simply, mail. Later versions of Unix System V adopted the BSD mail utility and renamed it mailx. It now simply referred to as Mail. Mail functions as a de facto default mailer on Unix and Linux systems. All systems will have the Mail mailer, whereas they may not have other mailers.

To send a message with Mail, type **mail** along with the address of the person to whom you are sending the message. Press ENTER and you will be prompted for a subject. Enter the subject of the message and press ENTER again. At this point, you are placed in input mode. Anything typed in is taken as the contents of the message. Pressing ENTER adds a new line to the text. When you have finished typing your message, press CTRL-D on a line of its own to end the message and send it. You will see EOT (end-of-transmission) displayed after you press CTRL-D. In the next example, the user sends a message to another user whose address is **robert**. The subject of the message is Birthday. After typing in the text of the message, the user presses CTRL-D.

```
$ mail robert
Subject: Birthday
    Your present is in the mail
really.

^D
EOT
$
```

The Mail utility receives input from the standard input. By default, the standard input is taken from what the user enters on the keyboard. However, with redirection, you can use the contents of a file as the message for the Mail program. In the next example, the file **mydata** is redirected as input for the Mail utility and sent to **robert**.

```
$ mail robert < mydata
```

You can send a message to several users at the same time by listing those users' addresses as arguments on the command line following the **mail** command. In the next example, the user sends the same message to both **chris** and **aleina**.

```
$ mail chris aleina
```

You may also want to save a copy of the message you are sending for yourself. You can copy a mail message to a file in your account by specifying a file name on the command line after the addresses. The file name must be a relative or full pathname, containing a slash (/). A pathname identifies an argument as a file name to which Mail will save a copy of the message being sent. In the next example, the user saves a copy of the message to a file called **birthnote**. A relative pathname is used, with the period denoting the current working directory: **./birthnote**.

```
$ mail robert ./birthnote
```

To receive mail, you enter just the **mail** command and press ENTER. This invokes a Mail shell with its own prompt and mail commands. A list of message headers is displayed. Header information is arranged into fields beginning with the status of the message and the message number. The status of a message is indicated by a single uppercase letter, usually **N**, for "new," or **U**, for "unread." A message number, used for easy reference to your messages, follows the status field. The next field is the address of the sender, followed by the date and time it was received, and then the number of lines and characters in the message. The last field contains the subject the sender gave for the message. After the headers, the Mail shell displays its prompt, a question mark, **?**. At the Mail prompt, you enter commands that operate on the messages. The commonly used Mail commands are listed in Table 11-1. An example of a Mail headers and prompt follows:

```
$ mail
Mail version 5.5-kw 5/30/95. Type ? for help.
"/var/spool/mail/chris": 3 messages 3 new
>N  1 valerie    Tue Feb 11 10:14:32 5/44    "Budget"
 N  2 aleina     Wed Feb 12 12:30:17 28/537 "Birthday"
 N  3 robert     Fri Feb 14  8:15:24 16/293 "Homework"
?
```

Mail references messages either through a message list or through the current message marker (**>**). The greater-than sign is placed before a message that is considered the current message. The current message is referenced by default when no message number is included with a Mail command. You can also reference messages using a message list consisting of several message numbers. Given the messages in the previous example, you can reference all three messages with **1-3**. The **^** references the first message; for example, **^-3** specifies the range of messages from the first message to the third message. The **$** references the last message. The period, **.**, references the current message. And the asterisk, *****, references all messages. Simply entering the number of the message by itself will display that message. The message will then be output screen by screen. Press the SPACEBAR or the ENTER key to continue to the next screen.

You use the **R** and **r** commands to reply to a message you have received. The **R** command entered with a message number will generate a header for sending a message and then place you into the input mode to type in the message. The **q** command quits Mail. When you quit, messages that you have read are placed in a file called **mbox** in your **home** directory. Instead of saving messages in the **mbox** file, you can use the **s** command to explicitly save a message to a file of your choice. However, the **s** command saves a message with its header, in effect, creating another mailbox file. You can then later access a mailbox file either by invoking the Mail utility with the **-f** option and the mailbox file name, or, if you are already using Mail, by executing the **folder** command that switches to a specified mailbox file. For example, the command **mail -f family_msgs** accesses the mailbox file **family_msgs**. Each message in the **family_msgs** mailbox file will then be displayed in a message list.

Mail has its own initialization file, called **.mailrc**, that is executed each time Mail is invoked, either for sending or receiving messages. Within it, you can define Mail options and create Mail aliases. You can set options that add different features to mail, such as changing the prompt or saving copies of messages that you send. To define an alias, you enter the keyword **alias**, followed by the alias you have chosen, and then the list of addresses it represents. In the next example, the alias **myclass** is defined in the **.mailrc** file.

.mailrc

```
alias myclass chris dylan aleina justin larisa
```

In the next example, the contents of the file **homework** are sent to all the users whose addresses are aliased by **myclass**.

```
$ mail myclass < homework
```

Status Codes	Description
N	Newly received messages
U	Previously unread messages
R	Reads messages in the current session
P	Preserved messages, read in previous session and kept in incoming mailbox
D	Deleted messages; messages marked for deletion
O	Old messages
*	Messages that you have saved to another mailbox file
Display Messages	**Description**
h	Redisplay the message headers
z+ z-	If header list takes up more than one screen, scrolls header list forward and backward
t *message-list*	Displays a message referenced by the message list; if no message list is used, the current message is displayed
p *message-list*	Displays a message referenced by the message list; if no message list is used, the current message is displayed

Table 11-1.   *Mail Commands*

Display Messages	Description
n or **+**	Displays next message
-	Displays previous message
top *message-list*	Displays the top few lines of a message referenced by the message list; if no message list is used, the current message is displayed
Message Lists	**Description**
message-number	References message with message number
num1-num2	References a range of messages beginning with *num1* and ending with *num2*
.	Current message
^	First message
$	Last message
*	All the messages waiting in the mailbox
/pattern	All messages with pattern in the subject field
address	All messages sent from user with address
: *c*	All messages of the type indicated by *c*; message types are as follows: **n** newly received messages **o** old messages previously received **r** read messages **u** unread messages **d** deleted messages
Deleting and Restoring Messages	**Description**
d *message-list*	Deletes a message referenced by the indicated message list from your mailbox
u *message-list*	Undeletes a message referenced by the indicated message list that has been previously deleted

Table 11-1.   *Mail Commands* (continued)

Deleting and Restoring Messages	Description
q	Quits the Mail utility and saves any read messages in the **mbox** file
x	Quits the Mail utility and does *not* erase any messages you deleted; this is equivalent to executing a **u** command on all deleted messages before quitting
pre *message-list*	Preserves messages in your waiting mailbox even if you have already read them

Sending and Editing Messages	Description
r	Sends a reply to all persons who received a message
R	Sends a reply to the person who sent you a message
m *address*	Sends a message to someone while in the Mail utility
v *message-list*	Edits a message with the Vi editor

Saving Messages	Description
s *message-list filename*	Saves a message referenced by the message list in a file, including the header of the message
S *message-list*	Saves a message referenced by the message list in a file named for the sender of the message
w *message-list filename*	Saves a message referenced by the message list in a file without the header; only the text of the message is saved
folder *mailbox-filename*	Switches to another mailbox file
%	Represents the name of incoming mailbox file: **folder %** switches to incoming mailbox file
#	Represents name of previously accessed mailbox file: **folder #** switches to previous mailbox file

Table 11-1.   *Mail Commands* (continued)

Saving Messages	Description
&	Represents name of mailbox file used to save your read messages automatically; usually called **mbox**: **folder** & switches to **mbox** file
General Commands	**Description**
?	Displays a list of all the Mail commands
! *command*	Executes a user shell command from within the Mail shell

Table 11-1. *Mail Commands* (continued)

The Mail Handler Utility: MH

The Mail Handler mailer, commonly known as MH, takes a different approach to managing mail than most other mailers. MH consists of a set of commands that you execute within your user shell just as you would execute any other Unix command. There is no special mail shell, as there is for Mail. One MH command will send a message, another will display your incoming messages, and still another will save a message. The MH commands and their options are listed in Table 11-2. A set of environment variables provides a context for the MH commands that you execute, such as keeping track of the current messages or mail folders. Instead of working from a command line interface, you can use xmh or ezmh, which provide an X Windows interface for accessing MH messages.

To send a message using MH, you first need to compose the message using the **comp** command, and then send the message with the **send** command. To compose a message, you type in the word **comp** on the command line by itself and press RETURN. Then, you are prompted for each header component, beginning with the address of the user to whom you are sending the message. After entering a subject, you are placed in an input mode for the default editor used for MH (usually the Vi editor). You then type the contents of the message and then save and quit the editor as you normally would (ESC-SHIFT-**ZZ** for Vi). At the **What now?** prompt, you can then send the message, edit it, save it to a file, display it again, or just quit without sending the message. The **send** command will send the message. Pressing ENTER at the **What now?** prompt will display a list of commands you can enter. In the next example, the user composes a message for another user whose address is **robert**.

```
$ comp
To: robert
cc:
Subject: Birthday
----------
Your present is in the mail
really.

What now? send
$
```

To read your mail with MH, you first need to store newly received mail into a designated MH mailbox file with **inc** command. The **inc** command will display a list of headers for each mail message in your incoming mailbox. A MH message header consists only of the message number, the month and year, the address of the sender, and the beginning of the message text.

```
$ inc
1+  02/97  To:valerie    budget <<You are way under
2   02/97  To:aleina     birthday <<Yes, I did remember
$
```

If you want to redisplay the headers, you need to use another MH command called **scan**.

```
$ scan
1+  02/97  To:valerie    budget <<You are way under
2   02/97  To:aleina     birthday <<Yes, I did remember
$
```

You use the **show, next**, and **prev** commands to display a message. The **show** command displays the current message, the **next** command displays the message after the current one, and the **prev** command displays the message before the current one. Initially, the current message is the first of the newly received messages. If you want to display a particular message, you can use the **show** command with the number of the message. **show 2** will display message 2. You can also reference several messages at once by listing their message numbers. The command **show 1 3** will display messages 1 and 3. You can also designate a range of messages by specifying the first message number in the range, and the last number, separated by a minus sign. The **show 1-3** command displays messages 1, 2, and 3.

```
$ show
$ next
```

To print a message you first output it with **show** and then pipe the output to a printer. You save a message to a text file in much the same way. First you output the message using the **show** command, and then redirect that output to a file.

```
$ show | lpr
$ show > myfile
```

You reply to the current message using the **repl** command. You need to know either the message number or the address and subject of the message in order to reply to it. You delete the current message using the **rmm** command. To delete a specific message, use the message number with **rmm**. **rmm 2** will delete the second message. You can create your own mailbox files for MH using the **folder** command. MH mailbox files are commonly referred to as *folders*. To create a new folder, enter in the **folder** command followed by the name of your folder preceded by a **+** sign. The **+** sign identifies an argument as a folder name.

Commands	Descriptions
inc	Places received mail in your incoming mailbox and display message headers
show *num*	Displays current message or specified messages
prev	Displays the previous message
next	Displays the next message
scan	Redisplays message headers
mhl	Displays formatted listing of messages
folders	Lists all mail folders
forw	Forwards a message
repl	Replies to a message
send	Resends a message or send a file as a message
pick	Selects message by specified criteria and assigns it a sequence
folder	Changes to another mailbox file (folder)

Table 11-2.   *MH Commands*

```
$ repl 2
$ rmm 2
$ folder +mybox
```

Mailing Binaries and Archives

Internet mail operations are set up to handle only text messages; that is, those consisting of a sequence of characters. Binary files such as programs, archives, and pictures can be sent through mail services as attachments. Most of the newer mailer such as Pine and Netscape support attached files. Older mailers such as Mail do not. Mailers that support attached files automatically encode and decode attachments, translating them into character equivalents that can then be transmitted as mail messages. The actual material transmitted through Internet mail services can only be in character format.

Should you need to do this manually—say, for sending a file through Mail—then you first have to encode the file using an encoding utility such as uuencode. The **uuencode** program translates a binary file into one that is character equivalent, which can then be sent through a mailer like Mail. The person receiving such an encoded file can then convert it back to a binary file using the **uudecode** program. The **uuencode** program is designed to work on either the standard input or on a particular file. In either case, you have to provide a name for the file that will be created when the encoded data is converted back to binary. The **uuencode** program outputs the encoded binary data to the standard output. The **uuencode** program has the following syntax:

```
uuencode file   name
```

where *name* is the name to be given to the decoded binary data and *file* is the name of a binary file to be encoded. Keep in mind that since **uuencode** sends the encoded data to the standard output, you should redirect this output to a file; then, you can send that file. The **uudecode** program takes as its argument the file that holds the encoded data. It will generate a binary file using the name you provided in the **uuencode** operation.

In the next example, the user encodes the picture file called **dylan.gif**. Picture files such as GIF and JPEG files are binary files and have to be translated to character format before they can be mailed. In this case, the name of the binary file and the name to be used for the decoded version of the file are the same. The encoded output is redirected to a file called **dylanpic**:

```
$ uuencode dylan.gif  dylan.gif  > dylanpic
```

The **dylanpic** file contains only character data, although this character data is encoded binary data. The user can then send **dylanpic** through the mail system.

```
$ mail larisa@ix.com < dylanpic
```

Once received, you simply use **uudecode** to convert the encoded data back to its binary form. The **uudecode** program will create a binary file, giving it the name specified for **uuencode**. In the following example, the data from **dylanpic** file has been received as a message. The receiver then saves this message as **dylanpic**. The uudecode program then converts this message to the original binary format and places it in a file called **dylan.gif**. The name that the receiver saves the message as does not have to be the same as the one the sender used. You can use any name, but you must use that same name with **uudecode**.

```
$ mail
Mail version 5.5-kw 5/30/95.  Type ? for help.
"/var/spool/mail/chris": 1 message 1 unread
>U   1 robert                Mon Apr  8 00:06 236/14104
& s 1 dylanpic
"dylanpic" [New file]
& q
$ uudecode dylanpic
$ ls
dylan.gif
```

You can also use **uudecode** to decode binary articles listed in newsgroups. Certain newsgroups specialize in encoded binary files. In these newsgroups, articles consist of encoded binary files such as JPEG pictures in character form. Though many newsreaders such as Netscape and Pine can decode such files automatically, others such at **tin** and **trn** cannot. Those, you will have to decode manually with **uudecode**. Articles that you post with such newsreaders will have to be encoded with **uuencode**. Newsgroups as well as mail utilities cannot handle binary files. They can only handle character files.

Notifications of Received Mail: From and Biff

As your mail messages are received, they are automatically placed in your mailbox file, but you are not automatically notified when you receive a message. To find out if you have any messages waiting, you can either use a mailer to retrieve messages, or you can use the From and Biff utilities simply to tell you if you have any mail waiting.

The From utility tells what messages you have received and are waiting to be read. For each waiting message, it lists the senders' addresses and times that each message was received. To use From, you enter the keyword **from** and press ENTER.

```
$ from
1 From valerie Sun Feb 11 10:14:32 1996
```

```
   Subject: Budget
2 From aleina Mon Feb 12 12:30:17 1996
   Subject: Birthday
3 From robert Wed Feb 14  8:15:24 1996
   Subject: Homework
$
```

Biff notifies you immediately when a message is received. It is helpful when you are expecting a message and want to know as soon as it arrives. Biff automatically displays the header and beginning lines of messages as they are received. To turn on Biff, you enter **biff y** on the command line. To turn it off, you enter **biff n**. To find out if Biff is on or not, enter **biff** alone. It displays a message notification whenever a message arrives, no matter what you may be doing at the time. You could be in the middle of an editing session and Biff will interrupt it to display the notification on your screen. You can then return to your editing session. In the next example, the user first sets Biff on. Then Biff notifies the user that a message has been received. The user then checks to see if Biff is still on.

```
$ biff y
$
New mail for chris has arrived:

-Date: Sun Feb 11 12:30:21
From: dylan
To: chris
Subject: Food
    Chris,
         Have you tried the chocolate
...more...
$
$ biff
is y
$
```

You can temporarily block Biff by using the **mesg n** command to prevent any message displays on your screen. The **mesg n** command will not only stop any Write and Talk messages, it will also stop Biff and Notify messages. Later, you can unblock Biff with a **mesg y** command. A **mseg n** command comes in handy should you not want to be disturbed while working on some project.

If you are running a window manager such as fvwm or Afterstep, you can use the xbiff utility to perform the same function. The Biff utility will display an icon of a mailbox on your desktop. The mailbox has a flag on it. When mail arrives, the flag will go up. It can also beep or produce some other sound, if you prefer.

The K Desktop has a Biff utility called KBiff that performs much in the same way (see Figure 11-15). With KBiff there are numerous options you can set. KBiff can show an empty inbox tray when there is no mail and a tray with slanted letters in it when mail arrives. If there is old mail still in your mailbox, then letters are displayed in a neat square. You can set these icons to be any image you wish. You can also specify the mail client to use and the polling interval for checking for new mail. If you have several mail accounts, you can set up a KBiff profile for each one. There will be different icons for each account telling you when mail arrives in one of them.

Accessing Mail on Remote POP Mail Servers

Most newer mailers are equipped to access mail accounts on remote servers. For such mailers, you can specify a separate mail account with its own mailbox. For example, if you are using an ISP, most likely you will be using that ISP's mail server to receive mail. You will have set up a mail account with a user name and password for accessing your mail. Your e-mail address is usually your user name and the ISP's domain name. For example a user name of **larisa** for an ISP domain named **mynet.com** would have

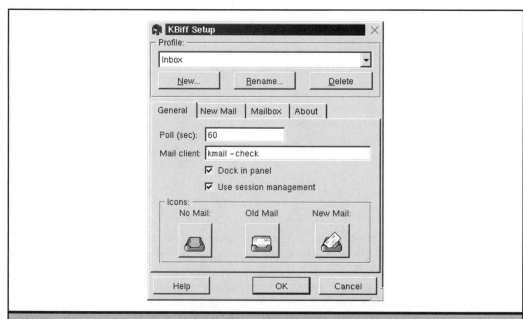

Figure 11-15. *KBiff configuration*

the address **larisa@mynet.com**. The user name would be **larisa**. The address of the actual mail server could be something like **mail.mynet.com**. The user **larisa** would login to the **mail.mynet.com** server using the user name **larisa** and password to access mail sent to the address **larisa@mynet.com**. Newer mailers such as kmail, Balsa, and Netscape will let you set up a mailbox for such an account and will access your ISP's mail server to check for and download received mail. You will have to specify what protocol a mail server uses. This is usually the Post Office Protocol (POP). This procedure is used for any remote mail server. Using a mail server address, you can access your account with your user name and password.

Instead of creating separate mailboxes in different mailers, you can arrange to have mail from different accounts sent directly to the inbox maintained by your Linux system for your Linux account. All your mail, whether from other users on your Linux system or from ISP mail servers, will appear in your local inbox. Such a feature is very helpful if you are using a mailer such as Elm or Mail that does not have the ability to access mail on your ISP's mail server. You can implement such as feature with Fetchmail. Fetchmail checks for mail on remote mail servers and downloads it to your local inbox, where it appears as newly received mail.

To use Fetchmail, you have to know a remote mail server's Internet address and mail protocol. Most remote mail servers use the POP3 protocol, but others may use IMAP, ETRM, or POP2 protocols. Enter **fetchmail** on the command line with the mail server address and any needed options. The mail protocol is indicated with the **-p** option and the mail server type, usually POP3. If your e-mail user name is different from your Linux login name, then you use the **-u** option and the e-mail name. Once you have executed the **fetchmail** command, you will be prompted for a password. The syntax for the **fetchmail** command for a POP3 mail server follows:

```
fetchmail -p POP3 -u username mail-server
```

To use Fetchmail just connect to your ISP and then enter the **fetchmail** commands with the options and the POP server name on the command line. You will see messages telling you if there is mail and, if so, how many messages are being downloaded. You can then use a mailer to read the messages from your inbox. You can run Fetchmail in daemon mode to have it automatically check for mail. You have to include an option specifying the interval in seconds for checking mail.

```
fetchmail -d  1200
```

You can specify options such as the server type, user name, and password in a **.fetchmailrc** file in your **home** directory. You can also have entries for other mail servers and accounts you may have.

Instead of entering option directly into the **.fetchmailrc** file, you can use the **fetchmailconf** program. This program provides an GUI interface for selecting

Fetchmail options and entering mail account information. The **fetchmailconf** program runs only under X Windows and requires that python and Tk be installed (most distributions automatically install these during installation). It will display windows for adding news servers, configuring a mail server, and configuring a user account on a particular mail server. The expert version will display the same kind of windows, but with many more options. Initially **fetchmailconf** displays a window with buttons for choosing a novice or expert version (see Figure 11-16). Choosing the novice version will display a window with an entry labeled "New Server." Type the address of your mail server in the adjoining box and press ENTER. The server address will appear in a list below. To configure that server, click on the server name and then the Edit button at the bottom of the window. A new window opens with entries such as user accounts and server protocols. You can add as many user accounts as you may have on that server. You can then further configure an individual account by selecting the user name and clicking on the Edit button. This opens another window for user account options. You can specify a password and specify any corresponding local users you want mail for this account downloaded to.

Once configured, you can enter **fetchmail** with no arguments; it will read entries from your **.fetchmailrc** file. Accounts you have specified will be checked and any new mail placed in your inbox. If you want Fetchmail to automatically check for new mail periodically, you can activate its daemon mode. To do so, place a daemon entry in the

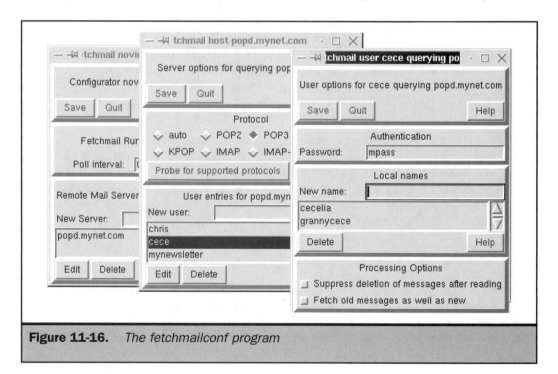

Figure 11-16. *The fetchmailconf program*

.fetchmailrc file. The following entry activates the Fetchmail daemon mode, checking for mail every 1,200 seconds:

```
Set daemon   1200
```

You can also make entries directly in the **.fetchmailrc** file. An entry in the **.fetchmailrc** file for a particular mail account consists of several fields and their values: poll, protocol, user name, and password. *Poll* is used to specify the mail server name, and *protocol* for the type of protocol used. Notice that you can also specify your password, instead of having to enter it in each time Fetchmail accesses the mail server. The syntax for an entry follows:

```
poll SERVERNAME protocol PROTOCOL username NAME password PASSWORD
```

You can use abbreviations for certain field names if you wish: proto for protocol, user for user name, and pass for password. An example follows for a POP3 server and an account with the user name chris and the password mypass:

```
poll popd.mynet.com proto pop3 user chris password mypass
```

You can specify a default entry for any of these fields and not have to repeat them for each account entry. The default has to be placed before the mail server entries. The following example sets the default protocol to POP3 and the user name to chris:

```
defaults protocol pop3 user chris
```

This next example would reference the chris account with the password newpass on the **popd.train.com** mail server using the POP3 protocol. The missing fields are filled in by default.

```
poll popd.train.com password newpass
```

Fetchmail lets you download messages to a specific user on your local system. In fact, you can access several accounts on the remote system and have them downloaded to specific users on the your local system. This is useful when running Fetchmail in daemon mode. Essentially, Fetchmail is transferring mail from one set of remote accounts to corresponding ones on your local system. You could even have Fetchmail download from one remote account to several local ones, sending copies of the same mail to each. This is helpful if you are using several accounts on your Linux system, or if a group of users is using an account on the remote server for group mail. Local users are specified with the keyword **is** or **to** followed by the user names, terminating with the keyword **here**. The following examples show different ways of specifying local users. The last entry will send all mail retrieved from the mynewsletter account to the users **larisa, aleina,** and **dylan**.

```
poll popd.mynet.com proto pop3 user chris password mypass is chris here
poll popd.othernet.com proto pop3 user neil password mypass is chris here
poll popd.mynet.com proto pop3 user cece password mypass to cecelia
    grannycece here
poll popd.mynet.com proto pop3 user mynewsletter password mypass to larisa
    dylan aleina here
```

Fetchmail also supports a multidrop mailbox feature. You can have several users' mail sent to one mailbox on the mail server, and then download it from there to the inboxes for their Linux accounts.

Chapter 12

Usenet and Newsreaders

U senet is an open mail system on which users post news and opinions. It operates like a system-wide mailbox that any user on your Linux system can read or send messages to. Users' messages are incorporated into Usenet files, which are distributed to any system signed up to receive them. Each system that receives Usenet files is referred to as a *site*. Certain sites perform organizational and distribution operations for Usenet, receiving messages from other sites and organizing them into Usenet files that are then broadcast to many other sites. Such sites are called *backbone sites* and they operate like publishers, receiving articles and organizing them into different groups.

To access Usenet news, you need access to a news server. A news server receives the daily Usenet news feeds and makes them accesible to other systems. Your network may have a system that operates as a news server. If you are using an Internet service provider, a news server is probably maintained for your use. To read Usenet articles, you use a *newsreader*—a client program that connects to a news server and accesses the articles. On the Internet and in TCP/IP networks, news servers communicate with newsreaders using the Network News Transfer Protocol (NNTP), and are often referred to as NNTP news servers. Alternatively, you could also create your own news server on your Linux system to run a local Usenet news service or to download and maintain the full set of Usenet articles. Several Linux programs, called News Transport Agents, can be used to create such a server.

Usenet News

Usenet files were originally designed to function like journals. Messages contained in the files are referred to as *articles*. A user could write an article, post it in Usenet, and have it immediately distributed to other systems around the world. Someone could then read the article on Usenet instead of waiting for a journal publication. Usenet files themselves were organized as journal publications. Since journals are designed to address specific groups, Usenet files were organized according to groups called *newsgroups*. When a user posts an article, it is assigned to a specific newsgroup. If another user wants to read that article, he or she looks at the articles in that newsgroup. You can think of each newsgroup as a constantly updated magazine. For example, to read articles on computer science, you would access the Usenet newsgroup on computer science. More recently, Usenet files have also been used as bulletin boards on which people carry on debates. Again, such files are classified into newsgroups, though their articles read more like conversations than journal articles. You can also create articles of your own that you can then add to a newsgroup for others to read. Adding an article to a newsgroup is called *posting* the article.

Each newsgroup has its own name, which is often segmented in order to classify newsgroups. Usually, the names are divided into three segments: a general topic, a subtopic, and a specific topic. The segments are delimited by periods, (.). For example, you may have several newsgroups that deal with the general topic **rec**, which stands for recreation. Of those, some newsgroups may deal with only the subtopic **food**.

Again, of those, there may be a group that only discusses a specific topic, such as **recipes**. In this case, the newsgroup name would be **rec.food.recipes**.

Many of the bulletin board groups are designed for discussion only, lacking any journal-like articles. Many of these begin with either **alt** or **talk** as their general topic. For example, **talk.food.chocolate** may contain conversations about how wonderful or awful chocolate is thought to be, and **alt.food.chocolate** may contain informal speculations about the importance of chocolate to the basic structure of civilization as we know it. Here are some examples of Usenet newsgroup names:

```
comp.ai.neural-nets
comp.lang.pascal
sci.physics.fusion
rec.arts.movies
rec.food.recipes
talk.politics.theory
```

Linux has newsgroups on various topics. Some are for discussion, others are sources of information about recent developments. On some, you can ask for help for specific problems. A current list of some of the popular Linux newsgroups is provided here.

Newsgroup	Topic
comp.os.linux.announce	Announcements of Linux developments
comp.os.linux.admin	System administration questions
comp.os.linux.misc	Special questions and issues
comp.os.linux.setup	Installation problems
comp.os.linux.help	Questions and answers for particular problems

You read Usenet articles with a newsreader, such as krn, Collabra, **trn** or **tin**, which allows you first to select a specific newsgroup and then read the articles in it. A newsreader operates like a user interface, allowing you to browse through and select available articles for reading, saving, or printing. The **trn** newsreader, perhaps the most widely used today, is a more recent and powerful version of an earlier newsreader called **rn**. It employs a sophisticated retrieval feature called *threads* that pulls together articles on the same discussion or topic. Collabra, the Netscape newsreader, provides many of the same features and will operate on any X Windows window manager. Currently krn is the only newsreader for the K Desktop, though several other are planned as of this printing. You can check for other newsreaders on the software list on the K Desktop Web site at **www.kde.org**. For Gnome-based newsreaders, check the software map on the Gnome Web site at **www.gnome.org**. You can use a newsreader to create and post articles, or post them separately using a separate utility called Pnews.

Most newsreaders can read Usenet news provided on remote news servers that use the Network News Transfer Protocol (NNTP). Many such remote news servers are available through the Internet. Desktop newsreaders such as krn and Netscape Collabra have you specify the Internet address for the remote newsreader in their own configuration settings. However, several shell-based newsreaders such as **trn**, **tin**, and Pine obtain the newsreader's Internet address from the **NNTPSERVER** shell variable. Before you can connect to a remote news server with such newsreaders, you first have to assign the Internet address of the news server to the **NNTPSERVER** shell variable, and then export that variable. You can place the assignment and export of **NNTPSERVER** in a login initialization file such as **.bash_profile** so that it will be performed automatically for you whenever you log in.

```
$ NNTPSERVER=news.servdomain.com
$ export NNTPSERVER
```

News Transport Agents

Usenet news is provided over the Internet as a daily news feed of articles for thousands of newsgroups. This news feed is sent to sites that can then provide access to the news for other systems through newsreaders. These sites operate as news servers, and the newsreaders used to access them are their clients. The news server software, called News Transport Agents, is what provides newsreaders with news, allowing you to read newsgroups and post articles. For Linux, three of the popular News Transport Agents are INN, nntp, and Cnews. Both Cnews and nntp are smaller and simpler, and useful for small networks. INN is more powerful and complex, and was designed with large systems in mind (see **www.isc.org** for more details).

Daily news feeds on Usenet are often very large and consume much of a news server's resources in both time and memory. For this reason, you may not want to set up your own Linux system to receive such news feeds. If you are operating in a network of Linux systems, you can designate one of them as the news server and install the News Transport Agent on it to receive and manage the Usenet news feeds. Users on other systems on your network can then access that news server with their own newsreaders.

If your network already has a news server, you do not need to install a News Transport Agent at all. You just have to use your newsreaders to remotely access that server (see **NNTPSERVER** in the previous section, "Usenet News"). In the case of an Internet service provider, such providers will often operate their own news server, which you can also remotely access using your own newsreaders, such as **trn** and **tin**. Bear in mind, though, that **trn** and **tin** will have to take the time to download all the articles for selected newsgroups as well as updated information on all the newsgroups.

You can also use News Transport Agents to run local versions of news for just the users on your system or your local network. To do this, you would install INN or Cnews and configure them just to manage local newsgroups. Users on your system could then post articles and read local news. You could also use INN, though the other agents would be adequate for local networks.

Mailing Lists

As an alternative to newsgroups, you can subscribe to a mailing list. Users on a mailing lists automatically receive messages and articles sent to it. It works much like an e-mail alias, broadcasting a message to all users on the list. Mailing lists were designed to serve small specialized groups of people. Instead of posting articles for anyone to see, only those subscribed receive them. Numerous mailing lists are available for Linux, as well as other subjects. For example, at the **www.gnome.org** site you can subscribe to any of several mailing lists on Gnome topics such as **gnome-themes-list@gnome.org** which deals with Gnome desktop themes. At **www.liszt.com** you can search for mailing lists on various topics. By convention, to subscribe to a list, you send a request to the mailing list address with a –request term added to its user name. For example, to subscribe to **gnome-themes-list@gnome.org**, you send a request to **gnome-themes-list-request@gnome.org**. At **www.linux.org** you can link to sites that support Linux-oriented mailing lists such as Majordomo and the Linux Mailing Lists Web site. There are lists for such topics as the Linux kernel, administration, and different distributions.

The K Desktop Newsreader: krn

The krn newsreader is for the K Desktop. To start krn, select the news entry in the K Internet submenu located on the K menu. When you first use krn, you will have to configure the Internet settings. A window will be displayed titled KRN-NNTP Settings. In the Servers section, enter the NNTP and SMTP server Internet addresses. Specify any of the other options as you wish. You can enter more than one NNTP server address and it will be added to a pop-up menu on the NNTP entry box. You can then use the pop-up menu to change news servers.

The krn newsreader window will display two folders, one for subscribed newsgroups and one for all newsgroups (see Figure 12-1). You can expand or contract either by clicking on their Folder icon. There is a menu bar at the top of the window for newsgroup and configuration operations. An icon bar just below the menus lists several common newsgroup operations. To connect to your news server, click on the first icon on this list. The second icon will disconnect. The icon with several lines will download a current, complete list of newsgroups. The Curved Arrow icon will check to see if new articles have been posted for your newsgroups. The icon of a sheet of paper with a small blue line partway through its left side is used to subscribe or unsubscribe to a newsgroup. To subscribe to a newsgroup, you first select it from the list of All Newsgroups. Then, you click on the Subscribe icon on the icon bar. It will automatically appear in your list of subscribed-to newsgroups.

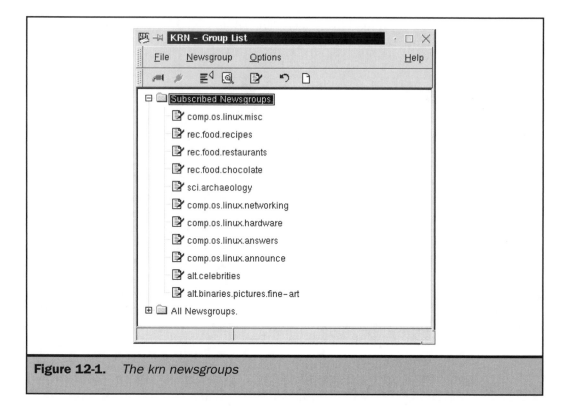

Figure 12-1. *The krn newsgroups*

To display articles in a newsgroup, just double-click on the newsgroup entry. A window opens up consisting of two panes. The top pane will list the headers for articles in the newsgroup. You can scroll through the list using the scroll bar to the right. Articles you have read will appear in blue type. If you right-click on an article header, a pop-up menu will display options for moving or copying it to another folder, or deleting it. Buttons appear at the top of the header pane for each of the header fields. There are fields for subject, sender, and date. Clicking on a button will sort the headers by that field. For example, clicking on the date field will sort all headers by date. There is another field named score. This is for score rules that you can set up for the newsgroup. A score rule will search for keywords in certain fields and give a score you specified to the articles if the keywords are found.

To read an article, just click on its header. The text of the article will appear in the pane below (see Figure 12-2). A menu bar at the top of the window holds commands for accessing articles. Two icon bars below let you execute commonly used commands. In the top icon bar, the arrows move through the list of articles. The icon with a looking glass opens a find window for searching articles by subject, sender, text, or other fields. The blank page will post a new article, and the icon with lines in it will download a current list of articles for the group. To the left is a box for adjusting the number of articles you want displayed.

If you want to post an article of your own to this newsgroup, you click on the icon of a blank paper. This opens a new window with the news group name already entered. Enter your own address and then the text of the article. You can add other newsgroups you want the article posted to. To attach a file, click on the Attach entry in the Attach menu. To post a follow-up article, you click on the icon of a page with lines in it. This opens a similar window with entries for Subject, Newsgroup, and a Follow-up-to entry. Enter in your message and then click the Envelope icon to send it. If, instead, you want to just send a reply to the author, then click on the Envelope icon. A window opens a kmail message window with entries already filled for the address and subject. The article will be displayed in the window with preceding **>>** signs. You can edit and add to the message as you wish.

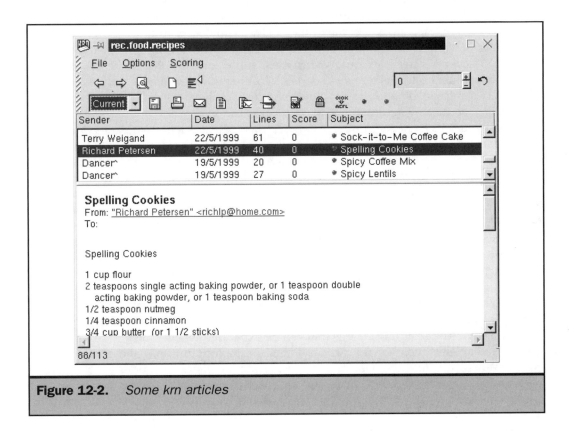

Figure 12-2.   *Some krn articles*

Articles that are encoded pictures or sound files, are not automatically decoded. To decode, them you first mark them for decoding by selecting them and then click on the Decode button in the icon bar. Then, you select the Decode entry in the File menu. This brings up a window listing the article marked for decoding. A button bar at the bottom includes a button for decoding the files. When decoded, the resulting binary files are placed in your current working directory. You can then examine them with other appropriate applications such as xv or kpic that can display images.

Netscape Newsreader

The Netscape newsreader is called Collabra Discussions and is part of the Netscape Communicator package. You can configure Collabra by editing the Netscape Preferences for news. From the Edit menu in Netscape Navigator, select the Preferences entry. Then, select News from the list on the left. This displays a pane that includes an entry for your news server. Here, you enter the address of your news server. You can set other options here also, such as the number of articles to display at a time for a newsgroup.

To access a newsgroup, select the Collabra Discussion entry from the Communicator window on Netscape Navigator or the Collabra icon in the Communicator window. This opens a Netscape Messenger window with the mailbox folders listed to the left. Below the mailbox folders is the list of news servers. Most likely you will have only one. Click on this entry to expand to a list of newsgroups you have subscribed to. Then, double-click on the newsgroup name to see its articles.

When you select a newsgroup, a new window opens up with two panes. The one on top lists the headers for articles in the newsgroup. Use the scroll bar to the right to move through the list. To display the contents of the article, click on it and it will be displayed in the large pane in the lower half of the window. Header information will be shown first. If the article is a picture file, then the picture will be automatically decoded and displayed in the pane. If it is a video file, then the appropriate program for running video will start up and run it. You can search for articles by subject or sender by selecting the Search Messages entry in the Edit menu. Figure 12-3 shows the Netscape discussion window. The icons in the icon bar at the top can be used to post new articles or follow-ups to the current newsgroup. A new window will open up that appears much like a Netscape Mail message window.

You can subscribe to newsgroups by selecting the Subscribe entry in the File menu. This opens a window that will show a list of all available newsgroups. The list is compressed, with beginning strings that can be expanded by clicking on the + signs next to them. Select the one you want and click on the Join button in the upper-right corner. When you close the window, the newsgroups will appear under your newsgroup server name.

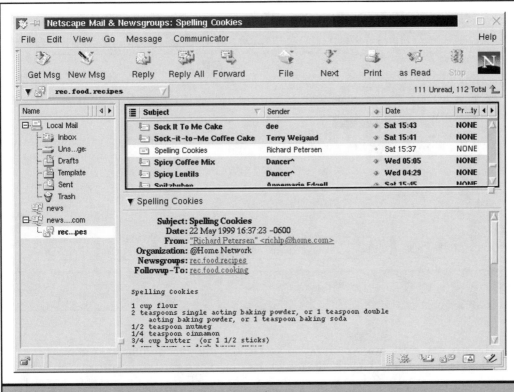

Figure 12-3.   *Netscape Collabra newsreader*

Pine and slrn

Pine is designed to work with the Internet and is capable of reading Internet newsgroups. The Config entry listed on the Setup screen will open an options list in which you can place entries for your Internet mail server or news server. If you are using an ISP or LAN, you can enter the domain names for your news server or mail server. Newsgroups are treated by Pine as just another mail folder (see Figure 12-4). To list a newsgroup, select the Folder List entry and use the **A** command to add the name of the newsgroup. It will then be listed as another folder. When you select it, the newsgroup headers are listed instead of mail headers. You can also post news using Pine, just as you would send a message. Pine has an extensive list of options with which you can customize its operations. These options are accessed through the Config selection in the Setup screen that is accessible from the main menu. The options you change are saved in a **.pinrc** file in your **home** directory.

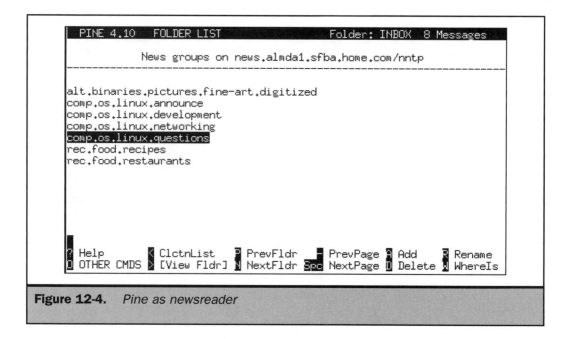

```
  PINE 4.10    FOLDER LIST                    Folder: INBOX  8 Messages

                  News groups on news.almda1.sfba.home.com/nntp
  ------------------------------------------------------------------------

  alt.binaries.pictures.fine-art.digitized
  comp.os.linux.announce
  comp.os.linux.development
  comp.os.linux.networking
  comp.os.linux.questions
  rec.food.recipes
  rec.food.restaurants




  ? Help         < ClctnList    P PrevFldr    - PrevPage A Add       R Rename
  O OTHER CMDS   > [View Fldr]  N NextFldr  Spc NextPage D Delete     W WhereIs
```

Figure 12-4.   *Pine as newsreader*

The **slrn** newsreader is screen-based and has an interface similar to Pine's. Commands are displayed across the top of the screen and can be executed using the listed keys. There are different types of screens for the newsgroup list, article list, and article content, each with its own set of commands. An initial screen lists your subscribed newsgroups with commands for posting, listing, and subscribing to your newsgroups. Selecting a newsgroup opens a screen that initially displays just the newsgroup's articles. Article headers are listed with different colors for the article number, author, and subject fields. Selecting an article will split the screen, showing the contents of the article in a larger portion below, and a smaller portion showing the article list. The ARROW keys as well as the PAGE UP and PAGE DOWN keys will move you through the article list, whereas the SPACEBAR and **b** keys move you forward and backward through the currently displayed article text. Selecting a new article displays it in the lower section of the screen. Commands you can perform on an article are shown at the bottom of the screen. They include commands for posting follow-ups and paging operations.

Emacs News

The GNU version of Emacs also includes a newsreader along with other components such as a mailer and editor. GNU Emacs is included on Red Hat distributions. Check the Emacs Web site at **www.emacs.org** for more information. When you start up GNU Emacs, menu buttons are displayed across the top of the screen. If you are running

Emacs in an X Windows environment, then you will have full GUI capabilities and can select menus using your mouse. Be sure that the **NNTPSERVER** variable is set to your news server address in your **.bash_profile** file and that it is exported.

To access the Emacs newsreader, select from the Read Net News entry in the Tools menu. A listing of newsgroups is displayed. The menus across the top of the screen change, adding Misc, Groups, and Groups menu. The Groups menu holds entries for managing newsgroups such as sorting and searching for groups as well as subscribing to new ones or listing only subscribed or unsubscribed groups. To select a group, click on it or move to it with the arrow keys, and then press the SPACEBAR.

When you select a newsgroup, a split screen is displayed where the headers for the newsgroup articles are listed in the top screen, and the contents of the currently selected article are shown in the bottom screen. Use the Tab key or the mouse to select the screen you want. When you select the header screen, the menus change listing Search, Misc, Post, Threads, and Article menus. These hold commands for managing the headers. For example, you can post a follow-up by selecting the article and choosing the Follow-up entry in the Post menu. In the Article menu you can move to the bottom of the header list or the top, highlight selected headers, and save articles. In the Thread menu you can move to the header for the next thread or toggle threads on or off. From the Search menu you can search for headers using patterns and regular expressions. When you are finished with a newsgroup, choose Exit from the Misc menu.

On the bottom screen, an article is displayed. When you select this screen, the menus change to Search, Misc, Post, Treatment, and Article. Here the Article menu lets you page forward and backward through the article. The Treatment menu has entries for hiding or showing headers and signatures. From the Post menu you can post follow-ups and replies for this particular article. The Search menu now performs searches on the article text.

GNU Emacs is really a working environment in which each task has its own buffer. When you read news, a buffer is opened to hold the newsgroup and article headers, and when you read an article, another buffer will hold the contents; when you compose a article, yet another buffer will hold the text you wrote. The buffers you have opened for mail, news, or editing notes or files will be listed in the Buffers menu. You can use this menu to switch between them.

XEmacs is the complete Emacs editor with a graphical user interface and Internet applications. The Internet applications, which you can easily access from the main XEmacs button bar, include a Web Browser, a mail utility, and a newsreader. Clicking the News button brings up another window that displays the newsreader, listing your Usenet newsgroups. If you are using an ISP, it will use the name of the news server in the **NNTPSERVER** variable.You can then access newsgroups, displaying articles.

trn

With the **trn** newsreader, you can display and search articles by subject, article, or threads. To use **trn** to access remote news servers, be sure the **NNTPSERVER** variable is set in your **.bash_profile** file. The **trn** interface has several powerful features, such as pattern searches for groups of articles. The *t* in **trn** stands for *threaded*. A *thread* is any connection between articles, such as articles that share the same subject or follow-up articles to a previously posted article. The **trn** newsreader has a special interface, called a *selector*, which allows you to move through a threaded set of articles. For example, if you are reading an article on a particular subject and you give an **n** command to go to the next article, you go to the next article on that subject (in the thread), not to the next sequentially posted article as you would normally do. Instead of moving through a newsgroup's articles according to their posted order, you can move through them using different threads, examining articles according to different subjects. The same is true for an article and its follow-up articles. An article and its follow-ups are threaded so that upon reading an article, pressing the **n** command will move you to the first follow-up to that article, not to the next sequentially posted article. Using threads, you can use the **n** command to read an article with all of its follow-ups, instead of searching separately for each one. The **trn** newsreader commands are listed in Table 12-1.

The **trn** newsreader operates on two levels: the newsgroup list and the article list. When you first execute **trn**, you select a newsgroup from a list of newsgroups. Commands move you from one newsgroup to another in the list. Once you have found the one you want, you can then select articles to read in that newsgroup. When you have finished reading, you can leave that newsgroup and select another in the newsgroup list. You use the **trn** selector to display, organize, and move through the article list, though you can also use the standard **rn** commands to manage the article list.

You enter the **trn** newsreader by typing the **trn** command at your Linux prompt. The **trn** newsreader will initially display a short list of newsgroup headers. However, before doing so, **trn** will first check an official list of new newsgroups with those listed in your **.newsrc** file. If there are any new newsgroups not yet listed in your **.newsrc** file, then **trn** will ask, one by one, if you want to subscribe to them. At each prompt, you can enter **y** to add the newsgroup and **n** not to add it. With **-q**, **trn** will go directly to displaying the newsgroup headers, skipping any new newsgroup queries.

```
$ trn -q
```

After the subscription phase, **trn** checks to see if there are any newsgroups listed in your **.newsrc** file that have unread news in them. If so, the newsgroup headers for the first few of these are displayed. Each newsgroup header tells how many unread articles remain in a given newsgroup. The **trn** newsreader then prompts you as to whether you want to read articles in the first newsgroup. If not, you can enter the **n** command to move to the next newsgroup. The **p** command moves you back to the previous newsgroup.

To list articles in a newsgroup, you enter **+** at the prompt. This displays the **trn** selector from which you can select the article you want to display. If you enter **y**, you will skip the list of articles and display the first article in the newsgroup. You will then be prompted to read the next article or quit and return to the newsgroup list. You can leave the newsgroup and return to the newsgroup list by entering **q** at the prompt.

In the next example, the user enters the **trn** interface and a list of newsgroup headers is displayed. The user is then prompted for the first header, which the user skips with the **n** command. At the next header, the user enters a **+** command to list articles in the **comp.os.linux.misc** newsgroup.

```
$ trn
comp.ai.language                    3 articles
comp.os.linux.misc                  1   article
rec.arts.movies                     7   articles
rec.food.recipes                  245 articles
sci.physics.fusion                 32   articles
talk.politics.theory              126 articles
 etc.

====== 3 unread articles in comp.ai.language — read now? [+ynq] n
====== 1 unread articles in comp.os.linux.misc — read now? [ynq] +
```

The **trn** newsreader has a variety of commands for moving through the list of newsgroups. You can move to the first or last newsgroup, the next or previous newsgroup, or the newsgroup whose name has a specific pattern. For example, a **$** will place you at the end of the newsgroup list. Many commands are designed to distinguish between read and unread newsgroups. The **^** places you at the first newsgroup with unread news, whereas the number 1 places you at the first newsgroup in the list, whether it is read or not. The lowercase **n** and **p** commands place you at the next and previous unread newsgroups. To move to the next or previous newsgroup regardless of whether it is read or not, you use the uppercase **N** and **P** commands. The pattern searching commands give **trn** great versatility in locating newsgroups. To perform a pattern search for a newsgroup, at the prompt you enter a **/** followed by the pattern. The **/** performs a forward search through the list of newsgroups. The **?** performs a backward search.

As mentioned earlier, typing **+** at the **trn** prompt enters the selector, which allows you to use threads. The selector consists of a screen that lists each article's author, thread count, and subject. Any follow-up articles are preceded by a **>** symbol. Articles are grouped according to the threads they belong to. The first article in each thread is preceded by an ID consisting of a lowercase alphabetic character or a single digit, starting from *a*. A sample **trn** selector screen is shown here:

```
rec.food.recipes       258 articles (moderated)

a     Dylan Chris           1     Fruit Salad
b     Cecelia Petersen      1     Fudge Cake
d     Richard Leland        2     Chocolate News
      Larisa@atlash
      Aleina Petersen       1     >White chocolate
      Maryann Price         1     >Chocolate Fudge
```

```
        mark@pacific        1    >
        Justin G.           1    >Chocolate
    e   George Petersen     1    Apple Muffins
    f   Marylou Carrion     1    REQUEST: romantic dinners
    g   Valerie Fuller      1    REQUEST: Dehydrated Goodies
    i   Carolyn Blacklock   1    REQUEST: Devonshire Cream
        Bill Bode           1    >
    j   Bonnie Matoza       1    Sauces
    l   Gabriel Matoza      1    Passion Fruit
    o   Ken Blacklock       1    REQUEST: blackened (red)fish
        augie@napa          3    >blackened (red)fish
        John Carrion
        Anntoinnete

-- Select threads (date order) -- 24%
```

Upon entering the selector, the first screen of articles is displayed, and the first thread is preceded with an *a*. To display the next screen of articles, you press either the SPACEBAR or the > key. You can display the previous screen by pressing the < key. Upon displaying the next screen, threads will again be listed beginning from *a*. The ID preceding a thread is unique to that thread only for that screen; it is simply a screen device for referencing threads displayed on the screen at that time. To read an article, you first select the thread for that article and then instruct the selector to display it. You select a thread by pressing the key corresponding to its ID. Once you have selected the thread, you can then display its articles by pressing either the ENTER key or uppercase **z**. The first article in the thread will be displayed. Pressing the **n** key moves you to the next article in the thread. Once you have found the article you want, you can read it using any of the standard **trn** commands for displaying articles. If the article takes up more than one screen, you can display the next screen by pressing the SPACEBAR. You can return to the selector any time by pressing the + key.

The selector has three display modes—article, subject, and thread—which correspond to how the selector displays articles. You can easily choose the mode you want by pressing the **s** command and entering **a** for article, **s** for subject, or **t** for thread. You can also switch back and forth between the different modes by pressing the = key. A subject is whatever a user enters into the subject field of an article's header. Articles with the same subject entry are threaded together. When using the thread mode, articles are grouped with any posted follow-ups, as well as with articles of the same subject. The follow-up articles are preceded by a > symbol. The article mode does not display threads. Articles are listed individually, each preceded by its own ID, in posted sequence.

When you select an article, its header is displayed followed by a **(more)** prompt and the first page of the text. The article will be displayed screen by screen, just as files are displayed screen by screen with the **more** utility. To continue to the next screen, you press the SPACEBAR. You can move backward one page at a time by pressing the **b** key. The

q command allows you to quit before reading the whole article. You can also search the text of the article for a pattern. The **g** command followed by a pattern will locate the first occurrence of that pattern in the text. You can repeat the search with the **G** command.

At the end of the article, you will be presented with a prompt asking what you want to do next. The choices **n**, **p**, and **q** will be displayed in brackets. Pressing **n** will display the next article in the newsgroup, and **p** will display the previous article. To return to your selector screen of newsgroup articles, you press **+**, as shown in the next example. Pressing **q** will return to the newsgroup list.

```
End of article 7155 (of 7158) -- what next? [npq] +
```

When you display the first article in a thread, a thread tree will appear in the upper-right corner of the screen. A thread tree represents the connections between articles in a thread. Each unread article is represented by a number starting from 1, with each enclosed in brackets. Lines connect the different article numbers. The number representing the article you are currently displaying is highlighted in the thread tree. Once you read an article and move on to another, the read article's number is enclosed in parentheses, and the next article's number is highlighted.

Table 12-1 lists the **trn** newsreader commands.

Commands	Description
N	Moves to the next newsgroup
p	Moves to the previous newsgroup with unread articles
P	Moves to the previous newsgroup
-	Moves to the previously selected newsgroup
^	Moves to the first newsgroup with unread articles
num	Moves to newsgroup with that number
$	Moves to the last newsgroup
g*newsgroup-name*	Moves to newsgroup with that name
/*pattern*	Searches forward to the newsgroup with that pattern
?*pattern*	Searches backward to the newsgroup with that pattern
L	Lists subscribed newsgroups
l*pattern*	Lists unsubscribed newsgroups

Table 12-1. *The* **trn** *Newsreader Commands*

Commands	Description
u *newsgroup-name*	Unsubscribed newsgroups
a *newsgroup-name*	Subscribed to a newsgroup
c	Marks articles in a newsgroup as read
Displaying Selector	
+	Enters the selector from the **trn** line prompt, or leaves the selector and returns to the **trn** line prompt
s	Selects selector mode: subject, thread, or article
=	Switches between article and subject/thread selector
o	Sorts selector items by date, author, thread count, or subject. User is prompted to enter **d, a, n**, or **s**.
L	Sets selector item display to short, medium, or long forms
E	Exclusive mode; displays only selected articles
k	Removes an article or subject from the selector display
U	Displays unread articles
Moving through Selector	
SPACEBAR	Displays the next screen of articles
>	Displays the next screen of threads
<	Displays the previous screen of articles
$	Displays the last screen of articles
^	Displays the first screen of articles
Selecting Articles in the Selector	
id	Selects/deselects an article thread
id*	Selects/deselects articles with the same subject as ID
n	Moves to the next thread ID
p	Moves to the previous thread ID

Table 12-1.   *The* **trn** *Newsreader Commands* (continued)

Commands	Description
z	Begins displaying selected articles; returns to newsgroup screen when finished
x	Begins displaying selected articles, but moves to the next newsgroup when finished
/pattern	Searches forward to the article with that pattern in each article's subject field
?pattern?	Searches backward to the article with that pattern in each article's subject field
/	Repeats previous forward search
?	Repeats previous backward search
/pattern:command	Selects a group of articles matching the pattern and applies the **trn** command to all
id,id:command	Selects a group of articles referenced by the numbers and applies the **trn** command to all
Displaying Articles	
SPACEBAR	Displays the next screen of the article
ENTER	Scrolls to the next line of the article
d	Scrolls to the next half-screen of the article
b	Displays the previous screen of the article
v	Redisplays article from the beginning
q	Displays last screen of the article
g pattern	Searches for a pattern in the text
G	Repeats pattern search in the text
Replying to Articles	
r	Replies to current article
R	Replies to current article and includes article text in the reply
f	Posts a follow-up to the current article
F	Posts a follow-up including the text of the current article

Table 12-1. *The* **trn** *Newsreader Commands* (continued)

INTERNET

tin

The **tin** newsreader operates using a selector that is much like the one used in the **trn** newsreader. However, **tin** has a screen selector for both newsgroups and articles. When you enter **tin**, the selector displays the screen listing your newsgroups. You can then select the newsgroup you want and display a screen for its articles. One set of screen movement commands is used for all screens, whether for newsgroups, article lists, or article text. CTRL-D, CTRL-F, and SPACEBAR all move you forward to the next screen. CTRL-U, CTRL-B, and **b** all move you backward to the previous screen. The UP ARROW and the **k** key move you up a line on the screen, and the DOWN ARROW and **j** key move you down a line. The **q** command will move you back from one selector to another. For example, if you are in the article selector, pressing **q** will move you back to the newsgroup selector. **Q** will quit the **tin** newsreader entirely.

The **tin** newsreader also has a set of editing and history commands that you can use to edit any commands that you enter. ESC will always erase a command you have entered and let you start over. The editing commands are a subset of the Emacs commands. CTRL-D deletes a character, CTRL-F and the RIGHT ARROW key move right one character. CTRL-B and the LEFT ARROW key move back one character. To insert new text, move your cursor to the position you want and start typing. The **tin** newsreader also keeps a history of the commands you enter. You can recall the previous commands with CTRL-P, moving back, one by one, through a list of your previously entered commands. CTRL-N moves you forward through the list. You can find a complete listing of all **tin** commands in the **tin** manual pages, which you can invoke by typing **man tin**. The **tin** newsreader commands are listed in Table 12-2.

When you start **tin**, it first displays a screen of newsgroups. The term "Group Selection" will be shown at the top of the screen. To its right will be "h=help." Pressing the **h** key will bring up a Help menu. The newsgroups are listed with a selection number that identifies the newsgroup, followed by the number of unread articles, and then the name of the newsgroup. To select a newsgroup, you must first move to it. You can do this in a variety of ways. If you see your newsgroup displayed on the screen, you can just use your UP ARRROW and DOWN ARROW keys to move to it. CTRL-D will move you to the next screen, and CTRL-U will move you back. Instead of using the arrow keys, you can move directly to a newsgroup by entering its index number. You can also locate a newsgroup by using pattern searches. You enter the **/** followed by a pattern. **?** performs a backward search.

Once you have located the newsgroup you want, press ENTER to display a list of its articles. A list of commonly used commands are displayed at the bottom of the screen. The **s** command will subscribe to a new newsgroup, and the **u** command will unsubscribe.

```
Group Selection (turlle.mytrek.com 3230)        h=help

     1    3      comp.ai.language
     2    1      comp.os.linux.misc
```

```
3     7      rec.arts.movies
4    24      rec.food.recipes
5    32      sci.physics.fusion
6   126      talk.politics.theory

 <n>=set current to n, TAB=next unread, /=search pattern, c)atchup,
g)oto, j=line down, k=line up, h)elp, m)ove, q)uit, r=toggle all/unread,
   s)ubscribe, S)ub pattern, u)nsubscribe, U)nsub pattern, y)ank in/out
```

search forwards > **rec.food**

The **tin** newsreader displays the subject and author of each article in the newsgroup preceded by an index number and, if unread, a **+**. The **+** sign indicates all unread articles. Working from the selector, you can choose articles you want to display. You select an article by moving the cursor to that article and pressing ENTER. Both the newsgroup and article selector screens use many of the same commands. The UP ARROW and DOWN ARROW keys will move you from one article to the next. If there is more than one screen of articles, you can move back and forth through them using CTRL-U or CTRL-D. You can also move to an article by typing its index number. An example of the **tin** article selector screen follows:

```
rec.food.recipes (119T 124A 0K 0H R)          h=help

65   +     Fruit Salad                  Dylan Chris
66   +     Fudge Cake                   Cecelia Petersen
67   +     Chocolate News               Richard Leland
68   +     Chocolate News               Larisa@atlash
69   +     Apple Muffins                George Petersen
70   +     REQUEST: romantic dinners    Marylou Carrion
71   +     REQUEST: Dehydrated Goodies  Valerie Fuller
72   +     REQUEST: Devonshire Cream    Carolyn Blacklock
73   +     Sauces                       Bonnie Matoza
74   +     Passion Fruit                Gabriel Matoza
75   +     REQUEST: blackened (red)fish Ken Blacklock
76   +     REQUEST: Cheese Toast        dylan@sf
77   +     REQUEST: Sausage Recipes     Penny Bode
78   +     Biscuit Recipe               gloria@stlake
79   +     >blackened (red)fish         augie@napa
80   +     Oatmeal Cookies              John Gunther
```

```
81    +    REQUEST: Potato Salad          Margaret
82    +    REQUEST: Sesame Chicken        Frank Moitoza
83    +    >Summer desserts               maryann@sebast

    <n>=set current to n, TAB=next unread, /=search pattern, ^K)ill/select,
 a)uthor search, c)atchup, j=line down, k=line up, K=mark read, l)ist thread,
  |=pipe, m)ail, o=print, q)uit, r=toggle all/unread, s)ave, t)ag, w=post
```

The commonly used commands for accessing articles are displayed at the bottom of the screen. You can search articles for a specified pattern with the **/** command. The **a** command allows you to search for articles by a specified author. The **s** command will save an article. You can post an article of your own to the newsgroup by pressing the **w** command. You will be prompted for header information, and then you enter the text of your message. Once you have selected an article, it is displayed. If the article takes up more than one screen, you can move forward by pressing the SPACEBAR and backward by pressing the **b** key. With the **B** command, you can search the article for a specified pattern, and with the **s** command you can save it. With the **f** command you can post a follow-up to the article, and with the **r** command you can send a message to the author.

The **tin** newsreader supports an extensive set of options, features, attributes, and variables. Configuration files are placed in the **.tin** directory maintained in your **home** directory. Options can be set using the **tin** Global Options menu or by entering them directly in the **tinrc** file in the **.tin** directory. Attributes for particular newsgroups can be set in the **.tin** attributes file. For accessing remote news servers, be sure the **NNTPSERVER** variable is set in your **.bash_profile** file.

Table 12-2 lists the **tin** newsreader screen-movement commands.

Screen-Movement Commands	Effect/Description
DOWN ARROW, **j**	Moves down a line
UP ARROW, **k**	Moves up a line
$	Goes to last line
CTRL-U, CTRL-B, **b**, PAGE UP	Goes to previous screen

Table 12-2.   *The tin Newsreader*

Screen-Movement Commands	Effect/Description
CTRL-D, CTRL-F, SPACEBAR, PAGE DOWN	Goes to next screen
CTRL-L	Redraws screen
q	Returns to previous level
Q	Quits **tin**
Command Editing and History	
CTRL-F, RIGHT ARROW	Moves to next character
CTRL-B, LEFT ARROW	Moves to previous character
CTRL-D, BACKSPACE, DEL	Deletes character
CTRL-P	Previously entered command in history list
CTRL-N	Next entered command in history list
ESC	Erases command entered
Newsgroup Selector	
num	Goes to newsgroup with that index number
ENTER	Selects current newsgroup
TAB	Goes to next unread newsgroup
/	Searches forward
?	Searches backward
g	Chooses a new group by name
K	Marks article/thread as read and goes to next unread
l	Lists articles within current thread
C	Marks all articles as read and goes to next unread group
c	Marks all articles as read and goes to group selection menu

Table 12-2.   *The tin Newsreader* (continued)

Screen-Movement Commands	Effect/Description
s	Subscribes to a newsgroup
u	Unsubscribes from a newsgroup
S *pattern*	Subscribes from newsgroups with *pattern*
U *pattern*	Unsubscribes to newsgroups with *pattern*
M	Displays menu of configurable options
v	Shows version information
h	Help command
CTRL-K	Kill/auto-select current newsgroup
H	Toggles mini Help menu
I	Toggles inverse video
Article Selector	
num	Goes to article with that index number
$	Goes to last article
ENTER	Selects current article
TAB	Goes to next unread article
a	Author forward search
A	Author backward search
/	Subject forward search
?	Subject backward search
n	Goes to next group
p	Goes to previous group
N	Goes to next unread article
P	Goes to previous unread article
d	Toggles display of subject or subject and author
r	Toggles display to show all/only unread articles

Table 12-2. *The tin Newsreader* (continued)

Screen-Movement Commands	Effect/Description
u	Toggles display of unthreaded and threaded articles
z	Marks article as unread
Z	Marks thread as unread
X	Marks all unread articles that have not been selected as read
t	Tags current article for cross-posting/mailing /piping/printing/saving
U	Untags all tagged articles
s	Saves article/thread/hot/pattern/tagged articles to file
m	Mails article/thread/hot/pattern/tagged articles to someone
o	Outputs article/thread/hot/pattern/tagged articles to printer
w	Posts an article to current group
W	Lists articles posted by user
x	Cross-posts current article to another group
*	Selects thread
.	Toggles selection of thread
@	Reverses all selections (all articles)
~	Undoes all selections (all articles)
+	Performs auto-selection on groups or articles creating hot items; these items will have a * displayed before them
=	Marks threads selected if at least one unread article is selected
!	Escapes shell
-	Shows last message
|	Pipes article/thread/hot/pattern/tagged articles into command

Table 12-2. *The tin Newsreader* (continued)

INTERNET

Screen-Movement Commands	Effect/Description
Displaying Article	
b	Moves back a page
SPACEBAR	Moves forward a page
B	Article body search
;	Marks threads selected if at least one unread article is selected
s	Saves article/thread/hot/pattern/tagged articles to file
m	Mails article/thread/hot/pattern/tagged articles to someone
o	Outputs article/thread/hot/pattern/tagged articles to printer
w	Posts an article to current group
f	Posts follow-up for current article
r	Sends reply to author of article

Table 12-2. *The tin Newsreader* (continued)

Posting Articles with Pnews

Though most newsreaders let you post news, some such as **trn**, do not. You can post articles directly using Pnews. Pnews prompts you for certain header information, places you in an editor in which you can type in your article, and then prompts you either to send, edit, save, or quit the article. It operates directly from the command line, providing you with a full-screen interface much like other screen-based applications such as Pine, **mutt**, and **tin**. To begin, enter the **Pnews** command at your Linux shell prompt. You are then prompted to enter the newsgroup for the article. To see the full list of newsgroups, enter a **?** at the newsgroups prompt. It is, however, a good idea to have already decided on what newsgroups you want. You can obtain a listing of newsgroups at any time from the newsgroup file located in the **news** directory on your system.

After selecting your newsgroups, you are asked to specify distribution. Distribution can be made at ever-widening areas. You can post your article for local viewing for users on your own system, or you can post it for worldwide viewing. There are various intermediate levels of distribution, such as North America, the United States, or a specific state or city. Pnews will first list possible prefixes, and then you enter the one you want at the distribution prompt. For the United States, you would enter **usa**.

Next, you are asked to enter a title or subject of the article. This will be used to classify the article and will be searched in pattern searches. You are then asked if you really want to post the article. To continue, enter **y**. You are then asked if you have a prepared file to include in your article. Often, it is easier to write your article and save it to a file first, using a standard editor. Once it is ready, you can post the contents of that file. The contents of the file you specify are then read into the article that is being posted. If you do not enter a file name at this point, Pnews will automatically place you in an editor where you can type in your article.

Finally, Pnews prompts you either to send, abort, edit, or list the article. You need enter only the first character of a command to execute it. For example, if you change your mind and decide not to post the article, you just enter **a** at this prompt, quitting Pnews without sending the article. On the other hand, you can enter **e** at the prompt to edit the article, in case you notice any mistakes or want to add something. You would then be placed in the standard editor with the contents of the article displayed. Here, you can make the changes you want and return to the Pnews prompt upon exiting the standard editor (**ZZ** for Vi). To post the article, enter **s**, for send, at this prompt. The article is sent to the Usenet manager and posted in the appropriate newsgroup.

If you want to use the standard editor to type the text of the article, you simply press ENTER when asked for a prepared file to include. You are then asked to enter an editor. Within brackets, Pnews will display the default standard editor it uses—often Vi—and you can simply press ENTER to use it. Pnews then places you in the default editor and displays the header information. You are free to change fields in the header if you want. You can change your subject or even your newsgroup. You then use standard editing commands to type the text of your article. When finished, exit the editor (if you are using Vi, press **ZZ**). Pnews prompts you to send, abort, edit, or list your article. You can, of course, edit your article again by typing **e** at this prompt. To finally post the article, you enter **s** at the prompt.

You usually end an article with the same standard signature information, such as your name, Internet address or addresses, and a polite sign-off. As you write more articles, it is helpful to have your signature information automatically added to your articles. To do so, you need to create a file called **.signature** in your **home** directory and enter your signature information in it. Pnews will read the contents of the **.signature** file and place them at the end of your article. You can use any standard editor to create your **.signature** file.

Chapter 13

FTP and Gopher

The Internet is a network of computers around the world that you can access with an Internet address and a set of Internet tools. Many computers on the Internet are configured to operate as servers, providing information to anyone who requests it. The information is contained in files that you can access and copy. Each server, often referred to as a *site*, has its own Internet address by which it can be located. Linux provides a set of Internet tools that you can use to access sites on the Internet and then locate and download information from them. These tools are known as *clients*. A client application such as an FTP client can communicate with a corresponding server application running on a remote system. An FTP client can communicate with an FTP server program on another system. The server will let the client access certain specified resources on its system. An FTP server will let an FTP client transfer certain files.

To access Internet sites, your computer must be connected to the Internet. You may be part of a network that is already connected to the Internet. If you have a standalone computer, such as a personal computer, you can obtain an Internet connection from an Internet service provider (ISP). Once you have an Internet address of your own, you can configure your Linux system to connect to the Internet and use various Internet tools to access different sites. The Network Administration chapter describes how to configure your Linux system to make such a connection.

The primary tools for accessing Internet sites are FTP clients and Web browsers. With FTP clients you can connect to a corresponding FTP site and download files from it. FTP clients are commonly used to download software from FTP sites that operate as software repositories. Most Linux software applications can be downloaded to your Linux system from such sites. The **contrib.redhat.com** site is an example of one such FTP site, holding an extensive set of packaged Linux applications that you can download using an FTP client and then easily install on your system. In the last few years, the Web browsers have become the primary tool for accessing information on the Internet. Most of the tasks you perform on the Internet may be done easily with a Web browser. You only need to use an FTP client to download or upload files from or to a specific FTP site.

Other Internet tools are also available for your use, such as Gopher, telnet, and IRC clients. Gopher is a kind of hybrid of FTP and Web clients. It provides you with a series of menus listing different topics. You move from one menu to the other, narrowing your topic until you find the information you want. Often this is in the form of a file that you download by just selecting its menu entry. The telnet protocol lets you directly log into an account on another system. IRC clients set up chat rooms through which you can communicate with other users over the Internet. Gopher is discussed later in this chapter, and Web clients are discussed in Chapter 14. Telnet and IRC clients are discussed in Chapter 15.

Internet Addresses

The Internet uses a set of network protocols called TCP/IP, which stands for Transmission Control Protocol/Internet Protocol. In a TCP/IP network, messages are broken into small components called datagrams that are then transmitted through various interlocking routes and delivered to their destination computers. Once received, the datagrams are reassembled into the original message. Datagrams are also referred to as packets. Sending messages as small components has proved to be far more reliable and faster than sending them as one large bulky transmission. With small components, if one is lost or damaged, only that component has to be re-sent, whereas if any part of a large transmission is corrupted or lost, the entire message has to be re-sent.

On a TCP/IP network such as the Internet, each computer is given a unique address called an *IP address*. The IP address is used to identify and locate a particular host—a computer connected to the network. An IP address consists of a set of four segments, each pair separated by a period. The segments consist of numbers that range from 0 to 255, with certain values reserved for special use. The IP address is divided into two parts, one that identifies the network and the other that identifies a particular host. The number of segments used for each is determined by the class of the network. On the Internet, networks are organized into three classes depending on their size—classes A, B, and C. A class A network will use only the first segment for the IP address and the remaining three for the host, allowing a great many computers to be connected to the same network. Most IP addresses reference smaller, class C, networks. For a class C network, the first three segments are used to identify the network, and only the last segment identifies the host. The syntax looks like this:

```
net.net.net.host
```

In a class C network, the first three numbers identify the network part of the IP address. This part is divided into three network numbers, each identifying a subnet. Networks on the Internet are organized into subnets beginning with the largest and narrowing to small subnetworks. The last number is used to identify a particular computer that is referred to as a host. You can think of the Internet as a series of networks with subnetworks, and these subnetworks have their own subnetworks. The rightmost number identifies the host computer, and the number preceding it identifies the subnetwork that the computer is a part of. The number to the left of that identifies the network that the subnetwork is part of, and so on. The Internet address 192.168.187.4 references the fourth computer connected to the network identified by the number 187.

INTERNET

Network 187 is a subnet to a larger network identified as 168. This larger network is itself a subnet of the network identified as 192. Here's how it breaks down:

192.168.187.4	IP address
192.168.187	Network identification
4	Host identification

An IP address is officially provided by the Network Information Center (NIC) that administers the Internet. You can obtain your own Internet address from the NIC, or if you are on a network already connected to the Internet, your network administrator can assign you one. If you are using an Internet service provider, the ISP may obtain one for you or, each time you connect, may temporarily assign one from a pool they have on hand.

Certain numbers are reserved. The numbers 127, 0, or 255 cannot be part of an official IP address. The address 127.0.0.0 is the loopback address that allows users on your computer to communicate with each other. The number 255 is a special broadcast identifier that you can use to broadcast messages to all sites on a network. Using 225 for any part of the IP address references all nodes connected at that level. For example, 192.168.255.255 broadcasts a message to all computers on network 142.168, all its subnetworks, and their hosts. The address 192.168.187.255 broadcasts to every computer on the local network. If you use 0 for the network part of the address, the host number will reference a computer within your local network. For example, 0.0.0.6 references the sixth computer in your local network. If you want to broadcast to all computers on your local network, you can use the number 0.0.0.255.

A special set of numbers is reserved for use on non-Internet local area networks. These are numbers that begin with the special network number 192.168., as used in these examples. If you are setting up a local area network such as a small business or home network, you are free to use these numbers for your local machines. You can set up an intranet using network cards such as Ethernet cards and Ethernet hubs, and then configure your machines with IP addresses starting from 192.168.1.1. The host segment can go up to 256. If you have three machines on your home network, you could give them the addresses 192.168.1.1, 192.168.1.2, 192.168.1.3. You can implement "Internet" services such as FTP, Web, and mail services on your local machines and use any of the "Internet" tools to make use of those services. They all use the same TCP/IP protocols as used on the Internet. For example, with FTP tools you can transfer files between the machines on your network, with mail tools you can send messages from one machine to the other, and with a Web browser you can access local "Web" sites that may be installed on a machine running its own "Web" servers. If you want to have one of your machines connected to the Internet or some other network, you can set it up to be a gateway machine. By conventions, the gateway machine is usually given the address 192.168.1.1. With a method called *IP masquerading* you can have any of the non-Internet machines use a gateway to connect to the Internet.

All hosts on the Internet are identified by their IP addresses. When you send a message to a host on the Internet, you must provide its IP address. However, using a sequence of four numbers of an IP address can be very difficult. They are hard to remember, and it's easy to make mistakes when typing them. To make it easier to identify a computer on the Internet, the Domain Name Service (DNS) was implemented. The DNS establishes a domain name address for each IP address. The domain name address is a series of names separated by periods. Whenever you use a domain name address, it is automatically converted to an IP address that is then used to identify that Internet host. The domain name address is far easier to use than its corresponding IP address.

A domain name address needs to be registered with the NIC so that each computer on the Internet will have a unique name. Creating a name follows specified naming conventions, as discussed earlier, in Chapter 11. The domain name address consists of the hostname, the name you gave to your computer; a domain name, the name that identifies your network; and an extension that identifies the type of network you are on. Here is the syntax for domain addresses:

```
host-name.domain-name.extension
```

In the following example, the domain address references a computer called metalab on a network referred to as unc, and it is part of an educational institution, as indicated by the extension edu.

```
metalab.unc.edu
```

The conversion of domain addresses to IP addresses used to be performed by each individual host. And for a few frequently used addresses for which you know the IP address, this can still be done. However, so many computers are now connected to the Internet that domain name conversion has to be performed by special servers known as domain name servers or simply name servers. A name server holds a database of domain name addresses and their IP addresses. Local networks will sometimes have their own name servers. If a name server does not have the address, then it may call on other name servers to perform the conversion. A program on your computer called a resolver will obtain the IP address from a name server and then use it in the application where you specified the domain name address.

With the **whois** and **nslookup** commands, you can obtain information for domain name servers about different networks and hosts connected to the Internet. Enter **whois** and the domain name address of the host or network, and **whois** will display information about the host, such as the street address and phone number as well as contact persons.

```
$ whois  domain-address
```

The **nslookup** command takes a domain address and finds its corresponding IP address.

```
$ nslookup   domain-address
```

The **nslookup** command has an interactive mode that you enter by not specifying any domain name. You can then use **nslookup** to search for other kinds of information about a host. For example, the HINFO option will find out what type of operating system a host uses. The **nslookup** Man page specifies a list of different options and how to use them.

Network File Transfer: FTP

You can use FTP clients to directly transfer very large files from one site to another. It can handle both text and binary files. FTP stands for File Transfer Protocol. This is one of the TCP/IP protocols, and it operates on systems connected to networks that use the TCP/IP protocols, such as the Internet. FTP performs a remote login to another account on another system connected to you on a network such as the Internet. Once logged into that other system, you can transfer files to and from it. To log in, you will need to know the login name and password for the account on the remote system. For example, if you have accounts at two different sites on the Internet, you can use FTP to transfer files from one to the other. However, many sites on the Internet allow public access using FTP. Many sites serve as depositories for very large files that anyone can access and download. Such sites are often referred to as FTP sites, and in many cases their Internet address will begin with the word "ftp" such as **ftp.calderasystems.com** or **ftp.redhat.com**. Others begin with other names such as **contrib.redhat.com** or **metalab.unc.edu**. These public sites allow anonymous FTP login from any user. For the login name you use the word "anonymous," and for the password you use your Internet address. You can then transfer files from that site to your own system.

You can perform FTP operations using any one of a number of FTP client programs. For Linux systems, you can choose from several FTP clients. Many now operate using GUI interfaces such as Gnome. Some, such as Netscape, have limited capabilities, whereas others such as IglooFTP and ncftp include an extensive set of enhancements. The original FTP client is just as effective, though not as easy to use. It operates using a simple command line interface and requires no GUI or cursor support as other clients do.

Web Browser-Based FTP: Netscape

You access an FTP site and download files from it with any Web browser. A Web browser is very effective for checking out an FTP site to see what files are listed there. When you access an FTP site with a Web browser, the entire list of files in a directory will be listed as a Web page. You can move to a subdirectory by just clicking its entry. Click the .. entry at the top of the page to move back up to the parent directory. With Netscape Navigator you can easily browse through an FTP site to download files, as shown in Figure 13-1. To download a file, you left-click its entry (not right-click). This opens a box for selecting your local directory and name for the file. The default name is the same as on the remote system. Netscape Navigator has some important limitations. You cannot upload a file, and you cannot download more than one at a time. Navigator is very useful for locating individual files, though not for downloading a large set of files as is usually required for a system update.

The K Desktop File Manager: kfm

On the K Desktop, the desktop file manager has a built-in FTP capability as shown in Figure 13-2. The FTP operation has been seamlessly integrated into standard desktop file operations. Downloading files from an FTP site is as simple as copying files from one directory to another, but one of the directories happens to be located on a remote FTP site. On the K Desktop you can use a file manager window to access a remote FTP site. Enter the FTP site's URL in the location box. Be sure to include the FTP protocol, **ftp://**. Files in the remote directory are listed just as your local files are. To download files from an FTP site, you open a window to access that site. Open the directory you want. Then open another window for the local directory you want the remote files copied to. In the

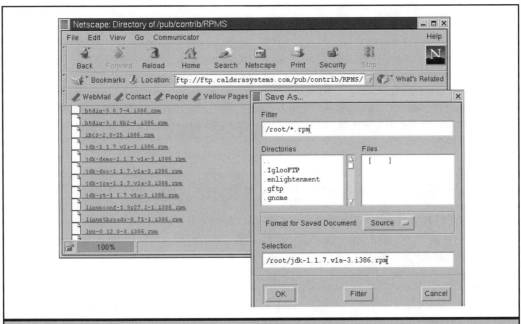

Figure 13-1. *FTP operations using Netscape*

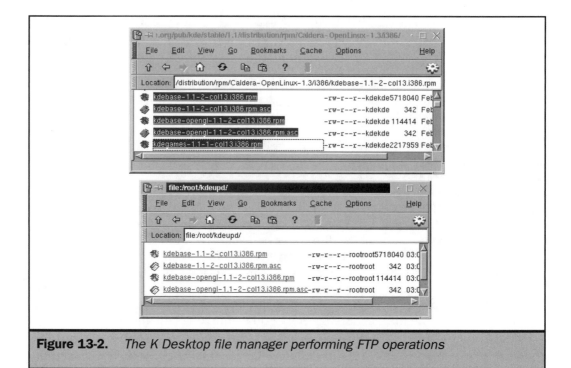

Figure 13-2. *The K Desktop file manager performing FTP operations*

window showing the FTP files, select the ones you want to download. Then simply click and drag those files to the window for the local directory. A pop-up menu will appear with choices for copy or move. Select move. The selected files are then downloaded. Another window will open that shows the download progress, displaying the name of each file in turn and a bar indicating the percentage downloaded so far.

Gnome FTP: Gnome File Manager, gFTP, and IglooFTP

The easiest way to download files in Gnome is to use the built-in FTP capabilities of the Gnome file manager, Midnight Commander. There are also several Gnome-based FTP clients that you can use that will offer more features, including gFTP and IglooFTP. Check the Gnome Web site at **www.gnome.org** for more. The client gFTP is included with the current Gnome release. IglooFTP can be downloaded from its Web site at **www.littleigloo.org**. You can link to it through the Gnome software map on the Gnome Web site.

Gnome File Manager

On Gnome, the desktop file manager, Midnight Commander, has a built-in FTP capability much like the KDE file manager. The FTP operation has been seamlessly integrated into standard desktop file operations. Downloading files from an FTP site is as simple as dragging files from one directory window to another, where one of the directories happens to be located on a remote FTP site. Use the Gnome file manager to access a remote FTP site, listing files in the remote directory just as local files are. Then open another window for the local directory you want the remote files copied to. In the window showing the FTP files, select the ones you want to download. Then use a CTRL-click and drag those files to the window for the local directory. A CTRL-click performs a copy operation, not a move. As files are downloaded, a dialog window appears showing the progress (see Chapter 4 for an illustration).

IglooFTP

IglooFTP is designed to be a Linux version of Bullet-proof FTP, used on Windows systems. It has an extensive set of features with an easy-to-use interface. FTP operations can be performed graphically, selecting files with your mouse and clicking a button or menu for a specified task. IglooFTP download features include recursive downloading, queue transfers, and firewall support. You can download a directory with all its subdirectories with just one operation, as well as download from different sites at the same time. Queue transfers feature auto-resume support in case of interruptions. IglooFTP provides operations managing files and directories on your remote site, provided you have the permission to do so. It supports directory creation and deletion, recursive deletion and moving, and **chmod** operations, as well as others.

The IglooFTP window shown in Figure 13-3 consists of several panes. A top pane displays a log of messages and commands for your IglooFTP's interactions with the remote site as they take place. Below this pane are two large panes side by side. A left-side pane shows your local directory. To change directories, you can use a drop-down menu and box at the top to specify a directory, or click displayed directories. Clicking an up arrow at the top of the directory list moves you to the parent directory. The right-side pane shows the remote directory or the FTP site you are connected to. When you are not connected to a system, this pane will show a listing of your bookmarked sites. The pane at the bottom of the window is for listing queued downloads. There is an icon bar at the top of the window for common FTP operations. The first three icons govern connection operations. The first connects, the second stops connection attempts, and the third disconnects. If a connection attempt fails, then IglooFTP will automatically attempt to reconnect until you click the Stop icon. The icon of a drive and a down arrow at the end of the bar performs downloads. The one with the up arrow and the drive performs uploads. Above the icon bar are boxes for entering login information for the remote site.

You choose an FTP site to connect to either by entering the site address in the FTP box at the top of the window or by selecting its entry from the bookmarks. There are

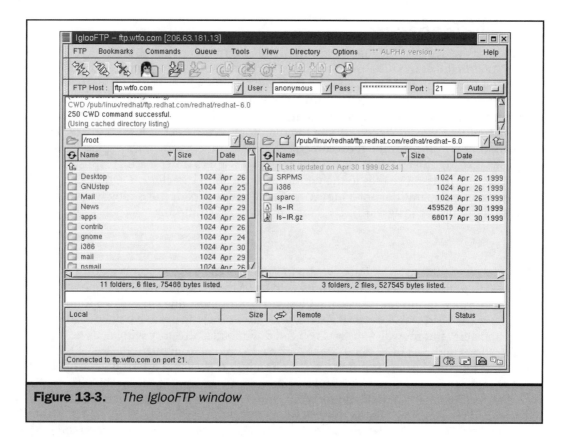

Figure 13-3.   *The IglooFTP window*

also boxes at the top for FTP login information for user name, password, and the default remote directory. For the user name a drop-down menu initially includes anonymous. Password entries are not shown. For an anonymous FTP site you would enter "anonymous" for the user name, your e-mail address for the password, and, in most cases, **/pub** for the remote directory, though you can leave this blank. To connect, click the Connect icon in the icon bar. If you will be connecting to this site again, you can bookmark it by selecting the Add Site entry in the Site Manager menu. The bookmark will include all the login information you specified. To connect again later, you just have to select the bookmark.

Once you are connected, files and directories for the remote site will be displayed in the right pane. Small icons are displayed next to each entry to indicate what it is. A directory will have a folder icon, text files will have a page icon, and links will have a folder with an arrow in it. At the top of the list is an up-arrow icon that indicates the parent directory. Click this to move up to the parent. To download a file, select the file and then click the Download icon in the icon bar. You can also just click its entry and drag it from the right-side pane to left-side pane listing your local directory. To download several files just SHIFT-click or CTRL-click to select them and then click the

Download icon. IglooFTP also supports recursive downloads. This means that you can download a directory and all its subdirectories at once. This is very helpful for system updates that may have several subdirectories. To download an entire directory, just select it and click the Download icon.

IglooFTP features a graphical directory browser for both local and remote file systems to locate directories and files easily. As shown in Figure 13-4, the graphical directory browser displays files and directories in a tree-like structure whose directories (folders) can be shrunk or expanded. On your local system, you can use the tree display to locate and open the directory you want to download files to. You can do the same for the remote system. To activate the directory browser, you click the folder icons located above the left corner for each pane. Clicking the folder icon above the left-hand pane will display a graphical tree for your local system. You can expand or shrink directories with a preceding + or – symbol. The folder icon above the right-hand pane displays the graphical directory browser for the remote system. Next to this folder icon is an icon for the site manager. Clicking it displays the site manager, and clicking the folder icon returns you to the remote directory.

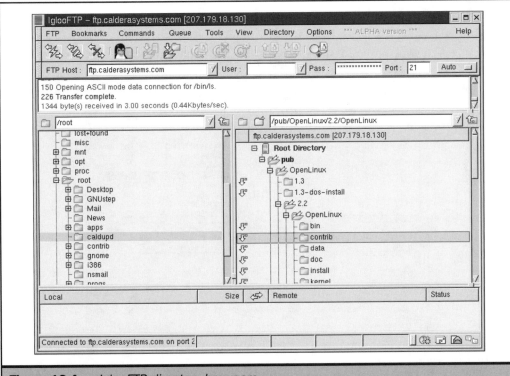

Figure 13-4. *IglooFTP directory browsers*

INTERNET

The IglooFTP site manager lets you easily access and configure bookmarked sites. The site manager uses a graphical tree display similar to the graphical directory browser. The format is similar to the Netscape bookmark editor. You can create folders within this tree and place site entries in them, further organizing your sites. The site manager directory browser is displayed in the right pane whenever you are not connected to a site. To display the directory browser while connected, you can click its icon located above the right-hand pane. A right-click on the graphical tree displays a pop-up menu with manager options for adding, editing, or deleting a site entry.

gFTP

The gFTP program shown in Figure 13-5 is a simpler Gnome FTP client designed to let you standardize FTP file transfers. It has an interface similar to WS_FTP used on Windows. The gFTP window consists of several panes. The top-left pane lists files in your local directory, and the top-right pane lists your remote directory. Subdirectories have a folder icon preceding their name. The parent directory can be referenced by a .. entry with an up-arrow at the top of each list. Double-click a directory entry to access it. The pathnames for all directories are displayed in boxes above each pane. You can enter a new pathname for a different directory to change to it, if you wish.

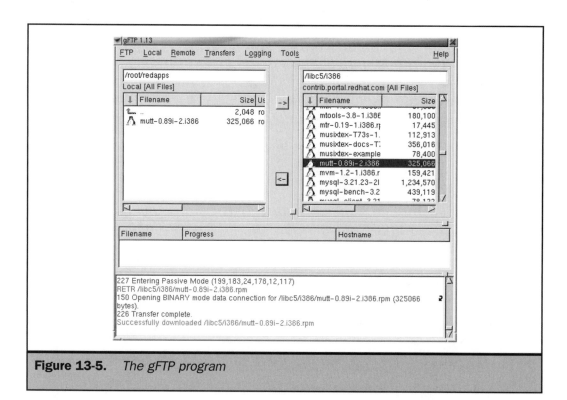

Figure 13-5. *The gFTP program*

Two buttons between the panes are used for transferring files. The <- button will
download selected files in the remote directory, and the -> button will upload files
from the local directory. To download a file, just click it in the right-side pane and then
click the <- button. When the file is downloaded, its name will appear in the left-side
pane, your local directory. Menus across the top of the window can be used to manage
your transfers. A connection manager lets you enter login information about a specific
site. You can specify whether to perform an anonymous login or to provide a user
name and password. Click the Connect button to connect to that site. A drop-down
menu for sites lets you choose the site you want.

ncftp

The ncftp program shown in Figure 13-6 has a screen-based interface that can be run
from any shell command line. It does not use a desktop interface. FTP operations are
executed using commands that you enter at a prompt. Options and bookmarks can be
selected using cursor-based menus. To start up ncftp, you enter the **ncftp** command
on the command line. If you are working in a window manager such as KDE, Gnome,
or FVWM, just open a shell terminal window and enter the command at its prompt.
The main ncftp screen consists of an input line at the bottom of the screen with a status
line above it. The remainder of the screen is used to display commands and responses
from remote systems. For example, when you download a file, a message specifying
the download files is displayed in the status line. The ncftp program lets you set

```
> ls

README  SRPMS/  alpha/  i386/   sparc/

> lcd gnomeupd

Current local directory is /root/gnomeupd.

> get -R i386

Receiving file: /root/gnomeupd/i386/README
100%  0 ======================================> 237 bytes. ETA:  0:00
README:  237 bytes received in 0.00 seconds, 91.44 kB/s.
Receiving file: /root/gnomeupd/i386/Base/GXedit-1.23-1.i386.rpm
100%  0 ======================================> 167911 bytes. ETA:  0:00
GXedit-1.23-1.i386.rpm:  167911 bytes received in 0.93 seconds, 175.86 kB/s.
Receiving file: /root/gnomeupd/i386/Base/ORBit-0.4.3-1.i386.rpm
100%  0 ======================================> 308434 bytes. ETA:  0:00
ORBit-0.4.3-1.i386.rpm:  308434 bytes received in 1.67 seconds, 179.97 kB/s.
Receiving file: /root/gnomeupd/i386/Base/audiofile-0.1.6-2.i386.rpm
ftp.gnome.org                                    /pub/GNOME/gnome-1.0/redhat
gnome> get -R i386
```

Figure 13-6.   *The ncftp program*

preferences for different features such as anonymous login, progress meters, or a download directory. Enter the **pref** command to open the preferences screen. From there you can select and modify the listed preferences.

To connect to an FTP site, you enter the **open** command on the input line followed by the site's address. The address can be either an IP address or a domain name such as **ftp.gnome.org**. If you don't supply an address, then a list of your bookmarked sites is displayed, and you can choose one from there. By default, ncftp will attempt an anonymous login, using the term "anonymous" as your user name and your e-mail address as the password. When you successfully connect, the status bar will display the remote site's name on the left and the remote directory name on the right.

```
open ftp.gnome.org
```

If you want to log into a specific account on a remote site, have yourself prompted for the user name and password by using the **-u** option with the **open** command. The **open** command will remember the last kind of login you performed for a specific site and will repeat it. If you want to change back to an anonymous login from a user login, you use the **-a** option with the **open** command. For busy sites you may not connect on the first try and will have to repeat the open process. The ncftp program has a redial capability that you turn on with the **-r** option. The **-d** option sets the delay for the next attempt, and the **-g** option sets the maximum number of connection attempts. With the **lookup** command you can obtain the IP and domain name addresses for an FTP site. The **lookup** command takes as an argument either the IP or domain name address and then displays both. This is useful for finding a site's IP address. With the **-v** option more information such as aliases are retrieved. Options are shown in Table 13-1.

Options	Description
-a	Connect anonymously
-u	Connect with user name and password prompts
-p *num*	Use specified port number when connecting
-r	Redial until connected
-d *num*	Set delay (*num*) in number of seconds for redial option
-g *num*	Specify the maximum number of redials

Table 13-1.   *The ncftp Open*

Once connected, you enter commands on the input line to perform FTP operations such as displaying file lists, changing directories, or downloading files. With the **ls** command you can list the contents of the current remote directory. Use the **cd** command to change to another remote directory. The **dir** command will display a detailed listing of files. With the **page** command you view the contents of a remote file, a screen at a time. To download files, you use the **get** command, and to upload files you use the **put** command. During a download a progress meter above the status bar will display how much of the file has been downloaded so far. The **get** command has several features that are described in more detail in the following section. When you are finished, you can disconnect from the site with the **close** command. You can then use **open** to connect to another site, or quit the ncftp program with the **quit** command. The **help** command will list all ncftp commands. You can use **help** followed by the name of a command to display specific information on it.

The ncftp program supports several commands that operate on your local system. These are usually standard FTP command names preceded by an *l*. The **lcd** command changes your local working directory, **lls** lists the contents of your local directory, **lpage** displays the contents of a remote file a screen at a time, and **lpwd** displays the local directory's full pathname. For any other local commands or scripts you need to execute, use the shell escape command, **!**. Just precede the shell command or script with a **!**.

The ncftp program also provides commands for managing files and directories on your remote site, provided you have the permission to do so. You can use **mkdir** to create a remote directory, and **rmdir** to remove one. Use the **rm** command to erase remote files. With the **rename** command you can change their names. Commands are listed in Table 13-2.

The ncftp program also has a colon mode of operation that lets you issue a single **ncftp** command to download a file. You simply enter the **ncftp** command followed by a URL for the file you want. You can enter the command on the shell command line or place it within a script. For example, the following command will download the README file on the Caldera FTP site.

```
$ ncftp ftp.calderasystems.com/pub/README
```

In the colon mode, the **-c** option will send the file to the standard output and the **-m** option will pipe it to your pager, usually the **more** program.

```
$ ncftp -c ftp.calderasystems.com/pub/README > ~/caldinfo/readme
$ ncftp -m ftp.calderasystems.com/pub/README
```

The ncftp Download Features

The ncftp **get** command differs significantly from the original FTP client's **get** command. Whereas the original FTP client uses two commands, **get** and **mget**, to

Commands	Description
help [*command*]	Lists names of ncftp commands
cd [*directory*]	Changes the working directory on the remote host
create [*file-name*]	Creates an empty file on the remote host, letting you use the file name as a message
debug	Turns debugging on or off
version	Displays version information
dir	Displays a detailed directory listing
echo	Displays a string, useful for macros
get	Downloads files from a remote host to your working directory
lcd [*directory*]	Changes the local working directory
lls	Lists files in your local working directory
lookup [*host*]	Looks up entries for remote hosts
lpage [*file name*]	Displays contents of local file, a page at a time
lpwd	Displays the local current working directory
mkdir [*directory name*]	Creates a directory on the remote host
mode [*mode*]	Specifies transfer mode (b for block mode, s for stream mode)
open [*option*] [*hostname*]	Connects to a remote host. If no hostname is specified, then the bookmark editor displays a host list from which you can choose one (**-a** forces anonymous login, **-u** forces user login, **-r** redials automatically, **-d** specifies time delay before redial—used with **-r**, **-g** specifies the maximum number of redials—used with **-r**)
page *file-name*	Displays the contents of a remote file
pdir	Same as **dir**, but outputs to your pager, letting you display remote file list a page at a time. Used for command line interface

Table 13-2. *The ncftp Commands*

Commands	Description
pls	Same as **ls**, but outputs to your pager. Used for command line interface
redir	Redisplays the last directory listing
predir	Redisplays the last directory listing and outputs to pager if working in command line interface
put *file-name*	Uploads a file to a remote host
pwd	Displays the remote current working directory
rename *orig-name new-name*	Changes the name of a remote file
quit	Quits ncftp
quote	Sends an FTP protocol command to the remote server
rhelp [*command*]	Sends a help request to the remote host
rm *file-names*	Erases remote files
rmdir *directories*	Removes remote directories
Site *command*	Executes site-specific commands
Type *type*	Changes transfer type (ASCII, binary, image)
! *command*	Escapes to the shell and executes the following shell command or script

Table 13-2.   *The ncftp Commands* (continued)

perform download operations, ncftp uses only the **get** command. However, ncftp **get** combines the capabilities of both **mget** and **get** into the **get** command, as well as adding several new features. By default, the ncftp **get** command performs wildcard matching for file names. If you enter just part of a file name, the **get** command will try to download all files beginning with that name. You can turn off wildcard matching with the **-G** option, in which case you will have to enter the full names of the files you want. The following example downloads all files with names beginning with "XFree86" and is similar to using **mget XFree86*** in the original FTP.

```
get Xfree86
```

The **get** command will check to see if you already have a file you are trying to download. If so, it skips the download. It will also check if the file you already have is a newer version, in which case it will also skip the download. This is a very helpful feature for easily maintaining upgrade files. You can just access the update directory on the remote site and then use the **get** command with the ***** to download to the directory you are using to keep your upgrade file. Only newer versions or newly added upgrade files will be download, instead of the entire set. Should you want to download a file, even though you have it already, you can force the download with the **-f** option. For example, to download upgrades for OpenLinux, you can connect to the OpenLinux upgrade directory in the Caldera FTP site and then simply issue the following **get** command:

```
get *
```

If you were interrupted during a download, you can restart the download from where you left off. This feature is built into ncftp. (On other FTP programs it can be invoked with the **reget** command.) The ncftp program will check to see if you have already started to download a file and then continue from where you left off.

Certain features require that you enter an option on the command line after the **get** command. For example, adding the **-R** command specifies a recursive capability, letting you download and create subdirectories and their files. This command is particularly helpful in downloading upgrade directories such as Red Hat that contain several subdirectories. The following example downloads the **i386** directory and all its subdirectories.

```
get -R i386
```

If you want to give a file a different name on your local system, then you use the **-z** option. Enter the local file name you want after the remote file name. The following example downloads the **readme** file and renames it **calinfo**. If you did not use the **-z** option, then both names would be taken as files to be downloaded, instead of just the first.

```
get -z readme calinfo
```

To obtain very recent files only, you can use the **-n** option. It takes as its argument a number of days. Files older than the specified number of days are not retrieved. The following example downloads files that have been posted within the last 30 days. See Table 13-3 for a description of the options.

```
get -n 30 *
```

Options	Desccription
–G	Turn wildcard matching for file names on or off
–R *directory*	Download a directory and all its subdirectories (recursive)
–f *file names*	Force the download of all specified files, even if older or the same as local ones
–C	Force resumption of a download from where it was interrupted
–z *remote-file local-file*	Rename a remote file on your local system
–n *num*	Download files that are no older than the specified number of days

Table 13-3.   *The ncftp Get Options*

Bookmarks and Macros

When you disconnect (close) from a site, ncftp automatically saves information about it. This includes the site address, the directory you were in, and the login information. This information is placed in a file called **bookmarks** in your **.ncftp** directory. The site information is given a bookmark name that you can use to easily access the site again. The bookmark name is usually just the key name in the site's address. You can use this name to connect to the site. For example **ftp.calderasystems.com** could be named calderasystems. You could then connect to it with the command

```
open calderasystems
```

You can edit your bookmark entries using the bookmark editor. Enter the command **bookmarks** to bring up the editor. Remote systems you have accessed are listed on the right side of the screen. Bookmark commands are listed on the left. You can change the bookmark name, or edit login information such as the user name or password, the remote directory, or the transfer mode.

INTERNET

The ncftp program supports macros for simple operations. You create macros by entering macro definitions in the macros file located in your **.ncftp** directory. Initially there will be no such file, so you have to create one using any text editor. The macros file is a simple text file that you can edit with any text editor. The syntax for a macro definition follows:

```
macro macro-name
    ftp-commands
end
```

A macro executes ncftp commands. However, bear in mind that the **!** is an ncftp command that lets you execute any Linux command or script. With a preceding **!** you can define an ncftp macro that executes any shell command or any script you have written. A simple example of a macro is

```
macro ascii
    type ascii
end
```

Macros support parameters similar to those used by shell programs. Arguments entered after a macro name can be referenced in the macro using a **$** sign and the number of the argument in the argument list. **$1** references the first argument; **$2**, the second and so on. **$*** is a special parameter that references all arguments, and **$@** references all arguments, encasing each in double quotes.

```
macro cdls
   cd $1
   ls
end
```

The ncftp program also supports a limited number of event macros. These are macros that are executed when a certain event is detected, such as when the program starts or shuts down. For example, a macro defined with the name **.start.ncftp** will have its commands executed every time you start ncftp; **.quit.ncftp** executes its commands when you quit. There are also site-specific macros that execute whenever it is necessary to access or disconnect from certain sites. These macros begin with either the open or close event followed by the site's bookmark. For example, a macro defined with the name **.open.redhat** would execute its commands whenever you connected to the Red Hat site. A macro named **.open.any** will have its commands executed whenever you connect to any site, and one named **.close.any** will execute whenever you disconnect from a site.

ftp

The name ftp designates the original FTP client used on Unix and Linux systems. It uses a command line interface and has an extensive set of commands and options you can use to manage your FTP transfers. You start the ftp client by entering the command **ftp** at a shell prompt. If you have a specific site that you want to connect to, you can include the name of that site on the command line after the **ftp** keyword. Otherwise, you will need to connect to the remote system with the ftp command **open**. You are then prompted for the name of the remote system with the prompt **(to)**. Upon entering the remote system name, ftp connects you to the system and then prompts you for a login name. The prompt for the login name will consist of the word "Name" and, in parentheses, the system name and your local login name. Sometimes the login name on the remote system is the same as the login name on your own system. If they are the same, just press ENTER at the prompt. If they are different, enter the remote system's login name. After entering the login name, you are prompted for the password. In the next example, the user connects to the remote system **garnet** and logs into the **robert** account.

```
$ ftp
ftp> open
(to) garnet
Connected to garnet.berkeley.edu.
220 Garnet.Berkeley.Edu Ftp Server (Ultrix Version 4.1 Sun May 16 10:23:46 Edt 1999) Ready.
Name (garnet.berkeley.edu:root): robert
password required
Password:
user robert logged in
ftp>
```

To save a step, you can directly specify the remote system on the command line when you invoke ftp. This connects you to that system without need of the **open** command. The login procedure then begins.

```
$ ftp garnet.berkeley.edu
Connected to garnet.berkeley.edu.
220 garnet.berkeley.edu FTP server (ULTRIX Version 4.1 Sun May 16 10:23:46 EDT 1999) ready.
Name (garnet.berkeley.edu:root):
```

Once logged in, you can execute Linux commands on either the remote system or your local system. You execute a command on your local system in ftp by preceding the command with an exclamation point. Any Linux commands without an exclamation point are executed on the remote system. There is one exception to this rule. Whereas you can change directories on the remote system with the **cd** command, to change directories on your local system, you need to use a special ftp command called **lcd** (local **cd**). In the next example, the first command lists files in the remote system, and the second command lists files in the local system.

```
ftp> ls
ftp> !ls
```

The ftp program provides a basic set of commands for managing files and directories on your remote site, provided you have the permission to do so. You can use **mkdir** to create a remote directory, and **rmdir** to remove one. Use the **delete** command to erase a remote file. With the **rename** command you can change their names. You close your connection to a system with the **close** command. You can then open another connection if you wish. To end the ftp session, use the **quit** or **bye** command.

```
ftp> close
ftp> bye
Good-bye
$
```

File Transfer

To transfer files to and from the remote system, use the **get** and **put** commands. The **get** command will receive files from the remote system to your local system, and the **put** command will send files from your local system to the remote system. In a sense, your local system **get**s files *from* the remote and **put**s files *to* the remote. In the next example, the file **weather** is sent from the local system to the remote system using the **put** command.

```
ftp> put weather
PORT command successful.
ASCII data connection
ASCII Transfer complete.
ftp>
```

If a download is ever interrupted, you can resume the download with **reget**. This is very helpful for a very large file. The download will resume from where it left off, so the whole file does not have to be downloaded again. Also, be sure to download binary files in binary mode. For most FTP sites, the binary mode is the default, but some sites might have ASCII (text) as the default. The command **ascii** sets the character mode, and the command **binary** sets the binary mode. Most software packages available at Internet sites are archived and compressed files, which are binary files. In the next

example, the transfer mode is set to binary, and the archived software package
mydata.tar.gz is sent from the remote system to your local system using the **get**
command.

```
ftp> binary
ftp> get mydata.tar.gz
PORT command successful.
Binary data connection
Binary Transfer complete.
ftp>
```

Often you may want to send several files, specifying their names with wildcard
characters. The commands **put** and **get**, however, operate only on a single file and do
not work with special characters. To transfer several files at a time, you have to use two
other commands, **mput** and **mget**. When you use **mput** or **mget**, you will be prompted
for a file list. You can then either enter the list of files or a file-list specification using
special characters. For example, ***.c** would specify all the files with a .c extension, and
* would specify all files in the current directory. In the case of **mget**, each file will be
sent, one by one, from the remote system to your local system. Each time, you will
be prompted with the name of the file being sent. You can type **y** to send the file or
n to cancel the transmission. You will then be prompted for the next file. The **mput**
command works in the same way but sends files from your local system to the remote
system. In the next example, all files with a .c extension are sent to your local system
using **mget**.

```
ftp> mget
(remote-files) *.c
mget calc.c? y
PORT command successful
ASCII data connection
ASCII transfer complete
mget main.c? y
PORT command successful
ASCII data connection
ASCII transfer complete
ftp>
```

Answering the **prompt** for each file can be a very tedious prospect if you are planning
to download a large number of files, such as those for a system update. In this case you
can turn off the prompt with the **prompt** command, which will toggle the interactive
mode on and off. The **mget** operation will then download all files it matches, one after
the other.

```
ftp> prompt
Interactive mode off.
ftp> mget
(remote-files) *.c
 PORT command successful
ASCII data connection
ASCII transfer complete
PORT command successful
ASCII data connection
ASCII transfer complete
ftp>
```

To access a public FTP site, you have to perform an anonymous login. Instead of a login name, you enter the keyword **anonymous**. Then for the password, you enter your Internet address. Once the ftp prompt is displayed, you are ready to transfer files. You may need to change to the appropriate directory first or set the transfer mode to binary. The following example is a complete ftp session in which the user performs an anonymous login and then downloads the updates for the current Red Hat distribution for a PC. The site access is the **updates.redhat.com** site. After changing to the **/current/i386** directory, the user changes to the appropriate local directory and then turns off the interactive prompts with the **prompt** command. The **mget *** command then downloads all the files at once. See Table 13-4 for ftp commands.

```
$ ftp updates.redhat.com
Connected to updates.portal.redhat.com.
220 ProFTPD 1.2.0pre1 Server ready.
Name (updates.redhat.com:root): anonymous
331 Anonymous login ok, send your complete e-mail address as password.
Password: email-address
230 Anonymous access granted, restrictions apply.
Remote system type is UNIX.
Using binary mode to transfer files.
ftp> ls
200 PORT command successful.
150 Opening ASCII mode data connection for file list.
total 0
-rw-r--r--   1 root     root        4664 Jan 26 11:21 00README.errata
..................
drwxrwxr-x   6 root     root        1024 Feb 10 13:43 5.0
drwxrwxr-x   8 root     root        1024 Feb 14 07:01 5.1
drwxrwxr-x   9 root     root        1024 Apr 14 15:19 5.2
drwxrwxr-x   4 root     root        1024 Feb 14 07:01 bru
drwxrwxr-x   3 root     root        1024 Feb 14 07:01 cde
lrwxrwxrwx   1 root     root           3 Feb 12 14:48 current -> 5.2
drwxr-xr-x   2 root     root        1024 Feb 26 14:54 lacd
-rw-r--r--   1 root     root      189645 Apr 20 04:06 ls-lR
```

```
-rw-r--r--    1 root      root        22987 Apr 20 04:06 ls-lR.gz
drwxrwxr-x    3 root      root         1024 Feb 14 07:01 motif
drwxrwxr-x    3 root      root         1024 Feb 14 07:01 real
drwxrwxr-x    4 root      root         1024 Feb 14 07:01 secureweb
226 Transfer complete.
ftp> cd current
250 CWD command successful.
ftp> ls
200 PORT command successful.
150 Opening ASCII mode data connection for file list.
total 0
-rw-r--r--    1 root      root        23599 Jan 26 11:22 00README.errata
drwxrwxr-x    2 root      root         1024 Apr 14 18:23 SRPMS
drwxrwxr-x    2 root      root         2048 Apr 14 18:23 alpha
drwxrwxr-x    2 root      root         3072 Apr 14 18:23 i386
drwxrwxr-x    5 root      root         1024 Feb 14 07:01 images
drwxrwxr-x    7 root      root         1024 Mar 30 14:30 kernel-2.2
-rw-r--r--    1 root      root        20734 Apr 20 04:06 ls-lR
-rw-r--r--    1 root      root         3125 Apr 20 04:06 ls-lR.gz
drwxrwxr-x    2 root      root         1024 Feb 14 07:01 noarch
drwxrwxr-x    2 root      root         2048 Apr 14 18:23 sparc
226 Transfer complete.
ftp> cd i386
250 CWD command successful.
ftp> ls
200 PORT command successful.
150 Opening ASCII mode data connection for file list.
total 0
-rw-r--r-- 1 root root 5675      00README.errata
-rw-r--r-- 1 root root 1268938 XFree86-100dpi-fonts-3.3.3.1-1.1.i386.rpm
-rw-r--r-- 1 root root 7093877 XFree86-3.3.3.1-1.1.i386.rpm
-rw-r--r-- 1 root root 873365   XFree86-3DLabs-3.3.3.1-1.1.i386.rpm
-rw-r--r-- 1 root root 1095957 XFree86-75dpi-fonts-3.3.3.1-1.1.i386.rpm
-rw-r--r-- 1 root root 697774   XFree86-8514-3.3.3.1-1.1.i386.rpm

.....................................
-rw-r--r-- 1 root root 50746    syslogd-1.3.31-0.5.i386.rpm
-rw-r--r-- 1 root root 119573  wu-ftpd-2.4.2b18-2.1.i386.rpm
-rw-r--r-- 1 root root 70402    zgv-3.0-7.i386.rpm
226 Transfer complete.
ftp> lcd redhatupd
Local directory now /root/redhatupd
ftp> prompt
Interactive mode off.
ftp> mget *
local: 00README.errata remote: 00README.errata
200 PORT command successful.
150 Opening BINARY mode data connection for 00README.errata (5675 bytes).
```

```
226 Transfer complete.
5675 bytes received in 0.717 secs (7.7 Kbytes/sec)
local: XFree86-100dpi-fonts-3.3.3.1-1.1.i386.rpm
        remote: XFree86-100dpi-fonts-3.3.3.1-1.1.i386.rpm
200 PORT command successful.
150 Opening BINARY mode data connection for
        XFree86-100dpi-fonts-3.3.3.1-1.1.i386.rpm (1268938 bytes).
226 Transfer complete.
1268938 bytes received in 57.7 secs (21 Kbytes/sec)
local: XFree86-3.3.3.1-1.1.i386.rpm remote: XFree86-3.3.3.1-1.1.i386.rpm
200 PORT command successful.
.............................................
local: zgv-3.0-7.i386.rpm remote: zgv-3.0-7.i386.rpm
200 PORT command successful.
150 Opening BINARY mode data connection for zgv-3.0-7.i386.rpm (70402 bytes).
226 Transfer complete.
70402 bytes received in 6.46 secs (11 Kbytes/sec)
ftp> close
221 Goodbye.
ftp> quit
```

Command	Effect
ftp	Invokes ftp program
open *site-address*	Opens a connection to another system
close	Closes connection to a system
quit or **bye**	Ends ftp session
ls	Lists the contents of a directory
dir	Lists the contents of a directory in long form
get *file name*	Sends file from remote system to local system
put *file name*	Sends file from local system to remote system
mget *regular-expression*	Allows you to download several files at once from a remote system; you can use special characters to specify the files; you will be prompted one by one for each file transfer in turn
mput *regular-expression*	Allows you to send several files at once to a remote system; you can use special characters to specify the files; you will be prompted one by one for each file to be transferred

Table 13-4.   *The ftp Client Commands*

Command	Effect
runique	Toggles storing of files with unique file names. If there is a file with the same file name already on the local system, a new file name is generated
reget *file name*	Resumes transfer of an interrupted file from where you left off
binary	Transfers files in binary mode
ascii	Transfers files in ASCII mode
cd *directory*	Changes directories on the remote system
lcd *directory*	Changes directories on the local system
help or **?**	Lists ftp commands
mkdir *directory*	Creates a directory on the remote system
rmdir	Deletes a remote directory
delete *file name*	Deletes a file on the remote system
mdelete *file-list*	Deletes several remote files at once
rename	Renames a file on a remote system
hash	Displays progressive hash signs during download
status	Displays current status of ftp

Table 13-4.   *The ftp Client Commands* (continued)

Automatic Login and Macros: .netrc

The ftp client has an automatic login capability and support for macros. Both are entered in a user's ftp configuration file called **.netrc**. Each time you connect to a site, the **.netrc** file is checked for connection information such as a login name and password. In this way, you do not have to enter a login name and password each time you connect to a site. This feature is particularly useful for anonymous logins. Instead of your having to enter the user name anonymous and your e-mail address as your password, they can be automatically read from the **.netrc** file. You can even make anonymous login information your default, so that, unless otherwise specified, an anonymous login will be attempted for any FTP site you try to connect to. If you have sites that you have to log into, you can specify them in the **.netrc** file and, when you connect, either automatically log in with your user name and password for that site or be prompted for them.

Entries in the **.netrc** file have the following syntax. An entry for a site begins with the term *machine* followed by the network or Internet address and then the login and password information.

```
machine system-address  login  remote-login-name   password password
```

The following example shows an entry for logging into the **dylan** account on the **turtle.trek.com** system.

```
machine golf.mygames.com  login   dylan  password  legogolf
```

For a site you would anonymously log into, you enter the word "anonymous" for the login name and your e-mail address for the password.

```
machine  ftp.calderasystems.com  login anonymous  password dylan@turtle.trek.com
```

In most cases, you will be using ftp to access anonymous FTP sites. Instead of trying to make an entry for each one, you can make a default entry for anonymous FTP login. When you connect to a site, ftp will look for a machine entry for it in the **.netrc** file. If there is none, then it will look for a default entry and use that. A default entry begins with just the term "default" with no network address. To make anonymous logins your default, just enter "anonymous" and your e-mail address as your login and password.

```
default  login anonymous  password dylan@turtle.trek.com
```

.netrc

```
machine golf.mygames.com  login   dylan  password  legogolf
default  login anonymous  password dylan@turtle.trek.com
```

You can also define macros in your **.netrc** file. With a macro you can execute several ftp operations at once using just the macro name. Macros remain in effect during a connection. When you close a connection, the macros are undefined. Though a macro can be defined on your **ftp** command line, it makes more sense to define them in **.netrc** entries. That way you do not have to redefine them again. They will be read automatically from the **.netrc** file and defined for you. You can place macro definitions within a particular machine entry in the **.netrc** file or in the default entry. Macros defined in machine entries will be defined only when you connect to that site. Macros in the default entry are defined whenever you make a connection to any site.

The syntax for a macro definition follows. It begins with the keyword **macdef** followed by the macro name you want to give it, and ends with an empty line. The ftp macros can take arguments, referenced within the macro with **$n**, where **$1** references the first argument, and **$2** the second, and so on. If you need to use a $ character in a macro, you have to quote it using the backslash, **\$**.

```
macdef   macro-name
ftp commands
empty-line
```

The **redupd** macro defined next changes to a directory where it then downloads Red Hat updates for the current release. It also changes to a local directory where the update files are to be placed. The **prompt** command will turn off the download prompts for each file. The **mget** command then downloads the files. The macro assumes that you are connected to the Red Hat FTP site.

```
defmac redupd
cd pub/redhat/current
lcd /root/redupdate
prompt
mget *
```

A sample **.netrc** file follows with macros defined for both specific and default entries. An empty line is placed after each macro definition. You can define several macros for a machine or the default entry. The macro definitions following a machine entry up to the next machine entry are automatically defined for that machine connection.

.netrc

```
machine updates.redhat.com  login   anonymous  password  dylan@turtle.trek.com
defmac redupd
cd pub/redhat/current
lcd /root/redupdate
prompt
mget *

default login anonymous password dylan@turtle.trek.com
defmac lls
!ls
```

Online FTP Resources

The Internet has a great many sites that are open to public access. They contain files that anyone can obtain using file transfer programs such as ftp. Unless you already know where a file is located, however, it can be very difficult to find it. To search for files on FTP sites, you can use search engines provided by Web sites such as Yahoo, Excite, AltaVista, or Lycos. These will usually search for both Web pages and FTP files. Normally you would have to use a Web browser to access such sites and perform searches. However, Linux utilities are being developed that can access sites directly and list the results. Ganesha is one such utility. It is a Gnome-based application that accesses the Lycos FTP search service at **ftpsearch.lycos.com**, performs a search, and displays the results, as in Figure 13-7. You just enter the search string and press ENTER. Results are listed showing round-trip times, number of hops, the FTP site, and the full pathname of the file. You can then select items and save them to your disk. The number of hops to a location indicates how far away the site is. You can also drag Netscape URLs into the Ganesha window to check the round-trip times and number of hops to a Web site.

Another utility you can use for locating files is Archie. Xarchie is an X Windows program that lets you use menus and list boxes to perform an Archie search and display its results. You can even use Xarchie to perform an FTP operation for a file you select, downloading it to your system. Xarchie has three menus, File, Settings, and Query. The

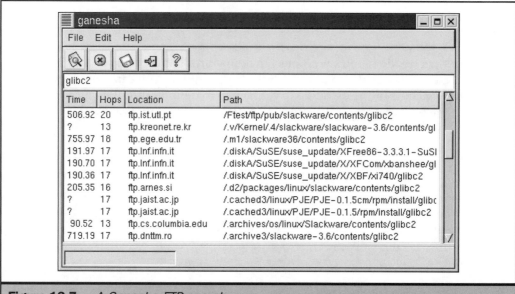

Figure 13-7. *A Ganesha FTP search*

fourth item on the menu bar is an Abort button that you can use to stop an Archie search. The last item is a Help button that starts a window displaying various Xarchie help files. Xarchie operates by accessing an Archie server to perform a search and then displays the results. The list of Archie servers is displayed by selecting the Archie Host item in the Settings menu. The Settings menu also contains items for configuring your search, letting you determine the sorting sequence or the pattern-matching method. To perform a search, enter the search term in the box labeled Search Term, and then select the Item entry in the Query menu. The display window is separated into several list boxes, the first of which lists the Internet sites found. When you click a particular site, the pathname for the file you are looking for is displayed in the second list box (there can be more than one). The third list box shows the item found, which can be either a file or a directory. If it is a directory, you can double-click it to display the list of files in it. To download a file, click the file name and select the Get item from the File menu.

Gopher

Gopher is designed to place at your fingertips information distributed throughout a network. It was originally created at the University of Minnesota to provide a campus-wide distributed information service connecting different university departments. Each department maintained its own Gopher information server that anyone using a Gopher client could access. This distributed model was quickly adopted for use across the Internet to provide easy access to the numerous information services available there. Many universities maintain Gopher servers that can be used both within their campuses and across the Internet.

To access Gopher servers, you need to use a Gopher client program. The Gopher client provides a menu interface through which you make your requests and then carries out your requests, whether they be to connect to another service or to transfer a file. Several Gopher clients are commonly available, such as Xgopher, an X-Windows-based Gopher client with buttons and drop-down menus that allow you to move through Gopher menus. You can also download the University of Minnesota line-based Gopher client from **boombox.micro.umn.edu**. When you invoke the Gopher client, you can specify the Gopher server to access. The following example accesses the **gopher.tc.umn.edu** Gopher server.

```
$ gopher gopher.tc.umn.edu
```

The names of many Gopher servers begin with the word *gopher*. If you do not specify a Gopher server, then the default server will be accessed. In this case you just enter the term **gopher** on the command line. You can determine the default server by pressing the **O** command once you have started your Gopher program. This will bring up an options menu from which you can configure your Gopher client. The options menu saves its information in a configuration file called **.gopherrc** that is kept in your home directory. Table 13-5 lists Gopher options and commands.

A Gopher menu consists of a list of menu items that can represent files, other menus, databases, or telnet connections. Each type of item is indicated by a qualifier placed at the end of the entry. Items that are files end with a period qualifier. Items that are other menus end with a slash. Database items end with the symbols **<?>**. The qualifier **<CSO>** indicates a CSO name server used to search for user addresses and information. The **<TEL>** qualifier indicates a telnet connection. The **<Picture>**, **<Movie>**, and **<)** qualifiers reference images, video, and sound files, respectively. Gopher can perform a pattern search on the text of each menu item. To perform a search, you press the slash key, /. A box will open in the middle of the screen, prompting you to enter a search pattern. The Xgopher client works much the same way with just a few differences. Instead of positioning an arrow, you can use your mouse to click a menu item. A double-click will select an item. Buttons and drop-down menus move you back and forth through the Gopher menus.

Option	Effect
gopher [**-sb**] [**-t** *title*] [**-p** *path*] [*hostname port*]	
-p *string*	Specifies a selector string to send to the root-level server on startup
-t *string*	Sets the title of the initial screen for the Gopher client
Menu Item Qualifiers	
.	File
/	Menu
<CSO>	CSO name server
<TEL>	Telnet connection
<Picture>	Graphic, such as GIF or JPEG
<)	Sound file
<Move>	Video, such as MOV or AVI

Table 13-5.   *Gopher Options and Commands*

Option	Effect
\<HTML\>	Hypertext document
\<Bin\>	Binary file
\<HCX\>	Macintosh BinHexed file
\<PC Bin\>	DOS binary file
\<MIME\>	Multipurpose Internet Mail extensions file
\<?\>	Database with keyword search
Moving to and Selecting Menu Items	
k and UP ARROW	Moves up to previous menu item
j and DOWN ARROW	Moves down to next menu item
num	Moves to *num* item in menu
l, RIGHT ARROW, ENTER	Press one of these to select the current menu item
Searching a Menu for an Item	
/pattern	Searches menu items for pattern and moves to first item with that pattern
n	Repeats previous search of menu items
Operations Performed on Menu Items	
=	Displays information about a menu item
s	Saves the current item to a file
m	Mails the current item to a user
p	Prints the current item
Moving Through Menu Screens	
\>, **+**, SPACEBAR	Moves to next menu screen
\<, **-**, **b**	Moves to previous menu screen

Table 13-5.   *Gopher Options and Commands* (continued)

INTERNET

Option	Effect
Return to Previous Menus	
u, .	Moves to previous menu
m	Returns to top main menu
Bookmark Commands	
a	Adds selected item to bookmark list
A	Adds current menu to bookmark list
d	Removes a bookmark from the bookmark list
v	Displays bookmark list
Options, Quit, and Help Commands	
q	Quits Gopher
Q	Quits Gopher without prompt
?	Help
O	Displays and changes options for Gopher
Environment Variables	
PAGER	Client will use that to display files to the user
GOPHER_MAIL	Program to send mail (must understand **-s** option)
GOPHER_PLAY	Program to play sound
GOPHER_TELNET	Program to contact telnet services
GOPHER_HTML	Program to display HTML documents
GOPHER_PRINTER	Program to print from a pipe

Table 13-5.   *Gopher Options and Commands* (continued)

The
Complete
Reference

Chapter 14

The World Wide Web

The World Wide Web (WWW) is a hypertext database of different types of information distributed across many different sites on the Internet. A *hypertext database* consists of items that are linked to other items, that in turn may be linked to yet other items, and so on. Upon retrieving an item, you can then use that item to retrieve any related items. For example, you could retrieve an article on the Amazon rain forest and then use it to retrieve a map of the rain forest or a picture of the rain forest. In this respect, a hypertext database is like a web of interconnected data that you can trace from one data item to another. Information is displayed in pages known as Web pages. On a Web page certain keywords are highlighted that form links to other Web pages or to items such as pictures, articles, or files.

The World Wide Web links data across different sites on the Internet throughout the world. It is often referred to as WWW or simply as the Web. The World Wide Web originated in Europe at CERN research laboratories. CERN remains the original WWW server. An Internet site that operates as a Web server is known as a Web site. Such Web sites are often dedicated to specialized topics or institutions, for example, the Smithsonian Web site or the NASA Web site. These Web sites usually have an Internet address that begins with www, as in **www.redhat.com**, the Web site for Red Hat, Inc. Once connected to a Web site, you can use hypertext links to move from one Web page to another.

To access the Web, you use a client program called a *browser*. There are many different Web browsers to choose from. Browsers are available for use on Unix, Windows, the Mac, and Linux. Certain browsers, such as Netscape and Mosaic, have versions that operate on all such systems. On your Linux system you can choose from several Web browsers, including Netscape Navigator. Navigator is available as part of all Linux distributions. Netscape and Mosaic are X-Windows-based browsers that provide full picture, sound, and video display capabilities. Most distributions also include the Lynx browser, a line-mode browser that displays only lines of text. The K Desktop incorporates Web browser capabilities into its file manager, letting a directory window operate as a Web browser. There are also Gnome-based browsers such as Express and Mnemonic that are designed to be easily enhanced.

URL Addresses

An Internet resource is accessed using a Universal Resource Locator (URL), as shown in Figure 14-1. A URL is composed of three elements: the transfer protocol, the hostname, and the pathname. The transfer protocol and hostname are separated by a colon and two slashes, **://**. The path name always begins with a single slash.

```
transfer-protocol://host-name/path-name
```

The transfer protocol is usually **http** (Hypertext Transfer Protocol), indicating a Web page. Other possible values for transfer protocols are **gopher**, **ftp**, and **file**. As their names suggest, **gopher** and **ftp** initiate Gopher and FTP sessions, whereas **file** displays a local file on your own system such as a text or an HTML file. Table 14-1 lists the various transfer protocols.

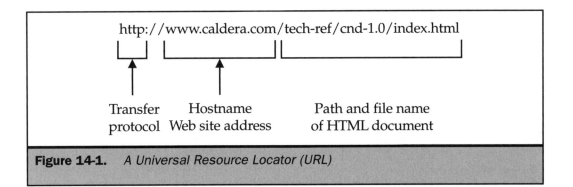

Figure 14-1. *A Universal Resource Locator (URL)*

The *hostname* is the computer that a particular Web site is located on. You can think of this as the address of the Web site. By convention most hostnames begin with "www." In the next example, the URL locates a Web page called **toc.html** on the **home.netscape.com** Web site.

```
http://home.netscape.com/toc.html
```

If you do not want to access a particular Web page, you can leave it out, and you will automatically access the Web site's home page. To access a Web site directly, you can just use its hostname. The default name for a Web site's home page is **index.html**, located in the site's top directory. A Web site can override the default and specify a particular file as the home page. If no file is specified, however, the **index.html** file is taken to be the home page. In the next example, the user brings up the Caldera home page.

```
http://www.calderasystems.com/
```

Protocol	Description
http	Hypertext Transfer Protocol for Web site access
gopher	Access Gopher site
ftp	File Transfer Protocol for anonymous FTP connections
telnet	Makes a telnet connection
wais	Access WAIS site
news	Reading Usenet news; uses Net News Transfer Protocol (NNTP)

Table 14-1. *Web Protocols*

The pathname specifies the directory where the resource can be found on the host system, as well as the name of the resource's file. For example, **/pub/Linux/newdat.html** references an HTML document called *newdat* located in the **/pub/Linux** directory. As you move to other Web pages on a site, you may move more deeply into the directory tree. In the following example, the user accesses the **resources.html** document in the directory **/support.**

```
http://www.calderasystems.com/support/resources.html
```

As just explained, should you specify a directory pathname without a particular Web page file, your Web browser will look for a file called **index.html** in that directory. An **index.html** file in a directory operates as the default Web page for that directory. In the next example, the **index.html** Web page in the **/resources** directory is displayed.

```
http://www.calderasystems.com/resources/index.html
```

You can use this technique to access local Web pages on your system. For example, once installed, the demo Web pages for Java are located in **/usr/local/java/**. Since it is on your local system, you do not need to include a hostname. An **index.html** page in the **/usr/local/java/** directory will be automatically displayed when you specify the directory path. You can do the same for your system documentation, which is in Web-page format located in the **/usr/doc/HTML/ldp** directory.

```
file:/usr/doc/HTML/ldp
```

If you reference a directory that has no **index.html** file, the Web server will create one for you, and your browser will then display it. This index will simply list the different files and directories in that directory. You can click an entry to display a file or move to another directory. The first entry will be a special entry for the parent directory.

The resource file's extension indicates the type of action to be taken on it. A picture will have a **.gif** or **.jpg** extension and will be converted for display. A sound file will have a **.au** or **.wav** extension and will be played. The following URL references a **.gif** file. Instead of displaying a Web page, your browser will invoke a graphics viewer to display the picture. Table 14-2 provides a list of the different file extensions.

```
http://www.train.com/engine/engine1.gif
```

File Type	Description
.html	Web page document formatted using HTML, the Hypertext Markup Language
Graphics Files	
.gif	Graphics, using GIF compression
.jpg	Graphics, using JPEG compression
Sound Files	
.au	Sun (Unix) sound file
.wav	Microsoft Windows sound file
.aiff	Macintosh sound file
Video Files	
.QT	Quicktime video file, multiplatform
.mpeg	Video file
.avi	Microsoft Windows video file

Table 14-2. *Web File Types*

INTERNET

Web Pages

A Web page is a specially formatted document that can be displayed by any Web browser. You can think of a Web page as a word processing document that can display both text and graphics. Within the Web page, links can be embedded that call up other Internet resources. An Internet resource can be a graphic, a file, a telnet connection, or even another Web page. The Web page acts as an interface for accessing different Internet tools, such as FTP to download files, or telnet to connect to an online catalog or other remote service.

Web pages display both text and graphics. Text is formatted with paragraphs and can be organized with different headings. Graphics of various sizes may be placed anywhere in the page. Throughout the page there will usually be anchor points that you can use to call up other Internet resources. Each anchor point is associated with a particular Internet resource. One anchor point may reference a picture; another, a file;

others may reference other Web pages or even other Web sites. These anchor points are specially highlighted text or graphics that usually appear in a different color from the rest of the text. Whereas ordinary text may be black, text used for anchor points may be green, blue, or red. You select a particular anchor point by moving your mouse pointer to that text or picture and then clicking it. The Internet resource associated with that anchor point will then be called up. If it is a picture, the picture will be displayed. If it is another Web page, that Web page is displayed. If the Internet resource is on another Web site, that site will be accessed. The color of an anchor point indicates its status and the particular Web browser you are using. Both Mosaic and Netscape use blue for anchors that you have not yet accessed. Netscape uses purple for anchors you have already accessed, and Mosaic uses red. All these colors can be overridden by a particular Web page.

Your Web browser will keep a list of the different Web pages that you accessed for each session. You will be able to move back and forth easily in that list. Having called up another Web page, you can use your browser to move back to the previous one. Web browsers construct their lists according to the sequence in which you displayed your Web pages. They keep track of the Web pages you are accessing, whatever they may be. However, on many Web sites, several Web pages are meant to be connected in a particular order, like chapters in a book. Such pages usually have buttons displayed at the bottom of the page that reference the next and previous pages in the sequence. Clicking Next will display the next Web page for this site. The Home button will return you to the first page for this sequence.

Web Browsers

Most Web browsers are designed to access several different kinds of information. They can access a Web page on a remote Web site or a file on your own system. Some browsers can also access a remote news server or an FTP site. The type of information for a site is specified by the keyword **http** for Web sites, **nntp** for news servers, **ftp** for FTP sites, and **file** for files on your own system.

To access a Web site, you enter **http://** followed by the Internet address of the Web site. If you know a particular Web page you want to access on that Web site, you can add the pathname for that page, attaching it to the Internet address. Then simply press ENTER. The browser will connect you to that Web site and display its home page or the page you specified.

You can just as easily use a Web browser to display Web pages on your own system by entering the term **file** followed by a colon, **file:**, with the pathname of the Web page you want to display. You do not specify an Internet site. Remember, all Web pages have the extension **.html**. Links within a Web page on your own system can connect you to other Web pages on your system or to Web pages on remote systems. When you first start a Web browser your browser displays a local Web page on your own system. The default page is usually a page for your particular distribution such as OpenLinux or Red Hat. Such pages will have links to a distribution's Web site where you can obtain online support. If you wish, you can create your own Web pages, with their own links, and make one of them your default Web page.

Web pages on a Web site will often contain links to other Web pages, some on the same site and others at other Web sites. Through these links you can move from one page to another. As you move from Web page to Web page, using the anchor points or buttons, your browser will display the URL for the current page. Your browser keeps a list of the different Web pages you have accessed in a given session. Most browsers have buttons that allow you to move back and forth through this list. You can move to the Web page you displayed before the current one, and then move back further to the one before that. You can move forward again to the next page and so on.

To get to a particular page, you may have moved through a series of pages, using links in each to finally reach the Web page you want. To access any Web page, all you need is its URL address. If you want to access a particular page again, you can enter its URL address and move directly to it, without moving through the intervening pages as you did the first time. Instead of writing down the URL addresses and entering them yourself, most Web browsers can keep a *hotlist*—a list of favorite Web pages you want to access directly. When you are displaying a Web page you want to access later, just instruct your browser to place it on the hotlist. The Web page will usually be listed in the hotlist by its title, not its URL. To access that Web page later, select the entry in the hotlist.

Most Web browsers can also access FTP and Gopher sites. You may find that using a Web browser to access an FTP site is easier than using the FTP utility. Directories and files are automatically listed, and selecting a file or directory is just a matter of clicking its name. First enter **ftp://** and then the Internet address of the FTP site. The contents of a directory will be displayed, listing files and subdirectories. To move to another directory, just click it. To download a file, click its name. You will see an entry listed as . ., representing the parent directory. You can move down the file structure from one subdirectory to another and move back up one directory at a time by selecting ... To leave the FTP site, just return to your own home page. You can also use your browser to access Gopher sites. Enter **gopher://** followed by the Internet address of the Gopher site. Your Web browser will display the main Gopher menu for that site. You can then move from one Gopher menu to the next.

Most browsers can connect to your news server to access specified newsgroups or articles. This is a local operation, accessing the news server you are already connected to. You enter **nntp** followed by a colon and the newsgroup or news article. Some browsers, such as Netscape, have an added newsreader browser that allows them to access any remote news servers.

As noted previously, several popular browsers are available for Linux. Three distinctive ones are described here: Netscape Navigator, Mosaic, and Lynx. Netscape and Mosaic are X-Windows-based Web browsers capable of displaying graphics, video, and sound, as well as operating as newsreaders and mailers. Lynx is a command line–based browser with no graphics capabilities. But in every other respect it is a fully functional Web browser.

Netscape Navigator

Hypertext databases are designed to access any kind of data, whether it is text, graphics, sound, or even video. Whether you can actually access such data depends to a large extent on the type of browser you use. One of the more popular Web browsers is the Netscape Navigator. Versions of Netscape operate on different graphical user interfaces such as X Windows, Microsoft Windows, and the Macintosh. Using X Windows, the Netscape browser can display graphics, sound, video, and Java-based programs (you will learn about Java a little later in the chapter). You can obtain more information about Netscape on its Web site: **www.netscape.com**.

Netscape Navigator is now included on most Linux distributions' CD-ROMs. Both OpenLinux and Red Hat CD-ROMs contain Netscape Navigator. For more recent versions as they come out, you can access your Linux distribution's FTP site, such as the Caldera FTP site at **ftp.calderasystems.com** or the Red Hat FTP site at **updates.redhat.com**. You can also obtain compressed archive versions (**.tar.gz**) from Netscape FTP sites such as **ftp8.netscape.com**. A compressed archive version has to be decompressed and unpacked with the **gunzip** and **tar xvf** commands, once the archive has been placed in an install directory such as **/usr/local**.

Netscape Navigator is an X Windows application that you operate from your desktop. Many distributions will have a desktop icon for Netscape or an entry for it in the desktop's menu. Netscape Navigator displays an area at the top of the screen for entering a URL address and a series of buttons for various Web page operations (see Figure 14-2). Drop-down menus provide access to Netscape features. To access a Web site, you enter its address in the URL area and press ENTER.

The icon bar across the top of the browser holds buttons for moving from one page to another and performing other operations. The Back-Arrow and Forward-Arrow buttons move you back and forth through the list of Web pages you have already accessed in a given session. The Home button (picture of house) exits a Web site and places you back in your own system. There is also a Stop button, in the form of a stop sign, that becomes active when you are linking to and displaying a new Web page. If the Web page is taking too long to display, you may want to click Stop to stop the process.

Netscape refers to the URLs of Web pages you want to keep in a hotlist as bookmarks, marking pages you want to access directly. The Bookmarks menu lets you add your favorite Web pages to a hotlist. You can then view your bookmarks and select one to move to. Items in the Windows menu enhance your Web browser operations. In the address book you can keep a list of Web site URLs. The Bookmarks item lets you edit your list of bookmarks, adding new ones or removing old ones. The History item is a list of previous URLs you have accessed. If you want to go back to a Web page that you did not save as a bookmark, you can find it in the history list. Additionally, you can use Netscape to receive and send mail as well as access Usenet newsgroups.

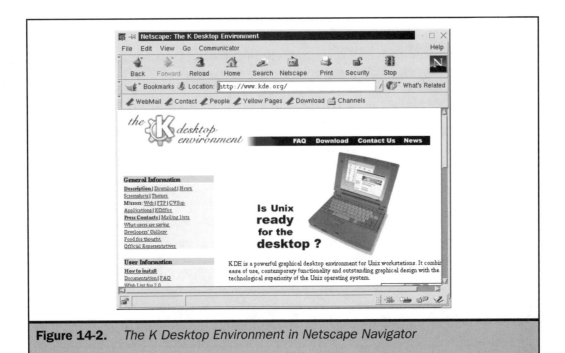

Figure 14-2.   *The K Desktop Environment in Netscape Navigator*

The Options menu in the Netscape Navigator lets you set several different kinds of preferences for your browser. You can set preferences for mail and news, the network, and security, as well as general preferences. In general preferences you can determine your home page and how you want the toolbar displayed. For mail and news you can enter the mail and news servers you use on the Internet. Netscape can be set to access any number of news servers that you subscribe to and that use the NNTP transfer protocols. You can switch from one news server to another if you wish.

If you are on a network that connects to the Internet through a firewall, you will have to use the Proxies screen to enter the address of your network's firewall gateway computer. A *firewall* is a computer that operates as a controlled gateway to the Internet for your network. There are several types of firewalls. One of the most restrictive uses programs called *proxies* that receive Internet requests from users and then makes those requests on their behalf. There is no direct connection to the Internet. From the Options menu select Network, then choose the Proxies screen. Here, enter the IP address of your network's firewall gateway computer.

To save a Web page, select the Save As entry in the File menu. This opens a dialog box with a default directory specified. There are three boxes. The top box is for a filter.

The bottom box is the name of the file. The middle box lists different directories in the current directory. You can enter a path and file name of your own, or you can click the .. entry in the middle box to move back through the directory tree, and then click directory names to move into those directories. When you have reached the directory you want, you can save your Web page.

Through the Mail item in the Windows menu you can open a fully functional mail client with which you can send and receive messages over the Internet. The News item, also in the Windows menu, opens a fully functional newsreader with which you can read and post articles in Usenet newsgroups. In this respect, your Netscape Navigator is more than just a Web browser. It is also a mail program and a newsreader.

K Desktop File Manager

If you are using the K Desktop, then you can use a file manager window as a Web browser, as shown in Figure 14-3. The K Desktop's file manager is automatically configured to act as a Web browser. It can display Web pages, including graphics and links. It supports standard Web page operation such as moving forward and backward through accessed pages. Clicking a link will access and display the Web page referenced. In this respect, the Web becomes seamlessly integrated into the K Desktop.

Figure 14-3. *The K Desktop file manager as a Web browser*

Express and Mnemonic: Gnome

Unlike the K Desktop, the Gnome file manager does not currently display Web pages. You use a Web browser such as Netscape, Express, or Mnemonic. Express and Mnemonic are Gnome-based Web browsers that support standard Web operations. Express is designed to rely on plugins for Web features. This way the browser can be made as complex or simple as you want. All major operations such as viewers and protocols are handled as plugins. This design allows new features to be easily added in this way. Mnemonic is an extensible and modular Web browser that integrates a set of Object Implementation Libraries (OILs) into a Web browser with a Gnome interface.

Lynx: Line-Mode Browser

Lynx is a line-mode browser that you can use without X Windows (see Figure 14-4). A Web page is displayed as text only. A text page can contain links to other Internet resources, but will not display any graphics, video, or sound. Except for the display limitations, Lynx is a fully functional Web browser. You can use Lynx to download files or make telnet connections. All information on the Web is still accessible to you. Since it does not require much of the overhead that graphics-based browsers need, Lynx can operate much faster, quickly displaying Web page text. To start the Lynx browser, you enter **lynx** on the command line and press ENTER.

```
$ lynx
```

The links are displayed in bold and dispersed throughout the text of the Web page. A selected link is highlighted in reverse video with a shaded rectangle around the link text. The first link is automatically selected. You can then move sequentially from one link to the next on a page by pressing the DOWN ARROW key. The UP ARROW key moves you back to a previous link. To choose a link, you first highlight it and then press either ENTER or the RIGHT ARROW key. If you want to go to a specific site, press G. This opens a line at the bottom of the screen with the prompt **URL to open:**. There, you can enter the URL for the site you want. Pressing M will return you to your Home page. The text of a Web page is displayed one screen at a time. To move to the next screen of text, you can either press SPACEBAR or PAGE DOWN. PAGE UP displays the previous screen of text. Pressing DOWN ARROW and UP ARROW will move to the next or previous links in the text, displaying the full screen of text around the link. To display a description of the current Web page with its URL, press the = key.

Lynx keeps a list of all the Web pages you access in a session. LEFT ARROW moves you back to a previously displayed page. RIGHT ARROW moves you forward to the next page in the list. Lynx refers to this list of Web pages as a *history list*. You can directly

```
                              The K Desktop Environment (p1 of 6)

     The K Desktop Environment [USEMAP:nav_bar3.gif]

     General Information
     Description | Download | News
     Screenshots | Themes
     Mirrors: Web | FTP | CVSup
     Applications | KOffice
     Press Contacts | Mailing lists
     What users are saying
     Developers' Gallery
     Food for thought
     Official Representatives
     User Information
     How to install
     Documentation | FAQ
     Wish List for 2.0
     Bug Reports
     -- press space for next page --
      Arrow keys: Up and Down to move. Right to follow a link; Left to go ba
     H)elp O)ptions P)rint G)o M)ain screen Q)uit /=search [delete]=history█
```

Figure 14-4.   *The Lynx Web browser*

display this history list by pressing DEL. You can then use your UP ARROW and DOWN ARROW keys to select a particular Web page link and use RIGHT ARROW or ENTER to access it. Lynx also supports bookmarks. By pressing A, you automatically add the current Web page to a bookmark file. Press V to display the list of bookmarks. As with a history list, you can use the UP ARROW and DOWN ARROW keys to select a bookmark link. Pressing either RIGHT ARROW or ENTER will move to and display that Web page.

Lynx uses a set of one letter commands to perform various browser functions. By pressing the ? key at any time, you can display a list of these commands. For example, pressing the D key will download a file. The H key will bring up a help menu. To search the text of your current Web page, you press the / key. This opens up a line at the bottom of the screen where you enter your search pattern. Lynx will then highlight the next instance of that pattern in the text. If you press N, Lynx will display the next instance. The \ key will toggle you between a source and rendered version of the current Web page, showing you the HTML tags or the formatted text.

HotJava

The Linux version of the HotJava browser is currently available. You can download it directly from the **java.sun.com** Web site. Follow the instructions there for installing HotJava on Linux. You can then start the HotJava browser with the command.

```
# hotjava
```

The current HotJava version uses JDK 1.1.*x*. You should first have JDK 1.1.*x* installed and set the **JDK_HOME** variable to whatever the location of JDK 1.1.*x* is on your system, for example, **/usr/local/jdk1.1.1**. You can obtain the JDK 1.1.*x* from the Blackdown Web site at **www.blackdown.org**.

The HotJava browser can be easily customized to your particular needs. Its Places menu allows you to collect Web page addresses or use Netscape bookmarks. It can also display both frames and tables. It has a very small footprint and can be used to complement Netscape browsers or other software designed to access the Web. HotJava includes support for security features such as signed applets. It is more flexible in its reading of HTML code, allowing the browser to recover successfully from errors. HotJava also supports the Unicode 2.0 character set, which allows it to display both Latin and non-Latin characters such as Chinese, Japanese, and Korean.

Mosaic

Mosaic, which can display graphics, sound, and video data, was the first graphics-based browser developed for the Web. Unlike Netscape, it is available free to anyone. There are versions of Mosaic for different graphical user interfaces such as X Windows, Microsoft Windows, and the Macintosh. It was developed by the National Center for Supercomputing Applications (NCSA) at the University of Illinois at Champaign-Urbana. More information about Mosaic is available at the NCSA Web site: **www.ncsa.uiuc.edu**. You can download a copy of Mosaic from the Mosaic FTP site at **ftp.ncsa.uiuc.edu** in the directory **/Web/Mosaic/Unix**.

Like Netscape, Mosaic is an X Windows application. You must have your desktop running before you can use it. When you attempt to access a Web page, the globe image in the upper-right corner will spin. Once the Web page is displayed, the globe will stop spinning. Should you decide not to access the Web page while the globe is spinning, you can stop the access by clicking the globe. In this respect, the globe functions as a Stop button. Sometimes, attempts to access a Web page may take a great deal of time. You can simply cancel your request by clicking the spinning globe.

The menus across the top of the Mosaic window allow you to manage your Web searches. With the Navigate menu, you maintain a hotlist of favored Web sites. The Options menu has several entries for configuring your Mosaic browser. You can set your home page or specify mail or news servers. You can also set default colors used for the background and for URL links. The News menu lets you use your Mosaic browser to access Usenet newsgroups, displaying and saving articles. Mosaic also has built-in security features that can protect your system.

Java for Linux: Blackdown

To develop Java applications, use Java tools, and run many Java products, you must install the Java Development Kit (JDK) and the Java Runtime Environment (JRE) on your system. Sun does not support or develop Linux versions of these products. However, they have been ported to Linux by the Blackdown project, and you can download the Blackdown ports of the JDK and JRE and install them on your system. More information and documentation is available at the Blackdown Web site at **www.blackdown.org**.

Numerous Java-based products and tools are currently adaptable for Linux. There are Linux versions of the HotJava browser and the Java Web server. Tools include IDE development environments, Just In Time compilers (JIT), and Java virtual machines. Most of the products and some of the tools are free. You can download most of the products and tools through links in the Blackdown Web page located at **www.blackdown.org**. Select the Javasoft Products entry for a list of links to available Java products; select Java Tools for Linux for a list of tools. Many of the products run directly as provided by Sun. You can download several directly from the Sun Java Web site at **java.sun.com**. A few of the currently available products are listed below in Table 14.3.

Product	Description
Java Development Kit (JDK) and Java Runtime Environment (JRE)	A Java development environment with a compiler, interpreters, debugger, and more. Download the Linux port from your distribution's update through **www.blackdown.org**.
HotJava browser 3.0	Sun's HTML 3.2- and JDK 1.1-compliant Web browser. Download the Linux version from **java.sun.com**.
Java Foundation Classes (Swing Set)	Swing is a new set of GUI components being developed by JavaSoft.
The Java Servlet Development Kit	Provides resources for running, testing, and operating servlets with Netscape, Microsoft, and Apache Web servers.
Java Web Server	A Web server implemented with Java. Available at Java Web site at **java.sun.com**.
The JDBC Database Access API	A SQL database access interface for Java.

Table 14-3.   *Java Applications*

The Java Development Kit: JDK and JRE

The Java Development Kit provides tools for creating and debugging your own Java applets and provides support for Java applications such as the HotJava browser. The kit includes demonstration applets with source code. You can obtain detailed documentation about the JDK from the Sun Web site at **java.sun.com**. There are three major releases of the JDK currently available, 1.0, 1.1.*x*, and 1.2, with corresponding versions for the Java Runtime Environment (JRE) for 1.1 and 1.2. JDK 1.0 is an earlier version of the JDK that is compatible with older browsers. JDK 1.1.*x* includes standard features such as JavaBeans and database connectivity. The current version of JDK 1.1.*x* is 1.1.7. JAVA 2 adds capabilities for security, Swing, and running Java enhancements such as Java3D and Java Sound. JDK 1.2 is also known as JAVA 2 (SDK). All JDK and JRE releases are available for Linux. You can download them from a Java-Linux mirror site that you can link to through the Blackdown Web page (**www.blackdown.org**) mentioned earlier. JDK and JRE 1.1 are not usually included on Linux distribution CD-ROMs. You can, however, download RPM versions from OpenLinux and Red Hat contrib sites, **ftp.calderasystems.com/pub/contrib** and **contrib.redhat.com**, respectively. JKD and JRE 1.2 currently have to be downloaded through **www.blackdown.org** as a compressed archive, **.tar.gz** file.

JDK 1.1

JDK 1.1 includes features such as Internationalization, signed applets, JAR file format, AWT (window toolkit) enhancements, JavaBeans component model, networking enhancements, Math package for large numbers, database connectivity (JDBC), Object Serialization, and Inner Classes. Detailed descriptions of these features can be found in the JDK documentation. The JDK package installs the Java applications, libraries, and demos in the specified directory. Java applications include a Java compiler, **javac**, a Java debugger, **jdb**, and an applet viewer, **appletviewer**. To use these applications, you have to add the directory to your **PATH** in either the **/etc/profile** or **.profile** initialization files.

JAVA 2 SDK (JDK 1.2)

JAVA 2 offers numerous capabilities over JDK 1.1 such as integrated Swing, Java 2d, the new security model, the Collections framework, CORBA, and JDBC 2.0. The Blackdown port of Java 2 has support for both native threads and green threads, and it includes a Just In Time dynamic bytecode compiler. With JAVA 2 you can run the Blackdown port of Java 3D, Java Advanced Imaging, Java Media Framework, and Java Sound. Detailed descriptions of these features can be found in the JAVA 2 documentation.

The Linux version of JAVA 2 is currently packaged as compressed archives. You need to download, decompress, and unpack the **.tar.gz** file. Once you download the

INTERNET

archive, place it in the directory that you want the JDK 1.2 installed in, usually a directory such as **/usr/local**. You then decompress it with gunzip and unpack it with **tar xvf**, or combine both operations with **tar xvzf**. A directory will be created for the JDK where you'll find the **bin** and **lib** subdirectories holding the Java applications and libraries. You should add that directory to your **PATH** in the **/etc/profile** or **.profile** script (**.login** for the TCSH shell). Also, in either **/etc/profile** or **.profile**, you should add an entry that assigns the respective directory to the **JDK_HOME** variable. This variable is used by various Java application such as HotJava to locate the Java interpreter. Check the readme file for details.

Java Applets

You create a Java applet much as you would create a program using a standard programming language. You first use a text editor to create the source code, which is saved in a file with a **.java** extension. Then you can use the **javac** compiler to compile the source code file, generating a Java applet. This applet file will have the extension **.class**. For example, the JDK demo directory includes the Java source code for a Blink applet called **Blink.java**. You can go to that directory and then compile the **Blink.java** file, generating a **Blink.class** file. The **example1.html** file in that directory runs the **Blink.class** applet. Start up your browser and access this file to run the Blink applet.

```
# javac Blink.java
```

An applet is called within a Web page using the **<applet>** HTML tag. This tag can contain several attributes, one of which is required: **code**. You assign to **code** the name of the compiled applet. There are several optional attributes you can use to set features such as the region used to display the applet and its alignment. You can even access applets on a remote Web site. In the following example, the applet called **Blink.class** will be displayed in a box on the Web browser that has a height of 140 pixels and a width of 100 pixels and is aligned in the center.

```
<applet code="Blink.class" width=100 height=140
align=center></applet>
```

To invoke the debugger you use the **appletviewer** command with the **-debug** option and the name of the HTML file that runs the applet.

```
appletviewer -debug mypage.html
```

Numerous Interface Development Environments (IDE) applications are available for composing Java applets and applications. Though most are commercial, some provide free shareware versions. An IDE provides a GUI interface for constructing Java applets. You can link to and download several IDE applications through the Blackdown Web page.

Web Search Utilities

To search for files on FTP sites you can use search engines provided by Web sites such as Yahoo, Excite, AltaVista, or Lycos. These will usually search for both Web pages and FTP files. To find a particular Web page that you want on the Internet you can use any number of online search sites such as Yahoo, Excite, AltaVista, or Lycos. You can use their Web sites, or perform searches from any number of Web portals such as Netscape or Linux online. Web searches have become a standard service of most Web sites. Searches carried out on documents within a Web site, may use local search indexes set up and maintained by indexing programs like ht:/Dig and WAIS. Sites using ht:/Dig use a standard Web page search interface, where WAIS provides its own specialized client programs like **swais** and **xwais**. You can find out more about ht:/Dig at **www.htdig.org**. WAIS is an older indexing program that is currently being supplanted by newer search applications like ht:/Dig. You can still obtain a free version of WAIS called freeWAIS from **ftp.cnidr.org.**

Creating Your Own Web Site

To create your own Web site, you will need access to a Web server. Most Linux distributions such as OpenLinux and Red Hat automatically install the Apache Web server on their Linux systems. You can also rent Web page space on a remote server, a service many ISPs provide, some for free. On Red Hat and OpenLinux systems the directory set up by your Apache Web server for your Web site pages is **/home/httpd/html**. Other servers will provide you with a directory for your home page. Place the Web pages that you create in that directory. It is here that you place your home page. You can make other subdirectories with their own Web pages to which these can link. Web pages are not difficult to create. Links from one page to another will move users through your Web site. You can even create links to Web pages or resources on other sites. Many excellent texts are available on Web page creation and management.

Web Page Composers

Web pages are created using HTML, the Hypertext Markup Language, which is a subset of SGML (Standard Generalized Markup Language). Creating an HTML document is a matter of inserting HTML tags in a text file. In this respect, creating a Web page is as simple as using a tag-based word processor. You use the HTML tags to format text for display as a Web page. The Web page itself is a text file that you can create using any text editor, such as Vi. If you are familiar with tag-based word processing on Unix systems, you will find it conceptually similar to nroff. There are HTML tags to indicate headings, lists, and paragraphs, as well as to reference Web resources.

Instead of manually entering HTML code, you can use Web page composers. A Web page composer provides a graphical interface for constructing Web pages. The Linux version of WordPerfect can automatically generate a Web page from a WordPerfect document. You can create Web pages using all the word processing features of WordPerfect. There are also special Web page creation programs such as Netscape Composer that easily help you create very complex Web pages without ever having to explicitly type any HTML tags. Keep in mind, though, that no matter what tool you use to create your Web page, the Web page itself will be an HTML document.

Many of the standard editors for the K Desktop and Gnome include Web page construction features. Many will let you insert links or format headings. The kedit program supports basic text-based Web page components. You can add headings, links, or lines, but not graphics. The gXedit program can also compose and edit Web pages. You can easily insert HTTP elements such as links, image references, or headings. The gXedit program can then access Netscape to preview the page. The gnotepad+ editor is very simple for making small text files. It does, however, have a toolbar for Web page composition containing several of the more common HTML elements. You can insert links, headings, and lists, as well as other basic Web page components.

Common Gateway Interfaces

A *Common Gateway Interface (CGI)* script is a program that a Web server at a Web site can use to interact with Web browsers. When a browser displays a Web page at a particular Web site, the Web page may call up CGI programs to provide you with certain real-time information or to receive information from you. For example, a Web page may execute the server's **date** command to display the current date whenever the Web page is accessed.

A CGI script can be a Linux shell script, Perl script, Tcl/Tk program, or a program developed using a programming language such as C. There are also two special HTML operations that are considered CGI scripts: query text and forms. Both receive and process interactive responses from particular users. You have seen how a user can use a browser to display Web pages at a given Web site. In effect, the user is receiving information in the form of Web pages from the Web site. A user can also, to a limited extent, send information back to the Web site. This is usually information specifically prompted for in a Web page displayed by your browser. The Web server then receives and processes that information using the CGI programs.

A *form* is a Web page that holds several input fields of various types. These can be input boxes for entering text or check boxes and radio buttons that users simply click. The text boxes can be structured, allowing a certain number of characters to be entered, as in a phone number. They can also be unstructured, allowing users to type in sentences as they would for a comment. Forms are referred to as form-based queries. After entering information into a form, the user sends it back to the server by clicking a Submit button. The server receives the form and, along with it, instructions to run a specific CGI program to process the form.

Chapter 15

Network Tools

Yｏu can use a variety of network tools to perform tasks such as obtaining information about other systems on your network, accessing other systems, and communicating directly with other users. Network information can be obtained using utilities such as **ping**, **finger**, and **host**. Talk, ICQ, and IRC clients let you communicate directly with other users on your network. Telnet performs a remote login to an account you may have on another system connected on your network. Each has a corresponding K Desktop or Gnome version. These provide a GUI interface so that you no longer have to use the shell command line to run these tools. In addition your network may make use of older remote access commands. These are useful for smaller networks and let you directly access remote systems to copy files or execute commands.

Network Information: ping, finger, and host

You can use the **ping**, **finger**, and **host** commands to find out status information about systems and users on your network. The **ping** command is used to check if a remote system is up and running. You use **finger** to find out information about other users on your network, seeing if they are logged in or if they have received mail.The **host** command will display address information about a system on your network, giving you a system's IP and domain name addresses.

ping

The **ping** command detects whether or not a system is up and running. It takes as its argument the name of the system you want to check. If the system you want to check is down, **ping** will issue a timeout message, indicating that a connection could not be made. The next example checks to see if **ftp.calderasystems.com** is up and connected to the network.

```
$ ping ftp.calderasystems.com
PING locutus.calderasystems.com (207.179.18.130): 56 data bytes
64 bytes from 207.179.18.130: icmp_seq=0 ttl=56 time=146.0 ms
64 bytes from 207.179.18.130: icmp_seq=2 ttl=56 time=104.5 ms
64 bytes from 207.179.18.130: icmp_seq=3 ttl=56 time=105.5 ms
64 bytes from 207.179.18.130: icmp_seq=4 ttl=56 time=203.2 ms
-- locutus.calderasystems.com ping statistics --
5 packets transmitted, 4 packets received, 20% packet loss
round-trip min/avg/max = 104.5/139.8/203.2 ms
```

On the K Desktop you can use the KDE network utilities to issue **ping** commands. Select the Ping panel, enter the address of the remote system at the box labeled Host, and click Go. The results will be displayed in the pane below, as shown in Figure 15-1.

finger and who

You can use the **finger** command to obtain information about other users on your network and the **who** command to check and see what users are currently online on your system. The **who** command will list all users currently connected along with when, how long, and where they logged in. It has several options for specifying the level of detail and is meant to operate on a local system or network. The **finger** command operates on very large networks including the Internet. As shown in Figure 15-2, **finger** will check to see when a user last logged in, the type of shell they are using, the pathname of their home directory, and whether any mail has been received. It will then check for a **.plan** file in a user's home directory that may contain information about the user. The **.plan** file is a file you create yourself on your own home directory; you can place in it information you want made publicly available. You can enter the command **finger** on the command line with the login name of the user you want to check on.

On the K Desktop you can use the KDE network utilities to issue **finger** commands. Click the Finger panel and enter the address of the host you want to check. On the K Desktop, the **kfinger** tool shown in Figure 15-3 also provides a GUI for easily sending finger queries. It features entries for users and remote servers. You can search for users on specific remote systems. With **kfinger** you can also access the K Desktop **talk** utility to talk with selected users online. You can start **kfinger** by selecting the "User Information" entry in the K Desktop's Internet menu.

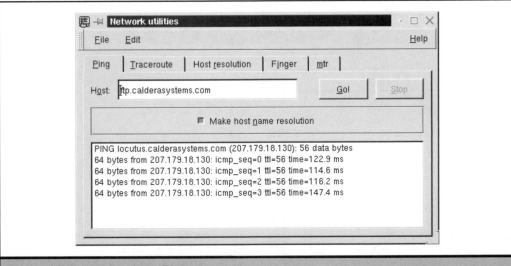

Figure 15-1.   *K Desktop Ping*

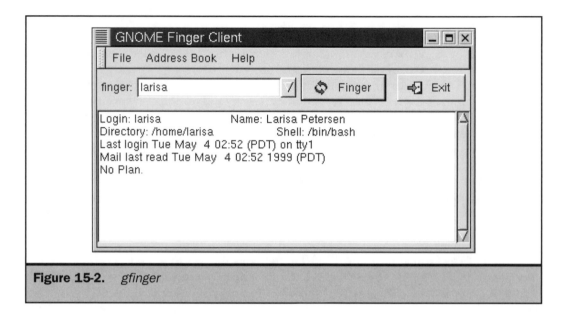

Figure 15-2. *gfinger*

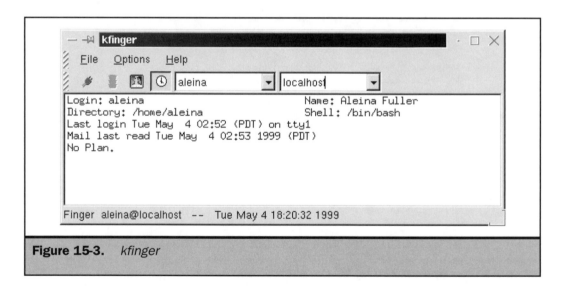

Figure 15-3. *kfinger*

host

With the **host** command you can find network address information about a remote system that is connected to your network. This information usually consists of a system's IP address, domain name address, domain name nicknames, and mail server. This information is obtained from your network's domain name server. For the Internet, this includes all systems you can connect to over the Internet.

The **host** command is an effective way to find out a remote site's IP address, or vice versa. If you have only the IP address of a site, you can use **host** to find out what its domain name is. For network administration, an IP address can be helpful for making your own domain name entries in your **/etc/host** file. That way you would not have to rely on a remote domain name server for locating a site. On the K Desktop you can use the KDE network utilities for running host commands. Click the Host resolution panel and enter the address of the host you want to check. On Gnome you can use the **gHostLookup** utility.

```
$ host www.gnome.org
www.gnome.org is a nickname for gnome.labs.redhat.com
gnome.labs.redhat.com has address 199.183.24.235
gnome.labs.redhat.com mail is handled (pri=10) by mail.redhat.com

$ host 199.183.24.235
235.24.183.199.IN-ADDR.ARPA domain name pointer
gnome.labs.redhat.com
```

The Xwhois program is a Gnome-based client that displays information obtained from NIC network services. Xwhois provides an X Windows interface with a list of NIC servers to choose from.

Network Talk Clients

You may, at times, want to communicate directly with other users on your network. You can do so with **talk** and IRC utilities, provided that the other user is also logged into a connected system at the same time. The *talk* utility operates like a telephone, allowing you to have a direct two-way conversation with another user. It is designed for users on the same system or connected on a local network. ICQ ("I Seek You") is an Internet tool that notifies you when other users are online and lets you communicate with them. It works much like an instant messenger. With an Internet Relay Chat utility (IRC) you can connect to a remote server where other users are also connected and talk with them.

INTERNET

Talk

You can use the **talk** utility to set up an interactive two-way communication between you and another user. The **talk** utility operates more like a phone call—both you and the other user can type in messages simultaneously. It operates like a phone call where two people are constantly talking back and forth to each other. You initiate the communication by entering the **talk** command followed by the other user's address, usually the login name. This displays a message on the other user's screen asking if he or she wants to talk and giving your address. The user then responds with a **talk** command of his or her own using your address. Both your screen and the other user's screen then split into two segments. The top segment displays what you type, and the bottom segment displays what the other user types. Either user can end the session with an interrupt character, usually CTRL-C.

A K Desktop version of **talk** called **ktalk** will display user screens as panes in a K Desktop window. It includes an address book and supports word wrap and file transfer features. The **ktalkd** utility is a KDE-aware Talk daemon with answering machine features and forwarding capabilities. GNU Talk is a Gnome version of Talk that supports multiple clients, file transfers, encryption, shared applications, autoanswer, and call-forwarding. GNU Talk includes both clients and a daemon. The client can operate using different front ends such as Emacs, screen-based cursors (curses), X Window System, Motif, and Gnome. Among applications included with GNU Talk is one that lets you draw pictures with another user.

ICQ clients

The ICQ ("I Seek You") protocol lets you communicate directly with other users online, but like an instant messenger utility. Using an ICQ client, you can send users messages, chat with them, or send files. You can set up a contact list of users who you may want to contact when they are online. You will be notified in real time when they connect, and you can communicate with them if you wish. Several modes of communication are supported, include chat, message, e-mail, file transfer, or games. To use ICQ, you register with an ICQ server that will provide you with an ICQ number, also known as a UIN (Universal Internet Number). You can find out more about the ICQ protocol at **www.mirabilis.com**.

Several Gnome-based ICQ clients are available for your use. Check the Gnome software map at **www.gnome.org** for new versions and recent updates. GnomeICU (formerly GtkICQ) is an ICQ client that can communicate with other ICQ users on any platform, whether Linux, Windows, or the Mac. You can find out more about GnomeICU at **gnomeicu.gdev.net**. Currently, GnomeICU features include message history for individual users, chat, messages, and sound events. File transfers will be supported in future updates. Gicq is a Gnome ICQ instant messenger client. Currently you can use it to send and receive messages and to search for users to add to your client list. K Desktop ICQ clients currently under development are kicq and KXicq. They will support instant messaging, client lists, and other ICQ features.

Internet Relay Chat

Internet Relay Chat (IRC) operates like a chat room, where you can enter channels and talk to other users already there. First you select an IRC server to connect to. Various servers are available for different locals and topics. Once connected to a server, you can choose from a list of channels to enter. The interface works much like a chat room. When you connect to the server, you can choose a nickname by which you will be referred to. Several Internet Relay Chat clients are available for use on Linux systems. Most operate on either X Windows, KDE, or Gnome platforms. Irssi, X-Chat, and yaggIRC are Gnome IRC clients, though there are versions for other platforms. All have support for multiple concurrent server connections, multiple windows, DCC (Send Chat Voice and Resume), and Perl scripts. X-Chat has a plugin interface for adding new features (see **xchat.linuxpower.org** for more details). Irssi has a very easy-to-use interface with support for the Gnome panel. The Kvirc and kSirc are K Desktop IRC clients. Kvirc features an alias and events editor, DCC, and scripting. Xirc is an X Windows client.

Telnet

You use the **telnet** command to log in remotely to another system on your network. The system can be on your local area network or available through an Internet connection. Telnet operates as if you were logging into another system from a remote terminal. You will be asked for a login name and, in some cases, a password. In effect, you are logging into another account on another system. In fact, if you have an account on another system, you could use telnet to log into it. You invoke the **telnet** utility with the keyword **telnet**. If you know the name of the site you want to connect with, you can just enter **telnet** and the name of the site on the Linux command line. As an alternative you can use the K Desktop kTelnet utility. This provides a GUI interface to connecting and logging into remote systems.

```
$ telnet garnet.berkeley.edu
Connected to garnet
login:
```

The telnet program also has a command mode with a series of commands that you can use to configure your connection. You can enter the **telnet** command mode either by invoking telnet with the keyword **telnet** or by pressing CTRL-] during a session. The telnet **help** command will list all the telnet commands that you can use. A comprehensive list is available on the man pages (**man telnet**). In the next example, the user first invokes the **telnet** utility. Then a prompt is displayed, indicating the command mode, **telnet>**. The telnet command **open** then connects to another system.

```
$ telnet
telnet> open garnet.berkeley.edu
Connected to garnet.berkeley.edu
login:
```

Once connected, you follow the login procedure for that system. If you are logging into a regular system, you will have to provide a login name and password. Once logged in, you will be provided with the operating system prompt that, in the case of Linux or Unix, will either be **$** or **%**. You are then directly connected to an account on that system and can issue any commands you want. When you have finished your work, you log out. This will break the connection and return you to the telnet prompt on your own system. You can then quit telnet with the **quit** command.

```
telnet> quit
```

When using telnet to connect to a site that provides public access, you will not need to provide a login name or password. Access is usually controlled by a series of menus that restricts what you can do on that system.

If you are logging into a specific account on another system, you can use the **-l** option to specify the login name of that account. This allows you to skip the login prompt. You can use the **-l** option either with the telnet invocation on the command line or with the **open** command, as shown in the next examples. Here the user is logging into a specific account called **dylan** on the **rose.berkeley.edu** system.

```
$ telnet rose.berkeley.edu -l dylan
telnet> open rose.berkeley.edu -l dylan
```

Remote Access Commands: rwho, rlogin, rcp, and rsh

The remote access commands were designed for smaller networks such as intranets. They allow you to log in remotely to another account on another system and to copy files from one system to another. You can also obtain information about another system, such as who is currently logged on. Many of the remote commands have comparable network communication utilities used for the Internet. For example, **rlogin**, which remotely logs into a system, is similar to telnet. The **rcp** command, which remotely copies files, performs much the same function as FTP.

You can use several commands to obtain information about different systems on your network. You can find out who is logged in, get information about a user on another system, or find out if a system is up and running. For example, the **rwho** command functions in the same way as the **who** command. It displays all the users currently logged into each system in your network.

```
$ rwho
violet     robert:tty1     Sept 10 10:34
garnet     chris:tty2      Sept 10 09:22
```

The **ruptime** command displays information about each system on your network. The information shows how each system has been performing. The **ruptime** command shows whether a system is up or down, how long it has been up or down, the number of users on the system, and the average load on the system for the last 5, 10, and 15 minutes.

```
$ ruptime
violet     up     11+04:10,      8 users,   load 1.20 1.10     1.00
garnet     up     11+04:10,     20 users,   load 1.50 1.40     1.30
```

Remote Access Permission: .rhosts

You use a **.rhosts** file to control access to your account by users using TCP/IP commands. Users create the **.rhosts** file on their own accounts using a standard editor such as Vi. It must be located in the user's home directory. In the next example, the user displays the contents of a **.rhosts** file.

```
$ cat .rhosts
garnet chris
violet robert
```

The **.rhosts** file is a simple way to allow other people access to your account without giving out your password. To deny access to a user, simply delete the system's name and the user's login name from your **.rhosts** file. If a user's login name and system are in a **.rhosts** file, then that user can directly access that account without knowing the password. This type of access is not necessary for remote login operations to work (you could use a password instead); the **.rhosts** file is required for other remote commands, such as remotely copying files or remotely executing Linux commands. If you want to execute such commands on an account in a remote system, that account must have your login name and system name in its **.rhosts** file.

The type of access **.rhosts** provides allows you to use TCP/IP commands to access other accounts directly that you may have on other systems. You do not have to log into them first. In effect, you can treat your accounts on other systems as extensions of the one you are currently logged into. Using the **rcp** command, you can copy any files from one directory to another no matter what account they are on. With the **rsh** command, you can execute any Linux command you wish on any of your other accounts.

rlogin, rcp, and rsh

You may have accounts on different systems in your network, or you may be permitted to access someone else's account on another system. You could access an account on another system by first logging into your own and then remotely logging in across your network to the account on the other system. You can perform such a remote login using the **rlogin** command, which takes as its argument a system name. The command will connect you to the other system and begin login procedures.

Login procedures using **rlogin** differ from regular login procedures in that the user is not prompted for a login name. The **rlogin** comand assumes that the login name on your local system is the same as the login name on the remote system. Upon executing the **rlogin** command, you are immediately prompted for a password. After entering the password, you are logged into the account on the remote system. Once logged into a remote system, you can execute any command you wish. You can end the connection with either **exit**, CTRL-D, **~.**, or **logout** (TCSH or C-shell). The **rlogin** command assumes the login name on the remote system is the same as the one on the local system because most people use **rlogin** to access accounts they have on other systems with their own login name. However, when the login name on the remote system is different from the one on the local system, the **-1** option allows you to enter it. The syntax is shown here:

```
$ rlogin system-name -1 login-name
```

You can use the **rcp** command to copy files to and from remote and local systems. It is a file transfer utility that operates like the **cp** command, but across a network connection to a remote system. The **rcp** command requires that the remote system have your local system and login name in its **.rhosts** file. The **rcp** command begins with the keyword **rcp** and has as its arguments the source file and copy file names. To specify the file on the remote system, you need to place the remote system name before the file name, separated by a colon. When you are copying a file on the remote system to your own, the source file is a remote file and will require the remote system's name. The copy file will be a file on your own system and does not require a system name:

```
$ rcp remote-system-name:source-file   copy-file
```

In the next example, the user copies the file **wednesday** from the remote system violet to his own system and renames the file **today**.

```
$ rcp violet:wednesday today
```

You can also use **rcp** to copy whole directories to or from a remote system. The **rcp** command with the **-r** option will copy a directory and all its subdirectories from one system to another. Like the **cp** command, **rcp** requires source and copy directories. The directory on the remote system requires the system name and colon placed before the directory name. When you copy a directory from your own system to a remote system, the copied directory will be on the remote system and requires the remote system's name. In the next example, the user copies the directory **letters** to the directory **oldnotes** on the remote system violet.

```
$ rcp -r letters violet:oldnotes
```

At times, you may need to execute a single command on a remote system. The **rsh** command will execute a Linux command on another system and display the results on your own. Your system name and login name must, of course, be in the remote system's **.rhosts** file. The **rsh** command takes two general arguments, a system name and a Linux command. The syntax is as follows:

```
$ rsh remote-system-name  Linux-command
```

In the next example, the **rsh** command executes an **ls** command on the remote system violet to list the files in the **/home/robert** directory on violet.

```
$ rsh violet ls /home/robert
```

Special characters are evaluated by the local system unless quoted. This is particularly true of special characters that control the standard output, such as redirection operators or pipes. The next example lists the files on the remote system and sends them to the standard output on the local system. The redirection operator is evaluated by the local system and redirects the output to **myfiles**, which is a file on the local system.

```
$ rsh violet ls /home/robert > myfiles
```

If you quote a special character, it becomes part of the Linux command evaluated on the remote system. Quoting redirection operators will allow you to perform redirection operations on the remote system. In the next example, the redirection operator is quoted. It becomes part of the Linux command, including its argument, the file name **myfiles**. The **ls** command then generates a list of file names that is redirected on the remote system to a file called **myfiles**, also located on the remote system.

```
$ rsh violet ls /home/robert '>' myfiles
```

The same is true for pipes. The first command shown next prints out the list of files on the local system's printer. The standard output is piped to your own line printer. In the second command, the list of files is printed on the remote system's printer. The pipe is quoted and evaluated by the remote system, piping the standard output to the printer on the remote system.

```
$ rsh violet ls /home/robert | lpr
$ rsh violet ls /home/robert '|' lpr
```

Unix to Unix CoPy: UUCP

The UUCP protocols are an alternative set of protocols to those of the Internet (TCP/IP) that provide network communication between Linux and Unix systems. However, UUCP is an older protocol that was designed to operate between systems that were not already connected on a network. With UUCP, one system can connect to another across phone lines at a predetermined time, sending a batched set of communications all at once. UUCP is very helpful for making a direct connection to a particular system, transferring data, and then cutting the connection. UUCP allows you to set up direct modem-to-modem communication with another system.

UUCP has its own set of remote access commands: **uuto**, **uupick**, **uucp**, and **uux**. The **uuto** command mails files to other systems, and **uupick** receives those files. These commands are used for sending and receiving large files. The **uucp** command copies files from one system to another. The **uux** command remotely executes a Linux command on another system. Many of the UUCP commands correspond to the TCP/IP remote access commands. The **uucp** command operates much like **rcp** and **uux** like **rsh**. UUCP commands are subject to the same permission restrictions as your own local commands. Protected files and directories cannot be accessed. Only files and directories with the other user permission set can be accessed.

You can think of UUCP commands as referencing files on other Linux systems through a mail system. These commands are designed to operate using point-to-point communication. It is as if you were using the mail capabilities of different systems to implement a network. When you issue a UUCP command for a given system, the command is queued and collected with other commands for that same system. The commands are then mailed to that system for execution. Once that system receives the commands and executes them, it mails back any results. Several systems can arrange to receive and send commands to each other, forming a UUCP network. The entire process then depends on each system in the network sending and receiving commands to and from other systems. In this respect, the network is only as strong as its weakest link. On the other hand, it requires no special structure, only the sending and receiving of what are essentially messages.

The Complete Reference

Linux

Part IV

Servers

The
Complete
Reference

Linux

Chapter 16

Internet Servers

Reflecting the close relationship between Unix and the development of the Internet, Linux is particularly good at providing Internet services such as the Web, FTP, and Gopher. In the case of the Web, instead of just accessing other sites, you can set up your own Linux system to be a Web site. Other people can then access your system using Web pages you created, or download files you provide for them. A system that operates this way is called a *server*, and is known by the service it provides. You can set up your system to be a Web server or an FTP server, connecting it to the Internet and turning it into a site that others can access. A single Linux system can provide several different services. Your Linux system can be a Web server and an FTP server as well as a Gopher and WAIS server, all at the same time. One user could download files using your FTP services while another reads your Web pages. All you have to do is install and run the appropriate server software for each service. Each one operates as a continually running daemon looking for requests for its particular services from remote users.

The Red Hat and OpenLinux systems install and run Web and FTP servers. They were designed with Internet servers in mind. When you install any of these distributions, the server software for these services is automatically installed and configured for you. Every time you start your system, you also start the Web and FTP server daemons. To turn your Linux system into a Web server, all you have to do is create Web pages. For an FTP server, you only have to place the files you want to make available in the FTP directories.

You can operate your Linux system as a server on the Internet, an intranet (local area network), or to service just the users on your own system. To operate servers as Internet servers, you must obtain a connection to the Internet and provide access to your system for remote users. Access is usually a matter of allowing anonymous logins to directories reserved for server resources. OpenLinux and Red Hat systems are already configured to allow such access for Web and FTP users. Connections to the Internet that can accommodate server activity can be difficult to come by. You may need a dedicated connection, or you may need to use a connection set up by an Internet service provider. You are no longer connecting only yourself to the Internet, but you are allowing many other users to make what could be a great many connections to you through the Internet. If you only want to provide the services to a local area network, you will not need a special connection. Also, you can provide these services to users by allowing them to connect over a modem and log in directly. Users could dial into your system and use your Web pages or use FTP to download files. Furthermore, users with accounts on your own machine can also make use of the servers. In whatever situation you want to use these services, you will need the appropriate server software installed and running. This chapter examines how servers are started and stopped on your system, as well different ways of accessing the servers.

Starting Servers: standalone and inetd

A *server* is a daemon that runs concurrently with your other programs, continuously looking for a request for its services either from other users on your system or from remote users connecting to your system through a network. When it receives a request from a user, it starts up a session to provide its services. For example, if users want to download a file from your system, they can use their own FTP client to request that your FTP server start a session for them. In the session, they can access and download files from your system. Your server needs to be running for a user to access its services. For example, if you set up a Web site on your system with HTML files, you must have the **httpd** Web server program running before users can access your Web site and display those files. See Chapters 17, 18, and 19 on how to install FTP, Web, and Gopher servers.

There are several ways to start a server. One way is to do it manually from the command line by entering the name of the server program and its arguments. Upon pressing ENTER, the server will start, although your command line prompt will reappear. The server will run concurrently as you perform other tasks. To see if your server is running, you can enter the following command to list all currently running processes. You should see a process for the server program you started up. To refine the list, you can add a **grep** operation with a pattern for the server name you want. The second command will list the process for the Web server.

```
# ps -aux
# ps -aux | grep 'httpd'
```

On OpenLinux and Red Hat systems, you can also use special start up scripts to manually start and stop your server. These scripts are located in the /**etc/rc.d/init.d** directory and have the same name as the server programs. For example, the /**etc/rc.d/init.d/httpd** script with the start option will start the Web server. Using it with the stop option will stop it. These scripts are explained in greater detail later in this chapter.

```
/etc/rc.d/init.d/httpd stop
/etc/rc.d/init.d/httpd httpd start
```

Instead of manually executing all the server programs each time you boot your system, your system can automatically start the servers for you. There are two ways to do this, depending on how you want to use a server. You can have a server running continuously from the time you start your system until you shut it down, or you can have the server start only when it receives a request from a user for its services. If a server is being used frequently, you may want to have it running all the time. If it is used rarely, you may just want it to start when a request comes in. For example, if you are running a Web site, your Web server will be receiving requests all the time from remote hosts on the Internet. However, for an FTP site, you may receive requests infrequently, in which case you may want to have the FTP server start only when it receives a request. Of course, certain FTP sites receive frequent requests, which would warrant a continually running FTP server.

A server that starts automatically and runs continuously is referred to as a *standalone* server. Most distributions use the SysV Init procedure to automatically start servers whenever your system boots. This procedure uses special startup scripts for the servers located in the **/etc/rc.d/init.d** directory. Alternatively, you could directly invoke a server in system startup scripts such as **rc.local.**

To start the server only when a request for its services is received, you configure it using the **inetd** daemon, known as the "Internet Superserver." This daemon looks for server requests and then starts up the server when a request comes through. OpenLinux and Red Hat systems already configured the Web server to start automatically and run continuously. There is a script for it in the **/etc/rc.d/init.d** directory called **httpd**. The Washington University FTP server, **wu-ftpd**, is configured to run under **inetd**. It will start only when someone initiates an FTP session with your system. You will find an entry for the FTP server in the **inetd.conf** configuration file, but there is no script for it in **/etc/rc.d/init.d**, as there is for the Web server.

Standalone Server Tools

The System V Runlevel Editor, Linuxconf, COAS, and the KDE System V Editor all provide simple interfaces you can use to choose what servers you want started up and how you want them to run.

The System V Runlevel Editor is installed with most distributions, including Red Hat, and features a GUI interface to let you easily manage any daemons on your system—Internet servers as well as system daemons such as print servers. The Runlevel Editor window is divided in to three major panes. To the left is a scroll window labeled "available" that lists all the daemons available for use on your system. These will include the daemons for Internet servers such as **httpd**. Below are buttons for operations you can perform on the server daemons: add, remove, edit, and execute. To the right, taking up most of the window, are an upper and lower pane. The upper pane has four scroll windows, one for each run level. (See Chapter 27 for an explanation of system runloads.) These list the daemons currently configured to run in their respective run levels. The lower pane also holds four scroll windows, one for each run level. These are daemons that will be shut down should you switch to that respective run level. System administrators can switch form one level to another. All the servers that will start up under normal processing will be listed in the start runlevel 3 scroll window.

To manually start or stop a server, click on its entry in the available scroll window and then click on the Execute button. This displays a small window with the various options to start or stop the selected server. To stop the **httpd** server, just click on its entry in the available scroll window and then click on the Stop button in the displayed window. Do the same procedure to restart the server, clicking on the Start button. You can also configure a server to start automatically when you boot at a certain run level. To have a server start at a given run level, select its entry in the available scroll window and then click on the Add button. A window appears where you can select the run level and whether you want to start or stop the server. To have a server automatically start up when you boot normally, make sure it is listed in the runlevel 3 start scroll window. If not, click on its entry in the available window and select Start and runlevel 3 in the window displayed. The server will be added to the list in the runlevel 3 start scroll window. For example, should you not want your Web server to start when you boot, click on the **httpd** entry in the runlevel 3 start list and click on the Remove button. To have the Web server again start whenever you boot, click on its entry in the available window and then click on the Add button, selecting Start and runlevel 3 in the window that appears. The **httpd** will be added to the runlevel 3 start list. Figure 16-1 shows the System V Runlevel Editor with the Execute and Add windows.

Servers that operate under **inetd** are not listed by the System V Runlevel Editor. Both GN Gopher and wu-ftpd are installed to run under **inetd**, so you will not find

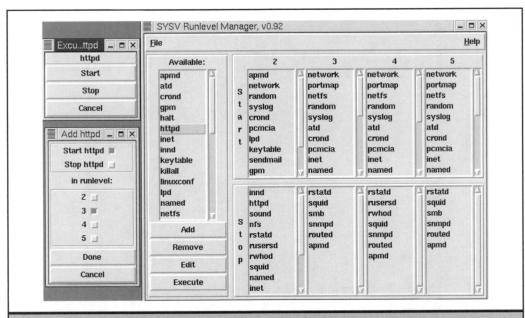

Figure 16-1. *System V Runlevel Editor with Execute and Add windows*

entries for them here. The System V Editor reads it list of servers from the server scripts in the **/etc/rc.d/init.d** directory. If you add a new script, you can have the System V Editor rescan that directory and you will see it appear in the available list. Removing a server from a runlevel window only removes its link in the corresponding runlevel **rc.d** directory. It does not touch the startup script in the **init.d** directory. Adding in the server to the Start runlevel window, just puts the link back in that runlevel directory. Adding a server to a Stop window will add a *K* link in the corresponding **rc.d** directory, which will stop a server when the system switches to that run level. For example, if you remove **httpd** from the runlevel 3 start window, then the **S85httpd** link in the **rc3.d** directory is deleted. Adding **httpd** back to the runlevel 3 start window will create the **S85htppd** link again in the **rc3.d** directory. Adding **httpd** to the runlevel 2 stop directory would create a **K85httpd** link in the **rc2.d** directory, shutting down the server when switching to runlevel 2.

You can also control the startup of a server using Linuxconf. The "Control service activity" panel, located in the "Control panel" list, will list various services available on your system (see Figure 16-2). You can click check boxes to enable or disable them. Disabling a service will remove its startup link in the **rc.d** directory. For example,

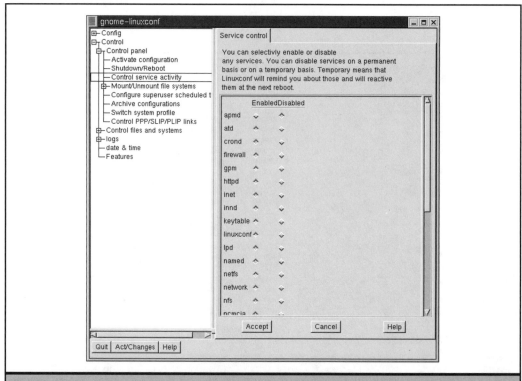

Figure 16-2. Linuxconf "Control service activity" panel

disabling the Web server will remove the **S85httpd** link in the **rc3.d** directory. Enabling the service will restore that link.

On OpenLinux, you can us COAS to select what servers you want to start up. Select "Enable/Disable System Services" from the "System Administration" menu. This lists the different services you can have start up. Those with a check in their check boxes are already selected. Click on a box to toggle the service on or off.

If you change the configuration of a server, you may need to start and stop it several times as you refine the configuration. Several servers provide special management tools that let you easily perform this task. The **apachectl** utility lets you easily start and stop the Apache Web server. For the domain name server, the **ndc** utility lets you start and stop the **named** server.

Linuxconf Server Configuration

Linuxconf provides configuration interfaces for most Internet servers. There are configuration interfaces for the Apache Web server, the BIND domain name server, the Washington University FTP server, and the sendmail mail server. Linuxconf has both a cursor-based interface that can be run from a shell command line and a Gnome and X Window System interface that uses an expandable tree to display entries for different panels. On Red Hat Linux, you can find an entry for Linuxconf in the Gnome start menu under Systems. You can also start it from the Red Hat Control Panel. If there is no menu entry, you can start a terminal window and enter in the command **linuxconf**. You can also use a **netconf** command to display a window with panels just for network and server tasks. Click on the server panel to display the list of buttons for servers you can configure. When using the main Linuxconf utility, select "Server tasks" under Networking.

Panels for various configuration components are displayed with entries for different features. Different panels will display buttons for basic operations such as accept, add, delete, and help. Clicking on the Help button will display a window providing detailed documentation for the current panel and the configuration process for that server. Once you make your entries and click on the "Act/changes" button to accept the configuration, Linuxconf will generate the appropriate configuration files for you. For example, if you use Linuxconf to configure your Domain Name Service server, it will generate the **named.conf** file and any needed zone files. Configuring the wu-ftpd FTP server will generate a new **/etc/ftpaccess** file. Configuring the Apache Web server will generate new **httpd.conf**, **srm.conf** and **access.conf** files. Many servers have an extensive set of features that just need to be turned on or off, rather than given a value. For these, Linuxconf provides check buttons, letting you include a feature just by clicking on its button. The server configurations currently require that certain Linuxconf modules be loaded: mailconf, dnsconf, apache, and wu-ftpd. Current distributions configure Linuxconf to do this automatically. You can manually add modules by selecting the "Linuxconf modules" panel in "Control files and systems" list and entering the module name. Figure 16-3 shows the panel for the FTP server (wu-ftpd) configuration.

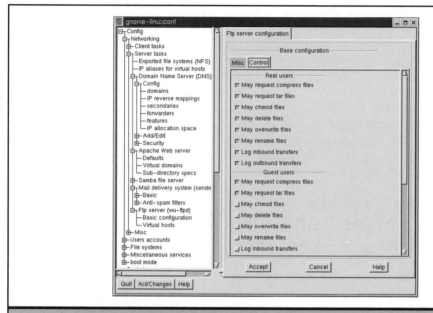

Figure 16-3. *Linuxconf server configuration*

SysV Init: init.d Scripts

Red Hat and OpenLinux manage the startup and shutdown of server daemons using special startup scripts located in the **/etc/rc.d/init.d directory**. These scripts often have the same name as the server's program. For example, for the **/usr/sbin/httpd** Web server program, there is a corresponding script called **/etc/rc.d/init.d/httpd**. It is this script that actually start and stops the Web server. This method of using **init.d** startup scripts to start servers is called SysV Init, after the method used in Unix System V. If your distribution does not use SysV Init scripts, you may have to place the server command in a system initialization file, such as **rc.local**.

The startup scripts in the **/etc/rc.d/init.d** directory can be executed automatically whenever you boot your system. However, be careful when accessing these scripts. These start essential programs such as your network interface and your printer daemon. These init scripts are accessed from links in subdirectories set up for each possible run level. In the **/etc/rc.d** directory, there is a set of subdirectories whose names have the format **rc$N$.d**, where N is a number referring to a run level. The **rc** script will detect the run level that the system was started in and then execute only the startup scripts specified in the subdirectory for that run level. The default run level is 3, the multiuser level. When you start your system, the **rc** script will execute the startup scripts specified in the **rc3.d** directory. The **rc3.d** directory holds symbolic links to certain startup scripts in the **/etc/rc.d/init.d** directory. So, the **httpd** script in the **/etc/rc.d/init.d** directory is actually called through a symbolic link in the **rc3.d** directory. The symbolic link for the **/etc/rc.d/httpd** script in the **rc3.d** directory is **S85httpd**. The *S* prefixing the link stands for startup and will call the corresponding **init.d** script with the start option. **S85httpd** will invoke **/etc/rc.d/init.d/httpd** with the option **start**. The numbers in these links are simply there for ordering purposes. If you change the name of the link to start with a *K*, then the script will be invoked with the **stop** option, stopping it. To have a server automatically start, you would first create a startup script for it in the **/etc/rc.d/init.d** directory and then create a symbolic link to that script in the **/etc/rc.d/rc3.d** directory. The startup script **httpd** used on Red Hat systems is shown here. You can see the different options listed under the case statement: start, stop, status, restart, and reload. If no option is provided (*), then the script usage syntax is displayed. The **httpd** script first executes a script to define functions used in these startup scripts. The daemon command with **httpd** will actually execute the **/usr/sbin/httpd** server program.

```
echo -n "Starting httpd: "
daemon httpd
echo
touch /var/lock/subsys/httpd
```

The **killproc** function will shut down the daemon. The lock file and process id file (**httpd.pid**) are then deleted.

```
killproc httpd
echo
rm -f /var/lock/subsys/httpd
rm -f /var/run/httpd.pid
```

Also located in the **inet.d** directory, **daemon**, **killproc**, and **status** are shell scripts defined in the **functions** script. The **functions** script is executed at the beginning of each startup script to activate these functions.

/etc/rc.d/init.d/httpd

```
#!/bin/sh
#
# Startup script for the Apache Web Server
#
```

```
# chkconfig: 345 85 15
# description: Apache is a World Wide Web server.  It is used to
serve \
#            HTML files and CGI.
# processname: httpd
# pidfile: /var/run/httpd.pid
# config: /etc/httpd/conf/access.conf
# config: /etc/httpd/conf/httpd.conf
# config: /etc/httpd/conf/srm.conf


# Source function library.
. /etc/rc.d/init.d/functions

# See how we were called.
case "$1" in
  start)
   echo -n "Starting httpd: "
   daemon httpd
   echo
   touch /var/lock/subsys/httpd
   ;;
  stop)
   killproc httpd
   echo
   rm -f /var/lock/subsys/httpd
   rm -f /var/run/httpd.pid
   ;;
  status)
   status httpd
   ;;
  restart)
   $0 stop
   $0 start
   ;;
  reload)
   echo -n "Reloading httpd: "
   killproc httpd -HUP
   echo
```

```
    ;;
  *)
    echo "Usage: $0 {start|stop|restart|reload|status}"
    exit 1
esac

exit 0
```

OpenLinux uses slightly different code but has the same functionality and the same start and stop arguments. The name of the Web server daemon and the type of Web server is assigned to a variable called **$VARIANT**. **$VARIANT** is used to check for the existence of the necessary configuration files. These variables are used in place of the daemon name, and this makes for a more modular program structure. The Web server is executed with the following line found in this script. The **$NAME** variable has been set to **httpd** and the **$DAEMON** to the Web server program, **/usr/sbin/httpd**. The **-f** option specifies this Web server's configuration file, where **$VARIANT** is the particular Web server used—in this case, Apache. The **ssd** function (start-stop-daemon) with the **-S** option will start up the daemon.

```
ssd -S -n $NAME -x $DAEMON -- -f
/etc/httpd/$VARIANT/conf/httpd.conf
```

The **ssd** function with the **-K** option will shut down the daemon, using the **-p** option to specify the process ID and the **-n** option for the name.

```
ssd -K -p /var/run/$NAME.pid -n $NAME
```

Creating Startup Scripts

Suppose you have installed the Gopher server on your system and now want to have it start automatically. The easiest way to create a startup script for **gopherd**, the University of Minnesota's Gopher server program, is to first make a copy of the **httpd** script, naming the copy **gopherd**. Both **httpd** and **gopherd** are network servers and use much of the same script.

```
# cp httpd gopherd
```

You then edit the **gopherd** script and replace all references to **httpd** with **gopherd**. For the standard startup scripts used on Red Hat systems, you can just replace **httpd** with **gopherd**. The start section would look something like this. Add whatever options to **gopherd** that you wish.

```
start)
echo -n "Starting gopherd: "
daemon gopherd
echo
touch /var/lock/subsys/gopherd
;;
```

The stop section would look like this:

```
stop)
    killproc gopherd
   echo
   rm -f /var/lock/subsys/gopherd
   rm -f /var/run/gopherd.pid
```

For an OpenLinux startup script, the **$DAEMON** variable should be assigned the path name for the **gopherd** server program, probably **/usr/sbin/gopherd**. OpenLinux also provides a file called *skeleton* in the **/etc/rc.d/init.d** directory that you can use as a basis for creating your own startup scripts. It already has start and stop entries and executes required scripts like **/etc/rc.d/init.d/functions**.

```
$NAME=gopherd
$DAEMON=/usr/sbin/gopherd
```

The following line executes the **gopherd** server. Notice that the command includes arguments such as the directory for Gopher files. Argument requirements vary from server to server. The **httpd** Web server program has no arguments. You can remove references to the **$VARIANT** variable.

```
ssd -S -n $NAME -x $DAEMON /usr/lib/gopher-data
```

Now you change to the **/etc/rc.d/rc3.d** directory and make a symbolic link to that **/etc/rc.d/init.d/gopherd** script. The **ln** command with the **-s** option creates a symbolic link. Alternatively, you could use the System V Runlevel Editor to create the link in the **/etc/rc.d/rc3.d** directory. Have the editor scan the **init.d** directory by selecting Re-scan from the File menu, then click on the entry in the Available listing, click on the Add button, and select the Runlevel and Start options in the Add window. Now when you start your system, the **gopherd** server is automatically started up, running concurrently and waiting for requests.

```
# ln -s /etc/rc.d/init.d/gopherd S94gopherd
```

If you want to change a server from using **inetd** to a standalone process, you have to first create a startup script for it in the **/etc/rc.d/init.d** directory with a link to it in the **rc3.d** directory. Then you have to remove or comment out its entry in the **/etc/inetd.conf** configuration file. To change a server from a standalone process to using **inetd**, you first remove its link in the **/etc/rc.d/rc3.d** directory and any other runlevel directory, then place an entry for it in the **inetd.conf** file. For example, the ProFTP FTP server can run as a standalone or **inetd** server. If it is running as an **inetd** server and want to run it as a standalone server, you first set up a Sys V Init script for it in the **/etc/rc.d/init.d** directory (ProFTP provides one). You then place a symbolic link for it in the **rc3.d** directory, just as described for the **gopherd** server. The name of the standalone ProFTP server program is **proftpd**. You then disable **inetd** management of the ProFTP server by commenting out or removing its entry in the **inetd.conf** file. The server name used in this file is **in.proftd**.

inetd Server Management

If your system averages only a few requests for a specific service, you do not need the server for that service running all the time. You only need it when a remote user is accessing its service. The **inetd** daemon manages Internet servers, invoking them only when your system receives a request for their services. The **inetd** daemon checks continuously for any requests by remote users for a particular Internet service, and when it receives a request it then starts the appropriate server daemon. For example, the Washington University FTP daemon, wu-ftpd, is installed by most distributions to run using **inetd** rather than as a standalone daemon. When **inetd** receives a request from a user to access FTP, it starts **in.ftpd**, the FTP daemon. The **in.ftpd** daemon then handles the request, allowing the remote user to download files.

For **inetd** to call the appropriate server daemon, it must be configured for that service. You place entries for that server in the **/etc/services** and the **/etc/inetd.conf** files. The **/etc/services** file lists services available on your system. An entry in **/etc/services** consists of the name of the service followed by its port and protocol, separated by a slash, /. Entries for FTP as they appear in your Red Hat **/etc/service** file are shown here. Other distributions may require only one entry for FTP.

```
ftp-data      20/tcp
ftp           21/tcp
```

The **/etc/inetd.conf** file is the **inetd** configuration file. For this entry, you specify the service, its protocol, and the server program to invoke. An entry for FTP is shown here. Server paths and arguments may vary according to different Linux distributions. Some programs will have a special script, link, or alternate program to use for **inet.d** activation, instead of directly using the program file. Such scripts or links begin with the prefix "in" and a period, followed by the program name. For example, the ProFTP server is called **proftpd**, but uses the **in.proftpd** as the program name in an **inetd.conf** entry. Other programs, such as the Apache Web server, just use the same program name—in this case, **httpd**.

```
# <service> <sock_type> <proto> <flags> <user> <server_path>     <args>
ftp          stream       tcp      nowait  root   /usr/sbin/in.ftpd in.ftpd
```

For some services, the configuration lines may be there, but they may be commented out with a preceding # symbol. Just remove the #. If there are no configuration entries, you will have to add them. The standard entries in **inetd.conf** for Internet services are shown here:

```
# These are standard services.
#
ftp        stream    tcp    nowait    root    /usr/sbin/tcpd    in.ftpd -l -a
telnet     stream    tcp    nowait    root    /usr/sbin/tcpd    in.telnetd
gopher     stream    tcp    nowait    root    /usr/sbin/tcpd    gn
```

tcpd

You can use the **tcpd** daemon to add another level of security to **inetd** managed servers. You can set up **tcpd** to monitor a server connection made through **inetd**. The **tcpd** daemon will verify remote user identities and check to make sure they are making valid requests. With **tcpd**, you can also restrict access to your system by remote hosts. Lists of hosts are kept in the **hosts.allow** and **hosts.deny** files. Entries in these files have the format **service:hostname:domain**. The domain is optional. For the service, you can specify a particular service such as FTP or you can enter **ALL** for all services. For the hostname, you can specify a particular host or **ALL** for all hosts. In the following example, the first entry allows access by all hosts to the Web service, **http**. The second entry allows access to all services by the **pango1.train.com** host. The third and fourth entries allow **rabbit.trek.com** and **caldera.com** FTP access.

```
http:ALL
ALL:pango1.train.com
ftp:rabbit.trek.com
ftp:caldera.com
```

The **hosts.allow** file holds hosts that you allow access to. If you want to allow access to all but a few specific hosts, you can specify **ALL** for a service in the **hosts.allow** file, but list the one you are denying access in the **hosts.deny** file. The **tcpd** Man pages (**man tcpd**) provide more detailed information about **tcpd**.

To have **tcpd** monitor a server, you have to place the pathname for **tcpd** in the path name field of a server's entry for the **inetd.conf** file. This is what has already done for the **ftpd** server entry in the OpenLinux and RedHat **inetd.conf** file. Instead of the path name for the **ftpd** program, **/usr/sbin/in.ftpd**, there is the path name for the **tcpd** daemon, **/usr/sbin/tcpd**. The argument field that follows then lists the **in.ftpd** server program.

```
# <service> <sock_type> <proto> <flags> <user>  <server_path>
<args>
ftp          stream     tcp      nowait  root     /usr/sbin/tcpd
in.ftpd
```

When **inetd** receives a request for an FTP service, it calls the **tcpd** daemon, which then takes over and monitors the connection. Then it starts up the **in.ftpd** server program. By default, **tcpd** will allow all requests. To allow all requests specifically for the FTP service, you would enter in the following in your **/etc/hosts.allow** file. The entry **ALL:ALL** opens up your system to all hosts for all services.

```
ftp:ALL
```

The
Complete
Reference

Linux

Chapter 17

FTP Servers

461

The File Transfer Protocol (FTP) is designed to transfer large files across a network from one system to another. Like most Internet operations, FTP works on a client/server model. FTP client programs can enable users to transfer files to and from a remote system running an FTP server program. Chapter 13 discusses FTP clients. Any Linux systems can operate as an FTP server. It only has to run the server software—an FTP daemon with the appropriate configuration. Transfers are made between user accounts on client and server systems. A user on the remote system has to log in to an account on a server and can then transfer files to and from that account's directories only. There is a special kind of user account called *FTP* that will allow any user to log into it with the user name *anonymous*. This account has its own set of directories and files that are considered public, available to anyone on the network who wants to download them. The numerous FTP sites on the Internet are just FTP servers supporting FTP user accounts with anonymous login. Any Linux system can be configured to support anonymous FTP access, turning them into network FTP sites. Such sites can work on an intranet or on the Internet. On Red Hat and OpenLinux systems, the configuration files for anonymous FTP are in a package beginning with the term *anonftp*. Installing this package sets up your FTP directories and configures the FTP account.

FTP Daemons

FTP server software consists of an FTP daemon and configuration files. The daemon is a program that continuously checks for FTP requests from remote users. When a request is received, it manages a login, sets up the connection to the requested user account, and executes any **ftp** commands the remote user sends. For anonymous FTP access, the FTP daemon allows the remote user to log into the FTP account using anonymous as the user name. The user then has access to the directories and files set up for the FTP account. However, as a further security measure, the daemon changes the root directory for that session to be the FTP **home** directory. This hides the rest of the system from the remote user. Normally, any user on a system can move around to any directories that are open to him or her. A user logging in with anonymous FTP can only see the FTP **home** directory and its subdirectories. The remainder of the system is hidden from that user. By default, the FTP server will also require that a user be using a valid shell. It checks for a list of valid shells in the **/etc/shells** file. Most daemons have options for turning off this feature.

There are several FTP server daemons available for use on Linux systems. Most Linux distributions come with the Washington University FTP server called wu-ftpd. You can download RPM package updates from **updates.redhat.com** and **ftp.calderasystems.com**. The daemon software begins with the term *wu-ftpd* You can obtain the original compressed archive from the Washington University archive at **http://wuarchive.wustl.edu/packages/wuarchive-ftpd**.

ProFTPD is a newer and very popular FTP daemon based on an Apache Web server design. It features simplified configuration and support for virtual FTP hosts. Though not currently included with most distributions, you can download RPM packages from **contrib.redhat.com**. The package begins with the term *proftpd*. The compressed archive of the most up-to-date version along with documentation is available at the ProFTPD Web site at **www.proftpd.org**. Another FTP daemon, ncftpd, is a commercial product produced by the same programmers that did the ncftp FTP client. It is free for academic use and features a reduced fee for small networks. Check **www.ncftpd.org** for more information.

Red Hat and OpenLinux distributions currently install the wu-ftpd server and the anon anonymous FTP package during installation. At that time, directories are created where you can place files for FTP access. The directories have already been configured to control access by remote users, restricting use to just the FTP directories and any subdirectories. The directory reserved for your FTP files is **/home/ftp**. You just have to place the files you want to allow access to in the **/home/ftp/pub** directory. You can also create subdirectories and place files there. Once connected to a network, a remote user can connect to your system and download files you have placed in **/home/ftp/pub** or any of its subdirectories. The Red Hat and OpenLinux FTP server installations implement a default configuration. You can change these if you wish. If you are installing an FTP server yourself, you will need to know the procedures detailed in the following sections to install an FTP server and create its data directories.

Anonymous FTP: anon

An anonymous FTP site is essentially a special kind of user on your system with publicly accessible directories and files in its **home** directory. Anyone can log into this account and access its files. Since anyone can log into an anonymous FTP account, you have to be careful to restrict a remote FTP user to just the files on that anonymous FTP directory. Normally, a user's files are interconnected to the entire file structure of your system. Normal users have write access that lets them create or delete files and directories. The anonymous FTP files and directories can be configured in such a way that the rest of the file system is hidden from them and remote users are given only read access. In ProFTPD, this is achieved through configuration directives placed in its configuration file. An older approach used by wu-ftpd involves having copies of certain system configuration, command, and library files placed within the FTP **home** directory. These are placed in directories that restrict access by other users. Within the FTP **home** directory, you then have a publicly accessible directory that holds the files you want to make available to remote users. It usually has the name **pub**, for public.

An FTP site is made up of an FTP user account, an FTP **home** directory, and certain copies of system directories containing selected configuration and support files. Newer FTP daemons such as ProFTPD will not need the system directories and support files. Most distributions, including Red Hat and OpenLinux, have already set up an FTP user account when you installed your system. On systems that support RPM package installation, such as Red Hat and OpenLinux, you can use the anon rpm package to set up the **home** directory and the copies of the system directories. If you do not have access to the anon package, you may have to create these system directories yourself.

The FTP User Account: anonymous

To allow anonymous FTP access by other users to your system, you must have a user account named ftp. Most distributions such as Red Hat and OpenLinux have already created this account for you. If your system does not have such an account, you will have to create one. You can then place restrictions on the ftp account to keep any remote FTP users from accessing any other part of your system. You must also modify the entry for this account in your **/etc/passwd** file to prevent normal user access to it. The following is the entry that you will find in your **/etc/passwd** file on OpenLinux or Red Hat systems that sets up an FTP login as an anonymous user:

```
ftp:*:14:50:FTP User:/home/ftp:
```

The asterisk in the password field blocks the account, which prevents any other users from gaining access to it and thereby gaining control over its files or access to other parts of your system. The user ID, 14, is a unique ID. The comment field is FTP User. The login directory is **/home/ftp**. When FTP users log into your system, this is the directory they will be placed in. If a **home** directory has not been set up, create one and then change its ownership to the FTP user with the **chown** command.

The group ID is the ID of the **ftp** group, which is set up just for anonymous FTP users. You can set up restrictions on the **ftp** group, thereby restricting any anonymous FTP users. Here is the entry for the **ftp** group that you will find in the **/etc/group** file. If your system does not have one, you should add it.

```
ftp::50:
```

Anonymous FTP Server Directories

On most distributions, the FTP **home** directory is **/home/ftp**. When users log in anonymously, they are placed in this directory. An important part of protecting your system is preventing remote users from using any commands or programs that are not in the restricted directories. For example, you would not let a user use your **ls** command to list file names since **ls** is located in your **/bin** directory. At the same time, you want to let the FTP user list file names using an **ls** command. Newer FTP daemons like ProFTPD solve this problem by creating secure access to needed system commands and files, while restricting remote users to just the FTP site's directories.

Another more traditional solution, used by wu-ftpd, is to create copies of certain system directories and files that will be needed by remote users and place them in the **/home/ftp** directory where users can access them. A **bin** directory is placed in the **/home/ftp** directory and remote users are restricted to it instead of the system's **bin** directory. Whenever they use the **ls** command, they are using the one in **/home/ftp/bin**, not the one you use in **/bin**.

On systems that support RPM installation, such as Red Hat and OpenLinux, you can use the **anon** rpm package to set up these copies of system directories and files. Otherwise you may have to create these directories and support files yourself. The **anon** package will install **etc**, **bin**, and **lib** directories in the **/home/ftp** directory. These contain localized versions of system files needed to let an FTP client execute certain FTP commands such as listing files or changing directories. The **/home/ftp/etc** directory contains versions of the password and group configuration files, the **/home/ftp/bin** directory contains copies of shell and compression commands, and the **lib** directory holds copies of system libraries. The directories set up by the **anon** package are shown here:

```
/home/ftp
/home/ftp/bin
/home/ftp/etc
/home/ftp/lib
/home/ftp/pub
```

The **/home/ftp/etc** directory holds a copy of your **passwd** and **group** files. Again, the idea is to prevent any access to the original files in the **/etc** directory by FTP users. The **/home/ftp/etc/passwd** file should not include any entries for regular users on your system. All entries should have their passwords set to ***** to block access. The **group** file should not include any user groups and all passwords should be set to *****.

```
/home/ftp/etc/passwd
root:*:0:0:::
bin:*:1:1:::
operator:*:11:0:::
ftp:*:14:50:::
nobody:*:99:99:::

/home/ftp/etc/group
root::0:
bin::1:
daemon::2:
sys::3:
adm::4:
ftp::50:
```

SERVERS

If, for some reason, you do not have access to the **anon** package, you can set up the anonymous FTP directories yourself. Again, keep in mind that if you are using ProFTPD, you do not need any of these files except for the **home** directory. You will have to use the **chmod** command to change the access permissions for the directories so that remote users cannot access the rest of your system. Create a **/home/ftp** directory and use the **chmod** command with the permission 555 to turn off write access: **chmod 555 /home/ftp**. Then make a new **bin** directory in the **/home/ftp** directory, and then make a copy of the **ls** command and place it in **/home/ftp/bin**. Do this for any commands you want to make available to FTP users. Then create a **/home/ftp/etc** directory to hold a copy of your **passwd** and **group** files. Again the idea is to prevent any access to the original files in the **/etc** directory by FTP users. The **/home/ftp/etc/passwd** file should be edited to remove any entries for regular users on your system. All other entries should have their passwords set to * to block access. For the **group** file, remove all user groups and set all passwords to *. Then create a **/home/ftp/lib** directory, and then make copies of the libraries you will need to run the commands you placed in the **bin** directory. Some libraries make use of the **/dev/zero** file. For these, you have to create a **/home/ftp/dev** directory and a copy of the **/dev/zero** device file and place it in this directory.

Anonymous FTP Files

A directory named **/home/ftp/pub** usually holds the files you are making available for downloading by remote FTP users. When FTP users log in, they will be placed in the **/home/ftp** directory and can then change to the **/home/ftp/pub** directory to start accessing those files. Within **/home/ftp/pub**, you can add as many files and directories as you wish. You can even designate some directories as upload directories, allowing FTP users to transfer files to your system.

In each directory set up under **/home/ftp/pub** to hold FTP files, you should create a **readme** file and an **index** file as a courtesy to FTP users. The **readme** file contains a brief description of the kind of files held in this directory. The **index** file should contain a listing of the files and a description of what each one holds.

Permissions

Technically, any remote FTP user gaining access to your system is considered a user and, unless restricted, could access other parts of your file system, create directories and files, or delete the ones already there. Permissions can be used to restrict remote users to simple read access, and the rest of your file system can be hidden from the FTP directories. The **anon** package and the ProFTPD daemon already implement these restrictions. If you are manually creating your anonymous FTP files, you have to be sure to set the permission correctly to restrict access.

Normally, a Linux file structure interconnects all the directories and files on its system. Except where prevented by permissions set on a directory or file, any user can access any directory or file on your system. Technically, any remote FTP user gaining anonymous access is an anonymous user and, as a user, could theoretically access an unrestricted directory or file on your system. To restrict FTP users to the **/home/ftp** directory and its subdirectories, the rest of the file structure has to be hidden from them. In effect, the **/home/ftp** directory should appear to be the root directory as far as FTP users are concerned. The real root directory, **/**, and the rest of the directory structure remain hidden. The FTP daemon attains this effect by using the **chroot** command to make the **/home/ftp** directory appear as a root directory, with the FTP user as the argument. When a remote FTP user issues a **cd /** command to change to the root, they will always change to the **/home/ftp** directory.

As a further restriction, all the directories that hold commands in **/home/ftp**, as well as the commands themselves, should be owned by the root, not by the FTP user. In other words, no FTP user should have any control over these directories. The root has to own **/home/ftp/bin**, **/home/ftp/etc**, and all the files they contain. The **anon** package already has set the ownership of these directories to the root. If you need to set them manually, you can use the **chown** command. The following example changes the ownership of the **/home/ftp/bin** directory to the root:

```
# chown root  /home/ftp/bin
```

Permissions for the FTP directories should be set to allow access for FTP users. Recall that there are three sets of permissions—read, write, and execute for the owner, the group, and others. To allow access by FTP users, the group and other permissions for directories should be set to both read and execute. The execute permission allows FTP users to access that directory, and the read permission allows listing the contents of the directory. Directories should not allow write permission by FTP users. You don't want them to be able to delete your directories or make new ones. For example, the **/home/ftp/bin** directory needs both read and execute permissions since FTP users have to access and execute its commands. This is particularly true for directories such as **/home/ftp/pub**, which holds the files for downloading. It must have both read and execute permissions set.

You, as the owner of the directories, may need write permission to be able to add new files or subdirectories. Of course, you only need this when you are making changes. To add further security, you could set these directories at just read and execute even for the owner when you are not making changes. You can set all permissions to read and execute with the **chmod** command and the number 555 followed by the directory name. This sets the owner, group, and other permissions to read and execute. The permissions currently in place for the FTP directories set up by the **anon** package are designated by the number 755, giving the owner write permission.

```
# chmod 555 /home/ftp/bin
```

Permissions for files within the **/home/ftp/bin** and other special FTP directories can be more restrictive. Some files only need to be read, while others have to be executed. Files in the **/home/ftp/bin** or **/home/ftp/lib** directories only have to be executed. These could have their permissions set to 555. Files in the **/home/ftp/etc** directory such as **passwd** and **group** should have their permissions set to 111. They only have to be read. You always use the **chmod** command to set permissions for files, as shown in the following example. The **anon** package sets these permissions at read and execute, 555.

```
# chmod 111 /home/ftp/etc/passwd
```

FTP Server Tools

Both the wu-ftpd and ProFTPD daemons provide a set of FTP tools that you can use to manage your FTP server. With the **ftpshut** command, you can smoothly shut down a running server, warning users of the shutdown well before it happens. The **ftpwho** can tell you who is currently connected and what they are doing. The **ftpcount** can give you the number of connections currently in effect. Though each daemon has its own set of tools, they perform the same action with much the same set of options. Tools provided by both ProFTPD and wu-ftpd have the same name and options, though ProFTPD provides more information on virtual hosts and has some added options.

ftpshut

With the **ftpshut** command, you can have the FTP server shut down at a given time, rather than suddenly shutting it down by killing its process. This gives you the chance to warn users that the server will be shutting down and not to start any long downloads. The **ftpshut** takes several options for specifying the time and including a warning message. The **ftpshut** takes as its arguments the time until the shutdown followed by a warning message you want sent to users. The time can be a word such as "now" that effects an immediate shutdown, a + sign with the number of minutes remaining, or a specific time of day indicated by an HHMM format, where HH is the hour in a 24-hour cycle and MM is the minute. Shutdown will disable new FTP access 10 minutes before a scheduled shutdown, though this can be changed using the **-l** option with the number of minutes you want. Five minutes before a scheduled shutdown, all current connections will be disconnected. You can adjust the time with the **-d** option. The warning message will be formatted at 75 characters and you can use special formatting symbols for in-place substitutions of certain values in the warning message, such as the shutdown time. These symbols are called magic cookies. For example, **%s** is the shutdown time, **%r** is the time when new connections are refused, **%d** is the time when current connections are cut, **%M** is the maximum number of users, and **%L** is the local hostname.

ftpwho and ftpcount

With the **ftpwho** command, you can find out who is currently connected to your FTP server. It shows the current process information for each user. The output displays five fields: the process ID, the tty connection, status of the connection, the amount of CPU time used so far for the process, and the connection details. The status of the connection will be R for running, S for sleeping, and Z for crashed. The connection details will include the Internet address from where the connection is made, the user making the connection, and the task currently to be performed, such as downloading a file. The field begins with the name of the FTP daemon, usually **ftpd**, followed by the different segments separated by colons.

The **ftpcount** command displays the number of users connected to your FTP server, broken down according to the classes specified in your **.ftpaccess** file. Along with the number of users, it shows the maximum number allowed to connect.

The Washington University FTP Daemon: wu-ftpd

The Washington University FTP daemon is currently the most widely used FTP server on Linux systems. It is the FTP server installed by most Linux distributions. The name of the Washington University FTP daemon is **wu-ftpd**. The wu-ftpd options are shown in Table 17-1. The wu-ftpd must be running to allow FTP access by remote users. As with other servers, you can start the FTP server at boot time, through **inetd** when a request is received, or directly from the command line. By default, the wu-ftpd server is installed to run using **inetd**. The use of inetd for the servers is described in detail in the previous chapter. The command name for the FTP server invoked by inetd is **in.ftpd**. If you want to run your server continually (like a Web server), you have to set up an init script for it in the **/etc/rc.d/init.d** directory so that it will start when you boot your system. You can also start the FTP server directly from the command line by entering the **wu.ftpd** command with any options or arguments. The wu-ftpd server can be called with several options. Usually, it is called with the **-l** option that allows logins. The **-t** and **-T** options set timeouts for users, cutting off those that have no activity after a certain period of time. The **-d** option displays debugging information, and **-u** sets the umask value for uploaded files.

wu-ftpd Server Configuration Files

There are numerous configuration options you can use to tailor your FTP server to your site's particular needs. The wu-ftpd makes use of several configuration files located in the **/etc** directory. All begin with the pattern **ftp**. The primary configuration file is named **ftpaccess**. Here, you provide basic server information and access for specified directories. The **ftphosts**, **ftpusers**, and **ftpgroups** control access by systems,

SERVERS

Option	Effect
-d	Writes debugging information to the syslog
-l	Logs each FTP session in the syslog
-t*seconds*	Sets the inactivity timeout period to specified seconds (default is 15 minutes)
-T*seconds*	The maximum timeout period allowed when timeout is set by user (default is two hours)
-a	Enables use of the **ftpaccess(5)** configuration file
-A	Disables use of the **ftpaccess(5)** configuration file
-L	Logs commands sent to the **ftpd** server to the syslog
-i	Logs files received by **ftpd** to **xferlog**
-o	Logs files transmitted by **ftpd** to the syslog

Table 17-1.   *ftpd Options*

particularly users, and groups. The **ftpconversions** specifies how archive and compression operations are to be performed on files before or after they are transferred. The **xferlog** is the log file that stores a running log of all transactions performed by the server. You can also configure your wu-ftpd server using Linuxconf (see Chapter 16).

ftpaccess

The **ftpaccess** file determines capabilities that users will have when they gain access to your FTP site. Access, information, permissions, logging, and several miscellaneous capabilities can be designated. You can have entries that create aliases for certain directories, display a message when FTP users log in, or prevent anonymous users from deleting files. A **loginfails** entry determines the number of login tries a user can make before being cut off, and the **email** entry specifies the e-mail address of the FTP administrator. The Man page for **ftpaccess** lists the possible entries. The **ftpaccess** file with the configuration used on Red Hat and OpenLinux systems is shown in this section. For commonly used **ftpaccess** entries, see Table 17-2. For more detailed information, check the **ftpaccess** Man page and wu-ftpd documentation.

In the **ftpaccess** file, you set capabilities for different types of users, called *classes*. There are three different types of users: anonymous, guest, and real. Anonymous users are any users using the anonymous login name. Guest users can be those with special guest accounts or access. A real user is one who has an account on the system and is using an FTP connection to access it. You can define your own class using the **class** option. In the **ftpaccess** file shown here, a class called **all** is created that consists of all users of the anonymous, guest, and real types.

The message entry specifies a file with the message to be displayed and when that message is to appear. You can have one message appear when users log in and other messages displayed when users enter certain directories. For example, the following entry will display the message in the **/welcome.msg** file when a user logs in:

```
message /welcome.msg              login
```

To set permissions, you use the command followed by a yes or no and then a list of the user types or classes. In the **ftpaccess** file shown here, all users can perform **tar** and **compress** operations, but anonymous and guest users are prohibited from using **chmod**, **delete**, **overwrite**, and **rename** operations. They also cannot erase files, modify them, or change their names or permissions.

/etc/ftpaccess

```
class   all    real,guest,anonymous   *
email root@localhost
loginfails 5
readme    README*       login
readme    README*       cwd=*
message   /welcome.msg login
message   .message      cwd=*
compress yes          all

tar       yes          all

chmod     no           guest,anonymous

delet     no           guest,anonymous
overwrite no           guest,anonymous
rename    no           guest,anonymous

log transfers anonymous,real inbound,outbound
shutdown /etc/shutmsg
passwd-check rfc822 warn
```

Options	Description
Access Capabilities	
autogroup *group classglob* [*classglob...*]	This allows access to a group's read only files and directories by particular classes of anonymous users. The *group* is a valid group from **/etc/group**.
class *class typelist addrglob* [*addrglob...*]	Defines *class* of users, with source addresses of the form *addrglob*. The *typelist* is a comma-separated list of the user types: anonymous, guest, and real.
deny *host-addrglob message_file*	Always deny access to host(s) matching *host-addrglob*. The *message_file* is displayed.
guestgroup *groupname* [*groupname...*]	Allow guest access by a real user, where the user is a member of the specified group. A password entry for the guest user will specify a **home** directory within the FTP site directories.
limit *class n times message_file*	Limit class to *n* users at times *times*, displaying *message_file* if access is denied.
noretrieve *file-list*	Deny retrieval ability of these files.
loginfails *number*	After *number* login failures, terminate the FTP connection. Default value is 5.
private *yes|no*	The user becomes a member of the group specified in the group access file **ftpgroups**.
Informational Capabilities	
banner *file*	The banner is displayed before login. File requires full pathname.
email *email-address*	Defines the e-mail address of the FTP manager.
message *file { when { class ...}}*	FTP displays the contents of the *file* at login time or upon changing directories. The **when** parameter may be LOGIN or CWD=*dir*; *dir* specifies the directory that will display the message when entered. There can be magic cookies in the message file that cause the FTP server to replace the cookie with a specified text string such as the date or the user name.

Table 17-2.   */etc/ftpaccess wu-ftpd Configuration File*

Options	Description
Access Capabilities	
readme *file* { *when* { *class*}}	The user is notified at login time or upon using a change working directory command (**cd**) that *file* exists and was modified on such-and-such date.
Logging Capabilities	
log commands *typelist*	Enables logging of individual commands by users.
log transfers *typelist directions*	Enables logging of file transfers. The *directions* is a comma-separated list of the terms "inbound" and "outbound," and will log transfers for files sent to the server and sent from the server.
Miscellaneous Capabilities	
alias *string dir*	Defines an alias, string, for a directory.
cdpath *dir*	Defines an entry in **cdpath**. This defines a search path that is used when changing directories.
compress yes|no *classglob* [*classglob* **tar** yes|no *classglob* [*classglob...*]...]	Enables **compress** or **tar** capabilities for any class matching of *classglob*. The actual conversions are defined in the external file **ftconversion**.
shutdown *path*	If the file pointed to by *path* exists, the server will check the file regularly to see if the server is going to be shut down.
virtual *address* root|banner|logfile *path*	Enables the virtual FTP server capabilities.
Permission Capabilities	Allows or disallows the ability to perform the specified function. By default, all users are allowed.
chmod yes | no *typelist*	Allow or disallow changing file permissions.
delete yes | no *typelist*	Allow or disallow deleting files, **rm**.
overwrite yes | no *typelist*	Allow or disallow modifying files.
rename yes | no *typelist*	Allow or disallow re-naming files, **mv**.

SERVERS

Table 17-2.   */etc/ftpaccess wu-ftpd Configuration File* (continued)

Options **Access Capabilities**	Description
umask yes | no *typelist*	Allow or disallow file creation permissions.
passwd-check *none* | *trivial* | *rfc822* (*enforce* | *warn*)	Define the level and enforcement of password checking done by the server for anonymous FTP.
path-filter *typelist mesg allowed_charset* { *disallowed regexp...*}	For users in *typelist*, `path-filter` defines regular expressions that control what a file name can or cannot be. There may be multiple disallowed *regexps*.
upload *root-dir dirglob* yes|no *owner group mode* ["dirs" | "nodirs"]	Define a directory with *dirglob* that permits or denies uploads.

Table 17-2.   */etc/ftpaccess wu-ftpd Configuration File* (continued)

ftphosts

You use the **ftphosts** file to allow or deny access by other host computers to your FTP site. When the remote system accesses your systems, it does so by logging in as a registered user. Access is made through a user account already set up on your system. You allow the remote host to log in as a certain specific user, or deny access as a certain user. You could use this kind of control to allow or deny anonymous access to the FTP user by a remote host.

The file **ftphosts** has two kinds of entries, one for allowing access and the other for denying access. Entries to allow access begin with the keyword **allow**, then the user account on your system to which the host is allowed access, followed by the address of the remote host. The address can be a pattern that can be used to match several hosts. You can use any of the file name generation symbols (see Chapter 9). Entries to deny access begin with the keyword **deny**, then the user account on your system to which the host is denied access, followed by the address of the remote host. The terms **deny** and **allow** can be misleading. The **allow** is a much more restrictive control, whereas **deny** is a much more open control. The **allow** will only allow access by the remote host to the specified account. No other access is permitted. You could use **allow** to permit a remote host anonymous access only. The **deny**, on the other hand, only denies access to the specified account. You could use it to deny anonymous access by a certain system, but not any direct FTP access from one user to another.

ftpusers and ftpgroups

The **ftpusers** files list users that cannot be accessed through FTP. For example, the root user should not be accessible through an FTP connection even if you knew the password. The **ftpgroups** is a group access file that allows FTP users to become members of specified groups on your system. This file lists special group passwords. For these to work, the private entry must be set to yes in the **ftpaccess** file.

ftpconversions

The **ftpconversions** file holds possible FTP conversions for compression and archive operations. It operates as an FTP conversions database, listing all possible conversions. A default **ftpconversions** file is included with the installation package that already has entries for the most common conversion operations. Each line in the file is a record of eight fields, with the fields separated by colons. The fields are strip prefix and postfix, addon prefix and postfix, external command, types, options, and a description. The prefix and postfix fields refer to changes that are made to the file name after the specified action is performed. The strip postfix will remove a specified suffix from a file name, and the add postfix will add a suffix. For example, a gzipped compressed file will have a suffix of **.gz**. If the command is to compress a file with gzip, then the add postfix entry should have the **.gz** placed in it. When the file is compressed, **.gz** is added to the end. If you were decompressing a file with **gunzip**, then you would want to remove the **.gz** suffix. For this, you would place **.gz** in the strip postfix field. The strip and add prefixes perform the same kind of action, but for prefixes.

The external command is the command you would use to convert the file. You can list command options after the command. The file name you are operating on is specified with **%s**, usually placed after any options. For example, you would use the **tar** command to extract a **.tar** archived file and gunzip to decompress **.gz** file. The type field lists the type of files that can be operated on by the command. These can be regular files, character files, or directories as indicated by the entries **T_REG**, **T_ASCII**, and **T_DIR**. You can specify more that one entry by placing a | between them. The options field specifies the type of operation the command performs. Currently there are options for compression, decompression, and use of the **tar** command: **O_COMPRESS**, **O_UNCOMPRESS**, and **O_TAR**. You can list more than one by separating them with a | symbol. The description provides some documentation as to what the conversion operation does. Here is the **ftpconversion** file used on Red Hat systems:

```
:.Z:  :  :/bin/compress -d -c %s:T_REG|T_ASCII:O_UNCOMPRESS:UNCOMPRESS
:   :  :.Z:/bin/compress -c %s:T_REG:O_COMPRESS:COMPRESS
:.gz: :  :/bin/gzip -cd %s:T_REG|T_ASCII:O_UNCOMPRESS:GUNZIP
```

```
:    : :.gz:/bin/gzip -9 -c %s:T_REG:O_COMPRESS:GZIP
:    : :.tar:/bin/tar -c -f - %s:T_REG|T_DIR:O_TAR:TAR
:    : :.tar.Z:/bin/tar -c -Z -f -
                    %s:T_REG|T_DIR:O_COMPRESS|O_TAR:TAR+COMPRESS
:    : :.tar.gz:/bin/tar -c -z -f -
                    %s:T_REG|T_DIR:O_COMPRESS|O_TAR:TAR+GZIP
```

FTP Log File: xferlog

This file contains log information about connections and tasks performed by your FTP server. On Red Hat and OpenLinux systems, this file is found in the **/var/log** directory. On other systems, it may be on the **/usr/adm** directory. The file is made up of server entries, one on each line. The entry is divided into several fields separated by spaces. The fields are: current-time, transfer-time, remote-host, file-size, filename, transfer-type, special-action-flag, direction, access-mode, username, service-name, authentication-method, and authenticated-user-id. The transfer-time is the time in seconds for the transfer. The remote-host is the address of the remote system making the connection and username is the name of the user on that system. The transfer-type is either an *a* for ASCII or *b* for binary. The access-mode is the method by which the user logged in: *a* for anonymous, *g* for guest, and *r* for a real login (to another account on your system). The direction is either *o* for outgoing or *i* for incoming.

Professional FTP Daemon: ProFTPD

ProFTPD is based on the same design as the Apache Web server, implementing a similar simplified configuration structure and supporting such flexible features as virtual hosting. ProFTPD RPM packages are available from the Red Hat contrib site at **contrib.redhat.com** and contrib mirror sites. Unlike other FTP daemons, you do not have to include directories of system files for FTP commands. No special **bin** or **etc** files are needed. You can set it up to automatically alternate between inetd startups or as a standalone server constantly running, depending upon the system load.

ProFTPD's tools operate in the same way as the wu-ftpd tools. The **ftpshut** shuts down the system at specified times with warnings. With ProFTPD, you can shut down a virtual host while the main server continues to run. The **ftpwho** displays a list of all remote users currently connected, broken down according to virtual hosts and servers. The **ftpcount** shows the number of current connections by server and virtual hosts. See the previous section on FTP tools for more information.

install and startup

If you install ProFTPD using Red Hat or OpenLinux RPM packages, then the required configuration entries are made in your **proftpd.conf** file. If you installed from compiled source code, then you may have to modify the entries in the default **proftpd.conf** file provided. Make sure that the FTP user and group specified in the **proftpd.conf** file actually exist.

You can run ProFTPD either as a standalone process or from **inetd**. Make sure that the appropriate entry is made in the ServerType directive in your **proftpd.conf** file. Unlike wu-ftpd, by default the RPM package will install **proftpd** to run as a standalone server, setting the ServerType to standalone. Table 17-3 lists **proftpd** options. A startup script named **proftpd** is placed in the **/etc/rc.d/inet.d** directory that will start up the daemon when you boot your system. A standalone process is continually running. If you want to run **proftpd** as an **inetd** process, then you have to first change the ServerType to **inetd** and disable the **proftpd** startup script in the **/etc/rc.d/inet.d** directory (see Chapter 16).

When you run ProFTPD from inetd, make sure the appropriate entry is in the **inetd.conf** file. If you were running wu-ftpd previously, you will have to change this entry to run proftpd. The **in.proftpd** is a link to the **proftpd** daemon. Use this link to invoke ProFTPD in the **inetd.conf** file. The ProFTPD inetd entry would look like this:

```
ftp stream tcp nowait root     /usr/sbin/in.proftpd in.proftpd
```

OpenLinux and Red Hat systems use TCP wrappers for their inetd entries. The inetd entry would look like this.

```
ftp stream tcp nowait root     /usr/sbin/tcpd     in.proftpd
```

Options	Description
–h,--help	Usage description including options
–n,--nodaemon	Runs the proftpd process in standalone mode (must also specify standalone as ServerType in the configuration file)
–v, --version	Display ProFTPD version number

Table 17-3.   *ProFTPD Daemon Startup Options*

Options	Description
–d, --debug *debuglevel*	Sets proftpd's internal debug level (1–5)
–c, --config *config-file*	Specify alternate configuration file
–p, --persistent 0 l 1	Disables (0) or enables (1) the default persistent password support, which is determined at configure time for each platform
–l, --list	Lists all modules compiled into proftpd

Table 17-3. *ProFTPD Daemon Startup Options* (continued)

proftpd.conf and .ftpaccess

ProFTPD uses just one configuration file named **proftpd.conf**, located in the **/etc** directory. Configuration entries take the form of directives. This format is purposely modeled on Apache configuration directives. With the directives, you can enter basic configuration information such as your server name or perform more complex operations such as implementing virtual FTP hosts. The design is flexible enough to let you define configuration features for particular directories, users, or groups.

To configure a particular directory, you can use an **.ftpaccess** file with configuration options placed within that directory. These **.ftpaccess** options will take precedence over those in your **proftpd.conf** directory. It is designed to operate like **.htaccess** files in the Apache Web server that configure particular Web site directories. You can find a complete listing of ProFTPD configuration parameters at the ProFTPD Web site (**www.proftpd.org**) and in the ProFTPD documentation installed in **/usr/doc** as part of the ProFTPD software package. Several of the more commonly used parameters are listed in Table 17-4 at the end of this chapter. When creating a new configuration, you should make a copy of the **proftpd.conf** configuration file and modify it. Then you can test its syntax using the **proftpd** command with the **-c** option and the name of the file.

```
proftpd -c newfile.conf
```

There are different kinds of directives. Many set values such as MaxClients that sets the maximum number of clients, or NameServer that sets the name of the FTP server. Others create blocks that can hold directives that apply to specific FTP server components. Block directives are entered in pairs, a beginning directive and a terminating directive. The terminating directive defines the end of the block and consists of the same name beginning with a slash. Block directives take an argument that specifies the particular object that the directives will apply to. For the Directory block directive, you have to specify a directory name that it will apply to. The <Directory *mydir*> block directive creates a block whose directives within it apply to the *mydir* directory. The block is terminated by a </Directory> directive. <Anonymous *ftp-dir*> configures the anonymous service for your FTP server. You need to specify the directory on your system used for your anonymous FTP service, such as **/home/ftp**. The block is terminated with the </Anonymous> directive. The <VirtualHost *hostaddress*> block directive is used to configure a specific virtual FTP server and must include the IP or domain name address used for that server. </VirtualHost> is its terminating directive. Any Directives you place within this block are applied to that virtual FTP server. The <Limit *permission*> directive specifies the kind of access you want to limit. It takes as its argument one of several keywords indicating the kind of permission to be controlled: **WRITE** for write access, **READ** for read access, **STOR** for transfer access (uploading), and **LOGIN** to control user login.

A sample of the standard **proftpd.conf** file installed as part of the ProFTPD software package is shown here. Notice that the default ServerType is standalone. Should you want to use inetd to run your server, you will have to change this entry to inetd. Detailed examples of **proftpd.conf** files showing various anonymous FTP and virtual host configurations can be found with the ProFTPD documentation, located in **/usr/doc**, and on the ProFTPD Web site at **www.proftpd.org**.

```
# This is a basic ProFTPD configuration file (rename it to
# 'proftpd.conf' for actual use.  It establishes a single server
# and a single anonymous login.  It assumes that you have a user/group
# "nobody" and "ftp" for normal operation and anon.

ServerName           "ProFTPD Default Installation"
ServerType           standalone
DefaultServer           on

# Port 21 is the standard FTP port.
Port            21
Umask          022
MaxInstances           30

# Set the user and group that the server normally runs at.
User            nobody
Group          nobody

# Normally, we want files to be overwriteable.
<Directory /*>
  AllowOverwrite        on
</Directory>
```

```
# A basic anonymous configuration, with one incoming directory.
<Anonymous ~ftp>
  User                ftp
  Group               ftp
  RequireValidShell       off
  MaxClients            10
  # We want clients to be able to login with "anonymous" as well as "ftp"
  UserAlias           anonymous ftp

  # We want 'welcome.msg' displayed at login, and '.message' displayed
  # in each newly chdired directory.
  DisplayLogin          welcome.msg
  DisplayFirstChdir       .message

  # Limit WRITE everywhere in the anonymous chroot except incoming
  <Directory *>
     <Limit WRITE>
         DenyAll
     </Limit>
  </Directory>

  <Directory incoming>
     <Limit WRITE>
       AllowAll
     </Limit>
     <Limit READ>
       DenyAll
     </Limit>
  </Directory>

</Anonymous>
```

Anonymous Access

You use the Anonymous configuration directive to create an anonymous configuration block in which you can place directives that configure your anonymous FTP service. The directive includes the directory on your system used for the anonymous FTP service. The ProFTPD daemon will execute a **chroot** operation on this directory, making it the root directory for the remote user accessing the service. By default, anonymous logins are supported, expecting users to enter their e-mail address as a password. You can modify an anonymous configuration to construct more controlled anonymous services such as guest logins and required passwords. For ProFTPD, your anonymous FTP directory does not require any system files. Before ProFTPD executes a **chroot** operation, hiding the rest of the system from the directory, it accesses and keeps open any needed system files that are outside the directory.

The following example shows a standard anonymous FTP configuration. The initial Anonymous directive specifies **/home/ftp** as the anonymous FTP **home** directory. The User directive specifies the user that the Anonymous FTP daemon will run as and Group indicates its group. In both cases it is FTP, the standard user name used on most systems for anonymous FTP. A Directory directive with the * file matching character then defines a Directory block that will apply to all directories and files in **/home/ftp**. The * symbol matches on all file names and directories. Within the Directory directive is a Limit directive that will place restrictions on the **WRITE** capabilities of users. Within the Limit directive, the DenyAll directive denies write permission, preventing users from creating or deleting files, effectively giving them only read access. A second Directory directive creates an exception to this rule for the **incoming** directory. An **incoming** directory is usually set up on FTP sites to let users upload files. For this Directory, the first Limit directive prevents both **READ** and **WRITE** access by users with its DenyAll directive, effectively preventing users from deleting or reading files here. However, the second Limit directive allows users to upload files, permitting transfers only (**STOR**) with the AllowAll directive.

One very important directive for anonymous FTP configurations is the RequireValidShell. By default, the FTP daemon will first check to see if the remote user is attempting to log in using a valid shell such as the BASH shell or C-shell. It obtains the list of valid shells from the **/etc/shells** file. If the remote user does not have a valid shell, a connection is denied. You can turn off the check using the RequireValidShell directive and the **off** option. The remote user can then log in using any kind of shell. The following is a sample segment from the **proftpd.conf** file.

```
<Anonymous /home/ftp>
    User ftp
    Group ftp
    UserAlias anonymous ftp
    RequireValidShell off
<Directory *>
        <Limit WRITE>
            DenyAll
        </Limit>
    </Directory>
    # The only command allowed in incoming is STOR
    # (transfer file from client to server)
```

```
<Directory incoming>
   <Limit READ WRITE>
      DenyAll
   </Limit>
   <Limit STOR>
      AllowAll
   </Limit>
</Directory>
</Anonymous>
```

Recall that FTP was originally designed to let a remote user connect to an account of his or her own on the system. Users can log into different accounts on your system using the FTP service. Anonymous users are restricted to the anonymous user account. However, you can create other users and their **home** directories that also function as anonymous FTP accounts with the same restrictions. Such accounts are known as guest accounts. Remote users are required to know the user name and, usually, the password. Once connected, they only have read access to that account's files, and the rest of the file system is hidden from them. In effect, you are creating a separate anonymous FTP site at the same location that has more restricted access.

To create a guest account you first create a user and the home directory for it. You then create an Anonymous block in the **proftpd.conf** file for that account. The Anonymous directive will include the **home** directory of the guest user you set up. You can specify this directory with a ~ for the path and the directory name, usually the same as the user name. Within the Anonymous block, you use the USER and GROUP directives to specify the user and group name for the user account. If you want remote users to provide a password, you set the AnonRequirePassword directive to on. A UserAlias directive defines aliases for the user name. A remote user can use either the alias or the original user name to log in. You then enter the remaining directives for controlling access to the files and directories in the account's **home** directory. An example showing the initial directives is listed here. The USER directive specifies the user as **myproject**. The **home** directory is **~myproject**, which usually evaluates to **/home/myproject**. The UserAlias lets remote users log in either with the name **myproject** or **mydesert**.

```
<Anonymous ~myproject>
   User myproject
   Group other
   UserAlias mydesert myproject
   AnonRequirePassword on
   <Directory *>
```

You could just as easily create an account that requires no password, letting users enter in their e-mail addresses instead. The following example configures an anonymous user named **mypics**. No password is required, nor is a valid shell. The remote user still needs to know the user name, in this case **mypics**.

```
<Anonymous /home/mypics>
    AnonRequirePassword off
    User mypics
    Group nobody
    RequireValidShell off
    <Directory *>
```

The following example provides a more generic kind of guest login. The user name is guest with the **home** directory located at **~guest**. Remote users are required to know the password for the guest account. The first Limit directive allows all users to log in. The second Limit directive allows write access from users on a specific network as indicated by the network IP address, and denies write access by any others.

```
<Anonymous ~guest>
  User               guest
  Group              nobody
  AnonRequirePassword  on

  <Limit LOGIN>
    AllowAll
  </Limit>

  # Deny write access from all except trusted hosts.
  <Limit WRITE>
    Order          allow,deny
    Allow          from 10.0.0.
    Deny           from all
  </Limit>

</Anonymous>
```

Virtual FTP Servers

The ProFTPD daemon can manage more than one FTP site at once. Using a VirtualHost directive in the **proftpd.conf** file, you can create an independent set of directives that configure a separate FTP server. The VirtualHost directive is usually used to configure virtual servers as FTP sites. You can configure your system to support more than one IP address. The extra IP addresses can be used for virtual servers, not independent machines, but treated as such. You can use such an extra IP address to set up a virtual FTP server, giving you another FTP site on the same system. This added server would use the extra IP address as its own. Remote users could access it using that IP address, instead of the system's main IP address. Since such an FTP server is not running independently on a separate machine but on the same machine, it is known as a virtual FTP server or virtual host. This feature lets you run what appear to others as several different FTP servers on one machine. When a remote user uses the virtual FTP server's IP address to access it, the ProFTPD daemon detects that request and will operate as the FTP service for that site. ProFTPD can handle a great many virtual FTP sites at the same time on a single machine. Given its configuration capabilities, you can also tailor any of the virtual FTP sites to specific roles, such as a guest site, anonymous site for a particular group, or an anonymous site for a particular user.

You configure a virtual FTP server by entering a <VirtualHost> directive for it in your **proftpd.conf** file. Such an entry begins with the VirtualHost directive and the IP address and ends with a terminating VirtualHost directive, </VirtualHost>. Any directives placed within these are applied to the virtual host. For anonymous or guest sites, you would add anonymous and guest directives. You can even add Directory directives for specific directories. With the Port directive on a standalone configuration, you can create a virtual host that operates on the same system but connects on a different port.

```
<VirtualHost 10.0.0.1>
  ServerName "My virtual FTP server"
</VirtualHost>
```

Inetd and standalone configurations handle virtual hosts differently. Inetd detects a request for a virtual host and then hands it off to a FTP daemon. The FTP daemon then examines the address and port specified in the request and processes the request for the appropriate virtual host. In the standalone configuration, the FTP daemon continually listens for requests on all specified ports and generates child processes to handle ones for different virtual hosts as they come in. In the standalone configuration, ProFTPD can support a great many virtual hosts at the same time.

The following example shows a sample configuration of a virtual FTP host. The VirtualHost directives use domain name addresses for its arguments. When a domain name address is used, it has to be associated with an IP address in the network's domain name server. The IP address, in turn, has to reference the machine that the ProFTPD daemon is running on. On the **ftp.mypics.com** virtual FTP server, an anonymous guest account named robpics is configured that requires a password to log in. An anonymous FTP account is also configured that uses the **home** directory **/home/ftp/virtual/pics**. See Table 17-4.

```
<VirtualHost ftp.mypics.com>

  ServerName            "Mypics FTP Server"
  MaxClients            10
  MaxLoginAttempts      1
  DeferWelcome          on
  <Anonymous            ~robpics>
    User                robpics
    Group               robpics
    AnonRequirePassword on

<Anonymous /home/ftp/virtual/pics>

    User        ftp
    Group       ftp
    UserAlias   anonymous ftp


  </Anonymous>

</VirtualHost
```

Directive	Description
AccessGrantMsg *message*	Response message sent to an FTP client indicating that the user has logged in or that anonymous access has been granted. The magic cookie '**%u**' is replaced with the user name specified by the client. Default: Dependent on login type Context: server config, <VirtualHost>, <Anonymous>, <Global>
Allow *["from"]* *"all"*|*"none"*|*host*| *network[,host|network[,...]]*	Used inside a <Limit> context to explicitly specify which hosts and/or networks have access to the commands or operations being limited. Used with Order and Deny to create access control rules. Default: Allow from all Context: <Limit>

Table 17-4.   *ProFTPD Configuration Directives, proftpd.conf*

Directive	Description
AllowAll	Allows access to a <Directory>, <Anonymous> or <Limit> block Default: Default is to implicitly AllowAll, but not explicitly Context: <Directory>, <Anonymous>, <Limit>, **.ftpaccess**
AllowForeignAddress *on/off*	Allows clients to transmit foreign data connection addresses that do not match the client's address. Default: AllowForeignAddress off Context: server config, <VirtualHost>, <Anonymous>, <Global>
AllowGroup *group-expression*	List of groups allowed in a limit block. Default: None Context: <Limit>
AllowUser *user-expression*	Users allowed access. Default: None Context: <Limit>
AnonRequirePassword *on/off*	Requires anonymous logins to enter a valid password that must match the password of the user that the anonymous daemon runs as. This is used to create guest accounts that function like anonymous logins but require a valid password. Default: AnonRequirePassword off Context: <Anonymous>
<Anonymous *root-directory>*	Create an anonymous FTP login, terminated by a matching </Anonymous> directive. The root-directory parameter is the directory proftpd will first move to, and then **chroot**, hiding the rest of the file system. Default: None Context: server config, <VirtualHost>

Table 17-4. *ProFTPD Configuration Directives, proftpd.conf* (continued)

Directive	Description
AuthGroupFile *path*	Alternate group's file with the same format as the system **/etc/group** file. Default: None Context: server config, <VirtualHost>, <Global>
AuthUserFile *path*	Alternate **passwd** file with the same format as the system **/etc/passwd** file. Default: None Context: server config, <VirtualHost>, <Global>
Bind *address*	Allows additional IP addresses to be bound to a main or VirtualHost configuration. Multiple Bind directives can be used to bind multiple addresses. Default: None Context: server config, <VirtualHost>
DefaultRoot *directory* *[group-expression]*	Default root directory assigned to user on login. The group-expression argument restricts the DefaultRoot directive to a group or set of groups. Default: DefaultRoot Context: server config, <VirtualHost>, <Global>
Deny *["from"]* *"all"|"none"|host|network* *[,host|network[,...]]*	List of hosts and networks explicitly denied access to a given <Limit> context block. The **all** indicates that all hosts are denied access, and **none** indicates no hosts are explicitly denied. Default: None Context: <Limit>
DenyAll	Deny access to a directory, anonymous FTP, or limit block. Default: None Context: <Directory>, <Anonymous>, <Limit>, **.ftpaccess**

Table 17-4.   *ProFTPD Configuration Directives, proftpd.conf* (continued)

SERVERS

Directive	Description
DenyUser *user-expression*	Users denied access within a limit block. Default: None Context: <Limit>
<Directory *pathname>*	Directory-specific configuration. Used to create a block of directives that apply to the specified directory and its subdirectories. Default: None Context: server config, <VirtualHost>, <Anonymous>, <Global>
DisplayFirstChdir *filename*	Specifies the text file that will be displayed to a user the first time he or she changes into a given directory during an FTP session. Default: None Context: server config, <VirtualHost>, <Anonymous>, <Directory>, <Global>
DisplayLogin *filename*	Specifies the text file that will be displayed to a user that logs in. Default: None Context: server config, <VirtualHost>, <Anonymous>, <Global>
<Global>	Global configuration block is used to create a set of configuration directives that are applied universally to both the main server configuration and all VirtualHost configurations. Default: None Context: server config, <VirtualHost>

Table 17-4. *ProFTPD Configuration Directives, proftpd.conf* (continued)

Directive	Description
<Limit *command|command-group [command2 ..]>*	Access restrictions on FTP commands, within a given context. The **command-group** refers to groupings of commands as defined in the ProFTPD documentation. Default: None Context: server config, <VirtualHost>, <Directory>, <Anonymous>, <Global>, **.ftpaccess**
LsDefaultOptions *"options string"*	Default options for directory listings (as in the **ls** command). Default: None Context: server config, <VirtualHost>, <Global>
MaxClients *number|none message*	Maximum number of connected clients allowed. The message specified is displayed when a client is refused connection. Default: MaxClients none Context: server config, <Anonymous>, <VirtualHost>, <Global>
MaxLoginAttempts *number*	Maximum number of times a client may attempt to log in to the server during a given connection. Default: MaxLoginAttempts 3 Context: server config, <VirtualHost>, <Global>
Order *allow,deny|deny,allow*	Configures the order that Allow and Deny directives are checked inside of a <Limit> block. Default: Order allow, deny Context: <Limit>

Table 17-4.   *ProFTPD Configuration Directives, proftpd.conf* (continued)

SERVERS

Directive	Description
PersistentPasswd *on/off*	When on, proftpd, during login, opens the system-wide **/etc/passwd**, **/etc/group** files, accessing them even during a **chroot** operation that changes the root directory. Default: Platform dependent Context: server config
RequireValidShell *on/off*	Allow or deny logins that are not listed in **/etc/shells**. By default, proftpd disallows logins if the user's default shell is not listed in **/etc/shells**. Default: RequireValidShell on Context: server config, <VirtualHost>, <Anonymous>, <Global>
ScoreboardPath *path*	Directory that holds proftpd run-time Scoreboard files. Default: ScoreboardPath /var/run Context: server config
ServerAdmin *"admin-email-address"*	E-mail address of the server or virtual host administrator. Default: ServerAdmin root@[ServerName] Context: server config, <VirtualHost>
ServerType *type-identifier*	The server daemon's operating mode, either inetd or standalone. Default: ServerType standalone Context: server config
TimeoutIdle *seconds*	Maximum number of seconds that proftpd will allow clients to stay connected without any activity. Default: TimeoutIdle 600 Context: server config

Table 17-4.   *ProFTPD Configuration Directives, proftpd.conf* (continued)

Directive	Description
Umask octal-mask	Permissions applied to newly created file and directory within a given context. Default: None Context: server config, <Anonymous>, <VirtualHost>, <Directory>, <Global> **.ftpaccess**
User *userid*	The user that the proftpd daemon runs as. Default: None Context: server config, <VirtualHost>, <Anonymous>, <Global>
UserAlias *login-user userid*	Maps a login name used by a client to a userid on the server. A client logging in as login-user will be actually logged in as userid. Often used inside an <Anonymous> block to allow specified login-names to perform an anonymous login. Default: None Context: server config, <VirtualHost>, <Anonymous>, <Global>
<VirtualHost *address>*	Configuration directives that apply to a particular hostname or IP address. Often used with virtual servers that run on the same physical machine. The block is terminated with a </VirtualHost> directive. By utilizing the Port directive inside a VirtualHost block, it is possible to create a virtual server that uses the same address as the master server but listens on a separate TCP port. Default: None Context: server config

Table 17-4.   *ProFTPD Configuration Directives, proftpd.conf* (continued)

SERVERS

The Complete Reference

Linux

Chapter 18

Apache Web Server

The Apache Web server is a full-featured free HTTP (Web) server developed and maintained by the Apache Project. The aim of the project is to provide a reliable, efficient, and easily extensible Web server, with free open source code. The server software includes the server daemon, configuration files, management tools, and documentation. The Apache Project is maintained by a core group of volunteer programmers known as the Apache Group and supported by a great many contributors worldwide. Apache was originally based on the NCSA Web server developed at the National Center for Supercomputing Applications, University of Illinois, Urbana-Champaign. It has since emerged as a server in its own right and has become one of the most popular Web servers in use. Though originally developed for Linux and Unix systems, it has become a cross-platform application with Windows and OS/2 versions. Apache provides online support and documentation for its Web server at **www.apache.org**. An HTML-based manual is also provided with the server installation. Several GUI configuration tools are also available to help easily configure your Apache server. They will operate on any X Windows window manager including Gnome and KDE. You can link to these Apache GUI configuration tools at **gui.apache.org**.

Other Web servers available for Linux include the Red Hat Secure Server (**www.redhat.com**), Apache-SSL (**www.apache-ssl.org**), Stronghold (**www.c2.net**), and Netscape Enterprise Server (**home.netscape.com**). Apache-SSL is an encrypting Web server based on Apache and SSLeay. Stronghold is a commercial version of the Apache Web server featuring improved security and administration tools. You can also use the original NCSA Web server, though it is no longer supported (**hoohoo.ncsa.uiuc.edu**).

Linux Distribution Apache Installations

Most Linux distributions, including Red Hat and OpenLinux, automatically install the Apache Web server on your system during installation, with all the necessary directories and configuration files. If you use one of these distributions, then your system will already be a fully functional Web site. Every time you start your system, the Web server starts up also, running continuously. The directory reserved for your Web site data files is **/home/httpd/html**. Place your Web pages in this directory or in any subdirectories. Your system is already configured to operate as a Web server. All you need to do is perform the necessary network server configurations and then designate the files and directories open to remote users. There is nothing more you have to do. Once it is connected to a network, remote users will be able to access your Web site.

The Web server installed on OpenLinux and Red Hat systems sets up your Web site in the **/home/httpd** directory. It also sets up several directories for managing the site. The **/home/httpd/cgi-bin** directory holds the CGI scripts, and **/home/httpd/manual** holds the Apache manual in HTML format. You can use your browser to examine it. Your Web pages are to be placed in the **/home/httpd/html** directory. Place your Web site home page there. Your configuration files are located in a different directory, **/etc/httpd/conf**.

To upgrade your Apache server, just look for recent Apache RPM packages at the Caldera or Red Hat update sites. For Red Hat this is at **updates.redhat.com** (there are many mirror sites). For Caldera this is **ftp.calderasystems.com** in the **updates** directory. Download the package and use the **rpm** command with the **-Uvh** options to install the upgrade.

```
rpm -Uvh apache-1.3.4-4.i386.rpm
rpm -Uvh apache-docs-1.3.4-4.i386.rpm
```

Other Web servers are also freely available. The NCSA httpd Web server was one of the first servers developed. You can download server software from most Linux FTP sites. Check for RPM package versions if available. You can also download the source code version directly from Apache and compile it on your system. You will have to decompress the file and extract the archive. Many of the same directories will be created, with added ones for the source code. The server package will include installation instructions for creating your server directories and compiling your software. Make sure that the configuration files are set up and installed. If you are installing Apache from the source code, you will notice that versions of the configuration files ending with the extension **.conf-dist** are provided. You have to make copies of these with the same prefix but with just the extension **.conf** to set up a default configuration. The Web server reads configuration information only from files with a **.conf** extension.

Starting and Stopping the Web Server

On most systems Apache is installed as a standalone server, continually running. As noted in Chapter 16 in the discussion of **init** scripts, your system automatically starts up the Web server daemon, invoking it whenever you start your system. On OpenLinux and Red Hat systems, a startup script for the Web server called **httpd** is in the **/etc/rc.d/init.d** directory. A symbolic link through which the **rc** program runs is in the **/etc/rc.d/rc3.d** directory and is called **S85httpd**. For systems using other Linux distributions, you can place the Web server command in a system startup script such as **rc.local** or **rc.sysinit**.

You can use this **httpd** script in the **/etc/rc.d/init.d** directory to start and stop the server manually. This may be helpful when you are testing or modifying your server. The **httpd** script with the **start** option will start the server and with the **stop** option will stop it. You can also use the SysV Runlevel Manager, available on many systems, to start and stop the **httpd** daemon. Just click the **httpd** entry in the Available list and then click the Execute button. A menu is displayed with buttons to stop or start the daemon. It is not advisable to kill the Web process directly.

```
/etc/rc.d/init.d/httpd stop
/etc/rc.d/init.d/httpd start
```

Apache also provides a control tool called **apachectl** (Apache control) for managing your Web server. With **apachectl** you can start, stop, and restart the server from the command line. It takes several arguments: **start** to start the server, **stop** to stop it, **restart** to shut down and restart the server, and **graceful** to gracefully shut down and restart. You can also use **apachectl** to check the syntax of your configuration files with the **config** argument. You can also use **apachectl** as a system startup file for your server in the **/etc/rc.d** directory.

Bear in mind that **httpd** is a script that calls the actual **httpd** daemon. You could call the daemon directly using its full pathname. This daemon has several options. The **-d** option allows you to specify a directory for the **httpd** program if it is different from the default directory. With the **-f** option you can specify a configuration file different from **httpd.conf**. The **-v** option displays the version.

```
/usr/sbin/httpd -v
```

To check your Web server, just start your Web browser and enter the Internet domain name address of your system. For the system **turtle.mytrek.com** the user enters **http://myturtle.mytrek.com**. This should display the home page you placed in your Web root directory. A simple way to do this is to use **lynx**, the command-line Web browser. Just start **lynx** and then press **g** to open a line where you can enter a URL for your own system. Then **lynx** will display your Web site's home page. Be sure to first place an **index.html** file in the **/home/httpd/html** directory.

Once you have your server running, you can check its performance with the **ab** benchmarking tool, also provided by Apache. Then **ab** will tell you how many requests at a time that your server can handle. Options include **-v**, which lets you control the level of detail displayed, **-n** to specify the number of requests to handle (default is 1), and **-t** to specify a time limit.

Most distributions including Red Hat and OpenLinux do not configure the Web server to run from **inetd**. If you want this done, you will have to place the appropriate entries in **/etc/services** and **/etc/inetd.conf**. You will also have to remove your Web server from the list of startup daemons in your system's autostart list (see Chapter 16 for details). If you want to have **httpd** called by the **inetd** daemon, place an entry for **httpd** in the **/etc/services** and **/etc/inetd.conf** files. The **/etc/services** file lists the different services available on your system. For a Web server you enter **http** with a *port*/tcp specification.

```
http    80/tcp
```

The Web server entry in the **/etc/inetd.conf** file is similar to the entry for the FTP server. Use the pathname for the Web server installed on your system, usually **/usr/sbin/httpd**.

```
http stream tcp nowait nobody /usr/sbin/httpd  /usr/sbin/httpd
```

To have Web server requests monitored and controlled by **tcpd**, you place the **/usr/sbin/tcpd** pathname in place of the **/usr/sbin/httpd** pathname.

```
http stream tcp nowait nobody /usr/sbin/tcpd  /usr/sbin/httpd
```

You also have to specify the **inetd** value for the ServerType variable in your Apache **httpd.conf** file, **/etc/httpd/conf/httpd.conf**.

```
# ServerType is either inetd, or standalone.
ServerType inetd
```

Apache Configuration Files

Traditionally, configuration directives have been placed in there different configuration files: **httpd.conf**, **srm.conf**, and **access.conf**. These files are located in the **/etc/httpd/conf** directory. The **srm.conf** and **access.conf** files are designed to hold directives that configure your Web site documents; **httpd.conf** is used to configure your server. The **srm.conf** file handles document specifications, configuring file types, and locations. The **access.conf** file is designed to hold directives that control access to Web site directories and files. This three-file organization was originally implemented to maintain compatibility with the NCSA Web server that preceded Apache.

With version 1.3.4, Apache recommends that all configuration directives be placed in one file, the **httpd.conf** file. In fact, if you download the original source code version, both the **srm.conf** and **access.conf** files will be empty. Only the **httpd.conf** file is used. There are even directives that will prevent reading the **srm.conf** and **access.conf** files. By default, Apache still reads both the **srm.conf** and **access.conf** files in case there is anything in them, though **httpd.conf** is still considered the primary configuration file. The situation is complicated by the fact that most major distributions, including Red Hat and OpenLinux, still use all three configuration files. Placing directives all in one file (see Table 18-1 on pages 22–37) has the advantage that you have to maintain only the one configuration file.

Apache configuration directives ordinarily placed in the **srm.conf** or **access.conf** file can now be placed in the **httpd.conf** file, and those files could be left empty if you wish. Still, the three-files organization does help to categorize files into primary directives, resources, and access controls. On the other hand, Apache's capabilities have extended to the point that these categories no longer cover the current directives. For example, directives for virtual hosts are placed in the **httpd.conf** file along with their access control directives. Directives should be thought of as independent of any particular file. Table 18-2 on page 38 lists the different directives by the different files they are found in using the old configuration structure.

Any of the directives in the main configuration files can be overridden on a per-directory basis using an **.htaccess** file located within a directory. Though originally designed for just access directives, the **.htaccess** file can hold any resource directives as well, letting you tailor how Web pages are displayed in a particular directory.

Apache Directives

Apache configuration operations take the form of directives entered into the Apache configuration files. With the directives you can enter basic configuration information such as your server name or perform more complex operations such as implementing virtual hosts. The design is flexible enough to let you define configuration features for particular directories and different virtual hosts. Apache has a variety of different directives performing operations as diverse as controlling directory access, assigning file icon formats, and creating log files. Most set values such as DirectoryRoot, which holds the root directory for the server's Web pages, or Port, which holds the port on the system that the server will listen on for requests.

Certain directives create blocks that can hold directives that apply to specific server components. For example, the **Directory** directive is used to define a block within which you place directives that apply only to a particular directory. Block directives are entered in pairs, a beginning directive and a terminating directive. The terminating directive defines the end of the block and consists of the same name beginning with a slash. Block directives take an argument that specifies the particular object that the directives will apply to. For the **Directory** block directive you have to specify a directory name that it will apply to. The **<Directory *mydir*>** block directive creates a block whose directives within it apply to the *mydir* directory. The block is terminated by a **</Directory>** directive. The **<VirtualHost *hostaddress*>** block directive is used to configure a specific virtual Web server and must include the IP or domain name address used for that server; **</VirtualHost>** is its terminating directive. Any directives you place within this block are applied to that virtual Web server. The **<Limit *method*>** directive specifies the kind of access method, such as GET or POST, that you want to limit. Access control directives within the block list the controls you are placing on those methods.

Usually, directives are placed in one of the main configuration files. Directory directives in those files can be used to configure a particular directory. However, Apache also makes use of directory-based configuration files. Any directory may have its own **.htaccess** file that holds directives that configure just that directory. If your site has many directories or if any directories have special configuration needs, you can place their configuration directives in their **.htaccess** files, instead of filling up the main configuration files. You can control what directives in an **.htaccess** file will take precedence over those in the main configuration files.

Much of the power and flexibility of the Apache Web server comes from its use of modules to extend its capabilities. Apache is implemented with a core set of directives. Modules can be created that hold definitions of other directives. They can be loaded into Apache, allowing you to use those directives for your server. A standard set of modules is included with the Apache distribution, though you can download others and even create your own. For example, the **mod_autoindex** module holds the directives for automatically indexing directories (as described in the "Automatic Directory Index" section of this chapter). The **mod_mime** module holds the MIME type and handler directives. Modules are loaded with the **LoadModule** directive. On many Linux distributions you will find **LoadModule** directives in the **httpd.conf** configuration file for most of the standard modules.

```
LoadModule mime_module   modules/mod_mime.so
```

The **apxs** application provided with the Apache package can be used to build Apache extension modules. With it you can compile Apache module source code in C and create dynamically shared objects that can be loaded with the **LoadModule** directive. It requires that the **mod_so** module be part of your Apache application. It includes extensive options such as **-n** to specify the module name, **-a** to add an entry for it in the **httpd.conf** file, and **-i** to install the module on your Web server.

You can find a complete listing of Apache Web configuration directives at the Apache Web site, **www.apache.org,** and in the Apache manual located in your site's Web site root directory. On Red Hat and OpenLinux systems this is located at **/home/httpd/manual**. Many of the more commonly used directives are listed in Table 18-1.

Server Configuration

Certain directives are used to configure your server's overall operations. These are placed in the **httpd.conf** configuration file. Some require pathnames, whereas others just need to be turned on or off with the keywords **on** and **off**. On OpenLinux and Red Hat distributions you will already find that the **httpd.conf** file contains these directives. Some are commented out with a preceding pound sign (#) symbol. You can activate a directive by removing its # sign. Many of the entries are preceded by comments explaining their purpose. The following is an example of the **ServerAdmin** directive used to set the address where users can send mail for administrative issues. You replace the you@your.address entry with the address you want to use to receive system administration mail. On Red Hat and OpenLinux systems this will be set to root@localhost.

```
# ServerAdmin: Your address, where problems should be e-mailed.
ServerAdmin you@your.address
```

Some directives require specific information about your system. For example, **ServerName** holds the hostname for your Web server. It is important to specify a hostname to avoid unnecessary DNS lookup failures that can hang your server. Notice that the entry is commented with a preceding #. Just remove the # and type your Web server's hostname in place of **new.host.name**.

```
# ServerName allows you to set a hostname which is sent back to
# clients for your server if it's different than the one the
```

```
# program would get (i.e. use "www" instead of the host's real name).

#ServerName new.host.name
```

On OpenLinux and Red Hat systems, entries have already been made for the standard Web server installation using **/home/httpd** as your Web site directory. You can tailor your Web site to your own needs by changing the appropriate directives. The **DocumentRoot** directive determines the home directory for your Web pages, and the **ServerRoot** directive specifies where your Web server configuration, error, and log files are kept.

```
DocumentRoot /home/httpd/html
ServerRoot /etc/httpd
```

The **MaxClients** directive sets the maximum number of clients that can connect to your server at the same time.

```
MaxClients 150
```

Directory-Level Configuration: .htaccess and <Directory>

One of the most flexible aspects of Apache is its capability to configure individual directories. With the **Directory** directive you can define a block of directives that apply only to a particular directory. Such a directive can be placed in the **httpd.conf** or **access.conf** configuration file. You can also use an **.htaccess** file within a particular directory to hold configuration directives. Those directives will be applied to only that directory. The name ".htaccess" is actually set with the **AccessFileName** directive. You can change it if you wish.

```
AccessFileName .htaccess
```

A Directory block begins with a **<Directory *pathname*>** directive, where *pathname* is the directory to be configured. The ending directive uses the same angle brackets (<>) symbols but with a slash preceding the term "Directory": **</Directory>**. Directives placed within this block will apply only to the specified directory. The following example denies access to just the **mypics** directory by requests from **www.myvids.com**.

```
<Directory /home/httpd/html/mypics>
Order Deny,Allow
Deny from www.myvids.com
</Directory>
```

With the **Options** directive you can enable certain features in a directory such as use of symbolic links, automatic indexing, execution of CGI scripts, and content negotiation. The default is the All option, which turns on all features except for content negotiation (MultiViews). The following example enables automatic indexing (Indexes) and symbolic links (FollowSymLinks) and content negotiation (MultiViews).

```
Options Indexes FollowSymLinks MultiViews
```

Configurations made by directives in main configuration files or in upper-level directories are inherited by lower-level directories. Directives for a particular directory held in **.htaccess** files and Directory blocks can be allowed to override those configurations. This capability can be controlled by the **AllowOverride** directive. With the *all* argument, **.htaccess** files can override any previous configurations. The *none* argument will disallow overrides, effectively disabling the **.htaccess** file. You can further control the override of specific groups of directives. *AuthConfig* allows use of authorization directives, *FileInfo* is for type directives, *Indexes* is for indexing directives, *Limit is* for access control directives, and *Options* is for the **options** directive.

```
AllowOverride all
```

Access Control

With access control directives such as *allow* and *deny*, you can control access to your Web site by remote users and hosts. If you are using three configuration files, such directives are usually placed in the **access.conf** file. The **allow** directive followed by a list of hostnames restricts access to just those hosts. The **deny** directive with a list of hostnames denies access by those systems. The argument *all* will apply the directive to all hosts. The **order** directive specifies in what order the access control directives are to be applied. Other access control directives such as **require** can establish authentication controls, requiring users to log in. The access control directives can be used globally to control access to the entire site or placed within **Directory** directives to control access to individual directives. In the following example, all users are allowed access.

```
order allow,deny
allow from all
```

You can further qualify access control directives by limiting them to certain HTML access methods. *HTML access methods* are ways that a browser interacts with your Web site. For example, a browser could get information from a page (GET) or send information through it (POST). You can control such access methods by using the **<Limit>** directive. **Limit** takes as its argument a list of access methods to be controlled. The directive then pairs with a **</Limit>** directive to define a Limit block within which you can place access control directives. These directives will only apply to the specified access methods. You can place such Limit blocks with a Directory block to set up controls of access methods for a specific directory.

On Red Hat and OpenLinux distributions, will find a Directory block placed in your **access.conf** file that controls access methods for your Web site's home directory, **/home/httpd/html**.

```
# This should be changed to whatever you set DocumentRoot to.
<Directory /home/httpd/html>
Options Indexes FollowSymLinks
AllowOverride All
<Limit GET>
order allow,deny
allow from all
</Limit>
</Directory>
```

Controls are inherited from upper-level directories to lower-level ones. If you wanted to strictly control access on a per-directory basis to your entire Web site, you could use the following entry to deny access to all users. Then in individual directories you could allow access to certain users, groups, or hosts.

```
<Directory /home/htppd/html>
    Order Deny,Allow
    Deny from All
 </Directory>
```

URL Pathnames

Certain directives can modify or complete pathname segments of a URL used to access your site. The pathname segment of the URL specifies a particular directory or Web page on your site. There are directives that will let you alias or redirect pathnames as well as select a default Web page. With the **Alias** directive you can let users access resources located in other parts of your system, on other file systems, or on other Web sites. An alias can use a URL for sites on the Internet, instead of a pathname for a directory on your system. With the **Redirect** directive you can redirect a user to another site.

```
Alias /mytrain /home/dylan/trainproj
```

If Apache is given just a directory to access, rather than a specific Web page, it will look for an index Web page located in that directory and display it. The possible names for a default Web page are listed by the **DirectoryIndex** directive. The name usually used is **index.html**, but you can add others. The standard names are shown here.

When Apache is given just a Web directory to access, it will look for and display the **index.html** Web page located in it.

```
DirectoryIndex index.html index.shtml index.cgi
```

Apache also lets a user maintain Web pages located in a special subdirectory in the user's home directory, rather than in the main Web site directory. Using a tilde (~) followed by the user name will access this directory. The name of this directory is specified with the **UserDir** directive. The default name is **public_html**, as shown here. The entry **turtle.trek.com/~dylan** will access **turtle.trek.com/home/dylan/public_html**.

```
UserDir public_html
```

Types

When a browser accesses Web pages on a Web site, it is often accessing many different kinds of objects including HTML files, picture or sound files, and script files. To display these objects correctly, the browser must have some indication of what kind of object they are. A JPEG picture file is handled differently from a simple text file. The server provides this type information in the form of MIME types. *MIME types* are the same types used for sending attached files through Internet mailers like Pine. Each kind of object is associated with a given MIME type. Provided with the MIME type, the browser can correctly handle and display the object.

The MIME protocol associates a certain type with files of a given extension. For example, files with a **.jpg** extension would have the MIME type image/jpeg. The **TypesConfig** directive holds the location of the **mime.types** file, which lists all the MIME types and their associated file extensions. *DefaultType* is the default MIME type for any file whose type cannot be determined. *AddType* lets you modify the **mime.type** types list without editing the MIME file.

```
TypesConfig /etc/mime.types
DefaultType text/plain
```

Other type directives are used to specify actions to be taken on certain documents. **AddEncoding** lets browsers decompress compressed files on the fly. **AddHandler** maps file extensions to actions, and **AddLanguage** lets you specify the language for a document. The following example marks file names with the **.gz** extension as gzip-encoded files, and files with the **.fr** extension as French language files.

```
AddEncoding x-gzip gz
AddLanguage fr .fr
```

A Web server can display and execute many different types of files and programs. However, not all Web browsers are able to display all those files. Older browsers are the most limited. Some browsers, such as Lynx, are not designed to display even simple graphics. To allow a Web browser to display a page, the server negotiates with it to determine the type of files it can handle. To enable such negotiation, you need to enable the MultiViews option.

```
Option MultiViews
```

CGI Files

CGI (Common Gateway Interface) files are programs that can be executed by Web browsers accessing your site. They are usually initiated by Web pages that execute the program as part of the content they display. Traditionally, CGI programs were placed in a directory called **cgi-bin** and could only be executed if they resided in such a special directory. There is usually only one **cgi-bin** directory per Web site. Red Hat and OpenLinux systems set up a **cgi-bin** directory in the **/home/httpd** directory, **/home/httpd/cgi-bin**. Here you place any CGI programs that can be executed on your Web site. The **ScriptAlias** directive specifies an alias for your **cgi-bin** directory. Any Web pages or browsers can use the alias to reference this directory.

```
ScriptAlias /cgi-bin/ /home/httpd/cgi-bin/
```

Should you want to be able to execute CGI programs that reside anywhere on your Web site, you can specify that files with a **.cgi** extension are to be treated as executable CGI programs. You do this with the **AddHandler** directive. This directive will apply certain handlers to files of a given type. The handler directive to do this is included in the default **httpd.conf** file provided with the Apache source code files, though commented out. You can remove the comment symbol (#) to enable it.

```
AddHandler cgi-script cgi
```

Automatic Directory Indexing

When given a URL for a directory instead of an HTML file, and when there is no default Web page in the directory, then Apache will create a page on the fly and display it. This is usually just a listing of the different files in the directory. In effect, Apache indexes the items in the directory for you. You can set several options for generating and displaying such an index. If **FancyIndexing** is turned on, then Web page items will be displayed with icons and column headers that can be used to sort the listing.

```
FancyIndexing on
```

Icon directives tell Apache what icon to display for a certain type of file. The **AddIconByType** and **AddIconByEncoding** directives uses MIME-type information to determine the file's type and then associate the specified image with it. **AddIcon** uses the file's extension to determine its type. In the next example, the **text.gif** image will be displayed for text files that have the extension **.txt**. You can also use **AddIcon** to associate an image with a particular file. The **DefaultIcon** directive specifies the image used for files of undetermined type.

```
AddIcon /icons/text.gif .txt
DefaultIcon /icons/unknown.gif
AddIconByType (VID,/icons/movie.gif) video/*
```

With the **AddDescription** directive you can add a short descriptive phrase to the file name entry. The description can be applied to an individual file or to file names of a certain pattern.

```
AddDescription "Reunion pictures" /home/httpd/html/reunion.html
```

Within a directory you can place special files that can be used to display certain text before the generated listing and after it. The **HeaderName** directive is used to set the name of the file whose text is inserted before the listing, and the **ReadmeName** directive sets the name of the file whose text is placed at the end of the listing. You can use these directives in an **.htaccess** file or a **<Directory>** block to select particular files within a directory. Usually, the **ReadmeName** directive is set to README and **HeaderName**, to HEADER. In that case, Apache will search for files named **HEADER** and **README** in the directory.

```
HeaderName HEADER
ReadmeName README
```

With the **IndexOptions** directive you can set different options for displaying a generated index. There are options for setting the height and width of icons and file names. The **IconsAreLinks** option makes icons part of file name anchors. The **ScanHTMLTitles** will read the titles in HTML documents and use those to display entries in the index listing instead of file names. There are various options for suppressing different index display features such as sorting, descriptions, and header/readme inserts. You can set options for individual directories using a Directory block or an **.htaccess** file. Normally, options set in higher-level directories will be inherited by lower-level ones. However, if you use an **IndexOption** directive to set any new option, then all previously inherited options are cleared. If you want to keep the inherited options you can set options using the plus (+) or minus (–) symbols. These add or remove options. However, if you were also to set an option without the + or – symbols, then all inherited options would be cleared.

```
IndexOptions IconsAreLinks FancyIndexing
IndexOptions +ScanHTMLTitles
```

Authentication

Your Web server can also control access on a per-user or per-group basis to particular directories on your Web site. You can require various levels for authentication. Access can be limited to particular users and require passwords, or expanded to allow members of a group access. You can dispense with passwords altogether or set up an anonymous type of access as used with FTP.

To apply authentication directives to a certain directory, you place those directives either within a Directory block or the directory's **.htaccess** file. You use the **require** directive to determine what users can access the directory. You can list particular users or groups. The **AuthName** directive provides the authentication realm to the user, the name used to identify the particular set of resources accessed by this authentication process. The **AuthType** directive specifies the type of authentication such as basic or digest. A **require** directive requires also **AuthType**, **AuthName**, and directives specifying the locations of group and user authentication files. In the following example, only the users george, robert, and mark are allowed access to the **newpics** directory:

```
<Directory /home/httpd/html/newpics
AuthType Basic
AuthName Newpics
AuthUserFile /web/users
AuthGroupFile /web/groups
<Limit GET POST>
    require users george robert mark
</Limit>
</Directory>
```

The next example allows group access by administrators to the CGI directory:

```
<Directory /home/httpd/html/cgi-bin
AuthType Basic
AuthName CGI
AuthGroupFile /web/groups
<Limit GET POST>
    require groups admin
</Limit>
</Directory>
```

To set up anonymous access for a directory, you place the **Anonymous** directive with the user anonymous as its argument in the directory's Directory block or **.htaccess** file. You can also use the **Anonymous** directive to provide access to particular users without requiring passwords from them.

Apache maintains its own user and group authentication files specifying what users and groups are allowed to which directories. These files are normally simple flat files like your system's password and group files. However, they can become very large, possibly slowing down authentication lookups. As an alternative, many sites have used database management files in place of these flat files. Database methods are then used to access the files, providing a faster response time. Apache has directives for specifying the authentication files depending upon the type of file you are using. The **AuthUserfile** and **AuthGroupFile** directives are used to specify the location of authentication files that have a standard flat file format. The **AuthDBUserFile** and **AuthDBGroupFile** directives are used for DB database files, and **AuthDBMGUserFIle** and **AuthDBMGGroupFile** are used for DBMG database files.

Tools provided with the Apache software package such as **htdigest**, **htpasswd**, and **dbmmanage** are for creating and maintaining user authentication files. These are user password files listing users who have access to specific directories or resources on your Web site. The **htdigest** and **htpasswd** files manage a simple flat file of user authentication records, whereas **dbmmanage** uses a more complex database management format. If your user list is extensive, you may want to use a database file for fast lookups. The **htdigest** file takes as its arguments the authentication file, the realm, and the username, creating or updating the user entry. The **htpasswd** file can also employ encryption on the password. The **dbmmanage** file has an extensive set of options to add, delete, and update user entries. A variety of different database formats are used to set up such files. Three common ones are Berkeley DB2, NDBM, and GNU GBDM. The **dbmanage** file will look for the system libraries for these formats in that order. Be careful to be consistent in using the same format for your authentication files.

Log Files

Apache maintains logs of all requests by users to your Web site. By default, these logs include records using the Common Log Format (CLF). The record for each request takes up a line composed of several fields: host, identity check, authenticated user (for logins), the date, the request line submitted by the client, the status sent to the client, and the size of the object sent in bytes. You can customize your log record to add more fields with varying levels of detail using the **LogFormat** and **CustomLog** directives. These directives use a format string consisting of field specifiers to determine the fields to record in a log record. You add whatever fields you want, and in any order. A field specifier consists of a percent (%) symbol followed by an identifying character. For example %h is the field specifier for a remote host, %b, for the size in bytes, and %s for the status. See the documentation for the **mod_log_config** module for a complete listing. You should quote fields whose contents may take up more than one word. The quotes themselves have to be quoted with a backslash to be included in the format string. The following example is the Common Log Format implemented as a **FormatLog** directive.

```
FormatLog "%h %l %u %t \"%r\" %s %b"
```

Instead of maintaining one large log file, you can create several using the **CustomLog** or **TransferLog** directive. This is very helpful for virtual hosts where you may want to maintain a separate log file for each host. You use the **FormatLog** directive to define a default format for log records. The **TransferLog** then uses this default as its format when creating a new log file. **CustomLog** combines both operations, letting you create a new file and define a format for it.

```
FormatLog "%h %l %u %t \"%r\" %s %b"
TransferLog myprojlog
CustomLog mypicslog "%h %l %u %t \"%r\" %s %b"
```

Certain field specifiers in the log format can be qualified to record specific information. The %i specifier records header lines in requests the server receives. The reference for the specific header line to record is placed within braces between the % and the field specifier. For example, User-agent is the header line that indicates the browser software used in the request. To record User-agent header information, you would use the conversion specifier %{User-agent}i.

To maintain compatibility with NCSA servers, Apache originally implemented **AgentLog** and **RefererLog** directives to record User-agent and Referer headers. These have since been replaced by qualified %i field specifiers used for the **LogFormat** and **CustomLog** directives. A *Referer header* records link information from clients, detecting who may have links to your site. The following is an NCSA-compliant log format.

```
"%h %l %u %t \"%r\" %s %b\"%{Referer}i\" \"%{User-agent}i\"".
```

Apache provides two utilities for processing and managing log files. The **logresolve** utility resolves IP addresses in your logfile to host names. The **rotatelogs** utility will rotate log files without having to kill the server. You can specify the rotation time.

Virtual Hosting

Virtual hosting allows the Apache Web server to host multiple Web sites as part of its own. In effect the server can act as several servers, each hosted Web site appearing separate to outside users. Apache supports both IP address and name-based virtual hosting. IP address virtual hosts use valid registered IP addresses, whereas name-based virtual hosts use fully qualified domain addresses. These domain addresses are provided by the Host header from the requesting browser. The server can then determine the correct virtual host to use on the basis of the domain name alone.

IP-Address Virtual Hosts

In the IP address virtual hosting method, your server must have a different IP address for each virtual host. The IP addresses that you use have to be set up already to reference your system. Network system administration operations can set up your machine to support several IP addresses. Your machine could have separate physical network connections for each one or a particular connection could be configured to listen for several IP addresses at once. In effect, any of the IP addresses will access your system.

You can configure Apache to run a separate daemon for each virtual host, separately listening for each IP address, or you can have a single daemon running that listens for requests for all the virtual hosts. To set up a single daemon to manage all virtual hosts, you just use **VirtualHost** directives. To set up a separate daemon for each host, you also use the **Listen** and **BindAddress** directives.

A **VirtualHost** directive block needs to be set up for each virtual host. Within each **VirtualHost** block you place the appropriate directives for accessing a host. You should have **ServerAdmin**, **ServerName**, **DocumentRoot**, and **TransferLog** directives specifying the particular values for that host. You can use any directive within a **VirtualHost** block except for **ServerType**, **StartServers**, **MaxSpareServers**, **MinSpareServers**, **MaxRequestsPerChild**, **BindAddress**, **Listen**, **PidFile**, **TypesConfig**, **ServerRoot**, and **NameVirtualHost**.

Though you can use domain names for the address in the **VirtualHost** directive, it is preferable to use the actual IP address. That way you are not dependent on your domain name service to make the correct domain name associations. Be sure to leave an IP address for your main server. If you use all the available IP addresses for your machine for virtual hosts, then you can no longer access your main server. You could, of course, reconfigure your main server as a virtual host. The following example shows two IP-based virtual hosts blocks, one using an IP address and the other, a domain name that associates with an IP address:

```
<VirtualHost 192.168.1.23>
    ServerAdmin webmaster@mail.mypics.com
    DocumentRoot /groups/mypics/html
    ServerName www.mypics.com
    ErrorLog /groups/mypics/logs/error_log
    …..
</VirtualHost>

<VirtualHost www.myproj.org>
    ServerAdmin webmaster@mail.myproj.org
    DocumentRoot /groups/myproj/html
    ServerName www.myproj.org
    ErrorLog /groups/myproj/logs/error_log
    ....
</VirtualHost>
```

SERVERS

Name-Based Virtual Hosts

With IP-based virtual hosting, you are limited to the number of IP addresses officially registered to your system. With name-based virtual hosting, you can support any number of virtual hosts using no additional IP addresses. With just a single IP address for your machine, you can still support an unlimited number of virtual hosts. Such a capability is made possible by the HTTP/1.1 protocol, which lets a server identify the name that it is being accessed as. This method requires that the client, the remote user, is using a browser that supports the HTTP/1.1 protocol, as current browsers do (though older ones may not). A browser using such a protocol can send a host: header specifying the particular host to use on a machine.

To implement name-based virtual hosting, you use a **VirtualHost** directive for each host and a **NameVirtualHost** directive to specify the IP address you want to use for the virtual hosts. If your system has only one IP address, you need to use that. Within the **VirtualHost** directives you use the **ServerName** directive to specify the domain name you want to use for that host. It is important to use **ServerName** to specify the domain name in order to avoid a DNS lookup. A DNS lookup failure will disable the virtual host. The **VirtualHost** directives each take the same IP address specified in the **NameVirtualHost** directive as its argument. Within the **VirtualHost** blocks you use Apache directives to configure each host separately. Name-based virtual hosting uses the domain name address specified in a host: header to determine the virtual host to use. If there is no such information, then the first host is used as the default. The following example implements two name-based virtual hosts. Here **www.mypics.com** and **www.myproj.org** are implemented as name-based virtual hosts instead of IP-based hosts:

```
  ServerName turtle.mytrek.com

NameVirtualHost 192.168.1.5

<VirtualHost 192.168.1.5>
    ServerName www.mypics.com
    ServerAdmin webmaster@mail.mypics.com
    DocumentRoot /home/httpd/mypics/html
    ErrorLog /home/httpd/mypics/logs/error_log
    ...
</VirtualHost>

<VirtualHost 192.168.1.5>
    ServerName www.myproj.org
    ServerAdmin webmaster@mail.myproj.org
    DocumentRoot /home/httpd/myproj/html
    ErrorLog /home/httpd/myproj/logs/error_log
    ....
</VirtualHost>
```

If your system has only one IP address, then implementing virtual hosts will prevent access to your main server with that address. You could no longer use your main server as a Web server directly, only indirectly to manage your virtual host. You could just configure a virtual host to manage your main server's Web pages. You would then use your main server to support a set of virtual hosts that would function as Web sites, rather than the main server operating as one directly. Should your machine have two or more IP addresses, you can use one for the main server and the other for your virtual hosts. You can even mix IP-based virtual hosts and name-based virtual hosts on your server. You can also use separate IP addresses to support different sets of virtual hosts. You can further have several domain addresses access the same virtual host. To do so, you place a **ServerAlias** directive listing the domain names within the selected **VirtualHost** block.

```
ServerAlias www.mypics.com www.greatpics.com
```

Requests sent to the IP address used for your virtual hosts have to match one of the configured virtual domain names. To catch requests that do not match one of these virtual hosts, you can set up a default virtual host using *_default_:*. Unmatched requests will be handled by this virtual host.

```
<VirtualHost _default_:*>
```

Apache GUI Configuration Tools: Comanche

The Apache GUI Project (**gui.apache.org**) provides a set of GUI tools for configuring and managing your Apache Web server. Its currently active projects are Comanche and TkApache. An older Comanche module comes with the Red Hat distribution. In the Linuxconf utility you can activate a module to configure your Apache Web server.

Comanche (Configuration Manager for Apache) is an easy-to-use, full-featured Apache configuration utility that runs on any X Windows window manager. You can download the current version and documentation from the Comanche Web site at **comanche.com.dtu.dk**. Comanche uses a simple directory-tree-like structure to let you access and configure your main Web server and any virtual server you have set up (see Figure 18-1). Currently it can only configure the server on your local machine, but it may, in the future, be able to configure remote servers. The main window is divided into two panes: The upper pane is a tree of Apache servers, and the lower pane is a status display that will show the Apache directives and commands executed by actions you specify using the Comanche interface. Unlike in ordinary programs, the menus are in the form of pop-up menus activated on entries in the server-tree, not from the menu bar at the top of the window. This menu bar only has an entry for quitting the program and accessing help.

The server-tree in the upper pane of the Comanche main window will initially only show one entry, eComanche with a folder icon. Click the folder to expand the tree to show the different machines you can configure. Currently, Comanche can only configure your local machine, so there is only one entry, named Apache Machine with a computer icon next to it. Double-click the computer icon to expand the tree and display a Server Management entry and a list of servers. To perform actions on any of these entries, you use pop-up menus that you activate by right-clicking the entry. A right-click on the Server Management entry displays a pop-up menu with items to Start, Stop, Restart, and Query the server status, as well as save your configuration. Any changes that you make with Comanche are not made in your Apache configuration files until you explicitly save the configuration by selecting this item in the Server Management pop-up menu. Be sure to save before you quit. To see what actual entries will be made in the Apache configuration files, choose the server entry, right-click, and select the Conf entry in the pop-up menu. This will display a version of the **httpd.conf** configuration file that reflects your current configuration selections. When you save your configuration, this version will overwrite your **httpd.conf** file.

Initially, only one server will be listed, labeled Default Web Site. If you add virtual hosts, they will be listed at the same level. Servers have a blue ball icon placed next to them. You can use Comanche to create a virtual host. You first access the pop-up menu for the Apache Machine by doing a right-click on the computer icon. Select New on the pop-up menu. This activates a drop-down menu with a Virtual Host entry. Select it to create your virtual host.

If you double-click the server icon, the tree expands to list server locations. These are the root directory, your Web server home directory, the CGI program directory, and the documentation directory. To create new directories, you right-click the blue ball icon in the Web server entry and select the New item in the menu that pops up. Then select Directory in the drop-down menu that is displayed. Should you want to delete it later, just right-click its entry and select Delete from the pop-up menu.

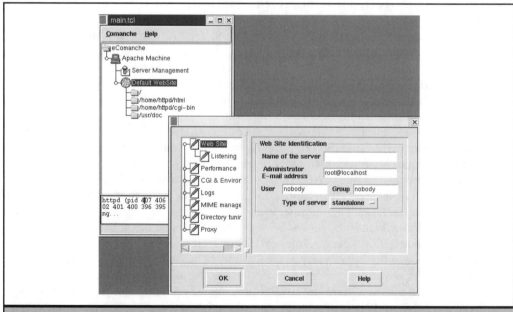

Figure 18-1.   *The Comanche Apache configuration tool*

To configure a server or directory, you just right-click its entry and select the Properties item from the pop-up menu displayed. This opens a new window for configuring your selection, as shown in Figure 18-2. The window is divided into two panes, a left one that shows a tree of configuration items, and a left pane that will display the configuration dialog windows for these items. The structure is similar to the Netscape preferences interface.

To use Linuxconf to configure your Apache server, first you may have to load the apache module into the Linuxconf utility. To do this, you select the Control entry, and then "Control files and systems," and finally the "Linuxconf modules" entry. This displays a panel where you can enter the name of various Linuxconf modules you want added. Enter in the name **apache** and click Add. When you restart Linuxconf, there will be an entry for "Apache Web server" under the "Server tasks" heading with the networking entries. Apache will have entries for defaults, directory configuration, and virtual domains. A panel is displayed for each entry with fields where you can enter in your value, or buttons to click to selected features. The defaults entry displays a panel listing fields for the directives used to configure your main server. The subdirectory entry lets you configure particular directories, using buttons to select controls you want to place on them. With virtual domains, you can create and configure virtual hosts, entering directive values into displayed fields and selecting controls from a list of buttons.

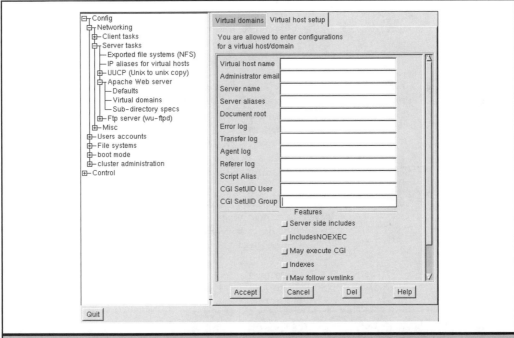

Figure 18-2.   *The Linuxconf Apache configuration module*

Directives	Description
AccessConfig *filename*	File to be read for more directives after reading the ResourceConfig file. *Filename* is relative to the ServerRoot. Default: AccessConfig conf/access.conf Context: server config, virtual host
AccessFileName *filename filename ...*	Default directory configuration file names located within directories. Default: AccessFileName **.htaccess** Context: server config, virtual host
Action *action-type cgi-script*	Adds an action, which will activate *cgi-script* when *action-type* is triggered by the request. Context: server config, virtual host, directory, **.htaccess** Override: FileInfo Module: mod_actions
AddDescription *string file file ...*	Sets the description to display for a file. Can be a file extension, partial file name, wildcard expression or full file name. String is enclosed in double quotes ("). Context: server config, virtual host, directory, **.htaccess** Override: Indexes Status: Base Module: mod_autoindex
AddHandler *handler-name extension extension ...*	Maps the file name extensions *extension* to the handler *handler-name*. Context: server config, virtual host, directory, **.htaccess** Override: FileInfo Status: Base Module: mod_mime
AddIcon *icon name name ...*	Specifies the icon to display next to a file ending in *name*. Context: server config, virtual host, directory, **.htaccess** Override: Indexes Status: Base Module: mod_autoindex

Table 18-1. *Apache Configuration Directives*

Directives	Description
AddIconByEncoding *icon MIME-encoding MIME-encoding ...*	Specifies the icon to display next to files with *MIME-encoding* (FancyIndexing). Context: server config, virtual host, directory, **.htaccess** Override: Indexes Status: Base Module: mod_autoindex
AddIconByType *icon MIME-type MIME-type ...*	Specifies the icon to display next to files of type *MIME-type* (FancyIndexing). Context: server config, virtual host, directory, **.htaccess** Override: Indexes Status: Base Module: mod_autoindex
AddLanguage *MIME-lang extension extension ...*	Maps the given file name extensions to the specified content language. Context: server config, virtual host, directory, **.htaccess** Override: FileInfo Status: Base Module: mod_mime
AddModule *module module ...*	Enables use of modules that are compiled but not in use. Context: server config
Alias *url-path directory-filename*	Allows access to documents stored in the local file system other than under the DocumentRoot. Context: server config, virtual host Status: Base Module: mod_alias
allow *from host host ...*	Determines which hosts can access a given directory: all, partial or full domain name or IP address. Context: directory, **.htaccess** Override: Limit Status: Base Module: mod_access

Table 18-1. *Apache Configuration Directives* (continued)

SERVERS

Directives	Description
AllowOverride *override override* ...	Directives that can be overridden by entries in an **.htaccess** file. All allows overrides, and none denies them. Default: AllowOverride All Context: directory
Anonymous *user user* ...	Users that are allowed access without password verification. *User* is usually anonymous (is case sensitive). Default: None Context: directory, **.htaccess** Override: AuthConfig Status: Extension Module: mod_auth_anon
Anonymous_Authoritative *on | off*	When on, there is no fall-through to other authorization methods. Default: Anonymous_Authoritative off Context: directory, **.htaccess** Override: AuthConfig Status: Extension Module: mod_auth_anon
AddType *MIME-type extension extension* ...	Maps the given file name extensions onto the specified content type. *MIME-type* is the MIME type to use for file names containing extension. Context: server config, virtual host, directory, **.htaccess** Override: FileInfo Status: Base Module: mod_mime
AuthGroupFile *filename*	Sets the name of the file with the list of user groups for user authentication. Context: directory, **.htaccess** Override: AuthConfig Status: Base Module: mod_auth

Table 18-1.   *Apache Configuration Directives* (continued)

Directives	Description
`AuthDBGroupFile filename`	DB file containing the list of groups for user authentication. Context: directory, **.htaccess** Override: AuthConfig Status: Extension Module: mod_auth_db
`AuthDBUserFile filename`	DB file containing the list of users and passwords for user authentication. Context: directory, **.htaccess** Override: AuthConfig Status: Extension Module: mod_auth_db
`AuthDBMGroupFile filename`	DBM file containing the list of groups for user authentication. Context: directory, **.htaccess** Override: AuthConfig Status: Extension Module: mod_auth_dbm
`AuthDBMUserFile filename`	DBM file containing the list of users and passwords for user authentication. Context: directory, **.htaccess** Override: AuthConfig Status: Extension Module: mod_auth_dbm
`AuthName auth-domain`	The authorization realm for a directory. A realm is given to the client so that the user knows which user name and password to send. Context: directory, **.htaccess** Override: AuthConfig

`AuthType type`
`Context: directory,`
`.htaccess`
`Override: AuthConfig`
	Type of user authentication for a directory. Only Basic and Digest are currently implemented.
	Context: directory, **.htaccess**
	Override: AuthConfig

Table 18-1.   *Apache Configuration Directives* (continued)

Directives	Description
AuthUserFile *filename*	Sets the name of the file with the list of users and passwords for user authentication. Context: directory, **.htaccess** Override: AuthConfig Status: Base Module: mod_auth
BindAddress *saddr*	Binds the server to specified IP address. If the value is *, then the server will listen for connections on every IP address; otherwise, it will only listen on the IP address specified. Only one BindAddress directive can be used. For more control over the address and ports listened to, use the **Listen** directive. Default: BindAddress * Context: server config
CheckSpelling *on/off*	Enables or disables the spelling module. This module tries to find a matching document by comparing each document name in the requested directory against the requested document name without regard to case and allowing up to one misspelling. Default: CheckSpelling off Context: server config, virtual host, directory, **.htaccess** Override: Options Status: Base Module: mod_spelling
ClearModuleList	Clears the built-in list of active modules. Context: server config
CustomLog *file-pipe format-or-nickname*	Creates a new log file with the specified format. Context: server config, virtual host Status: Base Compatibility: Nickname only available in Apache 1.3 or later Module: mod_log_config

Table 18-1.   *Apache Configuration Directives* (continued)

Directives	Description
`DefaultIcon url`	Specifies the icon to display for files when no specific icon is known (FancyIndexing). Context: server config, virtual host, directory, **.htaccess** Override: Indexes Status: Base Module: mod_autoindex
`DefaultLanguage MIME-lang`	Specifies *MIME-lang* as the default file language. Context: server config, virtual host, directory, **.htaccess** Override: FileInfo Status: Base Module: mod_mime
`DefaultType MIME-type`	Default type for documents whose types cannot be determined by their MIME types mappings. Default: DefaultType text/html Context: server config, virtual host, directory, **.htaccess** Override: FileInfo
`deny from host host ...`	Determines hosts that can access a given directory: all or partial, or full domain name or IP address. Context: directory, **.htaccess** Override: Limit Status: Base Module: mod_access
`<Directory directory> ...` `</Directory>`	**<Directory>** and **</Directory>** directives operate as tags that enclose a group of directives applying only to the named directory and subdirectories of that directory. Context: server config, virtual host
`<DirectoryMatch regex> ...` `</DirectoryMatch>`	**<DirectoryMatch>** and **</DirectoryMatch>** enclose a group of directives that apply only to the named directory. It operates the same as **<Directory>** but takes as an argument a regular expression. Context: server config, virtual host

Table 18-1.   *Apache Configuration Directives* (continued)

SERVERS

Directives	Description
DirectoryIndex *local-url* *local-url ...*	Specifies the list of resources to look for, when the client requests an index of the directory by specifying a slash (/) at the end of a directory name (usually index.html). Default: DirectoryIndex index.html Context: server config, virtual host, directory, **.htaccess** Override: Indexes Status: Base Module: mod_dir
DocumentRoot *directory-filename*	The directory from which httpd will serve files. Default: DocumentRoot /usr/local/apache/htdocs (/home/httpd/html on Red Hat and OpenLinux systems) Context: server config, virtual host
ErrorDocument *error-code* *document*	Redirects to a local or external URL to handle the problem/error. Context: server config, virtual host, directory, **.htaccess**
ErrorLog *filename|syslog[:facility]*	The file that the server will log errors on. Default: ErrorLog logs/error_log Context: server config, virtual host
FancyIndexing *Boolean*	Sets the FancyIndexing option for a directory. Boolean can be on or off. Context: server config, virtual host, directory, **.htaccess** Override: Indexes Status: Base Module: mod_autoindex
<Files *filename*> ... </Files>	Provides for access control by file name. It is similar to the **<Directory>** directive and **<Location>** directive. **<Files>** sections are processed in the order they appear in the configuration file, after the **<Directory>** sections and **.htaccess** files are read, but before **<Location>** sections. **<Files>** can be nested inside **<Directory>** sections to restrict the portion of the file system they apply to. Context: server config, virtual host, **.htaccess**

Table 18-1. *Apache Configuration Directives* (continued)

Directives	Description
`<FilesMatch regex> ...` `</FilesMatch>`	Provides for access control by file name like the **<Files>** directive but uses a regular expression. Context: server config, virtual host, **.htaccess**
`Group unix-group`	Sets the group for the server. The standalone server must be run initially as root. It is recommended that you set up a new group specifically for running the server. Default: Group #-1 Context: server config, virtual host
`HeaderName filename`	Specifies the name of the file that will be inserted at the top of the index listing (FancyIndexing). Context: server config, virtual host, directory, **.htaccess** Override: Indexes Status: Base Module: mod_autoindex
`HostNameLookups` `on | off | double`	Enables DNS lookups so that host names can be logged. The double option refers to double-reverse DNS. Default: HostNameLookups off Context: server config, virtual host, directory
`IdentityCheck Boolean`	Enables RFC 1413–compliant logging of the remote user name for each connection. Default: IdentityCheck off Context: server config, virtual host, directory
`<IfDefine [!]parameter-name>` `... </IfDefine>`	The **<IfDefine test>...</IfDefine>** section specifies conditional directives. Directives within an **IfDefine** section are processed if the test is true and ignored otherwise. The test consists of a parameter name and is true if the parameter is defined, false if undefined. An exclamation point (!) (not). placed before the parameter makes the test true if the parameter is undefined Default: NoneContext: all
`<IfModule [!]module-name>` `... </IfModule>`	The **<IfModule test>...</IfModule>** section specifies conditional directives. The test checks to see if a module is compiled in Apache and is true if present, false if not. A !module-name is true if the module is not present.

Table 18-1. *Apache Configuration Directives* (continued)

SERVERS

Directives	Description
Include *filename*	Inclusion of other configuration files. Context: server config
IndexOptions [+|-]*option* [+|-]*option* ...	Set options for directory indexing: FancyIndexing, IconHeight, IconsAreLinks, IconWidth, NameWidth, ScanHTMLTitles, SuppressDescription. Context: server config, virtual host, directory, **.htaccess** Override: Indexes Status: Base Module: mod_autoindex
KeepAlive on/off	Enables persistent connections, Specify Off to disable. Default: KeepAlive on Context: server config
KeepAliveTimeout *seconds*	The number of seconds Apache will wait for another request before closing the connection. Default: KeepAliveTimeout 15 Context: server config
<Limit *method method* ... > ... </Limit>	**<Limit>** and **</Limit>** specify a group of access control directives that will apply only to the specified access methods, any valid HTTP method. Access control directive appearing outside a **<Limit>** directive apply to all access methods. Method names are: GET, POST, PUT, DELETE, CONNECT, or OPTIONS.
<LimitExcept *method method* ... > ... </LimitExcept>	**<LimitExcept>** and **</LimitExcept>** specify a group of access control directives that will then apply to any HTTP access method not listed in the arguments.
LimitRequestBody *number*	Limits the size of an HTTP request message body. Default: LimitRequestBody 0 Context: server config, virtual host, directory, **.htaccess**

Table 18-1. *Apache Configuration Directives* (continued)

Directives	Description
`LimitRequestFields` *number*	Limits the number of request header fields allowed in an HTTP request. Default: LimitRequestFields 100 Context: server config
`Listen [`*IP address*`:]`*port number*	Listens to more than one IP address or port; by default it responds to requests on all IP interfaces, but only on the port given by the Port directive. Context: server config
`ListenBacklog` *backlog*	The maximum length of the queue of pending connections. Default: ListenBacklog 511 Context: server config
`LoadFile` *filename filename* `...`	Links in the named object files or libraries when the server is started or restarted; used to load additional code required for some module to work. Context: server config Status: Base Module: mod_so
`LoadModule` *module filename*	Links in the object file or library file name and adds the module structure named *module* to the list of active modules. Context: server config Status: Base Module: mod_so
`<Location `*URL*`> ...` `</Location>`	The **<Location>** directive provides for access control by URL. It is similar to the **<Directory>** directive. Context: server config, virtual host
`<LocationMatch `*regex*`> ...` `</LocationMatch>`	Provides access control by URL, in an identical manner to **<Location>**, using a regular expression an argument. Context: server config, virtual host

Table 18-1. *Apache Configuration Directives* (continued)

Directives	Description
LockFile *filename*	Path to the lockfile used when Apache is compiled. Default: LockFile logs/accept.lock Context: server config
LogFormat *format* [*nickname*]	Sets the format of the default logfile named by the TransferLog directive. Default: LogFormat "%h %l %u %t \"%r\" %s %b" Context: server config, virtual host Status: Base Module: mod_log_config
LogLevel *level*	Adjusts the verbosity of the messages recorded in the error logs. Default: LogLevel error Context: server config, virtual host
MaxClients *number*	Limits the number of simultaneous requests that can be supported. Any connection attempts over the MaxClients limit will normally be queued, up to a number based on the **ListenBacklog** directive. Default: MaxClients 256 Context: server config
MaxKeepAliveRequests *number*	Limits the number of requests allowed per connection when KeepAlive is on. Default: MaxKeepAliveRequests 100 Context: server config
NameVirtualHost *addr*[:*port*]	Specifies the address that a name-based virtual host name resolves. If you have multiple name-based hosts on multiple addresses, repeat the directive for each address. Required for configuring name-based virtual hosts. Though *addr* can be a hostname, it is recommended that you always use an IP address. Context: server config

Table 18-1.   *Apache Configuration Directives* (continued)

SERVERS

Directives	Description
`Options [+|-]option` `[+|-]option ...`	Controls the server features available in a particular directory. If set to None, then none of the extra features are enabled. **All** All options except for MultiViews. This is the default setting. **ExecCGI** Execution of CGI scripts is permitted. **FollowSymLinks** The server will follow symbolic links in this directory. **Includes** Server-side includes are permitted. **IncludesNOEXEC** Server-side includes are permitted, but the #exec command and #include of CGI scripts are disabled. **Indexes** Returns a formatted listing of the directory for directories with no DirectoryIndex. **MultiViews** Content negotiated MultiViews are allowed. **SymLinksIfOwnerMatch** The server will only follow symbolic links for which the target file or directory is owned by the same user ID as the link. Context: server config, virtual host, directory, **.htaccess** Override: Options
`order ordering`	Controls the order in which allow and deny directives are evaluated. Default: order deny, allow Context: directory, **.htaccess** Override: Limit Status: Base Module: mod_access

Table 18-1. *Apache Configuration Directives* (continued)

Directives	Description
PidFile *filename*	File that the server records the process ID of the daemon in. Default: PidFile logs/httpd.pid Context: server config
Port *number*	If there are no **Listen** or **BindAddress** directives, then a port directive sets the network port on which the server listens. Ports for a virtual host are set by the **VirtualHost** directive. Default: Port 80 Context: server config
ReadmeName *filename*	Specifies the name of the file to be appended to the end of the index listing. Context: server config, virtual host, directory, **.htaccess** Override: Indexes Status: Base Module: mod_autoindex
Redirect [*status*] *url-path url*	Maps an old URL into a new one Context: server config, virtual host, directory, **.htaccess** Override: FileInfo Status: Base Module: mod_alias
RemoveHandler *extension* *extension* ...	Removes handler associations for files with the given extensions. This allows **.htaccess** files in subdirectories to undo any associations inherited from parent directories or the server configuration files. Context: directory, **.htaccess** Status: Base Module: mod_mime
require *entity-name* *entity entity* ...	Selects the authenticated users that can access a directory. The *entity-name* is either user or group, followed by a list of users or groups. require user *userid userid* ... require *group group-name group-name* ... Context: directory, **.htaccess** Override: AuthConfig

Table 18-1.   *Apache Configuration Directives* (continued)

Directives	Description
ResourceConfig *filename*	Server will read this file for more directives after reading the **httpd.conf** file. Default: ResourceConfig conf/srm.conf Context: server config, virtual host
Satisfy *directive*	Access policy if both allow and require are used. The parameter can be either 'all' or 'any'. Syntax: Satisfy 'any' or 'all' Default: Satisfy all Context: directory, **.htaccess**
ScoreBoardFile *filename*	Specifies the ScoreBoardFile file. Default: ScoreBoardFile logs/apache_status Context: server config
Script *method cgi-script*	Adds an action, which will activate *cgi-script* when a file is requested using the method of *method*, which can be one of GET, POST, PUT, or DELETE. Context: server config, virtual host, directory Status: Base Module: mod_actions
ScriptAlias *url-path directory-filename*	Marks the target directory as containing CGI scripts. Context: server config, virtual host Status: Base Module: mod_alias
ScriptInterpreterSource 'registry' or 'script'	Finds the interpreter used to run CGI scripts. The default method is to use the interpreter pointed to by the #! line in the script. Default: ScriptInterpreterSource script Context: directory, **.htaccess**
ServerAdmin *e-mail-address*	The e-mail address included in any error messages sent to a client. Context: server config, virtual host
ServerAlias *host1 host2 ...*	Sets the alternate names for a host, for use with name-based virtual hosts. Context: virtual host
ServerName *fully qualified domain name*	Sets the hostname of the server; this is only used when creating redirection URLs. If it is not specified, then the server attempts to deduce it from its own IP address. Context: server config, virtual host

Table 18-1. *Apache Configuration Directives* (continued)

Directives	Description
ServerPath *pathname*	Sets the legacy URL path name for a host, for use with name-based virtual hosts. Context: virtual host
ServerRoot *directory-filename*	Sets the directory in which the server resides. Default: ServerRoot /usr/local/apache Context: server config
ServerSignature Off | On | EMail	Configures a trailing footer line under server-generated documents such as error messages. Default: ServerSignature Off Context: server config, virtual host, directory, **.htaccess**
ServerType *type*	Sets how the server is executed by the system. The *type* can be either inetd or standalone. Default: ServerType standalone Context: server config
SetHandler *handler-name*	Forces all matching files to be parsed through the handler given by *handler-name.* Context: directory, **.htaccess** Status: Base Module: mod_mime
StartServers *number*	Sets the number of child server processes created on startup. Default: StartServers 5 Context: server config
TimeOut *number*	Sets the timeout in seconds for receiving GET requests, receipt of TCP packets on POST and PUT, and TCP packet transmissions acknowledgments. Default: TimeOut 300 Context: server config
TransferLog *file-pipe*	Adds a log file in the format defined by the most recent **LogFormat** directive, or Common Log Format if a default is specified. Default: None Context: server config, virtual host Status: Base Module: mod_log_config

Table 18-1.   *Apache Configuration Directives* (continued)

Directives	Description
`TypesConfig filename`	Sets the location of the MIME types configuration file. Default: TypesConfig conf/MIME.types Context: server config Status: Base Module: mod_mime
`User unix-userid`	Specifies the userid for the server. The standalone server must be run as root initially. You can use a user name or a user ID number. The user should have no access to system files. It is recommended that you set up a new user and group specifically for running the server. Default: User #-1 Context: server config, virtual host
`UserDir directory/filename`	Sets the real directory in a user's home directory to use when a request for a document for a user is received. Default: UserDir public_html Context: server config, virtual host Status: Base Module: mod_userdir
`<VirtualHost addr[:port]` `...> ... </VirtualHost>`	**<VirtualHost>** and **</VirtualHost>** specify a group of directives that apply only to a particular virtual host. When the server receives a request for a document on a particular virtual host, it uses the configuration directives enclosed in the **<VirtualHost>** section. Addr can be an IP address of the virtual host or its fully qualified domain name. Each VirtualHost must correspond to a different IP address, a different port number, or a different host name for the server. Context: server config

Table 18-1. *Apache Configuration Directives* (continued)

srm.conf Directives	access.conf Directives
AccessFileName	<Directory *path-name*> </Directory>
AddDescription	
AddEncoding *extensions-list*	Options *feature-list*
AddIcon *image file file-extensions*	AllowOverride *feature-list*
AddIconByEncoding	<Limit> </Limit>
AddIconByType	
AddLanguage *language extension*	
AddType *type/subtype extension*	
Alias *alias-name path-name*	
DefaultType	
DefaultIcon	
DirectoryIndex	
DocumentRoot	
FancyIndexing	
HeaderName	
IndexIgnore *file-list*	
IndexOptions	
LanguagePriority *language-list*	
OldScriptAlias	
ReadmeName	
Redirect	
ScriptAlias *alias-name path-name*	
UserDir	

Table 18-2.   *Directives Used in **srm.conf** and **access.conf** Files*

Apache Web Server Configuration Files

The current Red Hat **httpd.conf** and **smf.conf** configuration files are shown here as
implemented on Red Hat systems:

httpd.conf

```
##
## httpd.conf -- Apache HTTP server configuration file
##

# This is the main server configuration file. # URL
# http://www.apache.org/ for instructions.

# Do NOT simply read the instructions in here without understanding
# what they do, if you are unsure consult the online docs. You have #
been warned.

# Originally by Rob McCool

# Dynamic Shared Object (DSO) Support
#
# To be able to use the functionality of a module which was built
# as a DSO you have to place corresponding 'LoadModule' lines
# at this location so the directives contained in it are actually
# available _before_ # they are used. Please read the file
# README.DSO in the Apache 1.3 distribution for more details
# about the DSO mechanism and run 'httpd -l' for the list of
# already built-in (statically linked and thus always available)
# modules in your httpd binary.
#
# Example:
# LoadModule foo_module libexec/mod_foo.so
#
# Documentation for modules is in "/home/httpd/manual/mod" in HTML.

#LoadModule mmap_static_module modules/mod_mmap_static.so
LoadModule env_module         modules/mod_env.so
LoadModule config_log_module  modules/mod_log_config.so
LoadModule agent_log_module   modules/mod_log_agent.so

................. .
#LoadModule example_module     modules/mod_example.so
#LoadModule unique_id_module   modules/mod_unique_id.so
```

```
LoadModule setenvif_module     modules/mod_setenvif.so

# Extra Modules
#LoadModule php_module          modules/mod_php.so
#LoadModule php3_module         modules/libphp3.so
#LoadModule perl_module         modules/libperl.so

#  Reconstruction of the complete module list from all available
#  modules (static and shared ones) to achieve correct module
#  execution order. [WHENEVER YOU CHANGE THE LOADMODULE SECTION
#  ABOVE UPDATE THIS, TOO]
ClearModuleList
#AddModule mod_mmap_static.c
AddModule mod_env.c
AddModule mod_log_config.c
...........................

#AddModule mod_example.c
#AddModule mod_unique_id.c
AddModule mod_so.c
AddModule mod_setenvif.c

# Extra Modules
#AddModule mod_php.c
#AddModule mod_php3.c
#AddModule mod_perl.c

# ServerType is either inetd, or standalone.

ServerType standalone

# If you are running from inetd, go to "ServerAdmin".

# Port: The port the standalone listens to. For ports < 1023, you
# will need httpd to be run as root initially.

Port 80

# HostnameLookups: Log the names of clients or just their IP numbers
#   e.g.   www.apache.org (on) or 204.62.129.132 (off)
# The default is off because it'd be overall better for the net if
# people had to knowingly turn this feature on.
```

```
HostnameLookups off

# If you wish httpd to run as a different user or group, you must
# run httpd as root initially and it will switch.

# User/Group: The name (or #number) of the user/group to run httpd as.
#   On SCO (ODT 3) use User nouser and Group nogroup
#   On HPUX you may not be able to use shared memory as nobody, and the
#   suggested workaround is to create a user www and use that user.
#   NOTE that some kernels refuse to setgid(Group) or semctl(IPC_SET)
#   when the value of (unsigned)Group is above 60000;
#   don't use Group nobody on these systems!

User nobody
Group nobody

# ServerAdmin: Your address, where problems with the server should be
# e-mailed.

ServerAdmin root@localhost

# ServerRoot: The directory the server's config, error, and log files
# are kept in.
# NOTE!  If you intend to place this on a NFS (or otherwise network)
# mounted filesystem then please read the LockFile documentation,
# you will save yourself a lot of trouble.

ServerRoot /etc/httpd

# BindAddress: You can support virtual hosts with this option. This
# option is used to tell the server which IP address to listen to. It
# can either contain "*", an IP address, or a fully qualified Internet
# domain name. See also the VirtualHost directive.

#BindAddress *

# ErrorLog: The location of the error log file. If this does not
# start with /, ServerRoot is prepended to it.

ErrorLog logs/error_log

# LogLevel: Control the number of messages logged to the error_log.
```

```
# Possible values include: debug, info, notice, warn, error, crit,
# alert, emerg.

LogLevel warn

# The following directives define some format nicknames for use with
# a CustomLog directive (see below).

LogFormat "%h %l %u %t \"%r\" %>s %b \"%{Referer}i\"
\"%{User-Agent}i\"" combined
LogFormat "%h %l %u %t \"%r\" %>s %b" common
LogFormat "%{Referer}i -> %U" referer
LogFormat "%{User-agent}i" agent

# The location of the access logfile (Common Logfile Format).
# If this does not start with /, ServerRoot is prepended to it.

CustomLog logs/access_log common

# If you would like to have an agent and referer logfile uncomment the
# following directives.

#CustomLog logs/referer_log referer
#CustomLog logs/agent_log agent

# If you prefer a single logfile with access, agent and referer
# information (Combined Logfile Format) you can use the following
# directive.

#CustomLog logs/access_log combined

# PidFile: The file the server should log its pid to
PidFile /var/run/httpd.pid

# ScoreBoardFile: File used to store internal server process
# information. Not all architectures require this.  But if yours does
# (you'll know because this file is created when you run Apache) then
# you *must* ensure that no two invocations of Apache share the same
# scoreboard file.
ScoreBoardFile /var/run/httpd.scoreboard

# The LockFile directive sets the path to the lockfile used when Apache
# is compiled with either USE_FCNTL_SERIALIZED_ACCEPT or
```

```
# USE_FLOCK_SERIALIZED_ACCEPT. This directive should normally be left
# at its default value. The main reason for changing it is if the logs
# directory is NFS mounted, since the lockfile MUST BE STORED ON A
# LOCAL DISK. The PID of the main server process is automatically
# appended to the filename.
#
#LockFile /var/lock/httpd.lock

# ServerName allows you to set a host name which is sent back to
# clients for your server if it's different than the one the program
# would get (i.e. use "www" instead of the host's real name).
#
# Note: You cannot just invent host names and hope they work. The name
# you define here must be a valid DNS name for your host. If you don't
# understand this, ask your network administrator.

#ServerName new.host.name

# UseCanonicalName:  (new for 1.3)  With this setting turned on,
# whenever Apache needs to construct a self-referencing URL (a url that
# refers back to the server the response is coming from) it will use
# ServerName and Port to form a "canonical" name.  With this setting
# off, Apache will use the hostname:port that the client supplied, when
# possible.  This also affects SERVER_NAME and SERVER_PORT in CGIs.
UseCanonicalName on

# CacheNegotiatedDocs: By default, Apache sends Pragma: no-cache with
# each document that was negotiated on the basis of content. This asks
# proxy servers not to cache the document. Uncommenting the following
# line disables this behavior, and proxies will be allowed to cache the
documents.

#CacheNegotiatedDocs

# Timeout: The number of seconds before receives and sends time out

Timeout 300

# KeepAlive: Whether or not to allow persistent connections (more than
# one request per connection). Set to "Off" to deactivate.

KeepAlive On
```

```
# MaxKeepAliveRequests: The maximum number of requests to allow
# during a persistent connection. Set to 0 to allow an unlimited
# amount. We recommend you leave this number high, for maximum
# performance.

MaxKeepAliveRequests 100

# KeepAliveTimeout: Number of seconds to wait for the next request

KeepAliveTimeout 15

# Server-pool size regulation.  Rather than making you guess how many
# server processes you need, Apache dynamically adapts to the load it
# sees --- that is, it tries to maintain enough server processes to
# handle the current load, plus a few spare servers to handle transient
# load spikes (e.g., multiple simultaneous requests from a single
# Netscape browser).

# It does this by periodically checking how many servers are waiting
# for a request.  If there are fewer than MinSpareServers, it creates
# a new spare.  If there are more than MaxSpareServers, some of the
# spares die off.  These values are probably OK for most sites ---

MinSpareServers 8
MaxSpareServers 20

# Number of servers to start --- should be a reasonable ballpark
# figure.

StartServers 10

# Limit on total number of servers running, i.e., limit on the number
# of clients who can simultaneously connect --- if this limit is ever
# reached, clients will be LOCKED OUT, so it should NOT BE SET TOO LOW.
# It is intended mainly as a brake to keep a runaway server from taking
# Unix with it as it spirals down...

MaxClients 150

# MaxRequestsPerChild: the number of requests each child process is
#  allowed to process before the child dies.
#  The child will exit so as to avoid problems after prolonged use when
```

```
#   Apache (and maybe the libraries it uses) leak.   On most systems,
#   this isn't really needed, but a few (such as Solaris) do have
#   notable leaks in the libraries.

MaxRequestsPerChild 100

# Proxy Server directives. Uncomment the following line to
# enable the proxy server:

#ProxyRequests On

# To enable the cache as well, edit and uncomment the following lines:

#CacheRoot /var/cache/httpd
#CacheSize 5
#CacheGcInterval 4
#CacheMaxExpire 24
#CacheLastModifiedFactor 0.1
#CacheDefaultExpire 1
#NoCache a_domain.com another_domain.edu joes.garage_sale.com

# Listen: Allows you to bind Apache to specific IP addresses and/or
# ports, in addition to the default. See also the VirtualHost command

#Listen 3000
#Listen 12.34.56.78:80

# VirtualHost: Allows the daemon to respond to requests for more than
# one server address, if your server machine is configured to accept IP
# packets for multiple addresses. This can be accomplished with the
# ifconfig alias flag, or through kernel patches like VIF.

# Any httpd.conf or srm.conf directive may go into a VirtualHost
# command. See also the BindAddress entry.

#<VirtualHost host.some_domain.com>
#ServerAdmin webmaster@host.some_domain.com
#DocumentRoot /www/docs/host.some_domain.com
#ServerName host.some_domain.com
#ErrorLog logs/host.some_domain.com-error_log
#TransferLog logs/host.some_domain.com-access_log
#</VirtualHost>
```

srm.conf

```
##
## srm.conf -- Apache HTTP server configuration file
##

# With this document, you define the name space that users see of
# your http server.  This file also defines server settings which
# affect how requests are serviced, and how results should be
# formatted.

# See the tutorials at http://www.apache.org/ for
# more information.

# Originally by Rob McCool; Adapted for Apache


# DocumentRoot: The directory out of which you will serve your
# documents. By default, all requests are taken from this
# directory, but symbolic links and aliases may be used to point to
# other locations.

DocumentRoot /home/httpd/html

# UserDir: The name of the directory which is appended onto a
# user's home directory if a ~user request is recieved.

UserDir public_html

# DirectoryIndex: Name of the file or files to use as a pre-written
# HTML directory index.  Separate multiple entries with spaces.

DirectoryIndex index.html index.shtml index.cgi

# FancyIndexing is whether you want fancy directory indexing or
# standard

FancyIndexing on

# AddIcon tells the server which icon to show for different files
# or filename extensions
```

```
AddIconByEncoding (CMP,/icons/compressed.gif) x-compress x-gzip

AddIconByType (TXT,/icons/text.gif) text/*
AddIconByType (IMG,/icons/image2.gif) image/*
AddIconByType (SND,/icons/sound2.gif) audio/*
AddIconByType (VID,/icons/movie.gif) video/*

AddIcon /icons/binary.gif .bin .exe
AddIcon /icons/binhex.gif .hqx
AddIcon /icons/tar.gif .tar
AddIcon /icons/world2.gif .wrl .wrl.gz .vrml .vrm .iv
AddIcon /icons/compressed.gif .Z .z .tgz .gz .zip
AddIcon /icons/a.gif .ps .ai .eps
AddIcon /icons/layout.gif .html .shtml .htm .pdf
AddIcon /icons/text.gif .txt
AddIcon /icons/c.gif .c
AddIcon /icons/p.gif .pl .py
AddIcon /icons/f.gif .for
AddIcon /icons/dvi.gif .dvi
AddIcon /icons/uuencoded.gif .uu
AddIcon /icons/script.gif .conf .sh .shar .csh .ksh .tcl
AddIcon /icons/tex.gif .tex
AddIcon /icons/bomb.gif core

AddIcon /icons/back.gif ..
AddIcon /icons/hand.right.gif README
AddIcon /icons/folder.gif ^^DIRECTORY^^
AddIcon /icons/blank.gif ^^BLANKICON^^

# DefaultIcon is which icon to show for files which do not have an
# icon explicitly set.

DefaultIcon /icons/unknown.gif

# AddDescription allows you to place a short description after a
# file in server-generated indexes.
# Format: AddDescription "description" filename

# ReadmeName is the name of the README file the server will look
# for by default. Format: ReadmeName name
#
# The server will first look for name.html, include it if found,
```

```
# and it will then look for name and include it as plaintext if
# found.
#
# HeaderName is the name of a file which should be prepended to
# directory indexes.

ReadmeName README
HeaderName HEADER

# IndexIgnore is a set of filenames which directory indexing should
# ignore Format: IndexIgnore name1 name2...

IndexIgnore .??* *~ *# HEADER* README* RCS

# AccessFileName: The name of the file to look for in each
# directory for access control information.

AccessFileName .htaccess

# TypesConfig describes where the mime.types file (or equivalent)
# is to be found.

TypesConfig /etc/mime.types

# DefaultType is the default MIME type for documents which the
# server cannot find the type of from filename extensions.

DefaultType text/plain

# AddEncoding allows you to have certain browsers (Mosaic/X 2.1+)
# uncompress information on the fly. Note: Not all browsers support
# this.

AddEncoding x-compress Z
AddEncoding x-gzip gz

# AddLanguage allows you to specify the language of a document. You
# can then use content negotiation to give a browser a file in a
# language it can understand.  Note that the suffix does not have
# to be the same as the language keyword --- those with documents
# in Polish (whose net-standard language code is pl) may wish to
```

```
# use "AddLanguage pl .po" to avoid the ambiguity with the common
# suffix for perl scripts.

AddLanguage en .en
AddLanguage fr .fr
AddLanguage de .de
AddLanguage da .da
AddLanguage el .el
AddLanguage it .it

# LanguagePriority allows you to give precedence to some languages
# in case of a tie during content negotiation.
# Just list the languages in decreasing order of preference.

LanguagePriority en fr de

# Redirect allows you to tell clients about documents which used to
# exist in your server's namespace, but do not anymore. This allows
# you to tell the clients where to look for the relocated document.
# Format: Redirect fakename url


# Aliases: Add here as many aliases as you need (with no limit).
# The format is Alias fakename realname

# Note that if you include a trailing / on fakename then the server
# will require it to be present in the URL.  So "/icons" isn't
# aliased in this example.

Alias /icons/ /home/httpd/icons/

# ScriptAlias: This controls which directories contain server
# scripts. Format: ScriptAlias fakename realname

ScriptAlias /cgi-bin/ /home/httpd/cgi-bin/

# If you want to use server side includes, or CGI outside
# ScriptAliased directories, uncomment the following lines.

# AddType allows you to tweak mime.types without actually editing
# it, or to make certain files to be certain types.
```

```
# Format: AddType type/subtype ext1

# For example, the PHP3 module (not part of the Apache
# distribution) will typically use:
#AddType application/x-httpd-php3 .php3
#AddType application/x-httpd-php3-source .phps
# The following is for PHP/FI (PHP2):
#AddType application/x-httpd-php .phtml

# AddHandler allows you to map certain file extensions to
# "handlers", actions unrelated to filetype. These can be either
# built into the server or added with the Action command (see
# below) Format: AddHandler action-name ext1

# To use CGI scripts:
#AddHandler cgi-script .cgi

# To use server-parsed HTML files
AddType text/html .shtml
AddHandler server-parsed .shtml

# Uncomment the following line to enable Apache's send-asis HTTP
# file feature
#AddHandler send-as-is asis

# If you wish to use server-parsed imagemap files, use
AddHandler imap-file map

# To enable type maps, you might want to use
#AddHandler type-map var

# To enable the perl module (if you have it installed), uncomment
# the following section
#
#Alias /perl/ /home/httpd/perl/
#<Location /perl>
#SetHandler perl-script
#PerlHandler Apache::Registry
#Options +ExecCGI
#</Location>
```

```
# Action lets you define media types that will execute a script
# whenever a matching file is called. This eliminates the need for
# repeated URL pathnames for oft-used CGI file processors.
# Format: Action media/type /cgi-script/location
# Format: Action handler-name /cgi-script/location

# MetaDir: specifies the name of the directory in which Apache can
# find meta information files. These files contain additional HTTP
# headers to include when sending the document

#MetaDir .web

# MetaSuffix: specifies the file name suffix for the file
# containing the meta information.

#MetaSuffix .meta

# Customizable error response (Apache style)
#   these come in three flavors
#
#     1) plain text
#ErrorDocument 500 "The server made a boo boo.
#   n.b.  the (") marks it as text, it does not get output
#
#     2) local redirects
#ErrorDocument 404 /missing.html
#   to redirect to local url /missing.html
#ErrorDocument 404 /cgi-bin/missing_handler.pl
#   n.b. can redirect to a script or a document using
#   server-side-includes.
#
#     3) external redirects
#ErrorDocument 402
http://some.other_server.com/subscription_info.html
#

# mod_mime_magic allows the server to use various hints from the
# file itself to determine its type.
#MimeMagicFile /etc/httpd/conf/magic

# The following directives disable keepalives and HTTP header
# flushes. The first directive disables it for Netscape 2.x and
```

```
# browsers which spoof it. There are known problems with these.
# The second directive is for Microsoft Internet Explorer 4.0b2
# which has a broken HTTP/1.1 implementation and does not properly
# support keepalive when it is used on 301 or 302 (redirect)
# responses.

BrowserMatch "Mozilla/2" nokeepalive
BrowserMatch "MSIE 4\.0b2;" nokeepalive downgrade-1.0
force-response-1.0

# The following directive disables HTTP/1.1 responses to browsers
# which are in violation of the HTTP/1.0 spec by not being able to
# grok a basic 1.1 response.

BrowserMatch "RealPlayer 4\.0" force-response-1.0
BrowserMatch "Java/1\.0" force-response-1.0
BrowserMatch "JDK/1\.0" force-response-1.0
```

Chapter 19

Gopher Server

A Gopher server presents a highly organized way to access Internet resources such as data files or graphics. Unlike FTP, with Gopher you can present users with a menu of items from which they can choose. One menu can lead to another menu or to another Gopher site. In this respect, Gopher is like the Web, allowing you to move from one site to another in search of resources, but it is only like FTP in that the resources are listed. There is no text or graphics to give you explanations. Gopher uses a TCP/IP protocol called the Gopher protocol. It provides for the very fast transmission of Gopher menu files. Gopher information is held in these files, which contain lists of items accessible at certain sites. Each item is organized into five fields specifying the information about the item and where it can be found. The fields are separated by tabs: type, display name, selector string, hostname, and port. The type can be one of several possible Gopher codes, as listed in Table 19-1. The *display name* is a description of the item as it will appear on the Gopher menu. The

File Type	Description
0	Text file
1	Gopher directory
2	CSO phone book server
3	Error
4	BinHex Macintosh file, HQX
5	Binary DOS file
6	Unix UUencoded file
7	Full text index (Gopher menu file)
8	Telnet session, includes the remote host's address
9	Binary file
g	GIF image file
h	HTML file
I	Graphic image file (other than GIF)
M	MIME multipart mixed message
P	Adobe PDF file
s	Sound file
T	TN3270 telnet session

Table 19-1. *Gopher File Types*

selector string is the item's unique identifier. The *hostname* is the hostname of the system where the item is located, and the *port* is the port to use when accessing this host system (usually 70).

Gopher was developed at the University of Minnesota, where it is currently supported—with new versions continually being developed. You can obtain a copy of Gopher from the University of Minnesota Gopher FTP site at **boombox.micro.umn.edu** or from other Linux FTP sites. There is also a GNU Public Licensed Gopher server available called GN Gopher. The University of Minnesota provides the Gopher software free to any educational institution and for noncommercial uses. It does ask a license fee for commercial users or anyone charging a fee for information accessed through a version of their Gopher server. The GN Gopher server is provided freely under the GNU public license to anyone, commercial or not. The University of Minnesota also has a more advanced version of Gopher called Gopher+ that it is currently provided as a commercial product.

You will have to have a data directory for your Gopher data files as well as a user account and group specifically for Gopher access. Although certain distributions such as OpenLinux and Red Hat will have already created the Gopher user, they have not created the data directory. On OpenLinux and Red Hat systems, the data directory for GN Gopher would be **/home/gopher**. To better control access by other Gopher users to your system, you should have a user named **gopher**. OpenLinux and Red Hat will have already created the Gopher user for you. The following is the entry that you will find in your **/etc/passwd** file on your OpenLinux for the Gopher user:

```
gopher:*:13:30:gopher:/home/gopher
```

The asterisk (*) in the password field blocks the account, which prevents any other users from gaining access to it and thereby gaining control over its files or access to other parts of your system. The user ID, 13, is a unique ID. The comment field is "gopher". The login directory is **/home/gopher**. When Gopher users log in to your system, this is the directory they will be placed in.

For other distributions, you will have to create the Gopher account. You can then place restrictions on it to keep any remote Gopher users from accessing any other part of your system. You would also have to modify the entry for this account in your **/etc/passwd** file to prevent normal user access to it by placing an asterisk in the password entry field of the Gopher password.

The group ID is the ID of the **gopher** group, which is set up just for Gopher users. You can set up restrictions on the **gopher** group, thereby restricting any Gopher users. Here is the entry for the **gopher** group that you will find in the **/etc/group** file. For other Linux distributions, if you do not have one, you should add it.

```
gopher::30:
```

The data directory for your Gopher files should be the same as the **home** directory for the Gopher user account. Should you want to use a different directory, change its ownership to that of the Gopher user with the **chown** command. When you configure your Gopher server software, be sure to specify that directory as your Gopher data directory. Otherwise, your server will not be able to find your Gopher files.

The University of Minnesota Gopher

In the following examples, the user has downloaded the University of Minnesota Gopher software package for Linux. Once extracted, the **gopherd** directory will hold your source code for the Gopher server. The **doc** directory has the documentation, including your Man documents. To install the Gopher server, you first specify options in certain configuration files located in the **gopherd** directory. You have to provide information such as the directory where you want to place your Gopher menu files. You then compile the Gopher software. Compiling the software is merely a matter of entering the command **./configure** and then the **make** and **make install** commands in your Gopher source code directory.

Before you create your Gopher server, you have to configure it using entries in the **gopherd.conf** and **gopherdlocal.conf** files (see Table 19-2). In the University of Minnesota Gopher version, these are found in the **gopherd** subdirectory. The **gopherd.conf** file is designed to configure system-specific features such as the number of connections permitted. The **gopherdlocal.conf** file customizes your Gopher server, providing information like the name of the administrator and controlling access by specified remote systems. The **gopherd.conf** and **gopherdlocal.conf** files contain the configuration specifications for your Gopher server. A set of commented default specifications are already listed in the file. You just need to uncomment the ones you want by deleting the **#** at the beginning of the line and then changing any values if you wish. You can set options such as the maximum number of users allowed or the compression method for transmitting files. Options are entered with the option's specification and a colon, followed by a space and the option's value.

You have to specify an alias for the Gopher service on your system. You do this with the **hostalias:** entry. Usually this is just the full hostname of your system, though some systems may identify it with the host part of the name as **gopher**. You may also have to set the full pathname for the **gopherdlocal.conf** file. There is an entry that begins with the **include** command and specifies the location of the **gopherdlocal.conf** file. Usually, the **gopherd** server along with the **gopherd.conf** and **gopherdlocal.conf** files should be installed in the **/usr/sbin** directory. When the **gopherd** server is run, it reads the **gopherd.conf** file for configuration information, which in turn reads the **gopherdlocal.conf** file for specific configuration information. The **include** operation in **gopherd.conf** may need to have the full pathname for **gopherdlocal.conf**, which in this case would be **/usr/sbin/gopherdlocal.conf**.

```
include: /usr/sbin/gopherdlocal.conf
```

The **gopherdlocal.conf** file is designed to hold local customizations (see Table 19-2). Its entries will override comparable entries in the **gopherd.conf** file. In the **gopherdlocal.conf** file, you specify management information such as the name of the system administrator and the description of your Gopher service. There are two entries in the **gopherdlocal.conf** file for the system administrator—**Admin:** and **AdminEmail:**. Use the **Admin:** entry to add the system administrator's name. You can also add other information, such as a phone number. With the **access:** option you can restrict access by other systems. An **access:** entry has the following format:

```
access: hostname permission-list num
```

The hostname is the domain name or IP address of either a network or a remote system. The *num* setting specifies how many users from that network or system can have access at any one time. The permission list sets the permissions for users from that network or system. There are four possible permissions: browse, FTP, read, and search. To turn off a permission, you precede it with an exclamation point (**!**). The browse permission allows users to list files in directories, FTP allows your system to be used as an FTP gateway, read allows access to files, and search allows access to indexes.

For the hostname, you can specify a network address, the address of a particular system, or a default entry that allows access by any system. The default entry uses the keyword **default** for the hostname. In the next example, the Gopher server is open to any user with the read and search permissions enabled, but with the browse and FTP permissions denied. No single network or system can have more than 15 of its users on your Gopher server at one time.

```
access: default  !ftp read search !browse  15
```

To control access from a particular network, you can use an **access:** entry with the network's domain name. In the next example, up to five users from the network **train.com** can access your Gopher server, but they have no browse capability.

```
access: train.com   ftp read search !browse  5
```

Instead of a domain name, you can use an IP address for a network or system. For the network, you specify only the network portion of an IP address. Don't forget to end the address with a period. In the next example, the network with the address **199.189** is denied use of your system as an FTP gateway. Only seven users are allowed on at one time.

```
access: 199.189.   !ftp read search browse  7
```

To provide access by a particular system you enter that system name for the host. In the next example, the system with the IP address of **192.166.1.21** has full access to your Gopher system. If the system is a stand-alone PC used by one person, you could specify that only one user from that system can have access.

```
access: 192.168.1.21 ftp read search browse  1
```

gopherd.conf	Description
hostalias: *DNS-alias-name*	Uses this hostname instead of the system's; hostname must be a valid DNS name; used to reference Gopher servers on a system such as: **gopher.ix.com** **hostalias: gopher.turnip.com**
cachetime: *seconds*	Seconds that a cache file used to cache Gopher directories remains valid.
viewext: *extension Gophertype Prefix Gopher+Type [Language]*	Maps a file name extension onto a particular Gopher type; most of these are already set for you in the **gopherd.conf** file. The first argument is an extension such **.gif**; the second argument is the single-character Gopher type (1, 0, I, etc.); the third argument is a prefix that will be appended to the normal file name path; the fourth argument is the Gopher+ view attribute or Internet Media Type (formerly called MIME Content Types), such as **image/gif**; the optional fifth argument is a language to use for the file instead of the default language: **viewext: .jpg I 9 image/JPEG** **viewext: .html h 0 text/html**
ignore: *extension*	Ignores files with specified extension; these files are not presented to Gopher users: **ignore: bin**
ignore_patt: *regular-expression*	Ignores files that match the regular expression; these files are not presented to Gopher users.
blockext: *extension*	Maps files with specified extension to attribute blocks.

Table 19-2.   *The gopherd.conf and gopherdlocal.conf Entries*

gopherd.conf	Description
decoder: *extension program*	The specified program will be run on files with the indicated extension when the file is retrieved; used with compressed files: **decoder: .gz /usr/gnu/bin/zcat**
pids_directory: *path-name*	A scratch directory to store **pid** files in.
maxconnections: *num*	The number of concurrent connections that the Gopher server can handle at the same time.
gopherdlocal.conf	
admin: *administrator-name-and-info*	The administrator's name and added information such as a phone number
adminemail: *email-address*	E-mail address of Gopher server administrator
site: *site-description*	Descriptive name of the site
loc: *address*	Address of site—street, city, etc.
geog:	Longitude and latitude for site
language: *default-language*	Default language used by the site
secureusers: *filename*	Specifies file listing authorized hosts and networks
bummermsg:	Message displayed when a client is denied access
access: *domain name access-list*	Allows you to determine who can browse directories, read files, and search your system. The first argument is a domain name, IP address, or default; the second argument is a list of comma-separated words determining access; the words are: browse, read, search, and ftp. Each can be preceded by a ! to deny access; **default !browse, read, search, !ftp** sets the default to deny browsing and ftp, but allow reading and searching. If you set the default first, it will be inherited by following entries and you only need to specify the access that differs. Optionally, you can base the access on the number of concurrent transactions in an added argument **access: default browse,read,search,ftp 5**

Table 19-3. *The gopherd.conf and gopherdlocal.conf Entries* (continued)

Before you compile your Gopher server, you should check your **Makefile.config** and **conf.h** files for certain configurations. In the **Makefile.config** file, first check the directory path that the Gopher program expects to operate from. This is assigned to a variable called **PREFIX**. If you want to operate Gopher out of a different directory, modify the default path name that is assigned to the **PREFIX** variable. You should also check the entries for the **DOMAIN**, **SERVERPORT**, **SERVERDATA**, and **SERVEROPTS** variables. The **DOMAIN** variable specifies the network portion of your hostname. For **richlp.ix.com,** the network portion would be **.ix.com**.

The **conf.h** file can be confusing. This is a C program file, not a shell script file. It looks different from other configuration files. In most configuration files, a **#** is a comment, but in the **conf.h** file it is the beginning of a define directive. In **conf.h**, a comment is anything encased by an opening **/*** and a closing ***/**. Such entries are commented out, disabling them. To enable them, you remove the **/*** and ***/** symbols around them.

Though the default entries for the **conf.h** file should work fine, you can change them if you wish. However, be careful when changing entries used for Linux systems. Linux uses any entries not reserved for other systems. If you see an entry preceded by a **#if defined(***system***)**, where system is the name of an operating system, then the following entries only apply to that operating system, until the next **#endif**. Thus, **#if defined(sun)** applies only to Sun systems. There is a large section devoted entirely to the VMS operating system. Most entries that apply to Linux are at the end of the **conf.h** file, with a few at the beginning.

You are now ready to compile your Gopher software. You can compile both the Gopher client and the Gopher server with the following command:

```
# make install
```

To compile just one or the other, use the **make** command with either the term "client" or "server".

```
# make client
# make server
```

This creates a server program called **gopherd**. You can then invoke **gopherd** directly or from **inetd**.

Starting the University of Minnesota Gopher

Before you start your Gopher server, you should first create some Gopher menu files as described in the later section, "Testing the Gopher Server." You may recall that you can start the Gopher server from the command line, or at boot time automatically using an **init** script, or through **inetd** when a request for the Gopher service is received.

Certain distributions such as OpenLinux may have already configured your system to run Gopher through **inetd**. This configuration expects to locate the Gopher data directory in **/home/gopher**. In the **/etc/services** file you will find an entry for Gopher, as shown here. It specifies the name of the service with the port number and the protocol. On other distributions, you may have to enter it.

```
gopher   70/tcp
```

On OpenLinux, there is already an entry for Gopher in the **/etc/inetd.conf** file. The entry currently references the GN Gopher server, **gn**. You will have to modify it for the **gopherd** server. In place of the entry for **gn**, you enter **gopherd** with the **-I** option and the path name for the Gopher data directory. The **-I** option specifies that **gopherd** is to be called with **inetd**. You can also add the port number, in this case, 70. This entry is also set up to use the **tcpd** to monitor and control access by remote users. Your entry should look like the following example. The Gopher data files are in **/home/gopher**, and the port is 70. The arguments, including the name of the **gopherd** program, are **gopherd -I /home/gopher 70**.

```
gopher stream tcp nowait root  /usr/sbin/tcpd  gopherd -I
/home/gopher 70
```

Should you not want to use **tcpd**, you can replace it with the pathname for the **gopherd** server program.

```
gopher stream tcp nowait root  /usr/sbin/gopherd gopherd -I
/home/gopher 70
```

If you want to start the **gopherd** server on the command line, you enter **gopherd** and as its arguments the path name of the directory for the Gopher data files and the port number. The **gopherd** program has several possible options. As a precaution you can use the **-u** option to specify an owner other than root to run **gopherd**. You have to first create the user and enter a * in the password field of its **passwd** entry. The user's **home** directory will be the **gopher** data directory. A user called **gopher** may have already been created by your distribution. In the following example, the full pathname for the **gopherd** server program is **/usr/sbin/gopherd**, the Gopher data files are in **/home/gopher**, and the port is 70.

```
/usr/sbin/gopherd -u gopher /home/gopher 70
```

SERVERS

To have the Gopher server start automatically whenever you boot, you can create an **init** script for it in the **/etc/rc.d/init.d** directory. The section on **init** scripts at the beginning of this chapter provides a detailed description on how to do this for the **gopherd** server.

GN Gopher Server

To begin, you download the GN Gopher server from its Web site or from **boombox.micro.umn.edu**. Check GN gopher's entry in the GNU Web page at **www.gnu.org** for a link to its Web site. The GN Gopher package contains source code that you need to configure for Linux before you compile it. There is one configuration file, **config.h**, and a **Makefile** that holds compiler directives. The **INSTALL** file in the **docs** subdirectory has detailed instructions on how to create your GN server, as well as setting up a Gopher site. The **docs/examples** directory has numerous examples of GN Gopher menus.

To configure the GN Gopher server, you modify entries in the **config.h** file and the **Makefile**. There are certain entries that are compulsory, that you have to specify. These are clearly indicated at the beginning of the file with the heading "Compulsory items to fill in." You have to enter your hostname and the pathname of the Gopher data directory, as well as specify that you are using a Linux system. You can make any other customizations you want. An entry in the **config.h** file has the format of a **#define** term followed by the item and then the value you want for it. You can change the value, not the item. The following entries are valid for the OpenLinux distribution of Linux. In place of the hostname **garnet.train.com**, you should have your own system's hostname.

```
#define GN_HOSTNAME      "garnet.train.com"
#define ROOT_DIR   "/home/gopher"
#define LINUX
#define MAINTAINER      "mailto:justin@garnet.train.com"
#define ROOT_MENU_NAME  "GN --  A Gopher/HTTP Server"
#define GN_LOGFILE  "/var/log/gn.log"        /* "/path/to/gn.log" */
#define MIME_TYPE_FILE  "/usr/local/gn_mime.types"
#define WAISGN  "/usr/sbin/waisgn"
```

Following the compulsory items, there are several other items that you also change if you wish, though the defaults should work fine. Should you want to use a different port you can specify it in the **DEFAULTPORT** entry. You can set the timeout with the **TIMEOUT** entry and set the maximum depth of menu searches in the **MAXDEPTH** entry (see Table 19-3). In the **Makefile**, you have to specify the type of C compiler you are using and the directories where you want your server program placed. You will find two entries for the **CC**, which designates the type of C compiler to use. The one specifying **gcc** will be commented out with a preceding **#**. The one for **cc** will not. You have to comment the **cc** entry by placing a **#** before it and remove the **#** from the **gcc** entry. This sets the **CC** entry to the **gcc** compiler. Also, in the **Makefile** you can set **SERVERBINDIR**, which holds the directory path where you want to place the server program. **BINDIR** is the directory for the **mkcache** an **uncache** programs. Set these to the directories where you want those programs placed, such as **/usr/sbin**. On OpenLinux and Red Hat distributions, the **SERVERFINDER** directory should be set to **/usr/sbin**, the directory that holds daemons. Though the **mkcache** and **uncache** programs can go anywhere, it may be best to also place them together with the GN server by also setting **BINDIR** to **/usr/sbin**.

Just below these variables, you will find the following entry for **include** directories. Uncomment the one for Linux by removing the preceding **#** so that it reads

```
# INCLUDES= -I.. -I../gn
# For Linux use
INCLUDES= -I.. -I../gn -I/usr/include/bsd
```

Further down in the **Makefile** you will find an empty entry for the libraries as shown here:

```
#     Libraries to be included.
LIBS    =
```

Following this entry will be comments specifying libraries for different systems. The Linux specification will look like this:

```
#For Linux use
#LIBS = -lbsd
```

You can either uncomment this **LIBS** entry by removing the preceding **#**, or type in the **-lbsd** value in the prior empty **LIBS** entry.

```
LIBS = -lbsd
```

Once configured, you can then create the server by entering **make**. This creates two executable server programs called **sgn** and **gn**. The **gn** program is for use with **inetd**, while **sgn** is the standalone daemon that you can run directly. It also creates two utility programs, **mkcache** and **uncache**. Then, enter **make install** to install these programs on your system.

GN Server config File	Description
GN_HOSTNAME	Sets the hostname for your server; this is the hostname of your system.
ROOT_DIR	Sets the Gopher data directory; for OpenLinux. This is **/home/gopher**.
LINUX	Defines Linux as your operating system; the default here will be SUN_OS; you have to replace it with LINUX.
MAINTAINER	Mail address of administrator.
ROOT_MENU_NAME	Name you want displayed as the title of your Gopher menu; default is "GN — A Gopher/HTTP Server."
GN_LOGFILE	Location for a GN log file.
MIME_TYPE_FILE	Location of MIME configuration file; default is **/usr/local/gn_mime.types**; you place this file anywhere, but be sure to set this pathname accordingly.
WAISGN	Pathname of the **waisgn** program that handles WAIS indexes **/usr/sbin/waisgn**.
DEFAULTPORT	Sets the default port for Gopher access, currently 70.
TIMEOUT	Sets the timeout waiting for requests.
MAXDEPTH	Sets the maximum depth of menu searches.
USERID	The user ID that the GN server will be run as for security purposes.
GROUPID	The group ID that the GN server will be run as for security purposes.
DECOMPRESS	Program used to decompress files; default is **/usr/local/bin/zcat**.
MENUFNAME	Sets the name used for menu files; the default is **menu**.

Table 19-3. *The GN Server config and Makefile File*

GN Server config File	Description
TEMPDIR	Sets the temporary directory; default is **/tmp**.
GN Server Makefile	
CC	Sets the C compiler; default setting is **cc**; you have to change it to **gcc**; **CC = gcc**.
INCLUDE	Sets Include directories; should be set to use **/usr/include/bsd**.
SERVBINDIR	Directory for your GN and SGN server programs; default is **../bin**; should be set to **/usr/sbin**.
BINDIR	Directory for cache support programs; default is **../b**; should be set to **/usr/sbin**.
LIBS=	Sets the library used; uncomment the one for Linux by removing **#**; should be set to **−lbsd**.

Table 19-3.   *The GN Server config and Makefile File* (continued)

Starting the GN Gopher Server

You are now ready to start the server. However, before you start your Gopher
server you should first create some Gopher menu files as described in the next section
"Testing the Gopher Server." You can either run the server as a standalone daemon or
through **inetd**. The OpenLinux and Red Hat distributions will have already configured
your system to run the GN Gopher server through **inetd**. After creating and installing
the GN Gopher server, all you have to do to have a fully functioning Gopher server is
create your Gopher data files and place them in the **/home/gopher** directory. To use
inetd, there have to be entries for the Gopher server in the **/etc/services** and
/etc/inetd.conf files. OpenLinux has already placed those entries. You will find the
following entry in the **/etc/services** file:

```
gopher 70/tcp
```

In the **/etc/inetd.conf** file, you will find the following entry for the GN Gopher
server. Notice that the GN Gopher server is invoked with **gn**. This is the version of

the GN server that works through **inetd**. Also, **tcpd** is used to monitor and control Gopher access.

```
gopher stream tcp nowait root /usr/sbin/tcpd  gn
```

You can also start the GN Gopher at boot time with an **init** script or directly from the command line. In both cases, the server has to be run as a standalone daemon using the **sgn** version of the GN Gopher. If you want to start Gopher at boot time, you have to create an **init** script for it in the **/etc/rc.d/init.d** directory, as described in a previous section, "Starting Servers." You enter **sgn** with arguments specifying the pathname of the directory for the Gopher data files and the port number (usually 70). The port number is specified with the **-p** option. As a precaution **sgn** will automatically run as the user specified in the **USERID** entry in the **config.h** file.

```
sgn -p 70 /home/gopher
```

Testing the Gopher Server

Once your Gopher server is running, you can test it using either telnet or a Gopher client. Add Gopher files and menus to the **/home/gopher** directory, and, for GN gopher, be sure to run **mkcache** to make your Gopher files accessible to Gopher clients. With telnet, you telnet into your own system specifying the port used for Gopher. The following command tests a Gopher server on the **garnet.train.com** system. Startup messages will be displayed.

```
telnet garnet.train.com 70
```

If you then press ENTER, the menu items for the main Gopher directory on your server will be displayed, output in the following format:

```
type display-name  selector  hostname  port
```

Here is an example of a test of a Gopher server:

```
# telnet garnet.train.com 70
Trying 127.0.0.1...
Connected to garnet.train.com.
Escape character is '^]'.
```

```
0About My Weather Site  0/intro      garnet.train.com   70    +
1California Weather Information    1/calif    garnet.train.com
70    +
1New York Weather this week    1/newyork    garnet.train.com    70
+
1The Weather in Hawaii    1/weather/hawaii/    garnet.train.com
70
```

You can also use your Gopher client to access your own Gopher server. In the next example, the Gopher client on **garnet.train.com** is used to access the Gopher server on the same system. The main Gopher menu for the Gopher server will be displayed and the user can then select and access items.

```
gopher garnet.train.com
```

Gopher Directories: .cap and .links Files

A Gopher menu that you see displayed when you access a Gopher site is generated using special files contained within a Gopher directory. Gopher menus are designed to operate by directory, listing the different files available within a directory or referencing another directory. Special Gopher menu configuration files within each directory provide information about the different data files available and how to access them. The University of Minnesota Gopher server uses **.cap** directories and link files to organize Gopher menus. The GN Gopher server uses a **menu** and a **.cache** file. However, the entries for the link and GN menu files are much the same.

By default, any files and subdirectories in a Gopher directory are automatically displayed in a Gopher menu in alphabetical order. Data files are given a type 0, and directories a type 1. The name used for each menu item is the name of the file or directory. You can override this listing by using **.cap** files.

Your Gopher data files can have any name you wish to give them. However, Gopher files are usually described in a Gopher menu using a descriptive sentence. By selecting that menu item, the file associated with that sentence is selected. The association between this descriptive sentence and the Gopher data file is carried out either by special files in a **.cap** directory or by entries in an extended link file.

Each directory of Gopher data files can have its own **.cap** directory, which holds files of the same name as those in the Gopher data directory. If you have a Gopher data file called **engine.1**, there will be a file in the **.cap** directory also called **engine.1**. A file in the **.cap** directory contains three entries: **Name**, **Type**, and **Numb**. **Name** is assigned the descriptive sentence used for the menu item that references the Gopher data file. The **Type** entry specifies the type of Gopher resource: 1 is a directory and 0 is a text file.

SERVERS

The **Numb** entry is assigned the number of your Gopher entry in the Gopher menu; for example, **Numb=3** indicates that this is the third item in the Gopher menu.)

```
.cap/engine.1
```

```
Name=The best engine in the world
Type=0
Numb=1
```

When displayed on the Gopher menu, this entry will appear as the first entry. Selecting it will select the **engine.1** Gopher data file.

```
1. The best engine in the world.
```

Although **.cap** files can be used to reference data files in your directory, they do not reference files in other directories or at other Gopher sites. For this, you use a link entry in a link file. A *link file* is any file beginning with a period. There is one link file in a directory that has several link entries to different Gopher resources. A common name for a link file is **.links**.

Each entry for a link has five variables set: **Name**, **Port**, **Type**, **Path**, and **Host**. You can also add an entry for the menu order, **NUMB**. The **Name** entry is the descriptive sentence used in the menu item. The **Port** is the port used for connection to a remote system and is usually set to 70. The **Type** is the type of resource that the menu item references. A resource could be a file, but it can also be a telnet session or a graphics file. Gopher can reference files other than data files. The **Path** variable holds the path name for the resource that the menu item references. The pathname here is the path starting from the Gopher data directory. The directory **/home/gopher/calif** would have a path name of **/calif**, where **/home/gopher** is the Gopher data directory. The path name can also be preceded by the **Type**. The **calif** directory could be entered as **1/calif**, 1 being the type for a directory. **Host** holds the hostname where the resource is to be found. For your own system, this will be your own hostname. If the resource is located on another system, it will have that system's hostname. A **+** sign for the **Port** and **Host** entries will indicate the current port and hostname. For files and directories on your own system, it is best to leave out the **Port** and **Host** name entries.

```
.links
```

```
Name=The best engine in the world
Type=1
Port=70
Path=1/engines
Host=richlp.ix.com
```

You may also use links to set up FTP or WAIS connections to other systems to access files or information from them. In this case, the service you are using and its arguments are specified in the **Path** entry. Both **Host** and **Port** have a **+** entry. The format for an FTP link is shown here:

```
Name=ftp-file-or-directory
Type=1
Path=ftp:hostname/path/
Host=+
Port=+
```

For example, to set up an FTP link to access the file **caboose1** on **chris.train.com**, you would set the path as shown in the following example. The current port and hostname are indicated by **+** for their entries.

```
Name=The last caboose
Type=0
Port=+
Path=ftp:pango1.train.com/usr/lib/gopher-data/caboose1
Host=+
```

For a WAIS link, you can access WAIS resources on your own system or on a remote system. For your own system, you use **waisrc:** followed by the path to the WAIS resource. For a remote system, you include the hostname after **waisrc:**. For example:

```
waisrc:pango1.train.com/usr/wais/data.
```

You can also set up a link to execute shell scripts, rather than just accessing a resource. In this case the **Path** variable is set to **exec:** followed by the script arguments and name. The arguments are enclosed in double quotes, ", and if there are none you just use an empty set of quotes. The argument and script are separated by a colon,

```
Path=exec:"arguments":script
```

Instead of maintaining separate **.cap** files in each directory along with a separate link file, you can use an extended link file to hold both the local file entries and the link entries. A common name for a link file is **.names**. The **.names** file would list each **Name** and **Numb** entry along with a Path entry to specify the location of the file. The **.names** file also has an **Abstract** entry that allows you to enter a brief description of the file's contents. In the **.names** file shown here, the first entry references a local file in the directory, whereas the second entry references a remote Gopher site.

```
.names


Path=/engines
Name=The best engine in the world
Numb=1
Abstract=A discussion of the best steam engine ever built.
Name=The oldest train running
Type=1
Port=70
Path=1/museums
Host=pango1.train.com
```

GN Gopher Directories: menu and .cache files

GN Gopher directories place their menu entries in a file called **menu**. Each Gopher directory will have its own **menu** file with the entries for each menu item. GN Gopher uses the same set of entries as described for the University of Minnesota Gopher, with a few exceptions. Within the **menu** file, you list the **Path**, **Name**, **Numb**, and **Abstract** for each menu item. However, before the pathname in the **Path** entry, you have to specify the Gopher type. This is usually a one-digit number such as 0 for text files and 1 for directories.

```
Name=About My Weather Site
Path=0/intro
Type=0
Numb=1
Abstract=Important Weather Information.
```

GN Gopher requires the creation of a **.cache** file for each directory. You make a **.cache** file by executing the **mkcache** program within that directory. You can do this to each **gopher** directory, or just execute **mkcache** with the **-r** option from the main **gopher-data** directory. The **mkcache -r** command will make the **.cache** files for the current directory and any of its nested subdirectories. You can run **mkcache -r** from your **/home/gopher** directory to create **.cache** files for all your Gopher directories.

The Complete Reference

Linux

Chapter 20

Domain Name System

The Domain Name System is an Internet service that converts domain names into their corresponding IP addresses. Recall that all computers connected to the Internet are using an Internet Protocol (IP) address. This consists of a number composed of four components separated by periods. The first three are the computer's network address and the last is the computer's host ID. For example, in the address 192.168.1.2, 192.168.1 is the network address and 2 is the computer's host ID within that network. Together they make up an IP address with which the computer can be addressed from anywhere on the Internet. IP addresses, though, are difficult to remember and easy to get wrong. Early on, IP addresses were associated with corresponding names called fully qualified domain names. A fully qualified domain name is composed of three or more segments, the first being the name to identify the host and the remaining for the network the host is in. The network segment of a fully qualified domain name is usually referred to simply as the domain name, and the host part is referred to as the hostname (though this is also used to refer to the complete fully qualified domain name). In effect, subnets are referred to as domains. The fully qualified domain name **www.linux.org** has an IP address 198.182.196.56 where 198.182.196 is the network address and 56 is the host ID. Computers can only be accessed with an IP address. So a fully qualified domain name first has to be translated into its corresponding IP address to be of any use.

Any computer on the Internet can maintain a file that manually associates IP addresses with domain names. On Linux and Unix systems, this file is called the **/etc/hosts** file. Here, you can enter the IP address and domain names of computers you commonly access. However, using this method, each computer would need a complete listing of all other computers on the Internet, and that listing would have to be updated constantly. Early on this became clearly impractical for the Internet, though it is still feasible for small isolated networks. The Domain Name System has been implemented to deal with the task of translating the domain name of any computer on the Internet to its IP address. The task is carried out by interconnecting domain name servers that keep lists of fully qualified domain names and their IP addresses. The Internet is composed of many connected subnets called *domains*, each with its own servers—such as mail servers. Each subnet also has its own domain name servers that keep track of all the fully qualified domain names and IP addresses for all the computers on their network. Domain name servers are hierarchically linked to root servers that in turn connect to other root servers and the domain name servers on their subnets throughout the Internet. The section of a network that a given domain name server is responsible for is called a *zone*. Though a zone may correspond to a domain, there may, in fact, be many zones within a domain, each with its own name server. This is true for very large domains where there are too many systems for one name server to manage.

When a user enters a fully qualified domain name to access a remote system, a resolver program will query the local network's domain name server requesting the corresponding IP address for that remote system. The names of the domain name servers that service a host's network are kept in the host's **/etc/resolv.conf** file.

If you are setting up a domain name server for a local area network that is not connected to the Internet, you should use a special set of IP numbers reserved for such non-Internet networks (also known as intranets). This is especially true if you are implementing IP masquerading, where only a gateway machine has an Internet address, and the others make use of that one address to connect to the Internet. These are numbers that belong with the special network number 192.168., as used in these examples. If you are setting up a local area network such as a small business or home network, you are free to use these numbers for your local machines. You can set up an intranet using network cards such as Ethernet cards and Ethernet hubs, then configure your machines with IP addresses starting from 192.168.1.1. The host segment can go up to 256. If you have three machines on your home network, you could give them the addresses 192.168.1.1, 192.168.1.2, 192.168.1.3. You can then set up Domain Name Service for your network by running a domain name server on one of the machines. This machine becomes your network's domain name server. You can then give your machines fully qualified domain names and configure your domain name server to translate the names to their corresponding IP addresses. For example, you could give the machine 192.168.1.1 the name **turtle.mytrek.com**, and the machine 192.168.1.2 the name **rabbit.mytrek.com**. You can also implement Internet services on your network such as FTP, Web, and mail services by setting up servers for them on your machines. You can then configure your domain name server to let users access those services using fully qualified domain names. For example, for **mytrek.com** network, the Web server could be accessed using the name **www.mytrek.com**. Instead of a domain name service, you could have the **/etc/host**s files in each machine contain the entire list of IP addresses and domain names for all the machines in your network. But for any changes, you would have to update each machine's **/etc/hosts** file.

BIND

The domain name server software currently in use on Linux systems is Berkeley Internet Name Domain (BIND). BIND was originally developed at UC Berkeley and is currently maintained and supported by the Internet Software Consortium (ISC). You can obtain BIND documentation and current software releases from their Web site at **www.isc.org**. The site includes online Web page documentation and manuals, including the BIND Operations Guide (BOG). RPM packages are available at both Caldera and Red Hat FTP sites. The BIND directory in **/usr/doc** contains extensive documentation, including Web page manuals and examples. The Linux HOW-TO for the Domain Name Service DNS-HOWTO, provides detailed examples. Documentation, news, and DNS tools can be obtained from the DNS Resource Directory at **www.dns.net/dnsrd**.

The BIND domain name server software consists of a name server daemon called **named**, several sample configuration files, and resolver libraries. As of 1998, a new version of BIND beginning with the series number 8.x implemented a new configuration file using a new syntax. Older versions, which begin with the number 4.x, use a different configuration file with an older syntax. In effect, there are now two versions in use with different configuration files. All Linux distributions currently install the newer 8.x version of BIND.

The name of the BIND name server daemon is **named**. To operate your machine as a name server, you simply run the **named** daemon with the appropriate configuration. The **named** daemon will listen for resolution requests and provide the correct IP address for the requested hostname. You can use the **ndc** utility provided with BIND to start, stop, restart, and check the status of the server as you test its configuration. **ndc** with the **stop** command will stop **named**, and with the **start** command will start it up again, reading your **named.conf** file. **ndc** with the **help** command will provide a list of all **ndc** commands. Once your name server is running, you can test it using the **nslookup** utility to query a name server, providing information about hosts and domains. If you start it with no arguments, it enters an interactive mode where you can issue different **nslookup** commands to refine your queries. Numerous other DNS tools are also available such as Dig and host. Check the DNS Resource Directory at **www.dns.net/dnsrd** for a listing.

On Red Hat and OpenLinux systems, the **named** daemon is started using a startup script in the **/etc/rc.d/init.d** directory called **named**. You can use this script to start and stop the daemon using the **stop** and **start** arguments. The **named** runs as a standalone daemon, constantly running. If you don't want it to run, you can use the System V Runlevel Editor, COAS, or Linuxconf to change its status.

Domain Name System Configuration

You configure a domain name server using a configuration file, several zone files, and a cache file. The part of a network that the name server is responsible for is called a *zone*. A zone is not the same as a domain in that in a very large domain you could have several zones, each with its own name server. You could also have one name server service several zones. In this case, each zone would have its own zone file. The zone files hold resource records that provide hostname and IP address associations for computers on the network that the domain name server is responsible for. There are zone files for the server's network and the local machine. In addition there is also a cache file that lists the root servers your domain server connects to.

As an alternative to manually making entries in the configuration files, you can use the Linuxconf domain name server configuration panels. You can use the **dnsconf** command to start up Linuxconf to perform just the domain name configuration tasks. This command will display a window with buttons for the different domain name server configuration panels. If you use the main Linuxconf window, select the "Domain Name Server" entry in the Servers Tasks list located under Networking. Linuxconf provides panels for primary (master), secondary (slave), reverse mapping, and fowarder zone entries. You can also configure features such as access control and logging. When you have finished configuration, Linuxconf will generate new **named.conf** and zone files. Use the "domain" panel to create zone files, and the "IP reverse mapping" panel to create corresponding reverse mapping zone files. In this panel, be sure to use only the network part of the IP address for the network number. Figure 20-1 shows the domain name server panel.

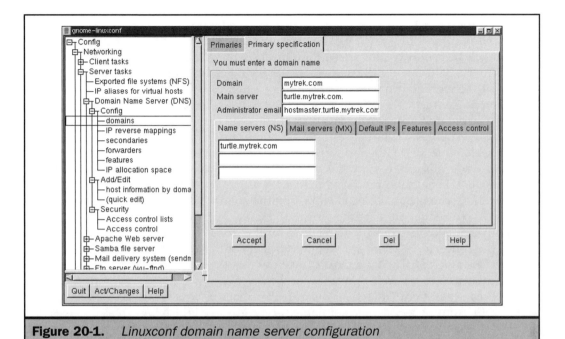

Figure 20-1.   *Linuxconf domain name server configuration*

named.conf

The configuration file for the **named** daemon is **named.conf**, located in the **/etc** directory. It uses a flexible syntax similar to C programs. The format enables easy configuration of selected zones, enabling features such as access control lists and categorized logging. The **named.conf** file consists of BIND configuration commands with attached blocks within which specific options are listed. A configuration command is followed by arguments and a block that is delimited with braces. Within the block are lines of option and feature entries. Each entry is terminated with a semicolon. Comments can use the C, C++, or Shell/Perl syntax: enclosing **/* */**, preceding **//**, or preceding **#**. The following example shows a **zone** command followed by the zone name and a block of options that begin with an opening brace, **{**. Each option entry ends with a semicolon. The entire block ends with a closing brace also followed by a semicolon.

```
// a caching only nameserver config
//
zone "." {
     type hint;
     file "named.ca";
};
```

The **named.conf** file is a new feature implemented with BIND version 8.*x*. The older BIND 4.*x* versions use a file called **named.boot**. This file is no longer used by version 8.*x*. The syntax used in these configuration files differs radically. If you upgrade to 8.*x*, you can use the **named-bootconf.pl** Perl script provided with the BIND software to convert your **named.boot** file to a **named.conf** file.

The **zone** command is used to specify the domains that the name server will service. You enter the keyword **zone** followed by the name of the domain placed within double quotes. Do not place a period at the end of the domain name. In the following example, there is a period within the domain name but not at the end, **"mytrek.com"**. This differs from the zone file, which requires a period at the end of a complete domain name. After the zone name, you can specify its class. By default this is the Internet whose class name is *in*. Within the zone block, you can place several options. Two essential ones are the type and the file. The **file** option is used to specify the name of the zone file to be used for this zone. The types entry is used to specify the zone's type. There are several types of zones to choose from: *master, slave, stub, forward,* and *hint*. The type master specifies that the zone holds master information and is authorized to act on it. A master server was called a primary server in the older 4.*x* BIND configuration. The type slave indicates that the zone needs to update its data periodically from a specified master name server. A slave is also known as a *secondary server*. You use this entry if your name server is operating as a secondary server for another primary (master) domain name server. A stub zone only copies other name server entries, instead of the entire zone. A forward zone will direct all queries to a specified name server. A hint zone specifies the set of root name servers used by all Internet domain name servers. You can also specify several options that will override any global options set with the **options** command. The following example shows a simple **zone** command for the **mytrek.com** domain. Its class is Internet, *in*, and type is *master*. The name of its zone file is usually the same as the zone name, in this case, **"mytrek.com"**.

```
zone "mytrek.com" in {
        type master;
        file "mytrek.com";
};
```

Other commands, such as **server**, **control**, **key**, and **logging**, let you configure different features for your name server. The **server** statement defines the characteristics to be associated with a remote name server, such as the transfer method and key ID for transaction security. The **control** statement defines special control channels. The **key** statement defines a key ID to be used in a **server** statement that associates an authentication method with a particular name server. The **logging** statement is used to configure logging options for the name server, such as the maximum size of the log file and a severity level for messages. To control access by other hosts, you use the **acl** command. The **allow** and **deny** options with access control host lists let you deny or allow access by specified hosts to the name server. Table 20-1 lists the BIND commands.

The **options** statement defines global options and can be used only once in the configuration file. There are an extensive number of options that cover such components as forwarding, name checking, directory path names, access control, and zone transfers, among others. A complete listing can be found in the BIND documentation. A critically important option found in most configuration files is the **directory** option, which holds the location of the name server's zone and cache files on your system. The following example is taken from the Red Hat **/etc/named.conf** file. It specifies that the zone files are located in the **/var/named** directory. In this directory, you will find your zone files and including those used for your local system.

```
options {
        directory "/var/named";
};
```

The following example is a simple **named.conf** file based on the example provided in the BIND documentation. It shows samples of several of the configuration commands. The file begins with comments using C++ syntax, **//**. The **options** command has a directory entry that sets the directory for the zone and cache files to **/var/named**. Here, you find your zone files such as **named.local** and reverse mapping files, along with the cache file, **named.ca**. The first **zone** command defines a zone for the **mytrek.com** domain. Its type is master and its zone file is named **"mytrek.com"**. The next zone is used for reverse IP mapping of the previous zone. Its name is made up of a reverse listing of the **mytrek.com** domain's IP address with the term **in-addr.arpa** appended. The domain address for **mytrek.com** is 192.168.1, so the reverse is 1.168.192. The **in-addr.arpa** domain is a special domain that supports gateway location and Internet address to host mapping. The next **zone** command defines a hint zone specifying the root name servers. The cache file listing these servers is **named.ca**. The second **zone** command defines a zone for the loopback interface, the method used by the system to address itself and allow communication between local users on the system. The zone file used for this local zone is **named.local**.

named.conf

```
//
// A simple BIND 8 configuration
//

logging {
        category cname { null; };
};
```

```
options {
   directory "/var/named";
   };
};

zone "." {
   type hint;
   file "named.ca";
};

zone "mytrek.com"{
   type master;
   file "mytrek.com";
   notify no;
};

zone "0.0.127.in-addr.arpa"{
   type master;
   file "named.local";
};

zone "1.168.192.IN-ADDR.ARPA"{
   type master;
   file "192.168.1";
   notify yes;
};
```

When BIND is initially installed it creates a default configuration for what is known as a *caching only server*. A caching only server will copy queries made by users and save them in a cache, for use later if the queries are repeated. This can save DNS lookup response times. The cache is held in memory and only lasts as long as **named** runs. The following example is the **named.conf** file initially installed for a caching only server. Only the local and cache zones are defined.

named.conf (caching only server)

```
// generated by named-bootconf.pl

options {
```

```
    directory "/var/named";
};

//
// a caching only nameserver config
//
zone "." {
    type hint;
    file "named.ca";
};

zone "0.0.127.in-addr.arpa" {
    type master;
    file "named.local";
};
```

Commands	Description
/* comment */	BIND comment in C syntax
// comment	BIND comment in C++ syntax
# comment	BIND comment in Unix shell and Perl syntax
acl	Defines a named IP address matching list
include	Includes a file
key	Specifies key information for use in authentication and authorization
logging	Specifies what the server logs, and where the log messages are sent
options	Global server configuration options and defaults for other statements
control	Declares control channels to be used by the ndc utility
server	Sets certain configuration options for the specified server basis
trusted-keys	Defines DNSSEC keys that are preconfigured into the server and implicitly trusted
zone	Defines a zone

Table 20-1.   *BIND Configuration Commands*

Resource Records

Your name server holds domain name information about the hosts on your network in resource records placed in zone and reverse mapping files. Resource records are used to associate IP addresses with fully qualified domain names. You need a record for every computer in the zone that the name server services. A record takes up one line, though you can use parentheses to use several lines for a record, as is the case usually with SOA records. A resource record uses the Standard Resource Record Format as shown here:

```
name [<ttl>] [<class>] <type> <rdata> [<comment>]
```

The name for this record is *name*. It can be a domain name for a fully qualified domain name. If you just specify the hostname, the default domain is appended. If there is no name entry, then the last specific name is used. If the **@** symbol is used then the name server's domain name is used. The **ttl** (time to live) is an optional entry that specifies how long the record will be cached. The class of the record is *class*. The class used in most resource record entries is IN, for Internet. By default it is the same as that specified for the domain in the **named.conf** file. Likewise, *type* is the type of the record, and *rdata* is the resource record data. The following is an example of a resource record entry. The name is **rabbit.mytrek.com**, the type is Internet (IN), its type is a host address record (A), and the data is the IP address 192.168.1.2.

```
rabbit.mytrek.com   IN   A      192.168.1.2
```

There are different types of resource records for different kinds of hosts and name server operations. See Table 20-2 (at the end of this section) for a listing of resource record types. A, NS, MX, PTR, and CNAME are the ones commonly used. A is used for host address records that match domain names with IP addresses. NS is used to reference a name server. MX specifies the host address of the mail server that services this zone. The name server will have mail messages sent to that host. The PTR type is used for records that point to other resource records. This is used for reverse mapping. CNAME is used to identify an alias for a host on your system.

A zone and reverse mapping files always begin with a special resource record called the *Start Of Authority record (SOA)*. This record specifies that all the following records are authoritative for this domain. It also holds information about the name server's domain, which is to be given to other name servers. An SOA record has the same format as other resource records, though its data segment is arranged differently. The format for an SOA record follows:

```
name   {ttl}   class   SOA Origin   Person-in-charge (
                                          Serial
                                          Refresh
                                          Retry
                                          Expire
                                          Minimum )
```

Each zone has its own SOA record. The SOA begins with the zone name specified in the **named.conf** zone entry. This is usually a domain name. An **@** symbol is usually used for the name. It acts like a macro expanding to the domain name. The class is usually the Internet class, IN. SOA is the type. *Origin* is the machine that is the origin of the records, usually the machine running your name server daemon. The *Person-in-charge* is the e-mail address for the person managing the name server (use dots, not **@**, for the e-mail address). Several configuration entries are placed in a block delimited with braces. The first is the serial number. You change it when you add or change records so they will be updated by other servers. *Refresh* specifies the time interval for refreshing SOA information. *Retry* is the frequency for trying to contact an authoritative server. *Expire* is the length of time a secondary name server keeps information about a zone without updating it. *Minimum* is the length of time records in a zone will live. The times are specified in the number of seconds. The following example shows an SOA record. The machine running the name server is **turtle.mytrek.com** and the e-mail address of the person responsible for the server is **hostmaster@turtle.mytrek.com**. Notice the periods at the end of these names. For names with no periods, the domain name is appended. For example, **turtle** would be the same as **turtle.mytrek.com**. When entering full hostnames, be sure to add the period so the domain is not appended.

```
@       IN      SOA     turtle.mytrek.com. hostmaster.turtle.mytrek.com.
(
                                1997022700 ; Serial
                                28800      ; Refresh
                                14400      ; Retry
                                3600000    ; Expire
                                86400 )    ; Minimum
```

The name server record specifies the name of the name server for this zone. These have a resource record type of NS. If you have more than one name server, list them in NS records. These records usually follow the SOA record. As they usually apply to the same domain as the SOA record, their name field is often left blank to inherit the server's domain name specified by the @ symbol in the previous SOA record.

```
IN          NS   turtle.mytrek.com.
```

Resource records of type A are address records that associate a fully qualified domain name with an IP address. Often, only their hostname is specified. Any domain names without a terminating period will automatically have the domain appended to it. Given the domain **mytrek.com**, the turtle name in the following example will be expanded to **turtle.mytrek.com**.

```
rabbit.mytrek.com   IN   A   192.168.1.2
turtle              IN   A   192.168.1.1
```

Resource records of type MX specify mail exchangers used for this host. The mail exchanger is the machine to which mail for the host is sent. In the following example, mail for **turtle.mytrek.com** is also sent to **turtle.mytrek.com**, but mail for **rabbit.mytrek.com** is sent to **turtle.mytrek.com**. An MX record recognizes an additional field that specifies the ranking for a mail exchanger. You can list several mail exchangers for a host with different rankings where the smaller number has a higher ranking. This way if mail cannot reach the first mail exchanger, it can be routed to an alternate exchanger to reach the host.

```
turtle.mytrek.com   IN                192.168.1.1
                    IN   MX   10       turtle.mytrek.com.
rabbit.mytrek.com   IN   A            192.168.1.2
                    IN   MX   10       turtle.mytrek.com.
```

Resource records of type CNAME are used to specify alias names for a host in the zone. Aliases are often used for machines running several different types of servers such as both Web and FTP servers. They are also used to locate a host when it changes its name. The old name becomes an alias for the new name. In the following example, **ftp.mytrek.com** is an alias for a machine actually called **turtle.mytrek.com**.

```
ftp.mytrek.com      IN          CNAME   turtle.mytrek.com.
```

A more stable way to implement aliases is to simply create another address record for it. You can have as many hostnames for the same IP address as you wish, provided they are certified. For example, to make **www.mytrek.com** an alias for **turtle.mytrek.com**, you just have to add another address record for it, giving it the same IP address as **turtle.mytrek.com**.

```
turtle.mytrek.com    IN    A    192.168.1.1
www.mytrek.com       IN    A    192.168.1.1
```

A PTR record is used to perform reverse mapping from an IP address to a host. They are used in the reverse mapping files. The name entry holds a reversed IP address and the data entry holds the name of the host. The following example maps the IP address 192.168.1.1 to **turtle.mytrek.com**:

```
1.1.168.192    IN    PTR    turtle.mytrek.com.
```

The HINFO, RP, MINFO, and TXT records are used to provide information about the host. The RP record lets you specify the person responsible for a certain host. The HINFO record provides basic hardware and operating system identification. The TXT record is used to enter any text you want. MINFO provides a host's mail and mailbox information.

Record Types	Description
A	Host address
NS	Authoritative name server
CNAME	Canonical name for an alias
SOA	Marks the start of a zone of authority
WKS	A well-known service description
PTR	Domain name pointer
HINFO	Host information
MINFO	Mailbox or mail list information
MX	Mail exchange
TXT	Text strings

Table 20-2.   *Domain Name System Resource Record Types*

Zone Files

A domain name server uses several zone files covering different components of the Domain Name System. Each zone uses two zone files: a zone file and a reverse mapping zone file. The zone file contains the resource records for hosts in the zone. A reverse mapping file contains records that provide reverse mapping of your domain name entries, letting you map from IP addresses to domain names. The name of the file used for the zone file can be any name. The name of the file is specified in the **zone** command's **file** entry in the **named.conf** file. If your server supports several zones, you may want to use a name that denotes the specific zone. Most systems use the domain name as the name of the zone file. For example, the zone **mytrek.com** would have a zone file also called **"mytrek.com"**. These could be placed in a subdirectory called **zones** or **master**. The zone file used in the following example is called **"mytrek.com"**. The reverse mapping file can also be any name, though it is usually the reverse IP address domain specified in its corresponding zone file. For example, in the case of the **"mytrek.com"** zone file, the reverse mapping file might be called 192.168.1, the IP address of the **mytrek.com** domain defined in the **"mytrek.com"** zone file. In addition, BIND sets up a cache file and a reverse mapping file for the localhost. The cache file holds the resource records for the root name servers that your name server connects to. It can be any name, though is usually called **named.ca**. The localhost reverse mapping file holds reverse IP resource records for the local loopback interface, **localhost**. Though it can be any name, it usually has the name **named.local**.

Zone Files for Internet Zones

A zone file holds resource records that follow a certain format. The file begins with general directives to define default domains or include other resource record files. These are followed by a single Start Of Authority record (SOA), name server and domain resource records, and then resource records for the different hosts. Comments begin with a semicolon and can be placed throughout the file. The @ symbol operates like a special macro representing the domain name of the zone the records apply to. It is used on the first field of resource and SOA records as the zone's domain name. Multiple names can be specified using the * matching character. The first field in a resource record is the name of the domain it applies to. If the name is left blank, the next previous explicit name entry in another resource record is automatically used. This way, you can list several entries that apply to the same host without having to repeat the hostname. Any host or domain name used throughout this file that is not terminated with a period will have the zone's domain appended to it. For example, if the zone's domain is **mytrek.com** and a resource record has only the name **rabbit** with no trailing period, the zone's domain is automatically appended to it, giving you **rabbit.mytrek.com**. Be sure to include the trailing period whenever you enter the complete fully qualified domain name as in "**turtle.mytrek.com**". There are also several directives that you can use to set global attributes. $ORIGIN sets a default domain name to append to address names that do not end in a period. $INCLUDE will include a file. $GENERATE can generate records where a part of a domain name or IP address will differ only by an iterated number.

A zone file begins with a Start Of Authority record specifying the machine the name server is running on, among other specifications. The @ symbol is used for the name of the SOA record, denoting the zone's domain name. After the SOA, the name server resource records (NS) are listed. Just below the name server record are resource records for the domain itself. Resource records for host addresses (A), aliases (CNAME), and mail exchangers (MX) follow. The following example shows a sample zone file. It begins with an SOA record and is followed by an NS record, resource records for the domain, and then resource records for individual hosts.

```
; Authoritative data for turtle.mytrek.com
;
@       IN   SOA turtle.mytrek.com. hostmaster.turtle.mytrek.com. (
                                  93071200    ; Serial number
                                  10800       ; Refresh 3 hours
                                  3600        ; Retry   1 hour
                                  3600000     ; Expire  1000 hours
                                  86400 )     ; Minimum 24 hours
             IN   NS                turtle.mytrek.com.
             IN   A                 192.168.1.1
             IN   MX      150       turtle.mytrek.com.

turtle       IN   A                 192.168.1.1
             IN   HINFO   PC-686    LINUX
             IN   MX      100       turtle
             IN   MX      150       fast.mytrek.com.
gopher       IN   CNAME             turtle.mytrek.com.
ftp          IN   CNAME             turtle.mytrek.com.
www          IN   A                 turtle.mytrek.com.

rabbit       IN   A                 192.168.1.2
             IN   HINFO   PC-586    LINUX
             IN   MX      100       turtle.mytrek.com.

lizard       IN   A                 192.168.1.3
             IN   HINFO   MAC       MACOS
             IN   MX      100       turtle.mytrek.com.
localhost    IN   A                 127.0.0.1
```

SERVERS

The first two lines are comments about the server this zone file is used for. Notice that they begin with a semicolon. The class for each of the resource records in this file is IN, indicating that these are Internet records. The Start Of Authority record begins with an **@** symbol that stands for the zone's domain. In this example, it is **mytrek.com**. Any host or domain name used throughout this file that is not terminated with a period will have this domain appended to it. For example, in the following resource record, **turtle** has no period so it will automatically expand to **turtle.mytrek.com**. The same will happen for **rabbit** and **lizard**. These will be read as **rabbit.mytrek.com** and **lizard.mytrek.com**. Also, in the SOA, notice that the e-mail address for hostmaster uses a period instead of **@**. **@** is a special symbol in zone files and cannot be used for any other purpose.

The next resource record specifies the name server for this zone. Here, it is **mytrek.com**. Notice that the name for this resource record is blank. If the name is blank, a resource record inherits the name from the previous record. In this case, the NS record inherits the value of **@** in the SOA record, its previous record. This is the zone's domain and the NS record specifies that **turtle.mytrek.com** is the name server for this zone.

```
        IN   NS      turtle.mytrek.com.
```

The following address records set up an address for the domain itself. This is often the same as the name server, in this case 192.168.1.1 (the IP address of **turtle.mytrek.com**). This allows users to reference the domain itself rather than a particular host in it. A mail exchanger record follows that will route mail for the domain to the name server. Users can send mail to the **mytrek.com** domain and it will be routed to **turtle.mytrek.com**.

The following resource record is an address record (A) that associates an IP address with the fully qualified domain name **turtle.mytrek.com**. The resource record name only holds **turtle** with no trailing period, so it is automatically expanded to **turtle.mytrek.com**. This record provides the IP address that **turtle.mytrek.com** can be mapped to.

```
turtle   IN    A        192.168.1.1
```

Several resource records immediately follow that have blank names. These will inherit their name from the previous record, in this case **turtle.mytrek.com**. In effect, these are records that apply also to that host. Using blank names is an easy way to list additional resource records for the same host (notice that there is an apparent indent). The first record is an information record, providing the hardware and operating system for the machine.

```
        IN   HINFO   PC-686    LINUX
```

The second record is a mail exchanger record listing **turtle.mytrek.com** as also capable of receiving mail for itself. You can have more than one mail exchanger record for host. There may be more than one host through which mail can be routed. These can be listed in mail exchanger records with a priority set where the smaller number ranks higher. In this example, if **turtle.mytrek.com** cannot be reached, its mail will be routed through **fast.mytrek.com**, which has been set up to also handle mail from **turtle.mytrek.com**.

```
IN    MX     100   turtle
IN    MX     150   fast.mytrek.com.
```

If you are using the same machine to run several different servers, such as a Web, FTP, and Gopher server, you may want to assign aliases to these servers to make it easier for users to access them. Instead of using the actual domain name such as **turtle.mytrek.com** to access the Web server running on it, users may find it easier to use **www.mytrek.com**; for the Gopher server, **gopher.mytrek.com**; and for the FTP server, **ftp.mytrek.com**. In the Domain Name System, you can implement such a feature using alias records. In the example zone file, there are two CNAME alias records for the **turtle.mytrek.com** machine: **ftp**, and **gopher**. The next record implements an alias for **www** using just another address record for the same machine. None of the name entries end in a period, so they are appended automatically with the domain name **mytrek.com**. The names **www.mytrek.com**, **ftp.mytrek.com**, and **gopher.mytrek.com** are all aliases for **turtle.mytrek.com**. Users entering those URLs will automatically access the respective servers on the **turtle.mytrek.com** machine.

Address and main exchanger records are then listed for the two other machines in this zone: **rabbit.mytrek.com** and **lizard.mytrek.com**. You could add HINFO, TXT, MINFO, or alias records for these entries. The file ends with an entry for localhost, the special loopback interface that allows your system to address itself.

Reverse Mapping File

Reverse name lookups are enabled using a reverse mapping file. They map fully qualified domain names to IP addresses. This reverse lookup capability is not necessary, but it is convenient to have. With reverse mapping, when users access remote hosts, their domain name address can be used to identify their own host, instead of just the IP address. The name of the file can be anything you want. On most current distributions, it is the zone's domain address (the network part of a zone's IP address). For example, the reverse mapping file for a zone with the IP address of 192.168.1.1 would be 192.168.1. Its full pathname would be something like **/var/named/192.168.1**. On some systems using older implementations of BIND, the reverse mapping file name may consist of the root name of the zone file with the extension **.rev**. For example, if the zone file is called **mytrek.com**, the reverse mapping file would be called something like **mytrek.rev**. The zone entry for a reverse mapping in the **named.conf** file uses a special domain name consisting of the IP address in reverse with an **in-addr.arpa** extension. This reverse IP address will become the zone domain referenced by the **@** symbol in the reverse mapping file. For example, the reverse mapping zone name for a domain with the IP address of 192.168.43 would be **43.168.192.in-addr.arpa**. In the following example, the reverse domain name for the domain address 192.168.1 is **1.168.192.in-addr.arpa**.

```
zone "1.168.192.in-addr.arpa " in {
        type master;
        file "192.168.1";
};
```

A reverse mapping file begins with the Start Of Authority record that is the same as that used in a forward mapping file. Resource records for each machine defined in the forward mapping file then follow. These resource records are PTR records that point to hosts in the zone. These must be actual hosts, not aliases that were defined with CNAME records. Records for reverse mapping begin with a reversed IP address. Each segment in the IP address is sequentially reversed. They begin with the host ID, followed by reversed network numbers. If you list only the host ID with no trailing period, the zone domain will be automatically attached. In the case of a reverse mapping file, the zone domain as specified in the **zone** command will be the domain IP address backwards. The 1 will expand to 1.1.168.192. In the following example, **turtle** and **lizard** inherit the domain IP address, whereas **rabbit** has its explicitly entered.

```
;    reverse mapping of domain names 1.168.192.in-addr.arpa
;
@       IN    SOA turtle.mytrek.com. hostmaster.turtle.mytrek.com. (
                                92050300    ; Serial (yymmddxx format)
                                10800      ; Refresh   3 hours
                                3600     ; Retry      1 hour
                                3600000     ; Expire    1000 hours
                                86400 )      ; Minimum   24 hours
@                  IN    NS    turtle.mytrek.com
1                  IN    PTR   turtle.mytrek.com
2.1.168.192        IN    PTR   rabbit.mytrek.com.
3                  IN    PTR   lizard.mytrek.com.
```

Localhost Reverse Mapping

A localhost reverse mapping file implements reverse mapping for the local loopback interface known as *localhost*, whose network address is 127.0.0.1. This file can be any name. On OpenLinux and Red Hat systems, it is given the name **named.local**. On other systems, it may use the network part of the IP address, 127.0.0. This file allows mapping the domain name localhost to the localhost IP address, which is always 127.0.0.1 on every machine. The address 127.0.0.1 is a special address that functions as the local address for your machine. It allows a machine to address itself. In the **zone** command for this file, the name of the zone is **0.0.127.in-addr.arpa**. The domain part of the IP address is entered in reverse order, with **in-addr.arpa** appended to it, **0.0.127.in-addr.arpa**. The **named.conf** entry is shown here:

```
zone "0.0.127.in-addr.arpa" {
    type master;
    file "named.local";
};
```

The name of the file used for the localhost reverse mapping file is usually **named.local**, though it can be any name. The NS record specifies the name server that localhost should use. This file has a PTR record that maps the IP address to the localhost. The 1 used as the name will expand to append the zone domain, in this case giving you 1.0.0.127, a reverse IP address. The contents of the **named.local** file are shown here. Notice the trailing periods for localhost.

```
@       IN      SOA     localhost. root.localhost. (
                                1997022700 ; Serial
                                28800      ; Refresh
                                14400      ; Retry
                                3600000    ; Expire
                                86400 )    ; Minimum
        IN      NS      turtle.mytrek.com.
1       IN      PTR     localhost.
```

IP Virtual Domains

IP-based virtual hosting allows more than one IP address to be used for a single machine. If a machine has two registered IP addresses, either one can be used to address the machine. If you want to just treat the extra IP address as another host in your domain, you need only create an address record for it in your domain's zone file. The domain name for the host would be the same as your domain name. However, if you want to use a different domain name for the extra IP, you have to set up a virtual domain for it. This entails creating a new **zone** command for it with its own zone file. For example, if the extra IP address is 192.168.1.42 and you want to give it the domain name **sail.com**, you would have to create a new **zone** command for it in your

named.conf file with a new zone file. The **zone** command would look something like this. The zone file is called **sail.com**.

```
zone "sail.com" in {
        type master;
        file "sail.com";
};
```

In the **"sail.com"** file, the name server name is still **turtle.mytrek.com** and the e-mail address is **hostmaster@turtle.mytrek.com**. In the name server record (NS), the name server is **turtle.mytrek.com**, the same machine using its original address that the name server is running as. The machine **turtle.mytrek.com** is also the host that handles mail addressed to **jib.sail.com** (MX). An address record then associates the extra IP address 192.168.1.42 with the **jib.sail.com** domain name. The aliases **www** and **ftp** are created for the new domain, creating **www.sail.com** and **ftp.sail.com** virtual hosts.

```
; Authoritative data for jib.sail.com
;
@       IN    SOA    turtle.mytrek.com. hostmaster.turtle.mytrek.com. (
                                   93071200    ; Serial (yymmddxx)
                                   10800       ; Refresh 3 hours
                                   3600        ; Retry   1 hour
                                   3600000     ; Expire  1000 hours
                                   86400 )     ; Minimum 24 hours
        IN    NS            turtle.mytrek.com
        IN    MX    100     turtle.mytrek.com
        IN    A             192.168.1.42      ;address of the sail.com domain

jib     IN    A             192.168.1.42
        IN    MX    100     turtle.mytrek.com
www     IN    A             jib.sail.com.
ftp     IN    CNAME         jib.sail.com.
```

In your reverse mapping file (**/var/named/1.168.192**), add PTR records for any virtual domains.

```
42.1.168.192    IN    PTR    jib.sail.com
```

You will also have to configure your network connection to listen for both IP addresses on your machine (see Chapter 28).

Cache File

The cache file is used to connect the domain name server to root servers on the Internet. The file can be any name. On Red Hat and OpenLinux systems, it is called **named.ca**. Other systems may call it **named.cache** or **roots.hints**. This is usually a standard file installed by your BIND software. It lists resource records for designated root servers for the Internet. The following example shows sample entries taken from the **named.ca** file:

```
; formerly NS.INTERNIC.NET
;
.                          3600000  IN  NS   A.ROOT-SERVERS.NET.
A.ROOT-SERVERS.NET.        3600000      A    198.41.0.4
;
; formerly NS1.ISI.EDU
;
.                          3600000      NS   B.ROOT-SERVERS.NET.
B.ROOT-SERVERS.NET.        3600000      A    128.9.0.107
```

If you are creating an isolated intranet, you need to create your own root domain name server until you connect to the Internet. In effect, you are creating a fake root server. This can be another server on your system pretending to be the root, or the same name server.

BIND Version 4.x

BIND version 4.x uses a different kind of configuration file called the **named.boot** file. The entries in this file consist of one-line records similar to that in a **named** zone file. Records begin with keywords for the type of entry followed by the associated values. For example, the directory record specifies the directory for zone files, just like the directory entry in the **options** command used in the **named.conf** file in BIND 8.x. The primary record specifies the zone and the data domain host file used for it. A secondary record specifies that the name server will operate as a secondary name server in the given domain. The cache record specifies the file name used for the cache. You can always convert a **name.boot** file to a **named.conf** file using the **named-bootconf.pl** Perl script provided with BIND 8.x. You can find out more about

BIND version 4.*x* from **www.isc.org** and BIND documentation. A sample **named.boot** file is shown here:

```
;
; nameserver config
;
directory        /var/named
cache            .                        named.ca
primary          mytrek.com               mytrek.com
primary          1.168.192.in-addr.arpa   "192.168.1"
primary          0.0.127.in-addr.arpa     named.local
```

The Complete Reference

Chapter 21

Mail, News, Proxy, and Search Servers

Mail and news servers provide Internet users with electronic mail and Usenet news services. They have their own TCP/IP protocols just as FTP and Web servers have theirs. *Mail servers* use the Small Mail Transfer Protocol (SMTP) and news servers using the Network News Transfer Protocol (NNTP). In addition, there are servers that provide better access to Internet resources. *Proxy servers* speed up Web access by maintaining current copies of commonly accessed Web pages, speeding access times by eliminating the need to constantly access the original site. Search servers such as ht:/Dig and WAIS enable document searches of Web and FTP sites. They can index documents and provide search engines for carrying out complex search requests.

Mail Servers: SMTP and POP

Messages are sent across the Internet through mail servers that service local domains. A domain can be seen as subnet of the larger Internet, with its own server to handle mail messages sent from or received for users on that subnet. When a user mails a message, it is first sent from his or her host system to the mail server. The mail server then sends it to another mail server on the Internet, the one servicing the subnet that the recipient user is on. The receiving mail server then sends the message to the recipient's host system. At each stage, a different type of operation takes place using different agents (programs). A Mail User Agent (MUA) is a mail client program such as **mail** or **Elm**. With an MUA, a user composes a mail message and sends it. A Mail Transport Agent (MTA) then transports the messages over the Internet. MTAs are mail servers that use the Simple Mail Transfer Protocol (SMTP) to send messages across the Internet from one mail server to another, transporting them from one subnet to another. On Linux and Unix systems, the commonly used MTA is **sendmail**. The **sendmail** MTA is a mail server daemon that constantly checks for incoming messages from other mail servers, and sends outgoing messages to appropriate servers. Incoming messages received by a mail server are then distributed to a user with Mail Delivery Agents (MDA). Most Linux systems use **procmail** as their MDA, taking messages received by the mail server and delivering them to user accounts (see **www.procmail.org** for more information).

Most Linux distributions such as Red Hat and OpenLinux will automatically install and configure **sendmail** for you. Upon starting up your system, you can send and receive messages over the Internet using **sendmail**. You can also set up your Linux system to run a POP server. POP servers hold users' mail until they log in to access their messages, instead of having mail sent to their accounts directly.

Messages exchanged with a system require a loopback interface. Most Linux distributions do this automatically for you during the installation process. A *loopback interface* enables your system to address itself, allowing it to send mail to and receive it from itself. A loopback interface uses the hostname **localhost** and a special IP address, 127.0.0.1, that is reserved for use by local systems. You can examine your **/etc/hosts** file to see if your loopback interface has been configured as the local host. You will see

localhost 127.0.0.1 listed as the first entry. If for some reason there is no entry for "localhost", you may have to create a loopback interface yourself using the `ifconfig` and `route` commands as shown here. The term `lo` is used for loopback.

```
ifconfig lo 127.0.0.1
route add -net 127.0.0.0
```

The sendmail MTA

To both receive and send mail messages, **sendmail** operates as a server. It listens for any mail messages received from other hosts and addressed to users on the network hosts it serves. At the same time, it handles messages that users are sending out to remote users, determining what hosts to send them to. You can find out more about **sendmail** at **www.sendmail.org**, including online documentation and current software packages. The **sendmail** newsgroup is **comp.mail.sendmail**.

The domain name server for your network designates the host that runs the **sendmail** server. This is your mail host, and messages are sent to this host whose **sendmail** server then sends the message to the appropriate user and its host. On your domain name server configuration file, the mail host entry is specified with an **MX** entry. To print out the mail queue of messages for future delivery, you can use **mailq**. This runs **sendmail** with instructions to print the mail queue.

Your **sendmail** supports the use of aliases either for sent or received mail. It checks an aliases database file called **aliases.db** that holds alias names and their associated e-mail addresses. This is often used for administrator mail, where mail may be sent to the system's root user and then redirected to the mail address of the actual system administrator. You can also alias host addresses, letting you address hosts on your network using only their aliases. Alias entries are kept in the **/etc/aliases** file. This file consists of one-line alias records, beginning with the address of the user or host followed by a colon and a list of aliases for that entry. You can edit this file to add new entries or change old ones. They are then stored for lookup in the **aliases.db** file using the command **newaliases**. The **newaliases** command runs **sendmail** with instructions to update the **aliases.db** file. The following is an example of an alias entry for the system administrator address:

```
# Basic system aliases -- these MUST be present.
MAILER-DAEMON:   postmaster
postmaster:   root
# Person who should get root's mail
#root:       richlp
```

The main **sendmail** configuration file is **sendmail.cf** located in the **/etc** directory. This file consists of a sometimes lengthy list of mail definitions and address rewrite rules. A series of mail definitions set features such as maximum size of mail messages or the name of host files. The rewrite rules "rewrite" a mail address to route through the appropriate Internet connections to its destination. These rules can be very complex. See the **sendmail** HOW-TO, the online documentation, and books such as *Sendmail* by O'Reilly for more details.

```
# location of help file
O HelpFile=/usr/lib/sendmail.hf
# file containing names of hosts for which we receive email
Fw/etc/sendmail.cw
```

To further simplify the configuration process, sendmail supports the use of macros that you can use to generate the **sendmail.cf** file using the m4 preprocessor (this requires that the sendmail-cf package is installed). Macros are placed in the **sendmail.mf** file. Here, you can use macros to designate the definitions and features you want for sendmail, and then the macros are used to generate the appropriate definitions and rewrite rules in your **sendmail.cf** file.

You can also use Linuxconf to configure sendmail. This requires that Linuxconf has its mailconf module loaded. Under the Networking heading, open the Server Tasks listing and select the Mail Delivery System entry. This opens a lengthy list of entries for panels that configure sendmail on your system. Click on its entry to display a panel (see Figure 21-1). Once you have configured sendmail, you can then have Linuxconf generate a **sendmail.cf** file. You can also use the **mailconf** command to display a window with buttons for the different Linuxconf **sendmail** panels.

POP Servers

The Post Office Protocol (POP) allows a remote server to hold mail for users who can then log in to access their mail. Unlike **sendmail** and **procmail**, which will deliver mail messages directly to a user account on a Linux system, the POP protocol holds mail until a user accesses his or her account on the POP server. Servers are often used by ISPs to provide Internet mail services for users. Instead of sending mail directly to a user's machine, the mail resides in the POP server until retrieved.

Qpopper is the current version of the Berkeley POP server (popper). Qpopper is supported by Qualcom, makers of Eudora email software. The Qpopper Web page is **www.eudora.com/free/qpop.html**. You can obtain a current source code version from **ftp.qualcomm.com/eudora/servers/unix**. An RPM package for Red Hat is located in the Red Hat contrib site at **contrib.redhat.com**. You can install Qpopper software on your Linux system and have it operate as a POP server for your network. It consists of both the **qpopper** daemon and the **popauth** program, which manages an authentication database with password encryption for secure user access. The **popauth** program creates a database file called **/etc/pop.auth**. To add a user, you enter the **popauth** command with the options -user and user name. You are then prompted for a password with which the user can then access a POP account.

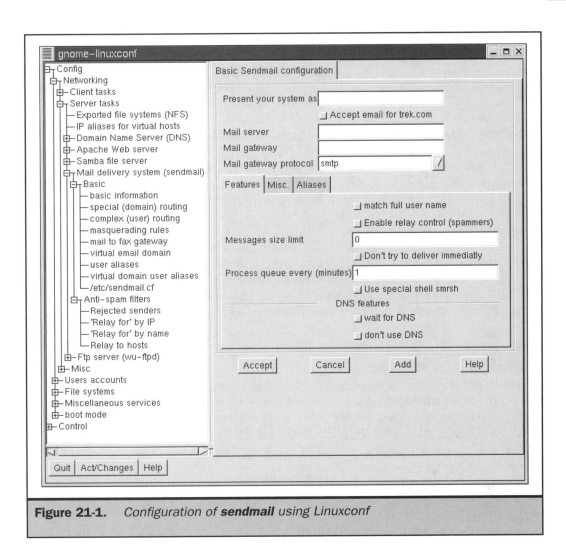

Figure 21-1. *Configuration of **sendmail** using Linuxconf*

News Servers: INN

The InterNetNews (INN) news server accesses Usenet newsfeeds, providing news clients on your network with the full range of newsgroups and their articles. Newsgroup articles are transferred using the Network News Transfer Protocol (NNTP), and servers that support this protocol are known as NNTP servers. INN was written by Rich Salz, and is currently maintained and supported by the Internet Software Consortium (ISC). You can download current versions from their Web site at **www.isc.org**. INN is also included with most Linux distributions, including Red

Hat and OpenLinux. The documentation directory for INN in **/usr/doc** contains extensive samples. The primary program for INN is the **innd** daemon. Various INN configuration files can be found in **/etc/news,** including **innd, inn.conf, rnews, nnrp.access,** and **hosts.nntp.** The **inn.conf** file sets options for INN, and the **hosts.nntp** file holds the hosts from which you receive newsfeeds. Place entries for remote hosts in the **nnrp.access** file to allow them access to your news server. Correct configuration of INN can be a complex and time-consuming process. Be sure to consult references and online resources such as the HOW-TO documents. There is an **innd** script in the **/etc/rc.d/init.d** directory that has similar arguments to the Web **httpd** script. You can use start and stop arguments with the **innd** script to start and stop the INN server.

Red Hat and OpenLinux systems have already created a **news** user with a newsgroup for use by your INN daemon. On other systems, you may have to create the **news** user and group. On all systems, you will have to create a news home directory, such as **/home/news.** INN software also installs **cron** scripts that are used to update your news server, removing old articles and fetching new ones. These are placed in the **/etc/cron.daily** directory. The **inn-cron-expire** file removes old articles and **inn-cron-rnews** will retrieve news ones. The **inn-cron-nntpsend** file sends articles posted from your system to other news servers.

Squid

Squid is a proxy caching server for Web clients, designed to speed up Internet access. It implements a proxy caching service for Web clients that will cache Web pages as users make requests. Copies of Web pages accessed by users are kept in the Squid cache. As requests are made, Squid checks to see if it has a current copy and, if so, returns the copy from its cache instead of querying the original site. In this way, Web browsers can then use the local Squid cache as a proxy HTTP server. Squid currently handles Web pages supporting the HTTP, FTP, Gopher, SSL, and WAIS protocols (it cannot be used with FTP clients). Replacement algorithms periodically replace old objects in the cache.

Squid is supported and distributed under a GNU public license by the National Laboratory for Applied Network Research (NLANR) at UC San Diego. The work is based on the Harvest Project. You can obtain current source code versions and online documentation from the Squid home page at **http://squid.nlanr.net** and the Squid FTP site at **ftp.nlanr.net.** The Squid software package consists of the Squid server, a domain name lookup program called **dnsserver,** an FTP client called **ftpget,** and a cache manager script called **cachemgr.cgi.** The **dnsserver** resolves IP addresses from domain names, and the **ftpget** program is an FTP client Squid uses to retrieve files from FTP servers.

The Squid configuration file is **squid.conf** located in the **/etc/squid** directory. The default version provided with Squid software includes detailed explanations of all standard entries along with commented default entries. Entries consist of tags that specify different attributes. For example, the **maximum_object_size** and **maximum_object** tags set limits on objects transferred.

```
#maximum_object_size 4096 KB
```

You can configure your Squid server to control access to and from other sites and by other users. Controls can list a specific URL or just a pattern. In the following example, the access is denied to any URL with the pattern "chocolate," and allows access from all others:

```
acl Choc1 url_regex chocolate
http_access deny Choc1
http_access allow all
```

Squid also supports ident and proxy authentication methods to control user access. The following example only allows the users dylan and chris to use the Squid cache:

```
ident_lookup on
acl goodusers user chris dylan
http_access allow goodusers
http_access deny all
```

Squid uses the Internet Cache Protocol (ICP) to implement the cache. Using the ICP protocols, your Squid cache can connect to other Squid caches or other cache servers such as Microsoft proxy server, Netscape proxy server, and Novell Bordermanager. This way, if your network's Squid cache does not have a copy of a requested Web page, it can contact another cache to see if it is there, instead of accessing the original site. You can configure Squid to connect to other Squid caches by connecting it to a cache hierarchy. Squid supports a hierarchy of caches denoted by the terms *child*, *sibling*, and *parent*. Sibling and child caches are accessible on the same level and are automatically queried whenever a request cannot be located in your own Squid's cache. If these queries fail, then a parent cache is queried which then will search its own child and sibling caches or it own parent cache, if needed, and so on. Use **cache_host** to set up parent and sibling hierarchical connections.

```
cache_host sd.cache.nlanr.net    parent 3128 3130
```

SERVERS

You can set up a cache hierarchy to connect to the main NLANR server by registering your cache using the following entries in your **squid.conf** file.

```
cache_announce 24
announce_to sd.cache.nlanr.net:3131
```

Squid keeps several logs. The **access.log** holds requests sent to your proxy, **cache.log** holds Squid server messages such as errors and startup messages, and **store.log** holds information about the Squid cache such as objects added or removed. You can use the cache manager (**cachemgr.cgi**) to manage the cache and view statistics on it as it runs. To run the cache manager, use your browser to execute the **cachemgr.cgi** script. This script should be placed in your Web server's **cgi-bin** directory. You can also monitor Squid using the Multi Router Traffic utility.

Dig Server

Dig, known officially as ht:/Dig, is a Web indexing and search system designed for small networks or intranets. It is not considered a replacement for full-scale Internet search systems like Lycos, Infoseek, or AltaVista. Unlike WAIS-based or Web-server-based search engines, ht:/Dig can span several Web servers at a site. Dig was developed at San Diego State University and is distributed free under the GNU public license. You can obtain information and documentation at **www.htdig.org**, and can download software packages—including RPM packages—from **ftp.htdig.org**. An RPM package version for Red Hat and OpenLinux can be found at the Red Hat contrib site, **contrib.redhat.com**.

The ht:/Dig system supports simple and complex searches, including complex Boolean and fuzzy search methods. *Fuzzy searching* supports a number of search algorithms, including exact, soundex, and synonyms. Searches can be carried out on both text and HTML documents. HTML documents can have keywords placed in them for more accurate retrieval. You can also use HTML templates to control how results are displayed.

Searches can be constrained by authentication requirements, location, and search depth. To protect documents in restricted directories, Dig can be informed to request a specific user name and password. You can also restrict a search to retrieve documents in a certain URL, search subsections of the database, or retrieve only documents that are a specified number of links away.

All the htdig programs use the same configuration file, **htdig.conf**, located in the **/etc/htdig** directory. The configuration file consists of attribute entries, each beginning with the attribute line and followed by the value after a colon. Each program will take only the attributes it needs.

```
max_head_length:    10000
```

You can specify attributes such as **allow_virtual_hosts**, which will index virtual hosts as separate servers, and **search_algorithm**, that specifies the search algorithms to use for searches.

The ht:/Dig system consists of five programs: **htdig**, **htmerge**, **htfuzzy**, **htnotify**, and **htsearch**. The **htdig**, **htmerge**, and **htfuzzy** programs generate the index, and htsearch performs the actual searches. First, htdig gathers information on your database, searching all URL connections in your domain and associating Web pages with terms. The **htmerge** program will use this information to create a searchable database, merging the information from any previously generated database. The **htfuzzy** program will create indexes to allow searches using fuzzy algorithms such as soundex and synonyms. Once the database is created, users can use Web pages that invoke htsearch to search this index. Results are listed on a Web page. You can use META tags in your HTML documents to enter specific htdig keywords, exclude a document from indexing, or provide notification information such as e-mail address and expiration dates. The htnotify program will use the e-mail and expiration date to notify Web page authors when their pages are out of date.

The **htsearch** program is a CGI program that expects to be invoked by an HTML form. It accepts both the GET and POST methods of passing data. The htsearch program can accept a search request from any form that contains the required configuration values. Values include search features such as config (configuration file), method (search method), and sort (sort criteria). For the Web page form that invokes htsearch, you can use the default page provided by htdig or create your own. Output is formatted using templates that you can modify. Several sample files are included with the htdig software. The **rundig** program is a sample script for creating a database. The **searchform.html** program is a sample html document that contains a search form for submitting htdig searches. The **header.html** progarm is a sample header for search headers, and **footer.html** is for search footers.

WAIS Server

WAIS (Wide Area Information Servers) searches a database of documents using keywords and displays the documents it finds with a ranking of their importance. It is a very effective way to make information available throughout a network. WAIS was developed by Thinking Machines and is now managed by WAIS, Inc. A free version of WAIS, called freeWAIS, is available through the Center for Networked Information Discovery and Retrieval (CNIDR). You can obtain a Linux version of freeWAIS from CNIDR and the FTP site (**ftp.cnidr.org**).

The freeWAIS package includes clients, a server, and an indexer program. The clients are called **swais**, **xwais**, and **waissearch**. They are used to enter requests and display results. The indexer is called **waisindex**. You use it to create indexes of keywords for your WAIS documents, providing fast and effective search capabilities. The server is called **waisserver**. With it, you can create your own WAIS site and allow other users to perform searches on your WAIS documents.

To use WAIS, you have to create indexes for the documents you want to make available. This indexing process is carried out by the **waisindex** command that creates a particular WAIS database. You can index a single file, a group of files, or whole directories and subdirectories of files. The data files together with their index form a WAIS database. You can separately index different files or groups of files, setting up several different WAIS databases on your server. The WAIS databases should be located in the WAIS data directory that was specified when the WAIS server was invoked.

The **waisindex** command creates an inverted file index, referencing every word in the designated files. This allows keyword searching on the full text of documents. The **waisindex** command takes several options followed by the name of the file, group of files, or directory to be indexed as the last argument. With the **-d** option you can specify a name for the index. The **waisindex** command creates several index files for a document that are used to manage the index. Each will have its own extension indicating its function, but all will have the index name specified by the **-d** option as the prefix. If you do not specify a name, the term "index" will be used as the prefix. Also, if you want to have your database accessible to other users on the Internet, you have to add the **-export** option. Without this option, your database is accessible only to other users on your system. The **-export** option is discussed in the next section. The **waisindex** options and the index files are listed in Table 21-1.

```
waisindex -d index-file -export file-list
```

If you list more than one file to be indexed, all those files will be referenced by the single index. If you want to index all the files in a subdirectory, you use the -r option followed by the directory name.

```
waisindex -d index-file -export -r directory-name
```

To add a file or directory to an existing database, you index it with the **-a** option. You also have to use the **-d** option and the database name to add the indexing of this file to that database. You can add several files by listing them on the command line. If you want to add a directory of files, you have to use the **-r** option followed by the directory name.

```
waisindex -d index-file -a -export file-list
```

In the next examples, the user first indexes the files **cookies** and **cakes**, creating an index called **recipes** for that group of files. Queries on **recipes** will search both **cookies** and **cakes**. In the next example, the user indexes the **pies** file and adds it to the **recipes** index. The WAIS **recipes** database now includes the files **cookies**, **cakes**, and **pies**. Now the user indexes the **snacks** directory, including all its files as well as files in any of its subdirectories. The name of the index is **junkfood**. In the final example, indexing is carried out again on the **snacks** array, but this time the indexing is added to the **recipes** database. The **junkfood** database still exists and references the **snacks** directory.

```
# waisindex -d recipes -export cookies cakes
# waisindex -d recipes -export -a pies
# waisindex -d junkfood -export -r snacks
# waisindex -d recipes -export -a -r snacks
```

With the **-t** option, you are able to index different types of files. You can index images, mailbox files, and even HTML pages, as well as standard text documents. The different document types are listed in Table 21-1. For text documents, you can refine your indexing by specifying the *one_line* type. If you index by line, WAIS will indicate the line in the document where a keyword is found. In the next example, the user indexes each line of the document **breads** and creates the index, called **cereals**.

```
#  waisindex -d cereals -t one_line breads
```

The **waisindex** command can also associate different types of files with a specified document. For example, if you have image, video, or sound files that you want to associate with a specific text document, you can have **waisindex** link those files together. When a user retrieves the text document, the associated image, video, or sound files will also be retrieved. As the user reads the text, she or he can also display a picture or play a sound. Associated files must have the same prefix as the document they are linked to. For example, if you have a document called **train.txt**, you can have a picture of a train in a file called **train.gif** and the sound of a train in **train.midi**. You use the **-M** option and a list of file types with the **-export** option to link a set of files to an index.

```
# waisindex -d train -M text, tiff, mpeg, midi  -export
/user/waisdata/train/*
```

To integrate WAIS with your Web resources, you need to create WAIS indexes for your Web pages. You use **waisindex** with the **-T HTML** option, specifying that the type of document being indexed is an HTML document. The name of the index could be something like **myweb**. This allows WAIS to search Web HTML documents. In the next example, the user indexes Web pages located in the **/home/httpd/html** directory. The name of the index is **myweb** and the type is HTML. The full contents of each Web page are indexed as specified by the **-contents** option. The **-export** option will include hostname information for easy Internet access.

```
# waisindex -d myweb -T HTML  -contents -export -r
/home/httpd/html/*.html
```

When you index files to make a database accessible, **waisindex** will create a source file for the database—the source file is the means by which other users can reach your database; it provides information, such as the name of the database. Some WAIS databases will charge for access, specifying a cost, and the source file will show this information. You will see the address of the maintainer where you can send comments. The source file ends with a short description of the WAIS database.

If you specified the **-export** option when the database was created with **waisindex**, several fields will be added to allow users on other systems access to your database. Two fields for Internet address information are added, one for the IP name and the other for the IP address of your host system. Another field is added to specify the port (usually 210) to be used to access the WAIS database on your computer (the host computer). If you did not use the **-export** option, these fields will be absent. In this case, only users on your system will be able to access the database.

If necessary, you can modify any of the fields in a source file. The entire source is enclosed in parentheses, with each field on a line of its own beginning with a colon and the field name. You can edit the source file and add more to the description. Notice that the description is enclosed in double quotes, with the first quote following the term "description" and the closing quote on a line by itself after the descriptive text. The following example is a source for zip codes in a file called **zipcodes.src**:

```
(:source
  :version  3
  :ip-address "192.31.181.1"
  :ip-name "quake.think.com"
  :tcp-port 210
  :database-name "/proj/wais/db/sources/zipcodes"
  :cost 0.00
  :cost-unit :free
  :maintainer "wais@quake.think.com"
  :description "
WAIS index of USA Zip Code database.
The full Zipcodes file may be obtained via FTP using the URL:
<ftp://obi.std.com/obi/ZIPCODES/zipcode.txt>
 "
)
```

Other users use the source file to access its WAIS database. The source file tells a user which host it is located on and what it is called. You can think of it as a URL for WAIS databases. The remote user first has to have the source file in order to access the database. You can either send the source file to a user, who then can insert their host's **wais-sources** directory, or register the source file with a WAIS server that maintains a directory of servers, such as **quake.think.com** and **cnidr.org**. Your source will be placed there with other sources. Using a WAIS client such as **swais**, users can access this directory of servers and find your WAIS database listed there. Then, they can select and query your database.

You register a database when you create it by including the **-register** option when indexing the files with **waisindex**. You can also wait and register it later, perhaps after you've tested it. Use the **waisindex** command with the **-d** option and the index name, followed by the **-register** option.

```
waisindex -d recipes -register
```

You can have WAIS run continuously or have it called by **inetd** when needed. To start the WAIS server, you use the command **waisserver** with several possible options. You can use the **-d** option to specify the default location of your WAIS indexes. You can also set the port with **-p** or the user name with **-u**. Be sure to add an ampersand (&) at the end of the command. When called directly, **waisserver** has to be run in the background. To run WAIS as a continuous daemon, you should enter the **waisserver** command in an **rc.d/init** initialization file, such as **wais.init**. The following is an example of the **waisserver** command:

```
waisserver -d /usr/wais/wais_index &
```

To provide your WAIS service with more security, it's a good idea to run **waisserver** as a user other than root. Create a user and place an * in its **passwd** entry. Then, use the **-u** option with that user name when you start **waisserver**. In the following example, **waisserver** runs as the user sports:

```
waisserver -u sports -d /usr/wais/wais_index &
```

To have **inetd** start the WAIS server, you must place the appropriate entries in the **/etc/services** and **/etc/inetd.conf** files. For the **/etc/services** file, you place the following entry:

```
z3590        210/tcp      # Z39_50 protocol for WAIS
```

Then, in the **inetd.conf** file you place the entry to invoke the WAIS server. When **waisserver** is called as **waisserver.d**, it knows it is being run under **inetd**. For this reason, the first argument in the argument list is **waisserver.d**.

```
z3590  stream  tcp  nowait  root  /usr/sbin/waisserver
waisserver.d  /home/wais -e server.log
```

waisindex Files	Description
index-name.**doc**	Information about the document, including the size and name
index-name.**dct**	Dictionary file with a list of each unique word cross-indexed to an inverted file
index-name.**fn**	List of all files created for the index
index-name.**hl**	Table of all headlines; headlines are the titles and are displayed when in retrieved results
index-name.**inv**	The inverted file containing a table of words, a ranking of their importance, and their connection to the indexed documents
index-name.**src**	A source description file that contains information about the index, what system it is located on, the topic it deals with, who maintains it, and so on.
index-name.**status**	Contains user-defined information
waisindex Options	**Description**
-a	Appends index to an existing one
-contents	Indexes the contents of a file (default)
-d *path-name*	Specifies a pathname for index files; the pathname will be appended to the front of the index's file name
-e *logfile*	Redirects error messages to *logfile*
-export	Adds hostname and TCP port to source description files to allow Internet access; otherwise, no connection information will be included and the files will be accessed locally
-l *num*	Sets logging level 0, 1, 5 and 10 0 logs nothing (silent) 1 logs only errors and warnings 5 logs messages of MEDIUM priority 10 logs everything

Table 21-1. The **waisindex** Files, Options, and Document Types

waisindex Options	Description
-mem	The amount of memory to use during indexing
-M	Links different types of files
-contents -nocontents	Determines whether to index the contents of a document; **-contents** indexes the entire document; **-nocontents** indexes only the header and file name, not the contents
-pairs -nopairs	How to treat consecutive capitalized words; **-pairs** (the default) treats capitalized words as one term; **-nopairs** treats them as separate terms
-pos -nopos	Whether to include word's position information in the index; **-pos** includes this information, allowing proximity searches but increasing the size of the index; **-nopos** does not include this information
-r	Recursively indexes subdirectories
-register	Registers indexes with WAIS directory of services
-t	Specifies the type of document file
-T	Sets the type of document

Document File Types	Description
filename	The text type that uses the file name as the headline
first_line	The text type that uses the first line in the file as the headline
one_line	The text type that indexes each sentence
text	The text type that indexes the document; headline is the pathname
ftp	Contains FTP code for accessing other systems
GIF	GIF image file
PICT	PICT image file
TIFF	TIFF image file

Table 21-1.   *The* `waisindex` *Files, Options, and Document Types* (continued)

SERVERS

waisindex Components	Description
MPEG	MPEG file
MIDI	MIDI file
HTML	HTML file used for Web pages
mail_or_rmail	Indexes the **mbox** mailbox file
mail_digest	Indexes e-mail using the subject as the headline
netnews	Indexes Usenet news

Table 21-1. *The* **waisindex** *Files, Options, and Document Types* (continued)

The Complete Reference

Part V

Applications

Chapter 22

Office Applications

variety of office suites are now available for Linux. These include professional-level word processors, presentation managers, drawing tools, and spreadsheets. The freely available versions are described in this chapter. Currently, you can download personal (noncommercial) versions for both WordPerfect and StarOffice from the Internet for free. KOffice is an entirely free office suite that is planned for release with KDE 2.0. The Gnome Workshop Project is integrating Gnome applications into a productivity suite that will be freely available. You can also purchase commercial office suites such as Applixware from Red Hat and Corel Office.

WordPerfect

The personal version of Corel's WordPerfect word processor is now available for Linux and is free (it is included with OpenLinux). The personal version is a fully functional word processor. However, it does not currently support TrueType fonts and it does not allow you to import other objects such as images. You can download WordPerfect from the Corel Web site at **linux.corel.com**. WordPerfect is more than just a word processor. You can use it to create drawings, spreadsheets, and charts, as well as edit and publish Web pages.

When you first start WordPerfect, a small window is displayed with the WordPerfect logo and four menus: Program, Preferences, Window, and Help. From the Program menu, you can select WordPerfect. In the Preferences menu, you can open a window with icons for configuring your printer, selecting fonts, choosing colors, and selecting conversion filters. The Window menu moves you to different open windows.

WordPerfect provides many of the standard word processing features, including cut and paste operations, font and paragraph styles, and document formatting. The extensive features for WordPerfect are indicated by its set of toolbars (see Figure 22-1). It includes such editing features as Grammar-As-You-Go, which checks and highlights suspicious phrases and will offer suggestions. With Spell-As-You-Go, words are identified that might be misspelled as you type them. Corel Versions will keep track of document revisions for workgroup collaboration.

WordPerfect includes a chart and drawing tool for creating figures. You can perform drawing operations such as sizing and rotating images, as well as contouring text over image shapes. The drawing tool supports features such as gradients, patterns, and groupings. You can create a variety of different charts, including 3-D, area, and line charts. WordPerfect supports a number of spreadsheet functions with which you can create tables with spreadsheet cells. You can use such data to generate charts.

You can also use WordPerfect as a Web page editor and publisher, adding or changing HTML components. Use WordPerfect to create your HTML document with hyperlinks and bookmarks, and then place them on your Web site. Any text beginning with an Internet protocol such as **www**, **ftp**, and **http**, is automatically set up as a hyperlink. You can also save Web pages as WordPerfect documents for easy editing.

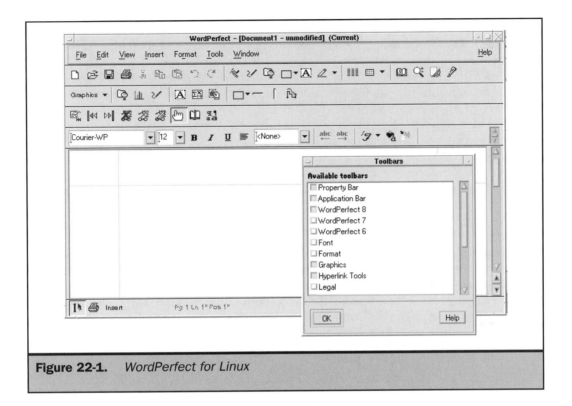

Figure 22-1. *WordPerfect for Linux*

WordPerfect supports an extensive number of file formats, including Microsoft Word 97 files. With WordPerfect, you can effectively edit your Word files. WordPerfect also has its own file manager. You can use it to locate and open files, but it will also perform other file manager operations. You can create directories and modify file permissions, as well as move and copy files.

KOffice

KOffice is an integrated office suite for the KDE (K Desktop Environment) consisting of several office applications, including a word processor, a spreadsheet, and graphic applications. All applications are written for the KOM/OP component model, which allows components from any one application to be used in another. This means that you can embed a spreadsheet from KSpread or a drawing from KIllustrator in a KWord document. You can obtain more information about KOffice from the KOffice Web site at **koffice.kde.org**. The first release of KOffice is scheduled as part of KDE version 2.0.

Currently, KOffice includes KSpread, KPresenter, KDiagramm, KImage, KIllustrator, KFormula, Kword, Katabase, KImageShop, and KoHTML (see Table 22-1). KSpread is a spreadsheet, KPresenter is a presentation application, KIllustrator is a vector drawing program, KWord is a Publisher-like word processor, KDiagram charts and diagrams, KFormula is a formula editor, and KImage is a simple image viewer, and KoHTML is an HTML viewer.

Embedded components support real time updates. For example, if you use KDiagram to generate a chart in a KWord document using data in a KSpread spreadsheet, and then change the selected data in the spreadsheet, the KDiagram automatically updates the chart in the KWord document. In effect, you are creating a compound document, one made up of several applications. This capability is implemented by the KDE object model known as K Object Model/OpenParts (KOM/OP). KOM/OP is based on CORBA 2.2, the industry standard for communication between distributed objects. KOM/OP is not dependent on the K Desktop, and can be used by any application designed for it on any interface, including Gnome. A Gnome application can be written to use KOM/OP and operate entirely on the Gnome GUI. This feature makes KOffice a possible candidate for a Linux and Unix standard.

With KOffice, you create one kind of document rather than separate ones for different applications. The different applications become views of this document, adding their components to it. KWord sets up the publishing and word processing

Application	Description
KSpread	Spreadsheet
KPresenter	Presentation program
KIllustrator	Vector drawing program
KWord	Word processor (desktop publisher)
KFormula	Mathematical formula editor
KChart/KDiagram	Tool for drawing charts and diagrams
KImage	A simple image viewer
Katabase	A database not unlike Paradox and Access
KoHTML	An HTML viewer
KImageShop	An image manipulation program

Table 22-1. *KOffice Applications*

components, KIllustrator will add drawing components, and KSpread will add spreadsheet components. You use the appropriate application to view the different components in the single document. This means that you can have separate windows open at the same time for different components of the document.

KSpread is the spreadsheet application. It incorporates the basic operations found in most spreadsheets, with formulas similar to those used in Excel. You can extend KSpread capabilities with Python scripts. It supports features such as embedded buttons for customized functions, automatic completion for cell contents, and formatting options such as backgrounds, borders, and font styles. To generate a diagram using selected cells, you just select the Insert Diagram entry from the KSpread menu. This starts up KDiagram, which you then use to create the diagram—that is then embedded in the spreadsheet. You can also embed pictures or formulas using KImage, KIllustrator, or KFormula.

With KDiagram, you can create different kinds of charts such as bar graphs, pie charts, and line graphs. To generate a chart, you can use data in KSpread, or you can use KDiagram tables to enter your data.

With KPresenter, you can create presentations consisting of text and graphics modeled using different fonts, orientations, and attributes such as colors. You can add such elements as speech bubbles, arrows, and clip art, as well as embed any KOffice component. KPresenter supports standard editing operations such as shading, rotating, and coloring objects, as well as cut and paste and undo/redo capabilities. You can generate templates from a KPresenter document, in effect letting you use a document's configuration to create other documents. With KPresenter, you can also create special effects such as simple animation.

KIllustrator is a vector-based graphics program much like Adobe Illustrator and Corel Draw. It supports the standard graphic operations such as rotating, scaling, and aligning objects. KIllustrator also includes text formatting capabilities such as alignment to irregular boundaries. You can create complex illustrations using layers, using a layer manager to control the layers. KIllustrator also supports a number of import and export filters for image files of different types like **.jpg**, **.gif**, and **.eps**.

KWord can best be described as a desktop publisher, with many of the features found in publishing applications like Microsoft Publisher and FrameMaker. Though it is also a fully functional word processor, KWord is not page-based like Word or WordPerfect. Instead, text is set up in frames that are placed on the page like objects. Frames, like objects in a drawing program, can be moved, resized, and even reoriented. You can organize frames into a frame set, having text flow from one to the other. Formatting can be applied to a frame set, changing features in all the frames belonging to it at once. The default frame set up for you when you first create a document is the same size as the page. This gives you the effect of a page-based word processor, letting you work as if you were using standard word processor. You can, of course, change the size of your frame, and add new ones if you wish.

You can also insert images, illustrations, tables, and other KOffice components such as diagrams and spreadsheets. You can set up a frame to contain an image and place it on top of a text frame, configuring the text frame to flow its text around it.

KWord uses templates to set up a document. You have two different sets of templates to choose from, one for desktop publishing (DTP) and the other for standard word processing (Wordprocessing). The desktop publishing templates let you freely move frames, whereas in the word processing templates the frames are fixed to the size of the page.

KWord supports the standard word processing features for formatting paragraphs, text, and document elements such as headers and footers, as well as lists and multiple columns. You can also define your own paragraph layouts, specifying features such as indentation, fonts, borders, and alignment. Layouts are the same as styles used in other word processors. Tables are implemented as frames, where each cell is its own frame.

KFormula is a formula editor used to generate mathematical formulas. Though it does not have the power of TeX, you can use it to create fairly complex formulas. It supports standard components like roots, integral, and fractions, as well as fonts for Greek symbols.

Currently, KImage is used only to display images. Later, it will be enhanced with image editing capabilities. For now, you can use it to display images embedded in different KOffice applications. KoHTML is another applet that is used to display Web pages. It is useful for displaying Web pages embedded in KOffice applications.

KImageShop is an image editor, much like PhotoShop. It is currently under development. Katabase is a database application designed to work with KOffice applications. (See Chapter 23.)

Gnome Workshop Project

Office applications for Gnome have been developed independently, such as the Gnumeric spreadsheet. Currently, the Gnome Workshop Project is attempting to integrate the various office applications into a productivity suite. Though most are still under development, some have working stable versions you can download and install. You can find out more from the Gnome Workshop Project Web site at **www.gnome.org/gw.html**. Here, you can download current versions and view screen shots. A current listing is shown in Table 22-2. All implement the CORBA model for embedding components, ensuring drag-and-drop capability through the Gnome interface.

Gnumeric is the Gnome spreadsheet, a professional-level program meant to replace commercial spreadsheets. Like Gnome, it is freely available under the GNU Public License. Gnumeric is included with the Gnome release and you will find it installed with Gnome on the Red Hat and SuSE distributions. You can download current versions from **www.gnome.org/gnumeric**. It supports standard GUI spreadsheet features, including autofilling and cell formatting. Gnumeric provides an extensive number of formats. It supports drag-and-drop operations, letting you select and then move or copy cells to another location. Gnumeric also supports plugins, making it possible to easily extend and customize its capabilities.

Application	Description
Achtung	Presentation manager
GWP	Word processor
GO	Word processor
AbiWord	Cross-platform word processor
Gnumeric	Spreadsheet
Guppi	Statistical tool for plotting data
Genius	Scientific calculator
Dia	Diagram and flow chart editor
Electric Eyes	Image viewer
Gnome Help Browser	Enhanced for Web browsing
GYVE	Vector drawing package
GIMP	GNU image manipulation program
gnome-db	Database architecture for Gnome
GNOME Personal Information Manager	Calendar/organizer and an address book

Table 22-2. *Gnome Workshop Project*

StarOffice

StarOffice is a fully integrated and Microsoft Office–compatible suite of office applications. It includes Web-enabled word processing, spreadsheet, presentations, e-mail, news, charts, and graphic applications. There are versions for Linux, Windows, Mac, Solaris and OS/2. With StarOffice you can access Microsoft Office (including 2000) files and data to create spreadsheets, presentations, and word processing documents. You can save StarOffice documents in Microsoft formats or as HTML files that you can post on Web sites.

StarOffice is free for all noncommercial, private users, as well as students. You can download a free copy of StarOffice from its Web site at **www.startdivision.com** or its FTP site at **ftp.stardivision.com**. The package is about 50 megabytes. The Web site also contains information such as online manuals and FAQs.

StarOffice describes itself as implementing a task-oriented approach to office projects. You can complete an entire project using a variety of different tools in just one place, StarOffice. In addition, StarOffice applications are fully Internet-aware, letting you directly connect to Web sites and access information from your word processor, spreadsheet, or presenter.

When you start up StarOffice, you are presented with the StarOffice Desktop window. From here you can create documents and access other StarOffice applications. The left pane in this window is the Explorer. This is a tree menu that lists the different resources you can use such as an address book, a gallery of clip art, and FTP server URLs. The main window of the StarOffice Desktop shows icons for applications you can use, your StarOffice documents, and other tools.

To use StarOffice, you create projects. In a particular project you can place resources such as images, Internet links, e-mail messages, or office documents such as spreadsheets and word processing documents. To create a new document, click on the New button in the bottom status bar and select the application you want to use from the pop-up menu. You can create spreadsheets, word processing documents, presentation files, mail messages, charts, images, mathematical formulas, and even Web pages (see Table 22-3 at the end of this section). You can also create frame sets for use in Web page frames. Initially, windows are attached (docked) to the Desktop window. You can unattach them to their own floating windows by double-clicking on the gray area between them.

StarOffice has its own mail and news clients. With StarMail you can define mail accounts and access your e-mail as well as compose and send messages. With StarDiscussion, you can access newsgroups, saving articles and posting your own. You can set up icons and entries for mail accounts and newsgroups on your Desktop and Explorer window.

The StarWriter word processor supports standard word processing features such as cut and paste, spell checking, and text formatting, as well as paragraph styles. You can also insert objects in your text such as images, diagrams, or text frames. Text can be configured to flow around them. A text frame can be further edited to create banner-like text, coloring, blending, and shaping text. The Navigator lets you move through the document by page or by object, such as from one image to another.

You can open and save documents in the MS Office, WordPerfect, Lotus 1-2-3, and AmiPro formats. This means you can effectively edit MS Word documents with StarOffice. StarWriter also functions as a Web browser—capable of displaying HTML pages—and supports Java, JavaScript, Navigator, and Explorer plugins. At the same time, you can edit a Web page, turning StarWriter into a Web page editor.

You can embed objects within documents, such as using StarChart to create a bar chart using data in the spreadsheet. With StarMath, you can create formulas that you can then embed in a text document.

With the presentation manager (StarImpress), you can create images for presentations, such as circles, rectangles, and connecting elements like arrows, as well as vector-based illustrations. StarImpress supports advanced features like morphing objects, grouping objects, and defining gradients. You can also create animation effects and use layers to generate complex images. Any components from other StarOffice applications can be embedded in a presentation document. You can also import Microsoft PowerPoint files and save presentation files as HTML files. An AutoPilot Wizard for StarImpress will walk you through the steps for creating a presentation.

StarDraw is a sophisticated drawing tool that includes 3-D modeling tools. You can create very simple or complex images, including animation text aligned on curves. You can use it to create buttons and icons for your Web page.

StarSchedule provides scheduling and task management that can be used to coordinate efforts by a group of users. You can use it to track events and to-do lists, connecting automatically to the address book. It includes a reminder system to display pop-up alerts and send e-mail reminders. The StarSchedule server operates independently from StarOffice to provide scheduling services to any client on your network. StarBase is a relational database somewhat like MS Access. It supports drag-and-drop operations for importing data to your StarOffice applications.

Application	Description
StarDesktop	Main desktop window for StarOffice applications
StarWriter	Word processor
StarImpress	Presentation manager
StarDraw	Drawing tool
StarChart	Chart and graph creator
StarMail	E-mail client
StarDiscussion	Newsgroup client
StarMath	Mathematical formulas
StarImage	Image editor
StarCalc	Spreadsheet
StarSchedule	Schedule manager
StarBase	Relational database

Table 22-3. *StarOffice Applications*

APPLICATIONS

The Complete Reference

Linux

Chapter 23

Database Management Systems and Graphic Tools

A variety of database management systems are now available for Linux. These include very high-powered, commercial-level database management systems such as Oracle, IBM, and Sybase. Most of the database management systems available for Linux are designed to support large relational databases. For small personal databases you can use the desktop database management systems begin developed for KDE and Gnome. In addition, some software is available for databases accessed with the xBase database programming language. These are smaller databases using formats originally developed for dBase on the PC. Various database management systems available to run under Linux are listed in Table 23-1.

You can also use a wide range of graphic tools, ranging from simple image viewers like kimage to sophisticated image manipulation programs like the GIMP. You also have newer graphic tools for Gnome and KDE desktops, as well as older X Window System, to choose from. Graphics tools available for use under Linux are listed in Table 23-2.

Database Management Systems

Database software can be generally organized into three categories, SQL, xBase, and desktop databases. SQL-based databases are professional-level relational databases, whose files are managed by a central database server program. Applications that use the database do not access the files directly. Instead, they send requests to the database server, which then performs the actual access. SQL is the query language used on these industrial-strength databases.

The xBase language is an enhanced version of the dBase programming language used to access database files whose formats were originally developed for dBase on the PC. With xBase, database management systems can directly access the database files. It is used mainly for smaller personal databases, with database files often located on a user's own system.

Desktop databases are being developed for both Gnome and KDE. Currently these are personal databases, designed for individual users. Katabase is meant to be used with a user's KOffice applications, and Gaby, for a user's personal records. Both, however, are designed with a plugin structure that can easily extend their capabilities.

SQL Databases (RDMS)

SQL databases are relational database management systems (RDMS) designed for extensive database management tasks. Many of the major SQL databases now have Linux versions, including Oracle, Informix, Sybase, and IBM (but, of course, not Microsoft). In addition, there are many free SQL databases available for Linux that offer much the same functionality. Most commercial database also provide a free personal version, as is the case with DB2, Adabas D, and MySQL.

Oracle

Oracle offers a fully functional version of its Oracle 8 database management system for Linux, as well as the Oracle Application Server. You can download trial versions effective for 30 days from the Oracle Web site at **www.oracle.com**. Oracle 8 is a professional database designed for large databases. Expect to use a gigabyte of memory just to install it. The Oracle Application Server provides support for real-time and commerce applications on the Web. As Linux is a fully functional version of Unix, Oracle is particularly effective on it. Oracle was originally designed to operate on Unix, and Linux is a far better platform for it than other PC operating systems.

Oracle offers extensive documentation for its Linux version that you can download from its Documentation page, which you can link to from the Support pages on its Web site. The documentation available includes an installation guide, administrator's reference, and release notes, as well as the generic documentation. You can find specific information on installing and configuring Oracle for Linux in the Oracle Database HOW-TO, available at **www.linux.org**.

Informix

Informix offers an entire line of database products for Linux, including its Dynamic Server, Informix SE, Informix 4GL, and C-ISAM. Informix Dynamic Server features Dynamic Scalable Architecture, making it capable of effectively using any hardware setup. Informix SE (special edition) is a user-friendly and reliable database server that requires little database administration, while providing fast and consistent access supporting SQL. Informix 4GL includes database tools such as a debugger and compiler. C-ISAM is a library of C functions for indexed sequential access methods. Informix database systems provide flexible indexing, data consistency, integrity constraints, and security. Informix only provides commercial products. There are no free versions, though the company currently provides special promotions for Linux products. You can find out more about Informix at **www.informix.com/linux**.

Informix strongly supports Linux development of its Informix line. It provides developer support through its Informix Developer Network (**www.informix.com/idn**). It has a close working relationship with Red Hat and plan to provide joint technical support for their products.

Sybase

Sybase offers a line of database products ported to Linux for free. You can download them through the Sybase Web site at **www.sybase.com** or from its FTP site at **ftp.sybase.com/linux**. The free products include the Adaptive Server Enterprise server, the Open Client/C library (unsupported), and SQL Anywhere Studio (evaluation version). Currently you can download the Adaptive Server Enterprise server from Web page **www.sybase.com:80/products/databaseservers/linux/**, or from the Sybase FTP

APPLICATIONS

site at **ftp.sybase.com/linux**. The Sybase Enterprise database features data integration that coordinates all information resources on a network. SQL Anywhere is a database system designed for smaller databases, though with the same level of complexity found in larger databases.

DB2

IBM provides a Linux version of its DB2 Universal Database software. You can download it for free from the IBM DB2 Web page for Linux, **www.software.ibm.com/data/db2/linux/**. DB2 Universal Database for Linux includes Internet functionality along with support for Java and Perl. With the Web Control Center, administrators can maintain databases from a Web browser. DB2 features scalability to easily expand the database, support for Binary Large Objects, and cost-based optimization for fast access. DB2 is still very much a mainframe database, though IBM is currently working on refining its Unix/Linux version.

Ingres II

Ingres II is an industrial-strength relational database provided by Computer Associates. You can download a free copy of Ingres II as part of the Computer Associates Open Beta program for Linux. You can find a link for the download at the Computer Associates Web site at **www.cai.com/products/ingres.htm** or at **www.ingres.com**. The Beta version include the complete Ingres II database engine, with features like variable page size, support for Binary Large Objects, interfaces for C, compatibility with IngPerl (database access with the Perl scripting language), and Internet publishing capabilities. A complete set of online documentation is also included.

Adabas D

Adabas D is an intermediate relational database meant for use on smaller networks of personal databases. It still provides the flexibility and power found in all relational databases. Adabas D provides a personal version for Linux for free. For commercial uses you have to purchase a copy. You can find online documentation, including manuals and FAQs, at the Caldera Web site at **www.calderasystems.com**. You can also check the Adabas D Web site at **www.softwareag.com**.

MySQL

MySQL is a true multiuser, multithreaded SQL database server, developed by TcX. MySQL is free for personal and noncommercial use. You can download a copy from its Web site at **www.mysql.com**. The site also includes detailed documentation including manuals and FAQs. RPM packages are available for Red Hat and OpenLinux at the Red Hat contrib site at **contrib.redhat.com**.

MySQL is structured on a client/server model with a server daemon (`mysqld`) filling requests from client programs. MySQL is designed for speed, reliability, and ease of use. It is meant to be a very fast database management system for very large databases and, at the same time, very reliable with intensive use.

GNU SQL

GNU SQL is the GNU relational database developed by a group at the Institute for System Programming of the Russian Academy of Sciences and supported by the GNU organization. It is a portable multiuser database management system with a client/server structure that supports SQL. The server processes requests and performs basic administrative operations such as unloading parts of the database not frequently used. The clients can reside on any computer of a local network. GNU-SQL uses a dialect of SQL based on the SQL-89 standard and designed for use on a Unix-like environment. You can download the database software from the GNU FTP site at **ftp.gnu.org**. For more information contact the GNU-SQL Web site at **www.ispras.ru/~kml/gss**.

PostgreSQL

PostgreSQL is based on the POSTGRES database management system, though it uses SQL as its query language. POSTGRES is a next-generation research prototype developed at the University of California, Berkeley. A Linux version is available free of charge from its Web site at **www.postgresql.org**. Development is being managed by a team of developers over the Internet.

xBase Databases

Databases accessed with xBase are smaller in scale, designed for small networks or for personal use. Many are originally PC database programs such as dBaseIII, Clipper, FoxPro, and Quicksilver. Currently only Flagship provides an interface for accessing xBase database files, although the Harmony project is currently developing a Clipper clone that may run on Linux systems.

Flagship is a compiler with which you can create interfaces for querying xBase database files. The interfaces support menus and dialog boxes and have function calls that execute certain database queries. It can compile dBaseIII+ code and up. It is compatible with dBase and Clipper and can access most xBase file formats such as **.dbf**, **.dbt**, **.fmt**, and **.frm**. One of its key features is that its interfaces can be attached to a Web page, letting users update databases. Flagship is commercial software, though you can download a free personal version from its Web site at **www.fship.com/free.html**.

Desktop Database

Both Gnome and KDE also have database management applications that take advantage of their respective desktops. KDE's Katabase is part of KOffice and is fully integrated with its other applications. Gnome's Gaby takes advantage of the interface to display and search user databases.

Katabase (KOffice)

Katabase is a database management system that is part of the K Desktop's KOffice suite of programs. It is a desktop database somewhat like Microsoft Access and Paradox; however, it makes full use of its integration with other KOffice programs by means of

KOM/OpenParts. As part of KOffice, any part of Katabase can be embedded into another KOffice application, and Koffice components can be embedded into Katabase. You can find out more about Katabase at **koffice.kde.org**.

The main structure of Katabase is a plugin framework that operates as a base manager. The database is composed of different parts serviced by a KOM application that plugs into the base manager. Kdataparse is where the methods plug in to access different data type. The interface will look the same to the user no matter what method is being used. At Kdataparse you enter a SQL query. Kforms will display forms, Kreports will generate reports, Ktable will display tables, and Kscripts will run scripts. Katabase's modular design allows the addition of other components, expanding its capabilities.

Gaby

Gaby is a small personal database manager using GTK+ and Gnome. It provides access to user databases such as those for addresses, books, even photos. Its plugin design makes it easily extensible. You can find out more about Gaby at **gaby.netpedia.net**. Its interface has the same browser-like tools found in most Gnome applications. You can download the current version of Gaby from the Gnome software map at **www.gnome.org**.

Graphic Tools

Gnome, KDE, and the X Window System support an impressive number of graphic tools, including image viewers, window grabbers, image editors, and paint tools. On the KDE and Gnome desktops, these tools can be found under either a Graphics submenu or the Utilities menu.

KDE Graphic Tools

The kview program is a simple image viewer for GIF and JPEG image files. The ksnapshot program is a simple screen grabber for KDE. It currently supports only a few image formats. The kfourier program is an image processing tool that uses the Fourier transform to apply several filters to an image at once. The kshow program is a simple image viewer. The kuickShow program is an easy-to-use comfortable image browser and viewer, based on imlib. The kpaint program is a simple paint program with brushes, shapes, and color effects.

Gnome Graphic Tools

ImageShaker is a digital image processing tool that includes an extensive set of graphic filters such as alpha blending and median. It uses a stream-like approach that allows batch processing.

Electric Eyes is a simple image viewer. Right-click its window to display a pop-up menu with options. You can load images and also move back and forth through previously viewed ones. You can even make an image your background.

User Database	Title	Location on Web
Oracle	Oracle database	**www.oracle.com**
Sybase	Sybase database	**www.sybase.com**
DB2	IBM database	**www.software.ibm.com/data/db2/linux**
Informix	Informix database	**www.informix.com/linux**
Ingres II	Computer Associates database	**www.cai.com/products/ingres.htm**
Adabas D	Adabas D database	**www.softwareag.com**
MySQl	MySQL database	**www.mysql.com**
GNU SQL	The GNU SQL database	**www.ispras.ru/~kml/gss**
PostgreSQL	The PostgreSQL database	**www.postgresql.org**
Flagship	Interface for xBase database files	**www.fship.com/free.html**
Katabase	KOffice desktop database	**koffice.kde.org**
Gaby	Gnome desktop personal database	**gaby.netpedia.net**

Table 23-1. *Database Management Systems for Linux*

GQview is a simple image viewer supporting features like click file viewing, thumbnail preview, zoom, drag and drop, and external editor support, as well as slide show and full screen options. Multiple files can selected for moving, copying, deleting, renaming, or dragging. See **gqview.netpedia.net** for more information.

The GIMP is the GNU Image Manipulation Program. It is a very sophisticated image application much like Adobe Photoshop. You can use it for such tasks as photo retouching, image composition, and image authoring. It supports features like layers, channels, blends, and gradients. It makes particular use of the GTK+ widget set. You can find out more about the GIMP from its Web site at **www.gimp.org**. You can also download the newest versions from here. GIMP if freely distributed under the GNU public license.

X Graphic

The xv program is a screen capture and image editing program. After displaying the main screen, right-click it to display its control screen. Use the Grab button to scan a window or a section you select with a drag operation using your middle mouse button. Once you have scanned a window or screen section, you can crop it with a drag operation with your left mouse key and then use crop to reduce to that selected section. With xv you can also convert an image file from one format to another. Just load the image and then save it as another file using a different image format.

The xpaint program is a painting program much like MacPaint. You can load paint pictures or photographs and then create shapes, add text, and add colors. You can use brush tools with various sizes and colors. The xfig program is a drawing program, and xmorph lets you morph images, changing their shapes.

KDE	Description
kview	Simple image viewer for GIF and JPEG image files
ksnapshot	Screen grabber
kfourier	Image processing tool that uses the Fourier transform
kuickShow	Image browser and viewer
kshow	Simple image viewer
kpaint	Paint program
Gnome	
Gqview	Image viewer
ImageShaker	Digital image processing
GIMP	GNU Image Manipulation Program
Electric Eyes	Image viewer
X Window System	
xv	Screen grabber and image conversion
xpaint	Paint program
xfig	Drawing program
xmorph	Morphs images
xfractals	Generates fractal images

Table 23-2. *Graphic Tools for Linux*

Chapter 24

Software Management

Installing or updating software packages has become a very simple process in Linux. Software for the major distributions such as Red Hat and OpenLinux use package software in special archives called RPMs. RPM stands for the Red Hat Package Manager. An RPM archive will contain all the program files, configuration files, data files, and even documentation that constitute a software application. With one simple operation, the Red Hat Package Manager will install all these for you from an RPM software package. You can even create your own RPM packages. You can use any of several RPM window-based utilities to manage your RPM packages, installing new ones or uninstalling ones you have. These utilities provide an easy-to-use interface for managing your packages, letting you easily obtain detailed information on a package, including a complete listing of the files it installs. Also, as part of their administration tools, distributions like Red Hat and OpenLinux also provide software management for packages on their CD-ROMs.

You can also download source code versions of applications, and then compile and install them on your system. Where this process once was complex, it has since been significantly streamlined with the addition of *configure scripts.* Most current source code, including GNU software, is distributed with a configure script. The configure script automatically detects your system configuration and generates a **Makefile** with which a binary will be created compatible to your system. With just three simple commands you can compile and install complex source code on any system.

There are extensive online sources for downloading Linux software. There are sites for particular kinds of applications such as Gnome and KDE, as well as for particular distributions like Red Hat. Some are repositories for RPM packages like **rpmfind.net** and others like **freshmeat.net** refer you to original development sites where you can download software packages. The **freshmeat.net** site is particularly useful for finding out about new software available. The Linux Applications and Utilities page lists one of the most extensive collections of Linux software. For particular database and office applications you can download software packages directly from the company's Web site, such as **www.stardivision.com** for the StarOffice office suite and **www.oracle.com** for the Oracle database (see Chapters 22 and 23). For particular RPM packages for Red Hat you can use the **contrib.redhat.com** site. Here you find Red Hat RPM packages for applications like ProFTPD and ht:/Dig. Table 24-1 lists several popular Linux software sites.

Red Hat Package Manager (RPM)

Several Linux distributions, including Red Hat, OpenLinux, and SuSE, use the Red Hat Package Manager (RPM) to organize Linux software into packages that you can automatically install or remove. An RPM software package operates like its own installation program for a software application. A Linux software application will often consist of several files that need to be installed in different directories. The program

FTP and Web Sites	Applications
contrib.redhat.com	Software packaged in RPM packages for Red Hat
updates.redhat.com	Red Hat update packages
ftp.calderasystems.com	Check the contrib directory for contributed software
freshmeat.net	New Linux software
rpmfind.net	RPM package repository
www.gnome.org	Gnome software
www.kde.org	KDE software
http://www.xnet.com/ ~blatura/linapps.shtml	Linux Applications and Utilities Page
www.filewatcher.org	Linux FTP site watcher
www.gnu.org	GNU Archive
www.opensound.com	Open Sound System drivers
www.uk.linux.org/Commercial.html	Linux Commercial Vendors Index
linuxwww.db.erau.edu/	Linux archive
metalab.unc.edu	Extensive Linux archive (formerly **sunsite.unc.edu**)
happypenguin.org	Linux Game Tome
www.linuxgames.org	Linux games
www.linuxquake.com	Quake

Table 24-1. *Linux Software Sites*

itself will most likely be placed in a directory called **/usr/bin**, online manual files will go in another directory, and library files, in yet another. In addition, the installation may require modification of certain configuration files on your system. The RPM software packages will perform all these tasks for you. Also, if you should later decide that you don't want a specific application, you can uninstall packages to remove all the files and configuration information from your system. RPM works very similar to the

Windows install wizard, automatically installing software, including configuration, documentation, image, sample, and program files, along with any other files an application may use. All are installed in their appropriate directories on your system. RPM maintains a database of installed software, keeping track of all the files installed. This lets you use RPM to also uninstall software, automatically removing all files that are part of the application.

To install and uninstall RPM packages you can use the **rpm** command on a shell command line or use any available RPM window-based program such as kpackage or GnomeRPM. Also, distribution install and management utilities such as COAS, Lisa, and YaST let you install or uninstall your distribution software packages. These are usually the RPM packages on your CD-ROM. Though you should download RPM packages for your particular distribution, numerous RPM software packages are designed to run on any Linux system. Many of these are located at distribution contrib sites or directories such as **contrib.redhat.com**. You can find out more about RPM at its Web site at **www.rpm.org**. The site contains up-to-date versions for RPM, documentation, and RPM support programs such as **rpm2html** and **rpm2cpio**. The former will take a directory containing RPM packages and generate a Web page listing those packages as links that can be used to download them. The latter is a Perl script to extract RPMs.

The RPM packages on your CD-ROMs only represent a small portion of the software packages available for Linux. You can download additional software in the form of RPM packages from distribution contrib sites, such as **contrib.redhat.com** for Red Hat packages and the **contrib** directory in the OpenLinux FTP site at **ftp.calderasystems.com**. In addition, these packages are organized into **lib5** and **lib6** directories. The **lib5** directory refers to the packages using the older libraries, whereas **lib6** refers to those using the new GNU 2.x libraries. For Red Hat 6.0 and OpenLinux 2.2 you should use the **lib6** versions, though **lib5** versions will also work.

There is also an extensive repository for RPM packages located at **http://rpmfind.net/linux/RPM**. Here packages are indexed according to distribution, group, and name. It includes packages for every distribution including previous versions of those distributions. From **http://rpmfind.net** you can download the **rpmfind** command that will let you search for RPM packages either on your local system or on the RPM repository at **rpmfind.net**. You can even use **rpmfind** to download and update packages. It will detect your system's distribution and list RPM packages for it. Search results will also tell what other packages a given RPM will depend on. With the **--appropos** option you can use more general terms to locate a package, instead of file name patterns. With the **--upgrade** option you can download and install newer versions of installed packages. The **rpmfind** command also sets up a **.rpmfind** configuration file where you can specify such features as a download directory, the remote servers to search, and the location of local RPM packages on your system.

Distributions such as the one for Red Hat 6.0 or OpenLinux 2.2 include an extensive set of applications. These are located in an **RPMS** directory. On the Red Hat 6.0 CD-ROM these are in the **RedHat/RPMS** directory, and on OpenLinux they are in

col/install/RPMS. You can install any of these packages using an **rpm** command, a GUI RPM utility, or the software manager screen on your distribution administration tool. To install a software package from your CD-ROM using the **rpm** command, it is easier to move first to the **RPMS** directory and then install the package you want. Be sure to first mount the CD-ROM before you try to access it.

You will have to download additional RPM packages not on your CD-ROM from distribution contrib sites or directories such as **contrib.redhat.com**. Web sites for the particular software you want may also have RPM packages already set up for you for your distribution. For example, you can obtain the ProFTPD RPM package for Red Hat from **contrib.redhat.com**, and the current Red Hat or OpenLinux Linuxconf RPM packages from the Linuxconf Web site (see Chapter 27). You could place these packages in a directory on your system and then use either **rpm** or a GUI RPM utility like GnomeRPM to install it. Normally, you should always try to use the version of the RPM package setup for your distribution. In many cases, attempting to install an RPM meant for a different distribution will fail. There are some exceptions. For example, the WordPerfect RPM package on the OpenLinux CD-ROM provided with this book will install on Red Hat 6.0, also included with this book. Popular RPM package managers are listed in Table 24-2.

The K Desktop Package Manager: kpackage

The KDE desktop provides a very powerful and easy-to-use RPM package manager called kpackage (see Figure 24-1). You run kpackage under any window manager or desktop (including Gnome), as long as you have installed the K Desktop on your system. You can start kpackage by selecting its entry in the K menu utility menu, or by entering the **kpackage** command in a terminal window.

Package Managers	Description
Kpackage	K Desktop RPM package manager
GnomeRPM	Gnome RPM package manager
rpm	The shell command to manage RPM packages
Xrpm	X Window System RPM package manager
Glint	Older X Window System RPM package manager

Table 24-2.   *RPM Package Managers*

APPLICATIONS

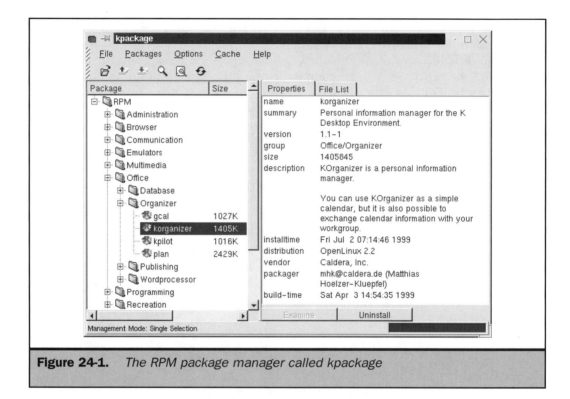

Figure 24-1. *The RPM package manager called kpackage*

The right side of kpackage contains two tabbed panels, one for Properties and the other for the File List. The Properties panel displays information about the software in the currently selected RPM package, including the version number and the authors. The File List lists all the files that are contained in the software package, including README files. If you are using kpackage on the K Desktop, you can click any text file in the File List and it will be displayed by the text editor. This is a very convenient way to read installation files such as README or INSTALL files. To uninstall a package, just select it and click Uninstall.

Often the list of installed packages is extensive. To locate a particular package, you select the Find entry in the File menu. If the Substring check box is selected, you can use a pattern to search for your package instead of a complete name. The package list in the left pane will move to the first package found, highlighting it. If you used a pattern and there are more choices, you can move to the next one by selecting the Find menu item again. The kpackage application also lets you search for a particular file in a package. Select the Find File entry in the File menu and enter the name of the file to search for. You have to use the full pathname for the file. Patterns are not supported.

You can also use kpackage to install RPM packages. You will have to know where on the system the packages are located. For example, on OpenLinux systems, the RPM packages on the CD-ROM are located in the **col/install/RPMS** directory. For Red Hat they are in the **RedHat/RPMS** directory. If you mounted the CD-ROM at **/mnt/cdrom**, then the full pathname under OpenLinux should be **/mnt/cdrom/col/install/RPMS**, and that for Red Hat should be **/mnt/cdrom/RedHat/RPMS**. Packages that you download from FTP sites would be in whatever directory you downloaded them to, say **/root/ download**. To install a package, select Open from the File menu. This opens a file browser dialog where you can move to the directory you want and select the RPM package. An Installation dialog is displayed with options that include updating and testing the package. You select Update for packages that are updated versions of ones already installed. With the Test option you can test an installation without having to actually install it.

GnomeRPM

Though not written by Red Hat, GnomeRPM provides an effective and easy-to-use interface for managing RPM packages on your Gnome desktop. It will run on any window manager, provided that Gnome is installed on your system. As Figure 24-2 shows, the GnomeRPM window displays two panes, the left one showing a tree listing categories of different installed RPM packages. Expand a category to display the packages in the right pane. You can query a package by selecting it and clicking the Uninstall icon in the icon bar, or by right-clicking it and selecting Uninstall from the pop-up menu. You can use the same method for querying packages and for displaying information and file listings. You can select several packages at once from different categories by Ctrl-clicking their icons. A selected package will darken. When you select uninstall, all of those packages will be uninstalled. Just Ctrl-click the package again to deselect it. Click Unselect to deselect all the packages you selected. The number of selected packages is shown in the lower-left corner of the window. The GnomeRPM package also features a find utility that you can use to locate RPM packages easily. In the find window you can then query or uninstall the package.

To install new packages with GnomeRPM, click the Install icon. This opens a window that will display the selected packages to install. You then click Add to open a window for locating packages on your system. You can add as many as you wish to the list. Click Install to install the packages. To upgrade a package that is already installed, click Upgrade and follow the same procedure.

GnomeRPM supports drag-and-drop operations from the desktop and file manager. You can drag one or more RPM packages from a file manager window to the GnomeRPM install dialog window. You can then install or query selected packages. GnomeRPM also lets you browse through packages available with the rpmfind system. Click on the Web Find button. The listing of packages will be downloaded and displayed in the treemenu. Use the treemenu to navigate to the package you want.

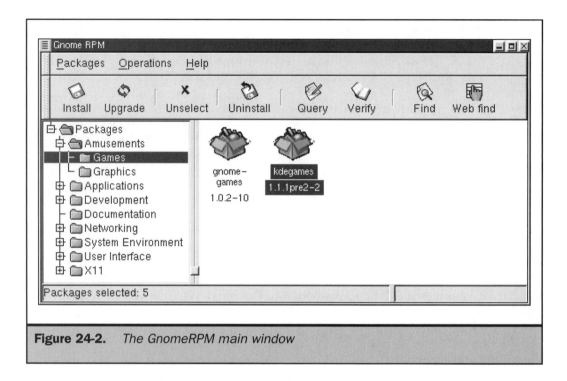

Figure 24-2. *The GnomeRPM main window*

KDE and Gnome File Managers

On Gnome, you can install RPM packages directly from the file manager, without using any special utility such as GnomeRPM. Use the file manager window to access the directory with your package, such as your distribution CD-ROM. Then right-click on the package name or icon. In the pop-up menu you can select the Install option to install the package. You can use this same method for FTP sites. The Gnome file manager is Internet aware. You can enter a URL for an FTP site in its location box to access the site. Be sure to include the FTP protocol in the URL, `ftp://`. When you have located the package, right-click on it and select Install or Update. The file is downloaded and then automatically installed on your system. (See Chapters 4, 6, and 13.)

The KDE file manager also lets you install RPM packages, though it uses kpackage to perform the actual installation. Just locate an RPM file on your system using the file manager, then single-click on its icon or name. This will automatically open kpackage with the RPM package loaded. It will be displayed on a window with panels for the package information and the list of files in it. At the bottom of the panels is an Install button. Click it to install the package. As the KDE file manager is Internet aware, you can use this same method to both download and install RPM packages from FTP sites. Locate the FTP site with the file manager (enter the URL in the location box), then locate your package. Once it is listed in the file manager window, just click on it. It will be automatically downloaded and then kpackage will start up showing the package. Just click the Install button to install it. (See Chapters 4, 5, and 14.)

Distribution CD-ROMs: COAS, Lisa, and YaST

COAS, Lisa, and YaST provide a simple software management interface for adding and removing RPM packages that come with a distribution release. This interface allows you to install or uninstall the software packages included with the distribution. If you choose anything other than a full installation when you installed your Linux system, then uninstalled packages will remain on your distribution CD-ROM. You can use the software management screen to install these packages or uninstall ones you don't want.

For OpenLinux, you select Software Management from the main COAS menu. This displays a series of columns that represent a hierarchical tree. Each column to the right is a sublisting of categories selected to the left. Each entry has a check box that toggles on and off. When the box is checked, the software will be installed, if it is not already. When the check is cleared, the software will be uninstalled. Checking categories to the left lets you select a whole range of software packages at once. You do not have to sort through and select them separately. With LISA, you select the Software Package Administration entry to display a menu from which you can choose to install or remove packages. To select a package, move to that package using the arrow keys and press SPACEBAR.

For SuSE, you select Choose/Install packages from the YaST main menu. Then select Change/Create Configuration to open a configuration window that displays a list of software packages. This window is divided into two panes, the upper one showing the list of packages and the lower one showing a description of a selected package. Use the arrow and page keys to move through the list, and use the ENTER key to select a package. Entries are displayed with a status indicator enclosed in brackets, the name of the package, and a short description. The status indicator can be empty for not yet installed, X for packages to be installed, i for packages that are already installed, D for packages to be removed, and R for packages to be updated. Continually pressing ENTER on a package entry will move through this list. Stop at the one you want. YaST also organizes packages into categories called series. Pressing F4 opens a window listing these series from which you can select one. A series will show how much disk space it will take up. The F10 key returns to the configuration menu. When you return to the "Choose/Install packages" menu, you can then select "Start installation" to install your packages.

YaST also lets you install from sources other than your CD-ROM such as FTP sites or local directories. Select the Install Packages entry in the Choose/Install Packages menu. YaST supports several types of packages including .rpm, .spm, and .tgz. The default FTP site is SuSE's update FTP site holding package updates for the SuSE distribution. Select the packages you want with the SPACEBAR and then press F10 to download and install them.

Command Line Installation: rpm

If you do not have access to the desktop or would prefer to work from the command line interface, you can use the **rpm** command to manage and install software packages. It is the command that actually performs installation, removal, and queries of software packages. In fact, GnomeRPM, kpackage, and distribution utilities like COAS and YaST use the **rpm** command to install and remove packages. An RPM package is an archive of software files that include information about how to install those files. The file names for RPM packages end with **.rpm**, indicating software packages that can be installed by the Red Hat Package Manager.

With the **rpm** command you can maintain packages, query them, build your own, and verify the ones you have. Maintaining packages involve installing new ones, upgrading to new versions, and uninstalling packages. The **rpm** command uses a set of options to determine what action to take. In addition, certain tasks such as installing or querying packages have their own options that further qualify the kind of action they take. For example, the **-q** option queries a package, but when combined with the **-l** option, it will list all the files in that package. Table 24-2 lists the set of **rpm** options.

You use the **-i** option to install a new software package and the **-U** option to update a currently installed package with a newer version. With the **-e** option, **rpm** will uninstall the package. The **q** option will tell you if a package is already installed, and the **qa** option will display a list of all installed packages. It is best to pipe this output to a pager utility like **more**.

```
rpm -qa | more
```

In the next example, the user checks to see if **xv** is already installed on the system. Notice that the full file name of the **rpm** archive is not needed. If the package is installed, your system has already registered its name and where it is located.

```
# rpm -q xv
```

You can combine the **q** options with the **i** or **l** options to display information about the package. The options **-qi** display information about the software such as the version number or author (**-qpi** will query an uninstalled package file). The options **-ql** will display a listing of all the files in the software package. The **--h** option provides a complete list of **rpm** options. The syntax for the **rpm** command is as follows (*rpm-package-name* is the name of the software package that you want to install):

```
rpm options rpm-package-name
```

The software package name is usually very lengthy, including information about version and release date in its name. All end with **.rpm**.

An **ls** command will list all the software packages. If you know how the name of a package begins, you should include that with the **ls** command and an attached *****. The list of packages is extensive and will not all fit on one screen. This is helpful for displaying the detailed name of the package. The following example lists X Window System packages:

```
# ls x*
```

You use the **-i** option to install new packages and the **-U** option to update currently installed packages with new versions. If you try to use the **-i** option to install a newer version of an installed package, you will receive an error saying that the package is already installed. In the next example, the user first installs a new package with the **-i** option and then updates a package with the **-U** option. It is customary to include the **-v** and **-h** options. Here, **-v** is the verbose option that will display all files as they are installed, and **-h** displays a cross-hatch symbol periodically to show RPM is still working.

In the following example, the user installs the software package for ht:/Dig (Chapter 21). Notice that the full file name is entered. To list the full name, you can use the **ls** command with the first few characters and an asterisk, **ls htdig***. The **h** option will display # symbols as the installation takes place. The **rpm** command with the **-q** option is then used to check that the software was installed. For installed packages only the software name needs to be used, in this case htdig.

```
[root@turtle mypackages]# ls ht*
htdig-3.1.2-0glibc.i386.rpm
[root@turtle mypackages]# rpm -ivh htdig-3.1.2-0glibc.i386.rpm
htdig                        #############################################
[root@turtle mypackages]# rpm -q htdig
htdig-3.1.2-0glibc
```

To display information about the installed package, you use **-qi**, and **-ql** will display a listing of the files a given RPM package contains.

```
# rpm -qi htdig
# rpm -ql htdig
```

To display information taken directly from an RPM package, you add the **p** qualifier to the **q** options. The **-qpi** combination will display information about a specific package, and **-qpl** will display a listing of the files a given RPM package contains. In this case you will have to specify the entire file name of the RPM package.

You can avoid having to enter the entire name by just entering a unique part of the name and using the * file name matching character to generate the rest.

```
[root@turtle mypackages]# ls proftp*
proftpd-1.2.0pre3-2.i386.rpm
[root@turtle mypackages]# rpm -qp proftpd-1.2.0pre3-2.i386.rpm
proftpd-1.2.0pre3-2
[root@turtle mypackages]# rpm - qpi proftpd-1.2*.rpm
Name        : proftpd              Relocations: (not relocateable)
Version     : 1.2.0pre3                 Vendor: (none)
.................................................
[root@turtle mypackages]# rpm -qpl proftpd*
/etc/logrotate.d/proftpd
/etc/pam.d/ftp
/etc/proftpd.conf
.................................................
```

Remember that if you are installing an upgrade, you need to use the **-U** option instead of the **-i** option. If you try to use **-i** to upgrade a package, you receive an error saying that the package is already installed. If you receive an error stating that there are dependency conflicts, the package may require other packages or their updated versions to be installed first. In some cases you may have to install with the no dependency check options, **--nodeps** (notice the two dashes before the option). In some rare cases, installation instructions for a particular package may require you to use **--nodeps**. Another risky option is the **--force** option. This forces installation, overwriting any current files. This is a brute-force approach that should be used with care.

To remove a software package from your system, first use **rpm -q** to make sure it is actually installed. Then, use the **-e** option to uninstall it. You do not have to use the full name of the installed file. You only need the name of the application. For example, if you decide that you do not need ht:/Dig, you can remove it using the **-e** option and just the software name as shown here.

```
# rpm  -e  htdig
```

If there are direct conflicts with another software package, you may have to uninstall the other package first. This is the case with wu-ftpd and ProFTP on many distributions. Distributions such as Red Hat and OpenLinux currently install wu-ftpd as the default FTP server. You will have to first uninstall the wu-ftpd with the **-e** option before you can install ProFTP. However, when you try to do that, you will receive a dependency error. You can overcome that error by using the **-nodeps** options. Once it is removed, you can then install ProFTP.

```
[root@turtle mypackages]# rpm -e --nodeps wu-ftpd
 [root@turtle mypackages]# rpm -ivh proftpd-1.2*rpm
proftpd                    ############################################
[root@turtle mypackages]# rpm -q proftpd
proftpd-1.2.0pre3-2
```

A complete description of **rpm** and its capabilities is provided in the online manual.

```
# man rpm
```

RPM maintains a record of the packages it has installed in its RPM database. You may, at times, have to rebuild this data base to ensure that RPM has current information on what is installed and what is not. Use the **-rebuild** options to rebuild your database file.

```
rpm --rebuild
```

To create a new RPM database, use the **-initdb** option. This can be combined with **-dbpath** to specify a location for the new database.

Mode of Operation	Effect
rpm **-i***options package-file*	Installs a package; the complete name of the package file is required
rpm **-e***options package-name*	Uninstalls (erases) a package; you only need the name of the package, often one word
rpm **-q***options package-name*	Queries a package; an option can be a package name or a further option and package name, or an option applied to all packages
rpm **-U***options package-name*	Upgrade; same as install, but any previous version is removed
rpm **-b0***options package-specifications*	Builds your own **rpm** package

Table 24-3. *Red Hat Package Manager (RPM) Options*

APPLICATIONS

Mode of Operation	Effect
`rpm -F`*options package-name*	Upgrade, but only if package is currently installed
`rpm -verify`*options*	Verifies that a package is correctly installed; uses same options as query; you can use **-V** or **-y** in place of **-verify**
`--nodeps`	Installs without doing any dependency checks
`--force`	Forces installation despite conflicts
`--percent`	Displays percentage of package during installation
`--test`	Tests installation; does not install, just checks for conflicts
`-h`	Displays # symbols as package is installed
`-excludedocs`	Excludes documentation files
Uninstall Options (to be used with -e)	
`--test`	Tests uninstall; does not remove, just checks for what will be removed
`--nodeps`	Uninstalls without checking for dependencies
`--allmatches`	Removes all versions of package
Query Options (to be used with -q)	
package-name	Queries package
`-a`	Queries all packages
`-f` *filename*	Queries package that owns *filename*
`-R`	Lists packages that this package depends on

Table 24-3.   *Red Hat Package Manager (RPM) Options* (continued)

Mode of Operation	Effect
-p *package-name*	Queries an uninstalled package
-i	Displays all package information
-l	Lists files in package
-d	Lists only documentation files in package
-c	Lists only configuration files in package
--dump	Lists only files with complete details
General Options (to be used with any option)	
-vv	Debug; displays descriptions of all actions taken
--quit	Displays only error messages
--version	Displays **rpm** version number
--help	Displays detailed usage message
--root*directory*	Uses directory as top-level directory for all operations (instead of root)
--dbpath*directory*	Uses RPM database in the specified directory
--dbpath *cmd*	Pipes output of RPM to the command *cmd*
--rebuild	Rebuilds the RPM database; can use with **–root** and **–dbpath** options
--initdb	Builds a new RPM database; **–root** and **–dbpath** options
Other Sources of Information	
`RPM-HOWTO` on **www.Red Hat.com**	More detailed information, particularly on how to build your own **rpm** packages
`man rpm`	Detailed list of options

Table 24-3.   *Red Hat Package Manager (RPM) Options* (continued)

Updating Distributions

In the period between major releases, distributions will post RPM package updates for software that was installed from your CD-ROM. Red Hat posts these packages at their update site at **updates.redhat.com**. OpenLinux posts them in the Updates directory on their FTP site at **ftp.calderasystems.com**. Such updates may range from single software packages to whole components, for instance, all the core, applications, and development packages issued when a new release of Gnome, KDE, or XFree86 are made available. For single packages, you can just download them from the distribution FTP site and then use the **rpm** command with the **-U** option to install them. You could also use an RPM utility such as kpackage. In fact, you can use both kpackage and GnomeRPM to directly access the distribution FTP sites, download the package, and automatically install it on your system. Just enter the FTP URL for the site in the Location box. In the following example, the **rpm** command with the **-Uvh** option installs an upgrade for Linuxconf.

```
$ rpm -Uvh  linuxconf-1.16r-1-1.i386.rpm
```

For a very large upgrade you will first have to download all the packages required and then install them. For example, to install new releases of the K Desktop you can download distribution versions of their packages from the KDE FTP site at **ftp.kde.org** or from distribution FTP sites, though you should always check the distribution FTP site first (like **redhat.com** updates). You can use an FTP client such as ncftp to download them all at once, including any subdirectories (see Chapter 5). Then change to that directory and use the **rpm -Uvh** command to install the packages.

Installing Software from Compressed Archives: .tar.gz

Linux software applications in the form of source code are available at different sites on the Internet. You can download any of this software and install it on your system. You download software using an FTP client as described in Chapter 12. Very recent and older software is usually downloaded in the form of a compressed archive file. This is particularly true for the very recent versions of Gnome or KDE packages. RPM packages are only intermittently generated. A compressed archive is an archive file that was created with **tar** and then compressed with **gzip**. To install such a file, you have to first decompress it with the **gunzip** utility and then use **tar** to extract the files and directories making up the software package. Instead of **gunzip**, you could also use **gzip -d**. The next example decompresses the **ganesha-0.6.tar.gz** file, replacing it with a decompressed version called **ganesha-0.6.tar**.

```
$ ls
 ganesha-0.6.tar.gz
$ gunzip ganesha-0.6.tar.gz
$ ls
ganesha-0.6.tar
```

First use **tar** with the **t** option to check the contents of the archive. If the first entry is a directory, that directory will be created and the extracted files will be placed in it. If the first entry is not a directory, you should first create one and then copy the archive file to it. Then extract the archive within that directory. If there is no directory as the first entry, files will be extracted to the current directory. You have to create a directory yourself to hold these files.

```
$ tar tf ganesha-0.6.tar
```

Now you are ready to extract the files from the tar archive. You use **tar** with the **x** option to extract files, the **v** option to display the pathnames of files as they are extracted, and the **f** option followed by the name of the archive file:

```
$ tar xvf ganesha-0.6.tar
```

You can combine the decompressing and unpacking operation into one **tar** command by adding a **z** option to the option list, **xzvf**. The following command both decompresses and unpacks the archive:

```
$ tar xzvf ganesha-0.6.tar.gz
```

Installation of your software may differ for each package. Instructions are usually provided along with an installation program.

Downloading Compressed Archives from Online Sites

Many software packages under development or designed for cross-platform implementation may not be in an RPM format. Instead, they may be archived and compressed. The file names for these files will end with the extensions **.tar.gz** or **.tar.Z**. In fact, most software with an RPM format also has a corresponding **.tar.gz** format. After you download such a package, you will first have to decompress it with **gunzip** and then unpack it with the **tar** command. Many RPM packages only contain binary versions of software applications. If you want the source code for the application, you will have to download and unpack the compressed archive for that application.

In the next example, the user uses **ftp** to connect to the **metalab.unc.edu** Linux FTP site. (You can use any FTP client; see Chapter 13.) For the login ID, the user enters **anonymous**, and for the password, the user enters his or her Internet address. The download mode can be set to binary by entering in the keyword **binary**. With the **cd** command, the user changes to the **pub/Linux/libs/X/xview** directory, where the Xview window manager software is located (see Chapter 3). The **get** command then downloads the package. The **close** command cuts the connection and **quit** leaves the **ftp** utility.

```
ftp> get xview-3.2p1.4.bin.tar.gz
>local: xview-3.2p1.4.bin.tar.gz remote: xview-3.2p1.4.bin.tar.gz
200 PORT command successful.
150 Opening BINARY mode data connection for xview-3.2p1.4.bin.tar.gz
226 Transfer complete.
2192197 bytes received in 728 secs (2.9 Kbytes/sec)
ftp>
```

Alternatively, you could just use Netscape or another Web Browser to access, browse through, and download software without having to bother with all the **ftp** commands. You can also use the Gnome and KDE file managers. Be sure to precede an FTP site name with the term **ftp://** instead of the usual **http://**. For Sunsite you would enter: **ftp://metalab.unc.edu**. Once you have selected the software you want, hold down the SHIFT key and click it to download it.

Once downloaded, any file that ends with a **.Z** , **bz**, **.zip**, or **.gz** is a compressed file that has to be decompressed. You would use the **gunzip** command followed by the name of the file.

```
# gunzip xview-3.2p1.4.bin.tar.gz
```

If the file then ends with **.tar**, it is an archived file that has to be unpacked using the **tar** command. Before you unpack the archive, you should move it to the directory you want it in. Source code that you intend to compile is usually placed in the **/usr/src** directory. Most archives will unpack to a subdirectory that they create, placing all those files or directories making up the software package into that subdirectory. For example, the file **xview-3.2p1.4.bin.tar** will unpack to a subdirectory called **usr**. To check if an archive will unpack to a directory, use **tar** with the **t** option to list its contents and see if the names are prefixed by a directory. If so, that directory will be created and the extracted files placed in it. If there is no directory name, you should first create one and then copy the archive file to it. Then extract the archive within that directory.

```
# tar tf xview-3.2p1.4.bin.tar
```

Now you are ready to extract the files from the tar archive. You use **tar** with the **x** option to extract files, the **v** option to display the pathnames of files as they are extracted, and the **f** option followed by the name of the archive file:

```
# tar xvf xview-3.2p1.4.bin.tar
```

Installation of your software may differ for each package. Instructions are usually provided along with an installation program. Downloaded software will usually include README files or other documentation. Be sure to consult them.

Compiling Software

Some software may be in the form of source code that you will need to compile before you can install it. This is particularly true of programs designed for cross-platform implementations. Programs designed to run on various Unix systems such as Sun, as well as on Linux, may be distributed as source code that is downloaded and compiled in those different systems. Compiling such software has been greatly simplified in recent years by the use of configuration scripts that will automatically detect a given system's configuration and compile the program accordingly. For example, the name of the C compiler on a system could be **gcc** or **cc**. Configuration scripts will detect which is present and use it to compile the program.

Before you compile software, you should first read the README or INSTALL files included with it. These will give you detailed instructions on how to compile and install this particular program. If the software used configuration scripts, then compiling and installing usually involves only the following three simple commands:

```
# ./configure
# make
# make install
```

The **./configure** command performs configuration detection. The **make** command performs the actual compiling, using a **Makefile** script generated by the **./configure** operation. The make install will install the program on your system, placing the executable program in a directory like **/usr/local/bin** and any configuration files in **/etc**. Any shared libraries it created may go into **/usr/lib**.

If you are compiling an X-, Gnome-, or KDE-based program, be sure that their development libraries have been installed. For X applications, also be sure that the **xmkmf** program is also installed. If you chose a standard install when you installed your distribution system, these will most likely not be installed. For distributions using RPM packages, these come in the form of a set of development RPM packages, usually having the word "development" or just "develop" in their name. You will have to install them using either RPM, kpackage, or GnomeRPM. Gnome in particular has an extensive set of RPM packages for development libraries. Many X applications may need special shared libraries. For example, some applications may need the xforms library or the Qt library. Some of these you will have to obtain from online sites.

Some older X applications use **xmkmf** directly instead of a configure script to generate the needed **Makefile**. In this case, you would enter the command **xmkmf** in place of **./configure**. Be sure to consult the INSTALL and README files for the software. Usually, you only need to issue the following commands within the directory that contains the source code files for the software.

```
xmkmf
make
make install
```

If there is no configure script and the program does not use **xmkmf**, you may just have to enter the **make** command, followed by a make install operation. Check the README or INSTALL files for details.

```
make
make install
```

Be sure to check the documentation for such software to see if there are any changes for you to make to the **Makefile**. There may be only a few, but more detailed changes require an understanding of C programming and how **make** works with it. If you successfully configure the **Makefile**, you may just have to enter the make and make install operations. One possible problem is locating the development libraries for C and X-Windows. X-Windows libraries are in the **/usr/X11R6/lib** directory. Standard C libraries are located in the **/usr/lib** directory.

Command and Program Directories: PATH

Programs and commands are usually installed in several standard system directories such as **/bin**, **/usr/bin**, **/usr/X11R6/bin**, or **/usr/local/bin**. However, some packages will place their commands in subdirectories that they create within one of these standard directories or in an entirely separate directory. In such cases, you may not be able to run those commands because your system may not be able to locate them in the new subdirectory. Your system maintains a set of directories that searches for commands each time you execute one. This set of directories is kept in a system variable called PATH that is created when you start your system. If a command is in a directory that is not in this list, then your system will not be able to locate it and run it. To use such commands, you first need to add the new directory to the set of directories in the PATH variable.

On the OpenLinux and Red Hat systems, the PATH variable is assigned its set of directories in the **/etc/profile** file, which is a script that is run when your system starts and is used to configure user's working environments. In this file you will find a line that begins with PATH followed by an = sign and then a list of directories, each separated by a colon. These are the directories that contain commands and programs.

To add a directory, carefully edit the **/etc/profile** file using a text editor such as kedit, gedit, Emacs, or Vi (you may want to make a backup copy first with the **cp** command). At the end of the list of directories, add the new directory with its full pathname before the closing double quote. Be sure a colon separates the new directory from the last one. You should also have a colon at the end. For example, if you install the **MH** mail utility, the **MH** commands will be installed in a subdirectory called **mh** in the **/usr/bin** directory. The full pathname for this directory is **/usr/bin/mh**. You need to add this directory to the list of directories assigned to PATH in the **/etc/profile** script. (The command **rpm -qpl** *package-name* will list all the directories where commands in an RPM software package are installed.) The following example shows the PATH variable with its list of directories and the **/usr/bin/mh** directory added (shown in bold).

```
PATH="/bin:/usr/bin:/opt/bin:/usr/X11R6/bin:/usr/openwin/bin:/usr/
local/bin:/usr/bin/mh:"
```

The **/etc/profile** script is a system script that is executed for each user when the user logs in. Individual users can customize their PATH variables by placing a PATH assignment in either their **.bashrc** or **.profile** files. In this way users can access commands and programs that they create or install for their own use in their own user directories (see Chapter 10 for more details). The following entry in the **.profile** file would add a user's **mybin** directory to the PATH variable. Use of $PATH keeps all the directories already listed in the **/etc/profile** script. Notice both the colon placed before the new directory and the use of the $HOME variable to specify the pathname for the user's home directory.

```
PATH=$PATH:$HOME/mybin:
```

Packaging Your Software: Autoconf and RPM

Once you have finished developing your software, you may then want to distribute it to others. Ordinarily you would pack your program into a **tar** archive file. People would then download the file and unpack it. You would have to include detailed instructions on how to install it and where to place any supporting documentation and libraries. If you were distributing the source code, users would have to figure out how to adapt the source code to their systems. There are any number of variations that may stop compilation of a program.

The Red Hat Package Manager (RPM) and Autoconf are designed to automate these tasks. The Autoconf program is used to automatically configure source code to a given system. RPM will automatically install software on a system in the designated directories, along with any documentation, libraries, or support programs. Both have very complex and powerful capabilities and are able to handle the most complex programs. Simple examples of their use are provided here.

Autoconf

A Unix system can compile any software written in the C programming language. However, different Unix systems have different configurations, some using different compilers or placing programs and libraries in different system directories. Different types of support libraries may be present. In the past, in order to compile software on different systems, the software had to be manually configured for each system. For example, if your system has the **gcc** compiler instead of the **cc** compiler, you would have to set that feature in the software's **Makefile**.

The Autoconf program is designed to automate the configuration process. It automatically detects the configuration of the current Unix system and generates an appropriate **Makefile** that can then be used to compile that software on this particular system. Much of the current software on the Internet in source form uses Autoconf. A detailed manual on Autoconf can be found in the **/usr/info** directory and is called **autoconf.info**. You can use the **info** command to view it. (You can also view the text with any text editor.) The general operations are described here.

Software that uses Autoconf performs the configuration without any need of the actual Autoconf software. Special shell scripts included with the software will detect the different system features that the software needs. The **./configure** command usually will automatically configure the software for your system. As the configuration is performed, it checks for different features one by one, displaying the result of each check. The operation is entirely automatic, not even requiring the identity of the system it is working on.

To create a configuration script for your own software, you use special Autoconf commands. The Autoconf applications package is available on your OpenLinux CD-ROM. Generating the configurations involves several stages, using several intermediate configuration files. Autoconf has many options designed to handle the requirements of a complex program. For a simple program you may only need to follow the basic steps.

The goal is to create a **configure** script. There are two phases in this process, using the **autoscan** and **autoconf** commands. The first phase creates a **configure.scan** file using the **autoscan** command. The **autoscan** command is applied directly to your source code files. You then check the **configure.scan** file for any errors, make any changes or additions you want, and then rename it as the **configure.in** file. This file is used as input for the **autoconf** command, which then generates the **configure** script. The **autoscan** step is an aid in the creation of the **configure.in** file, but **autoscan** and the **configure.scan** file it generates are optional. You can create your own **configure.in** file, entering various Autoconf macros. These are described in detail in the Autoconf info file.

In addition, you need to create a version of the **Makefile** for your program named **makefile.in**. This is essentially your original **Makefile** with reference to special Autoconf variables. When the software is compiled on another system, the **configure.in** will detect the system's features and then use this information with the **makefile.in** file to generate a **Makefile** for that particular system. It is this new **Makefile** that is used to compile the program.

Autoconf is designed to create values for different features that can then be used with **makefile.in** to create a new **Makefile** containing those features. The feature values are placed in special shell variables called *output* variables. You should place references to these shell variables in the **makefile.in** file wherever you want to use these values. For example, the **CC** variable will hold the name of the C compiler on your system (**cc** or **gcc**). The **AC_PROG_CC** macro in the **configure** script will detect the C compiler in use and place its name in the **CC** variable. A reference to this variable should be placed in the **makefile.in** file wherever you would invoke the C compiler. The variable name is bounded by two @ symbols. For example, @CC@ in **makefile.in** will reference the **CC** variable, and its value will be substituted in that place.

Once you have the **configure** file, you no longer need the **configure.in** file. You only need **configure**, **makefile.in**, and the source code files along with any header files. The **configure** file is a shell script designed to execute on its own. It does not need Autoconf.

Once another user has received the software package and unpacked all the source code files, there are only three steps to take: configuration, compilation, and installation. The **./configure** command will generate a customized **Makefile** for the user's system, **make** will compile the program using that **Makefile**, and **make install** will install the program on the user's system.

```
./configure
make
make install
```

RPM Build

The package creation process is designed to take the program through several stages, starting with unpacking it from an archive, then compiling its source code, and finally generating the RPM package. You can skip any of these stages, up to the last one. If your software is already unpacked, you can start with compiling it. If it is compiled, you can start with installation. If already installed, you can go directly to creating the RPM package.

RPM makes use of three components to build packages: the build tree, the **/etc/rpmrc** configuration file, and an **rpm** spec script. The build tree is a set of special instructions used to carry out the different stages of the packaging process. The **rpm** spec script contains instructions for creating the package as well as the list of files to be placed in it. The **/etc/rpmrc** file is used to set configuration features for RPM. RPM has several options you can set in the **/etc/rpmrc** file. To obtain a listing, enter

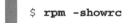

```
$ rpm -showrc
```

The build tree directories, listed in the following table, are used to hold the different files generated at each stage of the packaging process. The **SOURCES** directory holds the compressed archive. The **BUILD** directory holds the source code unpacked from that archive. The **RPMS** directory is where the RPM package containing the executable binary program is placed, and **SRPMS** is where the RPM package containing the source code is placed. If you are creating a package from software stored in a compressed archive, such as a **tar.gz** file, you will have to first copy that file to the build tree's **SOURCES** directory.

Directory Name	Description
BUILD	The directory where RPM does all its building
SOURCES	The directory where you should put your original source archive files and your patches
SPECS	The directory where all spec files should go
RPMS	The directory where RPM will put all binary RPMs when built
SRPMS	The directory where all source RPMs will be put

The following example copies the compressed archive for the **bookrec** software to the **SOURCES** directory:

```
# cp bookrec-1.0.tar.gz   /usr/src/redhat/SOURCES
```

The **topdir:** entry in the **/etc/rpmrc** file specifies the location of the build tree directories. In that file you will find an entry for **topdir:**. Currently the OpenLinux system has already set this directory to **/usr/src/OpenLinux**, and on Red Hat systems it is **/usr/src/redhat**. Here you will find the **SOURCES**, **BUILD**, **RPMS**, and **SRPMS** directories. You can specify a different directory for these subdirectories by changing the entry for **topdir:** in the **/etc/rpmrc** file.

```
topdir: /usr/src/Red Hat
```

By default, RPM is designed to work with source code placed in a directory consisting of its name and a release number, separated by a hyphen. For example, a program with the name *bookrec* and *release 1.0* should have its source-code files in a directory called **bookrec-1.0**. If RPM needs to compile the software, it will expect to find the source code in that directory within the **BUILD** directory, **BUILD/bookrec-1.0**. The same name and release number also need to be specified in the spec file.

To create a package you have to first create an **rpm** spec file for it. The **rpm** spec file specifies the files to be included, any actions to build the software, and information about the package. The spec file is designed to take the program through several stages, starting with unpacking it from an archive, then compiling its source code, and finally generating the RPM package. In the spec file, there are segments for the different stages and special RPM macros that perform actions at these stages. These are listed here:

File Segment or Macro	Description
%description	A detailed description of the software
%prep	The prep stage for archives and patches
%setup	The prep macro for unpacking archives. A **-n** *name* option resets the name of the build directory
%patch	The prep macro for updating patches
%build	The build stage for compiling software
%install	The install stage for installing software
%files	The files stage that lists the files to be included in the package. A **-f** *filename* option specifies a file that contains a list of files to be included in the package
%config *file-list*	A file macro that lists configuration files to be placed in the **/etc** directory
%doc *file-list*	A file macro that lists documentation files to be placed in the **/usr/doc** directory with the subdirectory of the name-version-release
%dir *directory-list*	The specification of a directory to be included as being owned by a package. (A directory in a file list refers to all files in it, not just the directory.)
%pre	A macro to do preinstall scripts
%preun	A macro to do preuninstall scripts
%post	A macro to do postinstall scripts
%postun	A macro to do postuninstall scripts

APPLICATIONS

A spec file is divided into five basic segments: the header, prep, build, install, and files. They are separated in the file by empty lines. The header segment contains several lines of information, each preceded by a tag and a semicolon. For example, the following tag is used for a short description of the software.

```
Summary: bookrec program to manage book records
```

The Name, Version, and Release tags are used to build the name of the RPM package. The name, version, and release are separated with hyphens. For example, the name *bookrec* with the *version 1.0* and *release 2* will have the following name:

```
bookrec-1.0-2
```

The Group entry is a list of categories for the software. It is used by the Red Hat **glint** utility to place the software in the correct **glint** display folder. The Source entry is the compressed archive where the software is stored on your system. Description is a detailed description of the software.

Following the header are the three stages for creating and installing the software on your system, indicated by the **%prep**, **%build**, and **%install rpm** macros. It is possible to skip any of these stages, say if the software is already installed. You can also leave any of them out of the spec file or comment them out with a preceding #. The spec file is capable of taking a compressed archive, unpacking it, compiling the source code files, and then installing the program on your system. Then the installed files can be used to create the RPM package.

The **%prep** macro begins the **prep** segment of the spec file. The **prep** segment's task is to generate the software's source code. This usually means unpacking archives, but it may also have to update the software with patches. The tasks themselves can be performed by shell scripts that you write. There are also special macros that will automatically perform these tasks. The **%setup** macro will decompress and unpack an archive in the **SOURCES** directory, placing the source code files in the **BUILD** directory. The **%patch** macro will apply any patches.

The **%build** segment contains the instructions for compiling the software. Usually this is a simple **make** command, depending on the complexity of your program. The **%install** segment contains the instructions for installing the program. You can use simple shell commands to copy the files or, as in the **bookspec** example that follows, the **install** command that installs files on systems. This could also be the **make install** command, provided your **Makefile** has the commands to install your program.

```
%build
make RPM_OPT_FLAGS="$RPM_OPT_FLAGS"

%install
```

```
install -s -m 755 -o 0 -g 0 bookrec /usr/bin/bookrec
install -m 644 -o 0 -g 0 bookrec.1 /usr/man/man1
```

The **%files** segment contains the list of files you want placed in the **rpm** package. Following the **%files** macro you list the different files, including their full pathnames. The macro **%config** can be used to list configuration files. Any files listed here are placed in the **/etc** directory. The **%doc** macro is used for documentation such as README files. These will be placed in the **/usr/doc** directory under a subdirectory consisting of the software's name, version, and release number. In the **bookspec** example, the **README** file will be placed in the **/usr/doc/bookrec-1.0-2** directory.

To create an **rpm** software package, you use the **rpm** build options (listed in Table 24-4) with the **rpm** command, followed by the name of a spec file. The **-bl** option checks to see if all the files used for the software are present. The **-bb** option builds just the binary package, whereas **-ba** builds both binary and source packages. They expect to find the compressed archive for the software in the build tree's **SOURCES** directory. The **-ba** and **-bb** options will execute every stage specified in the **rpm** spec script, starting from the prep stage to unpacking an archive and then compiling the program, followed by installation on the system and then creation of the package. The completed **rpm** package for executable binaries is placed in a subdirectory of the build tree's **RPMS** directory. This subdirectory will have a name representing the current platform. For a PC this will be **i386**, and the package will be placed in the **RPMS/i386** subdirectory. The source-code package is placed directly in the **SRPMS** directory.

The following program generates both a binary and a software package, placing them in the build tree's **RPMS/i386** and **SRPMS** directories. The name of the spec file in this example is **bookspec**.

```
rpm -ba bookspec
```

An executable binary package will have a name consisting of the software name, the version number, the release number, the platform name (**i386**), and the term **rpm**. The name, version, and release are separated by hyphens, whereas the release, platform name, and the **rpm** term are separated by periods. The name of the binary package generated by the previous example, using the **bookspec** spec script, will generate the following name:

```
bookrec-1.0-2.i386.rpm
```

The source code package will have the same name, but with the term **src** in place of the platform name:

```
bookrec-1.0-2.src.rpm
```

Option	Description
-ba	Create both the executable binary and source-code packages. Perform all stages in the spec file: prep, build, install, and create the packages.
-bb	Create just the executable binary package. Perform all stages in the spec file: prep, build, install, and create the package.
-bp	Run just the prep stage from the spec file (**%prep**).
-bl	Do a "list check." The **%files** section from the spec file is macro-expanded, and checks are made to ensure the files exist.
-bc	Do both the prep and build stages, unpacking and compiling the software (**%prep** and **%build**)
-bi	Do the prep, build, and install stages, unpacking, compiling, and installing the software (**%prep**, **%build**, and **%install**).
--short-circuit	Skip to specified stage, not executing any previous stages. Only valid with **-bc** and **-bi .**
--clean	Remove the build tree after the packages are made.
--test	Do not execute any build stages. Used to test out spec files.
--recompile *source_package_file*	RPM installs the source-code package and performs a prep, compile, and install.
--rebuild *source_package_file*	RPM first installs the named source package and does a prep, compile, and install; it then rebuilds a new binary package.
--showrc	List the configuration variables for the /**etc/rpmrc** file.

Table 24-4. *The RPM Build Options*

Chapter 25

Editors

Linux distributions include many text editors. These range from simple text editors for simple notes to editors with more complex features such as spell-checking, buffers, or pattern matching. All generate character text files and can be used to edit any Linux text files. Text editors are often used to change or add entries in Linux configuration files found in the **/etc** directory or a user's initialization or application dot files located in a **home** directory. You can use any text editor to work on source code files for any of the programming languages or shell program scripts.

Traditionally, most Linux distributions include the cursor-based editors Vim or Emacs. *Vim* is an enhanced version of the Vi text editor used on Unix system. These editors use simple cursor-based operations to give you a full-screen format. You can start these editors from the shell command line without any kind of X Window System support. In this mode, their cursor-based operations do not have the ease of use that is normally found in window-based editors. There are no menus, scroll bars, or mouse-click features. However, the K Desktop and Gnome do support powerful GUI text editors with all these features. These editors operate much more like those found on Mac and Windows systems. They have full mouse support, scroll bars, and menus. You may find them much easier to use than the Vi and Emacs editors. These editors operate from their respective desktops, requiring that you first have either KDE or Gnome installed, though the editors can run on either desktop. Vi and Emacs, on the other hand, have very powerful editing features that have been refined over the years. Emacs, in particular, is extensible to a full development environment for programming new applications. Newer versions of Emacs such as GNU Emacs and XEmacs provide X Window System support with mouse, menu, and window operations. They can run on any window manager or desktop. In addition, the gvim version of Vim editor also provides basic window operations. Table 25-1 lists several GUI-based editors for Linux.

K Desktop Editors: KEdit, KWrite, and KJots

All the K Desktop editors provide full mouse support, implementing standard GUI operations such as cut and paste to move text, and click and drag to select text. The KEdit program is the default editor for the K Desktop (see Figure 25-1). It is a simple text editor meant for editing simple text files like configuration files. A toolbar of buttons at the top of the KEdit window lets you easily execute common editing commands using just a mouse click. With KEdit, you can also mail files you are editing over a network. The entry for KEdit in the K menu is listed simply as "Text Editor." You can also start up KEdit by entering the **kedit** command in a terminal window.

A more advanced editor is KWrite, with features like spell-checking (see Figure 25-2). Formatting options can be set in the options menu and implemented using CTRL-J. Most

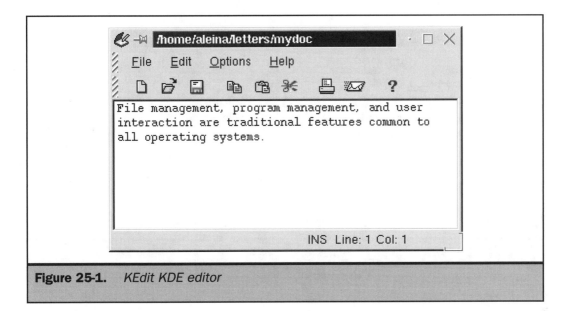

Figure 25-1. *KEdit KDE editor*

commands can be selected using menus. A toolbar of icons for common operations is displayed across the top of the kwrite window. A click on the right mouse button will display a pop-up menu with entries for Cut, Copy, and Paste, as well as Open and Save. At the bottom of the KWrite menu is a message box that displays the current operation or any error messages. The entry for KWrite in the K menu is "Advanced Editor." You can also start up KWrite by entering the **kwrite** command in a terminal window.

What is more, KWrite is designed to be a program editor for editing source code files. It does not have all the features of Emacs or Vi, but can handle most major tasks. The Highlight entry in the Options menu will let you set syntax highlighting for different programming languages such as C, Perl, Java, and HTML. In addition, KWrite also has the capability to access and edit files on an FTP or Web site.

The editor KJots is designed to let you jot down notes in a notebook. It organizes notes you write into notebooks, called simply "books." You can select the one you want to view or add to from the Books menu (see Figure 25-3). To start KJots, select its entry in the Utilities menu or enter the **kjots** command in a terminal window.

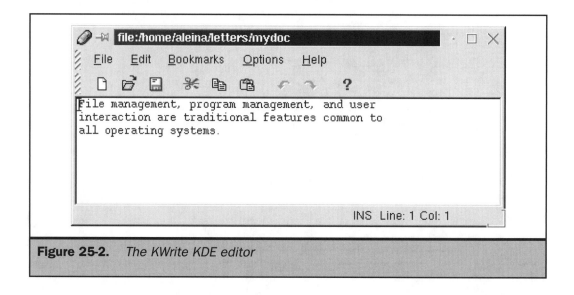

Figure 25-2. *The KWrite KDE editor*

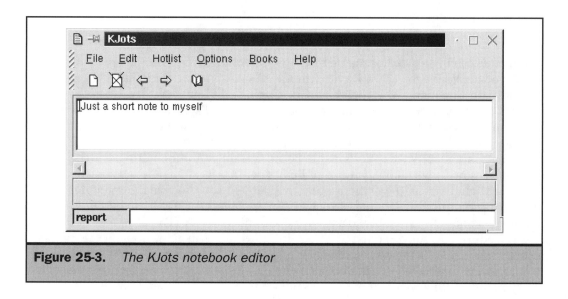

Figure 25-3. *The KJots notebook editor*

Gnome Editors: gEdit, GXedit, gnotepad+

All the Gnome editors provide full mouse support, implementing standard GUI operations such as cut and paste to move text, and click and drag to select text. The gEdit text editor is a basic one for the Gnome desktop (see Figure 25-4). You can use it to perform most text editing tasks such as modifying configuration files. It features a plugin menu that provides it added functionality. There are plugins for spell-checking, project management, encryption, and e-mail.

A more powerful editor, GXedit, includes standard features such as spell-checking, formatting, autosave, and encryption. Menus contain all of the GXedit commands, and a toolbar of icons for commonly used commands is displayed across the top of the GXedit window(see Figure 25-5). The GXedit editor supports a full range of file

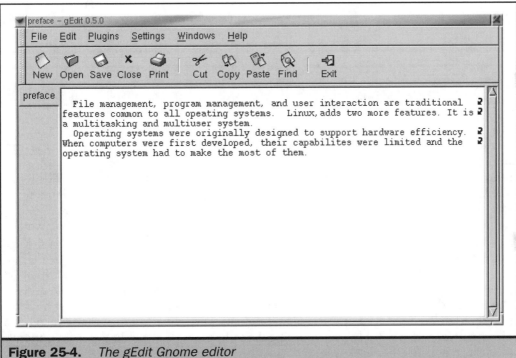

Figure 25-4. *The gEdit Gnome editor*

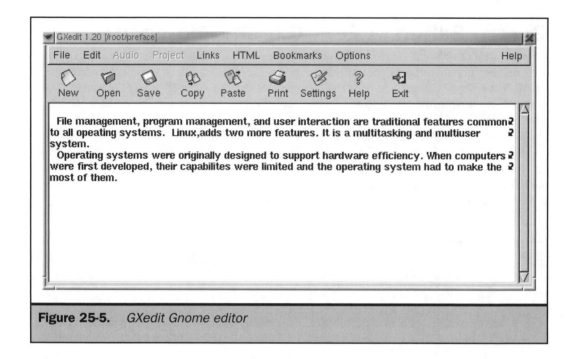

Figure 25-5. *GXedit Gnome editor*

operations, letting you merge, sort, or compare files. You can easily insert the date and the contents of your signature file. You can also use GXedit to compose Man pages, inserting the Man tags for the header, synopsis, description, and options. In addition, GXedit can also compose and edit Web pages. You can easily insert HTTP elements such as links, image references, or headings, and GXedit can then access Netscape to preview the page. You configure GXedit using the Settings window, which has panels for display, network, macro, and command settings. Settings are saved in the user's **home** directory in the file **.gxedit**.

The GXedit editor is network-aware. You can compose files and then send them as e-mail messages, edit news articles obtained from your news server directly, and access and edit files located on FTP or Web sites. The network setting will first have to be entered in the network panel in the Setting's window. In addition, GXedit also has a mirror function that works somewhat like the talk utility. You can have GXedit operate as a server, letting other users connect to your program and view everything you type in your GXedit window. You could also connect to someone else running GXedit to view what they are displaying.

The editor, gnotepad+ is a very simple editor for making small text files. It does, however, have a toolbar for Web page composition containing several of the more common HTML elements (see Figure 25-6). You can insert links, headings, and lists, as well as other basic Web page components.

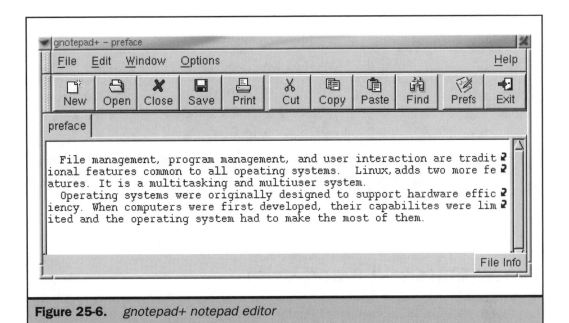

Figure 25-6. *gnotepad+ notepad editor*

The K Desktop	Description
KEdit	Text editor, default for K Desktop
KWrite	Text and program editor
KJots	Notebook editor
KWord	Desktop publisher, part of KOffice (See Chapter 22.)
Gnome	
gEdit	Text editor
GXedit	Text and HTML editor
gnotepad+	Notebook editor

Table 25-1. *Desktop Editors*

X-Windows	Description
Xemacs	X Window System version of Emacs editor
GNU Emacs	Emacs editor with X Window System support
gvim	Vim version with X Window System support
WordPerfect	Word processor that can edit text files

Table 25-1.   *Desktop Editors* (continued)

The Vi Editor: Vim and gvim

The Vim editor included with most Linux distributions is an enhanced version of the Vi editor. It includes all the commands and features of the Vi editor. Vi, which stands for "visual," remains one of the most widely used editors in Linux. Keyboard-based editors like Vim and Emacs use a keyboard for two very different operations: to specify editing commands and to receive character input. As editing commands, certain keys will perform deletions, some will execute changes, and others will perform cursor movement. As character input, keys will represent characters that can be entered into the file that is being edited. Usually, these two different functions are divided among different keys on the keyboard. Alphabetic keys are reserved for character input. Function keys and control keys specify editing commands such as deleting text or moving the cursor. Such editors can rely on the existence of an extended keyboard that includes function and control keys. Editors in Unix, however, were designed to assume a minimal keyboard with alphabetic characters, some control characters, as well as the ESC and ENTER keys. Instead of dividing the command and input functions among different keys, the Vi editor has two separate modes of operation for the keyboard: command mode and input mode. In *command mode*, all the keys on the keyboard become editing commands. In *input mode*, the keys on the keyboard become input characters. Some of the editing commands, such as **a** or **i**, enter the input mode. Upon pressing the **i** key, you leave the command mode and enter the input mode. Each key now represents a character to be input to the text. Pressing ESC automatically returns you to the command mode, and the keys once again become editor commands. As you edit text, you will find yourself constantly moving from the command mode to the input mode and back again. With Vim, you can use the CTRL-O command to jump quickly to the command mode and enter a command, and then automatically return to the input mode. Table 25-2 lists the basic set of Vi commands that you need to get started in Vi.

Though the Vi command mode handles most editing operations, there are some, such as file saving and global substitutions, that it cannot perform. For such operations you need to execute line editing commands. You enter the line editing mode using the Vi colon command, **:**. The colon is a special command that allows you to perform one line editing operation. Upon pressing the colon, a line opens up at the bottom of the screen with the cursor placed at the beginning of the line. You are now in the line editing mode. In this mode, you enter an editing command on a line, press ENTER, and the command is executed. Entry into this mode is only temporary. Upon pressing ENTER, you are automatically returned to the Vi command mode, and the cursor returns to its previous position on the screen.

Though with the Vi editor you can create, save, close, and quit files, the commands for each are not all that similar. Saving and quitting a file involves the use of special line editing commands, whereas closing a file is a Vi editing command. Creation of a file is usually specified on the same shell command line that invokes the Vi editor. To edit a file, type **vi** or **vim** and the name of a file on the shell command line. If a file by that name does not exist, the system will create it. In effect, giving the name of a file that does not yet exist instructs the Vi editor to create that file. The following command invokes the Vi editor, working on the file **booklist**. If **booklist** does not yet exist, the Vi editor will create it.

```
$ vim booklist
```

After executing the **vim** command, you enter Vi's command mode. Each key becomes a Vi editing command, and the screen becomes a window onto the text file. Text is displayed screen by screen. The first screen of text is displayed, and the cursor is positioned in the upper-left corner. With a newly created file, there is no text to display. This fact is indicated by a column of tildes (~) at the left-hand side of the screen. The tildes represent that part of a screen that is not part of the file.

Remember that when you first enter the Vi editor, you are in the command mode. To enter text, you need to enter the input mode. In the command mode, the **a** key is the editor command for appending text. Pressing this key places you in the input mode. Now, the keyboard operates like a typewriter and you can input text to the file. If you press ENTER, you will merely start a new line of text. With Vim, you can use the arrow keys to move from one part of the entered text to another and work on different parts of it. After entering text, you can leave the input mode and return to the command mode by pressing ESC. Once finished with the editing session, you exit Vi by typing two capital Z's, **ZZ**. You hold down the SHIFT key and press **z** twice. This sequence first saves the file and then exits the Vi editor, returning you to the Linux shell. To save a file while editing, you use the line editing command **w**, which writes a file to the disk. It is equivalent to the Save command found in other word processors. You first press the colon key to access the line editing mode, then type in a **w** and press ENTER.

You can use the **:q** command to quit an editing session. Unlike the **ZZ** command, the **:q** command does not perform any save operation before it quits. In this respect, it has one major constraint. If there have been any modifications to your file since the last save operation, then the **:q** command will fail and you will not leave the editor. However, you can override this restriction by placing a **!** qualifier after the **:q** command. The command **:q!** will quit the Vi editor without saving any modifications made to the file in that session since the last save.

To obtain online help you enter the **:help** command. This is a line editing command. You first press the colon, then enter the word **help** on the line that opens up at the bottom of the screen, and then press ENTER. You can add the name of a specific command after the word **help**. The F1 key will also bring up online help.

gvim

As an alternative to using Vim in a command-line interface, you can use gvim, which provides X-Windows-based menus for basic file, editing, and window operations. To use gvim, enter the **gvim** command at an X Windows terminal prompt or select it from a Window manager menu. The standard Vi interface is displayed, but with several menu buttons displayed across the top. All the standard Vi commands will work just as they are described here. However, you can use your mouse to select items on these menus. You can open and close a file, or open several files using split windows or different windows. The editing menu lets you cut, copy, and paste text as well as undo or redo operations. In the editing mode, you can select text with your mouse with a click-and-drag operation and then use the Editing menu to cut or copy and then paste the selected text. Text entry however, is still performed using the **a**, **i**, or **o** commands to enter the input mode.

Moving Through the Text in Vi

While in command mode, you can move the cursor across the text by using the keys for movement commands. The **h**, **j**, **k**, and **1** commands and the arrow keys perform the basic cursor movement operations. The **h** and **1** as well as the left and right arrow keys move the cursor horizontally across characters in a line. The **j** and **k** keys as well as the up and down arrow keys move the cursor up and down lines. The **j** key moves down one line and the **k** key moves up one line. In addition, you can use ENTER in place of the **j** key to move the cursor down a line. The SPACEBAR can be used in place of the **1** key to move the cursor left one character.

Each text line begins at the left column of the screen and ends when you press ENTER. If the cursor is at the end of the line and you press the **1** key to move right, the computer will beep and the cursor will not move. The same is true if the cursor is on the first character of a line and you press the **h** key to move left. The beep indicates that the cursor has reached a text boundary.

You also can move through the text a whole screen at a time using the CTRL-F and CTRL-B keys. The CTRL-F key moves forward one screen of text, and CTRL-B moves backward one screen of text. Once you have moved forward in your file, you may want to move back toward the beginning of your text. You can do so, screen by screen, by pressing CTRL-B.

You can move to a particular line using the **G** command and a line number. Vi sequentially numbers each line of text. The **G** command (it must be uppercase *G*) moves the cursor to a particular line. You first enter the line number and then press the **G** key. The cursor then moves to that line. You can also use the **G** command to move quickly to the end of your file. If no line number is entered before you press the **G** key, then the cursor moves directly to the end of the file. The **G** key by itself is a quick way to locate the end of a very large file.

Modifying Text in Vi: Input, Deletions, and Changes

Editing your text usually involves modifying it in some way. You can add more text at different places in your file. You may decide to delete text that you have already entered. Or, you may need to change part of your text. Vi has an extensive set of commands for inputting text in different ways as well as deleting or changing different text segments, such as characters, lines, sentences, words, and paragraphs. Vi also allows you to undo any changes you make to your file, even text that you have input. The undo command, **u**, will undo the previous Vi command. Pressing **u** repeatedly undoes previous operations.

There are several input commands, each of which enters the input mode at a different point in the text relative to the cursor. The most common input commands are **a** (append), **i** (insert), and **o** (open). The **a** key places the user into input after the character the cursor is on. The **i** key places the user into input before the character the cursor is on. The **o** key opens a new line below the line the cursor is on and places the user into input at the beginning of that new line. Because the **i** command inserts before the character the cursor is on, it is often used to insert text before a word. If the cursor is on the first character of a word, the **i** command will enter the insert mode before the word. The **a** command can be used to add text after a word. If the cursor is on the last character of a word, the **a** command will enter the input mode after the word. The difference between the **i** and **a** commands becomes significant when you want to add text to either the beginning or end of a line. You use the **i** command to insert text at the beginning of a line, and the **a** command to add text to the end of a line. Instead of just adding text on a given line, you may want to insert a whole new line. For this, you use the **o** command. It can be thought of as inserting a line between two lines. You are not limited to input on that line. The new line is only a starting point for entering the input mode. Once in the input mode, pressing ENTER will add as many lines as you wish.

The simplest deletion operations are those to delete single characters or whole lines of text. Pressing the **x** key deletes a single character. Whatever character the cursor is on will be deleted. The **dd** sequence of keys deletes the line that the cursor is on. The traditional way to change text is to first delete it with deletion commands and then enter the input mode to enter new text. To change a word, you could first repeatedly use the **x** command to delete the word and then use the **i** or **a** command to enter input and type in the new word. The Vi editor has a set of change commands that streamlines this process, automatically deleting words, lines, sentences, and paragraphs and placing you into the input mode. The **cc** sequence of keys changes an entire line. First, **cc** deletes the text on the line, and then it enters input mode. You use the **r** command to change a single character. The **r** command deletes whatever character the cursor is on and then waits for you to enter a replacement character. The character the cursor is on will be replaced by whatever character you enter. The **r** command, unlike other change commands, does not place you in the input mode. The **R** key is a replacement command that overwrites text until you press ESC. You are placed in the input mode, but for every character you type in, a corresponding character is deleted from the text. This command may appear similar to an overwrite mode used in other types of word processors, but it is not.

As you delete and change text, you may accidentally delete or change the wrong text and want to restore the text to its original condition. The undo command, **u**, lets you restore the text to its condition before the most recent editing command was executed. The **u** command will undo any modifications made by the input, deletion, and change commands. The Vim version of Vi supports multiple undo operations. Repeatedly pressing the **u** key will sequentially undo your previous operations.

The process of breaking or joining lines using Vi is more complex than that of PC-style editors. In a PC-style editor, you simply press ENTER to break a line, or use BACKSPACE to join lines. In Vi, breaking a line requires the use of an input command to first enter the input mode in which you can then press ENTER. Joining a line requires a whole new Vi command, the uppercase **J** key. You cannot use BACKSPACE to join lines.

To break a line into two lines, place the cursor at the point in the line where you want it to be broken. Then, enter the input command **i** or **a**. Remember that **i** inserts before the cursor and **a** appends after the cursor. Once in the input mode, press ENTER. Pressing ESC returns you to command mode. There are now two lines, the first terminated when you press ENTER. To join two lines, press **J**, and the line below the cursor is joined to the line that the cursor is on. It is as if you never pressed ENTER.

Copying, Moving, and Searching Text in Vi

The easiest way to copy, move, or delete text with Vim is to use the visual mode. Visual mode lets you select the text by moving your cursor, then pressing a single-letter command for the operation you want to perform. You enter visual mode with the **v** or **V** commands. The **v** command operates on single characters, and **V** will operate on lines. Move the cursor to extend the selection. To extend backward from the starting point, first press the **o** key. Once selected, you can then press **d** to delete the text, **c** to change it, or **y** to copy it. The Visual mode supports several operations, including **:** to enter a command that can be applied to the selected text.

You can also select text the traditional Vi way by entering commands tailored to specific text components such as words, lines, sentences, or paragraphs. To move text, you first delete the text that you want to move. The **dd** command will delete a line.

A number entered before the **dd** command will delete that many lines from and including the line that the cursor is on. These deleted lines are placed in the temporary buffer. Next, you move the cursor to the line where you want text inserted. Finally, press the **p** command, and the editor inserts the deleted lines after the line on which the cursor rests.

The **yy** command will copy a line of text. Preceding the **yy** command with a number will copy that many lines, including the line that the cursor is on. To copy lines of text, place the cursor on the first line to be copied. Enter the number of lines you want copied, followed immediately with the **yy** command. This command copies the lines to the temporary buffer. Then, move the cursor to the line where the copied lines are to be inserted and press the **p** command. The copied lines are inserted after the line the cursor is on. An uppercase **Y** is the same as the **yy** command and will also copy lines.

As you work on your text, you may need to search for and locate certain words or parts of words. The Vi editor has the ability to search forward and backward in a file for a given pattern. The slash key (**/**) is the Vi editing command for pattern searches. Pressing the slash key opens up a line at the bottom of the screen. A slash appears at the beginning of the line, and the cursor is positioned after the slash. You then enter the pattern you want to search for. When you press ENTER, the editor will search for the pattern, starting where the cursor was when the slash command was executed, and continuing toward the end of the file. The slash command is a forward search. If the pattern is found, the cursor is positioned at that instance of the pattern. The question mark key (**?**) performs a pattern search, moving backward in a file. Pressing the question mark key also opens up a line at the bottom of the screen. After you type in a pattern, the search is conducted from the position of the cursor back toward the beginning of the file. The **n** key is a command to repeat a search. A pattern is first entered and searched with the slash or question mark key. Pressing the **n** key initiates a search for the next instance of the pattern in the file.

Vi contains two special characters for designating the beginning and end of a word in a pattern. The beginning of a word is represented with a **\<**, and the end of a word is represented with a **\>**. The pattern **/\<make\>/** only searches for the line with the word "make." The pattern **/\<make/** searches for lines with a word beginning with "make," such as "makeup."

You can mark lines and use the marks as line references in other commands. The command **m** followed by a letter marks that line with the letter. A single quote placed before the letter references the line. You can use a mark in any command in place of a line number. **mb** marks a line with the letter *b*. The command **`bG** then goes to that line. The mark alone will also move to that line. The command **`b** moves to the line marked with a *b*. You can use a mark to reference lines to be deleted or changed. The command **`bd** deletes all lines from the current line to the line marked *b*.

The single quote is also used to reference your previous position in the text. You can move the cursor back to its previous location using two single quotes, **``**. In a sense, the second single quote is a mark that references the previous position to the cursor. Repeatedly pressing two single quotes moves you back and forth from your previous position to your current position.

You can also reference your text according to different text segments, such as a word, sentence, or paragraph. In the previous section, you only learned how to reference single characters or whole lines. For example, the **l** command moves the cursor left a character, and the **j** command moves the cursor down a line. However, you can also move across text segments using the **w**, **)**, and **}** commands. A **w** command moves left one word; the right parenthesis, **)**, moves one sentence; and the right brace, **}**, moves one paragraph. You can use these commands to qualify other Vi commands to operate on these text segments. For example, you can qualify the change command, **c**, with a word command, **w**, to change a word, **cw**. You can qualify a **d** command with a **)** command, **d)**, to delete a sentence. The qualifier is entered after the primary command. Table 25-2 lists the commonly used Vi and Vim editing commands.

Line Editing Commands

As previously noted, the colon, **:**, is a Vi editing command that opens up a line at the bottom of the screen and allows you to enter a line editing command. After entering the line editing command, the cursor returns to its Vi position on the screen, and you continue working in the Vi editing mode. The line-editing mode in Vim supports the standard editing capabilities that you use for the BASH command line. You can use the right and left arrow keys to move anywhere on the command line and insert or delete characters (a SHIFT-right or -left character moves right or left by words). Using CTRL-B moves to the beginning of the command line, and CTRL-E to the end. A history function is also supported using the up and down arrows to display previously entered commands. You can then edit a previous command and execute it. The TAB key performs command line completion, letting you enter the first part of a command and then having the program complete the rest for you.

The line editing mode in Vi is most often used for global operations. These are usually entered within Vi as one line editing command using the colon. If you want to reference text using their line numbers, you will need to use the line editing commands. For example, suppose you want to delete lines 9 through 17. With Vi screen commands you can locate line 9 and then figure out that you need to delete the next eight lines. With the line editing commands, you simply reference the range of lines 9–17 in a delete command, **d: 9,17 d**. The line referencing capability of the line editing commands is especially helpful when you want to make global operations. You can reference the entire text with the range **1,$**. The **$** is a special character that references the last line in a file.

You perform a global substitution by referencing all lines in the file and executing a substitution command on each one. The **$** references the last line in the file, and the range **1,$** references all lines in the file. A substitution command will substitute a matched pattern with a replacement pattern, and, when modified with a **g**, will replace text throughout the entire line. All instances of the pattern on the line will be replaced.

The global line reference combined with the substitution command will perform a global substitution. Here is the format for such a command:

```
: 1,$ s/pattern/text/g
```

The next command replaces all instances of the pattern "milk" with the pattern "yogurt":

```
: 1,$ s/milk/yogurt/g
```

All special characters are operative in Vi line editing operations. In the next example, the first word in each line is replaced by a minus sign. The circumflex, ^, when used in a pattern, is a special character indicating the beginning of a line. The brackets indicate a range of possible characters. The **[a-z]** matches on any lowercase characters. The * is a special character that matches on repeated instances of the preceding character. The **[a-z]*** will match on any sequence of alphabetic characters. A space follows. The pattern searches for any set of alphabetic characters at the beginning of a line and ending with a space. The replacement text of the substitution command consists only of a minus sign and a space.

```
: 1,$ s/^[a-z]* /- /
```

Options in Vi: set and .exrc

Vi has a set of options with which to configure your editor. You set an option with the **set** line editing command. You can set options within Vi using the Vi line editing mode. The **set** command followed by the option name sets the option on. If the characters "no" are attached to the beginning of the option name, then the option is set off. For example, the command **set number** sets the number option, which numbers your lines; whereas the command **set nonumber** turns off the number option. The command **set** by itself provides a list of all options the user has set. If an option is already set, the command **set** followed by that option's name will display the value of the option. The command **set all** will display the settings of all the options.

Vi options can be used to control search operation, text display, and text input. If you set the **ignorecase** option, then searches will ignore upper- or lowercase characters in making matches. A search for **/There** will retrieve both "there" and "There." You can abbreviate the **ignorecase** option with **ic**. The commands **set ignorecase** and **set ic** turn the option on, whereas **set noignorecase** and **set noic** turn it off. The **wrapscan** option allows a search to wrap around the file. While in the input mode,

- You can automatically start a new line at a specified margin (**wrapmargin**).
- You can automatically indent a new line (**autoindent**).

- You can check for an opening parenthesis when entering a closing parenthesis.
- You can determine the number of spaces you can backtab when in input.

You may want to set certain options for every file you edit. Instead of setting these options manually for each file each time you edit them, you can place these options in your **EXINIT** shell variable, or in editor initialization files, and have them automatically set for you. To use the **EXINIT** variable to set your options automatically, you need to assign the **EXINIT** variable a quoted **set** command specifying what options you want set. Whenever you invoke Vi, the **set** command stored in **EXINIT** is automatically executed. In the next example, the user assigns to the **EXINIT** variable the quoted **set** command to set both the **nu** option for numbering lines and the **ic** option for ignoring case in searches:

```
$ EXINIT='set nu ic'
```

Though you can assign the **set** command to the **EXINIT** variable in your shell, you would normally assign it in your login or shell initialization files. Then, whenever you log in, the **EXINIT** variable is automatically assigned its **set** command. In the next example, the quoted **set** command is assigned to **EXINIT** in the user's **.bash_profile** initialization file. Options set in this way will be set for every file you edit. However, there are options that you may need for only a selected set of files. For example, you may want to number lines in only your C source code files, and word wrap your lines only in your document files. You can tailor your options for a selected set of files by using an editor initialization file called **.exrc**. The **.exrc** file contains commands to configure your editor. When Vi is invoked, the shell first searches for an **.exrc** file in the current working directory. If there is one, the shell runs it, executing the commands. These are usually **set** commands setting the options for the editor. If there is no **.exrc** file in your working directory, the shell searches your **home** directory for an **.exrc** file. You can have a separate **.exrc** file in as many directories as you wish. This allows you to customize the editor according to the files you have in a given directory.

Here is Table 25-2 listing the commonly used Vi and Vim editing commands.

Key	Cursor Movement
h	Moves cursor left one character
l	Moves cursor right one character
k	Moves cursor up one line

Table 25-2. *Vi Editor Commands*

Key	Cursor Movement
j	Moves cursor down one line
w	Moves cursor forward one word
W	Moves cursor forward one space-delimited word
b	Moves cursor back one word
B	Moves cursor back one space-delimited word
e	Moves cursor to the end of the next word
E	Moves cursor to the end of the next space-delimited word
0	Moves cursor to the beginning of the line
$	Moves cursor to the end of the line
ENTER	Moves cursor to beginning of next line
-	Moves cursor to beginning of previous line
(	Moves cursor to beginning of sentence
)	Moves cursor to end of sentence; successive command moves to beginning of next sentence
{	Moves cursor to beginning of paragraph
}	Moves cursor to end of paragraph
CTRL-F	Moves forward by a screen of text; the next screen of text is displayed
CTRL-B	Moves backward by a screen of text; the previous screen of text is displayed
CTRL-D	Moves forward by one-half screen of text
CTRL-U	Moves backward by one-half screen of text
G	Moves cursor to last line in the text
*num*G	Moves cursor to specific line number: **45G** will place the cursor on line 45
H	Moves cursor to line displayed on screen
M	Moves cursor to middle line displayed on screen

Table 25-2. *Vi Editor Commands* (continued)

Key	Cursor Movement
L	Moves cursor to bottom line displayed on screen
` `	Moves the cursor to its previous location in the text
m*mark*	Places a mark on a line of text; the mark can be any alphabetic character
`*mark*	Moves the cursor to the line with the mark
Input	All input commands place the user in input; the user leaves input with ESC
a	Enters input after the cursor
A	Enters input at the end of a line
i	Enters input before the cursor
I	Enters input at the beginning of a line
o	Enters input below the line the cursor is on; inserts a new empty line below the one the cursor is currently on
O	Enters input above the line the cursor is on; inserts a new empty line above the one the cursor is currently on
Text selection (Vim)	
v	Visual mode; move cursor to expand selected text by character. Once selected, press key to execute action: c change, d delete, y copy, : line editing command, J join lines, U uppercase, u lowercase.
V	Visual mode; move cursor to expand selected text by line
o	Expand selected text backward
Delete	
x	Deletes the character the cursor is on
X	Deletes the character before the character the cursor is on
dw	Deletes the word the cursor is on

Table 25-2. *Vi Editor Commands* (continued)

Delete	Cursor Movement
dd	Deletes the line the cursor is on
D	Deletes the rest of the line the cursor is on
d0	Deletes text from cursor to beginning of line
dc	Deletes specified component, c
J	Joins the line below the cursor to the end of the current line; in effect, deleting the newline character of the line the cursor is on
Change	**Except for the replace command, r, all change commands place the user into input after deleting text**
s	Deletes the character the cursor is on and places the user into the input mode
c	Deletes the rest of the line the cursor is on and places the user into input mode
cw	Deletes the word the cursor is on and places the user into the input mode
c0	Changes text from cursor to beginning of line
r	Replaces the character the cursor is on; after pressing r, the user enters the replacement character; the change is made without entering input; the user remains in the Vi command mode
R	First places into the input mode, then overwrites character by character; appears as an overwrite mode on the screen but actually is in input mode
cc	Changes the specified component, c
Move	**Moves text by first deleting it, moving the cursor to desired place of insertion, and then pressing the p command. (When text is deleted, it is automatically held in a special buffer.)**
p	Inserts deleted or copied text after the character or line the cursor is on

Table 25-2. *Vi Editor Commands* (continued)

APPLICATIONS

Move	Cursor Movement
P	Inserts deleted or copied text before the character or line the cursor is on
dw p	Deletes a word, then moves it to the place you indicate with the cursor (press **p** to insert the word *after* the word the cursor is on)
d*c* **p**	Deletes specified component, *c*, then moves it to the place you indicate with the cursor (press **p** to insert the word *after* the word the cursor is on)
yy or **Y**	Copies the line the cursor is on
y*c*	Copies component specified, *c*
Component references	
w	Word the cursor is on
b	To beginning of a word
W	Space-delimited word
B	Beginning of a space-delimited word
)	Sentence
}	Paragraph
G	Rest of the file
m	The *m* is a mark
L	To bottom of the screen
yH	To top of the screen
Search	**The two search commands open up a line at the bottom of the screen and allow the user to enter a pattern to be searched for; press ENTER after typing in the pattern**
/*pattern*	Searches forward in the text for a pattern
?*pattern*	Searches backward in the text for a pattern
n	Repeats the previous search, whether it was forward or backward
N	Repeats the previous search in opposite direction

Table 25-2. *Vi Editor Commands* (continued)

Move	Cursor Movement
/	Repeats the previous search in forward direction
?	Repeats the previous search in backward direction
Buffers	**Description**
	There are 9 numbered buffers and 26 named buffers; named buffers are named with each lowercase letter in the alphabet, *a-z*. You use the double quote to reference a specific buffer
"*buf-letter*	Named buffer—references a specific named buffer, **a**, **b**, and so on.
"*num*	Numbered buffer—references a numbered buffer with a number 1–9
Help (vim)	
:help *command*	Starts help utility; you can specify a command
F1	Same as **:help**
Line Editing Commands	
w	Saves file
r *filename*	Inserts file text
q	Quits editor, **q!** quits without saving
d	Deletes a line or set of lines
m*Num*	Moves a line or set of lines by deleting them and then inserting them after line *Num*
co*Num*	Copies a line or set of lines by copying them and then inserting the copied text after line *Num*
Line Reference	
Num	A number references that line number
Num, Num	Two numbers separated by a comma references a set of lines
Num-Num	Two numbers separated by a dash references a range of lines

Table 25-2. *Vi Editor Commands* (continued)

Line Reference	Description
–Num	The minus sign preceding a number offsets to a line before the current line
+Num	The plus sign preceding a number offsets to a line after the current line
$	The dollar sign symbol references the last line in the file
/Pattern/	A line can be located and referenced by a pattern; the slash searches forward
?*Pattern***?**	A line can be located and referenced by a pattern; the question mark searches backward
g*/Pattern/*	A set of lines can be located and referenced by a repeated pattern reference; all lines with a pattern in it are referenced
Special Character	
.	Matches on any one possible character in a pattern
*	Matches on repeated characters in a pattern
[ ]	Matches on classes of characters, a set of characters, in the pattern
^	References the beginning of a line
$	References the end of a line
/<	References the start of a word
>/	References the end of a word
Substitution Command	
s*/pattern/ replacement/*	Locates pattern on a line and substitutes pattern with replacement pattern
s*/pattern/ replacement/***g**	Substitutes all instances of a pattern on a line with the replacement pattern
Num-Num **s***/pattern/ replacement/*	Performs substitutions on the range of lines specified
1,$ s*/pattern/ replacement/***g**	Substitutes all instances of a pattern in the file with the replacement pattern

Table 25-2.   *Vi Editor Commands* (continued)

The Emacs Editor

Emacs can best be described as working environment featuring an editor, a mailer, a newsreader, and a Lisp interpreter. The editor is tailored for program development, letting you format source code according to the programming language you use. There are currently many versions of Emacs available for use on Unix and Linux systems. The versions usually included with Linux distributions are either GNU Emacs or XEmacs. The current version for GNU Emacs is 20.*x* and is X Windows system capable, enabling GUI features such as menus, scrollbars, and mouse-based Editing operations. See Chapter 11 for a discussion of the GNU Emacs mailer, and Chapter 12 for one on its newsreader. Check the update FTP sites for your distribution for new versions as they come out. You can also check the GNU Web site at **www.gnu.org** and the Emacs Web site at **www.emacs.org**. You can find out more information about XEmacs at its Web site, **www.xemacs.org**. Currently, GNU Emacs is distributed with Red Hat systems, and XEmacs with OpenLinux.

Emacs derives much of its power and flexibility from its ability to manipulate buffers. Emacs can be described as a buffer-oriented editor. Whenever you edit a file in any editor, the file is copied into a work buffer, and editing operations are made on the work buffer. In many editors, there is only one work buffer, allowing you to open only one file. Emacs can manage many work buffers at once, allowing you to edit several files at the same time. You can edit buffers that hold deleted or copied text. You can even create buffers of your own, fill them with text, and later save them to a file. Emacs extends the concept of buffers to cover any task. When you compose mail, you open a mail buffer; and when you read news, you open a news buffer. Switching from one task to another is simply a matter of switching to another buffer.

The Emacs editor operates much like a standard word processor. The keys on your keyboard are input characters. Commands are implemented with special keys such as control (CTRL) keys and meta (ALT) keys. There is no special input mode, as there is in Vi or Ed. You type in your text, and if you need to execute an editing command, such as moving the cursor or saving text, you use a CTRL key. Such an organization makes the Emacs editor easy to use. However, Emacs is anything but simple—it is a sophisticated and flexible editor with several hundred commands. Emacs also has special features, such as multiple windows. You can display two windows for text at the same time. You can also open and work on more than one file at a time, and display each on the screen in its own window. You invoke the Emacs editor with the command **emacs**. You can enter the name of the file you want to edit, or if the file does not exist, it will be created. In the next example, the user prepares to edit the file **mydata** with Emacs:

$ emacs mydata

Emacs is a full-screen editor that supports menus even when used on the command line. In the case of a newly created file, the screen will be empty except for the bottom two lines. The cursor will be positioned in the upper-left corner. The bottom line is called the *Echo area*, and it functions as a kind of Emacs command line. It is also used to display Emacs messages. The line above it is called the mode line and is used to display status information about the text being edited. The mode line will be highlighted in reverse video. The GNU version of Emacs will also display a list of menus at the top of the screen. If you are working from the shell, you can access the menu entries by pressing the F10 key. If you are working on a desktop, you can use your mouse (see Figure 25-7).

To enter text, you simply start typing—you are always in the input mode. Editing commands, such as movement commands, are implemented with CTRL keys. For example, to move the cursor right, use CTRL-F, and to move the cursor left, use CTRL-B. To move up one line, use CTRL-P, and to move down one line, use CTRL-N. You can save your text at any time with the CTRL-X-CTRL-S command sequence. Many Emacs commands are made up of CTRL key combinations. The command sequence to quit the editor is CTRL-X-CTRL-C. When you have finished editing the file, you should first save the file with CTRL-X-CTRL-S before quitting the editor with CTRL-X-CTRL-C.

Emacs provides several help utilities, such as an online manual and a tutorial. You access the help utilities through a CTRL-H sequence. CTRL-H followed by another CTRL-H lists the many possible options. An option of special note is the tutorial. CTRL-H-T places you into an online tutorial that provides you with special lessons on Emacs. Table 25-3 (located at the end of this chapter) lists the Emacs help commands.

GNU Emacs

You can run GNU Emacs either from window manager desktop, or from the shell command line. Many window managers or desktops may already have an entry for it in their main menu. If not, you can open a terminal window and enter the command **emacs**. When run on a desktop or window manager, Emacs will operate with X

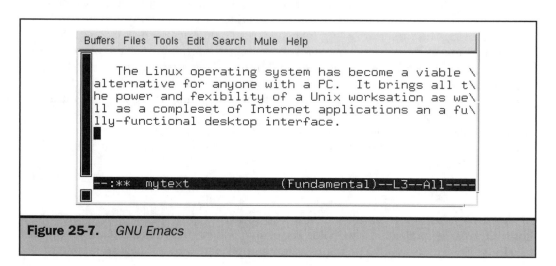

Figure 25-7. *GNU Emacs*

Windows support, enabling mouse-based editing and menu selection. You can also run Emacs from a standard shell command line, without X Windows. In this case, mouse-based operations are not enabled. However, the Emacs menu headings are still displayed at the top of the screen. You can access a menu by pressing F10. The screen will split, with the lower section listing menus and keys you press to access them. Once you select a menu, the items for that menu are listed with keys to press to select one. For example, to open a file you press F10, then **f** to list the file menu items, and then **o** to select the open item.

To enable X Window System support, just start Emacs within an X Windows environment such as a KDE, Gnome, or FVWM. The basic GUI editing operations are supported: selection of text with click-and-drag mouse operations; cut, copy, and paste; and a scroll bar for moving through text. The Mode line and Echo areas are displayed at the bottom of the window, where you can enter keyboard commands. The scroll bar is located on the left side. To move it down, click on it with the left mouse button. To move it up, click on it with the right mouse button (see Figure 27-7).

From the menus at the top of the window, you can execute most file, edit, and buffer operations. The Buffers menu lists your active buffers. You can use it to switch to another buffer, in effect switching to other files you are editing or to other tasks such as composing mail messages. The File menu manages buffers, windows, and frames. The Edit menu handles edit operations like cut, copy, and paste, as well as search and replace. The Search menu will list search operations such as searching with regular expressions. An Options menu lets you set options for editing and printing. From the Tools menu, you can access mail and the newsreader. The Help menu lists several help documents, including FAQs and Web pages. The menus are very helpful for more complicated Emacs operations such as opening multiple frames or windows on a text, as well as managing buffers and file buffers. When you execute an operation through a menu item, its equivalent keyboard command will appear in the Echo area.

XEmacs

XEmacs is the complete Emacs editor with a graphical user interface and Internet applications. The Internet applications, which you can easily access from the main XEmacs button bar, include a Web Browser, a mail utility, and a newsreader. If there is an entry for XEmacs in the Desktop menu, you can use that to start it. Otherwise, you can open a terminal window and enter the **xmacs** command at the prompt. The main XEmacs window is displayed with a button bar across the top for basic editing operations and for Internet applications. XEmacs supports the basic GUI editing operations. Selection of text is done with click-and-drag mouse operations: cut, copy, and paste; and a scroll bar for moving through text. At the bottom of the XEmacs window, the Mode line and Echo areas are displayed as on the standard Emacs editor. You can enter keyboard commands in the Echo area just as you would in the Emacs editor. From the XEmacs menus at the top of the window, you can execute most file, edit, and buffer operations. The File menu manages buffers, windows, and frames.

The Edit menu handles edit operations like cut, copy, and paste, as well as search and replace. An Options menu lets you set options for editing and printing. From the Apps menu, you can access other applications like mail, the newsreader, and the Web Browser. The Buffers menu lists your active buffers. The Help menu lists several help documents including FAQs and Web pages. The XEmacs menus are very helpful for more complicated Emacs operations such as opening multiple frames or windows on a text, as well as managing buffers and file buffers. When you execute an operation through a menu item, its equivalent keyboard command will appear in the Echo area. Figure 25-8 shows the XEmacs window.

Meta-Keys, Line Commands, and Modes

The Emacs editor operates much like any normal word processor. There is only one mode, the input mode. If you hit any character key, you are entering data into the file. All character keys are input characters, not commands. A character key can be thought of as any key you type in directly, as opposed to CTRL keys or ALT keys. Character keys

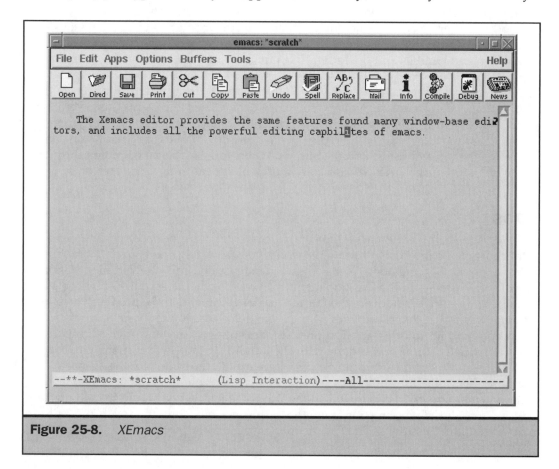

Figure 25-8.   *XEmacs*

are any keys you could type in at a typewriter. Commands are assigned to CTRL keys as well as meta-keys. In this version of Emacs, a meta-key may be either an ALT key sequence or escape (ESC) key sequence. On other systems, they may be one or the other. ALT key sequences operate like CTRL keys. While you hold down the ALT key, you press another key, and then let up on both. The ESC key sequence is slightly different. First, you press ESC and let up on it. Then you press another key. CTRL keys and meta-keys constitute only a part of the many commands available in Emacs. All commands can be entered using command words typed in the Echo area. The meta-key commands ALT-X or ESC-X will place you in the Echo area. Once in the Echo area, you execute a command by typing in the command and any of its arguments and pressing ENTER. Table 25-3 (at the end of this chapter) lists the Emacs editing commands.

The mode line displays status information about the text being edited. The mode line is made up of several components, with the following form:

```
-ST-Emacs: BufferName   (major minor)------Place--
```

The first field, ST, indicates whether the file has been saved or not since the last change to the text. If the field displays two asterisks, **, the text has been changed, but not yet saved. If the field displays two dashes, - -, the text has not been changed since the last save. If the field displays two percent signs, %%, the file is read-only and cannot be modified.

The NAME field is the name of the buffer. In the case of files, this will be the name of the file. The PLACE field indicates how far you are positioned in the file. For example, if the PLACE field is 40 percent, the text being displayed is 40 percent of the way through the file. In the next example, the mode line indicates that the file has not been saved since the last change, the name of the buffer is **mytext**, and the cursor is positioned at the top of the file.

```
-**-Emacs: mytext      (text fill)----  --Top--
```

The MAJOR/MINOR field indicates the major and minor modes for editing the file. Emacs recognizes several major modes, the most common of which is the text mode. Different types of files require special editing configurations. A C program file, for example, may need special indentation features. For this reason, there is a special editing mode for C programs. Emacs recognizes other standard modes, such as nroff and Lisp. Emacs determines the mode by examining the extension used in the file name. A **.c** extension indicates a C program file. In that case, Emacs will use the C mode. If there is no extension, Emacs will use the text mode. If, for some reason, Emacs cannot determine the mode for the file, it will use the fundamental mode, which offers no special features. Emacs has three minor modes: fill, overwrite, and abbrev. The fill mode is usually the default. It automatically wraps long lines in the file. The overwrite mode allows you to overwrite text, and the abbrev mode allows you to use abbreviations when entering text.

APPLICATIONS

Emacs Editing Commands

The Emacs editing commands perform many of the same operations found in other editors. GNU Emacs and XEmacs support standard mouse based editing operations such as click and drag to select text. You can use scroll bars to move through the text. All Emacs versions have an extensive set of keyboard commands (see Table 25-3 at the end of this chapter). CTRL-F moves the cursor forward one character, and CTRL-B moves the cursor back one character. The CTRL-F and CTRL-B commands can be thought of as right and left cursor movement on a line. The CTRL-N and CTRL-P commands move the cursor down and up lines respectively. CTRL-N moves the cursor down to the next line. If the line is the last line on the screen, the screen will scroll to display the next line. CTRL-P moves the cursor up to the previous line respectively. The CTRL-V and CTRL-Z commands move you through the text, screen by screen. CTRL-V moves you forward to the next screen of text. CTRL-Z moves you backward to the previous screen of text. There are also movement commands that position you in particular places in the text. The CTRL-A command positions you at the beginning of a line. The CTRL-E command positions you at the end of a line. CTRL-L moves you to the center of the screen. ALT-< moves you to the beginning of the file, and ALT-> moves you to the end of the file.

Deleting text permanently removes the text from the file. There are two basic deletion operations: one to delete the character before the cursor and one to delete the character after the cursor. CTRL-D deletes the character after the cursor. The DEL key deletes the character before the cursor. They are comparable to pressing BACKSPACE. You can remove (kill) different segments of text, such as words or lines. The ALT-DEL command removes the word before the cursor, and the ALT-D command removes a word after the cursor. You can precede these kill commands with the repeat command, ALT-*num*, to delete several words. For example, ALT-3-ALT-D will delete three words.

Emacs makes a distinction between deleting and killing text. Deleting text permanently removes the text from the file. Killing text removes the text from the file buffer, but copies it into what is called a kill buffer from which it can later be retrieved. Killing text works much like the deletion process in Vi. Killed text is placed in one of a set of kill buffers set up by the editor. As you kill text, each kill buffer is filled in turn. The kill buffers are circularly linked. When all are filled, the first one used is overwritten with the next text that is killed. At any time, you can insert the contents of any kill buffer back into the text. In this sense, the kill commands are meant to be one part of a text movement operation. You kill and thereby remove text from one place in your file. Then you can move to a different location and insert the removed text.

Once you have removed text to a kill buffer, you can reinsert it in the file with the CTRL-Y command. CTRL-Y is often referred to as the yank command. Whatever text has been placed in the kill buffer will be inserted into the text. If the kill buffer contains words, CTRL-Y will insert words. If the kill buffer contains lines, CTRL-Y will insert lines. Moving text involves first removing text to a kill buffer with a kill command and then inserting the text with the yank command, CTRL-Y. In the next example, the command sequence moves the current line of text up five lines. Notice the use of the repeat command before the cursor movement command.

```
Ctrl-k Ctrl-k
Alt-5 Ctrl-p
Ctrl-y
```

If you accidentally remove too many lines or insert text in the wrong place, you can undo it with CTRL-X-U. Emacs even allows you to undo all changes to the text since the editing session began with the ALT-X command.

Regions and Searches

You can select a block of text by creating a region relative to the cursor. A region is any text between the character the cursor is on and any previously marked text. You mark a place in the text with the CTRL-@ command. That marked place is the end of your region. Then, move the cursor to any other point in the file. The text between the marked character and the cursor is your region. Technically, the cursor position is referred to as the point and the marked character is referred to as the mark.

There are commands that perform operations on regions. For example, you can copy or remove regions. CTRL-W kills a region, removing it to a kill buffer. The ALT-W command copies a region to a kill buffer. You could remove a region with CTRL-W, and then use CTRL-Y to reinsert the region in the file—in effect, moving the region. Emacs does not display a mark in the file. If you forget where you placed the mark, you can use the CTRL-X-CTRL-X command sequence to locate the mark. The CTRL-X-CTRL-X command interchanges the point and the mark, moving the cursor to the position where you placed the mark. You can move the cursor back to its original position with another CTRL-X-CTRL-X sequence.

You can also define different text segments as regions. The mark-paragraph command, ALT-H, selects a paragraph the cursor is on as a region. The point is the beginning of the paragraph and the mark is placed at the end of the paragraph. CTRL-X-CTRL-P selects the page the cursor is on, making the page a region. The mark-whole-buffer command, CTRL-X-H, selects the entire buffer, making the whole text a region. Here are examples of these region commands:

```
Alt-h  Ctrl-w           Delete a paragraph
Alt-h  Alt-w            Copy a paragraph
Ctrl-x Ctrl-p  Alt-w    Copy a page
Ctrl-x h  Alt-g         Justify entire text
```

You enter searches with the CTRL-S command. The CTRL-S command places you in the Echo area where you type in the pattern to be searched for. The CTRL-S command performs an incremental search. Emacs begins the search as soon as you enter the first character. As you enter more characters in the pattern, Emacs locates text that matches the growing pattern. For example, if you are typing in the word "preface," upon typing **p**, the cursor moves to the next *p* in the text. Upon typing **r**, the cursor moves to "pr." You end the input by pressing ALT. Here is the basic form to search forward in a file for a pattern:

    Ctrl-s *pattern*

The CTRL-R command searches backward in a file. Neither command will wrap around. The CTRL-S command stops at the end of the file, and the CTRL-R command stops at the beginning of the file. Emacs remembers the last pattern searched. A CTRL-S or CTRL-R command entered without a pattern will search for the previous pattern.

The Emacs editor allows you to use any of the regular expression special characters used in the Vi, Ex, and Ed editors. To use a regular expression in a search, you precede CTRL-S or CTRL-R search commands with ALT. Thus, ALT-CTRL-S or ALT-CTRL-R allow you to use regular expressions in your search string.

You perform substitutions in Emacs using either a replace or query-replace operation. The replace operation performs global substitutions. Whereas the query-replace operation allows you to perform single substitutions. In fact, it will search for an instance of a pattern and then query you as to whether you want to replace it, skip it, or quit the query-replace operation. This gives you more control over the substitutions. Both operations have special commands for searching regular expressions. If want to use special characters, you need to use the command **query-replace-regexp**. You enter this command in the Echo area by first pressing ALT-X.

Using Windows in Emacs

Windows allow you to view different parts of the same file, or to view different files at the same time. On GNU Emacs, you can use the Window entries in the File menu to open and split windows. Window keyboard commands are usually a CTRL-X followed by a specified number. For example, CTRL-X-2 opens up a new window on the text. CTRL-X-0 (zero) closes the current window. The Emacs window commands are listed in Table 25-3 (located at the end of this chapter). When you have more than one window open, the one with the cursor is known as the current window. This is the one that is active. Any editing commands will operate on the text displayed in this window. You can move to another window with the CTRL-X-O ("oh") and CTRL-X-P commands. CTRL-X-O ("oh") will move from one window to the next, sequentially, in the order they were opened. CTRL-X-P moves to the previous window. You can close a window with CTRL-X-0 (zero) and close all but the current window with CTRL-X-1.

Buffers and Files

A *buffer* is a segment of memory used to hold characters. You can think of it as an array of characters. You then perform editing operations on the buffer. When you have finished editing the buffer, you save the contents of the buffer to the file. Emacs focuses on the fact that editors actually operate on buffers. You can edit buffers used for files or buffers used for other purposes. You can even create your own buffers, enter text into them; and, if you want, you can later save the contents to a file. The Vi editor, by contrast, allows you to edit only one file buffer.

Buffers used for files are created when you open a file. You can also simply open a buffer and then later save it to a file. In either case, the buffer becomes tied to that file. Such buffers are called *file buffers*. The command sequence CTRL-X-CTRL-F *filename* opens a file with its own buffer. The command sequence CTRL-X-CTRL-S saves the contents of the buffer to the file, and the command sequence CTRL-X-CTRL-C quits the file. The different file buffer commands are listed in Table 25-3 (at the end of this chapter).

You can have more than one file open at the same time, each with its own buffer. To display two file buffers at the same time on the screen, you need to use the window commands discussed in the previous section. CTRL-X-2 first creates a new window. Then, CTRL-X-CTRL-F *filename* displays that file buffer in the new window. The command CTRL-X-4F *filename* performs both operations, creating a new window and displaying another file buffer in it.

All versions of Emacs have a special utility called dired that interfaces with your directory and allows you to select files in your directory for editing, saving, and even deletion. On GNU Emacs, you can display a listing of files by selecting the Open Directory entry in the File menu. You can use your mouse or arrow keys to select a file and then execute any of the following dired commands. On all versions of Emacs, you can enter the dired utility with the command CTRL-X-D. A list of files in your directory is then displayed. The list is more like a menu. Each file name is really an item on the menu. You move from one item to the next and perform operations on it. The **n** command moves to the next file name and **p** to the previous one. The **s** command marks the file for saving, **d** marks the file for deletion, and **u** undoes a mark. Changes are not made until you leave dired. You leave the dired utility by changing back to your previous buffer with the CTRL-X-B command.

With the command CTRL-X-B, you can create buffers not associated with any files. When you press CTRL-X-B, Emacs prompts you for the name of the buffer. If the buffer does not already exist, a new one will be created. You can also use CTRL-X-B to change to a specific buffer. After the CTRL-X-B, simply enter the name of the buffer at the prompt. The buffer that you select will be displayed in the current window. In this way, you can use CTRL-X-B to change from one buffer to another. CTRL-X-B-CTRL-X-B displays a list of all buffers. The command **buffer-menu** places you into an interactive utility that displays all buffer names. Using the same commands as in dired, you can change to buffers, delete buffers, or save buffers. With GNU Emacs, you can access your buffers from the Buffers menu, which lists all your current buffers. To display a listing, select the List All Buffers entry in the Buffers menu. You can use your mouse or arrow keys to select a buffer and then execute any of the dired commands.

Cursor Movement	Effect
CTRL-B	Moves left one character (backward to the previous character)
CTRL-F	Moves right one character (forward to the next character)
CTRL-N	Moves down one line (the next line)
CTRL-P	Moves up one line (the previous line)
CTRL-V	Moves forward one screen
CTRL-Z	Moves backward one screen
CTRL-L	Moves to center of screen
ALT-F	Moves forward one word
ALT-B	Moves backward one word
ALT-]	Moves to next paragraph
ALT-[	Moves back to previous paragraph
CTRL-A	Moves to beginning of a line
CTRL-E	Moves to end of a line
ALT-<	Moves to beginning of buffer, usually beginning of file
ALT->	Moves to end of buffer, usually end of file
ALT-*num*	Repeats the following command *num* number of times
ALT-X	Moves to Echo area to enter a command

Table 25-3.   *Emacs Commands*

Deletions	Effect
DEL	Deletes the character before the cursor
CTRL-D	Deletes the character after the cursor
Kills and Yanks	
CTRL-K	Removes the remainder of a line (kills the rest of the line)
CTRL-K-CTRL-K	Removes the remainder of a line and the new line character at the end
ALT-D	Removes a word after the cursor
ALT-DEL	Removes the word before the cursor
ALT-K	Removes the remainder of a sentence
CTRL-W	Removes a region (deletes a block)
CTRL-Y	Inserts (yanks) the contents of a kill buffer into the text
CTRL-X-U	Undoes the previous command
Search and Replace	
CTRL-S	Searches for a pattern forward in the text
CTRL-R	Searches for a pattern backward in the text (reverse)
ALT-CTRL-S	Searches for a regular expression forward in the text
ALT-CTRL-R	Searches for a regular expression backward in the text
`replace string`	Performs a global substitution
`replace regexp`	Performs a global substitution using regular expression
`query-replace-regexp`	Searches for a regular expression in query and replace operation

Table 25-3. *Emacs Commands* (continued)

Search and Replace	Effect
ALT-% *pattern* ENTER *replacement* ENTER	Queries and replaces a pattern:

Key	Description
SPACEBAR	Replaces and moves to next instance
DEL	Does not replace and moves to next instance
ESC	Quits search-replace operation
.	Replaces and exits
!	Replaces all remaining instances
^	Moves back to previous replacement

Regions	
CTRL-@ or CTRL-SPACEBAR	Marks a region (block)
CTRL-X-CTRL-X	Exchanges cursor (point) and marks
ALT-H	Marks a paragraph as a region
CTRL-X-CTRL-P	Marks a page as a region
CTRL-X-H	Marks the entire text in buffer as a region

Text Format	
auto-fill-mode	Sets fill mode option
ALT-*num* CTRL-X-F	Sets position of right margin
ALT-Q	Justifies a paragraph
ALT-Q	Justifies a region

Window commands	
CTRL-X-2	Splits to new window vertically
CTRL-X-5	Splits to new window horizontally
CTRL-X-O	Selects other window
CTRL-X-P	Selects previous window
ALT-CTRL-V	Scrolls the other window
CTRL-X-0	Closes current window

Table 25-3. *Emacs Commands* (continued)

Window Command	Effect
CTRL-X-1	Closes all but the current window
CTRL-X-^	Extends the current window vertically
CTRL-X-}	Extends the current window horizontally

File Buffer Commands

CTRL-X-CTRL-F	Opens and reads a file into a buffer
CTRL-X-CTRL-S	Saves the contents of a buffer to a file
CTRL-X-CTRL-C	Quits editor
CTRL-X-CTRL-V	Closes the current file and opens a new one (visiting a new file)
CTRL-X-I	Inserts contents of a file to a buffer
CTRL-X-CTRL-Q	Opens a file as read-only; you cannot change it
CTRL-X-D	Enters the dired buffer that has a listing of your current directories; moves to different file and directory names; displays other directories; selects and opens files

Buffer Command

CTRL-X-B	Changes to another buffer; you are prompted for the name of the buffer to change to (to create a new buffer, enter a new name)
CTRL-X-K	Deletes (kills) a buffer
CTRL-X-CTRL-B	Displays a list of all buffers
ALT-X **buffer-menu**	Selects different buffers from a list of buffers

Help Commands

CTRL-H-CTRL-H	Lists possible help options
CTRL-H-I	Accesses the Emacs manual
CTRL-H-T	Runs the Emacs tutorial
CTRL-H-B	Displays keys and the commands they represent

Table 25-3.   *Emacs Commands* (continued)

APPLICATIONS

The Complete Reference

Part VI

System Administration

The Complete Reference

Linux

Chapter 26

File System Administration

Files reside on physical devices such as hard drives, CD-ROMs, or floppy disks. The files on each device are organized into a file system. To access files on a device, you attach its file system to a specified directory. This is called *mounting* the file system. For example, to access files on a floppy disk, you first mount its file system to a particular directory. This chapter discusses how you can access CD-ROMs, floppy disks, and hard disk partitions. You can even access an MS-DOS hard drive partition or floppy disk, as well as file systems on a remote server. Network access to files is implemented by a Network File System (NFS). With it, you can access files and devices on other remote Linux or Unix systems and use them as if they were your own. You can also access systems on Windows networks with Samba, server software that connects Linux systems to a Window network. With NetaTalk you can access Mac/OS systems on an AppleTalk network. You can also create your own compressed archives. Archives are used to back up files or to combine them into a package that can then be transferred as one file over the Internet or posted on an FTP site for easy downloading. The standard archive utility used on Linux and Unix systems is **tar**, for which there are several GUI front ends. You have several compression programs to choose from, including GNU zip (gzip), Zip, bzip, and compress.

Local File Systems

Your Linux system is capable of handling any number of storage devices that may be connected to it. You can configure your system to access multiple hard drives, partitions on a hard drive, CD-ROM disks, floppy disks, and even tapes. You can elect to manually attach these storage components or have them automatically mount when you boot. For example, the main partition holding your Linux system programs is automatically attached whenever you boot, whereas a floppy disk needs to be manually attached when you put one in your floppy drive. You can configure this access to different storage devices either by manually editing configuration files, such as **/etc/fstab**, or by using a file system configuration tool such as the Linuxconf's **fsconf** or OpenLinux's COAS. Currently, Red Hat uses Linuxconf to configure the file system.

File Systems

Although all the files in your Linux system are connected into one overall directory tree, the files themselves reside on storage devices such as hard drives or CD-ROMs. The Linux files on a particular storage device are organized into what is referred to as a *file system*. Your Linux directory tree may encompass several file systems, each on different storage devices. The files themselves are organized into one seamless tree of directories beginning from the root directory. Although the root may be located in a file system on your hard drive partition, there will be a pathname directly to files located on the file system for your CD-ROM.

The files in a file system remain separate from your directory tree until you specifically connect them to it. A file system has its files organized into its own directory tree. You can think of this as a subtree that must be attached to the main directory tree. For example, a floppy disk with Linux files will have its own tree of directories. You need to attach this subtree to the main tree on your hard drive partition. Until they are attached, you will not be able to access the files on your floppy disk.

Attaching a file system on a storage device to your main directory tree is called *mounting the device.* The mount operation will attach the directory tree on the storage device to a directory that you specify. You can then change to that directory and access those files. The directory in the file structure to which the new file system is attached is referred to as the *mountpoint.* For example, to access files on a CD-ROM, first you have to mount the CD-ROM.

Currently on Linux systems there are several ways to mount a file system. You can use Linuxconf to easily select and mount a file system. If you are using either Gnome or the K Desktop, you can use special desktop icons to mount a file system. From a shell command line, you can use the **mount** command. Mounting file systems can only be done as the root user. It is a system administration task and cannot be performed by a regular user. To mount a file system, be sure to log in as the root user. As the root user, you can, however, make a particular device like a CD-ROM user mountable. In that way, any user could put in a CD-ROM and mount it. You could do the same for a floppy drive.

For a file system to be accessible, it must be mounted. Even the file system on your hard disk partition has to be mounted with a **mount** command. When you installed your Linux system and create the Linux partition on your hard drive, your system was automatically configured to mount your main file system whenever it starts. Floppy disks and CD-ROMs, however, have to be explicitly mounted. Bear in mind that when you mount a CD-ROM or floppy disk, you cannot then just remove it to put in another one. You first have to unmount it. In fact, the CD-ROM drive will remain locked until you do so. Once you unmount a CD-ROM, you can then take it out and put in another one that you then have to mount before you can access it. When changing several CD-ROMs or floppy disks, you will be continually mounting and unmounting them.

The file systems on each storage device are formatted to take up a specified amount of space. For example, you may have formatted your hard drive partition to take up 1GB. Files installed or created on that file system will take up part of the space, and the remainder will be available for new files and directories. To find out how much space you have free on a file system, you can use the **df** command or, on Gnome, you can use Gnome disk free. Gnome disk free will display a list of meters showing how much space is used on each partition and how much you have left.

The **df** command lists all your file systems by their device names, how much memory they take up, and the percentage of the memory used, as well as where they are mounted. The **df** command is also a very safe way to obtain a listing of all your partitions, instead of using **fdisk**.

```
$ df
Filesystem      1024-blocks  Used Available Capacity Mounted on
/dev/hda3           297635  169499    112764     60%    /
/dev/hda1           205380  182320     23060     89%    /mnt/dos
/dev/hdc            637986  637986         0    100%    /mnt/cdrom
```

You can also use **df** to tell you what file system a given directory belongs to. Just enter **df** with the directory name, or **df .** for the current directory.

```
$ df .
Filesystem      1024-blocks  Used Available Capacity Mounted on
/dev/hda3           297635  169499    112764     60%    /
```

To make sure nothing is wrong with a given file system, you can use the **fsck** command to check it. Enter **fsck** and the device name that references the file system. Table 26-1 lists the **fsck** options. The following examples checks the disk in the floppy drive and the primary hard drive:

```
# fsck   /dev/fd0
# fsck   /dev/hda1
```

Device Files: /dev

To mount a file system, you have to specify its device name. The interfaces to devices that may be attached to your system are provided by special files known as device files. The names of these device files are the device names. Device files are located in the **/dev** directories and usually have abbreviated names ending with the number of the device. For example, **fd0** may reference the first floppy drive attached to your system. On Linux systems operating on PCs, the hard disk partitions have a prefix of **hd** followed by an alphabetic character that labels the hard drive and then a number for the partition. For example, **hda2** references the second partition on the first hard drive. In most cases, you can use the **man** command with a prefix to obtain more detailed information about that kind of device. For example, **man sd** displays the Man pages for SCSI devices. A complete listing of all device names can be found in the **devices** file located in the **linux/doc/device-list** directory at the **www.kernel.org** Web site. Table 26-2 lists several of the commonly used device names.

The device name for your floppy drive is **fd0**, and it is located in the directory **/dev**. The **/dev/fd0** references your floppy drive. Notice the number **0** after **fd**. If you have more than one floppy drive, they will be represented by **fd1**, **fd2**, and so on.

Options	Description
file-system	Specifies the file system to be checked. Use the file system's device name, such as **/dev/hda3**.
-A	Checks all file systems listed in the **/etc/fstab** file.
-V	Verbose mode. Lists actions that **fsck** takes.
-t *file-system-type*	Specifies the type of file system to be checked.
-a	Automatically repairs any problems.
-l	Lists the names of all files in the file system.
-r	Asks for confirmation before repairing file system.
-s	Lists superblock before checking file system.

Table 26-1.   *The fsck Options for Checking and Repairing File Systems*

IDE hard drives use the prefix **hd**, and SCSI hard drives use the prefix **sd**. The prefix for a hard disk is followed by an alphabetic character that labels the hard drive and then a number for the partition. For example, **hda2** references the second partition on the first IDE hard drive, and **sdb3** refers to the third partition on the second SCSI hard drive. To find the device name, you can use **df** to display your hard partitions or examine the **/etc/fstab** file.

The device name for your CD-ROM drive will vary depending upon the type of CD-ROM you have. The device name for an IDE CD-ROM has the same prefix as an IDE hard disk partition, **hd**. It is identified by a following character that distinguishes it from other IDE devices. For example, an IDE CD-ROM connected to your secondary IDE port may have the name **hdc**. An IDE CD-ROM connected as a slave to the secondary port may have the name **hdd**. The actual name will be determined when the CD-ROM is installed, as happened when you installed your Linux system. SCSI CD-ROM drives use a different nomenclature for their device names. They begin with **sd** for the SCSI drive and are followed by a distinguishing character. For example, the name of a SCSI CD-ROM could be **sdb** or **sda**. The name of your CD-ROM was determined when you installed your system. You can find out what it is by either examining the **/etc/fstab** file or using **Linuxconf** on your root user desktop.

Mount Configuration: /etc/fstab

Though you can mount a file system directly with just a **mount** command, you can simplify the process by placing mount information in the **/etc/fstab** configuration file.

Device Name	Description
hd	IDE hard drives, 1–4 are primary partitions, and 5 and up are logical partitions
sd	SCSI hard drives
sr	SCSI CD-ROM drives
fd	Floppy disks
st	SCSI tape drives
ht	IDE tape drives
tty	Terminals
lp	Printer ports
pty	Pseudoterminals (used for remote logins)
js	Analog joy sticks
midi	Midi ports
ttyS	Serial ports
cua	Callout devices (COM ports)
cdrom	Link to your CD-ROM device file
modem	Link to your modem device file

Table 26-2. *Device Name Prefixes*

Using entries in this file, you can have certain file systems automatically mounted whenever your system boots. For others, you can specify configuration information such as mountpoints and access permissions that can be automatically used whenever you mount a file system. You would not have to enter this information as arguments to a **mount** command as you otherwise would have to. This feature is what allows mount utilities on Gnome, KDE, and Linuxconf to let you mount a file system by just clicking on a button. All the mount information is already in the **/etc/fstab** file. For example, when adding a new hard disk partition to your Linux system, you will most likely want to have it automatically mounted on startup, and unmounted when you shut down. Otherwise, you will have to mount and unmount the partition explicitly each time you boot up and shut down your system. To have Linux automatically mount the file system on your new hard disk partition, you only need to add its name to the **fstab** file. You can do this by directly and carefully editing the **/etc/fstab** file to type in a new entry, or you can use the **Linuxconf** or, on OpenLinux, COAS, as described in the next section, "Mounting File Systems Using Linuxconf, KDE, Gnome, and COAS."

An entry in a **fstab** file contains several fields, each separated by a space or tab. The first field is the name of the file system to be mounted. This usually begins with **/dev**, such as **/dev/hda3** for the third hard disk partition. The next field is the directory in your file structure where you want the file system on this device to be attached. The third field is the type of file system being mounted. Table 26-3 provides a list of all the different types you can mount. The type for a standard Linux hard disk partition is **ext2**. The next example shows an entry for the main Linux hard disk partition. It is mounted at the root directory, /, and has a file type of **ext2**.

```
/dev/hda3  /  ext2  defaults  0  1
```

The field after the file system type lists the different options for mounting the file system. There is a default set of options that you can specify by simply entering **defaults**. You can list specific options next to each other separated by a comma (no spaces). The **defaults** option specifies that a device is read/write, asynchronous, block, that ordinary users cannot mount on it, and programs can be executed on it. By contrast, a CD-ROM only has a few options listed for it: **ro** and **noauto**. The **ro** option specifies that this is read-only, and **noauto** that it is not automatically mounted. The **noauto** option is used with both CD-ROMs and floppy drives, so they won't automatically mount since you do not know if you will have anything in them when you start up. At the same time, the entries for both the CD-ROM and the floppy drive specify where they are to be mounted when you do decide to mount them. Table 26-4 will list the options for mounting a file system. An example of CD-ROM and floppy drive entries follows. Notice that the type for a CD-ROM file system is different from a hard disk partition, **iso9660**. The floppy drive also has all the **default** options of the hard disk partitions.

```
/dev/fd0    /mnt/floppy   ext2      defaults,noauto  0  0
/dev/hdc    /mnt/cdrom    iso9660 ro,noauto          0  0
```

The last two fields consist of an integer value. The first one is used by the **dump** command to determine if a file system needs to be dumped, backing up the file system. The last one is used by **fsck** to see if a file system should be checked and in what order. If the field has a value of 1, it indicates a boot partition. The 0 value means that the **fsck** does not have to check the file system.

A copy of an **/etc/fstab** file is shown here. Notice that the first line is a comment. All comment lines begin with a **#**. The entry for the **/proc** file system is a special entry used by your Linux operating system for managing its processes. It is not an actual device. To make an entry in the **/etc/fstab** file, you can either edit the **/etc/fstab** file directly or use the utilities Linuxconf or COAS that will prompt you for information and then make the correct entries into your **/etc/fstab** file. You can use the **/etc/fstab** example here as a guide to show how your entries should look. The **/proc** and **swap** partition entries are particularly critical.

/etc/fstab

```
# <device>     <mountpoint>      <filesystemtype>  <options>          <dump>  <fsck>
/dev/hda3      /                 ext2              defaults            0       1
/dev/hdc       /mnt/cdrom        iso9660           ro,noauto           0       0
/dev/fd0       /mnt/floppy       ext2              defaults,noauto     0
/proc          /proc             proc              defaults
/dev/hda2      none              swap              sw
/dev/hda1      /mnt/dos          vfat              defaults            0       0
```

You can mount MS-DOS partitions used by your Windows operating system onto your Linux file structure, just as you would mount any Linux file system. You only have to specify the file type of **vfat**. You may find it convenient to have your MS-DOS partitions automatically mounted when you start up your Linux system. To do this, you just have to put an entry for your MS-DOS partitions in your **/etc/fstab** file. You make an entry for each MS-DOS partition you want to mount, and specify the device name for that partition followed by the directory that you want to mount it in. The **/mnt/dos** directory would be a logical choice (be sure that the **dos** directory has already been created in **/mnt**). For the file system type, enter **vfat**. The next example shows a standard MS-DOS partition entry for an **/etc/fstab** file. Notice that the last entry in the **/etc/fstab** file example was an entry for mounting an MS-DOS partition.

```
/dev/hda1 /mnt/dos  vfat  defaults  0  0
```

If your **/etc/fstab** file ever becomes corrupted—say a line gets deleted accidentally or changed—then your system will boot into a maintenance mode, giving you read-only access to your partitions. To gain read/write access so you can fix your **/etc/fstab** file, you have to remount your main partition. The following command performs such an operation:

```
# mount -n -o remount,rw  /
```

File systems listed in the **/etc/fstab** file are automatically mounted whenever you boot, unless this feature is explicitly turned off with the **noauto** option. Notice that the CD-ROM and floppy disks have a **noauto** option. Also, if you issue a **mount -a** command, all the file systems without a **noauto** option are mounted. If you would want to make the CD-ROM user mountable you would add the **user** option.

```
/dev/hdc    /mnt/cdrom    iso9660    ro,noauto,user    0    0
```

Linuxconf Configuration for Local File Systems

Unless you are very familiar with the **fstab** file, it is better to use Linuxconf to add and edit entries, instead of editing it directly. Linuxconf is available on Red Hat systems

Types	Description
Minux	Minux file systems. File names are limited to 30 characters.
ext	Earlier version of Linux file system, no longer in use.
ext2	Standard Linux file system supporting large file names and file sizes.
xiaf	**Xiaf** file system.
msdos	File system for MS-DOS partitions (16-bit).
vfat	File system for Windows partitions (32-bit).
hpfs	File system for OS/2 high-performance partitions.
proc	Used by operating system for processes.
nfs	NFS file system for mounting partitions from remote systems.
umsdos	UMS-DOS file system.
swap	Linux swap partition or swap file.
sysv	Unix System V file systems.
iso9660	File system for mounting CD-ROMs.

Table 26-3. *File System Types*

Options	Description
async	All I/O to the file system should be done asynchronously.
auto	Can be mounted with the **-a** option.
defaults	Use default options: **rw**, **suid**, **dev**, **exec**, **auto**, **nouser**, and **async**.
dev	Interpret character or block special devices on the file system.
noauto	Can only be mounted explicitly. The **-a** option will not cause the file system to be mounted.
exec	Permit execution of binaries.
nouser	Forbid an ordinary (i.e., nonroot) user to mount the file system.
remount	Attempt to remount an already-mounted file system. This is commonly used to change the mount flags for a file system, especially to make a read-only file system writable.
ro	Mount the file system read-only.
rw	Mount the file system read-write.
suid	Allow set-user-identifier or set-group-identifier bits to take effect.
sync	All I/O to the file system should be done synchronously.
user	Allow an ordinary user to mount the file system. Ordinary users always have the following options activated: **noexec**, **nosuid**, and **nodev**.
nodev	Do not interpret character or block special devices on the file system.
nosuid	Do not allow set-user-identifier or set-group-identifier bits to take effect.

Table 26-4. *Mount Options for File Systems –o and /etc/fstab*

and can be installed on any major distribution. With Linuxconf, you can choose many of the configuration options using drop-down menus and check boxes. Once you have finished making your entries, you can have Linuxconf generate a new **/etc/fstab** file incorporating your changes.

You can start Linuxconf either from a window manager, a desktop, or a shell command line. The figures here show Linuxconf panels as they are displayed in Gnome. Other desktops and window managers will show the same display. A Linuxconf shell command will show cursor-based lists and boxes. To access the Linuxconf file system configuration panels, you can select its entry in the main Linuxconf interface or you can use the **fsconf** command to invoke a specialized window showing only file system options (see Chapter 4 for an example of the **fsconf** interface). Using the main Linuxconf interface, you select the "Access local drive" entry in the file systems list under the Config heading. This will display the information about the different file systems accessible on your local system. The source is the device name for the storage device. The name will begin with **/dev**, the directory where device files are kept. For example, the name given to the first partition on the first hard drive is **hda1**. The device file name is **/dev/hda1**. On most Linux distributions, a CD-ROM is given the device name **/dev/cdrom**. Names for additional CD-ROMS will vary depending upon whether they are SCSI or IDE devices. On PCs, a second IDE CD-ROM could have the name **/dev/hdd**. The mountpoint and file system type are shown along with the size, partition type, and whether it is mounted or not. Figure 26-1 shows the Linuxconf "Access local drive" panel.

To add a new entry, click on the Add button. This will display panels for file system information and options. The Base tab prompts you to enter the file system's device name, its file system type, and its mountpoint, as shown in Figure 26-2. The box labeled Partition is where you enter the file system's device name. This box holds a drop-down menu listing the different hard disk partitions on your hard drive. If you

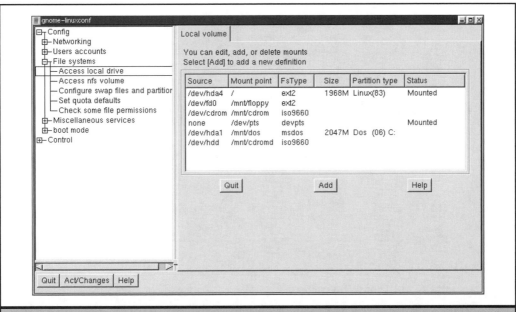

Figure 26-1.   *Linuxconf file system configuration*

are making an entry for one of those partitions, you can select it from there. If you are making an entry for a CD-ROM or floppy drive, you will have to enter the name yourself. The Type box is where you enter the file system type. The box contains a drop-down menu that lists the different file system types you can choose from. Select the type from this menu. See Table 26-3 for a listing of file system types supported. The "Mount point" box is where you enter the mountpoint—the directory on your main file system where you will attach this file system. For example, a floppy disk is usually attached to the **/mnt/floppy** directory. When you mount a floppy disk, you will find its files in that directory. The directory can actually be any directory on your file system. If it does not exist, then Linuxconf will ask to create it for you. Figure 26-2 shows an example of the Base tab for a CD-ROM. The device name in this example is **/dev/hdc**, the file system type is **iso9660** (standard for CD-ROMs), and the mountpoint is **/mnt/cdrom**. If you were mounting a Linux file system, you would use the **ext2** type, and for DOS partitions you would use **vfat**.

The Options tab will list different mount options in the form of check boxes. You can select options such as whether you don't want the file system automatically mounted at boot, or if you want to let normal users mount it. Figure 26-3 shows the

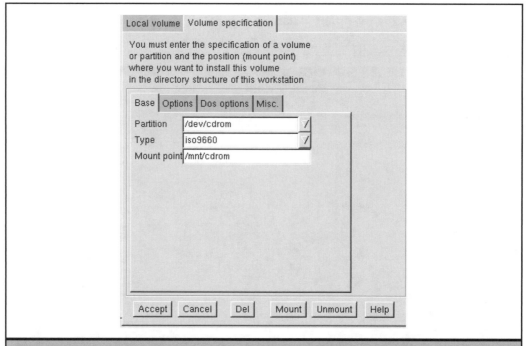

Figure 26-2.   *Linuxconf Base tab for adding or editing file systems*

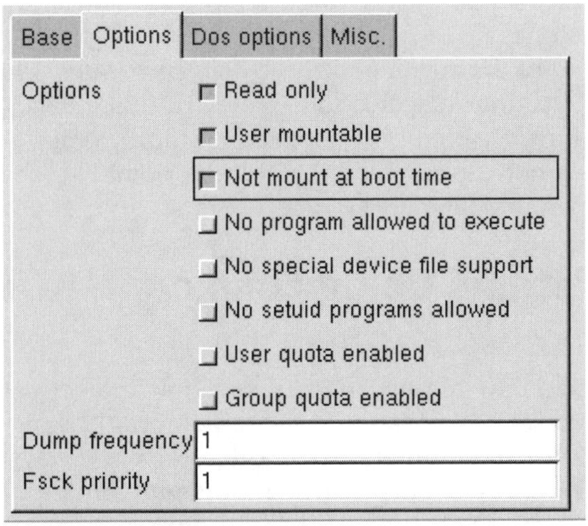

Figure 26-3.   *Linuxconf Options tab*

Options tab. The example here shows entries you may make for a CD-ROM. The CD-ROM is read-only, not mounted at boot time, and can be mounted by any user.

If your Linux system shares a hard drive with a Windows system, then you may want to add mount entries for the Windows partition. This way, those partitions would be accessible by your Linux system. Linux can access any file on a Windows partition, though not run its programs. For example, files could be downloaded by your Linux system and saved directly on a Windows partition. To create a mount entry for a Windows partition, you would enter its hard disk partition name in the Partition box, and **vfat** for its file system type. The following illustration shows a sample configuration of MS-DOS file systems on Linuxconf.

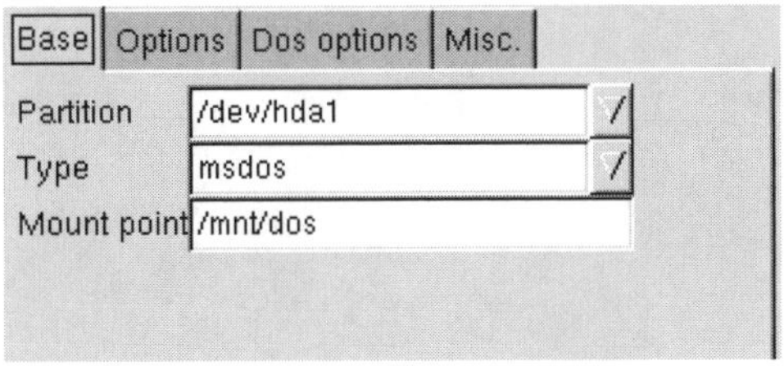

When you have finished, click the Accept button. This returns you to the "Local volume" panel and you will see the new entry displayed. Linuxconf does not actually implement these changes on your system until you click the Act/Changes button in the lower-left corner. When you do this, Linuxconf will generate a new **/etc/fstab** file, replacing the previous one.

You can change any of the current entries by simply double-clicking on its entry. This will display the "Volume specification" panel for that entry. You can then change any of the options or the base configuration. For example, to use a different mountpoint, just type a new directory in the "Mount point" box. Should you want to delete the entry, click on the DEL button.

Mounting File Systems Using Linuxconf, KDE, Gnome, and COAS

Once you have entered a new file system configuration and activated the changes to implement it on your system, you can then actually mount the file system. By default, file systems will be mounted automatically, though certain file systems such as CD-ROMs and floppy disks will normally be mounted manually. To manually mount a file system with Linuxconf, select the "Control configured local drives" in the "Mount/Unmount file systems" list that is under the Control Panel located in Config. This will display a listing of your local file systems, as shown in Figure 26-4. When you click on an entry, you will be asked if you want to mount the file system. You can also use this panel to unmount a file system. If a file system is already mounted, clicking on it will display a dialog box asking if you want to unmount the file system. Bear in mind that when you mount a CD-ROM or floppy disk, you cannot then just remove it to put in another one. You first have to unmount it before you can then take it out and put in another one.

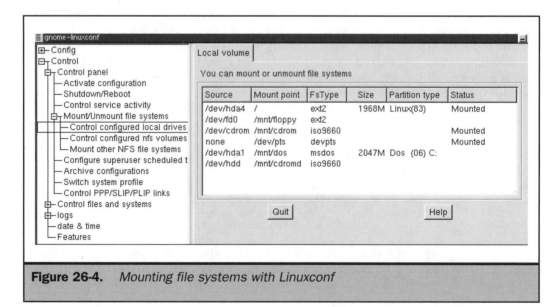

Figure 26-4.   *Mounting file systems with Linuxconf*

It is also possible to use the "Access local drive" configuration panel to mount a file system (refer to Figure 26-1). Just click on the Mount button in a file system's "Volume specification" panel. There is also an Unmount button to unmount it. You can use this method when checking to see if a new system mounts correctly.

Both the Gnome and K Desktop provide easy-to-use desktop icons for mounting and unmounting your file systems. Normally, these are used for manually mounted devices such as CD-ROMs, tapes, and floppy disks. Hard disk partitions are usually mounted automatically at boot time. On Gnome, an icon is automatically generated for your CD-ROM devices. A right-click on the icon will display a menu from which you can select an entry to mount or unmount the CD-ROM. You can also install a Mount applet in a Gnome panel that lets you mount a floppy, CD-ROM, or partition with a simple click on its Panel icon (see Chapter 6 for more details).

On the K Desktop, you can create a KDE **kdelink** file for a particular file system device. Right-click on the desktop and select File System from the New entry in the pop-up menu. Enter a name for the KDE link file with the extension **.kdelink**. Then, a Properties dialog box is displayed for the link file. In the Device tab, enter the device name, mountpoint, and file system type. You can also select a mount and unmount icon. Figure 26-5 shows a Device tab for a CD-ROM. The device name, in this example, could also be **/etc/cdrom**.

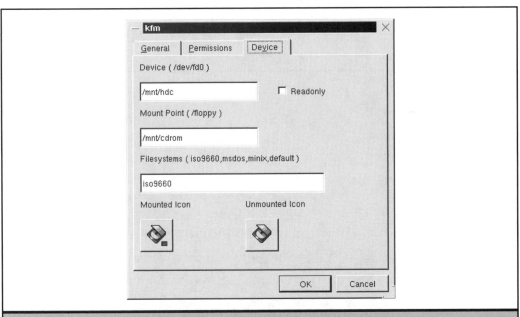

Figure 26-5. *KDE kdelink file dialog box for file systems*

On OpenLinux, you can use COAS to mount and unmount file systems. Select File System from the System Administration menu. This displays a File System window showing mountable devices on the left and the directories for mounted file systems on the right. To mount a file system, like a CD-ROM, select its device in the left list and click the Mount button. An IDE CD-ROM will often have a device name like **hdc** or **hdd**. To check what a device is used for, click on it and then click on the Info button. When you mount a file system, a window opens showing the device name, the directory it will be mounted on, and the file system type. For a new device, you will have to enter a directory and type. CD-ROMs have the type **iso9660** and Linux floppy disks use **ext2**. Windows partitions have a type of **vfat**. You can further set options such as read-only or user mountable. You can also elect to have it added to the **fstab** file, which then makes it a permanent entry and easier to mount again later.

The mount and umount Commands

You can also mount or unmount any file system using the **mount** and **umount** commands. You enter these commands on a shell command line. In a window manager or desktop, you can open a Terminal window and enter the command there, or you can simply use your login shell. The mount operations discussed in the previous sections use the **mount** command to actually mount a file system. Normally, mounting file systems can only be done as the root user (unless the device is user mountable). It is a system administration task and cannot be performed by a regular user. To mount a file system, be sure to log in as the root user. Table 26-5 lists the different options for the **mount** command.

Mount Options	Description
-f	Fakes the mounting of a file system. You use it to check if a file system can be mounted.
-v	Verbose mode. Mount displays descriptions of the actions it is taking. Use with **-f** to check for any problems mounting a file system, **-fv**.
-w	Mount the file system with read and write permission.
-r	Mount the file system with only read permission.
-n	Mount file system without placing an entry for it in the **mstab** file.
-t *type*	Specify the type of file system to be mounted. See Table 26-3 for valid file system types.

Table 26-5. *The mount Command*

Mount Options	Description
-a	Mount all file systems listed in **/etc/fstab**.
-o *option-list*	Mount the file system using list of options. This is a comma-separated list of options following **-o**. See Table 26-4 for a list of the options and the Man pages for **mount** for a complete listing.

Table 26-5.   *The mount Command* (continued)

The **mount** command takes two arguments: the storage device through which Linux accesses the file system, and the directory in the file structure to which the new file system is attached. The *mountpoint* is the directory on your main directory tree where you want the files on the storage device attached. The *device* is a special device file that connects your system to the hardware device. The syntax for the **mount** command follows:

```
# mount device mountpoint
```

Device files are located in the **/dev** directories and usually have abbreviated names ending with the number of the device. For example, **fd0** may reference the first floppy drive attached to your system. On Linux systems operating on PCs, the hard disk partitions have a prefix of **hd** followed by an alphabetic character that labels the hard drive and then a number for the partition. For example, **hda2** references the second partition on the first hard drive. In most cases, you can use the **man** command with a prefix to obtain more detailed information about that kind of device. For example, **man sd** displays the Man pages for SCSI devices. The following example mounts a floppy disk in the first floppy drive device (**fd0**) to the **/mydir** directory.

```
# mount /dev/fd0   /mydir
```

For any partition with an entry in the **/etc/fstab** file, you can mount it using only the mount directory specified in its **fstab** entry. You do not have to enter the device file name. The **mount** command will look up the entry for it in the **fstab** file, using the directory to identify the entry, and in that way find the device name. For example, to unmount the **/dev/hda1** DOS partition in the previous example, the **mount** command only needs to know the directory it is mounted to, in this case, **/mnt/dos**.

```
# mount /mnt/dos
```

Should you want to replace a mounted file system with another, you must first explicitly unmount the one already mounted. Say that you have mounted a floppy disk and now you want to take it out and put in a new one. You must unmount that floppy disk before you can put in and mount the new one. You unmount a file system with the **umount** command. The **umount** command can take as its argument either a device name or the directory where it was mounted. Here is the syntax:

```
# umount device-or-mountpoint
```

The following example unmounts the floppy disk mounted to the **/mydir** directory:

```
# umount /dev/fd0
```

Using the example where the device was mounted on the **/mydir** directory, you could just use that directory to unmount the file system.

```
# umount /mydir
```

There is one important constraint on the **umount** command. You can never unmount a file system that you are currently working in. If you change to a directory within a file system that you then try to unmount, you will receive an error message saying that the file system is busy. For example, suppose you mount the OpenLinux CD-ROM on the **/mnt/cdrom** directory, and then change to that **/mnt/cdrom** directory. If you decide to change CD-ROMs, you first have to unmount the current one with the **umount** command. This will fail because you are currently in the directory it is mounted to. You first have to leave that directory before you can unmount the CD-ROM.

```
# mount   /dev/hdc   /mnt/cdrom
# cd /mnt/cdrom
# umount /mnt/cdrom
umount: /dev/hdd: device is busy
# cd   /root
# umount /mnt/cdrom
```

Mounting Floppy Disks

To access a file on a floppy disk, you first have to mount that disk onto your Linux system. The device name for your floppy drive is **fd0**, and it is located in the directory **/dev**. Entering **/dev/fd0** references your floppy drive. Notice the number **0** after **fd**. If you have more than one floppy drive, they will be represented by **fd1**, **fd2**, and so on. You can mount to any directory you want. Many distributions like OpenLinux and Red

Hat create a convenient directory to use for floppy disks, **/mnt/floppy**. The following
example mounts the floppy disk in your floppy drive to the **/mnt/floppy** directory:

```
# mount /dev/fd0   /mnt/floppy
```

Bear in mind that you are mounting a particular floppy disk, not the floppy drive.
You cannot just remove the floppy disk and put in another one. The **mount** command
has attached those files to your main directory tree, and your system expects to find
those files on a floppy disk in your floppy drive. If you take out the disk and put
another one in, you will get an error message when you try to access it.

To change disks, you must first unmount the floppy disk already in your disk
drive; then, after putting in the new disk, you must explicitly mount that new disk. To
do this, use the **umount** command. Notice that there is no *n* in the **umount** command.

```
# umount   /dev/fd0
```

For the **unmount** operation, you can specify either the directory it is mounted on or
the **/dev/fd0** device.

```
# umount   /mnt/floppy
```

You can now remove the floppy disk, put in the new one and then mount it.

```
# mount   /mnt/floppy
```

When you shut down your system, any disk you have mounted will be
automatically unmounted. You do not have to explicitly unmount it.

Mounting CD-ROMs

You can also mount CD-ROM discs to your Linux system using the **mount** command.
On many distributions like OpenLinux and Red Hat, the directory **/mnt/cdrom** has
been reserved for CD-ROM file systems. You will see an entry for this in the **/etc/fstab**
file. With such an entry, to mount a CD-ROM, all you have to do is enter the command
mount and the directory **/mnt/cdrom**. You do not need to specify the device name.
Once mounted, you can access the CD-ROM through the **/mnt/cdrom** directory.

```
# mount /mnt/cdrom
```

As with floppy disks, keep in mind that you are mounting a particular CD-ROM,
not the CD-ROM drive. You cannot just remove the CD-ROM and put in a new one.
The **mount** command has attached those files to your main directory tree, and your

system expects to find them on a disc in your CD-ROM drive. To change discs, you have to first unmount the CD-ROM that is already in your CD-ROM drive with the **umount** command. Your CD-ROM drive will not open until you issue this command. Then, after putting in the new disc, you must explicitly mount that new CD-ROM. You can then remove the CD-ROM and put in the new one. Then, issue a **mount** command to mount it.

```
# umount   /mnt/cdrom
```

If you want to mount a CD-ROM to another directory, you have to include the device name in the **mount** command. The following example mounts the disc in your CD-ROM drive to the **/mydir** directory. The particular device name for the CD-ROM in this example is **/dev/hdc**.

```
# mount /dev/hdc   /mydir
```

To change discs, you have to unmount the CD-ROM that is already in your CD-ROM drive; then, after putting in the new disc, you must explicitly mount that new CD-ROM.

```
# umount /mydir
```

You can now remove the CD-ROM and put in the new one. Then, issue a **mount** command to mount it.

```
# mount   /dev/hdc      /mydir
```

Mounting Hard Drive Partitions: Linux and MS-DOS

You can mount both Linux and MS-DOS hard drive partitions with the **mount** command. However, it is much more practical to have them mounted automatically using the **/etc/fstab** file as described in the earlier section "Mount Configuration: **/etc/fstab**." The Linux hard disk partitions you created during installation are already automatically mounted for you. To mount a Linux hard disk partition, enter the **mount** command with the device name of the partition and the directory you want to mount it to. IDE hard drives use the prefix **hd**, and SCSI hard drives use the prefix **sd**. The next example mounts the Linux hard disk partition on **/dev/hda4** to the directory **/mnt/mydata**.

```
# mount -t ext2   /dev/hda4   /mnt/mydata
```

You can also mount an MS-DOS partition and directly access the files on it. As with a Linux partition, you use the **mount** command, but you also have to specify the file system type as MS-DOS. For that, use the **-t** option and then type **vfat**. In the next example, the user mounts the MS-DOS hard disk partition **/dev/hda1** to the Linux file structure at directory **/mnt/dos**. The **/mnt/dos** directory is a common designation for MS-DOS file systems, though you can mount it in any directory. Be sure that you have already created the directory.

```
# mount -t vfat  /dev/hda1  /mnt/dos
```

Formatting File Systems: mkfs

If you want to mount a new empty partition from either a new hard drive or your current drive, you must first create that partition using the Linux **fdisk** and format it with **mkfs**. Once created and formatted, you can then mount it on your system. To start **fdisk**, enter **fdisk** on the command line. This will bring up an interactive program that you can use to create your Linux partition. Be very careful using Linux **fdisk**. It can literally erase your entire hard disk if you are not careful. The Linux **fdisk** operates much as described in the installation process discussed in Chapter 2. The command **n** will create a new partition, and the command **t** will allow you to set its type to that of a Linux type, 83. Table 26-6 lists the **fdisk** commands.

Commands	Description
A	Sets and unsets the bootable flag for a partition.
C	Sets and unsets the DOS compatibility flag.
D	Deletes a partition.
L	Lists partition types.
M	Displays a listing of **fdisk** commands.
N	Creates a new partition.
P	Prints the partition table, listing all the partitions on your disk.
Q	Quits without saving changes. Use this to abort an **fdisk** session if you made a mistake.
T	Select the file system type for a partition.
V	Verify the partition table.

Table 26-6.   *The fdisk Commands*

Commands	Description
w	Write partition table to disk and exit. At this point the changes are made, irrevocably.
x	Displays a listing of advanced **fdisk** commands. With these, you can set the number of cylinders, sectors, and heads; print raw data; and change the location of data in the partition table.

Table 26-6. *The fdisk Commands* (continued)

Hard disk partitions are named with **hd** (IDE drive) or **sd** (SCSI drives), followed by an alphabetic letter indicating the hard drive and then a number for the partition on the hard drive. They can belong to any operating system such as MS-DOS, OS/2, or Windows NT, as well as Linux. The first partition created is called **hda1**—the first partition on the first IDE hard drive, *a*. If you add another partition, it will have the name **hda2**. If you add a new IDE hard drive, its first partition will have the name **hdb1**.

Once you have created your partition, you have to format it. For this, use the **mkfs** command and the name of the hard disk partition. A hard disk partition is a device with its own device name in the **/dev** directory. You have to specify its full pathname with the **mkfs** command. For example, the second partition on the first hard drive will have the device name **/dev/hda4**. You can now mount your new hard disk partition, attaching it to your file structure. The next example formats that partition:

```
# mkfs -t ext2   /dev/hda4
```

To format a floppy disk, use the **mkfs** command. This creates a Linux file system on that disk. Be sure to specify the **ext2** file system type with the **-t ext2** option. Once formatted, you can then mount that file system. The **mkfs** command takes as its arguments the device name and the number of memory blocks on the disk (see Table 26-7). At 1,000 bytes per block, 1,400 blocks format a 1.44MB disk. You do not first mount the blank disk; you simply put it in your floppy drive and enter the **mkfs** command with its arguments. The next example formats a 1.44MB floppy disk:

```
# mkfs -t ext2 /dev/fd0   1400
```

If you have the K Desktop installed, you can use the kfloppy utility to format your floppy disks. Kfloppy lets you choose an MS-DOS or Linux file system type (see Figure 26-6). For MS-DOS disks, you can choose a quick or full format.

Options	Description
Blocks	Number of blocks for the file system. There are 1,440 blocks for a 1.44MB floppy disk.
-t *file-system-type*	Specify the type of file system to format. The default is the standard Linux file system type, **ext2**.
fs *−options*	Options for the type of file system specified.
-V	Verbose mode. Displays description of each action **mkvfs** takes.
-v	Instructs the file system builder program that **mkvfs** invokes to show actions it takes.
-c	Check a partition for bad blocks before formatting it.
-1 *file-name*	Read list of bad blocks.

Table 26-7.   *The mkfs Options*

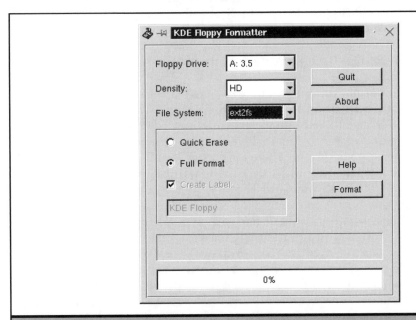

Figure 26-6.   *The kfloppy floppy disk formatter*

CD Images

With the **mkisofs** command, you can create a CD image file that you can then write to a CD write device. A CD image can be written to either a CDR or a CDR/W device. A CDR device is like a CD-ROM but can only write once to a CD disk, whereas a CDR/W can overwrite a CD disk. Each uses special CD media: CDR disks that can be written to only once and special CD read/write disks that can be overwritten like a floppy disk. Once you have created your CD image file, you can write it to a CD write device using the cdrecord or cdwrite applications. The cdrecord application is a more powerful application with many options. You could also copy the CD image file to an MS-DOS partition and then use Windows CD write software to create the CD-ROM.

One important use for a CD image is to create a CD-ROM for a Linux distribution's new release. Most Linux distributions such as OpenLinux and Red Hat will post the entire Linux version on their FTP sites for people to download. The release is the same as the one distributed on their CD-ROMs. The files are extensive, usually taking up about 600 megabytes. A CD image would also take up almost as much space. A fast connection, such as a cable modem or Ethernet connection, and a large hard drive can handle it easily. Be sure to download only the files you need. For example, the Red Hat distribution will include files for different systems such as Sun SPARC workstations, DEC alphas, and PCs. Their PC distribution will be under a directory labeled **i386** or **i686** (as in the Intel CPU). Use an FTP client like IglooFTP, gFTP, or even the KDE or Gnome file managers. If you use **ftp**, be sure to disable the **prompt** with the prompt command, and use the **mget *** to download the entire directory and all its subdirectories at once. This way, you do not have to be downloading individual files and subdirectories. The Red Hat CD Mini-HOWTO provides a simple shell script to change these permissions.

There is one very important change you may have to make to these files. Certain files have to have execute permission set for them. Sometimes, when files are downloaded with an FTP client, the original permissions are not preserved. This means that a file with execute permission on the remote system may have only read permission for the copy on your system. There are certain install programs that need to have execute permission in order to run off the CD-ROM during the installation process. The Linux Red Hat CD-ROM Mini-HOWTO provides a simple script you can use to change these permissions. You can find the Mini-HOWTOs at **www.linux.org**. Another needed change is required if you decide to incorporate any updated RPM packages in the distribution RPMS files, replacing ones from the original set. In this case, you need to generate a new **Red Hat/base/hdlist**. This list contains the names of the original set of RPM packages. You need to have a new list generated with the new names in order to have them installed. The Mini-HOWTO provides another script to do this for Red Hat distributions. The **misc/src/install/genhdlist** command will scan your RPMS files and create an updated list. It expects to find only RPM files in the **RPMS** directory. Remove any others such as ls-lR.gz.

Once you have the distribution files, you can use **mkisofs** to create an ISO CD image of them. You need to include several important options with **mkisofs** to properly create a distribution CD. The **-o** option is used to specify the name of the CD image file. This can be any name you want to give it. The **-r** option specifies Rockridge CD protocols, and the **-J** option provides for long Windows 95 names. The last argument is the directory that contains the files you want to make the CD image of. For this, you can specify a directory. If you downloaded the **i386** directory, then this would be **i386**. The top directory in the CD image will be the subdirectories of **i386**, not **i386** itself. You can also just change to that directory and then use **.** to indicate the current directory. One other important part of creating a distribution CD image is to specify the boot image and boot catalogue. Red Hat and OpenLinux CDs are boot CDs, allowing users to boot directly from the CD-ROM. With the **-c** option, you specify the boot catalogue. For Red Hat distributions, this is the **boot.cat** file. With the **-b** option, you specify the boot image. The boot image is a boot disk image, like that used to start up an installation procedure. On Red Hat systems, this is located in the images directory, **images/boot.img**. On other distributions, the boot catalogue and image files may be located in other directories and have different names.

```
mkisofs -v -r -T -J -V "Red6" -b images/boot.img -c boot.cat -o rd6.iso .
```

To test the CD image, you can mount it to a directory and then access it as if it were just another file system. Be sure to unmount it when you are done.

```
mount -t iso9660 -o ro,loop=/dev/loop0 redhat6.iso /mnt/cdrom
```

Once **mkisofs** has created the CD image file, you can use **cdrecord** or **cdwrite** to write it to a CD write disk. If your system mounts an MS-DOS partition, you could copy the CD image file to that partition and use Windows CD write software to write to a CD write disk. The **mkisofs** command creates an image of type ISO, and you may need to specify that type.

Network File Management

Linux provides several tools for accessing files on remote systems connected to a network. The Network File System (NFS) lets you connect to and directly access resources such as files or devices like CD-ROMs that reside on another machine. The Network Information System (NIS) maintains configuration files for all systems on a network. With Samba, you can connect your Linux system to a Microsoft Windows network, accessing any Windows PC as if your Linux system was just another Windows PC on the network. NetaTalk lets you connect your Linux system to an AppleTalk network, allowing you to directly access remote Macintosh file systems, as well as access any Apple printers such as LaserWriters.

Network File Systems: NFS and /etc/exports

The NFS allows you to mount a file system on a remote computer as if it were local to your own system. You can then directly access any of the files on that remote file system. This has the advantage of allowing different systems on a network to directly access the same files, without each having to keep its own copy. There would be just one copy on a remote file system that each computer could then access.

NFS operates over a TCP/IP network. The remote computer that holds the file system makes it available to other computers on the network. It does so by exporting the file system, which entails making entries in an NFS configuration file called **/etc/exports**, as well as running two daemons to support access by other systems: **rpc.mountd** and **rpc.nfsd**. An entry in the **/etc/exports** file specifies the file system to be exported and the computers on the network that can access it. For the file system, enter its mountpoint, the directory it was mounted to. This is followed by a list of computers that can access this file system. A comma-separated list of mount options placed within a set of parentheses may follow each computer. For example, you might want to give one computer read-only access and another read and write access. If only the options are listed, they are applied to anyone. A list of mount options is provided in Table 26-8. Examples of entries in an **/etc/exports** file are shown here. Read-only access with no security check is given to all computers to the file system mounted on the **/pub** directory, a common name used for public access. Read and write access is given to the **ant.trek.com** computer for the file system mounted on the **/home/foodstuff** directory. The next entry would allow access by **butterfly.trek.com** to your CD-ROM. The last entry denies anyone access to **/home/richlp**.

General Options	Description
`secure`	Requires authentication. This is on by default.
`ro`	Allow only read-only access.
`rw`	Allow read-write access. This is the default.
`noaccess`	This makes everything below the directory inaccessible for the named client.
`link_absolute`	Leave all symbolic links as they are. This is the default operation.
`link_relative`	Convert absolute symbolic links (where the link contents start with a slash) into relative links by prepending the necessary number of slashes (/) to get from the directory containing the link to the root on the server.

Table 26-8. *The /etc/exports Options*

General Options	Description
User ID Mapping	
`squash_uids` `squash_gids`	Specifies a list of uids and gids that should be subject to anonymous mapping.
`all_squash`	Map all uids and gids to the anonymous user. Useful for NFS-exported public FTP directories, news spool directories, etc.
`no_all_squash`	This is the opposite option to `all_squash`, and is the default setting.
`root_squash`	Map requests from uid/gid 0 to the anonymous uid/gid.
`no_root_squash`	Turns off root squashing. Does not map requests from uid/gid 0. This is the default.

Table 26-8. *The /etc/exports Options* (continued)

/etc/exports

```
/pub                   (ro,insecure,all_squash)
/home/foodstuff        ant.trek.com(rw)
/mnt/cdrom             butterfly.trek.com(ro)
/home/richlp           (noaccess)
```

Instead of editing the **/etc/exports** file directly, you can use Linuxconf's "Exported file systems" panel in the "Server tasks" list under the Networking heading in Config. Click the Add button to add a new entry. Figure 26-7 shows the panel with the **butterfly** example.

Once an NFS file system is made available, different computers on the network have to first mount it before they can use it. You can mount an NFS file system either by an entry in the **/etc/fstab** file or by an explicit **mount** command. An NFS entry in the **/etc/fstab** file has a mount type of **nfs**. An NFS file system name consists of the hostname of the computer it is located on, followed by the pathname of the directory where it is mounted. The two are separated by a colon. For example, **rabbit.trek.com:/home/project** specifies a file system mounted at **/home/project** on the **rabbit.trek.com** computer.

There are also several NFS-specific mount options that you can include with your NFS entry. You can specify the size of datagrams sent back and forth, and the amount of time your computer will wait for a response from the host system. You can also specify whether a file system is to be hard-mounted or soft-mounted. For a

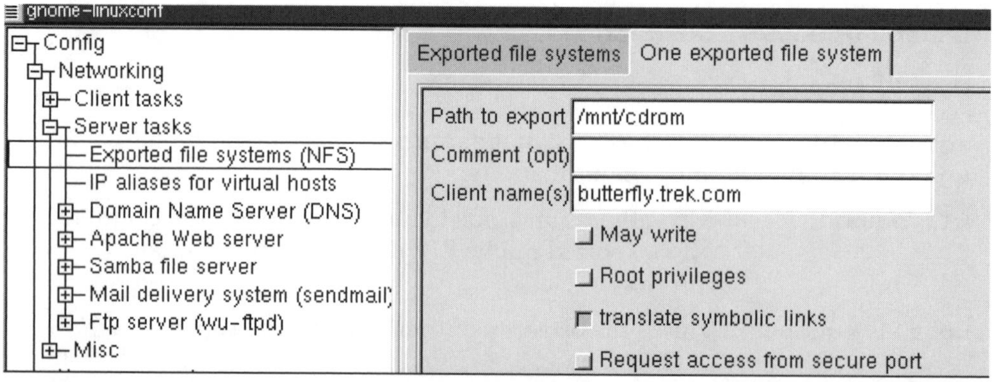

Figure 26-7. Linuxconf "Exported file systems" panel

hard-mounted file system, your computer will continually try to make contact if for some reason the remote system fails to respond. A soft mount, after a specified interval, will give up trying to make contact and issue an error message. A hard mount is the default. Table 26-9 and the Man pages for **mount** contain a listing of these NFS client options. They differ from the NFS server options indicated previously.

An example of an NFS entry follows. The remote system is **rabbit.trek.com** and the file system is mounted on **/home/projects**. This file system is to be mounted on the local system's **/home/dylan** directory. The type of system is NFS and the `timeo` option specifies that the local system will wait up to 20-tenths of a second for a response, two seconds.

```
rabbit.trek.com:/home/projects    /home/dylan    nfs    timeo=20
```

You can also use the **mount** command with the **-t nfs** option to explicitly mount an NFS file system. To explicitly mount the previous entry, use the following command:

```
# mount -t nfs -o timeo=20    rabbit.trek.com:/home/projects    /home/dylan
```

Instead of editing the **/etc/fstab** file directly, you can use Linuxconf's "Access nfs volume" in the "File systems" list under Config. Figure 26-8 shows the "Access nfs volume" panel.

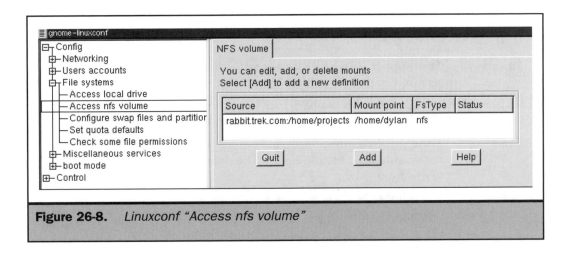

Figure 26-8.   *Linuxconf "Access nfs volume"*

Clicking the Add button displays "Volume specification" panels for Base entries, standard file options, and NFS options. In the Base tab, there are boxes for the remote server, the remote directory (volume), and the directory on your local system where the remote directory will be attached (mountpoint). Figure 26-9 shows the "Volume specification" panel where the remote server is **rabbit.trek.com** and the remote directory is **/home/projects**. The local mountpoint directory is **/home/dylan**.

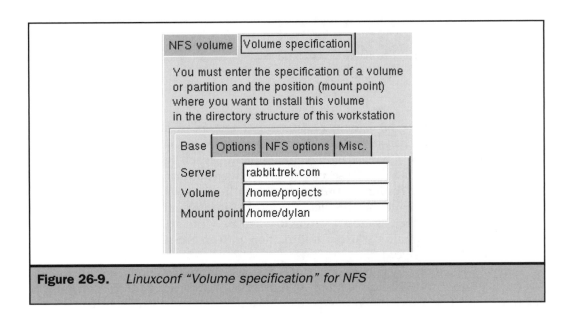

Figure 26-9.   *Linuxconf "Volume specification" for NFS*

Options	Description
rsize=*n*	The number of bytes NFS uses when reading files from an NFS server. The default is 1,024 bytes.
wsize=*n*	The number of bytes NFS uses when writing files to an NFS server. The default is 1,024 bytes.
timeo=*n*	The value in tenths of a second before sending the first retransmission after a timeout. The default value is seven-tenths of a second.
retry=*n*	The number of times to retry a backgrounded NFS **mount** operation before giving up. The default is 10,000 times.
soft	Mount system using soft mount.
hard	Mount system using hard mount. This is the default.
intr	Allow NFS to interrupt the file operation and return to the calling program. The default is to not allow file operations to be interrupted.
bg	If the first mount attempt times out, continue trying the mount in the background. The default is to fail without backgrounding.
tcp	Mount the NFS file system using the TCP protocol instead of the default UDP protocol.

Table 26-9. *NFS Options*

NIS

On networks supporting NFS, many resources and devices are shared by the same systems. Normally, each system would have to have its own configuration files for each device or resource. Changes would entail updating each system individually. However, NFS provides a special service called Network Information Services (NIS) that will maintain such configuration files for the entire network. For changes, you would only need to update the NIS files. NIS works for information required for most administrative tasks, such as those relating to users, network access, or devices. For example, you can maintain password information with an NIS service, having only to update those NIS password files.

NIS was developed by Sun Microsystems and was originally known as Sun's Yellow Pages (YP). NIS files are kept on an NIS server (NIS servers are still sometimes referred to as YP servers). Individual systems on a network use NIS clients to make requests from the NIS server. The NIS server maintains its information on special database files called *maps*. There are Linux versions for both NIS clients and servers. Linux NIS clients will easily connect to any network using NIS.

Most Linux distributions contain both the Linux NIS client and server software in RPM packages that install with default configurations. The NIS client is installed as part of the initial installation on most Linux distributions. You can use the Linuxconf Network Information System panel in the "Client tasks" list under Networking to specify the remote NIS server on your network. You can also use COAS to specify your NIS server. NIS client programs are ypbind (the NIS client daemon), ypwhich, ypcat, yppoll, ypmatch, yppasswd and ypset. Each has its own Man page with details of their use. The NIS server programs are ypserv, ypinit, yppasswd, yppush, ypxfr, and netgroup—each also with its own Man page. A detailed NIS-HOWTO document is available in the **/usr/doc/HOWTO** directory.

Samba

Two very different kinds of networks have evolved, one centered around Microsoft Windows operating systems and the other around Unix operating systems. Whereas most Unix systems use the TCP/IP protocol for networking, Microsoft Windows uses a different protocol, called the Session Message Block (SMB) protocol, that implements a local area network of PCs running Windows. SMB makes use of a network interface called NetBIOS (Network Basic Input Output System) that allows Windows PCs to share resources such as printers and disk space. One Windows PC on such a network can access part of another Windows PC's disk drive as if it were its own. SMB was originally designed for small local area networks. To connect it to larger networks, including those with Unix systems, Microsoft developed the Common Internet File System (CIFS). CIFS still uses SMB and NetBIOS for Windows networking.

Andrew Tridgell wrote a version of SMB that he called Samba. Samba allows Unix and Linux systems to connect to such a Windows network, as if they were Windows PCs. Unix systems can share resources on Windows systems as if they were just another Windows PC. Windows PCs can also access resources on Unix systems as if they were Windows systems. Samba, in effect, has become a professional level, open source, and free version of CIFS. It also runs twice as fast. Samba effectively allows you to use a Linux or Unix server as a network server for a group of Windows machines operating on a Windows network. You can also use it to share files on your Linux system with other Windows PCs, or access files on a Windows PC from your Linux system. On Linux systems, an **smbfs** file system lets you, in effect, mount a remote SMB shared directory onto your own file system. You can then access it as if it were a directory on your local system.

You can obtain extensive documentation and current releases from the Samba Web and FTP sites at **www.samba.org** and **ftp.samba.org**. RPM packages can be obtained from respective distribution FTP sites such as **ftp.redhat.com**. Samba is also included on most Linux distributions, including OpenLinux and Red Hat. Other information can be obtained from the SMB newsgroup, **comp.protocols.smb**. Extensive documentation is provided with the software package and installed on your system, usually in the **/usr/doc** directory under a subdirectory bearing the name of the Samba release. Here, you will find extensive documentation in HTML and text format, as well as numerous examples and the current FAQs. The examples include sample **smb.conf** files for different kinds of configuration.

The Samba software package consists of two server daemons and several utility programs: **smbd**, **nmbd**, **smbclient**, **smbstatus**, and **testparm**. One daemon, **smbd**, is a daemon that provides file and printer services to SMD clients and other systems such as Windows that support SMD. The **nmbd** utility is a daemon that provides NetBIOS name resolution and service browser support. The **smbclient** utility provides FTP-like access to any system on your network that supports SMD. The **smbstatus** utility displays the current status of the **smb** server and who is using it. The **smbsh** utility opens a connection to a Windows PC and lets you access its services using Unix commands such as **ls**. You use **testparm** to test your Samba configuration. The shell script **smbtar** backs up SMB/CIFS shared resources directly to a Unix tap drive. You use **nmblookup** to map the NetBIOS name of a Windows PC to its IP address. Included also with the package is swat, the Samba Web administration tool. This lets you use a Web page interface to create and maintain your Samba configuration file, **smb.conf**.

Samba provides four main services: file and printer services, authentication and authorization, name resolution, and service announcement. The SMB daemon, **smbd**, provides the file and printer services as well as authentication and authorization for those services. This means that users on the network can share files and printers. You can control access to these services by requiring users to provide a password. When users try to access a shared directory, they would be prompted for a password. Control can be implemented in share mode or user mode. The share mode sets up one password for the shared resource and then lets any user that has that password access it. The user mode provides a different password for each user. Samba maintains its own password file for this purpose, **smbpasswords**.

Name resolution and service announcements are handled by the **nmbd** server. Name resolution essentially resolves NetBIOS names with IP addresses (Microsoft plans to have this handled by DNS in the future). Service announcement, also known as browsing, is the way a list of services available on the network is made known to the connected Windows (and with Samba, Linux) PCs.

Samba Configuration: smb.conf

You configure the Samba daemon using the **smb.conf** file located in the **/etc** directory. The file is separated into different sections. Each section contains a service description for a particular SMB service. A service consists of the directory and the access rights allowed to users of the service. A service can be either a file space or a printer. Each service is given a service name by which it can be referenced. Special sections called global, printer, and home, provide default descriptions for SMB services. Following the special sections, sections are entered for specific services, namely access to specific directories or printers.

Most distributions will install a **smb.conf** file in your **/etc** directory. The file contains default settings used for that distribution. You can edit the file to customize your configuration to your own needs. Many entries are commented, and you can remove the initial semicolon to make them effective. The Man page for **smb.conf** contains a detailed list of all SMB parameters and their values, **man smb.conf**. Alternatively, you can generate this file using the Linuxconf "Samba file server" panel in the "Server tasks" list under Networking in Config. An extensive set of sample **smb.conf** files are located in the **/usr/doc/samba*** directory in the examples subdirectory. The **/usr/doc/samba*** directory also contains a standard Samba default file called **samba.conf.default**.

A section begins with the service name encased in brackets. Other than the special sections, the service name can be any name you want to give it. Following the section label, on separate lines, different parameters for this service are entered. The parameters define the access rights to be granted to the user of the service. For example, for a directory, you may want it to be browseable but read-only and use a certain printer. Parameters are entered in the format *parametername = value*. You can enter a comment by placing a semicolon at the beginning of the comment line.

A simple example of the service description follows. The service name is encased in brackets and followed by two parameter entries. The path parameter specifies the directory to which access is to be allowed. The writable parameter specifies whether the user will have write access to this directory and its file space.

```
[foo]
        path = /home/bar
        writable = true
```

A printer service has the same format, but will require certain other parameters. The path parameters specifies the location of the printer spool directory. The read-only and printable parameters are set to true, indicating that the service is read-only and printable. Public indicates that anyone with guest status can access it.

```
[aprinter
        path = /usr/spool/public
        read only = true
        printable = true
        public = true
```

The global segment determines configuration for the entire server, as well as specifying default entries to be used in the home and directory segments. The home segment specifies default controls for accessing a user **home** directory through the SMB protocols by remote users. The printer section specifies the default controls for accessing printers.

You can then list controls for specific directories on your system. To do so, enter a label for the system. Then, on separate lines enter options for its pathname and the different permissions you want to set. You can make a directory writable, public, or read-only. You can specify a printer or even the user that can have write access. For those options not set, the defaults entered in the global, home, and printer segments will be used. Initially, you will only need the following entries. This will let you connect to your **home** directory and use any printer supported by the host.

```
[homes]
     writable = yes

[printers]
     writable = no
     printable = yes
     path = /tmp
     public = yes
```

Once you have created your **smb.conf** file, you should test it using the **testparm** program. It takes as its argument the name of your configuration file. Once tested, you can add the hostname and host IP address of a remote system to see if you have access to that system.

```
testparm /etc/smb.conf
```

Both OpenLinux and Red Hat automatically install and start up the Samba server daemons. When configuring Samba, you will probably have to manually start up and stop these daemons. You can do so using the Samba **init** script with the arguments **stop** to stop it and **start** to start it up again. The Samba script is located in the **/etc/rc.d/init.d** directory.

```
/etc/rc.d/init.d/samba  stop
/etc/rc.d/init.d/samba  start
```

smbclient

The command **smbclient** operates like FTP to access systems using the SMB protocols. Whereas with an FTP client you can access other FTP severs or Unix systems, with **smbclient** you can access any Windows systems that use SMB. Many **smbclient** commands are similar to FTP such as **mget** to transfer a file or **del** to delete a file. The **smbclient** program has several options for querying a remote system as well as connecting to it. See the **smbclient** Man page for a complete list of options and commands. The **smbclient** program takes as its argument a server name and the service you want to access on that server. A double slash precedes the server name and single slash separates it from the service. The service can be any shared resource such as a directory or printer. The server name is its NetBIOS name, which may or may not be the same as its IP name. For example, to specify the **myreports** shared directory on the server named **dylan**, you wold use **//dylan/myreports**. If you have to specify a path name, you would use backslashes for Windows files and forward slashes for Unix/Linux files.

```
//server-name/service
```

With the **-I** option, you can specify the system using its Domain Name Service name. You use the **-U** option and a login name for the remote login name you want to use on the remote system. Attach **%** with the password if a password is required. With the **-L** option, you can obtain a list of the services provided on a server, such as shared directories or printers. To access a particular directory on a remote system, you enter the directory as an argument to the **smbclient** command, followed by any options. For Windows files, you use backslashes for the pathnames, and for Unix/Linux files you use forward slashes.

Once connected, an **smb** prompt is displayed and you can use **smbclient** commands such as **get** and **put** to transfer files. The **quit** or **exit** commands quit the **smbclient**. In the following example, **smbclient** accesses the directory **myreports** on the **dylanpc.trek.com** system using the george login name:

```
smbclient //dylan/myreports -I dylanpc.trek.com  -U george
```

A partial listing of the default sample Samba **smb.conf** file provided with the software package is shown here:

```
; The global setting for a default install
; Copyright(C) John H Terpstra - 1997
;
; smbd re-reads this file regularly, but if in doubt stop and restart it:
; /etc/rc.d/init.d/smb stop
; /etc/rc.d/init.d/smb start
;====================== Global Settings =====================================
[global]
```

```
; workgroup = NT-Domain-Name or Workgroup-Name, eg: REDHAT5
   workgroup = WORKGROUP

; comment is the equivalent of the NT Description field
   comment = Redhat Samba Server

; printing = BSD or SYSV or AIX, etc.
   printing = bsd
   printcap name = /etc/printcap
   load printers = yes

; Uncomment this if you want a guest account, you must add this to /etc/passwd
;  guest account = pcguest
   log file = /var/log/samba.d/%m

; Put a capping on the size of the log files (in Kb)
   max log size = 50


; Configuration Options ***** The location of this entry in your smb.conf
; hierarchy determines which parameters are overwritten - please watch out!
; Where %m is any SMBName (machine name, or computer name) for which a custom
; configuration is desired
;    include = /etc/smb.conf.%m

; Performance Related Options
; Before setting socket options read the smb.conf man page!!
   socket options = TCP_NODELAY
; Socket Address is used to specify which socket Samba
; will listen on (good for aliased systems)
;    socket address = aaa.bbb.ccc.ddd
; Use keep alive only if really needed!!!!
;    keep alive = 60
; Configure Samba to use multiple interfaces
;        Samba will auto-detect network interfaces - only use this if
;        the auto-detection does not deliver the needed results
;    interfaces = 192.168.12.2/24 176.16.111.22/19 10.11.13.14/255.255.252.0
```

```
; Browser Control Options:
; Local Master set to True causes Samba to participate in browser elections
;          the default setting is true, this causes Samba to behave like a
;          Windows NT server. Setting this to false turns off all browser
;          election participation.
;    local master = yes


; Windows Internet Name Serving Support Section:
; WINS Support - Tells the NMBD component of Samba to enable its WINS Server
;    the default is NO. If you have a Windows NT Server WINS use it!
;    Samba defaults to wins support = no
;    wins support = yes

; WINS Server - Tells the NMBD components of Samba to be a WINS Client
;    Note: Samba can be either a WINS Server, or a WINS Client, but NOT both
;    wins server = w.x.y.z

; WINS Proxy - Tells Samba to answer name resolution queries on behalf of a non
;    WINS Client capable client, for this to work there must be at least one
;    WINS Server on the network. The default is NO.
;    wins proxy = yes

;=========================== Share Definitions ===============================
[homes]
   comment = Home Directories
   browseable = no
   writable = yes

; Un-comment the following and create the netlogon directory for Domain Logons
; [netlogon]
;    comment = Samba Network Logon Service
;    path = /usr/local/samba/lib/netlogon
```

```
;   Case sensitivity breaks logon script processing!!!
;      case sensitive = no
;      guest ok = yes
;      locking = no
;      writable = no
;      For browseable say NO if you want to hide the NETLOGON share
;      browseable = yes

;   Un-comment the following to provide a specific roving profile share
;   the default is to use the user's home directory
;[Profiles]
;       path = /usr/local/samba/profiles
;       browseable = no
;       printable = no
;       guest ok = yes

;   NOTE: There is NO need to specifically define each individual printer
[printers]
     comment = All Printers
     path = /usr/spool/samba
     browseable = no
     printable = yes
;   Set public = yes to allow user 'guest account' to print
     guest ok = no
     writable = no
     create mask = 0700

;[tmp]
;      comment = Temporary file space
;      path = /var/tmp
;      read only = no
;      public = yes

;   A publicly accessible directory, but read only, except for people in
;   the staff group
;[public]
;      comment = Public Stuff
;      path = /home/samba
;      public = yes
;      writable = yes
```

```
;    printable = no
;    write list = @users
; Other examples.
;
; A private printer, usable only by fred. Spool data will be placed in fred's
; home directory. Note that fred must have write access to the spool directory,
; wherever it is.
;[fredsprn]
;    comment = Fred's Printer
;    valid users = fred
;    path = /homes/fred
;    printer = freds_printer
;    public = no
;    writable = no
;    printable = yes
;
; A private directory, usable only by fred. Note that fred requires write
; access to the directory.
;[fredsdir]
;    comment = Fred's Service
;    path = /usr/somewhere/private
;    valid users = fred
;    public = no
;    writable = yes
;    printable = no
;
; a service which has a different directory for each machine that connects
; this allows you to tailor configurations to incoming machines. You could
; also use the %u option to tailor it by user name.
; The %m gets replaced with the machine name that is connecting.
;[pchome]
;   comment = PC Directories
;   path = /usr/pc/%m
;   public = no
;   writable = yes
;
;
```

```
; A publicly accessible directory, read/write to all users. Note that all files
; created in the directory by users will be owned by the default user, so
; any user with access can delete any other user's files. Obviously this
; directory must be writable by the default user. Another user could of course
; be specified, in which case all files would be owned by that user instead.
;[public]
;    path = /usr/somewhere/else/public
;    public = yes
;    only guest = yes
;    writable = yes
;    printable = no
;
;
; The following two entries demonstrate how to share a directory so that two
; users can place files there that will be owned by the specific users. In this
; setup, the directory should be writable by both users and should have the
; sticky bit set on it to prevent abuse. Obviously this could be extended to
; as many users as required.
;[myshare]
;    comment = Mary's and Fred's stuff
;    path = /usr/somewhere/shared
;    valid users = mary fred
;    public = no
;    writable = yes
;    printable = no
;    create mask = 0765
```

NetaTalk: AppleTalk

NetaTalk implements the AppleTalk network protocol on Unix and Linux systems. It provides support for sharing file systems, accessing printers, and routing AppleTalk. It allows a Mac machine connected to an AppleTalk network to access a Linux system as if it were an AppleTalk file and print server. Linux systems can also use NetaTalk to access Mac machines connected to an AppleTalk network. AppleTalk is the network protocol used for Apple Macintosh computers. AppleTalk supports file sharing and network printing where different Macs can share each others file systems and printers. For example, if you have a LaserWriter connected to a Macintosh, you can have your Linux system access it and print on that LaserWriter. You can also access any shared file systems that may be set up on the Macintoshes on the network. The current NetaTalk Web site is **www.umich.edu/~rsug/netatalk/**, with a FAQ site at **threepio.hitchcock.org/netatalk/**.

The name of the NetaTalk daemon is **atalkd**. It performs much the same function as **routed** and **ifconfig**. Several programs manage printing. The **papd** program lets Macs spool to a Linux printer. The **pap** program lets Linux systems print to an AppleTalk printer. The **psf** program is a PostScript printer filter for **pap**, and **psorder** lets you print PostScript pages in reverse. The **apfd** program provides an interface to the Linux file system, while **nbplkup** will list all AppleTalk objects on the network. For example, **nbplkup :LaserWriter** will list the LaserWriters available. You would use **pap** to access and print to a LaserWriter. To use Linux commands to access a printer, you need to make an entry for it in the **/etc/printcap** file and create spool, status, and lock files for it.

NetaTalk requires kernel-level support for the AppleTalk Datagram Delivery Protocol (DDP). If your kernel does not currently support it, you will either have to rebuild the kernel including AppleTalk support or use a loadable module for AppleTalk. Current kernels for most distributions include AppleTalk support.

NetaTalk uses five configuration files as shown here. The software package will include default versions that you can modify. The RPM packages include the **config** file that contains documented default entries for use by the **atalk** startup script. Check the variable entries for any parameters you may want to change, such as the maximum number of allowed simultaneous users (default is 5).

Configuration files (see Table 26-10), are automatically installed for you by the RPM package versions of NetaTalk, such as those for Red Hat or OpenLinux. If you are installing from the source distribution, you need to install these from default files in the source directory. Also, make sure that the following lines are in your **/etc/services** file (RPM packages add these automatically):

```
rtmp 1/ddp # Routing Table Maintenance Protocol
nbp 2/ddp # Name Binding Protocol
echo 4/ddp # AppleTalk Echo Protocol
zip 6/ddp # Zone Information Protocol
```

File Name	Description
AppleVolumes.default	List of shared directories, including optional names.
AppleVolumes.system	Maps of file extensions to Mac OS types.
afpd.conf	Configuration file for **afpd** daemon (AppleTalk file system and printer daemon).
atalkd.conf	Controls the interfaces to which NetaTalk binds, letting you specify network numbers or zones. If empty, NetaTalk will detect the interfaces itself.
papd.conf	Provides AppleTalk access to Linux print queues. If empty, will use **/etc/printcap**.

Table 26-10.   *NetaTalk Configuration Files*

NetaTalk is started using a startup script called **atalk**. RPM packages such as those for Red Hat and OpenLinux will install **atalk** in the **/etc/rc.d/init.d** directory. You can also use a System V Init run-level editor to manage startup and shutdown operations. A link will be set up to start the **atalk** script when you boot. You can also use **start** and **stop** arguments directly with **atalk**. The source code distribution uses a startup script called **rc.atalk** and will install it in the **/usr/local/atalk/etc** directory.

```
/etc/rec.d/init.d/atalk  start
```

The mtools Utilities: msdos

Your Linux system provides a set of utilities known as mtools that let you easily access a floppy disk formatted for MS-DOS (see Table 26-11 at the end of this section). The **mcopy** command allows you to copy files to and from an MS-DOS floppy disk in your floppy drive. No special operations, such as mounting, are required. With mtools, you do not have to mount an MS-DOS partition to access it. For an MS-DOS floppy disk, just place the disk in your floppy drive, and you can then use mtool commands to access those files. For example, to copy a file from an MS-DOS floppy disk to your Linux system, use the **mcopy** command. You specify the MS-DOS disk with **a:** for the A drive. Unlike normal DOS pathnames, pathnames used with mtool commands use forward slashes instead of backslashes. The directory **docs** on the A drive would be referenced by the pathname **a:/docs**, not **a:\docs**. The next example copies the file **mydata** to the MS-DOS disk and then copies the **preface** file from the disk to the current Linux directory. Notice that, unlike DOS, mtools uses forward slashes instead of backward slashes.

```
$ mcopy mydata a:
$ mcopy a:/preface   .
```

You can use the **mdir** command to list files on your MS-DOS disk, and you can use the **mcd** command to change directories on it. The next example lists the files on the MS-DOS disk in your floppy drive and then changes to the **docs** directory on that drive.

```
$ mdir a:
$ mcd a:/docs
```

Most of the standard MS-DOS commands are available as mtool operations. You can create MS-DOS directories with **mmd** and erase MS-DOS files with **mdel**. A list of mtool commands is provided in Table 26-11. For example, to display a file on drive **b:** on an MS-DOS 5 1/4-inch floppy drive, use **mtype** and the name of the file preceded by **b:/**.

```
$ mtype b:/readme
```

Access to MS-DOS partitions is configured by the **/etc/mtools.conf** file. This file lists several different default MS-DOS partitions and disk drives. Each drive or partition is identified with a particular device name. Entries for your floppy drives are already entered, using the device names **/dev/fd0** and **/dev/fd1** for the first and second floppy drives. An entry in the **/etc/mtools.conf** file takes the form of the drive label followed by the term "file" and the equal sign, and then the device name of the drive or partition that you want identified with this label. The device name is encased in quotes. For example, assuming that the first hard disk partition is an MS-DOS partition and has the device name of **/dev/hda1**, the following entry would identify this as the **c:** drive on an MS-DOS system:

```
drive c: file="/dev/hda1"
```

It is important that you have the correct device name for your partition. These are listed in the **/etc/fstab** file and can also be viewed with the Linuxconf "Local drive access" panel on your root user desktop. If you have a SCSI hard disk, the hard disk partitions will have the form of **sd** followed by a character for the hard drive and a number for the partition in it. For example, **sda1** refers to the first partition on the SCSI hard drive. IDE hard drives have the form of **hd**, also followed by a character and a partition number—**hda1** refers to the first partition on an IDE hard drive.

On most distributions, a default **/etc/mtools.conf** file is installed for you. This file will have commented entries for the **c:** drive, one for a SCSI hard disk partition and one for an IDE partition. Both are commented out with a preceding **#**. If you have an IDE hard drive (as most users will), you need to remove the preceding **#** symbol from the entry for the IDE hard disk partition and leave the preceding **#** symbol in front of the entry for the SCSI partition. Also, if your MS-DOS partition on your IDE hard drive is not the first partition, you will have to change the device name. For example, if the MS-DOS partition is the second partition, the device name will be **/dev/hda2**. If you have several MS-DOS partitions, you can add entries for each one, assigning a different label to each. The following example assigns the **d:** label to the fifth hard disk partition on an IDE drive:

```
drive d: file="/dev/hda5"
```

/etc/mtools.conf

```
# Linux floppy drives
drive a: file="/dev/fd0" exclusive 1.44m
drive b: file="/dev/fd1" exclusive 1.44m
# First SCSI hard disk partition
#drive c: file="/dev/sda1"
# First IDE hard disk partition
drive c: file="/dev/hda1"
drive d: file="/dev/hda5"
#dosemu floppy image
drive m: file="/var/lib/dosemu/diskimage"
#dosemu hdimage
drive n: file="/var/lib/dosemu/diskimage" offset=3840
#Atari ramdisk image
drive o: file="/tmp/atari_rd" offset=136
mtools_lower_case=1
```

Once the DOS hard disk partitions are referenced, you can then use their drive letters to copy files to and from them to your Linux partitions. The following command copies the file **mydoc.html** to the **c:** partition in the directory **webstuff** and renames it **mypage.htm**. Notice the use of forward slashes instead of backward ones.

```
$ mcopy mydoc.html c:/webstuff/mypage.htm
```

Because of the differences in the way DOS and Linux handle newlines in text files, you should use the **-t** option whenever copying a DOS text file to a Linux partition.

The following command copies the **mydoc.txt** file from the **c:/project** directory to the **/newdocs** directory.

```
$ mcopy -t c:/project/mydoc.txt   /newdocs
```

Here, in Table 26-11, are some mtools access commands.

Commands	Execution
mcopy *filename filename*	Copies a file to and from an MS-DOS disk on your Linux system. The following copies a file from an MS-DOS diskette to your Linux system: mcopy **a:/***filename directory-or-filename* The following copies a file from Linux for an MS-DOS diskette in your floppy drive: **mcopy** *filename* **a:/***filename*
mcd *directory-name*	Changes directory on your MS-DOS file system. The following lists files on an MS-DOS disk in your floppy drive: **mdir a:**
mdir	Lists the files on an MS-DOS disk in your floppy drive.
mattrib	Change the attribute of an MS-DOS file.
mdel *filename*	Delete an MS-DOS file.
mformat	Add an MS-DOS file system to a diskette.
mlabel	Make a volume label.
mmd *directory-name*	Make an MS-DOS directory.
mrd *directory-name*	Remove an MS-DOS directory.
mread *filename filename*	Low-level read (copy) an MS-DOS file to Unix.
mren *filename filename*	Rename an MS-DOS file.
mtype *filename*	Display contents of an MS-DOS file.
mwrite *filename filename*	Low-level write (copy) a Unix file to MS-DOS.

Table 26-11.   *The mtools Access Commands*

Archive Files and Devices: tar

The **tar** utility creates archives for files and directories. With **tar**, you can archive specific files, update them in the archive, and add new files, as you wish, to that archive. You can even archive entire directories with all their files and subdirectories, all of which can be restored from the archive. The **tar** utility was originally designed to create archives on tapes. The term "tar" stands for tape archive. You can create archives on any device, such as a floppy disk, or you can create an archive file to hold the archive. The **tar** utility is ideal for making backups of your files or combining several files into a single file for transmission across a network.

On Linux, **tar** is often used to create archives on devices or files. You can direct **tar** to archive files to a specific device or a file by using the **f** option with the name of the device or file. The syntax for the **tar** command using the **f** option is shown in the next example. The device or file name is often referred to as the archive name. When creating a file for a **tar** archive, the file name is usually given the extension .**tar**. This is a convention only, and is not required. You can list as many file names as you wish. If a directory name is specified, then all of its subdirectories will be included in the archive.

```
$ tar optionsf archive-name.tar directory-and-file-names
```

To create an archive, use the **c** option. Combined with the **f** option, **c** will create an archive on a file or device. You enter this option before and right next to the **f** option. Notice that there is no preceding dash before a **tar** option. Table 26-12 lists the different options you can use with **tar**. In the next example, the directory **mydir** and all of its subdirectories are saved in the file **myarch.tar**.

```
$ tar cf myarch.tar mydir
```

The user can later extract the directories from the tape using the **x** option. The **xf** option extracts files from an archive file or device. The **tar** extraction operation will generate all subdirectories. In the next example, the **xf** option directs **tar** to extract all the files and subdirectories from the **tar** file **myarch.tar**.

```
$ tar xf myarch.tar
```

You use the **r** option to add files to an archive that has already been created. The **r** option appends the files to the archive. In the next example, the user appends the files in the **letters** directory to the **myarch.tar** archive.

```
$ tar rf myarch.tar letters
```

Commands	Execution
`tar` *options files*	Backs up files to tape, device, or archive file
`tar` *options***f** *archive_name filelist*	Backs up files to a specific file or device specified as *archive_name*. *filelist*; can be file names or directories

Options

`c`	Creates a new archive
`t`	Lists the names of files in an archive
`r`	Appends files to an archive
`u`	Updates an archive with new and changed files; adds only those files that have been modified since they were archived or files that are not already present in the archive
`w`	Waits for a confirmation from the user before archiving each file; allows you to update an archive selectively
`x`	Extracts files from an archive
`m`	When extracting a file from an archive, no new time stamp is assigned
`M`	Creates a multiple-volume archive that may be stored on several floppy disks
`f` *archive-name*	Saves the tape archive to the file *archive-name* instead of to the default tape device; when given an *archive-name*, the **f** option saves the **tar** archive in a file of that name
`f` *device-name*	Saves a **tar** archive to a device such as a floppy disk or tape; **/dev/fd0** is the device name for your floppy disk; the default device is held in **/etc/default/tar-file**
`v`	Displays each file name as it is archived
`z`	Compresses or decompresses archived files using gzip

Table 26-12. *File Backups: tar*

Should you change any of the files in your directories that you have previously archived, you can use the **u** option to instruct **tar** to update the archive with any modified files. The **tar** command compares the time of the last update for each archived file with those in the user's directory and copies into the archive any files that have been changed since they were last archived. Any newly created files in these directories will be added to the archive as well. In the next example, the user updates the **myarch.tar** file with any recently modified or newly created files in the **mydir** directory:

```
$ tar uf myarch.tar mydir
```

If you need to see what files are stored in an archive, you can use the **tar** command with the **t** option. The next example will list all the files stored in the **myarch.tar** archive:

```
$ tar tf myarch.tar
```

To back up the files to a specific device, specify the device as the archive. In the next example, the user creates an archive on the floppy disk in the **/dev/fd0** device and copies into it all the files in the **mydir** directory:

```
$ tar cf /dev/fd0 mydir
```

To extract the backed-up files on the disk in the device, use the **xf** option:

```
$ tar xf /dev/fd0
```

If the files you are archiving take up more space than would be available on a device such as a floppy disk, you can create a **tar** archive that uses multiple labels. The **M** option instructs **tar** to prompt you for a new storage component when the current one is filled. When archiving to a floppy drive with the **M** option, **tar** will prompt you to put in a new floppy disk when one becomes full. You can then save your **tar** archive on several floppy disks.

```
$ tar cMf /dev/fd0 mydir
```

To unpack the multiple-disk archive, place the first one in the floppy drive and then issue the following **tar** command using both the **x** and **M** options. You will be prompted to put in the other floppy disks as they are needed.

```
$ tar xMf /dev/fd0
```

The **tar** operation will not perform compression on archived files. If you want to compress the archived files, you can instruct **tar** to invoke the gzip utility to compress them. With the lowercase **z** option, **tar** will first use gzip to compress files before archiving them. The same **z** option will invoke gzip to decompress them when extracting files.

```
$ tar czf  myarch.tar mydir
```

Bear in mind that there is a difference between compressing individual files in an archive and compressing the entire archive as a whole. Often, an archive is created for transferring several files at once as one tar file. To shorten transmission time, the archive should be as small as possible. You can use the compression utility gzip on the archive **tar** file to compress it, reducing its size, and then send the compressed version. The person receiving it can decompress it, restoring the **tar** file. Using gzip on a **tar** file often results in a file with the extension **.tar.gz**. The extension **.gz** is added to a compressed **gzip** file. The next example creates a compressed version of **myarch.tar** using the same name with the extension **.gz**:

```
$ gzip myarch.tar
$ ls
$ myarch.tar.gz
```

If you have a default device specified, such as a tape, and you want to create an archive on it, you can simply use **tar** without the **f** option and a device or file name. This can be helpful for making backups of your files. The name of the default device is held in a file called **/etc/default/tar**. The syntax for the **tar** command using the default tape device is shown in the following example. If a directory name is specified, all of its subdirectories will be included in the archive.

```
$ tar option directory-and-file-names
```

In the next example, the directory **mydir** and all of its subdirectories are saved on a tape in the default tape device:

```
$ tar c mydir
```

In this example, the **mydir** directory and all of its files and subdirectories are extracted from the default tape device and placed in the user's working directory:

```
$ tar x mydir
```

Midnight Commander (Gnome) and Kfm (KDE)

Both file managers in Gnome and the K Desktop have the ability to automatically display the contents of a **tar** archive file. The contents are displayed as though they were files in a directory. Figure 26-10 shows the KDE file manager displaying files in a tar archive. You can list the files as icons or with details, sorting them by name, type, or other fields. You can even display the contents of files. Clicking on a text file will open it with a text editor, and an image will be displayed with an image viewer. If the file manager cannot determine what program to use to display the file, it will prompt you to select an application. Both file managers can perform the same kind of operation on archives residing on remote file systems, such as **tar** archives on FTP sites. You can obtain a listing of their contents and even read their README files. The Midnight Commander file manager (Gnome) can also extract an archive. Right-click on the Archive icon and select extract.

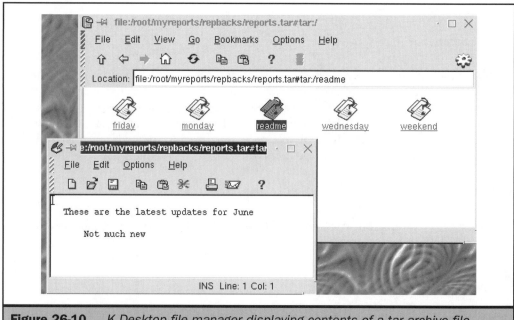

Figure 26-10.   *K Desktop file manager displaying contents of a tar archive file*

Desktop Archivers: guiTar, Ark, KDAT, and Xtar

There are several desktop applications that provide a GUI interface for creating and extracting archives. These archivers provide simple methods for managing archives, letting you easily select files and set options. The guiTAR archiver is Gnome-based. When creating an archive, you can choose from several of the compression methods including **tar**, **rar**, and **zip**. You can open an archive with a drag-and-drop operation, dragging an archive file from the file manager window to the guiTAR window (see Figure 26-11). Files listed in an archive can be sorted by different fields just by clicking on the buttons across the top of the list.

Ark is a K Desktop archiver. To open a new archive, you enter a name with the **.tar.gz** extension. Once an archive is open, you can add to it by simply dragging files from a file manager window to the Ark window. To extract an archive, first open it and then select Extract. KDAT is a tape archiver for the K Desktop. You can use it to back up files to a tape drive. You can specify a root directory or create a tape profile listing specific files and directories. The Xtar archiver is an X Window System application that can run on any file manager. It provides much the same functionality as the other archivers. Once you select the **tar** archive to open, all the files making up the **tar** archive are then listed in the main window. With XTar, you have the option of either

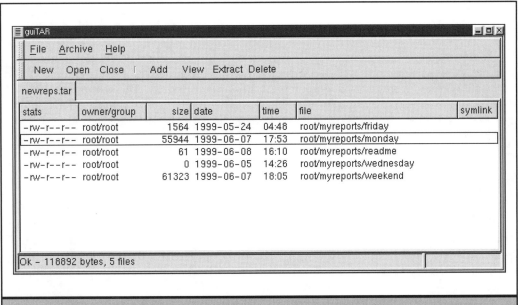

Figure 26-11.   *The guiTAR Gnome archiver*

unpacking the entire **tar** archive or just a few files within it. Options also has a View item for just displaying short text files such as a README file.

File Compression: gzip, bzip2, and zip

There are several reasons for reducing the size of a file. The two most common are to save space or, if you are transferring the file across a network, to save transmission time. You can effectively reduce a file size by creating a compressed copy of it. Anytime you need the file again, you just decompress it. Compression is used in combination with archiving to let you compress whole directories and their files at once. Decompression generates a copy of the archive file that can then be extracted, generating a copy of those files and directories.

There are several compression utilities available for use on Linux and Unix systems. Most software for Linux systems use the GNU **gzip** and **gunzip** utilities. The **gzip** utility compresses files and **gunzip** decompresses them. To compress a file, enter the command **gzip** and the file name. This will replace the file with a compressed version of it with the extension **.gz**.

```
$ gzip mydata
$ ls
mydata.gz
```

To decompress a **gzip** file, use either **gzip** with the **-d** option or the command **gunzip**. These commands will decompress a compressed file with the **.gz** extension and replace it with a decompressed version with the same root name, but without the **.gz** extension. When you use **gunzip**, you do not even have to type in the **.gz** extension; **gunzip** and **gzip -d** will assume it. Table 26-13 lists the different **gzip** options.

```
$ gunzip mydata.gz
$ ls
mydata
```

Suppose you want to display or print the contents of a compressed file without first having to decompress it. The command **zcat** will generate a decompressed version of a file and send it to the standard output. You can then redirect this output to a printer or display a utility such as **more**. The original file will remain in its compressed state.

```
$ zcat mydata.gz | more
```

Option	Execution
-c	Sends compressed version of a file to standard output; each file listed is separately compressed: $ gzip –c mydata preface > myfiles.gz

-d	Decompresses a compressed file; alternatively, you can use gunzip:
	$ gzip –d myfiles.gz
	$ gunzip myfiles.gz

-h	Displays help listing.
-l *file-list*	Displays compressed and uncompressed size of each file listed: $ gzip –l myfiles.gz
-r *directory-name*	Recursively searches for specified directories and compresses all the files in them; the search begins from the current working directory; when used with **gunzip**, compressed files of a specified directory will be uncompressed.
-v *file-list*	For each compressed or decompressed file, displays its name and the percentage of its reduction in size.
-num	Determines the speed and size of the compression; the range is from –1 to –9. A lower number gives greater speed but less compression, resulting in a larger file that compresses and decompresses quickly; –1 gives the quickest compression, but with the largest size; –9 results in a very small file that takes longer to compress and decompress. The default is –6.

Table 26-13. *The gzip Options*

You can also compress archived **tar** files. This will result in files with the extensions **.tar.gz**. Compressed archived files are often used for transmitting very large files across networks.

```
$ gzip myarch.tar
$ ls
myarch.tar.gz
```

You can compress **tar** file members individually using the **tar z** option that invokes **gzip**. With the **z** option, **tar** will invoke **gzip** to compress a file before placing it in an archive. However, archives with members compressed with the **z** option cannot be updated, nor can they be added to. All members have to be compressed and all have to be added at the same time.

You can also use the **compress** and **uncompress** commands to create compressed files. They generate a file that has a **.Z** extension and use a different compression format than **gzip**. The **compress** and **uncompress** commands are not that widely used, but you may run across **.Z** files from time to time. You can use the **uncompress** command to decompress a **.Z** file. The **gzip** utility is the standard GNU compression utility and should be used instead of **compress**.

Another popular compression utility is **bzip2**. It compresses files using the Burrows-Wheeler block-sorting text compression algorithm and Huffman coding. The command line options are very similar to **gzip** by design, but they are not exactly the same. See the **bzip2** Man page for a complete listing. You compress files using the **bzip2** command and decompress with **bunzip2**. The **bzip2** command creates files with the extension **.bz2**. You can use **bzcat** to output compressed data to the standard output. The **bzip2** command compresses files in blocks and lets you specify their size, larger blocks giving you greater compression. Like **gzip**, you can use **bzip2** to compress **tar** archive files. The following example compresses the **mydata** file into a **bzip** compressed file with the extension **.bz2**.

```
$ bzip2 mydata
$ ls
mydata.bz2
```

To decompress, use the **bunzip2** command on a **bzip** file.

```
$ bunzip2 mydata.bz2
```

Zip is a compression and archive utility modeled on pkzip, which was used originally on DOS systems. It is a cross-platform utility used on Windows, Mac, MSDOS, OS/2, Unix, and Linux systems. Zip commands can work with archives created by PKZIP and PKZIP programs and can use Zip archives. You compress a file using the **zip** command. This creates a Zip file with the **.zip** extension. If no files are listed, **zip** will output the compressed data to the standard output. You can also use the – argument to have **zip** read from the standard input. To zip a directory, you include the **-r** option. The first example archives and compresses a file:

```
$ zip mydata
$ ls
mydata.zip
```

The next example archives and compresses the **reports** directory.

```
$ zip -r reports
```

A full set of archive operations is supported. With the **-f** option, you can update a particular file in the Zip archive with a newer version. The **-u** option will replace or add files, and the **-d** option will delete files from the Zip archive. There are also options for encrypting files, and DOS to Unix end-of-line translations, and including hidden files.

To decompress and extract the Zip file, you use the **unzip** command.

```
$ unzip mydata.zip
```

DOS and Windows Emulators: DOSemu and Wine

Emulators are available for Linux that let you run DOS and Windows programs. These are projects still in development and their success is only partial, to date. As emulators, they run programs slower than DOS or Windows would. The DOS emulator is DOSemu. You can install it from your OpenLinux CD-ROM. It includes sample configuration files called **config.dist** located in the **examples** directory. This contains a long list of configuration options. All are commented out with a preceding **#** symbol. You need to copy this file to **dosemu.conf**. Edit the **dosemu.conf** file, removing the **#** from the entries that apply to your system. Explanations are given for each section in the file.

To create a bootable floppy DOS disk, use **mcopy** to copy the **command.com**, **sys.com**, **emufs.sys**, **ems.sy.cdrom.sys**, and **exitemu.com** files to that disk. To run the DOS emulator, enter **dos** on the command line. To exit the emulator, entering **exitemu. dos -?** gives you a list of **dos** command options.

The Wine emulator is designed to run Windows 3.1 and 32-bit programs. It is still in development, with new versions continually being released. At this point, it is considered very experimental. You can download a version from the Web site at **www.winehq.com**. The Windows FAQ provides detailed information.

Chapter 27

System Administration

L inux is designed to serve many users at the same time as well as provide an interface between the users and the computer with its storage media, such as hard disks and tapes. Users have their own shells through which they interact with the operating system. However, you may need to configure the operating system itself in different ways. You may need to add new users, printers, or terminals. You have already seen how to add new file systems. Such operations come under the heading of system administration. The person who performs such actions is referred to as either a system administrator or a superuser. In this sense there are two types of interaction with Linux: regular users' interaction and the superuser, performing system administration tasks. This chapter will cover only the basic operations in system administration. You will learn about system states, managing users, and configuring printers and compiling the kernel. You will perform most tasks rarely, such as adding a new printer or mounting a file system. Other tasks such as adding users, you will perform on a regular basis.

Though system administration can become very complex, basic administration tasks such as adding users or mounting file systems are easy to perform, particularly if you use a configuration tool such as COAS or Linuxconf. Both Red Hat and OpenLinux versions of the Linux system provide you with easy-to-use configuration interfaces that simplify many system administration tasks. Red Hat uses a configuration interface called Linuxconf along with other specialized tools, and OpenLinux uses one called COAS. Both have a cursor-based interface as well as an X-Windows-based interface that uses menus, windows, and buttons with which you can make entries. You can run the cursor-based interface from the command line, using arrow keys, the SPACEBAR, and the ENTER key to make choices. Both tools are simple front ends for making entries in Linux configuration files. You can edit these files and make entries directly if you wish. The underlying administration tasks are the same.

System Management: Superuser

To perform system administration operations, you must first have the correct password that allows you to log in as the root user, making you the superuser. Since a superuser has the power to change almost anything on the system, such a password is usually a carefully guarded secret given only to those whose job it is to manage the system. With the correct password you can log into the system as a system administrator and configure the system in different ways. You can start up and shut down the system as well as change to a different operating mode, such as a single-user mode. You can also add or remove users, add or remove whole file systems, back up and restore files, and even designate the system's name. To become a superuser, you log into the root user account. This is a special account reserved for system management operations with unrestricted access to all components of your Linux operating system. When you log into the system as the root user, you are placed in a shell from which you can issue administrative Linux commands. The prompt for this shell is a sharp sign, #. In the next example, the user logs into the system as the root user. The password is, of course, not displayed.

```
login: root
password:
#
```

As the root user you can use the **passwd** command to change the password for the root login as well as for any other user on the system.

```
# passwd root
New password:
Re-enter new password:
#
```

While you are logged into a regular user account, it may be necessary for you to log into the root and become a superuser. Ordinarily you would have to log out of your user account first and then log into the root. Instead, you can use the **su** command to log in directly to the root while remaining logged into your user account. A CTRL-D will return you to your own login. In fact, you can use **su** to log in as any user, should you know the password. In the next example, the user is already logged in. The **su** command then logs the user into the root, making the user a superuser. Some basic superuser commands are shown in Table 27-1.

```
$ pwd
/home/chris
$su
login: root
password:
# pwd
/root
# ^D
$
```

System Administration Tools

With system administration tools you can perform almost all your administration tasks with the user-friendly screen-based X Window System interfaces. Most tools are provided with specific distributions. Red Hat provides several X Window System configuration tools accessible from a Control Panel window. It also includes a setup utility that lets you change any of the settings you made during installation, such as specifying your keyboard or mouse type. It also lets you access Xconfigurator to

Command	Description
su root	Logs a superuser into the root from a user login; the superuser returns to the original login with a CTRL-D
passwd *login-name*	Sets a new password for the login name
crontab *options file-name*	With *file-name* as an argument, installs **crontab** entries in the file to a **crontab** file; these entries are operations executed at specified times Options: **-e** Edits the **crontab file** **-l** Lists the contents of the **crontab** file **-r** Deletes the **crontab** file
init *state*	Changes the system state (see Table 27-7)
lilo *options Config-file*	Re-install the Linux Loader (LILO)
shutdown *options time*	Shuts down the system; similar to CTRL-ALT-DEL
date	Sets the date and time for the system

Table 27-1. *Basic System Administration*

configure your X Window System. Caldera, on OpenLinux systems, provides the Caldera Open Administration System (COAS) tool. COAS is a comprehensive administration tool that covers most system administration tasks such as file system, user, and module configuration. LISA is an older version that covers many of the same operations. YaST is yet another comprehensive administration tool used on SuSE systems. Linuxconf is an independent effort available under the GNU public license, though it has been adopted by Red Hat as its official configuration tool. It aims to be a comprehensive administration tool covering tasks such as user and file system configuration as well as server configurations. Its modular design allows its capabilities to be enhanced easily. On Red Hat, most tasks have been integrated into the Linuxconf.

These tools are only available to the root user. You first have to log in as the root user and provide the password. You can run most of these tools either from the desktop or from a shell command line. On the shell command line, they use a screen-based interface from which you can select entries using the arrow keys and the TAB key. From a window manager or desktop, most tools provide an X Window interface with menus, icons, and buttons. Your root user's main menu will display entries for these tools, listed in Table 27-2.

Configuration Tool	Command	Description
Linuxconf	`linuxconf`	The Linuxconf configuration tool providing comprehensive configuration for users, networks, file systems, servers, and LILO. Designed for all Linux and Unix systems.
COAS	`coastool`	Caldera Open Administration System (COAS) provides time zone, network, user, group, printer, file system, and LILO configuration, as well as software package management. Used on OpenLinux.
YaST	`yast`	Yet Another System Administration Tool provides user, network, file system, module, and LILO configuration. Used on SuSE.
Control Panel	`control-panel`	Red Hat collection of X configuration tools for networking, modules, printers, time settings, etc.
Setup	`setup`	Collection of Red Hat setup utilities for specifying device types, time zone, and X Window configuration (screen-based only)
LISA	`lisa`	Linux Installation and System Administration, a Caldera tool that provides time zone, network, user, group, printer, file system, and LILO configuration, as well as software package management. Used on older OpenLinux systems (replaced by COAS) (screen-based only).

Table 27-2.   *Linux Configuration Tools*

Using Red Hat Control Panel and Setup

Red Hat provides both a set of X Window–based configuration tools and a screen-based setup utility for basic configuration tasks. Though these tools have been officially replaced by Red Hat with Linuxconf, many users still find them helpful. You can access the X Window–based configuration tools using the Control Panel window on your root user desktop. You will find an entry for the Control Panel in a window manager or desktop's main menu under System or Administration. As shown in the following illustration, the Control Panel provides icons for accessing a variety of configuration tools. Currently there are tools for such tasks as setting the time and date, network administration, and kernel module management. Many of these tools have their own entries in the System or Administration menus. You can also invoke them from a terminal window using their command names. The **netcfg** utility allows you to configure your network interfaces (discussed in detail in Chapter 28). With **timetool** you can set the system time and date (see "System Time and Date"). Using **printtool**, you can configure new printers, interfacing them with your system (see "Installing and Managing Printers"). The **helptool** lets you search for documentation on your system using a keyword search. It displays Man, HOW-TO, and info documentation. The Sys V Init Editor lets you start and stop servers and daemons (see Chapter 16). With the Kernel Configurator you can manually add and remove kernel modules. Many system tasks, including user, server, and file system management, are provided by the Linuxconf, which is accessible by clicking the icon labeled System. The icon shows a picture of a music conductor waving a baton. Table 27-3 lists these tools, and the following illustration shows the root user Control Panel.

Red Hat also provides a setup utility with which you can configure different devices and system settings such as your keyboard, mouse, and time zone. It features the same setup interfaces that you used when installing Red Hat. Setup is useful if you have changed any of your devices, for instance installed a new mouse, keyboard, or sound card. You start the setup utility with the command **setup** that you enter at a shell command line. On the desktop you can open a terminal window and enter the command. A menu of configuration choices is displayed. Use the arrow keys to select one, and then press the TAB key to move to the Run Tool and Quit buttons.

Setup is actually an interface for running several configuration tools (see the following illustration). You can call any of these tools separately using their commands. For example, the **kbdconfig** command starts the keyboard configuration utility that lets you select the type of keyboard. The **mouseconfig** command lets you select type of mouse. The **sndconfig** utility automatically detects your sound card and loads the appropriate module containing that soundcard's drivers.

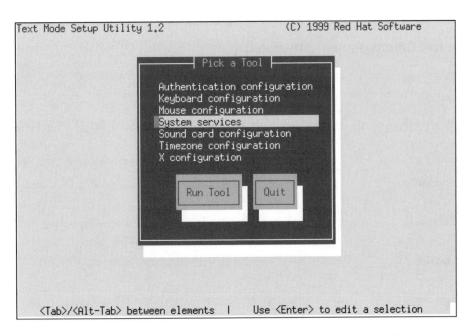

Text Mode Setup Utility 1.2   (C) 1999 Red Hat Software

One important utility is the X Window System setup provided by Xconfigurator. If you have trouble with your X Window System configuration, you can use this command to configure it again. It is also helpful for updating X-Windows should you change your video card. Just run Xconfigurator again and select the card. When you download a new version of XFree86, the packages will include a compatible version of Xconfigurator.

Using COAS and LISA

The Caldera Open Administration System (COAS) provides an effective and easy-to-use interface for performing most system and network administration functions. COAS is available for use by any distribution, although it currently is included with Caldera's OpenLinux. COAS has both a GUI interface and a cursor-based interface. You can operate the GUI interface on any window manager as well as the KDE or Gnome desktops. The cursor-based interface can be used in a command line shell and displays a series of screens on which you can use arrow and TAB keys to make selections.

On the OpenLinux KDE desktop you will find an entry for COAS on the main menu as well as an icon for it in the panel. Clicking either displays a main COAS menu from which you can select the kind of tasks you want to perform, including system administration, kernel configurations, and software management. Selecting System Administration displays entries for administration operations such as Account Administration, Filesystem Administration, and the System Clock. Here you can manage users or mount file systems, including CD-ROMs and floppy disks. Kernel Modules allows you to install modules for different devices and services that you are adding to your system. Menus at the top of COAS windows let you edit or delete

Red Hat Control Panel	Description
tksysv	Starts and stops servers and daemons
timetool	Sets the system date and time
printtool	Configures a printer, creating a printer device and printcap entry for the printer
netcfg	Configures your network interfaces (see Chapter 21)
kernelcfg	Kernel Configurator, loads and configures kernel modules
modemtool	Selects your modem's device name (sets the /etc/modem link to the modem's port)
helptool	Searches for documentation, Man pages, and info pages
Linuxconf	Linuxconf configuration tool for user, networking, LILO, servers, file systems, etc.
Red Hat Setup	**Description**
setup	Red Hat Setup interface listing configuration tools for system and device setting
authconfig	Authentication options such as enabling NIS, shadow passwords, and MD5 passwords
kbdconfig	Selects the keyboard type
mouseconfig	Selects the mouse type
ntsysv	Selects servers and daemons to start up at boot time
sndconfig	Detects and configures your sound card
timeconfig	Selects the time zone
xconfigurator	Configures your X Window System for your video card and monitor

Table 27-3. *Red Hat Control Panel and Setup Tools*

selected entries as well as add new ones. You can use the Exit entry in the File menu to close the window.

The COAS command is **coastool**. Entering this command in a shell command line will start the cursor-based COAS interface shown in the following illustration. You use the TAB and arrow keys to move to different entries. To access the menu, press the F8 key. You can then use the RIGHT ARROW and LEFT ARROW keys to move to the menu you want. Press ENTER to display the menu and use arrow keys to move to the entry you want. Press ESC to shift back to the main window. At any point you can press the F1 key to bring up a box with an explanation of the current choice.

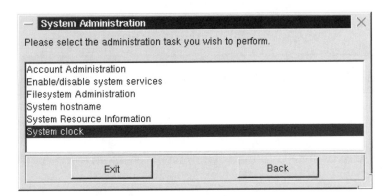

Currently Caldera also includes with OpenLinux an older administration utility called the Linux Installation and System Administration tool (LISA). Many prior users of OpenLinux will be familiar with it. It uses a cursor-based screen interface similar to COAS. As it was also designed as an installation utility, it contains some entries for installation procedures such as managing LILO. To perform administration tasks, you choose the System Configuration entry. Most LISA screens show buttons at the bottom. A Call button will start up a selection made on the menu. The Continue button will leave the screen, reverting to a previous one or, in the case of the main menu, ending the program. If there are two buttons, one will be selected, and the other will be deselected with its name in black. To choose the selected one, you just press ENTER. To access the other one, such as the Continue button, you use the RIGHT ARROW or LEFT ARROW keys (you can also use the TAB key). Press the RIGHT ARROW key to select the button on the right, and the LEFT ARROW key for the left button.

Using Linuxconf

Linuxconf is a comprehensive configuration tool for almost all your administrative tasks, including user and file system management as well as network services (see the list of features in Table 27-4). It is designed to work on any Linux distribution. Currently it is compatible with Caldera, Red Hat, SuSE, Slackware, and Debian. Both compressed archive and RPM versions of the software are provided. You can

Features	Description
User accounts and groups	User configuration, passwords, and permissions
Networking	TCP/IP, NIS, PPP, IPX, DHCP, DNS, IP-aliasing, UUCP, hosts, routing, and gateways
Servers	Apache, Squid, ProFTP, wu-ftpd, DHCPD, Samba, DNS, and sendmail
File systems	fstab, NFS
LILO	LILO boot options and entries

Table 27-4. *Linuxconf Configuration Features*

download the current version from the Linuxconf Web site at **www.solucorp.qc.ca/ linuxconf**. Here you can also find documentation and links to any added packages.

Linuxconf has three interfaces: text, GUI, and HTML. The text interface provides cursor-based full screens that can be run from any shell command line. You use the TAB key to move between boxes, lists, and buttons and the arrow keys to select entries in a list. The text mode also operates as a command line mode, letting you place Linuxconf commands in the shell scripts. The GUI interface is an X Window System interface that runs on any window manager or desktop, including Gnome and KDE. It provides a menu tree with which you can easily select panels for different configuration tasks. The HTML interface shown in Figure 27-1 is a Web page interface that lists options as links to other Web pages that provides boxes and check boxes with which you can make your entries. To access it, just enter your system's hostname with the port 98, written as :98 attached to the end of the hostname, for example **http://turtle.mytrek.com:98**. Be sure to first permit access by setting permissions for the user you want to use (such as **root**) in the Linuxconf Network Access panel in the Misc list under Networking. All the interfaces provide context-level help. On each screen, panel, or page is a Help button that will display detailed information about the current task.

In the GUI interface, the main Linuxconf window displays a window with two frames. On the left is a list of all the system administration operations. The list is organized into categories and subcategories that you can expand to list entries or shrink to show just the category heading. Small boxes to the left of the category headings show small – signs when expanded and + signs when entries are not displayed. Initially all entries for each category are displayed. Clicking a category box

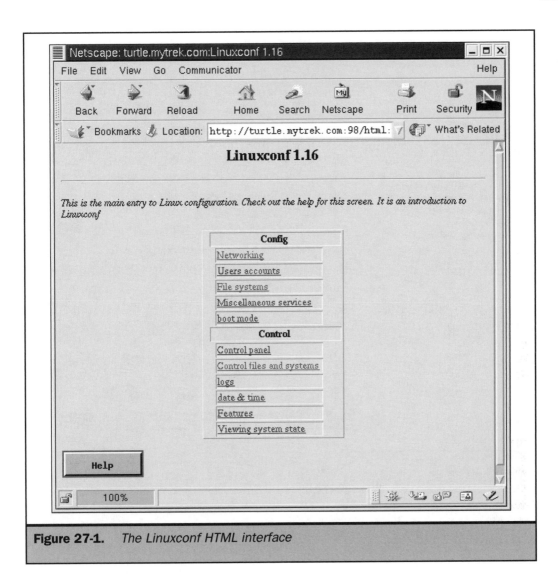

Netscape: turtle.mytrek.com:Linuxconf 1.16

File   Edit   View   Go   Communicator   Help

Back   Forward   Reload   Home   Search   Netscape   Print   Security   N

Bookmarks   Location: http://turtle.mytrek.com:98/html: What's Related

Linuxconf 1.16

This is the main entry to Linux configuration. Check out the help for this screen. It is an introduction to Linuxconf

Config

Networking

Users accounts

File systems

Miscellaneous services

boot mode

Control

Control panel

Control files and systems

logs

date & time

Features

Viewing system state

Help

100%

Figure 27-1.   _The Linuxconf HTML interface_

will display or hide the entries. Two major categories are shown, Config and Control. You use the Config entries to configure almost all components on your systems, including users, file systems, networking, servers, and LILO. Among the servers supported are Apache, Squid, ProFTP, wu-ftpd, DHCPD, Samba, and sendmail. The Control entries let you perform tasks such as setting the time, adding modules, mounting file systems, and selecting servers to start up.

Using the main window shown in Figure 27-2, you select an administration task by clicking its entry. A panel for that task is then displayed on the right frame. Most tasks

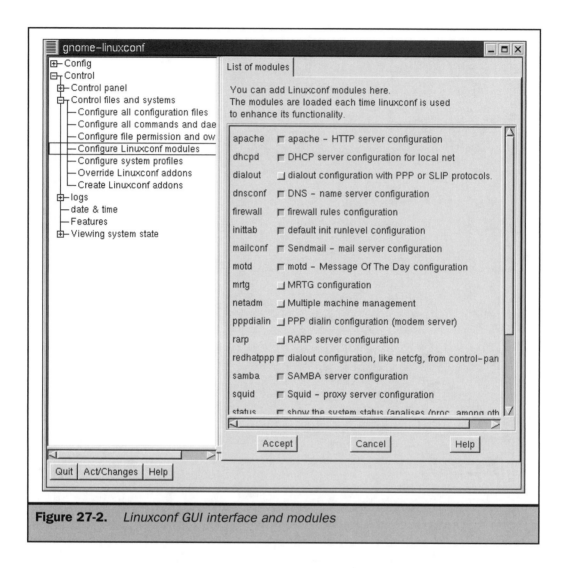

Figure 27-2. *Linuxconf GUI interface and modules*

have several panels with panel tabs displayed at the top of the window. Click a tab to display that panel. If you do not close the window before selecting another administration task, then a new window is opened on top of the current one. You can move from one task to another by clicking their respective entries.

Much of the configuration support for specific components such as the Apache Web server or Squid is implemented using modules. You can add or remove modules as you wish. Modules are usually included with the Linuxconf software package. You can then select which modules to load into Linuxconf using the Configure Linuxconf Modules panel in the Control Files And Systems list under Control Panel. In version

1.16, this panel shows all the available modules with check boxes you can use to toggle whether a module should be loaded or not. For example, to add firewall configuration panels to Linuxconf, make sure the firewall module check box is selected. On earlier versions of Linuxconf (as in 1.14 used on Red Hat 6.0), this panel shows boxes where you can type in the name of the modules to add. Table 27-5 shows a list of current Linuxconf modules. Those listed as core modules are included in the Linuxconf package. Those listed as pkg are packages installed separately and usually located at different sites. Links are available on the Linuxconf Web site; most are also kept on the FTP site, **ftp.solucorp.qc.ca/pub/linuxconf/modules**.

Module	Status	Description
apache	core	Configuration of the Apache Web server
dhcpd	core	Configuration of the ISC DHCPD server
dialout	core	PPP dialout configuration; alternative to redhatppp
dnsconf	core	Configuration of bind 4 and 8 DNS
firewall	core	Configuration of the kernel 2.0 packet filter, including support for masquerading, port redirection, and accounting
inittab	core	Controls editing of the **/etc/inittab** file
isdnadmin	pkg	Manages an ISDN adapter, **www.terminator.net/isdnadmin**
ldapconf	pkg	Configures an ldap server and clients, **www.terminator.net/ldapconf**
mailconf	core	Configuration of sendmail
managerpm	pkg	Manipulates RPM packages
mgettyconf	pkg	Configuration of the mgetty serial port manager
motd	core	Edits the message of the day file
mrtg	core	Configuration for the mrtg package
netadm	core	Configures PPP connections
pppdialin	core	Configures a PPP dialin session

Table 27-5. *Linuxconf Modules*

Module	Status	Description
proftpd	pkg	Manages the pro-ftp daemon, **http://lie-br.conectiva.com.br/~marcelo**
rarp	core	Configures the kernel RARP table
redhatppp	core	PPP/SLIP/PLIP configuration compatible with Red Hat netcfg utility
samba	core	Configuration of the Samba SMB file server
shellmod	pkg	Writes Linuxconf modules and standalone utilities using the shell (**/bin/sh**)
squid	core	In development, provides basic support for the configuration of the Squid
status	core	Reports various items of information about the system
treemenu	core	Pulls all menu/submenu options into a single large tree
updpass	pkg	Updates password
userinfo	pkg	Adds custom fields to the user account dialog
usermenu	core	Custom views of the Linuxconf menu access privileges
usersbygroup	pkg	Allows user account management by group
virtual	pkg	In development; this module provides a unified view of all services supporting virtual hosting, to configure a virtual host in one dialog
wuftpd	core	Configuration of the wu-ftpd FTP server
xterminals	core	Management of Linux-based X terminals

Table 27-5.   *Linuxconf Modules* (continued)

You can also access Linuxconf using specialized windows for just the particular service you want to configure: **userconf**, **fsconf**, **dnsconf**, **netconf**, **mailconf**. These are special Linuxconf commands that call Linuxconf using an interface listing option for a particular service. For example, to add a new user to your system, you could use the **userconf** command to display a special Linuxconf window. This window displays buttons and icons for accessing the different Linuxconf user and group configuration panels. These are the same panels that you can access through the main Linuxconf interface. The **netconf** command will display a window listing the icons for the different network configuration panels. Another panel on this same window lists icons for the different server configuration panels. The **dnsconf** command displays a window with buttons for accessing the Domain Name Service (named) configuration panels. The **mailconf** command lets you directly access panels for configuring your mail server (sendmail). Currently the Red Hat 6.0 distribution includes no menu entries for these specialized windows. You have to open a terminal window and then enter and execute their commands at the prompt.

Linuxconf saves its configuration information in files located in the **/etc/linuxconf/archive** directory. When you activate changes with new configuration information, Linuxconf both updates your system configuration files and saves the information in its own files. In effect, Linuxconf maintains its own set of your system's configuration files and can detect if its information does not correspond to your system's configuration files. It also includes a sophisticated translation system that lets you implement Linuxconf in the language of your choice.

Linuxconf allows you to create multiple system configurations that you can load, activating or deactivating features and services. You could have one set of configurations for your office and one for home, or even one for, say, your Web server. A home configuration might have your Web server turned off, whereas a Web server configuration might have it running. If you have Linux running on a portable PC, you could switch networking configurations just by switching Linuxconf system configurations. Different configurations are placed in subdirectories in the **/etc/linuxconf/archive** directory. Their names are the same as those subdirectories. Linuxconf provides two for you by default, Office and Home-Office. Various Linuxconf startup commands appear in Table 27-6.

Using YaST

The Yet Another System Tool (YaST) is an administrative tool for SuSE Linux. It has much the same interface as LISA but makes much more use of function keys. Use arrow keys to move from one selection to another. The TAB key moves you to the buttons at the bottom of the screen for OK, Cancel, or Continue to the next screen. From the main window you can click the System Administration entry to display a pop-up menu of administration functions. Use your arrow keys to move to the one you want and select it.

System Configuration

Though many different specialized components go into making up a system, such as servers, users, and devices, some operations apply to the system in general. These

Command	Description
`linuxconf`	Start Linuxconf in the main window
`netconf`	Network configuration window for configuring your network and servers, accesses network and server panels directly
`userconf`	User configuration window, accesses user and group configuration panels directly
`fsconf`	File system configuration window, accesses file system configuration panels directly
`dnsconf`	Domain Name Service configuration window, accesses DNS configuration panels directly
`mailconf`	Mail (sendmail) configuration window, accesses sendmail configuration panels directly

Table 27-6.   *Linuxconf Startup Commands*

include setting the system date and time, specifying shutdown procedures, and determining the services to start up and run whenever the system boots. In addition you can use numerous performance analysis tools to control processes and check on resource usage.

System Time and Date

You can use several different tools to set the system time and date, depending on the distribution you use. On all distributions you can set the system time and date using the shell **date** command. Most users prefer to use a configuration tool. On OpenLinux you can use COAS, on Red Hat and other distributions you can use Linuxconf or TimeTool, and SuSE users can use YaST. Recall that you set the time and date when you first installed your system. You should not need to do so again. However, if you entered the time incorrectly or moved to a different time zone, you could use this utility to change your time.

You can use the **date** command on your root user command line to set the date and time for the system. As an argument to **date**, you list (with no delimiters) the month, day, time, and year. In the next example the date is set to 2:30 P.M., September 18, 1996 (09 for September, 18 for the day, 1430 for the time, and 96 for the year):

```
# date 0918143096
Sat Sept 18 14:30:00 EDT 1999
```

To set the system time and date with Linuxconf, you select the Time and Date entry under Control. This displays a panel with boxes for the date and time (see Figure 27-3). Linuxconf is configured to read your system's time and date directly from the CMOS, the time and date set on your motherboard's BIOS.

You can also use the Red Hat TimeTool, included on many distributions. There is an icon for it in the Control Panel. Double-click the Timetool icon or select its menu entry to open the Time Configuration window. You can make changes to any part of the time you wish (see Figure 27-4). Move your mouse pointer to the hour, for example, and then click. The hour will be highlighted. You use the two triangles below the time and date display to increase or decrease the time or date entry. If you select the hour, then clicking the upper triangle will set the time forward to the next hour. The bottom inverted triangle will move the hour backward. The same is true for the date. Once you have set the new time and date, click the Set System Clock button at the bottom of the window. Then click the Exit Time Machine button to exit the Time Configuration window.

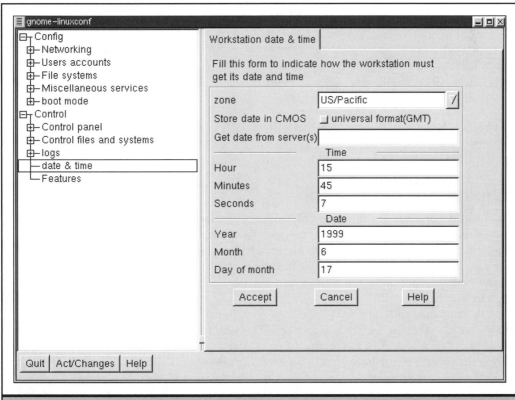

Figure 27-3. *Linuxconf system date and time*

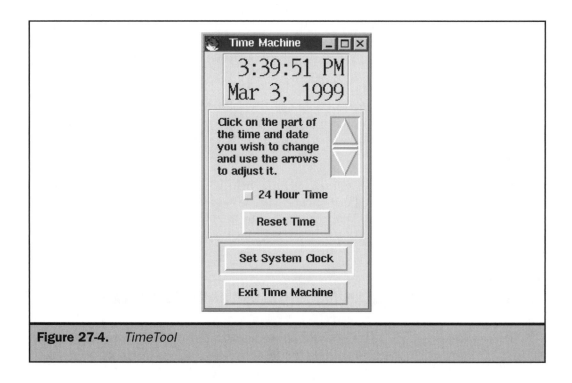

Figure 27-4. *TimeTool*

On COAS you can select the System Clock entry in the System Administration menu or window. This displays a System Time window with a box displaying the current time and a pop-up menu for selecting your time zone.

Scheduling Tasks: crontab

Though it is not a system file, you will find a crontab file very helpful in maintaining your system. A crontab file lists actions to take at a certain time. The cron daemon constantly checks the user's crontab file to see if it is time to take these actions. Any user can set up a crontab file of his or her own. The root user can set up a crontab file to take system administrative actions, such as backing up files at a certain time each week or month.

A crontab entry has six fields: The first five are used to specify the time for an action, and the last field is the action itself. The first field specifies minutes (0–59), the second field, the hour (0–23), the third field is the day of the month (1–31), the fourth field is the month of the year (1–12), and the fifth field is the day of the week (0–6), starting with 0 as Sunday. In each of the time fields you can specify a range, a set of values, or use the asterisk to indicate all values. For example, 1–5 for the day-of-week field would specify Monday through Friday. In the hour field, 8, 12, 17 would specify

8 A.M., 12 noon, and 5 P.M. An * in the month-of-year field would indicate every month. The following example backs up the **projects** directory at 2:00 A.M. every weekday.

```
0 2 1-5 * * tar cf  /home/chris/backp   /home/chris/projects
```

You use the **crontab** command to install your entries into a crontab file. To do this, you first create a text file and type your crontab entries. Save this file with any name you wish, such as **mycronfile**. Then to install these entries, enter **crontab** and the name of the text file. The **crontab** command takes the contents of the text file and creates a crontab file in the **/usr/spool/cron** directory, adding the name of the user that issued the command. In the next example, the root user installs the contents of the **mycronfile** as the root's crontab file. This will create a file called **/usr/spool/cron/root**. If a user named justin installed a crontab file, it would create a file called **/usr/spool/cron/justin**. You can control use of the **crontab** command by regular users with the **/etc/cron.allow** file. Only users with their names in this file can create crontab files of their own.

```
# crontab mycronfile
```

You should never try to edit your crontab file directly. Instead, use the **crontab** command with the **-e** option. This will open your crontab file in the **/usr/spool/cron** directory with the standard text editor, such as Vi. Running **crontab** with the **-l** option will display the contents of your crontab file, and the **-r** option will delete the entire file. Invoking **crontab** with another text file of crontab entries will overwrite your current crontab file, replacing it with the contents of the text file.

System States: init and shutdown

Your Linux system has several states, numbered from 0 to 6, and a single-user state represented by the letters **s** and **S**. When you power up your system, you enter the default state. You can then change to other states with the **init** command. For example, state 0 is the power down state. The command **init 0** will shut down your system. State 6 stops the system and reboots. Other states reflect how you want the system to be used. State 1 is the administrative state, allowing access only to the superuser. This allows you as administrator to perform administrative actions without interference from others. State **s** is a single-user state that allows use of the system by only one user. State 2 is a partial multiuser state, allowing access by many users, but with no remote file sharing. State 3, the default state, is the multiuser state that implements full remote file sharing. You can change the default state by editing the **/etc/inittab** file and changing the **init** default entry. The states are listed in Table 27-7.

No matter what state you start in, you can change from one state to another with the **init** command. If your default state is 2, you will power up in state 2, but you can

State	Description
init *state*	Changes the system state; you can use it to power up or power down a system, allow multiuser or single-user access; the **init** command takes as its argument a number representing a system state
System States	
0	Halt (do *not* set the default to this); shuts down the system completely
1	Administrative single-user mode; denies other users access to the system but allows root access to the entire multiuser file system
2	Multiuser, without NFS (the same as 3, if you do not have networking)
s or S	Single user; only one user has access to the system; used when you want all other users off the system or you have a single-user personal system
3	Full multiuser mode; allows remote file sharing with other systems on your network
4	Unused
5	X11 only
6	Reboots; shuts down and restarts the system (do *not* set the default to this)

Table 27-7. *Runlevel States*

change to, say, state 3 with **init 3**. In the next example, the **init** command changes to state **s**, the single-user state.

```
# init s
```

Though you can power down the system with the **init** command and the 0 state, you can also use the **shutdown** command or the Shutdown panel in Linuxconf. On Linuxconf select the Shutdown/Reboot entry in the Control Panel under Control. This displays a panel that shows the entries for entering a shutdown message and specifying how long to wait before shutting down.

The **shutdown** command has a time argument that gives users on the system a warning before you power down. You can specify an exact time to shut down or a period of minutes from the current time. The exact time is specified by *hh:mm* for the hour and minutes. The period of time is indicated by a + and the number of minutes. The **shutdown** command takes several options with which you can specify how you want your system shut down. The **–h** option simply shuts down the system, whereas the **–r** option shuts down the system and then reboots it. In the next example, the system is shut down after ten minutes. The shutdown options are listed in Table 27-8.

```
# shutdown -h +10
```

To shut down the system immediately, you can use **+0** or the word **now**. The following example has the same effect as the CTRL-ALT-DEL method of shutting down your system, as described in Chapter 4. It shuts down the system immediately and then reboots.

```
# shutdown -r now
```

With the **shutdown** command you can include a warning message to be sent to all users currently logged in, giving them time to finish what they are doing before you shut them down.

```
# shutdown -h +5   "System needs a rest"
```

If you do not specify either the **–h** or the **–r** options, the **shutdown** command will shut down the multiuser mode and shift you to an administrative single-user mode. In effect, your system state changes from 3 (multiuser state) to 1 (administrative single-user state). Only the root user is active, allowing the root user to perform any necessary system administrative operations that other users might interfere with.

You use the **runlevel** command to see what state you are currently running in. In the next example the system is running in state 3. The word "runlevel" is another term for state.

```
# runlevel
N 3
```

System Directories

Your Linux system is organized into directories whose files are used for different system functions. Directories with "bin" in the name are used to hold programs. The

Command	Description
shutdown [**-rkhncft**] *time* [*warning-message*]	Shuts the system down after the specified time period, issuing warnings to users; you can specify a warning message of your own after the time argument; if neither **-h** or **-r** are specified to shut down the system, the system sets to the administrative mode, runlevel state 1
Argument	
time	Has two possible formats: it can be an absolute time in the format *hh*:*mm*, with *hh* the hour (one or two digits) and *mm* the minute (in two digits); it can also be in the format **+***m*, with *m* the number of minutes to wait; the word **now** is an alias for **+0**
Option	
-t *sec*	Tells **init** to wait *sec* seconds between sending processes the warning and the kill signal, before changing to another runlevel
-k	Doesn't really shut down; only sends the warning messages to everybody
-r	Reboots after shutdown, runlevel state 6
-h	Halts after shutdown, runlevel state 0
-n	Doesn't call **init** to do the shutdown; you do it yourself
-f	Does a *fast* reboot
-c	Cancels an already running shutdown; no time argument

Table 27-8. *System Shutdown Options*

/bin directory holds basic user programs such as login, shells (BASH, TCSH, and ZSH), file commands (**cp**, **mv**, **rm**, **ln**, and so on). The **/sbin** directory holds specialized system programs for such tasks as file system management (**fsck**, **fdisk**, **mkfs**) and system operations like shutdown and startup (**lilo**, **init**). The **/usr/bin** directory holds program files designed for user tasks. The **/usr/sbin** directory holds user-related system operations such as **useradd** to add new users. The /**lib** directory holds all the libraries that your system makes use of, including the main Linux library, libc, and subdirectories such as **modules**, which holds all the current kernel modules.

```
# ls /
bin boot dev etc home lib lost+found mnt proc root sbin tmp usr var
```

The **/etc** directory holds your system, network, server, and application configuration files. Here you will find the **fstab** file listing your file systems, the **hosts** file with IP addresses for hosts on your system, and **lilo.conf** for the boot systems provided by LILO. This directory will include various subdirectories such as **apache** for the Apache Web server configuration files and **X11** for the X Window System and window manager configuration files.

The **/mnt** directory is usually used for mount points for your CD-ROM, floppy, or Zip drives. These are file systems that you may be changing frequently, unlike partitions on fixed disks. The **/home** directory holds user home directories. When a user account is set up, a home directory for it is set up here, usually with the same name as the user. On Red Hat and OpenLinux systems, the **/home** directory will also hold server data directories such as **/home/httpd** for the Apache Web server Web site files, or **/home/ftpd** for your FTP site files. The **/var** directory holds subdirectories for tasks whose files change frequently, such as lock files, log files, or printer spool files. The **/tmp** directory is simply a directory to hold any temporary files that programs may need to generate to perform a particular task.

The **/usr** directory holds programs for user-related operations. The **/usr/lib** directory holds many of the libraries for particular applications. The **/usr/X11R6** directory holds the X Window System programs and libraries for revision 6 of the X Window System. The **/usr/X11R6/lib/X11** directory is a link to the **/etc/X11** directory, which holds the X Window System configuration files. The **/usr/src** directory holds source files; in particular, **/usr/src/linux** holds the kernel source files you use to update the kernel. The **/usr/doc** directory holds documentation that is usually installed with different applications. Here you will also find HOW-TO documents. The **/usr/local** directory is used for programs that are meant to be used only on this particular system. The **/usr/opt** directory is where optional packages are installed. For example, this is where the K Desktop programs and files are installed on OpenLinux and Red Hat systems.

```
# ls /usr
X11R6 bin cgi-bin dict doc etc games include info lib libexec local
man sbin share src tmp
```

Directories	Description
/bin	System-related programs
/sbin	System programs for specialized tasks
/lib	System libraries
/etc	Configuration files for system and network services and applications
/home	The location of user home directories and server data directories such as Web and FTP site files
/mnt	The location where CD-ROM and floppy disk file systems are mounted
/var	The location of system directories whose files continually change, such as logs, printer spool files, and lock files
/usr	User-related programs and files; includes several key subdirectories such as **/usr/bin**, **/usr/X11**, and **/usr/doc**
/usr/bin	Programs for users
/usr/X11R6	X Window System programs and files
/usr/doc	Documentation for applications
/tmp	Directory for system temporary files

Table 27-9. *System Directories*

Standard system directories and configuration files are shown in Tables 27-9 and 27-10.

System Startup Files: /etc/rc.d

Each time you start your system, it reads a series of startup commands from system initialization files located in your **/etc/rc.d** directory. These initialization files are organized according to different tasks. Some are located in the **/etc/rc.d** directory itself, and others are located in a subdirectory called **init.d**. You should not have to change any of these files. The organization of system initialization files varies among Linux distributions. The Red Hat and OpenLinux organization is described here. Some of the files you will find in **/etc/rc.d** are listed in Table 27-11, in the next section, "Performance Analysis Tools and Processes."

File	Description
/etc/inittab	Sets the default state as well as terminal connections
/etc/passwd	Contains user password and login configurations
/etc/group	Contains a list of groups with configurations for each
/etc/fstab	Automatically mounts file systems when you start your system
/etc/lilo.conf	The LILO configuration file for your system
/etc/conf.modules	Modules on your system to be automatically loaded
/etc/printcap	Contains a list of each printer and its specifications
/etc/termcap	Contains a list of terminal type specifications for terminals that could be connected to the system
/etc/gettydefs	Contains configuration information on terminals connected to the system
/etc/skel	Directory that holds the versions of initialization files such as **.bash_profile** that are copied to new users' home directories
/etc/ttys	List of terminal types and the terminal devices to which they correspond

Table 27-10.   *Configuration Files*

The **/etc/rc.d/rc.boot** file holds the commands for initializing your system, including the mounting of your file systems. The **/etc/rc.d/rc.modules** file loads any kernel modules that may be needed to support certain features or devices on your system. The **/etc/rc.d/rc.local** file is the last initialization file executed. Here you can place commands of your own. If you look at this file, you will see the message that is displayed for you every time you start the system. You can change that message if you wish. When you shut down your system, the **halt** file, which contains the commands to do this, is called. The files in **init.d** will be called to shut down daemons, and the file systems will be unmounted. In the current distribution of Red Hat, **halt** is located in the **init.d** directory. For other distributions, it may be called **rc.halt** and located in the **/etc/rc.d** directory.

The **/etc/rc.d/init.d** directory is designed primarily to hold scripts that both start up and shut down different specialized daemons. It is here that network and printer daemons are started up. You will also find files to start font servers and Web site daemons. These files perform double duty, starting up a daemon when the system starts up and shutting down the daemon when the system shuts down. The files in **init.d** are designed in a way to make it easy to write scripts for starting up and shutting down specialized applications. On OpenLinux, the **skeleton** file is a sample file for how to write scripts for this directory. It uses functions defined in the **functions** file, as do many of the other **init.d** files. Many of these files are set up for you automatically. You will not need to change them. If you do, be sure you know how they work first. Chapter 16 describes this process in detail.

When your system starts up, several programs are automatically started and run continuously to provide services such as Web site operations. Depending upon what kind of services you want your system to provide, you can add or remove items in a list of services to be automatically started. In the installation process you were able to determine what services those would be. For example, the Web server is run automatically when your system starts up. If you are not running a Web site, you would have no need, as yet, for the Web server and could have the service not started, removing an extra task that the system does not need to perform. Several of the servers and daemons perform necessary tasks. The sendmail process enables you to send messages across networks, and the lpd server performs printing operations.

When your system starts up, it uses links in special runlevel directories in the **/etc/rc.d/** directory to run the startup scripts in the **/etc/rc.d/init.d** directory. A runlevel directory bears the number of its runlevel, as in **/etc/rc.d/rc3.d** for runlevel 3. To have a service not start up, remove its link from that runlevel directory. You can use any of these scripts to manually start and stop a daemon at any time by using the `stop` argument to stop it, the `start` argument to start it again, and the `restart` argument to restart the daemon.

You can use a System V Init utility to determine which servers and daemons are to start and stop at what runlevel. There are several System V Init utilities to choose from. Sys V Init Manager is an X-based utility that provides an easy-to-use GUI interface for managing the servers and daemons in your **/etc/rc.d/init.d** directory. You can stop, start, and assign servers to different runlevels. There is also a KDE System V Init utility called the Sys V Init Editor, with many of the same features (see Figure 27-5). It is easier to use in that it supports drag-and-drop operations. To assign a server to a particular runlevel, just drag its entry from the Services box to the appropriate Runlevel box. To remove it from a particular runlevel, just drag its entry out of that Runlevel box to the Trash icon. To manually start and stop a daemon, right-click it and select either the stop or start entry from the pop-up menu.

Most administration tools provide interfaces displaying a simple list of services from which you can select the ones you want to start up. On Linuxconf, the Control Service Activity panel lists different daemons and servers that you can have start by just clicking a check box (see Chapter 16 for more details). On COAS you select Enable/Disable System Services from the System Administration menu. This lists the different services you can have start up (see Figure 27-6). Those with checks in their check boxes are already selected. Click a box to toggle the service on or off. On the Red

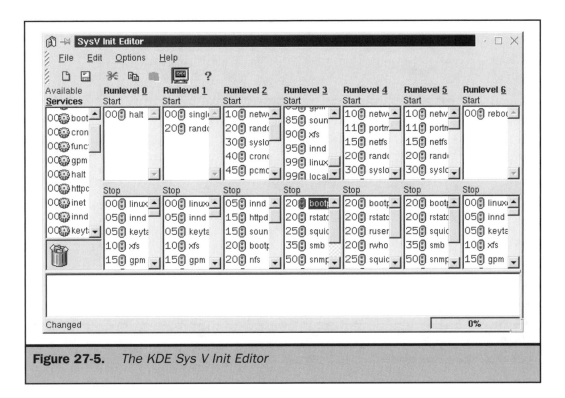

Figure 27-5. *The KDE Sys V Init Editor*

Hat Setup menu, select System Services and then choose from the list of servers and daemons provided. Toggle an entry on or off with the SPACEBAR. On LISA, you configure your startup servers using the Configure Daemon/Server Autostart list accessible from the System Configuration menu System Configuration entry. This displays a list of daemons and servers with an *x* next to the ones that will start up when you start your system. Moving to an item and pressing the SPACEBAR will toggle that selection.

Performance Analysis Tools and Processes

Each task performed on your system is treated by Linux as a process. It is assigned a number and a name. You can examine these processes and even stop them. From the command line you can use the **ps** command to list processes. With the **-aux** command you can list all processes. Piping the output to a **grep** command with a pattern lets you search for a particular process. The following command will list all X Window System processes.

```
ps -aux | grep 'X'
```

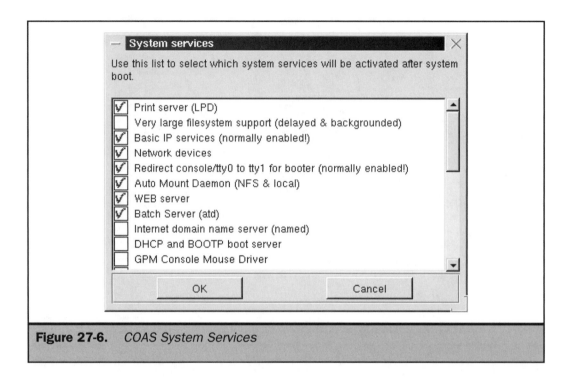

Figure 27-6.   *COAS System Services*

A number of utilities on your system provide detailed information on your processes, as well as other system information such as CPU and disk usage. Though these tools were designed to be used on a shell command line, displaying output in text lines, several now have KDE and Gnome versions that provide a GUI interface for displaying results and managing processes. The **vmstat** command outputs a detailed listing indicating the performance of different system components, including CPU, memory, I/O, and swap operations. A report is issued as a line with fields for the different components. It repeats at a specified interval, usually a few seconds. The **top** command provides a listing of the processes on your system that are the most CPU intensive, showing what processes are using most of your resources. The listing is in real time and updated every few seconds. Commands are provided for changing a process's status, such as its priority. The **free** command lists the amount of free RAM memory on your system, showing how much is used and how much is free, as well as what is used for buffers and swap memory. Xosview is a X Window System tool showing the load, CPU, and memory. You can also use Linuxconf to display basic system information such as memory and disk usage. Select Viewing System State under Control.

The K Desktop provides two utilities for viewing and managing your processes: the KDE Task Manager (KTop, shown in Figure 27-7) and the KDE Process Manager

File	Description
/etc/rc.d	Directory that holds system startup and shutdown files
/etc/rc.d/rc.sysinit	Initialization file for your system
/etc/rc.d/rc.local	Initialization file for your own commands; you can freely edit this file to add your own startup commands; it is the last startup file executed
/etc/rc.d/rc.modules	Loads kernel modules needed by your system
/etc/rc.d/init.d	Directory that holds many of the daemons, servers, and scripts such as httpd for Web servers and networks to start up network connections
/etc/rc.d/rc*num*.d	Directories for different runlevels where *num* is the runlevel and hold links to scripts in the **/etc/rc.d/init.d** directory.
/etc/rc.d/init.d/halt	Operations performed each time you shut down the system such as unmounting file systems; called **rc.halt** in other distributions
/etc/rc.d/init.d/lpd	Start up and shut down the lpd daemon
/etc/rc.d/init.d/inet	Operations to start up or shut down the inetd daemon
/etc/rc.d/init.d/network	Operations to start up or shut down your network connections
/etc/rc.d/init.d/httpd	Operations to start up or shut down your Web server daemon, httpd

Table 27-11.   *System Startup Files*

(kpm). On both utilities you can sort the processes according to their fields by clicking the field's button at the top of the process list. If you select a process, you can then choose to perform several different actions on it such as ending it (killing the process) or suspending it (putting it to sleep). A right-click on a process entry displays a pop-up menu with the different actions you can take. You can further refine your process list by choosing to view just your own processes, system processes, or all processes.

KTop provides both list and tree views. With the tree view you can see what processes are dependent on others. For example, the desktop will rely on the

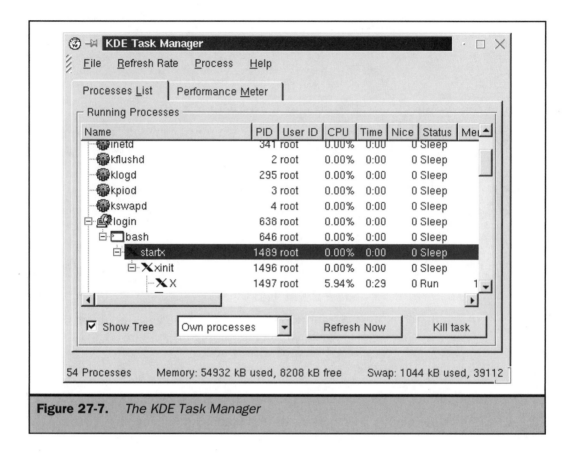

Figure 27-7. *The KDE Task Manager*

X Window System process. A Performance Meters panel displays system information such as memory usage and CPU load.

On the Gnome System Manager (GTop) you can also sort the processes according to their fields by clicking the field's button at the top of the process list. If you right-click an entry, a pop-up menu displays with actions you can perform on it (see Figure 27-8). System statistic summary graphs are displayed at the top of the window showing the CPU load, memory usage, and disk usage. You can add more graphs or change their display features such as the colors used. The GTop window displays three tabbed panels for detailed reports showing processes, memory usage, and file system usage. You can add more, showing customized reports such as just the user processes. Process lists can be further refined to show user, system, or all processes. To configure Gtop, you select the Preferences entry in the Settings menu. This displays a menu with tabbed panels for specifying the update frequency for different statistics, determining the summaries you want displayed, and what process fields to show. You will find the Gnome System Manager in the Utilities menu.

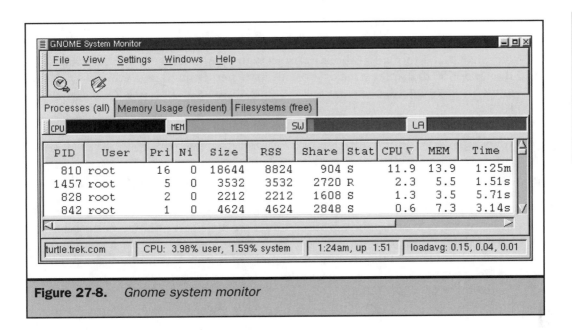

Figure 27-8. *Gnome system monitor*

System Logs: /var/log

Various system logs kept for tasks performed on your system are kept in the **/var/log** directory. Here you will find logs for mail, news, and all other system operations. The **/var/log/messages** file is a log of all system tasks not covered by other logs. This will usually include startup tasks such as loading drivers and mounting file systems. If a driver for a card failed to install at startup, you will find an error message for it here. Logins are also logged in this file, showing you who attempted to log into what account. The **/var/log/maillog** file logs mail message transmissions and news transfers.

The names and locations of system log files are specified in the **/etc/syslog.conf** file. Here you will find entries for **/ar/log/messages** and **/var/log/maillog**, among others. An entry consists of a specification of the service to be logged followed by the log file. You can further qualify the type of messages to be logged, saving error messages for a particular service in one file and notice messages in another. To exclude a service from a log, you follow it with a .none qualifier.

Managing Users

As a superuser you can manage user logins on your system. You can add or remove users as well as add and remove groups. You also have access to system initialization files that you can use to configure all user shells. And you have control over the default initialization files that are copied into an account when it is first created. With them, you can decide how accounts are to be initially configured.

You can obtain information about users on your system with the **who** command. Add the **-u** option to display a list of those users currently on the system. The command displays the login name, the login port, the date and time of login, the length of inactivity (if still active), and the process ID for the login shell. For example:

```
# who -u
root         console        Oct 12 10:34        .        1219
valerie      tty1           Oct 12 22:18        10       1492
```

Any utility to add a user, such as Linuxconf or COAS, makes use of certain default files and directories to set up the new account. There are a set of pathnames used to locate these default files or to know where to create certain user directories. For example, **/etc/skel** holds initialization files for a new user. A new user's home directory is placed in the **/home** directory. A list of the pathnames follows:

/home	Location of the user's own home directory
/mail	Location of the user's mail directory
/etc/skel	Holds the default initialization files for the login shell, such as **.bash_profile** and **.cshrc**
/etc/shell	Holds the login shells, such as BASH or TCSH

The /etc/passwd File

When you add a user, an entry for that user is made in the **/etc/passwd** file, commonly known as the password file. Each entry takes up one line that has several fields separated by colons. The fields are

Username	Login name of the user
Password	Encrypted password for the user's account
user id	Unique number assigned by the system
group id	Number used to identify the group the user belongs to
Comment	Any user information, such as the user's full name
home directory	The user's home directory
login shell	Shell to run when the user logs in; this is the default shell, usually **/bin/bash**

The following is an example of an **/etc/passwd** entry. The entry for **chris** has a * in its password field, indicating that a password has not yet been created for this user. For such entries you have to use **passwd** to create a password. Notice also that user IDs, in this particular system, start at 500 and increment by one.

```
dylan:YOTPd3Pyy9hAc:500:500:User:/home/dylan:/bin/bash
chris:*:501:501:User:/home/chris:/bin/bash
```

The **/etc/passwd** file is a text file that you can edit using a text editor. You can change fields in entries and even add new entries. The only field you cannot effectively change is the password. This has to be encrypted. To change the password field, you should always use the **passwd** command.

Though you can make entries directly to the **/etc/passwd** file, it is easier and safer to use the **userconf**, **adduser**, and **useradd** utilities. These programs will not only make entries in the **/etc/passwd** file but also create the home and mail directories for the user as well as install initialization files in the user's home directory.

The **/etc/passwd** file is a simple text file and as such is vulnerable to security breaches. Should anyone gain access to the **/etc/password** file, they might be able to decipher the passwords. On current Linux systems, the shadow suite of applications implements a greater level of security. These include versions of **useradd**, **groupadd**, and their corresponding update and delete programs. Most other user configuration tools support shadow security measures. With shadow security, passwords are no longer kept in the **/etc/password** file. Instead, passwords are kept in a separate file called **/etc/shadow** and heavily encrypted. Access is restricted to the root user. A corresponding password file called **/etc/gshadow** is also maintained for groups that require passwords.

Managing User Environments: /etc/skel

Each time a user logs in, two profile scripts are executed. There is a system profile script that is the same for every user, and there is the **.bash_profile** script that each user has in his or her home directory. The system profile script is located in the **/etc** directory and named **profile** with no preceding period. As a superuser, you can edit the profile script and put in any commands that you want executed for each user when he or she logs in. For example, you may want to define a default path for commands in case the user has not done so. Or you may wish to notify the user of recent system news or account charges.

When you first add a user to the system, you must provide the user with a skeleton **.bash_profile** file (**.profile** on OpenLinux). The **useradd** command will do this automatically by searching for a **.bash_profile** file in the directory **/etc/skel** and copying it to the user's new home directory. The **/etc/skel** directory contains a skeleton initialization file for **.bash_profile** files or, if you are using the C-shell as your login shell, **.login** and **.logout** files. It also provides initialization files for BASH and C-shell: **.bashrc** and **.cshrc**. On current OpenLinux systems, the **/etc/skel** directory will also contain the default file **.kderc**, providing a default configuration for a user's KDE desktop. Red Hat systems will include an **.Xdefaults** file, a **.kderc** file, and a Gnome Desktop directory, adding a default configuration for Gnome.

As the superuser, you can configure the **.bash_profile** file in the **/etc/skel** any way you wish. Usually, basic system variable assignments are included that define pathnames for commands, system prompts, mail pathnames, and terminal default definitions. In short, the **PATH**, **TERM**, **MAIL**, and **PS1** variables are defined. Once users have their own **.bash_profile** files, they can redefine variables or add new commands as they wish.

Login Access

You can control user login access to your system with the **/etc/login.access** file. The file consists of entries listing users, whether they are allowed access, and from where they can access the system. A record in this file consists of three colon delimited fields: a + or – sign indicating whether users are allowed access or not, user login names allowed access, and the remote system (host) or terminal (tty device) they are trying to log in from. The following allows the user dylan to access the system from the **rabbit.mytrek.com** remote system.

```
+:chris:rabbit.mytrek.com
```

You can list more than one user or location. You can also use the ALL option in place of either users or locations to allow access by all users and locations. The ALL option can be qualified with the EXCEPT option to allow access by all users except certain specified ones. The following entry allows any user to log into the system using the console, except for the users larisa and aleina.

```
+:ALL EXCEPT larisa aleina:console
```

Other access control files are used to control access for specific services such as the **hosts.deny** and **hosts.allow** files used for inetd-supported servers.

Managing Users with Linuxconf and kuser

You can easily add, remove, or change users with Linuxconf. Currently for Red Hat distributions, it is recommended that you use Linuxconf to manage user accounts. You can access Linuxconf user configuration panels either through the main Linuxconf interface or through a special user configuration interface invoked with the **userconf** command. With the main Linuxconf interface, select the User Accounts entry in the Normal list under the User Accounts heading under Config. This displays a panel listing all your user accounts, including those used for special system purposes such as FTP and news (see Figure 27-9). Each entry will have four fields: the account name, the login name, the account ID, and the group it belongs to. With **userconf**, you will first be presented with a window showing icons for user, group, and password configuration. Click the User icon to display a window with several tabbed panels, the first being a list of all users on the system.

To add a new user, click Add on this panel. This displays a User Information panel with tabbed Base Info and Privileges panels. In the Base Info panel you can enter the login name, the group the user will belong to, the user's home directory, and the login shell (command interpreter). The home directory will have the default consisting of **/home** and the user's login name, as in **/home/aleina**. Both the group and shell have drop-down menus listing available groups and shells to choose from. To give the user an initial password, click Passwd. A Changing Password panel is displayed where you can enter the new password. On the Privileges panel you can set certain user privileges, including giving the user superuser access, or permission to use Linuxconf, or shut down the system.

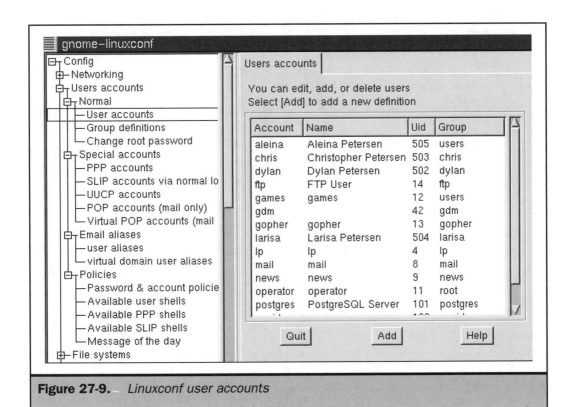

Figure 27-9.   _Linuxconf user accounts_

When you have finished, click Accept. You will now see the new user displayed in the User accounts panel. If you need to change or delete a user, just double-click its entry in this panel to display its User Information panel. To remove the user, just click Del. If you want to make some changes such as adding the user to a different group or giving the user a different home directory, just edit the appropriate entries and click Accept. The user information will be updated.

From the User Information panel shown in Figure 27-10 you can also schedule certain tasks you want performed for this user at specific times, such as backup or printing operations. Click Tasks to display the Schedule Jobs panel. You can then create job definitions. In the Schedule Job Definitions panel you can enter the command along with the time and date for the command to be executed. There are boxes for the month, day, hour, and minute. The scheduling operation works much like the Unix **at** command.

You can also deactivate an account, denying all access to it and its files. The files for this account remain intact, and when you decide to reactivate the account, the files can then be accessed. The check box labeled "The account is enabled" in the User

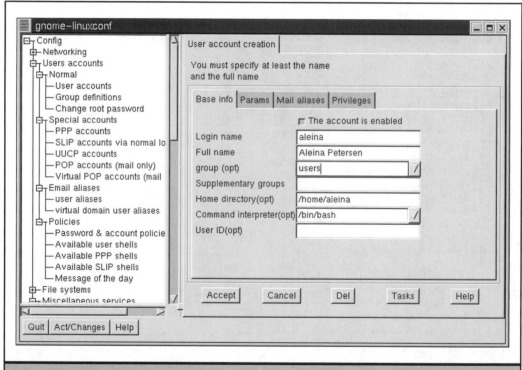

Figure 27-10. *Linuxconf user information*

Information panel is a toggle that activates and deactivates the user account. When recessed and dark, it is activated.

The K Desktop also provides a simple user management utility called kuser that works much like Linuxconf (see Figure 27-11). You can use it to manage both users and groups. The window is divided into two panes, one for users and the other for groups. Add, Edit, and Delete icons let you easily add new users, change their configuration, or remove them. When you add a new user, a new window opens with entries such as the shell and home directory. To add the password, click Password and enter the password in the window displayed.

Managing Users with COAS, LISA, and YaST

OpenLinux and SuSE provide user configuration as part of their configuration utilities, COAS, LISA, and YaST. With COAS, you select the Account Administration entry in the System Administration menu. This displays a User Accounts window listing all the users on your system, including special system users' setup for system tasks like FTP. From the View menu you can select display options such as displaying only regular users. To add a new user, select the Add entry from the Actions menu. This displays an

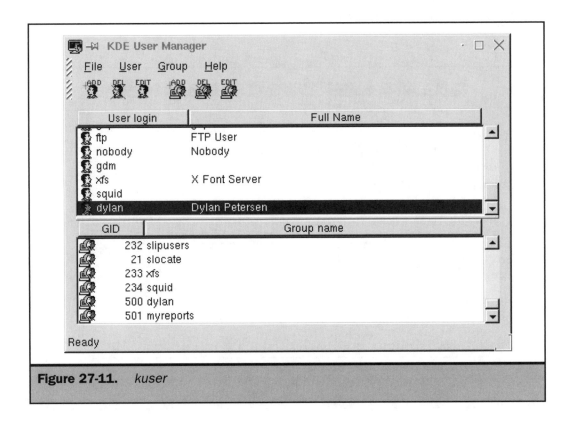

Figure 27-11. *kuser*

Edit User dialog with boxes for entering user information such as the login name, home directory, and password (see Figure 27-12). To change any user information, select its entry in the User Accounts window and choose Edit from the Actions menu. To remove a user, select it and choose Delete.

You can also add users with LISA. On the User Administration screen you can add or delete users and groups. Yet Another Setup Tool (YaST), used on SuSE, provides a similar interface, providing a full screen interface for adding, deleting, and editing users. Start up YaST and select Systems Administration and then User Administration. This displays a screen with fields for user information. Press F3 to display a selection list of users.

Adding Users with adduser

You can also add a new user to the system with the **adduser** command. This command is entered on your command line and is very easy to use. There are different versions of **adduser**. The one on Red Hat Linux comes from the Debian Linux distribution. It operates somewhat differently from other distributions, such as Slackware. This version of **adduser** takes as its argument the user name for the account you are creating. When you press ENTER, it then creates the new account using default values. You can use **passwd** to create a password for the new account. This

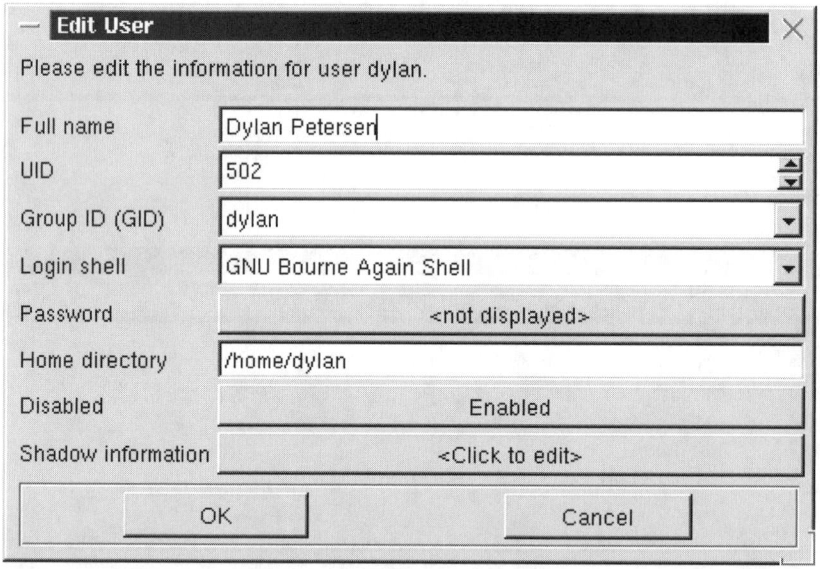

Figure 27-12. *COAS add users*

adduser program is a shell script located in the **/usr/sbin** directory. If you are familiar with shell programming, you can edit this script to change its default values.

With different versions of **adduser** found on other Linux distributions, it is best to enter the **adduser** command without any arguments. You will then be prompted for each piece of information needed to set up a new user. At the end of each prompt, within brackets, **adduser** will display a default value. To accept this default value as your entry, just press ENTER. After you have typed all your entries, **adduser** will create the new account. Once you have added a new user login, you need to give the new login a password. The login is inaccessible until you do.

Adding and Removing Users with useradd, usermod, and userdel

Most distributions of Linux also provide the **useradd**, **usermod**, and **userdel** commands to manage user accounts. All these commands take in all their information as options on the command line. If an option is not specified, they use predetermined default values. With the **useradd** command you enter values as options on the command line, such as the name of a user to create a user account. It will then create a new login and directory of that name using all the default features for a new account.

```
# useradd chris
```

The **useradd** utility has a set of predefined default values for creating a new account. The default values are the group name, the user ID, the home directory, the **skel** directory, and the login shell. The group name is the name of the group the new account is placed in. By default, this is "other," which means that the new account belongs to no group. The user ID is a number identifying the user account. This starts at 1 with the first account and increments automatically for each new account. The **skel** directory is the system directory that holds copies of initialization files. These initialization files are copied into the user's new home directory when it is created. The login shell is the pathname for the particular shell the user will use. You can display these defaults using the **useradd** command with the **-D** option. The **useradd** command has options that correspond to each default value. Table 27-12 holds a list of all the options that you can use with **useradd**. You can use specific values in place of any of these defaults when creating a particular account. Once you have added a new user login, you need to give the new login a password. The login is inaccessible until you do. In the next example, the group name for the chris account is set to intro1 and the user ID is set to 578.

```
# useradd chris -g intro1 -u 578
```

The **usermod** command allows you to change the values for any of these features. You can change the home directory or user ID. You can even change the user name for the account.

When you want to remove a user from the system, you can use the **userdel** command to delete the user's login. In the next example the user chris is removed from the system.

```
# userdel -r chris
```

Command	Description
adduser *username*	Adds a new user, creating a password file entry and home and mail directories with initialization files; uses the **passwd** command to create a password for the user
useradd *username options*	Adds new users to the system
usermod *username options*	Modifies a user's features
userdel -r *username*	Removes a user from the system
useradd, usermod Options	
-u *userid*	Sets the user ID of the new user; the default is the increment of the highest number used so far
-g *group*	Sets a group or name
-d *dir*	Sets the home directory of the new user
-s *shell*	Sets the login shell directory of the new user
-c *str*	Adds a comment to the user's entry in the system password file: **/etc/passwd**
-k *skl-dir*	Sets the skeleton directory that holds skeleton files, such as **.profile** files, that are copied to the user's home directory automatically when it is created; the default is **/etc/skel**

Table 27-12.   *User and Group Management Commands*

Command	Description
-D	Displays defaults for all settings
Group Management Commands	
groupadd	Creates a new group
groupdel	Removes a group
groupmod *option*	Modifies a group **-g** Changes a group ID **-n** Changes a group name

Table 27-12. *User and Group Management Commands* (continued)

Managing Groups

You can manage groups using either shell commands or window utilities like Linuxconf. The system file that holds group entries is called **/etc/group**. The file consists of group records, with one record per line and its fields separated by colons. A group record has four fields: a group name, password, its ID, and the users that are part of this group. The password field can be left blank. The fields for a group record are as follows:

group name	Name of the group; must be unique
password	Usually an asterisk to allow anyone to join the group; a password can be added to control access
group id	Number assigned by the system to identify this group
users	List of users that belong to the group

Here is an example of an entry in a **/etc/group** file. The group is called engines, there is no password, the group ID is 100, and the users that are part of this group are chris, robert, valerie, and aleina.

```
engines::100:chris,robert,valerie,aleina
```

As in the case of the **/etc/passwd** file, you can edit the **/etc/group** file directly using a text editor. Instead of using either Linuxconf or **groupdel**, you could just delete the entry for that group in the **/etc/group** file. However, this can be risky should you make accidental changes.

Managing Groups Using Linuxconf, COAS, LISA, and YaST

You can add, remove, and modify any groups easily with the Linuxconf utility on your root user desktop. To manage groups using Linuxconf, select the Group Definitions entry in the Normal list under User Accounts in Config. This displays a User Groups panel that lists all the groups currently on your system (see Figure 27-13). Each entry will have three fields: the group name, the group ID, and the list of users that are part of this group. To add a new group, click Add. This displays a Group Specification panel where you can enter the name for the new group and the group ID. A default group ID will already be listed.

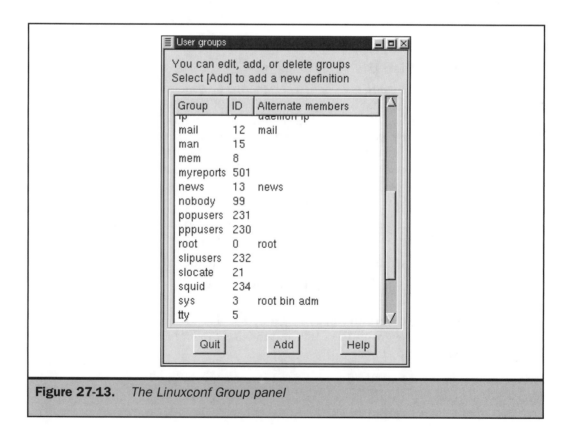

Figure 27-13.   *The Linuxconf Group panel*

You can edit or delete any group by first double-clicking its entry in the User Groups panel to display its Group Specification panel. To remove the group, click Del. For changes, edit any of the entries and click Accept. For example, to add certain users to a group, bring up the group's Group Specification panel and enter the users you want to add.

COAS and LISA (OpenLinux) have entries for adding, updating, and removing groups. LISA has a Group Administration menu from which you can create or delete groups. Yet Another Setup Tool (YaST), used on SuSE, provides a similar interface, providing a full-screen interface for adding, deleting, and editing groups. Start up YaST and select Systems Administration and then Group Administration. This displays a screen with fields for group information. Press F3 to display a selection list of groups.

Managing Groups Using groupadd, groupmod, and groupdel

On many Linux distributions you can manage groups with the **groupadd**, **groupmod**, and **groupdel** commands. With the **groupadd** command you can create new groups. When you add a group to the system, the system will place the group's name in the **/etc/group** file and give it a group ID number. The **groupadd** command only creates the group category. Users are individually added to the group. In the next example, the **groupadd** command creates the engines group.

```
# groupadd engines
```

You can delete a group with the **groupdel** command. In the next example, the **engines** group is deleted.

```
# groupdel engines
```

You can change the name of a group or its ID using the **groupmod** command. Just enter **groupmod -g** with the new ID number and the group name. To change the name of a group, you use the **-n** option. Enter **groupmod -n** with the new name of the group followed by the current name. In the next example, the engines group has its name changed to trains.

```
# groupmod -n trains engines
```

Installing and Managing Devices

All the devices, such as printers, terminals, and CD-ROMs, are connected to your Linux operating system through special files called device files. Such a file contains all the information your operating system needs to control the specified device. This design introduces great flexibility. The operating system is independent of the specific details for managing a particular device; the specifics are all handled by the device file. The operating system simply informs the device what task it is to perform, and the device file tells it how. If you change devices, you only have to change the device file, not the whole system.

To install a device on your Linux system, you need a device file for it, software configuration such as provided by a configuration tool, and kernel support, usually supplied by a module or already built into the kernel. An extensive number of device files are already set up for you for different kinds of devices. You usually just need to choose one of these. For kernel support, you may have to load a kernel module or recompile the kernel, both simple procedures. In most cases, support is already built into the kernel. Configuration of your device may be provided by desktop configurations tools such as the Gnome Control Center, system configuration tools like COAS or Linuxconf, or a module configuration interface such as that provided for sound modules.

Device Files

The name of a device file is designed to reflect the task of the device. Printer device files begin with **lp** for "line print." Since you could have more than one printer connected to your system, the particular printer device files are distinguished by two or more numbers or letters following the prefix **lp**, such as **lp0**, **lp1**, **lp2**. The same is true for terminal device files. They begin with the prefix **tty**, for "teletype," and are further distinguished by numbers or letters such as **tty0**, **tty1**, **ttyS0**, and so on. You can obtain a complete listing of the current device file names and the devices that are used from the **kernel.org** Web site at

```
http://www.kernel.org/pub/linux/docs/device-list/devices.txt
```

All of these file names will be implemented as device files in your **/dev** directory. Here you will find printer, CD-ROM, hard drive, SCSI, and sound device files along with many others. Certain link files bear common device names that are often linked to the actual device file used. For example, a **/dev/cdrom** symbolic link links to the actual device used for your CD-ROM. If your CD-ROM is an IDE device, it may use the device file **hdc**. In this case, **/dev/cdrom** would be a link to **/dev/hdc**. In effect, **/dev/cdrom** would be another name for **/dev/hdc**. You can use **/dev/cdrom** to reference your CD-ROM's device file, instead of **/dev/hdc**. There is also a **/dev/modem** link file for your modem. If your modem is connected to the second serial port, its device file would be **/dev/ttyS1**. In that case, **/dev/modem** would be a link to that device file. Applications can then use **/dev/modem** to access your modem, instead of having to know the actual device file used. A listing of commonly used device links is shown in Table 27-13.

In Linux there are two types of devices: block and character. A block device, such as a hard disk, transmits data a block at a time. A character device, such as a printer or modem, transmits data one character at a time, or rather as a continuous stream of data, not as separate blocks. Device driver files for character devices will have a **c** as the first character in the permissions segment displayed by the **ls** command. Device driver files for block devices will have a **b**. In the next example, **lp0** (the printer) is a character device and **hda1** (the hard disk) is a block device.

```
# ls -l hda1 lp0
brw-rw----  1 root     disk       3,   1 Sep  7  1999 hda1
crw-r-----  1 root     daemon     6,   0 Dec 31  1999 lp0
```

Though most distributions include an extensive set of device files already set up for you, it is possible for you to create your own. You use the **mknod** command to create a device file, either a character or block type. The **mknod** command has the following syntax:

```
mknod  options  device  device-type  major-num  minor-num
```

The device type can be either **b**, **c**, **p**, or **u**. As already mentioned, the **b** indicates a block device, and **c** is for a character device. The **u** is for an unbuffered character device, and **p** is for a FIFO device. Devices of the same type often have the same name; for example, Ethernet cards will all have the name **eth**. Devices of the same type are then uniquely identified by a number that is attached to the name. This number has

Links	Description
/dev/mouse	Current mouse device
/dev/tape	Current tape device
/dev/cdrom	Current CD-ROM device
/dev/cdwriter	Current CD-writer device
/dev/scanner	Current scanner device
/dev/modem	Current dialout device, modem port
/dev/root	Current root file system
/dev/swap	Current swap device

Table 27-13.   *Device Links*

two components, the major number and the minor number. Devices may further have the same major number, but if so, the minor number will always be different. This major and minor structure is designed to deal with situations in which several devices may be dependent on one larger device, such as several modems connected to the same I/O card. They would all have the same major number that would reference the card, but each modem would have a unique minor number. Both the minor and major numbers are required for block and character devices (**b**, **c**, and **u**). However, they are not used for FIFO devices.

For example, Linux systems usually provide device files for three parallel ports (lp0–2). If you need more, you can use the **mknod** command to create a new one. Printer devices are character devices and must be owned by the root and daemon. The permissions for printer devices are write and execute for the owner and read for the group, 620 (see Chapter 9 for a discussion of file permissions). The major device number is set to 6, and the minor device number is set to the port number of the printer, such as 0 for LPT1 and 1 for LPT2. Once the device is created, you use **chown** to change its ownership to **root.daemon**. In the next example, a parallel printer device is made on a fourth parallel port, **/dev/lp3**. The **–m** option specifies the permissions, in this case, 620. The device is a character device, as indicated by the **c** argument following the device name. The major number is 6, and the minor number is 3. If you were making a device at **/dev/lp4**, the major number would still be 6, but the minor number would be 4. Once the device is made, the **chown** command then changes the ownership of the parallel printer device to **root.daemon**. Be sure to check that a spool directory has been created for your device. If not, you will have to make one.

```
# mknod -m 620 /dev/lp3 c 6 3
# chown root.daemon /dev/lp3
```

Installing and Managing Printers

Setting up a printer interface is fairly simple. It is a matter of determining a device file to use and placing printer configuration entries in your **printcap** file. You may also have to set up printing filters. There are several configuration tools you can use that will let you easily set up and configure your printer. Red Hat systems provide the PrintTool utility. On OpenLinux you can use either COAS or LISA.

Most distributions of Linux create three device names for parallel printers automatically during installation. They are **lp0**, **lp1**, and **lp2**. The number used in these names corresponds to a parallel port on your PC. The **lp0** references the LPT1 parallel port usually located at address 0x03bc. The **lp1** references the LPT2 parallel port located at 0x0378, and **lp2** references LPT3 at address 0x0278. If you are not sure at what address your parallel port is located, you can use the **msd.exe** command on your DOS system to find out. The **lp0** connects to an XT bus, and **lp1** connects to an AT bus.

For a detailed explanation of printer installation, see the Printing HOWTO file in **/usr/doc/HOWTO**.

The PrintTool utility provided on Red Hat distributions is a very easy interface for setting up and managing your printers. Using just PrintTool, you can easily install a printer on your Linux system. You can start PrintTool either by selecting its entry in the System menu or clicking its icon in the Red Hat Control Panel. In the PrintTool window, select the Add button. This opens up an Edit window that displays several fields in which you enter printer configuration information. In the Names field, you enter the names you want to use for the printer. Each name is separated by a |. You should include **lp** as one of your names. The **lpr** command used without a specified printer name will use the printer named **lp**. In the Spool directory fields, the default spool directory will already be entered for you. You can change it to another directory if you wish. For the Device field, it's customary to enter **/dev/lp1**. This is the parallel printer device for computers that use an AT bus, which most computers today use. If you have a serial device, you will have to use a different device name.

For the Input Filter you can click Select to display a window with three fields. Each field has a Select button by it that will display a set of currently available options. The Select button for the PrinterType field opens a menu of printers that you can choose from. The Select button for the Resolution field lists several possible resolutions. The Select button for the PaperSize field lists paper sizes such as letter and legal. When you are finished, click OK to close the window and do the same for the Edit window. You will see your printer listed in the PrintTool window, as shown in Figure 27-14. Choose the Quit item from the PrintTool menu to quit PrintTool. You are now ready to print. For a detailed explanation of printer installation, see the Printing HOWTO file in **/usr/doc/HOWTO**.

On OpenLinux, you use COAS or LISA to configure printers. For COAS, select Printer Administration from the Peripherals Administration menu. This opens a Printer Attributes window with boxes for entering printer information such as device, speed, and type (see Figure 27-15). Many of the boxes have drop-down menus from which you can select entries. The Type drop-down list will list all the supported printers. The list for Device will list the currently available devices. You can also select features such as resolution, paper size, and speed.

With LISA you select the Configure Printer entry in the Hardware Configuration menu. Here a long list of printer types will be displayed, just as during installation. Upon selecting the one you want, you will be prompted for a series of printer features such as resolution and paper size.

Printer Devices and /etc/printcap

When your system prints a file, it makes use of special directories called spool directories. A print job is a file to be printed. When you print a file to a printer, a copy of it is made and placed in a spool directory set up for that printer. The location of the spool directory is obtained from the printer's entry in the **/etc/printcap** file. In the spool

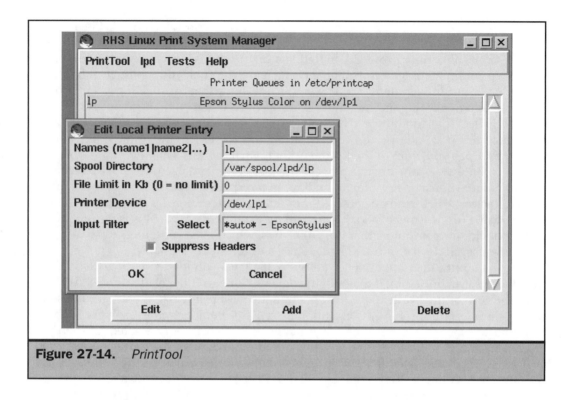

Figure 27-14. *PrintTool*

directory two files are made for each print job. One begins with **df** and is the data file containing the copy of the file to be printed. The other begins with **cf** and is the control file for the print job. It contains information about the print job, such as the user it belongs to.

The **/etc/printcap** file holds entries for each printer connected to your system. A printcap entry holds information such as the pathname for a printer's spool directory and the device name of the printer port that the printer uses. The first field in a printcap entry is a list of possible names for the printer. These are names you can make up yourself, and you can add others if you wish. Each name is separated by a |. You use these names to identify the printer when entering various printer commands or options, such as the **-P** option. They are also used for special shell variables, such as the **PRINTER** variable, used in many initialization scripts.

The fields following the list of names set different fields for your printer. The fields have two-letter names and are usually assigned a value using =. These assignments are separated by colons. Three of the more important fields are **lp**, **sd**, and **of**. The **lp** field is set to the device name that the printer uses. The **sd** field is set to the pathname of the spool directory, and **of** is set to the particular filter used for this printer. Some have Boolean values and will just list the field name with no assignment for a true value.

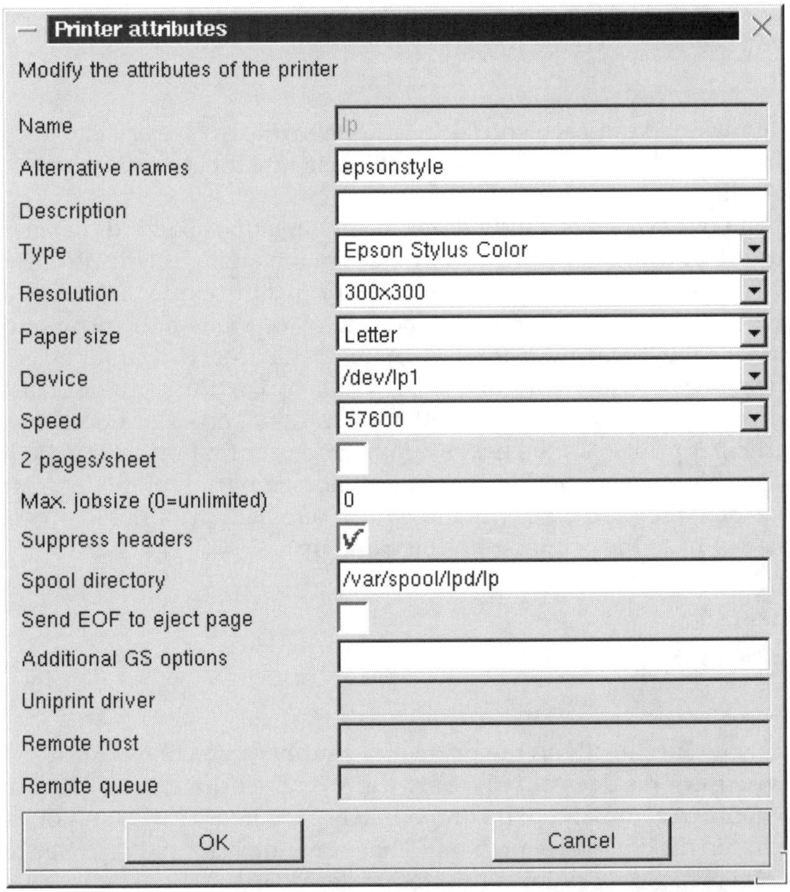

Figure 27-15. *COAS printer attributes*

You can find a complete listing of the printcap fields in the printcap man pages: **man 8
printcap.** An example of a printcap entry follows.

```
##PRINTTOOL## LOCAL djet500c 600x600 letter {}
hp1|lp:\
    :sd=/var/spool/lpd/lp:\
    :mx#0:\
```

```
:lp=/dev/lp1:\
:if=/var/spool/lpd/lp/filter:
```

Instead of making your own entries in the **/etc/printcap** file, you can use the Red Hat PrintTool utility, located on your root user desktop, to make them for you automatically.

Printing on your system is handled by a print daemon called lpd, which is constantly running, waiting for print jobs and then managing their printing procedures. The lpd daemon takes its print jobs from a print queue that you can list using the **lpq** command. The **lpr** command will place a job on the print queue, and lpd will then take it in turn and print it. As noted in Chapter 5, **lpr** takes as its argument the name of a file. You can also feed data to **lpr** through the standard input, piping in the data to be printed from another operation. The **-P** option allows you to specify a particular printer. In the next example, the user first prints the file **preface**. Then she uses the **cat** command to generate combined output of the files **intro** and **digest**. This is piped to the **lpr** command, which will then print it. Finally, the user prints the file **report** to the printer with the name **hp1**.

```
$ lpr preface
$ cat intro digest | lpr
$ lpr -Php1 report
```

You can also print directly to the printer by simply redirecting output to the printer's device file. This does not place anything on the print queue. The print operation becomes a command to be immediately executed. However, your system is occupied until the file completes printing. The following example uses this technique to print the **report** file to a printer connected to device **lp1**.

```
$ cat report > /dev/lp1
```

The Print Queue

To manage the printing jobs on your printer or printers, enter the command **lpc** and press ENTER. You are then given an LPC> prompt at which you can enter **lpc** commands to manage your printers and their jobs. The **status** command with the name of the printer displays whether the printer is ready, how many print jobs it has, and so on. The **stop** and **start** commands can stop a printer and start it back up. See Table 27-15 for a listing of **lpc** commands.

```
# lpc
lpc> status hp1
hp1|lp1:
    queuing is enabled
    printing is enabled
    1 entry in spool area
```

You can manage the print queue using the **lpq** and **lprm** commands. The **lpq** command lists the printing jobs currently on the print queue. With the **-P** option and the printer name you can list the jobs for a particular printer. If you specify a user name, you can list the print jobs for that user. With the **-l** option, **lpq** displays detailed information about each job. If you want information on a specific job, you can just use that job's ID number with **lpq**.

With the **lprm** command you can remove a printing job from the queue, erasing it before it can be printed. The **lprm** command takes many of the same options as **lpq**. To remove a specific job, just use **lprm** with the job number. To remove all printing jobs for a particular user, enter **lprm** with the user name. To remove all printing jobs for a particular printer, you use the **-P** option with the printer name.

The **lprm** command has a special argument indicated by a dash, (**-**), that references all print jobs for the user who issues the command. For example, to remove all your own print jobs, you can just enter **lprm -**. If you logged in as the root user, then **lprm -** will remove all print jobs for all printers and users from the print queue, emptying it completely.

You should not use **lprm** to kill a printing job that has already started printing. Instead, you may have to use the **kill** command on the print job process. You can display processes using the **ps -ax** command and then use **kill** and the number of the process to end it. For a job that is already printing, you will see a process for its filter. This is the process to kill.

Table 27-14 shows various printer commands; Table 27-15 includes **lpc** commands.

Installing and Managing Terminals and Modems

With a multiuser system such as Linux, you will probably have several users logged in at the same time. Each user would, of course, need his or her own terminal through which to access the Linux system. The monitor on your PC acts as a special terminal called the console, but you can add other terminals through either the serial ports on your PC or through a special multiport card installed on your PC. The other terminals can be standalone terminals or PCs using terminal emulation programs. For a detailed explanation of terminal installation, see the **Term-HOWTO** file in **/usr/doc/HOWTO**. A brief explanation is provided here.

Printer Management	Description
lpr *options file-list*	Prints a file; copies the file to the printer's spool directory and places it on the print queue to be printed in turn **-P***printer* Prints the file on the specified printer
lpq *options*	Displays the print jobs in the print queue **-P***printer* Prints queue for the specified printer **-1** Prints a detailed listing
lprm *options Printjob-id or User-id*	Removes a print job from the print queue; you identify a particular print job by its number as listed by **lpq**; if you use *User-id*, it will remove all print jobs for that user **-** Refers to all print jobs for the logged-in user; if the logged-in user is the root, it refers to all print jobs **-P***printer* Removes all print jobs for the specified printer
lpc	Manages your printers; at the LPC> prompt you can enter commands to check the status of your printers and take other actions

Table 27-14. *Printer Commands*

The serial ports on your PC are referred to as COM1, on up to COM4. They correspond to the terminal devices **/dev/ttyS0** through **/dev/ttyS3**. Note that several of these serial devices may already be used for other input devices such as your mouse and for communications devices such as your modem. If you have a serial printer, then one will already be used for that. If you've installed a multiport card, you will have many more ports to choose from. For each terminal you add, you must create a character device on your Linux system. As with printers, you use the **mknod** command to create terminal devices. The permissions for a terminal device are 660. Terminal devices are character devices with a major number of 4 and minor numbers usually beginning at 64.

Terminal devices are managed by your system using the **getty** program and a set of configuration files. When your system starts, it reads a list of connected terminals in the **inittab** file and then executes a **/etc/getty** program for each one. The **getty**

Commands	Operation
help [*command ...*]	Prints a short description of each command
abort *printers*	Terminates an active spooling daemon on the local host immediately and then disables printing for the specified printers; use **all** to indicate all printers
clean *printers*	Removes any temporary files, data files, and control files that cannot be printed
disable *printers*	Turns the specified printer queues off; new jobs will not be accepted
down *printers message*	Turns the specified printer queue off, disables printing, and puts a message in the printer status file
enable *printers*	Enables spooling for the listed printers; allows new jobs into the spool queue
quit or **exit**	Exits from **lpc**
restart *printers*	Starts a new printer daemon; used if the printer daemon, lpd, dies, leaving jobs yet to be printed
start *printers*	Enables printing and starts a spooling daemon for the listed printers
status *printers*	Displays the status of daemons and queues on the local machine
stop *printers*	Stops a spooling daemon after the current job completes and disables printing
topq *printer* [*jobnum ...*] [*user ...*]	Places the jobs in the order listed at the top of the printer queue
up *printers*	Enables everything and starts a new printer daemon; undoes the effects of **down**

Table 27-15.   *lpc Commands*

program sets up the communication between your Linux system and a specified terminal. It obtains from the **/etc/gettydefs** file certain parameters such as speed and the login prompt as well as any special instructions.

```
# Format: <speed># <init flags> # <final flags> #<login
   string>#<next-speed>
# 38400 fixed baud Dumb Terminal entry
DT38400# B38400 CS8 CLOCAL # B38400 SANE -ISTRIP CLOCAL #@S login:
   #DT38400
```

The **/etc/inittab** file holds instructions for your system on how to manage terminal devices. A line in the **/etc/inittab** file has four basic components: an ID, runlevel, action, and process. Terminal devices are identified by ID numbers, beginning with 1 for the first device. The runlevel at which the terminal operates is usually 1. The action is usually "respawn," which says to continually run the process. The process is a call to **/etc/getty** with the baud rate and terminal device name. The **/etc/ttys** file associates the type of terminal used with a certain device.

The **/etc/termcap** file holds the specifications for different terminal types. These are the different types of terminals users could use to log into your system. Your **/etc/termcap** file is already filled with specifications for most of the terminals currently produced. An entry in the **/etc/termcap** file consists of various names that can be used for a terminal separated by a | and then a series of parameter specifications, each ending in a colon. It is here that you find the name used for a specific terminal type. You can use **more** to display your **/etc/termcap** file and then use a search, **/**, to locate your terminal type. There are many options that you can set for a terminal device. To change these options, you can use the **stty** command instead of changing configuration files directly. The **stty** command with no arguments lists the current setting of the terminal.

When a user logs in, it is helpful to have the terminal device initialized using the **tset** command. Usually the **tset** command is placed in the user's **.bash_profile** file and is automatically executed whenever he or she logs into the system. You use the **tset** command to set the terminal type and any other options the terminal device requires. A common entry of **tset** for a **.bash_profile** file follows. The **-m dialup:** option prompts the user to enter a terminal type. The type specified here is a default type that will be displayed in parentheses. The user just presses ENTER to choose the default. The prompt will look like this: **TERM=(vt100)?**

```
eval 'tset -s -Q -m dialup:?vt00'
```

Installing Input Devices

Input devices such as mice and keyboards are displayed on several levels. Initial configuration is performed during installation where you select the mouse and keyboard types. You can change that configuration with your administration configuration tool such as COAS, LISA, YaST, or Red Hat Setup. There are also special configurations for mice and keyboard for X Window System and the KDE and Gnome

desktops. You select the keyboard layout and language as well as configure the speed
and display of the mouse.

Installing Sound, Network, and Other Cards

For you to install a new card, your kernel has to be configured to support it. Support
for most cards is provided in the form of modules that can be dynamically loaded in
and attached to the kernel, running as an extension of it. Installing support for a card is
usually a simple matter of loading a module that includes the drives for it. For
example, drivers for the SoundBlaster sound card are in the module **sb.o**. Loading this
module makes your sound card accessible to Linux. Most distributions automatically
detect the cards installed on your system and load the needed modules. If you change
cards, you may have to manually load the module you need, removing an older
conflicting one. For example, if you change your Ethernet card, you may have to
unload the module for your previous card and load in the one for your new card.
Certain utilities such as Linuxconf and **netcfg** let you choose a new module and will
have the module loaded for you. You can, however, load modules manually. The next
section describes this process.

Device files for most cards are already set up for you. The device name for your
sound card is **/dev/audio**. The device name for your Ethernet card begins with **eth** with
the numbering starting from 0, as in **eth0** for the first Ethernet card on your system.
For sound cards, you can tell what your current sound configuration is by listing the
contents of the **/dev/sndstat** file. You can test your card by simply redirecting a sound
file to it, as shown here.

```
cat sample.au  >  /dev/audio.
```

Modules

Beginning with Linux kernel 2.0, the Linux kernel adopted a modular structure. In
earlier kernel versions, support for specific features and devices had to be included
directly into the kernel program. Adding support for a new device, say a new kind of
sound card, required that you create a new version of your kernel program that
included the code for supporting that device. This involved a sometimes lengthy
configuration, followed by compiling and installing the new kernel program and
making sure it was called properly when your system booted up.

As an alternative to this rebuilding of the kernel, Linux now supports the use of
modules. Modules are components of the Linux kernel that can be loaded and attached
to it as needed. To add support for a new device, you can now just instruct a kernel to
load its module. In some cases, you may have to recompile just that module to provide
support for your device. The use of modules has the added advantage of reducing the
size of the kernel program. The kernel can load modules in memory only as they are

needed. For example, the module for the PPP network interface that is used for a modem needs only be used when you connect to an ISP.

The modules that your system will need are usually determined during installation, based on the kind of configuration information you provided. For example, if your system uses an Ethernet card whose type you specified during installation, then the system will load the module for that card. You can, however, manually control what modules are to be loaded for your system. This, in effect, lets you customize your kernel whatever way you want. There are several commands, configuration tools, and daemons that you can use to manage kernel modules. Most distributions provide the **kerneld** or **kmod** kernel daemons that will automatically load modules as they are needed. In addition, there are several tools that let you manually load and unload modules, should you need to. Red Hat provides a user interface for **kerneld** that lets you load and unload modules. On OpenLinux you can use COAS to manage modules. The **kerneld** and **kmod** processes actually use certain kernel commands to perform the actual task of loading or unloading modules. The **modprobe** command is a general-purpose command that calls **insmod** to load modules and **rmmod** to unload them. These commands are listed in Table 27-16 (see section "Managing Modules with the Module Commands").

The file name for a module has the extension **.o**. Modules reside in the **/lib/modules/**_version_ directory, where _version_ is the version number for your current kernel. The directory for the 2.2 kernel is **/lib/modules/2.2.5-15**. As you install new kernels on your system, new module directories will be generated for them. One trick used to always access the directory for the current kernel is to use the **uname -r** command to generate the kernel version number. This command needs to have backquotes.

```
cd /lib/modules/'uname -r'
```

In this directory there will be several subdirectories where the modules reside. These subdirectories serve to categorize your modules, making them easier to locate. For example, the **net** directory holds modules for your Ethernet cards, and the **misc** directory contains sound card modules.

Automatically Loading Modules: kerneld and kmod

With the **kerneld** daemon, you can have modules loaded into the kernel as they are needed. For example, when a user uses a sound application, **kerneld** will automatically load the appropriate sound modules. When **kerneld** detects a need for a module, it then invokes **modprobe** to load it.

The kerneld process is a daemon with its own startup script in the **/etc/rc.d/init.d** directory. You can use this script to start and stop the daemon from the command line. The command **/etc/rec.d/init.d/kerneld stop** will stop **kerneld**, and using the start argument will start it up again. You can also manually edit the **/etc/modules.conf** file to add or remove entries.

The **kmod** daemon is designed as a streamlined replacement of **kerneld**. It lacks many of the features of **kerneld** but performs essential module tasks faster and with lower overhead.

Managing Modules with COAS

On OpenLinux you can use COAS to unload and load modules. Select Kernel Modules from the COAS menu to display the Kernel Modules window shown in Figure 27-16. The window is divided into two scrollable lists. The left list consists of available modules not yet loaded. The right list shows modules already loaded. To load a module, just select it from the left list and click Load. Modules are listed by their file names, which can be obscure. To find out what a module is used for, select it and click Info. There is one for loaded and unloaded modules. If you should want to unload a module, select its name in the right list and click Unload.

If a module requires configuration, then a window opens up with entries for different configuration options (see the following illustration of the sound card module configuration). For example, with sound cards, you may have to specify the IRQ, DMA, and I/O settings. When you add the SoundBlaster sound module, **sb.o**, a window opens up with entries for the different sound card settings.

— Kernel Module Configuration		×
Please edit the configuration for module sb:		
Description	SoundBlaster/Compatible	
Driver Type	Sound Driver	
Load at boot time	Enabled	
I/O address	0x220	
IRQ	5	
DMA channel	1	

Managing Modules with Red Hat Kernel Configurator

The Red Hat Kernel Configurator utility shown in the following illustration provides an X interface for loading and unloading modules. On the Red Hat Control Panel, select the icon that looks like a heart. This opens the Kernel Configurator window that lists all the modules currently loaded. Each entry has three fields: its type, module name, and its arguments. For example, the module 3c595, which provides support for 3c595 3Com Ethernet cards, has the type eth0 (the Ethernet interface), 3c595 (its name), and no arguments. You can add new entries by clicking Add. A window opens where you can enter the module type, name, and any arguments. A new entry is not immediately loaded to the kernel. Entries are saved to the **/etc/conf.modules**. file. To load the new entry, you click the Restart **kerneld** button, forcing **kerneld**. The Kernel Configurator uses the **kerneld** daemon to load and unload modules. When **kerneld**

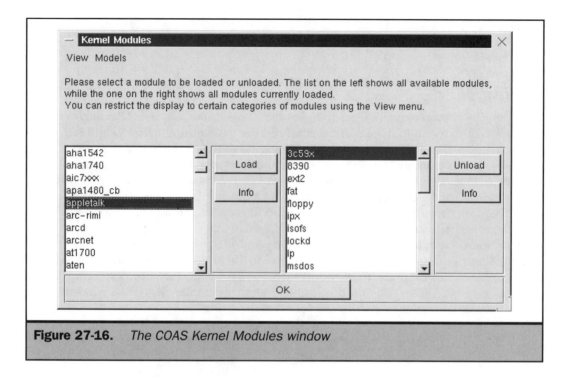

Figure 27-16.   *The COAS Kernel Modules window*

restarts, it reads the **/etc/conf.modules** file, which now has the new entry. To remove a module, select its entry and click Remove. To edit an entry, say to add arguments, select its entry and click Edit.

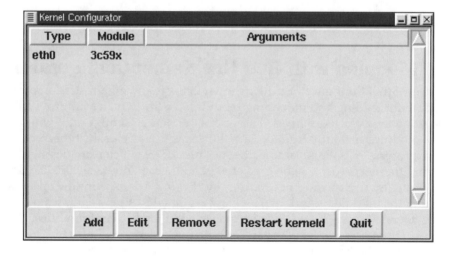

Managing Modules with the Module Commands

The **lsmod** command will list the modules currently loaded into your kernel. You can add a new one using the **insmod** command and the module name. With **rmmod** you can unload a module. (See Table 27-16 for kernel module commands.) It is often the case, however, that a given module will require that other modules be loaded. For example, the module for the SoundBlaster sound card, **sb.o**, requires that the **sound.o** module be also loaded. Instead of manually trying to determine what modules a given module depends on, you use the **modep** command to detect the dependencies for you. The **modep** command will generate a file that lists all the modules a given module depends on. It generates a hierarchical listing, noting what modules should be loaded first and in what order. Then to load the module, you use the **modprobe** command using that file. It reads the file generated by **modep** and loads any dependent modules in the correct order along with the module you want. You will need to execute **modep** with the **-a** option once, before you ever use **modprobe**. Entering **modep -a** will create a complete listing of all module dependencies. This command will create a file called **modules.deb** in the module directory for your current kernel version, **/lib/modules/**_version_.

```
modep -a
```

To install a module, you use the **modprobe** command and the module name. You can add any parameters that the module may require. The following command installs

Command	Description
lsmod	Lists modules currently loaded
insmod	Loads a module into the kernel
rmmod	Unloads a module currently loaded
depmod	Creates a dependency file listing all other modules that the specified module may rely on
modprobe	Loads a module with any dependent modules it may also need; uses the file of dependency listing generated by **depmod**

Table 27-16. _Kernel Module Commands_

the SoundBlaster sound module with the IO, IRQ, and DMA values. The **modprobe** command also supports use of the ∗ character to let you use a pattern to select several modules.

```
modprobe sb io=0x220 irq=5 dma=1
```

You can use the **-l** option to just list modules, and the **-t** option will look for modules in a specified subdirectory. In the next example the user lists all modules that begin with "sound" in the **misc** directory.

```
# modprobe -l -t misc sound*
/lib/modules/2.2.5-15/misc/soundlow.o
/lib/modules/2.2.5-15/misc/soundcore.o
/lib/modules/2.2.5-15/misc/sound.o
```

Options for the **modprobe** command are placed in the **/etc/conf.modules** file. Here you can enter configuration options such as default directories and aliases. An alias provides a simple name for a module. For example, the following entry would let you reference the 3c59x.o Ethernet card module as eth0.

```
alias eth0 3c59x
```

Installing New Modules for the Kernel

The source code for your Linux kernel contains an extensive set of modules, of which only a few are actually used on your system. When you install a new device, you may have to install the kernel module that provides the drivers for it. This involves selecting the module you need from a listing and then regenerating your kernel modules with the new module included. Then the new module is copied into the module library, installing it on your system. Then you can use **modprobe** to install it manually or place an entry for it in **conf.modules** to have it loaded automatically. First, make sure you have installed the kernel source code in the **/usr/src/linux** directory (see the following section, "The Linux Kernel," for details). Change to the **/usr/src/linux** directory. Then use the **xconfig** or **menuconfig** commands to display the kernel configuration menus, invoking them with the following commands. The **xconfig** command is an X Window System application that needs to be run on your desktop from a terminal window.

```
make xconfig
make menuconfig
```

Using the menus as described in the next section, "The Linux Kernel," select the modules you need. Make sure each is marked as a module, clicking the Module check box in **xconfig** or pressing M for **menuconfig**. Once the kernel is configured, you save and exit from the configuration menus. Then you create the modules with the following command.

```
make modules
```

This will place them in the kernel source modules directory: **/usr/src/linux/modules**. You can copy the one you want to the modules directory, **/lib/modules/***version*, where *version* is the version number of your Linux kernel. A simpler approach is to just reinstall all your modules; you can use the following command. This copies all the compiled modules to the **/lib/modules/***version* directory.

```
make modules-install
```

For example, if you wanted to provide AppleTalk support and your distribution did not create an AppleTalk module or incorporate the support into the kernel directly, then you can use this method to create and install the AppleTalk module. First check to see if your distribution has already included it. The **appletalk.o** module should be in the **/lib/modules/***version***/misc** directory. If not, you can move to the **/usr/src/linux** directory, run **make xconfig**, and select AppleTalk as a module. Then generate the modules with the **make modules** command. You could then use the **make modules-install** command to install the new module, along with your other modules. Alternatively, you can use the following command to copy **appletalk.o** to the module directory (**uname -r** is used here to generate the version number).

```
cp /usr/src/linux/modules/appletalk.o   /lib/modules/'uname -r'/misc
```

The Linux Kernel

The kernel is the core of the operating system. It is the program that performs operating system functions. The version number for a Linux kernel consists of three segments: the major, minor, and revision numbers. The major number increments with major changes in the kernel. The minor number indicates stability. Even numbers are used for stable releases, whereas odd numbers are reserved for development releases, which may be unstable. New features, of course, will first appear in the development versions. If stability is a concern, it is best to wait for the stable version. The revision number refers to the corrected versions. As bugs are discovered and corrected, new revisions of a kernel are released. A development kernel may have numerous revisions. For example, kernel 2.2-15 can be a major number of 2 and a minor number of 2, with a revision number of 15. On systems that support RPM packages, you can use a RPM query to find out what version is installed.

```
rpm -q kernel
```

The Linux kernel is continually being worked on, with new versions released when they are ready. Major distributors such as OpenLinux and Red Hat will include the most up-to-date kernel in their releases. In fact, the release number for an OpenLinux release is the same as its kernel. OpenLinux 2.2 contains the 2.2 Linux kernel. When a new kernel becomes available, you can download and install it yourself instead of waiting for a distribution's next release. Linux kernels are kept at **www.kernel.org**. Also, RPM packages for a new kernel will often be available at distribution update sites such as **updates.redhat.com**. One reason you may need to upgrade your kernel is to provide support for new hardware or for features not supported by the distribution's version. For example, you may need support for a new device not provided in the distribution's version of the kernel. Certain features may not be included in a distribution's version because they are considered experimental or a security risk. For example, IP masquerading is not supported by OpenLinux 2.2. If you want to run OpenLinux with support for IP masquerading, you have to configure and recompile the OpenLinux kernel to include support for IP masquerading. You then, in effect, have a different customized version of the OpenLinux kernel.

Note that you probably do not need to install a new kernel just to add support for a new device. Kernels provide most device support in the form of modules, of which only those needed are installed with the kernel. Most likely your current kernel will have the module you need. You just have to install it. For this task, see the previous section on "Installing New Modules for the Kernel."

You can find out more about the Linux kernel from **www.kernel.org**, the official repository for the current Linux kernels. Here you will find the most up-to-date source code as well as documentation. **www.kernelnotes.org** contains news about different releases. Different distribution Web sites such as **www.calderasystems.com** and **www.redhat.com** also provide online documentation for installing and compiling the kernel on their systems. There are also several Linux HOWTOs on the subject. You can find the HOWTOS online at **www.linux.org** and at distribution Web sites. The kernel source code software packages also include extensive documentation. Kernel source code files are always installed in the **/usr/src/linux** directory. In this directory you will also find a subdirectory named **Documentation** that contains an extensive set of files and directories documenting kernel features, modules, and commands.

To install a new kernel, you need to download the software packages for that kernel to your system. You can download them either from your Linux distribution's FTP sites or from **www.kernel.org**. You can install a new kernel either by downloading a binary version from your distribution's Web site and installing it, or by downloading the source code, compiling the kernel, and then installing the resulting binary file. The source code is available either from your distributor or from **www.kernel.org**. Wherever you download a kernel version from, it will always be the same. The source code downloaded for a particular kernel version from Red Hat is the same as the one for the same version from OpenLinux, and the same for **www.kernel.org** (though the configuration may differ). Patches for that version can be applied to any distribution.

Precautionary Steps

You should retain a copy of your current kernel, so that you can use it again in case
something goes wrong with the new one. This simply involves making a backup copy
of the kernel file. The kernel file will have different names on various distributions. On
Red Hat and OpenLinux it is called **vmlinuz**, but others may call it **zImage**. Even Red
Hat and OpenLinux, though they use the same name, place it in different directories.

On OpenLinux, the name of the kernel file is **/vmlinuz**. You can use the **cp**
command to make a copy of it, giving it a name like **/vmlinuz.back** (do not use
vmlinuz.old for a name). However, OpenLinux also stores a copy of the kernel file in
the **/boot** directory, giving it a name like **vmlinuz-2.2.5-modular**. You can use this file
as your backup file if you wish, or make one of your own as shown here.

```
cp /vmlinuz /vmlinuz.back
```

On Red Hat, **vmlinuz** is located in the **/boot** directory and is itself only a symbolic
link to the actual kernel file. The kernel file will be named something like
vmlinuz2.2-15. The name usually includes the kernel version number, already giving it a
unique file name. The new kernel will be installed with a file name using its own version
number. However, to be on the safe side it may be advisable to make a backup copy.

```
cp /boot/vmlinuz2.2-15  /boot/vmlinuz2.2-15.back
```

If you are using LILO, you should create a new entry for the old kernel in the
lilo.conf file. You then make an entry for the new kernel in the **lilo.conf** file. It is
advisable to leave the entry for the old kernel in case something should go wrong with
the new one. That way you could always reboot and select the old kernel. In **lilo.conf**
just add a new entry, similar to the one for the old kernel, that references the new
kernel in its image line. The **lilo.conf** entry would look something like the following.
Be sure to execute the **lilo** command to update LILO with the new **lilo.conf** entries.
You could then use the label "oldlinux2.2-5" at the LILO prompt to launch the
old kernel.

```
image = /boot/vmlinuz2.2-15.back
    label = oldlinux2.2-5
    root = /dev/hda3
    read-only
```

It is also advisable to have a boot disk ready just in case something goes wrong
with the installation. On OpenLinux and Red Hat systems you can create a boot disk
using the **mkbootdisk** utility.

Examine your **lilo.conf** file to find out the name of the boot image you are currently loading. It is in the line beginning with **image =** as in the following.

```
image = /boot/vmlinuz
```

On Red Hat systems the name of the boot file is **/boot/vmlinuz**, but on other systems, including OpenLinux, the name of the boot file is **/vmlinuz**. Use the boot image file to create your boot disk.

```
mkbootdisk --device /vmlinuz
```

Installing the Distribution Kernel Binaries and Source: RPM

You can obtain RPM packages for the Linux kernel from your distribution's update sites. For example, to download a new kernel for Red Hat, locate the kernel RPM packages from **updates.redhat.com** or its mirror sites. There will be a series of RPM packages, all beginning with the term "kernel." There are also nonkernel packages you may need that contain updated system configuration files used by the new kernel. As an example, the kernel packages for the 2.2 kernel are listed here. Only install one of the **kernel-**_version_**-ix86** packages. Choose the one for your machine, for example i686 for a Pentium II, i586 for a Pentium, and i386 for other PCs.

```
kernel-2.2.5-22.i386.rpm
kernel-2.2.5-22.i586.rpm
kernel-2.2.5-22.i686.rpm
kernel-BOOT-2.2.5-22.i386.rpm
kernel-doc-2.2.5-22.i386.rpm
kernel-headers-2.2.5-22.i386.rpm
kernel-ibcs-2.2.5-22.i386.rpm
kernel-pcmcia-cs-2.2.5-22.i386.rpm
kernel-smp-2.2.5-22.i586.rpm
kernel-smp-2.2.5-22.i686.rpm
kernel-source-2.2.5-22.i386.rpm
initscripts-4.16-1.i386.rpm.
mkinitrd-2.0-1.i386.rpm
SysVinit-2.74-11.i386.rpm.
```

You are now ready to install the new kernel. First install any nonkernel support packages. For Red Hat and OpenLinux these currently include mkinitrd, SysVinit, and iniscripts. Use the **-Uvh** option to update those packages.

```
# rpm -Uvh mkinitrd*rpm SysVinit*rpm initscripts*rpm
```

It is also essential that you install the source code and headers for the kernel. You use the source code to generate any modules and tailor the kernel to your own needs. For example, you can use the source code to generate modules containing devices drivers for any uncommon devices you may have installed.

```
# rpm -Uvh kernel-headers-2.0.36-1.i386.rpm
# rpm -Uvh kernel-source-2.0.36-1.i386.rpm
```

You can now install the kernel. On Red Hat systems you install the kernel, kernel-ibcs, and the kernel-pcmia-cs packages. As a safety precaution, it is advisable to preserve your old kernel, just in case the new one should not work out for some reason. This involves installing with the install (**-i**) instead of the update (**-U**) option, creating a separate RAM disk for the new kernel, and then modifying **lilo.conf** to have LILO start up using the new kernel.

```
# rpm -ivh kernel-2.0.36-1.i386.rpm kernel-ibcs-2.0.36-1.i386.rpm
kernel-pcmcia-cs-2.0.36-1.i386.rpm
```

On Red Hat Linux, kernels are installed in the **/boot** directory. Performing an **ls -l** operation on this directory will list all the currently installed kernels. There will be a file for your old kernel and a file for your new one, as well as a link file called **vmlinuz** that links to the new kernel file. If you took the precautions described in the previous section, "Precautionary Steps," you may have already renamed the older kernel. If you are using LILO, you will not have to change the **lilo.conf** file, as the entry to invoke the kernel still references the **/boot/vmlinuz** link, which now points to the new kernel. Red Hat boots the kernel using the **/boot/vmlinuz** link to the kernel file. In your **lilo.conf** file, the image line for the kernel file will reference this link.

```
image = /boot/vmlinuz
```

For OpenLinux, the binary and documentation kernel packages begin with the term "linux-kernel," and the source code files begin with "linux-source." The kernel-binary package contains the compiled kernel, ready to install. For the source code, be sure to download the **linux-include**, **linux-source-common**, and source code package for your platform. For PCs it is linux-source-i386, shown next. There are also kernel source versions for the Mac and Sun.

```
linux-kernel-binary-2.2.5-1.i386.rpm
linux-kernel-doc-2.2.5-1.i386.rpm
linux-kernel-include-2.2.5-1.i386.rpm
linux-source-common-2.2.5-1.i386.rpm
linux-source-i386-2.2.5-1.i386.rpm
SysVinit-2.77.3-1.i386.rpm
SysVinit-scripts.1.04-5.i386.rpm.
```

Download and install the packages with the **rpm** command. You may want to make a backup copy of the old kernel first.

```
rpm -Uvh linux-kernel-binary-vnum.i386.rpm
```

The kernel file is copied both to the **/boot** directory and to the root directory, where it is called **/vmlinuz**. It is from this file that OpenLinux will boot the kernel. In your **lilo.conf** file, the image line for the kernel file will reference this file.

```
image = /vmlinuz
```

In the **/boot** directory, the name of kernel is **vmlinuz-*Ver*-modular**, where *Ver* is the version number, as in **vmlinuz-2.2.5-modular**. Also in this directory is a file called **WHATSIN-*ver*-modular** that is a log of all the features included or not included in the kernel binary.

Installing Compressed Archives: tar.gz

You can also download the compressed archive from **www.kernel.org** and its mirror sites. In this case you first decompress and extract the archive with the following commands. The *vnum* is the version number.

```
cd /usr/src
gzip -cd linux-2.2.vnum.tar.gz | tar xfv -
```

For some releases, you can simply update your current kernel source code files using patches. A patch will modify a source code file, making required changes. To install a patch, download the patch file and then execute the following command. The patch file is first decompressed, and then the **patch** command implements the changes.

```
cd /usr/src
gzip -cd patchvnum.gz | patch -p0
```

You may have to implement several patches, depending upon how out of date your kernel is. In that case you have to execute a patch operation for each patch file needed. As an alternative, you can use the patch-kernel script, which determines your kernel version and applies the patches needed.

```
cd /usr/src
linux/scripts/patch-kernel
```

Before you can install the kernel, you have to configure and compile it, as discussed in the next section.

Compiling the Kernel

You can compile a kernel using the Linux kernel source code. One advantage to compiling the kernel is that you are able to customize its configuration, selecting particular devices you want supported by the kernel or the kind of networking support you want. You have more control over exactly what your operating system will support. You can obtain the most recent version of the source code from **www.kernel.org** or **www.linuxhq.com**. There are also RPM packages of kernel sources available. If you are downloading a compressed archive (**.tar.gz**) package, be sure to unpack it in the **/usr/src** directory. The archive extracts a directory named **linux** that holds the source code files. This way the files are located in the **/usr/src/linux** directory. There are links already set up in the **/usr/include** directory to source files in the **/usr/src/linux** directory. They expect to find the source code in **/usr/src/linux**.

Once the source is installed, you then have to configure the kernel. Configuration consists of determining the features that you want to provide kernel-level support for. This includes drivers for different devices such as sound cards and SCSI devices. This process is referred to as configuring the kernel. You can configure features as directly included in the kernel itself or as modules that the kernel can load as they are needed. You can also specifically exclude features. Features incorporated directly into the kernel will make for a larger kernel program. Features set up as separate modules can also be easily updated.

You can configure the kernel using one of several available configuration tools: **config**, **menuconfig**, and **xconfig**. They perform the same configuration tasks, but use different interfaces. The **config** tool is a simple configure script providing line-based prompts for different configuration options. The **menuconfig** tool provides a cursor-based menu that you can still run from the command line. There are menu entries for different configuration categories, and you can pick and choose the ones you want. To mark a feature for inclusion in the kernel, move to it and press the SPACEBAR. An asterisk will appear in the empty parenthesis to the left of the entry. If you want to make it a module, press M and an M will appear in the parenthesis. The **xconfig** tool runs on a window manager and provides a window interface with buttons and menus.

You can use your mouse to select entries. A menu of configuration categories are listed as buttons that you can click.

You start a configuration tool by preceding it with the **make** command. Be sure you are in the **/usr/src/linux** directory. The process of starting a configuration tool is a **make** operation that uses the Linux kernel Makefile. The **xconfig** tool should be started from a Terminal window on your window manager. The **menuconfig** and **config** tools are started on a shell command line. The following example lists commands to start **xconfig**, **menuconfig**, or **config**.

```
make xconfig
make menuconfig
make config
```

The **xconfig** tool will open a Linux Kernel Configuration window listing the different configuration categories (see Figure 27-17). Buttons at the right of the screen are used to save the configuration or copy it to a file as well as quit. Clicking an entry opens a window that lists different features you can include. There are three check boxes to the left of each entry that let you choose to have a feature compiled directly into the kernel, created as a separate module that can be loaded at run time, or not included at all. As a rule, features in continual use such as network and file system support should be compiled directly into the kernel. Features that could easily change such as sound cards, or features used less frequently, should be compiled as modules. The **xconfig** tool also provides context-sensitive help for each entry. To the right of an entry is a Help button. Click it to display a detailed explanation of what that feature does and why you would include it either directly or as a module, or even exclude it. When in doubt about a feature, always use the Help button to find out what exactly it does and why you would want to use it.

In most cases, you will want to make sure that your kernel can load modules. Click the Loadable Modules Support button to display a listing of several module management options. Make sure that Enable Loadable Module Support is set to Yes. This feature allows your kernel to load modules. Kernel Module Loader should also be Yes, as this allows your kernel to load any modules as they are needed. The Set Version Information entry allows you to use any modules that were set up for previous kernels.

The General Setup window lets you select general features such as math emulation, networking, and PCI BIOS support, as well as support for ELF and a.out binaries. The Block Devices window lists entries that enable support for your IDE floppy and hard drive. There are also special features such as RAM disk support and the loopback device for mounting CD-ROM image files.

The Networking Options window shown in Figure 27-18 lists an extensive set of networking capabilities. The TCP/IP Networking entry has to be set to enable any kind of Internet networking. Here you can specify features that will enable your system to operate as a gateway, firewall, or router. Network Aliasing will enable support for IP

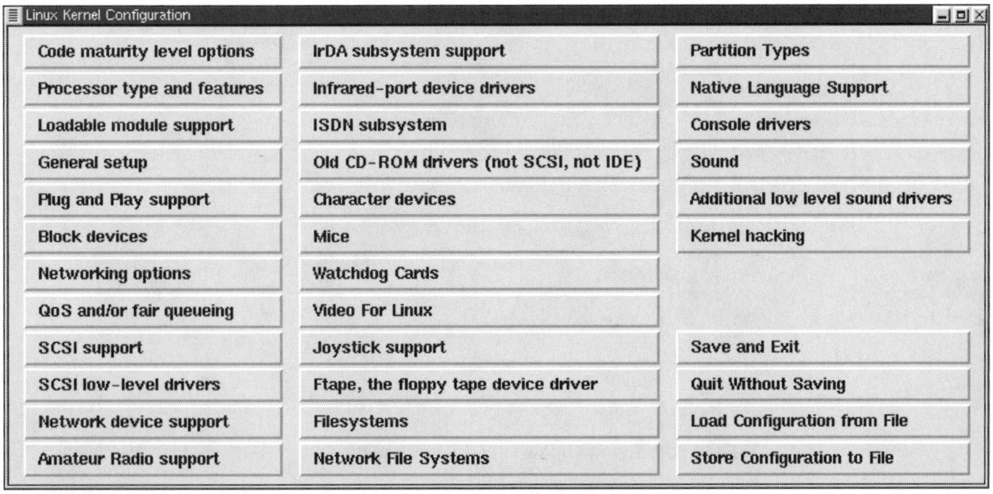

Figure 27-17. *The xconfig Linux kernel configuration tool*

aliases. There is also support for other kinds of networks including AppleTalk and IPX. AppleTalk has to be enabled if you want to use NetaTalk to connect to a Macintosh system on your network.

If you have any SCSI devices on your system, make sure that the entries in the SCSI support window are set to yes. Here you enable support for SCSI disks, tape drives, and CD-ROMs. The SCSI Low-Level Drivers window displays an extensive list of SCSI devices currently supported by Linux. Select the ones you have. The Network Device Support window lists several general features along with an extensive list of drivers for network devices such as Ethernet cards as well as PPP and SLIP connections. In the CD-ROM Drivers window, select the drivers for your CD-ROMs.

The Filesystems window shown in Figure 27-19 lists the different types of file systems that Linux can support. These include DOS, VFAT (Windows 95), and ISO9660 (CD-ROM) file systems. Network file systems such as NFS, SMB (Samba), and NCP (NetWare), HFS (Macintosh) and NTFS (Windows NT—read only with 2.2) are also listed.

The Character Devices window lists features for devices such as your keyboard, mouse, and serial ports. There is support for both serial and bus mice. The Sound window lists different sound cards supported by the kernel. Select the one on your system. You will also have to provide the IRQ, DMA, and Base I/O that your sound card uses. The Kernel Hacking window lists features of interest to programmers interested in modifying the kernel code. You can have the kernel include debugging information.

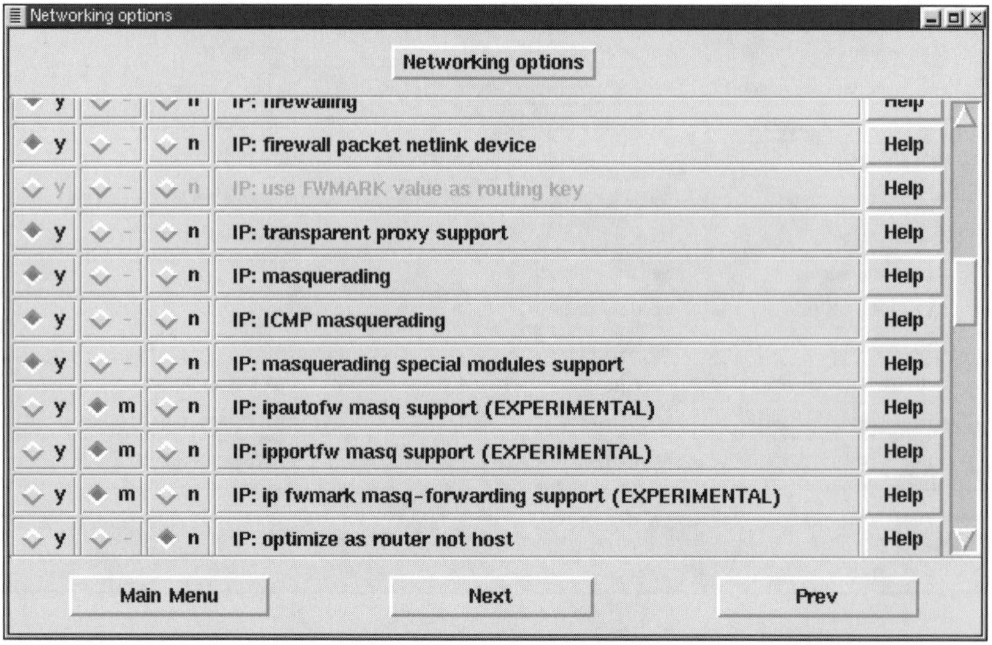

Figure 27-18.   *Networking Options in xconfig*

Once you have set your options, you then save your configuration. You can also make a backup copy by clicking Save To File. Now that the configuration is ready, you can compile your kernel. You first need to generate a dependency tree that will determine what part of the source code to compile based on your configuration. Use the following command:

```
make dep
```

It is a good idea to also clean up any stale object and dependency files that may remain from a previous compilation. Use the following command to remove such files.

```
make mrproper
```

There are several options you can use to compile the kernel. The **zImage** option simply generates a kernel file called **zImage** and places it in the **/usr/src/linux***Ver***/arch** directory. The **install** option will both generate the kernel file and install it on your system as either **vmlinuz** or **zImage**. The **zlilo** option will install the kernel file as

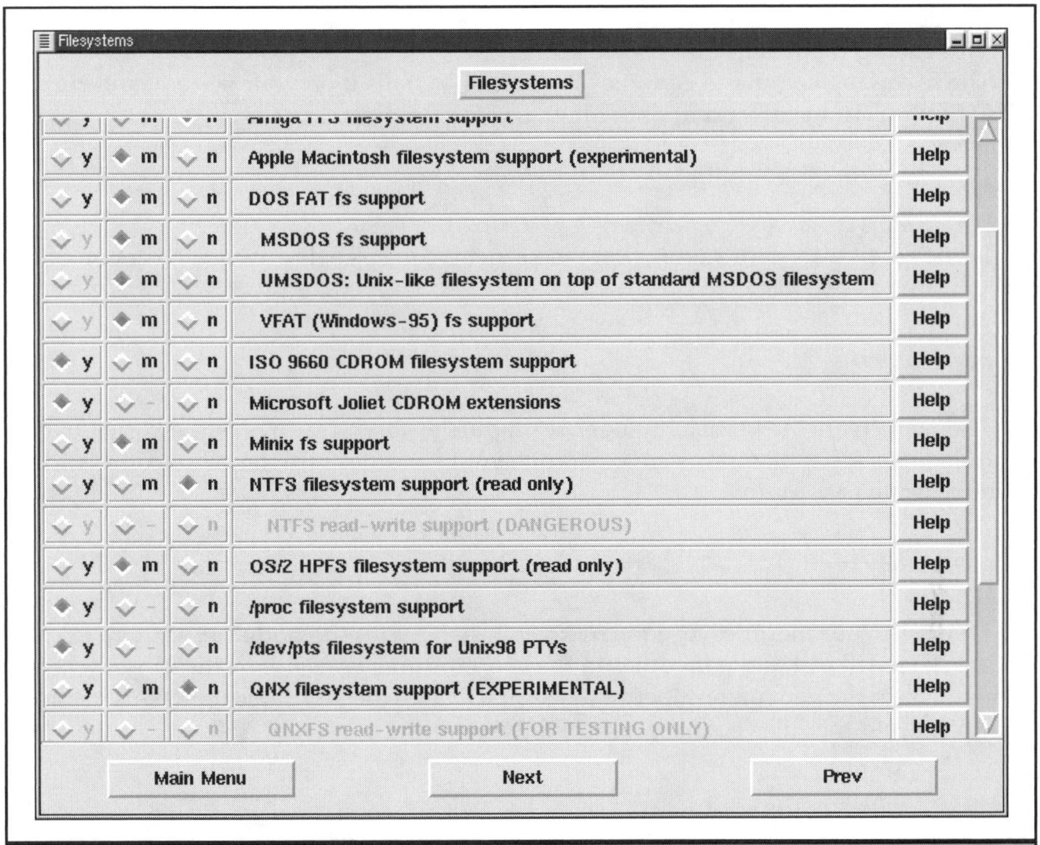

Figure 27-19.   *File systems*

well but will also run LILO to update LILO. It is designed for use with systems that run LILO. To manually install a kernel file generated by zImage, you have to copy the **zImage** file to the directory where the kernel resides and give it the name used on your distribution, such as **/vmlinuz** for OpenLinux. Be sure to back up the old kernel file first.

The compile options operate slightly differently depending on the distribution kernel source packages you downloaded. The OpenLinux kernel sources will install the kernel file to the **/vmlinuz** file for both the **install** and **zlilo** options. The Red Hat kernel sources will install the kernel file to the boot directory and set up a link to **/boot/vmlinuz** for both the **install** and **zlilo** options.

In addition, another set of corresponding options are available that allow you to generate a more efficient and larger kernel. These begin with the letter *b*. The **bzImage** option creates a kernel file called **bzImage**. The **bzlilo** option will both install the kernel file on your system and run LILO. You should use these options if you receive an error saying that your kernel is too big.

The following command compiles the kernel, installs it on your system, and runs LILO for you. To install and update LILO, use the following.

```
make zlilo
```

If you receive an error saying that the kernel is too large, try using a *b* version of the option, such as **bzlilo**.

```
make bzlilo
```

This will create the kernel, but not the modules—those features of the kernel to be compiled into separate modules. To compile your modules, use the **make** command with the **modules** argument.

```
make modules
```

To install your modules, use the **make** command with the **modules_install** option. This will install the modules in the **/lib/modules/**version-num directory, where *version-num* is the version number of the kernel. It may be advisable to make a backup copy of the old modules before you install the new ones.

```
make modules_install
```

Other **make** options are listed in Table 27-17.

LILO Configurations

If you are using LILO, you can configure your system to let you start any of your installed kernels. As seen in the "Precautionary Steps" section, you can create an added entry in the **lilo.conf** file for your old kernel. As you install new kernel versions, you could just add more entries, letting you use any of the previous kernels. For example, you could install a developmental version of the kernel, along with a current stable version, while keeping your old version. In the image line for each entry you would specify the file name of the kernel. Whenever you add a new entry, be sure to execute the **lilo** command to update LILO. In the next example, the **lilo.conf** file contains entries for two Linux kernels, as well as windows.

/etc/lilo.conf

```
boot = /dev/hda
install = /boot/boot.b
message = /boot/message
prompt
timeout = 200
default = win
image = /boot/vmlinuz-2.2.5-15
        label = linux
        root = /dev/hda3
        read-only
image = /boot/vmlinuz-2.0.36
        label = linux-2.0
        root = /dev/hda3
        read-only
other = /dev/hda1
        label = win
        table = /dev/hda
```

Module RAM Disks

If your system requires that certain modules be loaded when you boot, then you may have to create a RAM disk for them. For example, if you have SCSI hard drive or CD-ROMs, the SCSI drivers for them are often held in modules that are loaded whenever you start up your system. These modules are stored in a RAM disk that the startup process reads from. If you create a new kernel that needs to load modules to start up, then you have to create a new RAM disk for those modules. When you create a new kernel, you also need to create its modules. You place the modules needed for startup, such as SCSI hard drive modules, in a new RAM disk. In the **lilo.conf** file, add an entry to load this RAM disk. You only need to create a new RAM disk if your kernel has to load modules at startup. If, for example, you use a SCSI hard drive but you incorporated SCSI hard drive and CD-ROM support (including support for the specific model) directly into your kernel, you would not have to set up a RAM disk. Support for IDE hard drives and CD-ROMs is already incorporated directly into the kernel.

If you need to create a RAM disk, you can use the **mkinitrd** command to create a RAM disk image file, or create a RAM disk device. With no options **mkinitrd** will use modules listed in the **/etc/cont.modules** file. See the Man pages for **mkinitrd** and RAM disk documentation for more details. In the **lilo.conf** segment for the new kernel you would place an **initrd** entry specifying the new RAM disk.

```
# mkinitrd /boot/initrd-2.2.5-15.img 2.2.5-15
```

Configuration Tools	Description
config	Line-based interface for kernel configuration
menuconfig	Screen-based interface for kernel configuration
xconfig	X Window System interface for kernel configuration
Maintenance Options	
checkhelp	Checks configuration for options not documented
checkconfig	Checks source tree for missing header files
clean	Removes old object files and dependencies
mrproper	Removes old object files and dependencies
Compiling Options	
zImage	Creates the kernel file called **zImage** located in the **/usr/src/linux/arch** or **arch/i386/boot** directory
install	Creates the kernel and installs it on your system
zlilo	Creates the kernel, installs it on your system, and runs `lilo`
zdisk	Creates a kernel file and installs it on a floppy disk (creates a boot disk)
bzImage	Creates the kernel file and calls it **bzImage**
bzlilo	Creates and installs the kernel and runs `lilo`
bzdisk	Creates the kernel and installs it on a floppy disk (creates a boot disk)
Module Options	
modules	Creates kernel modules
modules-install	Installs kernel modules in the **/lib/modules** directory

Table 27-17.   *Kernel Compile Options, Use as Arguments to the Make Command in /usr/src/linux*

In your **lilo.conf** file there would be an **initrd** entry for the kernel, specifying the RAM disk to use.

```
image=/boot/vmlinuz-2.2.5-15
          label=linux
          root=/dev/hda3
          initrd=/boot/initrd-2.2.5-15.img
          read-only
```

LILO

You can configure your Linux Loader (LILO) using the **/etc/lilo.conf** file and the command **lilo**. If you examine your **/etc/lilo.conf** file, you will find it organized into different segments called stanzas, one for each operating system that LILO is to start up. If your Linux system shares your computer with a DOS system, you should see two stanzas listed in your **/etc/lilo.conf** file, one for Linux and one for DOS. Each stanza will indicate the hard disk partition that the respective operating system is located on. It will also include an entry for the label. This is the name you enter at the LILO prompt to start that operating system.

You can, if you wish, make changes directly to the **/etc/lilo.conf** file using a text editor. Whenever you make a change, you have to execute the **lilo** command to have it take effect. Type **lilo** and press ENTER.

```
# lilo
```

You can also configure LILO using the LILO panels in Linuxconf. There you can add segments and specify options. When you activate your changes in Linuxconf, the **/etc/lilo.conf** file will be updated and the **lilo** command will be run.

/etc/lilo.conf

```
# general section
boot = /dev/hda
# wait 20 seconds (200 10ths) for user to select the entry to load
timeout = 200
message = /boot/message
prompt
# default entry
default = win
vga = normal
map=/boot/map
install=/boot/boot.b
image = /boot/vmlinuz-2.2.5-15
        label = linux
        root = /dev/hda4
        read-only
```

```
other = /dev/hda1
        label = win
        table=/dev/hda
```

Unless specified by the **default** entry, the default operating system that LILO boots is the one whose segment is the first listed in the **lilo.conf** file. Should the Linux stanza is the first listed, this is the one that LILO will boot if you do not enter anything at the LILO prompt. If you would like to have your Windows system be the default, you can use **lilo** with the **-D** option to reset the default, or edit the **lilo.conf** file to assign a value to **default**. You could also use a text editor to place the Windows stanza first, before the Linux stanza. Be sure to execute **lilo** to have the change take effect. The next time you start your system, you could just press ENTER at the LILO prompt to have Windows loaded, instead of typing **dos**.

```
# lilo -D dos
```

Command Line Options	lilo.conf Options	Description
-b *bootdev*	**boot=***bootdev*	Boot device
-c	**compact**	Enable map compaction; speeds up booting
-d *dsec*	**delay=***dsec*	Timeout delay to wait for you to enter the label of an operating system at the LILO prompt when you boot up
-D *label*	**default=***label*	Use the kernel with the specified label, instead of the first one in the list, as the default kernel to boot
-i *bootsector*	**install=***bootsector*	File to be used as the new boot sector
-f *file*	**disktab=***file*	Disk geometry parameter file
-l	**linear**	Generate linear sector addresses instead of sector/head/cylinder addresses (for very large hard disks)
-m *mapfile*	**map=***mapfile*	Use specified map file instead of the default
-P fix	**fix-table**	Fix corrupt partition tables
-P ignore	**ignore-table**	Ignore corrupt partition tables

Table 27-18. *LILO Options for Command Line and lilo.conf*

You can set a number of LILO options using either command line options or options in the **lilo.conf** file. These are listed in Table 27-18.

If you are booting an operating system from a location other than the first hard disk, you need to include a loader line for the **chain.b** file in its stanza.

```
loader=/boot/chain.b
```

For a very large hard disk, be sure to enter the linear option in the general section.

```
linear
```

Command Line Options	lilo.conf Options	Description
-s *file*	**backup=***file*	Alternate save file for the boot sector
-S *file*	**force-backup=***file*	Allow overwriting of existing save file
-v	**verbose=***level*	Increase verbosity
-u		Uninstall LILO, by copying the saved boot sector back
-V		Print version number
-t		Test only. Do not really write a new boot sector or map file. Use together with **-v** to find out what LILO is about to do.
-I *label*		Display label and pathname of running kernel. Label is held in BOOT_IMAGE shell variable
	timeout=*dsec*	Timeout delay waits for you to enter the label of an operating system at the LILO prompt when you boot up
	image=*Linux-kernel*	Path name for boot image of a Linux kernel
	other=*os-boot-image*	Path name for boot image of a non-Linux operating system
	read-only	Boot Linux kernel as read only (system startup remounts as read/write)

Table 27-18.   *LILO Options for Command Line and lilo.conf* (continued)

Chapter 28

Network Administration

L inux systems are configured to connect into networks that use the TCP/IP
protocols. These are the same protocols that the Internet, as well as many local
networks, use. In Chapter 10 you were introduced to TCP/IP, a robust set of
protocols that are designed to provide communications between systems with different
operating systems and hardware. The protocols were developed in the 1970s as a
special DARPA project to enhance communications between universities and research
centers. The protocols were originally developed on Unix systems, with much of the
research carried out at the University of California, Berkeley. Linux, as a version of
Unix, benefits from much of this original focus on Unix.

The TCP/IP protocols actually consist of different protocols, each designed for
a specific task in a TCP/IP network. The two basic protocols are the Transmission
Control Protocol (TCP), which handles receiving and sending communications, and
the Internet Protocol (IP), which handles transmitting communications. Other protocols
provide various network services. The Domain Name Service (DNS) provides address
resolution. The File Transfer Protocol (FTP) provides file transmission, and Network
File Systems (NFS) provides access to remote file systems. Table 28-1 lists the different
TCP/IP protocols.

Administering and configuring a TCP/IP network on your Linux system is not
particularly complicated. There is a set of configuration files that your system uses to
set up and maintain your network. Later in this chapter (in the section called "TCP/IP
Configuration Files"), Table 28-2 will provide a complete listing. Many of these can be
managed using administrative programs such as Linuxconf or **netcfg** on your root user
desktop. You can also use the more specialized programs, such as **netstat**, **ifconfig**, and
route. Some configuration files are easy to modify yourself using a text editor. Also
later in this chapter (in the section called "Network Interfaces and Routes: ifconfig and
route"), Table 28-3 will list the commonly used network administration programs.

Most distributions, including Red Hat, OpenLinux, and SuSE, will let you configure
your network during installation. If you did so, then your system is ready to go. If you
need to later change your configuration, you may find the information in this chapter
helpful. On many distributions, including Red Hat and OpenLinux, your network
interface is started up using the network script in the **/etc/rc.d/init.d** directory. You can
manually shut down and restart your network interface using this script and the
start or **stop** options. The following commands will shut down and then start up
your network interface:

```
/etc/rc.d/init.d/network stop
/etc/rc.d/init.d/network start
```

To test if your interface is working, use the **ping** command with an IP address of a
system on your network, such as your gateway machine. The **ping** command will
continually repeat until you stop it with a CTRL-C.

Transport	Description
TCP	Transmission Control Protocol; places systems in direct communication
UDP	User Datagram Protocol
Routing	
IP	Internet Protocol; transmits data
ICMP	Internet Control Message Protocol; status messages for IP
RIP	Routing Information Protocol; determines routing
OSPF	Open Shortest Path First; determines routing
Network Addresses	
ARP	Address Resolution Protocol; determines unique IP address of systems
DNS	Domain Name Service; translates hostnames into IP addresses
RARP	Reverse Address Resolution Protocol; determines addresses of systems
User Services	
FTP	File Transfer Protocol; transmits files from one system to another using TCP
TFTP	Trivial File Transfer Protocol; transfers files using UDP
TELNET	Remote login to another system on the network
SMTP	Simple Mail Transfer Protocol; transfers e-mail between systems
Gateway	
EGP	Exterior Gateway Protocol; provides routing for external networks
GGP	Gateway-to-Gateway Protocol; provides routing between Internet gateways

Table 28-1. *TCP/IP Protocols*

Gateway	Description
IGP	Interior Gateway Protocol; provides routing for internal networks
Network Services	
NFS	Network File Systems; allows mounting of file systems on remote machines
NIS	Network Information Service; maintains user accounts across a network
RPC	Remote Procedure Call; allows programs on remote systems to communicate
BOOTP	Boot Protocol; starts system using boot information on server for network
SNMP	Single Network Management Protocol; provides status messages on TCP/IP configuration
DHCP	Dynamic Host Control Protocol; automatically provides network configuration information to host systems

Table 28-1.   *TCP/IP Protocols* (continued)

```
ping 192.168.1.42
```

TCP/IP networks are configured and managed with a set of utilities: **ifconfig**, **route**, and **netstat**. The **ifconfig** utility operates from your root user desktop and allows you to fully configure your network interfaces, adding new ones and modifying others. The **ifconfig** and **route** utilities are lower-level programs that require more specific knowledge of your network to use effectively. The **netstat** utility provides you with information about the status of your network connections. If your system does not have a direct hardware connection to a network, such as an Ethernet connection, and you dial into a network through a modem, you will probably have to set up a SLIP or PPP connection. If you are using an Internet service provider, you have to set up such a connection.

TCP/IP Network Addresses

As explained in Chapter 10, a TCP/IP address is organized into four segments consisting of numbers separated by periods. This is called the IP address. Part of this address is used for the network address, and the other part is used to identify a particular interface on a host in that network. It is important to realize that IP addresses are assigned to interfaces, like Ethernet cards or modems, not to the host computer as such. Often a computer has only one interface, and is accessed using only that interface's IP address. In that regard, an IP address can be thought of as identifying a particular host system on a network and, as such, the IP address is usually referred to as the host address.

In fact, though, a host system could have several interfaces, each with its own IP address. This is the case for computers that operate as gateways and firewalls from the local network to the Internet. There is usually one interface connecting to the local network and another to the Internet, as in two Ethernet cards. Each interface (such as an Ethernet card) will have its own IP address. For example, when you use Linuxconf to specify an IP address for an Ethernet card on your system, the panel for entering your IP address is labeled as Adapter 1, and there are three other panels for different adapters. These are for other Ethernet cards that have their own IP address. Currently, the Linux kernel can support up to four network adapters. If you use a modem to connect to an ISP, then you would set up a PPP interface that would also have its own IP address (usually dynamically assigned by the PPP). It is important to keep this distinction in mind if you plan to use Linux to set up a local or home network, using Linux as your gateway machine to the Internet (see "IP Masquerading" later in this chapter).

The network address identifies the network that a particular interface on a host is a part of. Usually, the network part of the address takes up the first three segments and the interface/host takes the last segment. Altogether, this forms a unique address with which to identify any computer on a TCP/IP network. For example, in the IP address 192.168.1.72, the network part is 192.168.1 and the interface/host part is **72**. The interface/host is a part of a network whose own address is 192.168.1.0. Currently, a new version of the IP protocol is available called IPv6 that will expand the number of possible IP addresses and provide greater security. Most systems, however, still use IPv4.

The IP address of the interface on a host, or host address, is only one of several addresses you will need in order to connect the host to a network. In addition, you will need the network address, broadcast address, gateway address (if there is one), name server address, and a network mask, or *netmask*. If you configured your network during installation, they will all be automatically entered into the appropriate configuration files. (Table 28-2 lists these network configuration addresses.)

Network Address

You can easily figure out the network address using your host address. It is the network part of your host address, with the host part set to **0**. So, the network address for the host address 192.168.1.72 is 192.168.1.0. Systems derive the network address from the host address using the netmask. For those familiar with computer programming, a bitwise AND operation on the netmask and the host address results in zeroing the host part, leaving you with the network part of the host address.

Broadcast Address

The *broadcast address* allows a system to send the same message to all systems on your network at once. As with the network address, you can easily figure it out using your host address; it has the host part of your address set to **255**. The network part remains untouched. So the broadcast address for the host address 192.168.1.72 is 192.168.1.255 (you combine the network part with **255** in the host part).

Gateway Address

Some networks will have a computer designated as the gateway to other networks. Every connection to and from a network to other networks passes through this gateway computer. Most local networks use gateways to establish a connection to the Internet. If you are on this type of network, you will have to provide the gateway address. If your network does not have a connection to the Internet, or you use a standalone system, or dial into an Internet service provider, you may not need a gateway address. The gateway address is the address of the host system providing the gateway service to the network. On many networks, this host is given a host id of **1**; so that, the gateway address for a network with the address 192.168.1 would be 192.168.1.1. However, this is just a convention. To be sure of your gateway address, ask your network administrator for it.

Name Server Addresses

Many networks, including the Internet, have computers that provide a Domain Name Service that translates the domain names of networks and hosts into IP addresses. These are known as the network's domain name servers. The Domain Name Service makes your computer identifiable on a network, using just your domain name rather than your IP address. You can also use the domain names of other systems to reference them, so you don't have to know their IP addresses. You do, however, have to know the IP addresses of any domain name servers for your network. You can obtain the addresses from your system administrator (there is often more than one). Even if you are using an Internet service provider, you will have to know the address of the domain name servers that your ISP operates for the Internet.

Netmask

The *netmask* is used to derive the address of the network you are connected to. The netmask is determined using your host address as a template. All the numbers in the network part of your host address are set to **255**, and the host part is set to **0**. This, then, is your netmask. So the netmask for the host address 192.168.1.72 is 255.255.255.0. The network part, 192.168.1, has been set to 255.255.255, and the host part, **72**, has been set to **0**. Systems can then use your netmask to derive your network address from your host address. They can determine what part of your host address makes up your network address and what those numbers are.

TCP/IP Configuration Files

A set of configuration files in the **/etc** directory, shown in Table 28-2, are used to set up and manage your TCP/IP network. They specify such network information as host and domain names, IP addresses, and interface options. It is in these files that the IP addresses and domain names of other Internet hosts that you want to access are entered. If you configured your network during installation, you will already find that information in these files. The **netcfg,** Linuxconf, and the **netconfig** configuration tools (later described in the section of the same name) provide easy interfaces for entering the configuration data for these files. In addition to the files discussed here, the **/etc/services** file will list network services available on your system, such as FTP and Telnet, and the **/etc/protocols** file will list the TCP/IP protocols supported by your system.

Identifying Hostnames: /etc/hosts

Without the unique IP address that the TCP/IP network uses to identify computers, a particular computer could not be located. Since IP addresses are difficult to use or remember, domain names are used instead. For each IP address, there is a domain name. When you use a domain name to reference a computer on the network, your system translates it into its associated IP address. This address can then be used by your network to locate that computer.

Originally, it was the responsibility of every computer on the network to maintain a list of the hostnames and their IP addresses. This list is still kept in the **/etc/hosts** file. When you use a domain name, your system looks up its IP address in the **hosts** file. It is the responsibility of the system administrator to maintain this list. Because of the explosive growth of the Internet and the development of more and more very large networks, the responsibility for associating domain names and IP addresses has been taken over by domain name servers. However, the **hosts** file is still used to hold the domain names and IP addresses of frequently accessed hosts. Your system will always check your **hosts** file for the IP address of a domain name before taking the added step of accessing a name server.

The format of a domain name entry in the **hosts** file is the IP address followed by the domain name, separated by a space. You can then add aliases for the hostname. After the entry, on the same line, you can enter a comment. A comment is always preceded by a **#** symbol. You will already find an entry in your **hosts** file for "localhost" with the IP address 127.0.0.1. Localhost is a special identification used by your computer to enable users on your system to communicate locally with each other.

Address	Description
Host address	IP address of your system; it has a network part to identify the network you are on and a host part to identify your own system.
Network address	IP address of your network (network part of your host IP address with host part set to **0**).
Broadcast address	IP address for sending messages to all hosts on your network at once (network part of your host IP address with host part set to **255**).
Gateway address	IP address of your gateway system if you have one (usually the network part of your host IP address with host part set to **1**).
Domain name server addresses	IP addresses of domain name servers that your network uses.
Netmask	Network part of your host IP address set to **255** with host part set to **0** (255.255.255.0).
Files	
/etc/hosts	Associates hostnames with IP addresses.
/etc/networks	Associates domain names with network addresses.
/etc/host.conf	Lists resolver options.
/etc/hosts	Lists domain names for remote hosts with their IP addresses.
/etc/resolv.conf	Lists domain name server names, IP addresses (nameserver), and domain names where remote hosts may be located (search).
/etc/protocols	Lists protocols available on your system.
/etc/services	Lists available network services such as FTP and telnet.
/etc/HOSTNAME	Holds the name of your system.

Table 28-2.   *TCP/IP Configuration Addresses and Files*

The IP address 127.0.0.1 is a special reserved address used by every computer for this purpose. It identifies what is technically referred to as a *loopback device*.

/etc/hosts

```
127.0.0.1            turtle.mytrek.com            localhost
192.168.1.72         turtle.mytrek.com
192.168.196.56       pango1.train.com
202.211.234.1        rose.berkeley.edu
```

Network Name: /etc/networks

The **/etc/networks** file holds the domain names and IP addresses of networks that you are connected to, not the domain names of particular computers. Networks have shortened IP addresses. Depending on the type of network, they will use one, two, or three numbers for their IP addresses. You will also have your localhost network IP address 127.0.0.0. This is the network address used for the loopback device.

The IP addresses are entered, followed by the network domain names. Recall that an IP address consists of a network part and a host part. The network part is the network address you will find in the **networks** file. You will always have an entry in this file for the network portion of your computer's IP address. This is the network address of the network your computer is connected to.

/etc/networks

```
loopback 127.0.0.0
mytrek.com 192.168.1.0
```

/etc/HOSTNAME

The **/etc/HOSTNAME** file holds your system's hostname. To change your hostname, you change this entry. The **netcfg** program allows you to change your hostname and will place the new name in **/etc/HOSTNAME**. Instead of displaying this file to find your hostname, you can use the **hostname** command.

```
$ hostname
turtle.mytrek.com
```

Domain Name Service (DNS)

Each computer connected to a TCP/IP network such as the Internet is identified by its own IP address. An *IP address* is a set of four numbers specifying the location of a network and of a host (a computer) within that network. IP addresses are difficult to remember, so a domain name version of each IP address is also used to identify a host. As described in Chapter 13, a domain name consists of two parts, the hostname and the domain. The hostname is the computer's specific name, and the domain identifies the network that the computer is a part of. The domains used for the United States usually have extensions that identify the type of host. For example, **.edu** is used for educational institutions and **.com** is used for businesses. International domains usually have extensions that indicate the country they are located in, such as **.du** for Germany or **.au** for Australia. The combination of a hostname, domain, and extension forms a unique name by which a computer can be referenced. The domain can, in turn, be split into further subdomains.

As you know, a computer on a network can still only be identified by its IP address, even if it has a domain name. You can use a domain name to reference a computer on a network, but this involves using the domain name to look up the corresponding IP address in a database. The network then uses the IP address, not the domain name, to access the computer. Before the advent of very large TCP/IP networks such as the Internet, it was feasible for each computer on a network to maintain a file with a list of all the domain names and IP addresses of the computers connected on its network. Whenever a domain name was used, it was looked up in this file and the corresponding IP address located. You can still do this on your own system for remote systems that you access frequently placing entries in the **/etc/hosts** file.

As networks became larger, it became impractical—and in the case of the Internet, impossible—for each computer to maintain its own list of all the domain names and IP addresses. To provide the service of translating domain addresses to IP addresses, databases of domain names were developed and placed on their own servers. To find the IP address of a domain name, a query is sent to a name server that then looks up the IP address for you and sends it back. In a large network, there can be several name servers covering different parts of the network. If a name server cannot find a particular IP address, it will send the query on to another name server that is more likely to have it.

If you are administering a network and you need to set up a name server for it, you can configure a Linux system to operate as a name server. To do so, you have to start up a name server daemon that then wait for domain name queries. It makes use of several configuration files that enable it to answer requests. The name server software used on Linux systems is the Berkeley Internet Name Domain (BIND) distributed by the Internet Software Consortium (**www.isc.org**). Chapter 20 describes in detail the process of setting up a domain name server.

Name servers are queried by *resolvers*. These are programs specially designed to obtain addresses from name servers. To use domain names on your system, you will have to configure your own resolver. Your local resolver is configured with your **/etc/host.conf** and **/etc/resolv.conf** files.

host.conf

Your **host.conf** file lists resolver options (shown in the following table). Each option can have several fields, separated by spaces or tabs. You can use a **#** at the beginning of a line to enter a comment. The options tell the resolver what services to use. The order of the list is important. The resolver will begin with the first option listed and move on to the next ones in turn. You will find the **host.conf** file in your **/etc** directory along with other configuration files.

Options	Description
order	Specifies sequence of name resolution methods: Options:
	hosts Checks for name in the local **/etc/host** file
	bind Queries a DNS name server for address
	nis Uses Network Information Service protocol to obtain address
alert	Checks addresses of remote sites attempting to access your system; you turn it on or off with the **on** and **off** options
nospoof	Confirms addresses of remote sites attempting to access your system
trim	For checking your local host's file; removes the domain name and checks only for the hostname; allows you to use just a hostname in your host file for an IP address
multi	For checking your local hosts file; allows a host to have several IP addresses; you turn it on or off with the **on** and **off** options

In the next example of a **host.conf** file, the **order** option instructs your resolver first to look up names in your local **/etc/hosts** file and then, if that fails, to query domain name servers. The system does not have multiple addresses.

/etc/host.conf

```
#  host.conf file
#  Lookup names in host file and then check DNS
order bind host
# There are no multiple addresses
multi off
```

/etc/resolv.conf

For the resolver to do its job, it must have access to domain name servers. In the **resolv.conf** file, you provide the resolver with the addresses of the domain name servers that your system has access to. There are three different types of entries that you can make in your **resolv.conf** file, each preceded by one of three keywords: **domain**, **nameserver**, and **search**. For the domain entry, you list the domain name of your system. You can, if you wish, add search entries. A search entry provides a list of domains to try if only a hostname is given. If there is a system that you access frequently, you could enter its domain name in a search entry and then just use its hostname as the address. Your resolver will then try to find the hostname using the domain name listed in the search entry.

Following the search entries, you place your name server entries. For each name server your system has access to, you enter **nameserver** and the name server's IP address. There may be several name servers that you can access. The order is important. Often, networks will have a primary name server, followed by several secondary ones. The primary one is expected to be queried first. To do this, you must have its IP address entered in the first name server entry.

The following is an example of a **resolv.conf** file. The domain of the host computer is **mytrek.com**. The IP addresses of the name servers for this domain are listed in the name server entries. The search entry will allow just the hostname for a computer in the **unc.edu** domain to be used as an address. For example, to access **metalab.unc.edu**, a user would only have to enter the hostname as an address, **metalab**.

/etc/resolv.conf

```
#  resolv.conf file
domain mytrek.com
search unc.edu
nameserver   192.168.1.8
nameserver   192.168.1.9
```

Hardware Specifications

In addition to your configuration files, you may have to also configure support for your networking hardware such as Ethernet cards and modems. Ethernet cards use different modules. During installation, most Linux systems will automatically detect your Ethernet card type and have the appropriate module loaded whenever you boot up. Should you change your Ethernet card, you may have to change the module. On most Linux distributions, you can use Linuxconf to select a new Ethernet module. You can also manually load a module using the **modprobe** command.

For a modem, you should make sure that there is a link by the name of **/dev/modem** to your modem device, which is usually one of the **/dev/cua***num* devices, where *num* is in the range of 0–3. For example, a modem on the second serial port would have a device name of **/dev/cua1**, and **/dev/modem** would be a link to the **/dev/cua1** device file. On most distributions, this is usually done for you during installation. On many systems, you can use a modem configuration tool called **modemtool** to create this link for you. Many modem programs and PPP configuration programs look for the **/dev/modem** file by default.

Network Configuration Tools

Instead of manually editing configuration files, many distributions provided GUI or cursor-based configuration tools that will prompt you for network information. Many distributions incorporate this kind of network configuration into the installation process. If you chose not to configure your network during configuration, or need to make changes to it, you may find it easier and safer to use a network configuration tool. Most distributions include the Linuxconf configuration tool that provides network configuration panels for adding or changing network information. Red Hat, along with other distributions, also provides the Red Hat Network configuration tool, **netcfg**. Certain distributions such as OpenLinux and SuSE include network configuration in their administration program, COAS for OpenLinux and YaST for SuSE.

netcfg (Red Hat)

Red Hat provides an very easy-to-use network configuration tool called **netcfg**. Other systems may also have this tool. On the Red Hat control panel, there is an icon labeled Network Configuration. You can also start it from desktop or window manager's program menus, usually with the entry Network Configuration. The **netcfg** window consists of four panels and a button bar at the top for each one: Names, Hosts, Interfaces, and Routing (see Figure 28-1). Clicking on a button will display its panel. Basic configuration of your network requires that you specify the hostname and IP address of your own system, the IP addresses of your network's name servers and gateway, the network netmask, and your network interfaces. Using the **netcfg** tool, you can enter all this information easily. The Name panel is where you enter your own system's hostname and your network's name server addresses. The Hosts panel lists host IP addresses and their domain names, including those for your own system. On the Interfaces panel, you add and configure your network interfaces such as an Ethernet or PPP interface. The Routing panel is where you specify special routing hosts, including your gateway system. If you already configured your network during installation, you will already find entries in these panels.

The Names panel has two boxes at the top labeled Hostname and Domain. Here, you enter your system's fully qualified domain name and your network's domain name. For example, **turtle.mytrek.com** would be the fully qualified domain name and **mytrek.com** would be the domain name. The panel has two panes, one for search domains and another for name server addresses. For the search domain, you would enter specific domains you want searched for an Internet address. In the name server pane you would enter the IP addresses for your network's name servers. Both the

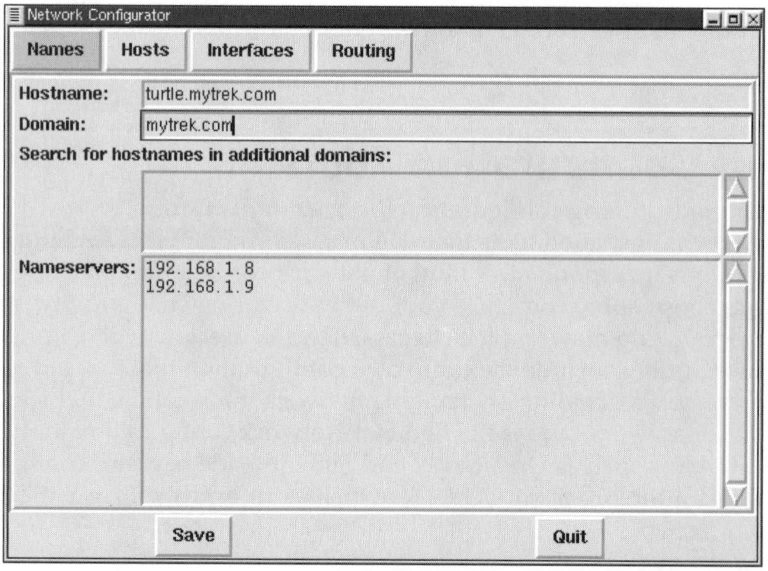

Figure 28-1.   *The netcfg Names panel*

search domain and name server addresses are saved in the **/etc/resolv.conf** file. The hostname is saved to your **/etc/HOSTNAME** file.

The Hosts panel has a single pane with Add, Edit, and Remove buttons (see Figure 28-2). This panel lists entries that associate hostnames with IP addresses. You can also add aliases (nicknames). The Hosts panel actually displays the contents of the **/etc/hosts** file, and will save any entries you make to that file. To add an entry, click on the Add button. A window opens up with boxes for the hostname, IP address, and nicknames. When you click OK, the entry is added to the Hosts list. To edit an entry, click on the Edit button and a similar window opens, letting you change any of the fields. To delete an entry, select it and click on the Remove button.

The Interfaces panel lists configured network interfaces on your system (see Figure 28-3). Making entries here performs the same function as **ifconfig**. An entry will show the interface name, its IP address, preferences, whether it is made active whenever you boot, and whether it is currently active. Use the Add, Edit, Alias, and Remove buttons to manage the interface entries. You use the Activate and Deactive buttons to connect or disconnect the interface with the network. To add an interface, click on the Add button. A window opens—the Choose Interface window—listing possible interfaces, including Ethernet or PPP. Select one and its appropriate interface window appears. For example, if you choose Ethernet, the Edit Ethernet Interface window appears. Here, you enter the IP address for your machine and your network's

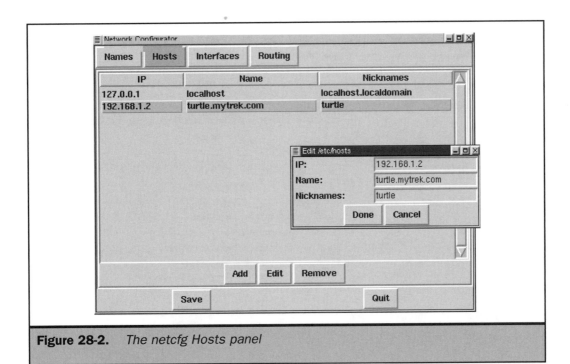

Figure 28-2. *The netcfg Hosts panel*

netmask. You can further choose if you want the interface to automatically start at boot time and whether you want to use the BOOTP or DHCP protocols to configure the interface. When you are finished, you will see your new entry displayed on the Interfaces panel. To activate it, you can click on the Activate button. To make any changes, select it and click on the Edit button. The Alias button lets you create IP aliases for the interface. This lets you assign two IP addresses to the same interface, instructing your system to listen on that interface for packets and messages addressed to either IP address. In effect, you are giving your system two IP addresses.

The Routing panel has boxes at the top for your network's gateway system. In the Default Gateway box, enter the IP address of gateway system, and in the Default Gateway Device box, specify the interface through which you connect to the network serviced by that gateway. This is usually the same interface you use to connect to your network. For example, the device for an Ethernet card would be **eth0**. Should your network use more than one gateway, you can add the others here by clicking on the Add button. If you are on a local area network with no connection to the Internet, you will not have a gateway and need not make any entries here.

When you are finished and ready to save your configuration, click on the Save button. Should you want to abandon the changes you made, you can just Quit without saving. You can run **netcfg** at any time to make changes in your network configuration

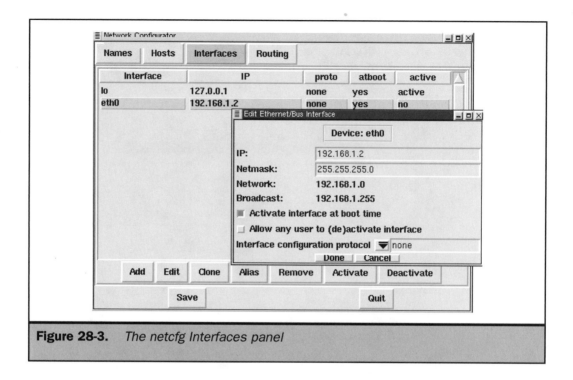

Figure 28-3. *The netcfg Interfaces panel*

or to connect or disconnect manually from a network using the Activate or Deactivate buttons on the Interfaces panel.

You can also use **netcfg** to configure a PPP interface. When you click Add and select PPP as the interface, a window opens up with four panels: Hardware, Communication, Networking, and PAP (see Figure 28-4). The Hardware panel lets you set hardware specifications such as the modem speed and the port used. Select the Communications panel to display entries for your ISP's dial-up phone number, your Expect/Send script entries, and modem initializations. To add or change an Expect/Send entry, click on the Append, Insert, or Edit buttons. A window opens up where you can enter the Expect and Send strings. When you are finished, you can have your modem dial up a connection by just selecting the PPP interface entry, usually ppp0, and clicking on the Activate button. Click on the Deactivate button to disconnect. If you need to edit your PPP configuration, just double-click on the ppp0 interface entry in the Interfaces panel to display the PPP window.

Linuxconf

Linuxconf provides panels for entering network configuration information that will be saved to the appropriate network configuration files when you activate the changes.

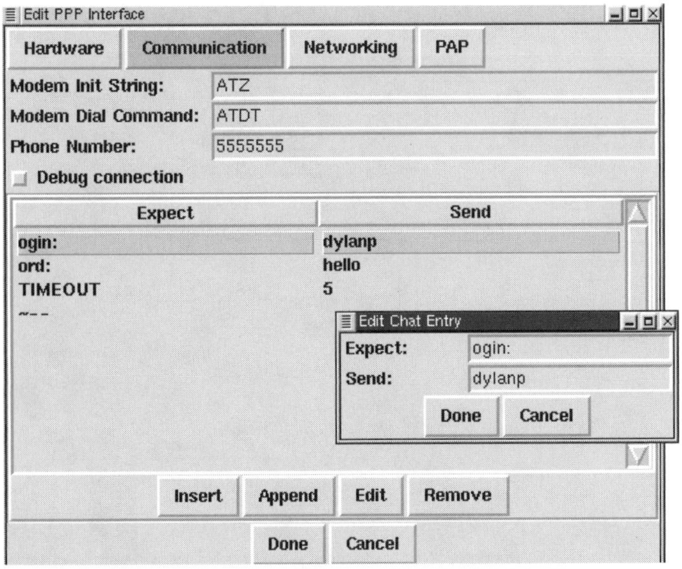

Figure 28-4. *The netcfg PPP configuration*

You use the "Basic host information" panel to enter your system's hostname and interface information. Select the panel from the "Client tasks" list under the Networking" heading under Config. This panel has several tabbed subpanels for the hostname and for different adapters. On the Hostname panel, enter your system's fully qualified domain name (see Figure 28-5). You can also enter the **netconfig** command in a terminal window to display a Linuxconf window for just the network configuration panels (see Chapter 4 and Chapter 27).

You then use a different Adaptor panel for each network interface on your system. Most systems have only one interface, usually an Ethernet or PPP interface. To configure an interface, click on an Adapter tab to display an Adapter panel (see Figure 28-6). On the Adaptor panel, you can use a BOOTP, DHCP, or manual configuration. If the network that this interface connects to provides BOOTP or DHCP configuration services, then your network information will be automatically set up for you. Your system will be configured with an IP address, name server and gateway addresses, and the network netmask. If such configuration services are not provided, you will have to enter your network information manually.

On the Adaptor panel there are several boxes for network interface information, some of which have drop-down menus for selecting entries. In the "Primary name +

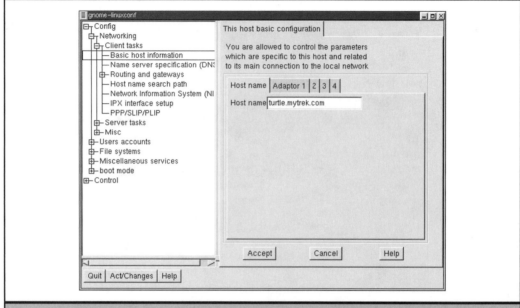

Figure 28-5. *The netcfg PPP configuration*

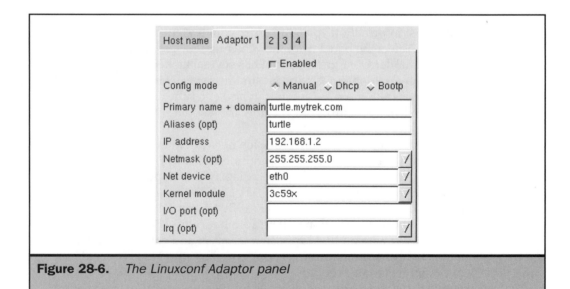

Figure 28-6. *The Linuxconf Adaptor panel*

domain" box enter your system's fully qualified domain name, and in the IP Address box enter your system's IP address. In the Aliases box, you can enter nicknames (these are not IP aliases). For the Netmask box, include your network's netmask. In the Net Device box, you enter the name of your network interface. This box has a drop-down menu listing the different interface devices available. You can select an entry from this menu to make your entry. For example, for an Ethernet card you can select **eth0** from the drop-down menu, or for a modem you could select **ppp0**. The Kernel module box is where you enter the name of the module used for your interface's device. This is usually used for the many modules available for different Ethernet cards. This box has a very long drop-down menu listing all the kernel modules available for your system. Choose the one appropriate for your card. When finished, click the Accept button. If the interface is active, the check box labeled Enabled at the top of the panel will be darkened and recessed. If inactive, it will be lighter and stand out. Click on this check box to toggle the interface on and off.

You will also have to specify your network's domain name servers and search domains. You enter this information in the "Resolver configuration" panel. Select "Name server specification (DNS)" from the "Client tasks" list under the Networking heading. You will find three boxes for name server Internet addresses, starting with the first name server for your network (see Figure 28-7). Enter the IP address for your primary name server in the "nameserver 1" box, and the secondary name sever in the 'nameserver 2" box. Enter your search domains in the "search domain" box. If your network is connected to the Internet it will have a gateway system. You enter the IP address for the gateway in the "Default gateway" box on the Defaults panel in the "Routing and gateways" list. This is located in the "Client tasks" list under the Networking heading.

Should you use a modem instead of an Ethernet card to connect to a network, you need to configure a dial-up interface. With Linuxconf, you can configure a PPP, SLIP, or PLIP interface. Most Internet service providers set up connections over a modem using PPP interfaces. To configure such an interface, click on the PPP/SLIP/PLIP entry in the "Routing and gateways" list under "Client tasks" in Networking. This displays a PPP/SLIP/PLIP panel. When you add an interface, it will display another panel where you can choose the interface you want. If you select PPP, a PPP interface panel is displayed with boxes for dial-up phone number, the interface device, and the login name and password you use to connect to your ISP (see Figure 28-8). If you click on the Customize button, four more tabbed panels are displayed for Hardware, Communications, Networking, and PAP. On the Hardware panel, you can set communication speeds and the modem port, along with PPP options. The Communications panel lets you set the modem initialization string, phone number, and dial-up command, as well as the Expect/Send script used for the ISP login operation. Here, you can specify what password and login prompt to expect. When you are finished, click Accept. When you click on the Linuxconf Activate/Changes

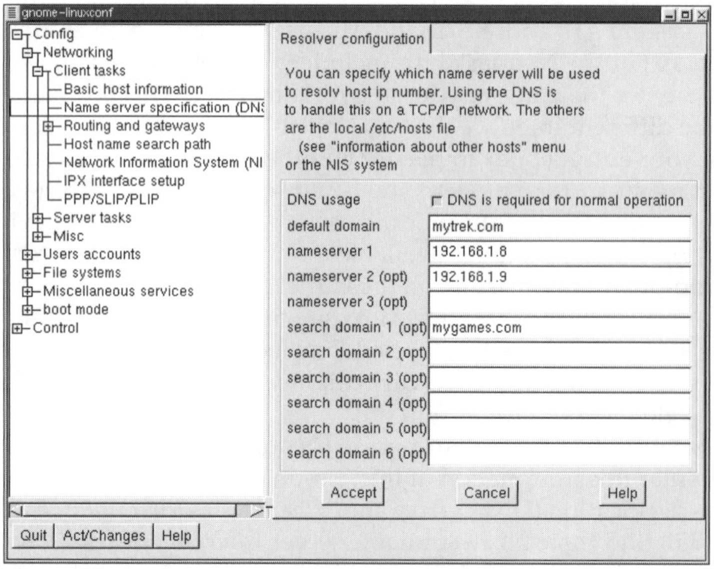

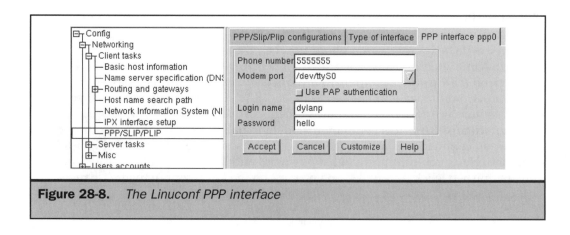

Figure 28-7. *The Linuxconf name server specification*

button, it will save your dial-up configuration to appropriate files, generating any needed scripts. For a PPP connection, it will generate a chat script to dial the connection, and an Expect/Send script for login. To use Linuxconf to connect to your ISP, click on the "Control PPP/SLIP/PLIP links" entry in the "Control panel" list under Control (not Config). This displays a panel in which you can click on a Connect

Figure 28-8. *The Linuconf PPP interface*

button to have your modem dial up and connect to the ISP. You can also use the PPP/SLIP/PLIP entry in the "Routing and gateways" list under "Client tasks" in Networking. For a PPP connection, select the PPP interface panel and click on the Connect button. When finished, click on the Disconnect button.

COAS, LISA (OpenLinux), and YaST (SuSE)

OpenLinux and SuSE provide network configuration as part of their configuration utilities, COAS, LISA, and YaST. To configure a network connection with COAS (Caldera Open Adminstration System), you select Network Administration from the COAS menu. You can then further select Ethernet Interfaces to enter your network settings. This displays a window where you can enter your IP, Gateway, Broadcast addresses, and Netmask, as well as the name of your Ethernet device. When finished, you can then select the Hostname Resolution entry in the Network Administration menu to open a window where you can enter your domain name server addresses. For PPP connections you use a PPP configuration tool like **kppp**.

Lisa (Linux Installation and System Administration tool), used for OpenLinux, has entries for letting you enter network information such as your host, name server, and gateway IP addresses. To use Lisa, just enter the command **lisa** at the command line and move to the Network Configuration menu from the System Configuration entry. You can then choose to configure general network services to enter your domain name server addresses, or choose to enter a hostname. Yet Another Setup Tool (YaST) used on SuSE, provides a similar interface, prompting you to enter various network addresses for your system. Start up YaST and select "Systems administration" and then "Network configuration." From here, you can select "Basic network configuration" to list your network interfaces that you can then configure with your host and gateway IP addresses.

Network Interfaces and Routes: ifconfig and route

Your connection to a network is made by your system through a particular hardware interface such as an Ethernet card or a modem. Data passing through this interface is then routed to your network. The **ifconfig** command configures your network interfaces, and the **route** command will route them accordingly. If you configure an interface with a network configuration tool such as **netcfg**, Linuxconf, or YaST, you do not have to use **ifconfig** or **route**. However, you can directly configure interfaces using **ifconfig** and **route**, if you wish. Every time you start your system, the network interfaces and their routes have to be established. This is done automatically for you when you boot up by **ifconfig** and **route** commands executed for each interface by the **/etc/rc.d/init.d/network** initialization file, which is executed whenever you start your system. If you are manually adding your own interfaces, you will have to set up the network script to perform the **ifconfig** and **route** operations for your new interfaces.

ifconfig

The **ifconfig** command takes as its arguments the name of an interface and an IP address, as well as options. The **ifconfig** command then assigns the IP address to the interface. Your system now knows that there is such an interface and that it references a particular IP address. In addition, you can specify whether the IP address is a host or network address. You can use a domain name for the IP address, provided the domain name is listed along with its IP address in the **/etc/hosts** file. The syntax for the **ifconfig** command is as follows:

```
# ifconfig  interface  -host_net_flag  address  options
```

The *host_net_flag* can be either **-host** or **-net** to indicate a host or network IP address. The **-host** flag is the default. The **ifconfig** command can have several options, which set different features of the interface, such as the maximum number of bytes it can transfer (**mtu**) or the broadcast address. The **up** and **down** options activate and deactivate the interface. In the next example, the **ifconfig** command configures an Ethernet interface:

```
# ifconfig eth0  192.168.1.2
```

For a simple configuration such as this, **ifconfig** automatically generates a standard broadcast address and netmask. The standard broadcast address is the network address with the number **255** for the host address. Remember that the standard netmask is 255.255.255.0. However, if you are connected to a network with a particular netmask and broadcast address, you will have to specify them when you use **ifconfig**. The option for specifying the broadcast address is **broadcast**; for the network mask, it is **netmask**. Table 28-3 at the end of this section lists the different **ifconfig** options. In the next example, **ifconfig** includes the netmask and broadcast address:

```
# ifconfig eth0 192.168.1.2  broadcast 192.168.1.2.55  netmask 255.255.255.0
```

Once you have configured your interface you can use **ifconfig** with the **up** option to activate it, and with the **down** option to deactivate it.

```
# ifconfig eth0 up
```

Point-to-point interfaces such as Parallel IP (PLIP), Serial Line IP (SLIP), and Point-to-Point Protocol (PPP) require that you include the **pointopoint** option. A PLIP interface name is identified with the name **plip** with an attached number; for example, **plip0** is the first PLIP interface. SLIP interfaces use **slip0**, and PPP interfaces start with **ppp0**. Point-to-point interfaces are those that usually operate between only two hosts, such as two computers connected over a modem. When you specify the **pointopoint** option, you need to include the IP address of the host. In the next example, a PLIP interface is configured that connects the computer at IP address 192.168.1.72 with one at 192.168.1.14. If there were domain addresses listed for these systems in **/etc/hosts**, those domain names could be used in place of the IP addresses.

```
# ifconfig  plip0  192.168.1.72  pointopoint 192.168.1.14
```

Should you need to, you can also use **ifconfig** to configure your loopback device. The name of the loopback device is **lo**, and its IP address is the special address 127.0.0.1. The following example shows the configuration:

```
# ifconfig lo 127.0.0.1
```

The **ifconfig** command is very useful for checking on the status of an interface. If you enter the **ifconfig** command alone with the name of the interface, information about that interface is displayed.

```
# ifconfig eth0
```

To see if your loopback interface is configured, you can use **ifconfig** with the loopback interface name, **lo**.

```
# ifconfig lo

lo          Link encap:Local Loopback
            inet addr:127.0.0.1  Bcast:127.255.255.255
Mask:255.0.0.0
            UP BROADCAST LOOPBACK RUNNING  MTU:2000  Metric:1
            RX packets:0 errors:0 dropped:0 overruns:0
            TX packets:12 errors:0 dropped:0 overruns:0
```

Table 28-3 lists the commonly used network administration programs.

Routing

A *packet* that is part of a transmission takes a certain route to reach its destination. On a large network, packets are transmitted from one computer to another until the destination computer is reached. The route determines where the process starts and what computer your system needs to send the packet to in order for it to reach its

Option	Description
interface	Name of the network interface; these are usually located in the **/dev** directory—for example, **/dev/eth0**.
aftype	Address family for decoding protocol addresses; default is inet, currently used by Linux.
up	Activates an interface.
down	Deactivates an interface.
arp	Turns on or off ARP; preceding – turns it off.
trailers	Turns on or off trailers in Ethernet frames; preceding – turns it off.
allmulti	Turns on or off the promiscuous mode; preceding – turns it off. This allows network monitoring.
metric *n*	Cost for interface routing (not currently supported).
mtu *n*	Maximum number of bytes that can be sent on this interface per transmission.
dstaddr *address*	Destination IP address on a point-to-point connection.
netmask *address*	IP network mask; preceding – turns it off.
broadcast *address*	Broadcast address; preceding – turns it off.
point-to-point *address*	Point-to-point mode for interface; if address is included, it is assigned to remote system.
hw	Sets hardware address of interface.
address	Hostname or IP address assigned to interface.

Table 28-3.   *The ifconfig Options*

destination. On small networks, routing may be static—that is, the route from one system to another is fixed. One system knows how to reach another, moving through fixed paths. However, on larger networks and on the Internet, routing is dynamic. Your system knows the first computer to send its packet off to, and then that computer takes it from there, passing it on to another that then determines where to pass it on to. For dynamic routing, your system needs to know very little. Static routing, however, can become very complex, since you have to keep track of all the network connections.

Your routes are listed in your routing table in the **/proc/net/route** file. To display
the routing table, enter **route** with no arguments.

```
# route
Kernel routing table
Destination      Gateway         Genmask        Flags Metric  Ref   Use Iface
loopback            *            255.0.0.0        U     0      0     12  lo
pango1.train.com    *            255.255.255.0    U     0      0      0  eth0
```

Each entry in the routing table has several fields, providing information such as the
route destination and the type of interface used. The different fields are listed in the
following table:

Field	Description
Destination	Destination IP address of the route
Gateway	IP address or hostname of the gateway the route uses; * indicates no gateway is used
Genmask	The netmask for the route
Flags	Type of route: U = up, H = host, G = gateway, D = dynamic, M = modified
Metric	Metric cost of route
Ref	Number of routes that depend on this one
Window	TCP window for AX.25 networks
Use	Number of times used
Iface	Type of interface this route uses

You should have at least one entry in the routing table for the loopback interface.
If not, you will have to route the loopback interface using the **route** command. The IP
address for an interface has to be added to the routing table before you can use that
interface. You add an address with the **route** command and the **add** option.

```
route  add  address
```

The next example adds the IP address for the loopback interface to the routing table:

```
route add 127.0.0.1
```

With the **add** argument, you can add routes either for networks with the **–net** option or with the **–host** option for IP interfaces (hosts). The **–host** option is the default. In addition, you can then specify several parameters for information such as the netmask (**netmask**), gateway (**gw**), interface device (**dev**), and the default route (**default**). If you have more than in IP interface, such as several Ethernet cards, you will have to specify the name of the interface using the **dev** parameter. If your network has a gateway host, you use the **gw** parameter to specify it. If your system is connected to a network, there should be at least one entry in your routing table that specifies the default route. This is the route taken by a message packet when no other route entry leads to its destination. The following example is the routing of an Ethernet interface:

```
# route add 192.168.1.2 dev eth0
```

If your system has only the single Ethernet device as your IP interface, you could leave out the **dev eth0** parameter.

```
# route add 192.168.1.2
```

You can delete any route you've established by invoking **ifconfig** with the **del** argument and the IP address of that route, as in this example:

```
# route del 192.168.1.2
```

You also need to add routes for networks that an IP interface can access. For that, you use the **–net** option. In this example, a route is set up for a system's local area network at 192.168.1.0:

```
# route add -net  192.168.1.0 dev eth0
```

For a gateway, you first add a route to the gateway interface, and then add a route specifying that it is a gateway. The address of the gateway interface in this example is 192.168.1.1:

```
# route add 192.168.1.1
# route add default gw  192.168.1.1
```

If you are using the gateway to access a subnet, add the network address for that network (in this example, 192.168.23.0).

```
# route add -net 192.168.23.0 gw dev eth1
```

To add another IP address to a different network interface on your system, you just use the **ifconfig** and **route** commands with the new IP address. The following command configures a second Ethernet card (eth1) with the IP address 192.168.1.3.

```
ifconfig eth1 192.168.1.3
route add 192.168.1.3 dev eth1
```

Network Startup Script: /etc/rc.d/init.d/network

On OpenLinux and Red Hat systems, the **/etc/rc.d/init.d/network** file performs the startup operations for configuring your network. The network script uses a script called **ifup** to activate a network connection, **ifdown** to shut it down. These scripts make use of special configuration files located in the **/etc/sysconfig/network-scripts** directory that bear the names of the network interfaces currently configured. These files define shell variables that hold information on the interface such as whether to start them at boot time. The **ifdown** and **ifup** scripts hold the **ifconfig** and **route** commands to activate scripts using these special variables. As noted previously, you can use the network script to activate and deactivate your network interfaces at any time. Use the **start** option to activate interfaces, and **stop** to deactivate them.

Monitoring Your Network: ping and netstat

With the ping program, you can check to see if you can actually access another host on your network. The ping program will send a request to the host for a reply. The host then sends a reply back, and it is displayed on your screen. The ping program will continually send such a request until you stop it with a **break** command, a CTRL-C. You will see one reply after another scroll by on your screen until you stop the program. If ping cannot access a host, it will issue a message saying that the host is unreachable. If ping fails, it is an indication that your network connection is not working. It may just be the particular interface, a basic configuration problem, or a bad physical connection. To use ping, enter **ping** and the name of the host. You can also use the KDE network utilities on the KDE desktop and gfinger on the Gnome desktop (see Chapter 15).

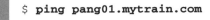

```
$ ping pang01.mytrain.com
```

The netstat program provides real-time information on the status of your network connections, as well as network statistics and the routing table. The netstat program has several options you can use to bring up different information about your network (see Table 28-4).

```
# netstat
Active Internet connections
Proto Recv-Q Send-Q Local Address        Foreign Address          (State)        User
tcp        0      0 turtle.mytrek.com:01 pango1.mytrain.com.:ftp ESTABLISHED dylan
Active UNIX domain sockets
Proto RefCnt Flags        Type         State          Path
unix  1      [ ACC ]      SOCK_STREAM  LISTENING       /dev/printer
unix  2      [ ]          SOCK_STREAM  CONNECTED      /dev/log
unix  1      [ ACC ]      SOCK_STREAM  LISTENING      /dev/nwapi
unix  2      [ ]          SOCK_STREAM  CONNECTED      /dev/log
unix  2      [ ]          SOCK_STREAM  CONNECTED
unix  1      [ ACC ]      SOCK_STREAM  LISTENING      /dev/log
```

The **netstat** command with no options will list the network connections on your system. First, active TCP connections are listed and then the active domain sockets. The domain sockets contain processes used to set up communications between your system and other systems. The various fields are described in the following table. You can use **netstat** with the **-r** option to display the routing table, and **netstat** with the **-i** option displays the usage for the different network interfaces.

Options	Description
-a	Displays information about all Internet sockets, including those sockets that are just listening.
-i	Displays statistics for all network devices.
-c	Continually displays network status every second until the program is interrupted.
-n	Displays remote and local address as IP addresses.
-o	Displays timer states, expiration times, and backoff state for network connections.
-r	Displays the kernel routing table.
-t	Displays information about TCP sockets only, including those that are listening.
-u	Displays information about UDP sockets only.
-v	Displays version information.
-w	Displays information about raw sockets only.
-x	Displays information about Unix domain sockets.

Table 28-4.   *The* netstat *Options*

IP Aliasing

In some cases, you may want to assign a single Linux system that has only one network interface two or more IP addresses. For example, you may want to run different Web sites on this same system that can be accessed with separate IP addresses. In effect, you are setting up an alias for your system, another address by which it can be accessed. In fact, you are assigning two IP addresses to the same network interface—for example, assigning a single Ethernet card two IP addresses. This procedure is referred to as *IP aliasing* and is used to set up multiple IP-based virtual hosts for Internet servers. This method can let you run several Web servers on the same machine using a single interface (or more than one on each of several interfaces). See Chapters 17 and 18 for FTP and Web server information about virtual hosts, and Chapter 20 for Domain Name Service configuration.

Setting up an IP alias is a simple matter of configuring a network interface on your system to listen for the added IP address. Your system needs to know what IP addresses it should listen for and on what network interface. You set up IP aliases using either Linuxconf, **netcfg**, or the **ifconfig** and **route** commands. For Linuxconf, select the IP aliases for virtual hosts under "Server tasks." This opens a panel that lists available interfaces. Click on one to open a panel where you can enter added IP addresses for it. On **netcfg** select the interface on the Interfaces panel and click the Alias button.

To add another address to the same interface, you need to qualify the interface by adding a colon and a number. For example, if you are adding another IP address to the first Ethernet card (**eth0**), you would add a **:0** to its interface name, **eth0:0**. The following example shows the **ifconfig** and **route** commands for the Ethernet interface 192.168.1.2 and two IP aliases add to it, 192.168.1.100 and 192.168.1.101.- To add yet another IP address to this same interface, you would use **eth0:1**, incrementing the qualifier, and so on. The first **ifconfig** command assigns the main IP address, 192.168.1.2, to the first Ethernet device, **eth0**. Then, two other IP addresses are assigned to that same device. In the first **route** command, the network route is set up for the Ethernet device and then routes are set up for each IP interface. The interfaces for the two aliases are indicated with **eth0:0** and **eth0:1**.

```
ifconfig eth0 192.168.1.2
ifconfig eth0:0 192.168.1.100
ifconfig eth0:1 192.168.1.101
route add -net 192.168.1.0 dev eth0
route add -host 192.168.1.2 dev eth0
route add -host 192.168.1.100 dev eth0:0
route add -host 192.168.1.101 dev eth0:1
```

IP aliasing has to be supported by the kernel before you can use it. If your kernel does not support it, you may have to rebuild the kernel including IP aliasing support or use loadable modules to add IP aliasing.

Firewalls: IP-Chains

The newest Linux kernel includes support for firewalls. This lets you set up a Linux system to operate as a firewall for your network, protecting it from unauthorized access. A firewall is simply the process of deciding whether a packet received by the firewall host should be passed on into the local network. Even if your system is not part of a network, but connected directly to the Internet, you can still use the firewall feature to control access to your system. Of course, this also provides you with much more security. With a firewall, you can restrict access to certain services, such as preventing any telnet access. The tool used to implement firewalls is **ipchains**. You can, however, do much more with this tool, such as implementing IP masquerading and proxies. The Linux Web site for **ipchains** is currently **www.rustcorp.com/linux/ipchains**. The **ipchains** tool is the successor to **ipfwadm** used on older versions of Linux.

The kernel uses chains to manage packets that it receives. A chain is just a checklist of rules. These rules specify what action to take for packets containing certain headers. The rules operate with an if-then-else structure. If a packet does not match the first rule, then the next rule is checked, and so on. If the packet does not match any rules, then it consults chain policy. Usually, at this point the packet is rejected. The kernel uses three firewall chains: input, output, and forward. When a packet is received through an interface the input chain is used to determine what to do with it. The kernel then uses its routing information to decide where to send it. If it sends it to another host, then the forward chain is checked. Before the packet is actually sent, the output chain is also checked.

To use **ipchains**, you have to have it compiled as part of the kernel. Red Hat already does this, but for OpenLinux you may have to recompile the kernel with that feature selected. You add and modify chain rules using the `ipchains` command. The process of setting up and maintaining firewall chains can be very complex. Linuxconf also provides a configuration interface for maintaining simple chain rules, as well loading special kernel modules for services like FTP, Quake, and IRC. (You may have to load the Linuxconf's own firewall module.) Select Firewalling under Networking and then choose the panel for the kind of chain rules you want to configure: Blocking, Forward, and Output. There are also several GUI configuration tools available—such as **fwconfig**, currently located at **www.mindstorm.com/~sparlin/fwconfig.shtml**.

IP Masquerading

On Linux systems, you can set up a network in which you could have one connection to the Internet that several systems on your network could use. This way, using only one IP address, several different systems could connect to the Internet. This method is called *IP masquerading*, where a system masquerades as another system, using that system's IP address. In such a network, one system is connected to the Internet with its own IP address and the other systems are connected on a local area network to this system. When a local system wants to access the network, it masquerades as the Internet-connected one, borrowing its IP address.

IP masquerading is implemented on Linux using the **ipchains** firewalling tool. In effect, you set up a firewall that you then configure to do IP masquerading. Currently IP masquerading, as does **ipchains** firewalling, supports all the common network services such as Web browsing, telnet, ping, and gopher. Other services like IRC, FTP, and Real Audio require the use of certain modules. Any services you want local systems to access must also be on the firewall system, as request and response will actually be handled by services on that system.

You can find out more information on IP masquerading at the IP Masquerade Resource Web site at **http://ipmasq.cjb.net/**. In particular, the Linux IP Masquerade mini-HOWTO provides a detailed step-by-step guide to setting up IP masquerading on your system. IP masquerading has to be supported by the kernel before you can use it. If your kernel does not support it, you may have to rebuild the kernel including IP masquerade support or use loadable modules to add IP masquerading. See the IP Masquerade mini-HOWTO for more information.

With IP masquerading, as implemented on Linux systems, the machine with the Internet address is also the firewall and gateway for the local area network of machines that will use the firewall's Internet address to connect to the Internet. Firewalls that also implement IP masquerading are sometimes referred to as *MASQ gates*. With IP masquerading, the Internet-connected system (the firewall) listens for Internet requests from hosts on its local network. It then replaces the requesting local host's IP address with the Internet IP address of the firewall and then passes the request out to the Internet as if the request were its own. Replies from the Internet will be sent to the firewall system. The replies that the firewall receives will be addressed to the firewall using its Internet address. The firewall then determines the local system whose request the reply is responding to. It then strips off its IP address and sends the response on to the local host across the local network. The connection from the perspective for the local machines is transparent. They appear to be connected directly to the Internet.

To implement IP masquerading you need to specify forwarding rules for use by **ipchains**. The following example assumes that the Internet connect host, the firewall, uses its first Ethernet device to connect to the Internet, **eth0**. If you are using a modem to dial up a connection to an ISP, then the interface used would probably be the first PPP interface, **ppp0**. The second command appends (**-A**) the forward rule to the target (**-j**) **MASQ** (masquerade) for the interface (**-I**) **eth0**. The host machines on the local network must specify the connected system as their gateway machine. The last command enables IP forwarding. To enable IP masquerading using Linuxconf's firewalling entries, select Forward Firewalling and click on the "Do masquerade" check box for any firewall forwarding rules you add that you want to apply to IP masquerading.

```
# ipchains -P forward DENY
# ipchains -A forward -i eth0 -j MASQ
# echo 1 > /proc/sys/net/ipv4/ip_forward
```

IP masquerading is often used to allow machines on a private network to access the Internet. These could be machines in a home network or a small local network, say for a small business. Such a network might have only one machine with Internet access and, as such, only the one Internet address. The local private network would have IP addresses chosen from the Private Network allocations (10., 172.16., or 192.168.). Ideally, the firewall will have two Ethernet cards, one for an interface to the local network (say, **eth1**) and one for an interface to the Internet such as **eth0** (for dial-up ISPs this would be **ppp0** for the modem). The card for the Internet connection (**eth0**) would be assigned the Internet IP address. The Ethernet interface for the local network (**eth1** in this example) is the firewall Ethernet interface. Your private local network would have a network address like 192.168.1. Its Ethernet firewall interface (**eth1**) would be assigned the IP address 192.168.1.1. In effect, the firewall interface lets the firewall operate as the local network's gateway. The firewall is then configured to masquerade any packets coming from the private network. Your local network needs to have its own domain name server, identifying the machines on your network including your firewall. Each local machine needs to have the firewall specified as its gateway. You should not try to use IP aliasing to assign both the firewall and Internet IP addresses to the same physical interface. Use separate interfaces for them such as two Ethernet cards or an Ethernet card and a modem (ppp0).

PPP

As an alternative to hardwired network connections such as Ethernet, you can use a modem with telephone lines to connect to a network. There are two protocols that can transmit IP communications across the telephone lines. These are the Point-to-Point Protocol (PPP) and the Serial Line Internet Protocol (SLIP). SLIP is an older protocol, whereas PPP is newer and has become predominant. Most high-speed connections used by current Internet service providers (ISPs) use PPP. The SLIP and PPP protocols are especially designed for users who connect their systems to the Internet over a modem and telephone line. Usually, a connection is made to an ISP that then connects the system to the Internet through its own systems. An Internet service provider will support either SLIP or PPP on a given line. Find out which protocol your ISP supports. You need to use one or the other. Setting up a SLIP or PPP connection can be a complicated process. For more detailed explanations, see the PPP-HOWTO and the Net-2-HOWTO documents in **/usr/doc/HOWTO**. There are also Web page instructions in **/usr/doc/HTML**. Also, check the **/usr/doc/ppp-***version* where version is the PPP package version.

PPP Connection Utilities: kppp, gnomeppp,

There are several graphical PPP configuration utilities that you can use on your Linux desktop to create and manage a PPP connection. There is a KDE PPP tool called **kppp**, a Gnome PPP tool called **gnomeppp**, as well as several X-Windows-based tools such as **xisp** and **easyppp**. All the tools offer the same kind of interface, providing panels for login information, modem configuration, and dial-up connections. This section discusses the kppp PPP utility. You can use it as a model for using the other PPP tools. As noted previously, you can also use netcfg and Linuxconf to manage a PPP connection. Though their interface is somewhat different, they do perform much the same tasks as described here for kppp.

During configuration, you are presented with a set of tabbed panels in which you enter Internet and modem information. Once configured, connecting is simply a matter of clicking on a button labeled Connect. The kppp tool will run fine from the root user, but needs permission set on certain files to allow use by other users on your system. See the documentation in the **/usr/doc/kppp*** directory. It also includes a detailed tutorial that you can view with your Web browser. The main screen will appear as shown in Figure 28-9.

To configure a connection, you click on the Setup button. This brings up the Configuration window, which has several panels. One panel will appear in the front, with tabs for the others showing at the top. In the Configuration window there are six panels, with one for accounts, other panels for device and modem settings, and one for PPP features. Accounts hold your Internet information. You can have more than one account, depending upon how many different Internet service providers you subscribe to (most users have only one). To create an account you click on the New button. This

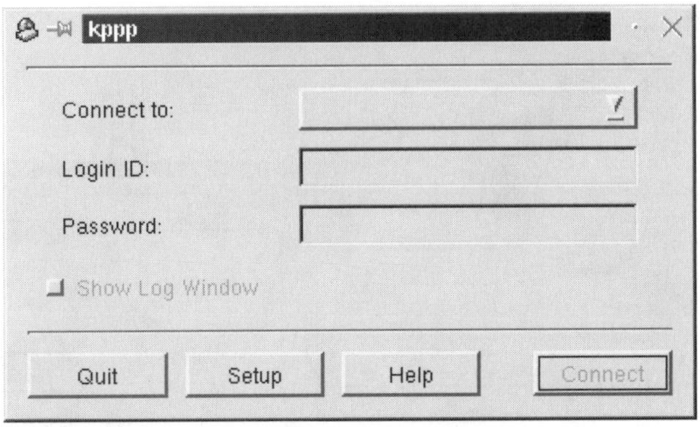

Figure 28-9. *The kppp window*

brings up a New Accounts window with a set of panels for Internet information. The Dial panel is where you enter connection information such as the phone number you use to connect to the provider. Be sure to enter a name for the connection. It can be anything you want. The Arguments button brings up another window for entering PPP arguments. These are options for the PPP daemon. Figure 28-10 shows the Configuration, New Account, and Arguments windows.

The IP panel is where you enter any local and remote IP addresses, as well as a netmask. Each entry has Dynamic and Static check buttons, and the Dynamic ones are already set by default. If your Internet service provider gives you dynamic addresses and a netmask, as most do these days, you can just leave this panel alone. If, on the other hand, you have a static local or remote address, you will have to bring up the panel and enter them. Click on the tab labeled DNS to bring up the Domain Name Server panel. Here, you enter in the IP addresses of your Internet service provider's domain name servers. Click on the box labeled IP Address and type the address. Then, click on Add to add it to the list of name servers.

You then have to create a login script in which you provide the user name and password that you use to connect to your Internet service provider. To do this, you click on the Login Script tab to bring up the Script panel. You will see a frame called Edit Script

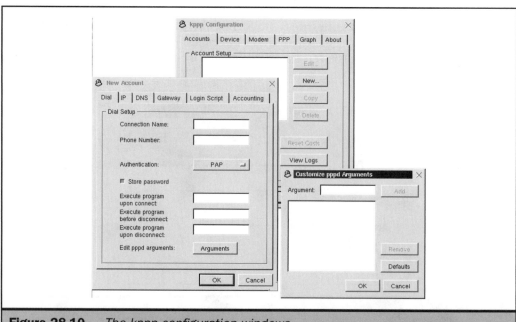

Figure 28-10. *The kppp configuration windows*

with several buttons and boxes (see Figure 28-11). You need to create a simple script that
will perform the following task using two instructions, send and receive:

```
receive      ogin:
send         username
receive      word:
send         password
```

You will see a button labeled Expect. This is actually a pop-up menu with several
entries listing possible login instructions. The entry you select will be shown when the
pop-up menu collapses. There are five entries: Expect, Send, Pause, Hangup, and Answer.
The instructions usually used to send a string or to expect receiving a string are Send and
Expect. If you want a send instruction, select the Send entry; for the receive instruction,
select the Expect entry. The box to the right of this button is where you enter text you want
that instruction to operate on. For example, for the instruction to receive the text "ogin:",
you would select the Expect entry and type **ogin:** into this box. To place it in the script,
you click the Add button. You will see both the term "expect" and the text "ogin:" appear
in the script frame below the Add button. If you make a mistake, you can click on the
entry and then click on the Remove button to delete it. If you need to insert an instruction
instead of having it placed at the end, use the Insert button.

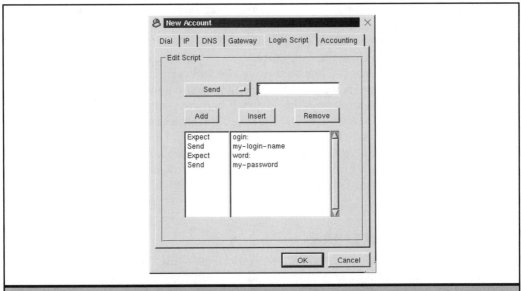

Figure 28-11.   *The kppp Send/Expect script*

Most login scripts only need two pairs of Send and Expect instructions; one for the login name and one for the password. The first instruction would expect the text "ogin:", and the second would send text consisting of the login name. The third instruction would expect the text "word:", and the fourth would send the text consisting of the password. This may vary depending upon how you connect to your Internet service provider. Figure 28-11 shows a sample login script, where "my-login-name" would be your user name, and "my-password" would be the password you use.

You have finished entering in the Internet information. Click OK to close the Script and New Accounts windows. At the Configure window, click on the Modem tab to bring up the Modem panel. Make sure the modem port is correct. Usually, this will be **/dev/modem**, where modem is a link to the actual modem port device. In most cases, you will not have to change this. Modem port devices begin with the name **/dev/cua** with an attached number from 0 to 3. On your PC, you have four ports to choose from, 1 through 4. Usually, a modem is connected to either 2 or 4. The names for these would be **/dev/cua1** and **/dev/cua3**. (The count is from 0, so port 1 is cua0 and port 2 is cua1.) If you already set up a modem alias for the port, you can just use **/dev/modem**.

You then need to check the dialing prefix as well as any special settings you may need for your modem. You can click on the Edit button to bring up a window with a long list of boxes with settings for your modem. They should already have default settings entered. The first box is where you would enter your modem initialization string, adding such instructions as M0 to turn off the connection sound. The third box, labeled Dial String, is where you enter your dialing prefix. ATDT is the default already entered, which most people use. Check also the Connect response entry and the Hangup string. The default connect response is CONNECT, which is valid for most ISPs. The Hangup string is a standard hang-up instruction for most modems.

Once you are finished, close the Configuration window by clicking on the OK button. You are then ready to use kppp. Click on the Connect button in the main window. If you have problems, click "show log window." This will bring up a window that will display the connection process and any errors that occur. When kppp makes a connection, it will display the amount of time connected and the speed it connected at. The Connect button will be changed to Disconnect. To end your session, just click Disconnect. Quit will end the kppp program. Each individual user creates their own accounts using the steps described previously. This information is held in a **.ppprc** file in the user's **home** directory. In fact, different users could use kppp to connect to different Internet service providers.

Manual PPP Connections

You can manually create your own PPP connection, invoking the PPP program directly on the command line with **chat** scripts to make the appropriate dial-up connections. The PPP program is called pppd. The pppd program does not make the initial connection. It does not dial up through your modem and provide login and password information. To use pppd, you first have to establish the connection to the remote host.

You can make such a connection using the chat program, which has its own options and format. The chat program first makes the connection, and then pppd configures it. However, you do not have to call chat first and then pppd. The pppd program is designed to take as its argument a program that will make the connection—in this case, chat. You simply specify **chat** along with its options on the command line with **pppd**.

SuSE also provides a script called **ppp-on** that invokes pppd using options specified in the **/etc/ppp/options** file and a **chat** script in the **/etc/ppp/ppp.chat** file. Once you have configured these files, you can use **ppp-on** to establish your PPP connection, instead of entering a **pppd** command yourself. You can use the companion script **ppp-off** to disconnect.

Static and dynamic IP addresses are distinguished by pppd by whether you include a set of IP addresses as an argument on the command line and the use of the noipdefault option. If you do include the IP addresses, then pppd assumes you have a static connection and these are the remote and local addresses to use to establish that connection. If you do not specify any addresses as arguments, then pppd assumes a default remote and local address. The default local address is the IP address of your systems as specified in your **/etc/hostname** file. A default remote address will try to be determined from remote addresses in your **/etc/hosts** file. The pppd program assumes you use dynamic addresses and will look for them when a connection is made. To have pppd assume dynamic addresses, you use the noipdefault option, as well as not specifying any addresses. The noipdefault option instructs pppd not to use default addresses. With no address is specified, pppd then assumes that dynamic addresses will be received from the remote host.

The local and remote static addresses are entered next to each other, separated by a colon. The local address is entered first. The following example specifies a local address of 192.168.1.72 and remote address of 163.179.4.22.

```
192.168.1.72:163.179.4.22
```

Should you use a dynamic remote address, but your own local address, you can specify just your local address followed by the colon, :. The pppd program will then use your local address and dynamically receive your remote address.

```
192.168.1.72:
```

Since your local address as specified in your **/etc/hostname** file is your default local address, you do not even have to enter it on the command line. You could just enter the **pppd** command with no addresses. The pppd program will use your hostname address as your local address and receive a remote address from the remote host.

Most Internet service providers that use dynamic addresses will provide you with both the local and remote address. In this case, you do not enter any addresses at all, and you have to specify the noipdefault option. The noipdefault option will prevent the use of the hostname address as the default local address. Lacking any addresses, **pppd** will obtain both from the remote host.

Chat Scripts

The best way to use chat is to invoke a **chat** script. To make a connection, **chat** has to specify all the connection information: the telephone number, login prompt and user ID, password prompt and password, and any connect strings. You could enter this as a string after the **chat** command on the command line, but this makes for a very long and complex command line. Instead, you can create a file with the chat information in it and then use the **-f** option and the file name with the **chat** command. Such files are called **chat** scripts.

A **chat** script consists of one line organized into different segments for the parts of the connection procedure. Each segment consists of an expect-reply pair of strings. The first string is what you expect to receive and the second string is what you are sending. If you expect to receive nothing, then you use a null string, **""**. Each expect-reply pair performs a specific task in the login process. You can start with an initialization of your modem, should you need to do this. Many users can just use the default settings. Then, the number is dialed to make the connection. You can then check to see if the connection was made. A login name is provided at the login prompt. And finally, a password is sent at the password prompt.

If you decide to initialize your modem, you need to start with an expect-reply entry to perform this task. You expect nothing at first, so the expect string is only an empty string, two double quotes, **""**. For the reply string, you specify the codes for your modem initialization. When entering the codes for your initialization string, you will have to escape any code beginning with **&**. For chat, the **&** is a break and will stop the process. See Table 28-5 for a list of chat options and special characters.

The next expect-reply entry dials the phone number. If you have an initialization string before it, then its expect string will be the word OK. This is the response from your modem indicating that there was no problem initializing your modem. You will usually receive a connect string indicating that you have connected to the remote system. This can vary from system to system. There may not even be a connect string at all. On many systems, the connect string is the word CONNECT; on others, it is the baud rate, or speed. In this example, the user receives the speed as the connect string. The response to a connect string is usually nothing, though it can also be a newline. Recall that you represent no response with an empty string—two double quotes, **""**. The newline is represented in a **chat** script with a \n.

After the connect string, the remote system usually sends the login prompt. This is often the word "login" with a colon. You only need the last few characters, **ogin:**. Don't forget the colon. In reply, you send your user ID. Depending on your ISP, you may have to add **\n** to the user ID to enter a newline, as in *mylogin\n*.

```
ogin:   mylogin
```

After the login, you can expect the password prompt. Again, you only need the last few characters, **word:**. In response, you send your password. If needed, be sure to add the **\n** to enter the newline.

```
word:  mypass
```

All this fits together on just one line. You have a sequence of words indicating alternating received and sent text.

```
""  AT\&F2V1L0 OK  ATDT8888888 CONNECT  \n  ogin: mylogin   word:  mypass
```

If you did not initialize your modem, it would look slightly different.

```
"" ATDT8888888 CONNECT  \n  ogin:   mylogin  word:  mypass
```

If your ISP does not require you to send a return character on receiving the connect string, you can leave that out, reducing the **chat** script as shown here:

```
"" ATDT8888888 ogin:  mylogin  word:  mypass
```

In a **chat** script, you can break the expect and reply pairs into separate lines, one pair to a line, with the strings for each pair separated by a space or tab. You could also put it all on the very first line if you wish. The file name for the script has the extension **.chat**. The next example shows the **/etc/ppp/ppp.chat** script with pairs entered on separate lines.

ppp.chat

```
"  "         AT\&F2V1L0
OK           ATDT4448888
CONNECT      \n
ogin:        mylogin
word:        mypass
```

You can then call the **chat** script with the **chat** command and the **-f** option, as shown here. The chat program will use the information in the **chat** script to initialize your modem, dial up your remote host, and then log in with your user ID and password.

```
chat -f  /etc/ppp/ppp.chat
```

Many remote systems and modes will send error messages if something should go wrong in the connection process. You can use the special expect string, **ABORT**, followed by a key term to detect such an error message. If such a term is received, chat cancels the connection procedure. If you are using a command line only, you can enter abort strings either where you would expect them to occur in the connection process or at the very beginning. Within a **chat** script, as shown here, the abort strings are placed at the beginning. The next example would expect a NO CARRIER or a BUSY response before the login prompt. In either case, an initial connection failed, and **chat** will cancel the remaining steps. Notice the quotes around NO CARRIER. If a string has a space in it, you have to quote it.

ppp.chat

```
ABORT       'NO CARRIER'
ABORT       BUSY
"  "        AT\&F2V1L0
OK          ATDT5558888
CONNECT     \n
ogin:       mylogin
word:       mypass
```

You need to incorporate the chat operation into your invocation of the **pppd** command. The entire chat operations will be encased in single quotes and entered on the same line as the **pppd** command. The chat program will use the information in the **chat** script to initialize your modem, dial up your remote host, and then log in with your user ID and password. The **chat** script will make the connection and then **pppd** will configure it. The Point-to-Point Protocol daemon (**pppd**) is invoked with several possible options. Its standard syntax is

pppd *options serial-device-name speed local:remote-addresses ppp-options*

The *serial-device-name* is the device name for your modem. This is likely to be **/dev/cua** with a number attached, usually from 0 to 3, depending on the port you are using for your modem. Port 1 is **cua0**, port 2 is **cua2**, and so on. The *speed* is the baud rate. For a 14.4 modem, this is 14,400. For a v.28 modem, this is 38,400, or even 56,700. Check with your ISP and your modem documentation for the highest speed you can support.

The options specify configuration features such as your MTU size and whether you are receiving a dynamic IP address. The **connect** option instructs **pppd** to make a connection. It takes as its argument a Linux command that will actually make the connection—usually the **chat** command. You enter **pppd** followed by the **connect**

option and the **chat** command with its **-f** option and **chat** script file name. The
chat command and its **-f** option with the chat file name are all enclosed in quotes to
distinguish them from other **pppd** options. In the next example, the user invokes **pppd**
with the **chat** command using the **mycon.chat chat** script. The modem is connected
to port 4, **/dev/cual**, and the speed is 57,600 baud.

```
# pppd connect 'chat -f /etc/ppp/ppp.chat' /dev/cual 57600
```

To disconnect your PPP connection, you invoke **pppd** with the **disconnect**
option. You must use **chat** to instruct your modem to hang up. For this, you may
have to send a modem command such as **H0**. You can also use the **ppp-off** script to
disconnect. You will probably find it more convenient to place the **chat** commands in
a chat file, as shown here:

```
# pppd disconnect 'chat -f turnoff.chat'
```

turnoff.chat

```
- \d+++\d\c   OK
  ATH0   OK
```

PPP Options

The **pppd** command has a great many options. The more commonly used ones are
listed in Table 28-6. See the **pppd** Man pages for a complete list. For example, the **mru**
option sets the "maximum receive unit" size. The **pppd** command instructs the remote
system to send packets no larger than this size. The default is 1,500, and 296 or 542 is
recommended for slower modems. The **defaultroute** option instructs **pppd** to set up
the PPP connection as the default route. The lack of any addresses combined with the
noipdefault option instructs **pppd** to detect and use a dynamic IP address from the
ISP remote system. You have to specify this option if you have an ISP that supplies
dynamic IP addresses. The **crtscts** option uses hardware flow control, and the **modem**
option uses the modem control lines. You can list the options after the speed on the
command line, as shown here:

```
# pppd connect 'chat -f /etc/ppp/ppp.chat' /dev/cual 57600
    mru 1500 defaultroute noipdefault crtscts modem
```

In the following command, the presence of addresses instructs **pppd** to use these
addresses to establish a static connection. The local address is 192.168.1.72 and the
remote address is 163.179.4.22.

Option	Description
-f *filename*	Executes **chat** commands in the **chat** script with name *filename*
-l *lockfile*	Makes UUCP style like file using *lockfile*
-t *num*	Timeout set to *num* seconds
-v	A description of all **chat** actions are output to the **/log/messages** file; use **tail**, **cat**, or **more** on this file to display the descriptions: `tail /log/messages`

Special Characters

BREAK	Sends break to modem
' '	Sends null string with single newline character
\b	BACKSPACE
\c	Suppresses newline sent after reply string
\d	Makes **chat** wait for one second
\K	Sends break; when specifying string for modem initialization, and codes beginning with *K* may have to be escaped
\n	Sends newline characters
\N	Sends null character
\p	Pauses for 1/10 of a second
\q	String does not appear in **syslog** file
\r	Sends or expects a new line
\s	Sends or expects a space
\t	Sends or expects a tab
****	Sends or expects a backslash
nnn	Specifies a character in octal
^*C*	Specifies a control character

Table 28-5.   *The **chat** Options and Special Characters*

```
# pppd connect 'chat -f /etc/ppp/ppp.chat' /dev/cua1 57600
192.168.1.72:163.179.4.22 mru 1500 defaultroute crtscts modem
```

This can make for a very lengthy and complex command line, depending on how many options you need. As an alternative, **pppd** allows you to enter options in the file **/etc/ppp/options** as well as in a **.ppprc** file. The **pppd** option will automatically read and use the options specified in these files each time it is invoked. You can specify as many options as you wish, entering each on a separate line. With the **#** symbol, you can also enter comments, explaining the options and their settings. The **/etc/ppp/options** file contains system default options for **pppd**. You create this file as the root user, and it is the first options file called when **pppd** is invoked. Each user can have a **.ppprc** file in his or her own **home** directory. These options are specified by a particular user and are read after the system's **/etc/ppp/options** file.

/etc/ppp/options

```
crtscts
defaultroute
modem
mru 542
asyncmap 0
netmask 255.255.255.0
noipdefault
```

Now when you invoke **pppd**, you do not have to enter any of these options on the command line. With your options specified in the **/etc/ppp/options** file, you then only need to enter the **pppd** command with the **chat** invocation, the device name for your modem, and the modem speed.

```
$ pppd connect 'chat -f /etc/ppp/ppp.chat' /dev/cua1 57600
```

You can reduce your entry even further by placing the **pppd** invocation in a shell script and then just executing the shell script. Recall that a shell script is a text file that you create with any text editor. You type the command invocation with all its arguments as you would on the command line. Be sure to precede the **pppd** command with an **exec** command. The **exec** command runs **pppd** from your command line shell, not the script's shell. You then make the script executable with the command **chmod 755** *script-name*. Now to execute your **pppd** operation, just enter the script name on the command line and press ENTER. In the next example, the **pppd** connect operation is placed in a shell script called **pppcon**, and the user simply enters **pppcon** to invoke **pppd**.

```
pppcon

exec pppd  connect  'chat -f /etc/ppp/ppp.chat'  /dev/cua1  57600
```

```
$ pppcon
```

You are now ready to try **pppd** to connect to your remote system. Any number of things may go wrong. You may not have the right connect string or the modem may be initializing wrong. The **pppd** command will log descriptions of all the steps it is taking in the **/var/log/messages** file. You can use **tail** to list these descriptions even as **pppd** is operating. For a successful connection, you will see the local and remote IP addresses listed at the end as shown here:

```
$ tail /var/log/messages
```

To receive an ongoing display of messages as they are entered in the **/var/log/messages** file, use the **tail** command with the **–f** option, as shown here. Use a CTRL-C to end the process.

```
$ tail -f /var/log/messages
Mar 23 20:01:03 richlp pppd[208]: Connected...
Mar 23 20:01:04 richlp pppd[208]: Using interface ppp0
Mar 23 20:01:04 richlp kernel: ppp: channel ppp0 mtu = 1500, mru = 1500
Mar 23 20:01:04 richlp kernel: ppp: channel ppp0 open
Mar 23 20:01:04 richlp pppd[208]: Connect: ppp0 ~ /dev/cua3
Mar 23 20:01:09 richlp pppd[208]: local  IP address 204.32.168.68
Mar 23 20:01:09 richlp pppd[208]: remote IP address 163.179.4.23
```

The ppp RPM package installed on Red Hat and OpenLinux systems includes a sample login PPP script called **ppp-on** in the **/usr/doc/ppp-*version*/scripts** directory, where version is the **pppd** version. You can use a text editor to set the correct values to certain variables such as TEPEPHONE, ACCOUNT, and PASSWORD. You also must be careful to set the correct arguments and options for both the **chat** and the **pppd** commands. If you have already set options in the **/etc/ppp/options** file, you can remove most of the options that you would normally specify on the command line. Also, be sure to set the correct speed and device name for the modem. The default used on the script is 38,400. For a 56k modem, change it to 57,600. Once working, all you then have to enter is **ppp-on** to establish your PPP connection. If you have trouble disconnecting, try the **ppp-off** command.

You can also configure your system to be a PPP server, allowing remote systems to dial into yours and make PPP connections. You only need to create one special account and a script to invoke **pppd** with the **–detach** and **silent** options. The script is usually called **ppplogin**—here is an example:

/etc/ppp/ppplogin

```
exec pppd -detach silent modem crtscts
```

With the **–detach** option, **pppd** won't detach itself from the line it is on. The **silent** option makes **pppd** wait for a remote system to make a link to your system. The **modem** option monitors the modem lines, and **crtscts** uses hardware flow control. The special account has the name **ppp**. The **/etc/passwd** entry for the **ppp** account would appear as follows:

```
ppp:*:501:300:PPP Account:/tmp:etc/ppp/ppplogin
```

Table 28-6 shows the **pppd** options.

PPP Security: CHAP

To ensure security for PPP connections you have to use additional protocols. Two have been developed for PPP, the Password Authentication Protocol (PAP) and the Challenge Handshake Authentication Protocol (CHAP). CHAP is considered a more secure protocol. It uses an encrypted challenge system that requires the two connected systems to authenticate each other continually. The keys for the encryption are kept in the **/etc/ppp/chap-secrets** file. To use CHAP in your PPP connections, you include the **auth** option when you invoke **pppd**. Also, you must enter the required information for the remote host into the **/etc/ppp/chap-secrets** file. The following is an example of a **/etc/ppp/chap-secrets** entry. Entries for the PAP in **/etc/ppp/pap-secrets** have the same format.

etc/ppp/chap-secrets

```
pango1.train.com       turtle.trek.com       "my new hat"
     *                 turtle.trek.com       "confirmed tickets"
turtle.trek.com        pango1.train.com      "trek on again"
```

A CHAP secrets entry has up to four fields: the client's hostname, the server's hostname, a secret key, and a list of IP possible addresses. For a particular computer trying to make a connection to your system, you can specify that it supply the indicated secret key. Instead of specifying a particular computer, you can use a * to indicate any computer. Any system that knows the designated secret key can connect to your

Option	Description
device-name	Uses the specified device; if the device name does not have **/dev** preceding it, **pppd** will add it for you
speed *num*	Sets the modem speed (baud rate)
asyncmap *map*	Sets the async character map that specifies what control characters cannot be sent and should be escaped
auth	Requires the remote host to authenticate itself
connect *Connection-operation*	Uses the connection operations to set up the connection; the Linux command here is usually **chat**, which makes the actual connection
crtscts	Uses hardware flow control
xonxoff	Uses software flow control
defaultroute	The **pppd** command sets a default route to the remote host
disconnect *Linux-command*	Runs the specified command after **pppd** cuts its connection; usually a **chat** operation
escape *c,c,...*	Causes the specified characters to be escaped when transmitted
file *filename*	Reads **pppd** options from the specified file
lock	Uses UUCP-style locking on the serial device
mru *num*	Sets the maximum receive units to *num*
netmask *mask*	Sets the PPP network interface mask
noipdefault	For dynamic IP addresses provided by ISP; searches the incoming data stream from the remote host for both the local and remote IP addresses assigned to your system for that Internet session; must have this option to connect with a dynamic IP address
passive	Makes **pppd** wait for a valid connection instead of failing when it can't make the connection immediately
silent	The **pppd** command waits for a connection to be made by a remote host

Table 28-6.   *The pppd Options*

system. In the first entry in the following example, the server is the user's own system, **turtle.trek.com**, and it allows **pango1.train.com** to connect to it if it provides the secret key specified. In the next entry, any remote system can connect to **turtle.trek.com** if they know the secret key "confirmed tickets".

```
pango1.train.com      turtle.trek.com    "my new hat"
    *                 turtle.trek.com    "confirmed tickets"
```

You also have to make entries for remote systems that you want to access. In that case, the remote system is the PPP server and you are the client. In the next example, **turtle** can connect to **pango1** with the secret key "trek on again".

```
turtle.trek.com pango1.train.com "trek on again"
```

SLIP: dip

There are two types of SLIP connections, the standard one referred to as just SLIP, and the newer Compress SLIP, referred to as CSLIP. Be sure you know which type of connection your Internet service provider is giving you. You will have to specify one or the other as your protocol mode when you connect. Except for specifying the mode, the connection procedure is the same for both. References to SLIP will apply to both SLIP and CSLIP unless specifically noted. You use the dip program to manage and set up your SLIP connection. The dip program operates like an interpreter. In a file called a **dip** script, you specify certain commands needed to log into the ISP and make the connection. The dip program then reads the commands in this file, executing them one by one. With Linux, not only can you make a SLIP connection to a remote system, but other systems can make their own SLIP connections to your system. Another system can dial into your system and make a SLIP connection. If you have provided an account for a user on that remote system, then the user could dial in a SLIP connection and log in to that account. Such remote dial-up SLIP connections are managed by **dip** with the **-i** option. This places dip in a dial-in mode to receive incoming connections. In the dial-in mode, dip will prompt a remote user for a user ID and a password, and then make the SLIP connection.

Dynamic Host Configuration Protocol (DHCP)

The Dynamic Host Configuration Protocol (DHCP) provides configuration information to systems connected to a TCP/IP network, whether it be the Internet or an intranet. The machines on the network operate as DHCP clients, obtaining their network configuration information from a DHCP server on their network. A machine on the network runs a DHCP client daemon that automatically downloads its network configuration information from its network's DHCP server. The information includes its IP address along with the network's name server, gateway, and proxy addresses, including the netmask. Nothing has to be entered manually on the local system. This has the added advantage of centralizing control over network configuration for the different systems on the network. A network administrator can manage the network configurations for all the systems on the network from the DHCP server.

A DHCP server also supports several methods for IP address allocation: automatic, manual, and dynamic. *Automatic allocation* assigns a permanent IP address for a host. *Manual allocation* assigns an IP address designated by the network administrator. With *dynamic allocation*, a DHCP server can allocate an IP address to a host on the network only when the host actually needs to use it. Allocation can be made from a pool of IP addresses that hosts can use when needed and release when they are finished.

There are a variety of DHCP servers and clients available for different operating systems. For Linux, you can obtain DHCP software from the Internet Software Consortium (ISC) at **www.isc.org**. The software package includes a DHCP server, client, and relay agent. Most Linux distributions include a DHCP server and client, including Red Hat and OpenLinux. The DHCP client is called **dhcpcd** and the server is called **dhcpd**. The network information that a DHCP client downloads is kept in its own network configuration files in the **/etc/dhcpc** directory. For example, here you will find a **resolv.conf** file for your network's name servers.

The Complete Reference

Chapter 29

The X Window System and XFree86

Most Linux and Unix systems use the same standard underlying graphics utility known as the X Window System, also known as X or X11. This means, in most cases, that an X-based program can run on any of the window managers and desktops. X-based software is often found at Linux or Unix FTP sites in directories labeled **X11**. You can download these packages and run them on any window manager running on your Linux system. Some may already be in the form of Linux binaries that you can download, install, and run directly. Netscape is an example. Others will be in the form of source code that can easily be configured, compiled, and installed on your system with a few simple commands. Some applications, such as Motif applications, may require special libraries. You can find out more about X Window Systems at **www.X11.org**.

The X Window System is designed for flexibility—there are various ways you can configure it. You can run it on almost all of the video cards currently available. The X Window System is not tied to any specific desktop interface. It provides an underlying set of graphical operations that user interface applications such as window managers, file managers, and even desktops can make use of. A window manager uses these operations to construct widgets for manipulating windows, such as scroll bars, resize boxes, and close boxes. Different window managers can construct them to appear differently, providing interfaces with very different appearances. All will work on the X Window System. There are a variety of different window managers for you to choose from. Each user on your system could run a different window manager, each using the same underlying X Window System graphic operations. You can even run X programs without any window or file managers.

To run the X Window System, you need to install an X Window System server that works for your video card. A free version of X Window System server software known as XFree86 is used on most Linux systems, though commercial versions are available from MetroLink (**www.metrolink.com**) and Accelerated X. Once you have installed the XFree86 server appropriate for your system's video card, you then have to provide configuration information about your monitor, mouse, and keyboard. This information will be used in a configuration file called **/etc/XF86Config**. The file includes technical information that is best generated by an X Window System configuration program such as Xconfigurator, XF86Setup, or SaX. When you configured the X Window System when you installed your system, this file was automatically generated.

You can also configure your own X interface using the configuration files **.xinitrc/etc/X11/xinit/xinitrc**, or Xsession where window managers, file managers, and initial X applications can be selected and started up. There is also a set of specialized X commands that you can use to configure your root window, load fonts, or configure X Window System resources such as setting the color of window borders. You can also download X utilities from online sources that serve as Linux mirror sites, usually in their **/pub/Linux/X11** directory. If you have to compile an X application, you may have to use special procedures as well as install support packages.

The X Window System was developed and is maintained by The Open Group (TOG), a consortium of over a hundred companies including Sun, HP, IBM, Motorola, Intel, and

Microsoft (**www.opengroup.org**). Development is currently managed by the X.org group (**www.X.org**) on behalf of the TOG. X.org is a nonprofit organization that maintains the existing X Window System code. X.Org periodically provides official Window System update releases to the general public for free. It controls the development of the X11R6 specifications, working with appropriate groups to revise and release updates to the standard as required. The newest release is currently X11R6.4. XFree86 is a free distributed version of X Window System servers used on most Linux systems. XFree86 has plans to incorporate X11R6.4 into their XFree86-4.0 release.

The X Protocol

The X protocol was developed for Unix systems in the mid-1980s to provide a network transparent graphical user interface. It organizes display operations into a client and server relationship, in which a client submits display requests to a server. The client is known as an X client, and the server, as an X server. The client, in this case, is an application and the server is a display. This relationship separates an application from the server. The application acts as a client sending request to the server, which then does the actual work of performing the requested display operation. This has the advantage of letting the server interact with the operating system and its devices, whereas the application need know nothing of these details. An application operating as an X client can display on any system that uses an X server. In fact, a remote X client can send requests to have an X server on a local machine perform certain display operations. In effect, the X server/client relationship is, in a sense, inverted from the way we normally think of servers. Usually, several client systems access a single server. In the X server model, you would have each system operating as an X server and they could access a single system that holds X client programs.

XFree86

The XFree86 Project (**www.xfree86.org**) is a nonprofit organization that provides free X Window System servers and supporting materials for several operating systems on PCs and other microcomputers. The X servers, client programs, and documentation supplied by the XFree86 Project are commonly referred to as XFree86. The XFree86 servers are available for free and include source code. The project is funded entirely by donations.

The XFree86 servers support a wide range of video cards and monitors. There are servers for monochrome, VGA, and Super VGA, and accelerated video cards. In addition, there are a series of servers designed for accelerated video cards, a server for each chipset. Table 29-1 lists XFree86 directories, and Table 29-2 lists the current XFree86 servers. For current updated information access the XFree86 Web site at

www.xfree86.org or **www.x11.org**. You can also consult the XFree86 documentation in the **/usr/X11R6/lib/X11/doc** directory. There you will find files for the specific servers available as well as types of cards supported. The **AccelCards** file lists all the hardware currently supported, including chipsets, and the **Monitors** file lists monitor configurations. Also, consult the man pages for the different driver types. The driver types and the associated man pages are listed here. XFree86 configuration tools such as Xconfigurator, XF86Setup, and SaX make configuring your video card and monitor a very simple process. They keep on hand an extensive list of video cards and monitors provided by Xfree86 from which you can select your own. However, if your video card or monitor are very new, they may not be on this list. In that case you will have to enter in certain hardware specifications like horizontal sync. If you have to do this, be very careful to enter in the correct information. The wrong settings could damage your card and monitor.

Video Cards	Man Pages
Accelerated cards	XF86_Accel
Monochrome cards	XF86_Mono
VGA cards	XF86_VGA16
SVGA cards	XF86_SVGA

The XFree86 servers that you specified when you installed your system are automatically installed. Most standard and accelerated graphics cards are supported by the SVGA server, XF86_SVGA. If you are using a simple monochrome or VGA card, you use the XF86_Mono or XF86_VGA generic server. A few accelerated graphics cards are supported by specialized servers such as the S3 and ATI's Mach64 chips. For these you first have to find out what chipset is used. Consult the manual or documentation that comes with the card. For example, if you have an S3 chipset on your graphics video card, you would use the XFree86_S3 package. In rare cases you may need to manually install such a server, say if you change your card (normally, just use a configurator like Xconfigurator). On distributions like Red Hat and OpenLinux that support RPM packages, you can use an RPM package manager such as kpackage, GnomeRPM, glint, or LISA. You can also use the **rpm -i** command to install the package from a shell command line. Compressed tar archives are also available. Each package that contains an XFree server starts with the term "XFree86." You have to install the package appropriate for your graphics card. Most recent video cards are included in the XF86_SVGA server. Older ones are continually being integrated into this server with new releases. For example, the S3 ViRGE chip (Diamond Stealth 3D series) now uses the SVGA server instead of the separate S3V server it once used. You can obtain a current listing of the graphics cards supported by XFree86 organized by the different server packages at the X11 and XFree86 Web sites, **www.X11.org** and **www.xfree86.org**.

```
rpm -i XFree86_S3-3.3-3.i386.rpm
```

Be sure to check periodically for new releases of XFree86 servers at the XFree86 Web site. You can download the new releases from there or from your distribution's update sites such as **updates.redhat.com**. If you have a recent card that is not yet supported by XFree86, you may find a server for it at the XSuSE Web site at **www.suse.de/ XSuSE/index.html**. XSuSE is a special service provided by the SuSE Linux distributor in close association with XFree86 to develop XFree86 servers for cards not yet supported by a current XFree86 release. When a new XFree86 release comes out, these servers are then incorporated into it. The server packages begin with the name Xfcom as in Xfcom_Matrox for Matrox graphics cards. You can obtain a current listing of these servers and the cards they support at the X11 and XSuSE Web sites.

In addition to the servers, XFree86 includes support programs and development libraries. The entire XFree86 collection is installed in various directories, beginning with the pathname **/usr/X11R6**. Here there are directories for X programs, development files, libraries, man pages, and documentation. Configuration files are placed in the **/etc/X11** directory. Applications written to support X will usually install in the **/usr/X11R6/bin** directory. Here you will also find the XFree86 servers and support programs.

XFree86 Servers	Support Programs
/usr/X11R6/bin	Programs (X Window System clients and servers)
/usr/X11R6/include	Development files
/usr/X11R6/lib	Libraries
/usr/X11R6/man	man pages
/usr/X11R6/lib/X11/doc	Documentation
/etc/X11	Configuration files
/usr/X11R6/lib/X11/	Configuration files (links to **/etc/X11** or Red Hat and OpenLinux)

Table 29-1.   *XFree86 Directories*

Server	Type
Xfree86_SVGA	Color SVGA server, includes drivers for most video cards
Xfree86_VGA16	16-color SVGA and VGA nonaccelerated server
Xfree86_Mono	Monochrome nonaccelerated server
Xfree86_S3	S3 accelerated server
Xfree86_S3V	Use SVGA
Xfree86_I128	Number 9 Imagine 128 accelerated server
Xfree86_8514	8514/A accelerated server
Xfree86_Mach8	ATI Mach8 accelerated server
Xfree86_Mach32	ATI Mach32 chipset accelerated server
Xfree86_Mach64	ATI Mach64 chipset accelerated server
Xfree86_P9000	Weitek accelerated server
Xfree86_W32	ET4000/W32 accelerated server
Xfree86_AGX	IIT AGX accelerated server
Xfree86_3Dlabs	3Dlabs server

Table 29-2.   *XFree86 Servers (version 3.3.3)*

XFree86 Configuration: /etc/XF86Config

The XFree86 servers provide a wide range of hardware support but can be challenging to configure. There is XFree86-HOWTO document that you can consult at **www.linux.org** or in the **/usr/doc/HOWTO** directory for most distributions. There are also man pages for XFree86 and XF86Config. Documentation and FAQs are available at **www.xfree86.org**. The configuration file used for your XFree86 server is called **XF86Config**, located in the **/etc** directory. It contains all the specifications for your graphics card, monitor, keyboard, and mouse. To configure the XF86Config file, you will need specific information on hand about your hardware. For your monitor, you will have to know the horizontal and vertical sync frequency ranges and bandwidth. For your graphics card, you have to know the chipset and you may even need to know the clocks. For your mouse, you should know whether it is Microsoft compatible or some other brand such as Logitech. Also, know the port that your mouse is connected to.

Although you could create and edit the file directly, it is better to use a configuration utility such as Xconfigurator, XF86Setup, SaX, or xf86config. (Table 29-3 lists these various configuration tools.) With these, you just answer questions about your hardware or select options on dialog window and the program will generate the appropriate **/etc/XF86Config** file. The xf86config utility provides line mode prompts where you type in responses or enter a menu selection. It provides explanations of each step. You can run it from any shell command line. Xconfigurator uses a cursor-based screen that also operates on a shell command line. You can use arrow keys, TAB, and the ENTER key to make your selections. It will also attempt to automatically detect your card, or you can select your monitor from a predetermined list. XF86Setup provides you with a full-screen interface where you can very easily select features for your mouse, keyboard, graphics card, and monitor. You will need the horizontal and vertical frequency for your monitor. XF86Setup is described in detail in Chapter 4. However, if you have problems configuring with XF86Setup, you can use xf86config, which presents you with a command line interface that prompts you for different settings. SaX (SuSE Advanced X Configuration) is another GUI X Window System configuration tool provided by the SuSE Linux distribution. It provides windows similar to XF86Setup for your mouse, keyboard, video card, and monitor. The monitor window will list supported monitor models.

The **/etc/XF86Config** file is organized into several parts as shown here. You can find a detailed discussion of all these sections and their entries in the XF86Config man page. All of these are set by the XF86Setup program. For example, the Monitor screen generates the Monitor section in the **XF86Config** file, the Mouse screen generates the

X Window System	Configuration Tools
XF86Setup	GUI X Window System configuration tool, use after installation process
Xconfigurator	Screen-based X Window System configuration tool (used in Red Hat install procedure)
xf86setup	Command line X Window System configuration tool, requires no screen-based support
SaX	SaX, the SuSE Advanced X Configuration tool, provides GUI interface for configuring X Window System
/etc/XF86Config	The X Window System configuration file; edited by the configuration tools

Table 29-3. *X Window System Configuration Tools*

Pointer section, and so on. A section in the file begins with the keyword **Section** followed by the name of the section in quotes. The section ends with the term **EndSection**. Comments have a # sign at the beginning of the line. Entries for each section begin with a data specification followed by a list of values. For example, in the Files section where the **rgb** color data is listed, a line begins with the data specification **RgbPath** followed by the pathname for that **rgb** color data file.

Sections	Descriptions
Files	Directories for font and rgb files
Module	Dynamic module loading
ServerFlags	Miscellaneous options
Keyboard	Keyboard specifications
Pointer	Mouse configuration
Monitor	Monitor configuration (set horizontal and vertical frequency)
Device	Video card configuration
Screen	Configures display, setting virtual screen, display colors, screen size, and other features

Although you can directly edit the file using a standard text editor, it's always best to rely on the setup programs such as XF86Setup to make changes. Most of the sections you will never have to touch. However, in some cases, you want to make changes to the Screen section, located at the end of the file. To do so, you would edit the file and add or change entries in the Screen section. In the Screen section you can configure your virtual screen display and set the number of colors supported. Since the Screen section is the one you would most likely change, it will be discussed first, even though it comes last, at the end of the file.

Screen

A Screen section begins with a Driver entry that specifies the driver name. There are five driver names, one for each type of XFree86 server: Accel, Mono, SVGA, VGA2, and VGA16. The Accel driver name is used for all accelerated X servers such as S3_XFree86. Mono is for non-VGA mono drivers supported by the XF86_Mono server. VGA2 and VGA16 are used for the VGA server, and SVGA is used for the XF86_SVGA server. If you are using the XFree86_SVGA server, the Driver entry would have "svga". If you are using any of the accelerated servers, this entry would be "Accel". Setup programs such as XF86Setup will generate Screen sections for each of these. If you are using the SVGA server, you would use the SVGA screen section.

After the Driver entry, the Device and Monitor entries specify the monitor and video card you are using. The name given in the Identifier entry in these sections is used to reference those components. A monitor given the Identifier name Nec3v will have the entry **Monitor Nec3v** in the Screen section.

```
Section "Screen"
    Driver          "Accel"
    Device          "Primary Card"
    Monitor         "Primary Monitor"
    DefaultColorDepth  16
    SubSection "Display"
       Depth        8
       Modes        "1152x864" "1024x768" "800x600" "640x480" "640x400"
                    "480x300" "400x300" "320x240" "320x200"
       Virtual 800 600
    EndSubSection
    SubSection "Display"
```

The Screen section has Display subsections, one for each depth supported. Whereas the previous sections were configuring hardware, the Display subsection configures display features such as the number of colors displayed and the virtual screen size. There are three main entries: Depth, Modes, and Virtual. The Depth entry is the screen resolution: 8, 16, and 24. You can add the DefaultColorDepth entry to set the default color depth to whatever your X server will support: 8 for 256K, 16 for 32K, and 24 for 16M. Modes are the modes allowed given the resolution. Virtual is the size of the virtual screen. You can have a virtual screen larger than your display area. When you move your mouse to the edge of the displayed screen, it will scroll to that hidden part of the screen. This way you can have a working screen much larger than the physical size of your monitor. The usual setting for a virtual screen is 1024 × 768, a 17-inch monitor size. You could also set it to 1152 × 864, a 21-inch monitor size. For a 15-inch monitor, the virtual screen is sometimes set to 1024 × 768. If you want to disable the virtual screen, you can set the Virtual entry to 800 × 600, making the display the same size as the physical screen.

Virtual 1024 768	17-inch virtual screen
Virtual 1152 864	21-inch virtual screen
Virtual 800 600	15-inch screen (disable virtual screen)

Any of these features in this section can be safely changed. In fact, to change the virtual screen size, you will have to modify this section. However, other sections in the **XF86Config** file should be left alone, unless you are certain of what you are doing.

Files, Modules, ServerFlags, and Keyboard

The Files section lists different directories for resources that XFree86 needs. These are mostly the fonts available on your system. A font entry begins with the data specification **FontPath** and is followed by the pathname for that font. A sample of these entries is shown here:

```
RgbPath      "/usr/X11R6/lib/X11/rgb"
FontPath     "/usr/X11R6/lib/X11/fonts/misc:unscaled"
```

The Module section specifies modules to be dynamically loaded. The **Load** entry will load a module. See the XF86Config man page for more details.

There are several flags that can be set for the XFree86 server. You can find a complete listing in the XF86Config man page. For example, the **NoTrapSignals** enables the core to be dumped for debugging purposes. **DontZap** disables the use of CTRL-ALT-BACKSPACE to shut down the server. **DontZoom** disables switching between graphic modes.

The keyboard section determines your keyboard type and sets the layout, model, and protocol used. For example, the following entry sets the layout. There are a large number of options for this section. Consult the XF86Config man pages for a complete listing.

```
XkbLayout        "us"
```

Pointer

The Pointer section configures your mouse and any other pointer devices. This section has only a few entries, with some tailored for specific types of mice. The Protocol entry specifies the protocol your mouse uses such as Microsoft or Logitech. The Device entry is the pathname for the mouse device. The following example shows a standard Pointer section for a Microsoft mouse at 1200 baud. The device file is **/dev/mouse**.

```
Section "Pointer"
   Protocol       "Microsoft"
   Device         "/dev/mouse"
   BaudRate       1200
EndSection
```

The following is a listing of the Pointer section entries.

Protocol	Mouse protocol (do man XF86Config for complete listing)
Device	Device path such as **/dev/mouse** or **/dev/cua0**
BaudRate	Baud rate for serial mouse

Emulate3Buttons	Enables two-button mouse to emulate third button by pressing both left and right buttons at once
ChordMiddle	Three-button mouse configuration on some Logitech mice
ClearDTR and ClearRTS	Clear DTR and RTS lines, valid only for Mouse Systems mice
SampleRate	Set the sampling rate (Logitech)

Monitor

There should be a Monitor section for each monitor used on your system. The vertical and horizontal frequencies have to be accurate, or you can damage your monitor if they are too high. A monitor section begins with entries that identify the monitor such as vendor and model names. The HorizSync and VerRefresh entries are where the vertical and horizontal frequencies are specified. Most monitors can support a variety of resolutions. Those resolutions are specified in the Monitor section by ModeLine entries. There is a ModeLine entry for each resolution. The entry has five values, the name of the resolution, its dotclock value, and then two sets of four values, one for the horizontal timing and one for the vertical timing, ending with flags. The flags specify different characteristics of the mode such as Interlace to indicate that the mode is interlaced, and +hsync and +vsync to select the polarity of the signal.

```
ModeLine "name"  dotclock  horizontal-freq vertical-freq  flags
```

A sample of a ModeLine is shown here. It is best to leave the entire Monitor section alone, relying on the entries generated by a configuration tool like XF86Setup.

```
Modeline  "800x600"   50.00 800 856 976 1040 600 637 643 666 +hsync +vsync
```

Commonly used entries for the Monitor section are listed here.

Identifier	A name to identify the monitor
VendorName	Manufacturer
ModelName	The make and model
HorizSync	The horizontal frequency; can be a range or series of values
VerRefresh	Vertical refresh frequency; can be a range or series of values
Gamma	Gamma correction
ModeLine	Specifies a resolution with dotclock, horizontal timing, and vertical timing for that resolution

Device

The Device section specifies your video card. It begins with entries that identify the card such as VendorName, BoardName, and Chipset. The amount of video RAM is indicated in the VideoRam entry. The Clocks entry lists your clock values. There are many different entries that can be made in this section such as Ramdac for a Ramdac chip, should the board have one, and MemBase for the base address of a frame buffer, should it be accessible. See the XF86Config man pages for a detailed list and descriptions.

Though you could safely change the VideoRam entry—for example, if you added more memory to your card—it is not safe to change the Clocks entry. If you get the clock values wrong, you could easily destroy your monitor. Rely on the clock values generated by XF86Setup or other XFree86 setup programs. If the clock values are missing, the server is able to automatically determine them. This may be the case for newer cards.

X Window System Command Line Arguments

You can start up any X Window System application either within an **.xinitrc** or **.xsession** script or on the command line in an Xterm window. Some distributions, including Red Hat, place X Window System startup applications in an **.Xclients** file that is read by the **.xinitrc** script. Most X Window System applications take a set of standard X Window System arguments used to configure the window and display that the application will use. You can set the color of the window bars, give the window a specific title, and specify the color and font for text, as well as position the window at a specific location on the screen. Table 29-4 lists these X Window System arguments. They are discussed in detail in the X man pages, man X.

One commonly used argument is **-geometry**. This takes an additional argument that specifies the location on the screen where you want an application's window displayed. In the next example, the xclock X Window System application is called with a geometry argument. A set of up to four numbers specifies the position. The value +0+0 references the upper left-hand corner. There, you will see the clock displayed when you start up the X Window System. The value –0–0 references the upper right-hand corner.

```
& xclock -geometry +0+0 &
```

With the **-title** option, you can set the title displayed on the application window. Notice the use of quotes for titles with more than one word. You set the font with the **-fn** argument and the text and graphics color with the **-fg** argument. **-bg** sets the background color. The following example starts up an Xterm window with the title "My New Window" in the title bar. The text and graphics color is green and the background color is gray. The font is Helvetica.

```
$ xterm -title "My New Window"  -fg green -bg gray  -fn /usr/fonts/helvetica  &
```

**X Window System
Application Description
Configuration Arguments**

Configuration Arguments	Description
	See **x** man pages for detailed explanations
-bw *num*	Borderwidth of pixels in frame
-bd *color*	Border color
-fg *color*	Foreground color (for text or graphics)
-bg *color*	Background color
-display *display-name*	Displays client to run on; displays name consisting of hostname, display number, and screen number (see X man pages)
-fn *font*	Font to use for text display
-geometry *offsets*	Location on screen where X Window System application window is placed; offsets are measured relative to screen display
-iconic	Starts application with icon, not with open window
-rv	Switches background and foreground colors
-title *string*	Title for the window's title bar
-name *string*	Name for the application
xrm *resource-string*	Specifies resource value

Table 29-4.   *Configuration Options for X Window System–Based Applications*

X Window System Commands
and Configuration Files

The X Window System uses several configuration files as well as X commands to configure your X Window System. Some of the configuration files belong to the system and should not be modified. However, each user can have his or her own set of configuration files such as **.xinitrc**, **.xsession**, and **.Xresources** that can be used to configure a personalized X Window System interface. Some distributions, like Red Hat, also use an **.Xclients** file to hold X Window System startup applications. These configuration files are automatically read and executed when the X Window System is started up with either the **startx** command or an X display manager like xdm, kdm, or gdm. Within these configuration files you can execute X commands used to configure your system. With commands such as **xset** and **setroot**, you can add fonts or control the display of your root window. Tables 29-5 and 29-6 provide lists of X Window System commands and configuration files, respectively. You can obtain a complete description of your current X configuration using the **xdypinfo** command. The X man page provide a detailed introduction to the X commands and configuration files.

X Resources

Several X commands such as **xrdb** and **xmodmap** configure your X Window System interface. X Window System graphic configurations are listed in a resource file called **.Xresources**. Each user can have a customized **.Xresources** file in his or her home directory, configuring the X Window System to particular specifications. The **.Xresources** file contains entries for configuring specific programs such as the color of certain widgets. There is also a systemwide version called **/etc/X11/xinit/.Xresources**. (Notice that, unlike **/etc/X11/xinit/xinitrc**, there is a period before Xresources in the **/etc/X11/xinit/.Xresources** file name.) The **.Xdefaults** file is a default configuration loaded by all programs. It contains the same kind of entries for configuring resources as **.Xresources**. An **.Xdefaults** file is accessible by programs on your system, but not by those running on other systems. The **/usr/X11R6/lib/X11/app-defaults** directory holds files that contain default resource configurations for particular X applications such as Xterm, Xclock, and Xmixer. The Xterm file will hold resource entries specifying how an Xterm window is displayed. Users can override any of these defaults with alternative entries in an **.Xresources** file in their **home** directory.

Many distributions install only with a system **.Xresources** file. You can create an **.Xresources** file of your own in your **home** directory, and add resource entries to it. You could also copy the **/etc/X11/xinit/.Xresources** file and edit the entries there or add new ones of your own. The configuration is carried out by the **xrdb** command, which reads both the system's **.Xresources** file and any **.Xresources** or **.Xdefaults** file in the user's **home** directory. The **xrdb** command is currently executed in the **/etc/X11/xinit/xinitrc** script and the **/etc/X11/xdm/Xsession** script. If you create your own **.xinitrc** script in your **home** directory, be sure it executes the **xrdb** command with at least your own **.Xresources** file or the **/etc/X11/xinit/.Xresources** file (preferably both). You can ensure this by simply using a copy of the system's **xinitrc** script as your own **.xinitrc** file and then modifying that copy as you wish. See the man pages on **xrdb** for more details on resources. Also, you can find a more detailed discussion of Xresources as well as other X commands in the man pages for X.

An entry in the **.Xresources** file consists of a value assigned to a resource, class, or resources for an application. Usually, these are resources used for widgets or classes of widgets in an application. The resource designation typically consists of three elements separated by a period: the application, an object in the application, and the resource. The entire designation is terminated by a colon, and the value follows. For example, suppose you want to change the color of the hour hand to blue in the oclock application. The application is oclock, the object is clock, and the resource is hour: oclock.clock.hour. The entry would look like this:

```
oclock.clock.hour: blue
```

The object element is actually a list of objects denoting the hierarchy leading to a particular object. In the oclock example there is only one object, but in many applications the object hierarchy can be very complex. This would require a lengthy set of objects listed to specify the one you want. To avoid this complexity, you can use the asterisk notation to reference the object you want directly, using an asterisk in place of the period. You just need to know the name of the resource you want to change. The following example sets the oclock minute and hour hands to green.

```
oclock*hour: green
oclock*minute: green
```

You can also use the asterisk to apply a value to whole classes of objects. Many individual resources are grouped into classes. You can reference all the resources in a class by their class name. Class names begin with an uppercase character. For example, in the Xterm application, the background and pointer color resources are both part of the Background class. The reference **XTerm*Background** would change all of these resources in an Xterm window. However, any specific references will always override the more general ones.

You can also use the asterisk to change the values of a resource in objects for all of your applications. In this case, you place an asterisk before the resource. For example, to change the foreground color to red for all the objects in every application, you would enter

```
*foreground: red
```

If you just wanted to change the foreground color of the scroll bars in all your applications you would use:

```
*scrollbar*foreground: blue
```

The **showrgb** command will list the different colors available on your system. You can use the descriptive name or a hexadecimal form. Values can also be fonts, bitmaps, and pixmaps. You could change the font displayed by certain objects in, or for graphic applications, change background or border graphics. Resources vary with each application. Applications may support very different kinds of objects and the resources for them. Check the man pages and documentation for an application to learn what resources it supports and the values accepted for them. Some resources take Boolean values that can turn features on or off. Others can specify options. Some applications will have a default set of resource values that will be automatically placed in your system's **.Xresources** or **.Xdefaults** files.

The **Xmodmap** file holds configurations for your input devices such as your mouse and keyboard (for example, you can bind keys such as BACKSPACE or reverse the click operations of your right and left mouse buttons). The **Xmodmap** file used by your display manager will be in the display manager configuration directory such as **/etc/X11/xdm**, whereas the one used by **startx** is located in **/etc/X11/xinit**. Each user can create a custom **.Xmodmap** file in his or her **home** directory to configure the system's input devices. This is helpful if users connect through their own terminals to your Linux system. The **.Xmodmap** file is read by the **xmodmap** command, which performs the configuration. The **xmodmap** command will first look for an **.Xmodmap** file in the user's **home** directory and use that. If there is no **.Xmodmap** in the **home** directory, it will use the one for your display manager or **startx** command. You will see entries for the **xmodmap** command in the **/etc/X11/xinit/xinitrc** file and the display manager's **Xsession** file. If you have your own **.xinitrc** or **.xsession** script in your **home** directory, it should execute the **xmodmap** command with either your own **.Xmodmap** file or the system's **Xmodmap** file. See the man pages on **xmodmap** for more details.

X Commands

Usually, an **.xinitrc** or **.xssesion** script will have X Window System commands like **xset** and **xsetroot** used to configure different features of your X Window System session. The **xset** command sets different options such as turning on the screen saver or setting the volume for the bell and speaker. You can also use **xset** to load fonts. See the **xset** man pages for specific details. With the **b** option and the **on** or **off** argument, **xset** will turn your speaker on or off. The following example turns on the speaker.

```
xset b on
```

You use **xset** with the **-s** option to set the screen saver. With the **on** and **off** arguments you can turn the screen saver on or off. Two numbers entered as arguments will specify the length and period in seconds. The length is the number of seconds the screen saver waits before activating. The period is how long it waits before regenerating the pattern.

The **xsetroot** command lets you set the features of your root window (setting the color or displaying a bitmap pattern—you can even use a cursor of your own design). Table 29-5 lists the different **xsetroot** options. See the man pages for **xsetroot** for options and details. The following **xsetroot** command uses the **-solid** option to set the background color of the root window to blue.

```
xsetroot -solid blue
```

Fonts

Your X Window System fonts are located in a directory called
/usr/X11R6/lib/X11/fonts. X Window System fonts are loaded using the **xfs** command.
This command reads the **/etc/X11/fs/config** configuration file that lists the font
directories in an entry for the term **catalogue**. The XMan pages provides a detailed
discussion on fonts. To install a set of fonts, place them in a directory whose path you
can add to the catalogue entry to have them automatically installed. You can also
separately install a particular font with the **xset** command and its **+fp** option. Fonts
for your system are specified in a font path. The font path is a set of file names, each
holding a font. The file names include their complete path. An example of the
catalogue entry in the **/etc/X11/config** file follows. This is a comma-delimited list of
directories. These are directories where the X Window System will first look for fonts.

```
catalogue =
/usr/X11R6/lib/X11/fonts/misc/,/usr/X11R6/lib/X11/fonts/Speedo/,/us
r/X11R6/lib/X11/fonts/Type1/,/usr/X11R6/lib/X11/fonts/75dpi/,/usr/X
11R6/lib/X11/fonts/100dpi/
```

Before you can access newly installed fonts, you have to first index them with
the **mkfontdir** command. From within the directory with the new fonts, enter
the **mkfontdir** command. You can also use the directory path as an argument to
mkfontdir. After indexing the fonts, you can then load them using the **xset**
command with the **fp rehash** option. To have the fonts automatically loaded, add the
directory with its full pathname to the catalogue entry in the **xfs** configuration file.
The following shows how to install a new font and then load it:

```
$ cp newfont.pcf  ~/myfonts
$ mkfontdir ~/myfonts
$ xset fp rehash
```

Within a **font** directory, there are several special files that hold information about
the fonts. The **fonts.dir** file lists all the fonts in that directory. In addition, you can set
up a **fonts.alias** file to give other names to a font. Font names tend to be very long and
complex. A **fonts.scale** file holds the names of scalable fonts. See the man pages for
xfs and **mkfontdir** for more details.

With the **xset +fp** and **−fp** options, you can specifically add or remove particular
fonts. The **fn** option with the **rehash** argument will then load the fonts. With the
default argument, the default set of fonts are restored. The **+fp** adds a font to this font
path. For your own fonts, you can place them in any directory and specify their file
names, including their complete path. The next example adds the **myfont** font in the
/usr/local/fonts directory to the font path. Then the **fp** option with the **rehash**
argument loads the font.

```
xset +fp /usr/local/fonts/myfont
xset fp rehash
```

To remove this font you would use **xset -fp /usr/home/*myfont*** and follow it with the **xset fp rehash** command. If you want to reset your system back to the set of default fonts, enter the following:

```
xset fp default
xset fp rehash
```

With **xlsfonts**, you can list the fonts currently installed on your system. To display an installed font to see what it looks like, use **xselfonts**. You can browse through your fonts, selecting the ones you like.

Table 29-5 lists common X Window System commands, whereas Table 29-6 lists the configuration files and directories associated with the X Window System.

X Window System Commands	Explanation
xterm	Opens up a new terminal window
xset	Sets X Window System options; see man pages for complete listing **-b** Configures bell **-c** Configures key click **+fp** *fontlist* Adds fonts **-fp** *fontlist* Removes fonts **led** Turns on or off keyboard LEDs **m** Configures mouse **p** Sets pixel color values **s** Sets the screen saver **q** Lists current settings

Table 29-5. *X Window System Commands*

X Window System Commands	Explanation
xsetroot	Configures the root window **-cursor** *cursorfile maskfile* Sets pointer to bitmap pictures when pointer is outside any window **-bitmap** *filename* Sets root window pattern to bitmap **-gray** Sets background to gray **-fg** *color* Sets color of foreground bitmap **-bg** *color* Sets color of background bitmap **-solid** *color* Sets background color **-name** *string* Sets name of root window to string
xmodmap	Configures input devices; reads the **.Xmodmap** file **-pk** Displays current keymap **-e** expression Sets key binding keycode NUMBER = KEYSYMNAME Sets key to specified key symbol keysym KEYSYMNAME = KEYSYMNAME Sets key to operate the same as specified key pointer = NUMBER Sets mouse button codes
xrdb	Configures X Window System resources; reads the **.Xresources** file
xdm	X Window System Display Manager; runs the XFree86 server for your system; usually called by **xinitrc**
startx	Starts up X Window System by executing **xinit** and instructing it to read the **.Xclients** file
xfs *config-file*	The X Window System font server
mkfontdir *font-directory*	Indexes new fonts, making them accessible by the font server

Table 29-5.   *X Window System Commands* (continued)

X Window System Commands	Explanation
xlsfonts	Lists fonts on your system
xfontsel	Displays installed fonts
xdpyinfo	Lists detailed information about your X Window System configuration
xinit	Starts up X Window System, first reading the system's **xinitrc** file; when invoked from **startx**, it also reads the user's **.Xclients** file; **xinit** is not called directly, but through **startx**
xmkmf	Creates a Makefile for an X Window System application using the application's Imakefile; invokes **imake** to generate the Makefile (never invoke **imake** directly)
xauth	Reads **.Xauthority** file to set access control to a user account through **xdm** from remote systems

Table 29-5. *X Window System Commands* (continued)

Configuration Files	
.Xmodmap	User's X Window System input devices configuration file
.Xresources	User's X Window System resource configuration file
.Xdefaults	User's X Window System resource configuration file

Table 29-6. *X Window System Configuration Files*

Configuration Files

.xinitrc	User's X Window System configuration file (read automatically by **xinit**, if it exists)
.Xclients or **.Xsessions**	User's X Window System configuration file (used on Red Hat and other Linux distributions)
.Xssession	User X Window System configuraion file read by X Display Manager.
.Xauthority	User's access controls through xdm GUI login interface
/usr/X11R6/	Directory where the X Window System release 6 commands, applications, and configuration files are held
/usr/X11R6/lib/X11/	Directory that holds X Window System configuration files and subdirectories for the version currently installed on your system. On Red Hat and OpenLinux this is a link to the **/etc/X11** directory
/etc/X11/xinit/xinitrc	System X Window System initialization file; automatically read by **xinit**
/etc/X11/xinit/Xclients	System X Window System configuration file (used on Red Hat and other Linux distributions)
/etc/X11/xinit/.Xresources	System X Window System resources file; read by **xinitrc**
/etc/X11/xinit/.Xmodmap	System X Window System input devices file; read by **xinitrc**
/etc/X11/rgb.txt	X Windows colors; each entry has four fields; the first three fields are numbers for red, green, and blue; the last field is the name given to the color
/etc/X11/xdm	X Display Manager
/etc/X11/gdm	Gnome Display Manager
/etc/X11/kdm	KDE Display Manager
/etc/X11/xdm/Xsession	X Display Manager Configuration file

Table 29-6.   *X Window System Configuration Files* (continued)

X Window System Startup Methods: startx and display managers

There are two different ways to start up your X Window System. You can start Linux with the command line interface and then, once you log in, use the **startx** command to start the X Window System and your window manager and desktop. You can also use a display manager that will automatically start the X Window System when you boot your computer, displaying a login window and a menu for selecting the window manager or desktop you want to use. There will also be options for shutting down your system. Currently there are three display managers you can use. The K Display Manager (kdm) is a display manager provided with the KDE. The Gnome Display Manager (gdm) comes with the Gnome desktop. The X Display Manager (xdm) is the original display manager used on Linux system.

Each method uses its own startup script. The **startx** command uses the **xinit** command to start the X Window System; its startup script is **/etc/X11/xinit/xinitrc**. Startup scripts for display managers are found in their respective directories. For **xdm** the startup script is **/etc/X11/xdm/Xsession**. The kdm and gdm display managers have their own configuration directories, **/etc/X11/kdm** and **/etc/X11/gdm**. Here you find files for configuring their login window and menus. The gdm application as currently implemented on Red Hat uses the xdm **Xsession** script, whereas kdm uses an **Xsession** script in its own directory.

As an enhancement to either **startx** or a display manager you can use the X session manager (xsm). You can use it to launch your X Window System with different sessions. A session is a specified group of X applications. Starting with one session might start Gnome and Netscape, and another might start KDE and KOffice. You can save it during a session or when you shut down. The applications you have running will become part of a saved session. When you start, xsm will display a session menu for you to choose from, listing previous sessions you saved. For xsm to work, it has to be the last entry in your **.xsessions** or **.Xclients** file, nor should you have any other applications started in these files.

startx, xinit, and .xinitrc

The X Window System can be started from the command line interface using the **xinit** command. You do not invoke the **xinit** command directly, but through the **startx** command that you always use to start the X Window System. Both of these commands are found in the **/usr/X11R6/bin** directory, along with many other X-based programs. The **startx** command is a shell script that executes the **xinit** command. The **xinit** command, in turn, will first look for an X Window System initialization script called **.xinitrc**, in the user's **home** directory. If there is no **.xinitrc** script in the home directory, then **xinit** will use **/etc/X11/xinit/xinitrc** as its initialization script. Both **.xinitrc** and **/etc/X11/xinit/xinitrc** have commands to configure your X Windows server and execute any initial X commands such as starting up the window manager. You can think of the **/etc/X11/xinit/xinitrc** script as a default script. In addition, many systems use a separate file named **Xclients** where particular X applications, desktop, or window manager can be specified. These entries can be directly listed in an **xinitrc** file, but a separate file makes for a more organized format. The **Xclients** file will be executed as shell scripts by the **xinitrc** file. There is a user version as well as a system version: **.Xclients** and **/etc/X11/init/Xclients**. On Red Hat systems, the user's home directory is checked for the **.Xclients** file, and if missing, the **/etc/X11/xinit/Xclients** file is used.

Most distributions do not initially set up any **.xinitrc** or **.Xclients** scripts in any of the home directories. These have to be created by a particular user who wants one. Each user can create a personalized **.xinitrc** script in his or her home directory, configuring and starting up the X Window System as desired. Until a user sets up an **.xinitrc** script, the **/etc/X11/xinit/xinitrc** script is used. You can examine this script to see how the X Window System starts up. Certain configuration operations required for the X Window System must be in the **.xinitrc** file. For a user to create his or her own **.xinitrc** script, it is best to first copy the **/etc/X11/xinit/xinitrc** to his or her home directory and name it **.xinitrc**. Then each user can modify the particular **.xinitrc** file as desired. (Notice that the system **xinitrc** file has no preceding period in its name, whereas the home directory **.xinitrc** file set up by a user does have a preceding period.) The following example shows a simple system **xinitrc** file that starts the Window Maker window manager and an Xterm window. System and user **.Xresources** and **.Xmodmap** files are executed first to configure the X Window System.

/etc/X11/xinit/xinitrc

```
#!/bin/sh
userresources=$HOME/.Xresources
usermodmap=$HOME/.Xmodmap
sysresources=/usr/X11R6/lib/X11/xinit/.Xresources
sysmodmap=/usr/X11R6/lib/X11/xinit/.Xmodmap

# merge in defaults and keymaps
if [ -f $sysresources ]; then
    xrdb -merge $sysresources
fi
if [ -f $sysmodmap ]; then
    xmodmap $sysmodmap
fi
if [ -f $userresources ]; then
    xrdb -merge $userresources
fi
if [ -f $usermodmap ]; then
    xmodmap $usermodmap
fi
```

```
# start some nice programs
xterm &
exec wmaker
```

OpenLinux provides both a system **xinitrc** and **kdeinitrc** file. The **kdeinitrc** file is a special **xinitrc** file used by OpenLinux to start KDE. On OpenLinux, you use the **kde** command to read this file and start KDE, whereas the **startx** command will use the **xinitrc** file and starts a simple window manager. The local version of the **/etc/X11/xinit/ kdeinitrc** file is **.kdeinitrc**. You can also consult the man pages on **xinit** and **startx** for more information. On Red Hat, if a user only wants to add startup applications, then the user can just create an **.Xclients** file instead of a complete **.xinitrc** file (OpenLinux does not implment Xclient files). Be sure that there are commands in the system **xinitrc** file to check for and run a user's **.Xclients** file. The following example shows the code used in the Red Hat **xinitrc** file to execute a user's **.Xclients** script, and failing that, the system **Xclients** script. If that fails, then the FVWM2 window manager is started, and should that fail, then the twm file manager is started.

```
if [ -f $HOME/.Xclients ]; then
    exec $HOME/.Xclients
elif [ -f /etc/X11/xinit/Xclients ]; then
    exec /etc/X11/xinit/Xclients
else
        # failsafe settings.  Although we should never get here
         xclock -geometry 100x100-5+5 &
        xterm -geometry 80x50-50+150 &
        if [ -f /usr/X11R6/bin/fvwm2 ]; then
                exec fvwm2
        else
                exec twm
        fi
fi
```

Display Managers: xdm, kdm, and gdm

When a system configured to run a display manager starts up, the X Window System starts up immediately and displays a login dialog. The dialog prompts the user to enter a login name and a password. Once they are entered, a selected X Windows interface starts up, say with Gnome, KDE, or some other desktop or window manager. When the user quits the window manager or desktop, the system returns to the login dialog and remains there until another user logs in. You can shift to a command line interface with the CTRL-ALT-F1 keys and return to the display manager login dialog with CTRL-ALT-F7.

A display manager can do much more than provide a GUI login window. You can also use it to control access to different hosts and users on your network. The **.Xauthority** file in each user's home directory contains authentication information for that user. A display manager like xdm supports the X Display Manager Control Protocol (XDMCP). They were originally designed for systems like workstations that are continually operating, but are also used to start up X Windows automatically on single user systems when the system boots.

A display manager refers to a user's login and startup of a window manager and desktop as a session. When the user quits the desktop and logs out, the session ends. When another user logs in, a new session starts. The X Window System never shuts down; only desktop or window manager programs do. Session menus on the display manager login window list different kinds of sessions you can start, in other words, different kinds of window managers or desktops. For each session, the startup script used to configure a user's X Window System display and execute the selected desktop or window manager is the **Xsession** script. Though this script is not necessary for gdm, it is still used in the gdm Red Hat implementation.

Xsession

Xsession is the display manager session startup script used by xdm, kdm, and also by the Red Hat implementation of gdm. It contains many of the X commands also used the **xinitrc** startup script. **Xsession** will usually execute the same **xmodmap** and **xrdb** commands using the **.Xmodmap** and **.Xresources** files in the **/etc/X11/xinit** directory. Shown here is the **Xsession** script used by gdm on Red Hat systems. It is located in the **/etc/X11/xdm** directory.

```
#!/bin/bash -login
# (c) 1999 Red Hat Software, Inc.

xsetroot -solid #356390

# redirect errors to a file in user's home directory if we can for errfile
# in "$HOME/.xsession-errors" "${TMPDIR-/tmp}/xses-$USER" "/tmp/xses-$USER"
do
    if ( cp /dev/null "$errfile" 2> /dev/null )
    then
    chmod 600 "$errfile"
    exec > "$errfile" 2>&1
    break
    fi
done

# clean up after xbanner
if [ -f /usr/X11R6/bin/freetemp ]; then
    freetemp
```

```
fi

userresources=$HOME/.Xresources
usermodmap=$HOME/.Xmodmap
sysresources=/usr/X11R6/lib/X11/xinit/.Xresources
sysmodmap=/usr/X11R6/lib/X11/xinit/.Xmodmap

# merge in defaults and keymaps
if [ -f $sysresources ]; then
    xrdb -merge $sysresources
fi

if [ -f $sysmodmap ]; then
    xmodmap $sysmodmap
fi

if [ -f $userresources ]; then
    xrdb -merge $userresources
fi

if [ -f $usermodmap ]; then
    xmodmap $usermodmap
fi

#see if xdm/gdm/kdm has asked for a specific environment case $# in 1
    case $1 in
    failsafe)
    exec xterm -geometry 80x24-0-0
    ;;
    gnome)
    exec gnome-session
    ;;
    kde)
    exec startkde
    ;;
    anotherlevel)
        # we assume that switchdesk is installed.
    exec /usr/share/apps/switchdesk/Xclients.anotherlevel
    ;;
    esac
esac
```

Should users want to set up their own startup files, you can reprogram the
Xsession file to first check for an .**Xsession** file in the user's **home** directory and
execute that. A user could copy the **Xsession** file to their own .**xsession** and edit it. The
user could replace the case statement with a single invocation of the desktop they

want. The following example shows a simple **Xsession** script that executes the user's
.Xsession script if it exists. The user's **.Xsession** script is expected to start a window
manager or desktop.

```
#
# Xsession
#
# This is the program that is run as the client
# for the display manager.


startup=$HOME/.xsession
resources=$HOME/.Xresources

if [ -f "$startup" ]; then
        exec "$startup"
    else
        if [ -f "$resources" ]; then
            xrdb -load "$resources"
        fi
        fvwn2 &
        exec xterm -geometry 80x24+10+10 -ls
  fi
```

The following example shows a simple **.Xsession** script to start Window Maker.

```
wmaker &
xrdb -merge "$HOME/.Xresources"
xterm -geometry -0+50 -ls
```

The X Display Manager (xdm)

The X Display Manager (xdm) manages a collection of X displays either on the local
system or remote servers. Its design is based on the X Consortium standard X Display
Manager Control Protocol (XDMCP). The xdm program manages user logins, providing
authentication and starting sessions. For character-based logins, a session is the lifetime
of the user shell that is started up when the user logs in and forms the command line
interface. For xdm and other display managers, the session is determined by the session
manager. The session is usually the duration of a window manager or desktop. When the
desktop or window manager terminates, so does the sesssion.

The xdm program displays a login window with boxes for a login name and
password. The user logs in, and a window manager or desktop starts up. When the
user quits the window manager, the X Window System is then restarted automatically,

displaying the login window again. Authentications to control access for particular users are kept in their **.Xauthority** file.

The xdm configuration files are located in the **/usr/X11R6/lib/X11/xdm/** directory, although on Red Hat and OpenLinux this is a link to the **/etc/X11/xdm** directory. The main xdm configuration file is **xdm-config**. There are also files such as **Xresources** to configure how the dialog is displayed, and **Xsetup**, which lets you specify a root-window image or other windows to display. You can use the **xbanner** program to choose a graphic to display with the login dialog. When the user starts up a session, the **Xsession** script is run to configure the user's X Window System and execute the user's window manager or desktop. This script usually calls the **.Xsession** script in the user's **home** directory, if there is one (thought this is not the case currently for OpenLinux and RedHat Xsession scripts). It holds any specific user X commands.

If you want to start xdm from the command line interface you can enter it with the **−nodaemon** option. CTRL-C will then shut down xdm.

```
xdm −nodaemon
```

Table 29-7 lists the configuration files and directories associated with xdm.

File Names	Description
/usr/X11R6/lib/X11/xdm	The xdm configuration directory; on Red Hat and OpenLinux this is **/etc/X11/xdm**
xdm-config	xdm configuration file
Xsession	Startup script for user session
Xresource	Resource features for xdm login window
Xsetup	Sets up the login window and xdm login screen
Xstartup	Session startup script
xdm-errors	Errors from xdm sessions
.Xsession	User's session script in the home directory, usually executed by **Xsession**
Xreset	Resets the X Window System after a session ends
.Xauthority	User authorization file where xdm stores keys for clients to read

Table 29-7. *The xdm Configuration Files and Directories*

The Gnome Display Manager (gdm)

The Gnome Display Manager (gdm) manages user login and GUI interface sessions. GdItm can service several displays and generates a process for each. The main gdm process listens for XDMCP requests from remote displays and monitors the local display sessions. gdItm displays a login window with boxes for entering a login name and password. It also displays a pop-up menu labeled options with entries for Sessions and Shutdown submenus. The Sessions menu displays different window mangers and desktops you can start up. On Red Hat you will find entries for Gnome, KDE, and AnotherLevel (fvwm2). You can easily add entries to this menu by adding files for them in the gdm configuration directory, **/etc/X11/gdm/Sessions**.

The gdm configuration files are located in the **/etc/X11/gdm** directory. Its main configuration file is **gdm.conf**, where you can set various options such as the logo image and welcome text to display. The **gdm** directory also contains four directories, **Init**, **Sessions**, **PostSession**, and **PreSession**. You can easily configure gdm by placing or editing files in these different directories. The **Init** directory contains scripts that are executed when gdm starts up. On Red Hat this directory contains a Default script that holds X commands such as setting the background. These are applied to the screen showing the gdm login window.

The Sessions directory hold session scripts. These become entries in the session menu displayed on the gdm login window options menu. For example, you could have a script called **kde** that contains the command **startkde** to run the KDE desktop. The term *kde* will appear in the gdm session menu. Selecting it will execute this script and start KDE. Currently on Red Hat, these scripts contain calls to the **/etc/X11/xdm/Xsession** script, using the file name as its argument. In the **Xsession** script, this name is used to start that particular kind of session. For example, when you select kde, the term kde it passed to the **Xsession** script, which then uses it to execute the **startkde** command to start KDE. For example, the **gnome** script consists of just the following lines. The term *gnome* is passed to the **Xsession** script, which then uses it to execute the **gnome-session** command to start Gnome. This design has the advantage of not having to repeat any X configuration commands such as **xmodmap**.

```
#!/bin/bash -login
/etc/X11/xdm/Xsession gnome
```

The **PreSession** directory holds any presession commands to execute, and the **PostSession** directory holds scripts for commands you want executed whenever a session ends. Neither the **Init**, **PreSession**, or **PostSession** scripts are necessary (Red Hat currently does not include **PreSession** or **PostSession** scripts).

For gdm, the login window is generated by a program called the *greeter*. Initially, the greeter will look for icons for every user on the system, located in the **.gnome/photo** file in users' **home** directories. Clicking the icon will automatically display the name of the user in the login box. The user can then enter the password and click the Login button to log in.

Table 29-8 lists the configuration files and directories associated with gdm.

The K Display Manager (kdm)

The K Display Manager (kdm) also manages user logins and start X Window System sessions. kdItm is derived from the xdm display manager, using the same configuration files. The kdm login window displays a list of user icons for users on the system. A user can click his or her icon and that user's name will appear in the login box. Just enter the password and click Go to log in. The session menu is a drop-down menu showing possible sessions. Click the Shutdown button to shut down the system.

You configure kdm using the KDM Configuration Manager located on the KDE root user desktop (see Chapter 4). Log in as the root user and start the KDM Configuration Manager by selecting KDM login manager in the Applications menu located in the Settings menu. There are panels for configuring the background, logo, and welcome message, as well as for adding icons for users on the system. To add a new session entry in the Session menu, enter the name for the entry in the New Type box on the Sessions panel and click Add. The name you enter will be passed as an argument to the kdm **Xsession** script.

When you select a session and click Go, kdm will run the **/etc/X11/kdm/Xsession** script, passing the name of the session as an argument. In the **Xsession** script, this name is used to start that particular kind of session. For example, when you select kde, the term kde it passed to the **Xsession** script, which then uses it to execute the **kde** command to start KDE. The following example shows the **Xsession** script used for kdm on OpenLinux.

The kdm program uses the same configuration files as xdm. On OpenLinux, a directory called **/etc/X11/kdm** is created with kdm versions of the xdm files. Here you will find an **xdm.conf** file along with **Xsession**, **Xresources**, and **Xsetup**, among others. The resources used to control how the kdm login window is displayed are set in the **/opt/kde/share/config/kdmrc** file.

File Names	Description
/etc/X11/gdm	gdm configuration directory
gdm.conf	gdm configuration file
Init	Startup scripts for configuring gdm display
Sessions	Holds session scripts whose names appear in session menu
PreSession	Scripts execute at start of session
PostSession	Scripts execute when session ends

Table 29-8. *The gdm Configuration Files and Directories*

Starting Window Managers

As noted in Chapter 4, the X Window System is started either automatically using a display manager with a login window, or from the command line by entering the **startx** command. Your X Window System server will then load, followed immediately by the window manager. You exit the window manager by choosing an exit or quit entry in the desktop workspace menu. The display manager and some window managers, like FVWM2 and Window Maker, will give you the option of starting other window managers. If you get into trouble and the window manager hangs, you can forcibly exit the X Window System with the keys CTRL-ALT-BACKSPACE.

The window manager that you will start is the default one set up by your Linux distribution when you installed your system. Many distributions now use as their default either Gnome or KDE. For Gnome and the K Desktop different window managers are used, kwm for the K Desktop and Enlightenment for Gnome. You can run Gnome or KDE applications on most window managers. To have Gnome use a particular window manager, you need to select it using the Gnome Control Center. It is also possible to use a window manager in place of kwm for KDE. Check the window manager's Web site for current information on Gnome and KDE compatibility. Currently, Enlightenment is fully Gnome compliant, and AfterStep and Window Maker are nearly so. Normally, distributions will include several window managers on their CD-ROM that you can install and run on your system. Red Hat and OpenLinux provide Window Maker, Enlightenment, AfterStep, kwm, and FVWM2, with FVWM2 being the default.

To use a different window manager, first install it. RPM packages will install with a default configuration for the window manager. If you are installing from source code you compiled, follow the included installation instructions. You can then configure Gnome or KDE to use that window manager, provided it is compliant with them. See Chapters 5 and 6 on how to configure the KDE and Gnome desktops. Alternatively, you can configure your system to start a particular window manager without either desktop. To do this, you have to place an entry for your window manager in an X Window System startup file. There are different startup files for the display manager and the **startx** command.

startx and .xinitrc

The system X Window System startup file is called **/etc/X11/xinit/xinitrc**. For **startx**, users can also set up their own **.xinitrc** files in their **home** directories in place of the system's **xinitrc** file. To create your own **xinitrc** file, you can copy the system one. In addition, Red Hat lets users specify their own X clients, such as window managers and desktops, in a startup file called **.Xclients**. This way you do not have to bother with a complex **.xinitrc** file.

The following command generates a user's **.xinitrc** file using the system's **xinitrc** file. Be sure you are in your **home** directory. Notice that the **.xinitrc** file has a preceding dot as part of its name, whereas the system's **xinitrc** file does not.

```
$ cp /etc/X11/xinit/xinitrc  .xinitrc
```

The invocation of the window manager is always the last command in the **.xinitrc** script. The X Window System will exit after finishing the execution of whatever the last command in the **.xinitrc** script is. By making the window manager the last command, exiting the window manager will shut down your X Window System session. Any other programs that you want to initially start up should be placed before the window manager command. You just have to place the command to start the window manager you want at the end of your **.xinitrc** file. Be sure to comment out any other window managers by placing a # at the beginning of the lines that hold their commands, or just remove them. It is also best to use the full pathname of a window manager program. They are usually located in the **/usr/X11R6/bin** directory or in the **/usr/bin** directory. Leave the rest of the file alone. The following example runs Window Maker.

```
exec /usr/X11R6/bin/wmaker
```

Should you also want to load other programs automatically such as a file manager, you can place their commands before the command for the window manager. Put an ampersand (&) after the command. The following example starts the Xterm window when the Window Maker window manager starts up.

```
xterm &
exec /usr/X11R6/bin/wmaker
```

If you are planning extensive changes, it is advisable to make them a few at a time, testing as you go. A very simple **.xinitrc** file is shown here:

.xinitrc

```
#!/bin/sh

userresources=$HOME/.Xresources
usermodmap=$HOME/.Xmodmap
sysresources=/usr/X11R6/lib/X11/xinit/.Xresources
sysmodmap=/usr/X11R6/lib/X11/xinit/.Xmodmap

# merge in defaults and keymaps

if [ -f $sysresources ]; then
xrdb -merge $sysresources
fi
```

```
if [ -f $sysmodmap ]; then
xmodmap $sysmodmap
fi

if [ -f $userresources ]; then
xrdb -merge $userresources
fi

if [ -f $usermodmap ]; then
xmodmap $usermodmap
fi


if [ -f /usr/X11R6/bin/wmaker ]; then
exec /usr/X11R6/bin/wmaker
else
exec fvwm2
fi
```

Red Hat uses a rather complex startup procedure that is designed to configure window managers automatically with the complete set of Red Hat menus for applications installed by its distribution. There is support for FVWM2, Window Maker, and AfterStep. Red Hat's global **Xclients** file will search for a file called **.wm_style** in a user's **home** directory. This is where the name of your preferred window manager is placed if you should select an alternative from the FVWM2 or AfterStep menus. You can also manually edit this file with a text editor and type one in. The **.wm_style** file holds a single name such as FVWM2, AfterStep, Window Maker, or LessTiff. **Xclients** then calls the **/usr/X11R6/bin/RunWM** script with an option for the window manager to start up. The RunWM script will check to see if the window manager is installed and then start it up with helpful options. As the system administrator you can edit this file to add new entries if you wish. Alternatively, you can create your own **.xinitrc** file to bypass this procedure.

Display Managers and Xsession

To invoke a window manager using a display manager like xdm, kdm, or gdm, you first have to create an entry for it in the login window's session menu. There are different ways to do this for kdm and gdm. You then have to edit the session startup script and add code to select and start up that window manager. The startup script used for the Red Hat implementation of gdm is **/etc/X11/xdm/Xsession**, and the one used for the OpenLinux implementation of kdm is **/etc/X11/kdm/Xsession**.

Gnome Display Manager: gdm

First create an entry for the window manager in the session menu displayed in the gdm login window's option's menu. Here you find files for other items listed in this menu. Then create a file with the name of the entry you want displayed in the **/etc/X11/gdm/Sessions** directory (you can simply copy one of the scripts already there). On Red Hat, these scripts simply invoke the **/etc/X11/xdm/Xsession** script with an option for the particular window manager or desktop chosen. For example, to create an entry for Window Maker, you can create a file called WinMaker as shown here.

/etc/X11/gdm/Sessions/winmaker

```
#!/bin/bash -login

/etc/X11/xdm/Xsession wmaker
```

You then have to edit the **/etc/X11/xdm/Xsession** file to insert the code for selecting and starting the new window manager. **Xsession** contains detailed code, most of which you can ignore. In it is a case statement that lists the different window managers and desktops. Here you can enter

```
# now, we see if xdm/gdm/kdm has asked for a specific environment
case $# in
1)
    case $1 in
    failsafe)
     exec xterm -geometry 80x24-0-0
     ;;
    gnome)
     exec gnome-session
     ;;
    kde)
     exec startkde
     ;;
    wmaker)
     exec wmaker
     ;;
    anotherlevel)
        # we assume that switchdesk is installed.
     exec /usr/share/apps/switchdesk/Xclients.anotherlevel
     ;;
    esac
esac
```

KDE Display Manager: kdm

To be able to start a new window manager or desktop from the kdm login window, you first have to add an entry for it to the session menu. You do this using the kdm configuration tool, described in Chapter 4. Log in as the root user and start the KDM Configuration Manager by selecting KDM login manager in the Applications menu located in the Settings menu. Then display the Sessions panel. Enter the new session entry in the box labeled New Type and click Add. The entry is added to the session menu on the kdm login window. The name you give the session entry will be the argument passed to the kdm **Xsession** script.

You then need to edit the kdm **Xsession** script and add code that will check for the name of this new session and then execute your new window manager. The KDE display manager (kdm) used on OpenLinux and SuSE uses its own **Xsession** file, **/etc/X11/kdm/Xsession**. The code is added to the case statement in the **Xsession** script that chooses which window manager or desktop to run for the user. The following example shows an entry for Window Maker added to the kdm **Xsession** script.

```
case $# in
1)
    case $1 in
    kde)
        KDEDIR=/opt/kde; export KDEDIR
        PATH=$KDEDIR/bin:$PATH
        exec /etc/X11/xinit/kdeinitrc
        ;;
    wmaker)
        exec wmaker
        ;;
    failsafe)
        exec xterm -geometry 80x24-0-0
        ;;
    esac
esac
```

Compiling X Window System Applications

To compile X Window System applications, you should first make sure that the XFree86 development package is installed along with any other development package you may need. These will contain header files and libraries used by X Window System programs. The name of such packages will contain the term **devel**, for example, **XFree86-devel**. Also, many X Window System applications may need special shared libraries. For example, some applications may need the **xforms** library or the **qt** library. Gnome applications will require the Gnome development libraries and KDE applications require the KDE development libraries. Some of these you will have to obtain from online sites, though most are available in the Red Hat **contrib** directory in RPM form.

Many X Window System applications use configure scripts that will automatically detect your system's configuration and generate a Makefile that can then be used to compile and install the program. An applications configure script is locate in its source code directory. Just change to that directory and execute the **configure** command. Be sure to include a preceding ./ to specify the configure script in that directory. Afterward the command **make** will compile the program, and **make install** will install it on your system. Check an application's readme and install files for any special instructions.

```
./configure
make
make install
```

For older applications that do not have configure scripts you will use the **xmkmf** command. A Makefile has to be generated that is configured to your system. This is done using an Imakefile provided with the application source code. The **xmkmf** command installed on your system can take an Imakefile and generate the appropriate Makefile. Once you have the Makefile, you can use the **make** command to compile the application. The **xmkmf** command actually uses a program called **imake** to generate the Makefile from the Imakefile; however, you should never use **imake** directly. Consult the man pages for **xmkmf** and **make** for more details.

The Complete Reference

Linux

Part VII

Appendix

The Complete Reference

Appendix A

About the CD-ROMs

907

Two Linux distribution CD-ROMs, Red Hat Linux 6.0 and Caldera OpenLinux 2.2, are included in this book. Standard installation installs and configures the Apache Web server and an FTP server, automatically configuring your Linux system to be a Web and FTP site. You can find recent information about Red Hat from **www.redhat.com** and about OpenLinux from **www.calderasystems.com**.

The CDs include both Gnome and the K Desktop Environment (KDE) GUI user interfaces, along with many Gnome and KDE applications. Red Hat 6.0 installs both Gnome and KDE, whereas OpenLinux installs KDE. OpenLinux also includes the current version of Corel's WordPerfect. It is also possible to install this package on Red Hat, though you can also download it directly from the Corel Web site at **linux.corel.com**.

Both distributions include a comprehensive set of Linux software applications including the GNU software packages (graphics, communications, publishing, editing, programming, games), as well as development tools, and Internet servers (FTP, Web, mail, news, and DNS). Both distributions install a complete set of Internet clients such as mail, news, FTP, and Web browsers, including Netscape Communicator. There are clients for both the Gnome and KDE desktops, as well as for shell and window manager interfaces. The CD-ROMs include extensive documentation including HOW-TO documents, tutorials in Web page format, and online manuals. The Red Hat CD-ROM contains the complete Red Hat manual in Web page format located in the **doc\rhmanual\manual** directory, and the OpenLinux CD-ROM holds the Getting Started Guide, also in Web page format. You can view either of these using a Windows Web browser.

For added functionality you can also download free personal editions of the Star Office office suite from **www.stardivision.com**, KOffice from **koffice.kde.org**, and WordPerfect from **linux.corel.com**. Also, the Java Development Kit is available for free through **www.blackdown.org**. Databases are available from their respective Web sites; Oracle, for instance, is available from **www.oracle.com**. Numerous applications, in the easy-to-install RPM package format, are available for download from the Red Hat contrib site and the Red Hat FTP site, **updates.redhat.com**, and its mirror sites. You can both download and install these applications using either the Gnome or KDE file manager. Several popular Internet sites where you can easily obtain Linux applications are listed here.

Linux Applications	Internet Site
Java Development Kit	**www.blackdown.org**
Window manager and desktop themes	**www.themes.org**
Gnome applications	**www.gnome.org**
KDE applications	**www.kde.org**
Netscape Communicator and Navigator	Any distribution site such as **ftp.redhat.com** or **ftp.calderasystems.com**
Star Office	**www.stardivision.com**
Tk/Tcl Applications	**www.scriptics.com**
Perl Applications	**www.perl.com**
Applications for Red Hat	**contrib.redhat.com**
Linux Applications	**www.xnet.com/~blatura/linapps.shtml/ www.linuxapps.com**
Linux World	**www.linuxworld.com**
Linux Journal	**www.linuxjournal.com**
Linux news	**www.linux.com**
Linux Online	**www.linux.org**
Linux Application RPM packages	**www.rpmfind.net**
New Linux Applications	**www.freshmeat.net**
Linux Documentation Project	**metalab.unc.edu/LDP/**
WordPerfect	**linux.corel.com**

Both the OpenLinux and Red Hat distributions install a professional-level and very stable Linux system with KDE and Gnome GUI interfaces, providing you with all the advantages of a Unix workstation on your PC combined with the same ease of use and versatility found on GUI systems such as Windows and Mac/OS. An extensive set of

Internet servers are also included that are automatically installed along with flexible and easy-to-use system configuration tools such as Linuxconf.

This book includes a copy of the Publisher's Edition of Red Hat Linux from Red Hat Software, Inc., which you may use in accordance with the GNU General Public License. The Official Red Hat Linux, which you may purchase from Red Hat Software, includes the complete Official Red Hat Linux distribution, Red Hat Software's documentation, and 90 days of free e-mail technical support regarding installation of Official Red Hat Linux. You also may purchase technical support from Red Hat Software on issues other than installation. You may purchase Official Red Hat Linux and technical support from Red Hat Software through the company's Web site (**www.redhat.com**) or its toll-free number: 1 (888) REDHAT1.

Index

U

V

redhat®

www.redhat.com

Batteries Included.

Just open it up and turn it on. The new Lizard installer guides you through the first point and click install in the industry, complete with PowerQuest partitioning (Caldera Edition) with Boot Magic 4.0. Tightly meshed with the new 2.2.x Linux kernel, OpenLinux 2.2 is the only proven, tested, stable, and supported Linux solution, with source and binaries that match. We've also included the new KDE 1.1 GUI, glibc 2.1 libraries, COAS, Netware client and admin, WordPerfect 8, StarOffice, 7x24 support, and much more. It's what Linux for Business is all about. Visit **www.calderasystems.com** for more information. Because batteries should always be included.

Proven.
Tested.
Stable.
Supported.™

LINUX FOR BUSINESS.™

Caldera® SYSTEMS

This book includes a copy of the Publisher's Edition of Red Hat Linux from Red Hat Software, Inc., which you may use in accordance with the GNU General Public License. The Official Red Hat Linux, which you may purchase from Red Hat Software, includes the complete Official Red Hat Linux distribution, Red Hat Software's documentation, and 90 days of free e-mail technical support regarding installation of Official Red Hat Linux. You also may purchase technical support from Red Hat Software on issues other than installation. You may purchase Official Red Hat Linux and technical support from Red Hat Software through the company's Web site (**www.redhat.com**) or its toll-free number: 1 (888) REDHAT1.

Due to space considerations on the Red Hat 6.0 CD-ROM, some rarely used files such as TeX, some foreign-language Xfree86 fonts, a DOS emulator, and some Alpha and Sparc source code files are not included. Check **README.publishers-edition** file on the CD-ROM for all listings. Should you happen to want any of these files, they can be downloaded from **ftp.redhat.com**.